JOHN STROUD

Airports
of the World

AIRPORTS OF THE WORLD

Dulles International Airport, Washington, on 24 May, 1976, immediately after the arrival of the first supersonic passenger services from London and Paris. The British Airways and Air France Concordes stand on the apron in front of Eero Saarinen's terminal and control tower. There is a Plane-Mate mobile lounge at the door of each Concorde and more Plane-Mates and first-generation mobile lounges are at the gate positions along the face of the terminal. (*Arthur Gibson, Image in Industry*)

AIRPORTS
OF THE WORLD

JOHN STROUD

PUTNAM
LONDON

BY THE SAME AUTHOR

Japanese Aircraft
Annals of British and Commonwealth
Air Transport 1919–1960
European Transport Aircraft since 1910
Soviet Transport Aircraft since 1945
The World's Airliners
The World's Airports
The World's Civil Marine Aircraft
The BP Books of IATA Airlines

©1980 John Stroud
ISBN 0 370 30037 8
Printed in Great Britain for
Putnam & Company Ltd
9 Bow Street London WC2E 7AL
by Thomson Litho Ltd,
East Kilbride, Scotland
set in Monophoto Times
by Willmer Brothers Ltd., Birkenhead
First published 1980

CONTENTS

Warning: Very great care was taken in the compilation of this book to ensure its accuracy at the time of going to press; nevertheless, it must be stressed that it is *not* to be used for OPERATIONAL PURPOSES

viii

INTRODUCTION

When, early in 1977, I was asked to write this book I had no idea of the form it would take nor which airports would be included. Neither did I appreciate the monumental task with which I was faced. The total number of airports is almost certainly unknown. Apart from the tight security in certain countries such as the USSR and China, the actual definition of the term airport imposes its own problems in assessing the numbers. For example, the Aircraft Owners and Pilots Association in Washington, DC, in its 1976 edition of *Listing of Airports*, gives a total of 12,936 landing sites and these are obviously not all airports as the term is generally understood. The FAA's 1974 *Statistical Handbook of Aviation* lists 13,062 airports of which 4,716 had paved runways, 3,999 had runway lights and 61 were designated points of entry to the United States.

ICAO, using the term aerodrome, has stated that in 1977 'The total number of civil aerodromes in ICAO [member] States is 30,251 of which at least 16,118 are open to public use.' The 1,012 aerodromes designated in the ICAO Air Navigation Plan as essential for international civil aviation represent 6.3 per cent of the aerodromes open to public use. These are broken down by ICAO as 639 regular aerodromes and 123 alternate aerodromes for international scheduled air transport, 37 regular and one alternate for international non-scheduled air transport, and 212 for international general aviation.

Obviously no single book can describe this enormous number of airports or civil aerodromes and therefore a selection had to be made. My original decision was to limit this work to airports handling one million or more passengers a year and initial research showed slightly over 100 airports in this category, but most published material on world airport traffic proved to be misleading or incomplete and further research showed that the true figure for this category exceeded 200 excluding airports in the USSR, while other airports achieved the one million status during the time this book has been compiled. The task of selecting the airports was not made any easier by the fact that the FAA and numerous United States airport authorities record only embarking passengers—using, as in the case of Dallas/Fort Worth, this figure doubled plus 10 per cent to arrive at a passenger total for planning purposes. Even where total figures are obtainable it is not always possible to ascertain whether these include transit passengers.

Furthermore, a book dealing only with the one million passenger category airports would exclude many airports of importance. My final decision on the choice was to give detailed coverage, with technical data, descriptions, histories and, where possible, illustrations of all airports known or reasonably thought to have handled one million or more passengers during 1975, 1976 or 1977. In order to include the many

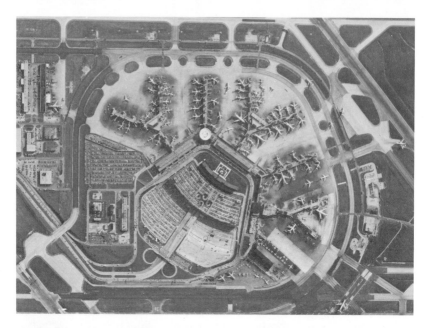

The modern airport. Terminal areas of the world's busiest airport, Chicago O'Hare International Airport with nearly 50 mn passengers in 1978 (top), and the world's busiest in terms of international passengers, London Heathrow Airport. 106 aircraft can be seen at Chicago and 67 at Heathrow.
(*City of Chicago and British Airports Authority*)

important airports which did not handle a million passengers in the years mentioned, I decided to give brief details of those known to have handled 250,000 or more passengers but less than one million.

However, in the case of the United States, including Alaska and Hawaii, the airports covered are only those designated by the FAA as 'larger and medium traffic hub airports'; and in the case of the USSR and China maximum information is given on all airports for which information is available because traffic figures cannot be obtained.

An appendix gives very brief details of international airports which handled between 100,000 and 250,000 passengers in 1975, 1976 or 1977.

By adopting this method it has been possible to cover some 495 airports overall.

The large areas which airports have to provide for car parking is well illustrated in this 1976 photograph of LaGuardia Airport, New York. There is a massive multi-storey car park in front of the terminal, with open car parks on each side.
(*Port Authority of New York & New Jersey*)

For each of the major airports there is a runway layout drawing except for those which have a single runway, and, as far as possible, a photograph has been included. Where some of the major airports are not illustrated it is because their owners claim that no photograph is available, although in some instances airlines and private individuals have come to my rescue and proved that photographs do exist.

My main purpose was to put on record a picture of the world's airports in the mid-to-late 1970s, not to produce an operational handbook. Each ICAO-member State produces its AIP (Aeronautical Information Publication) for the use of airlines and other operators, and I have made full use of these publications—but I regret to say that some AIPs, particularly Soviet and Chinese, by no means provide a record of those countries' airports.

Terminal development. Munich Airport main hall as restored after the Second World War represented the typical German airport architecture of the 1930s. Part of Düsseldorf Airport's Terminal 2 is typical of today.
(*John Stroud and Flughafen Düsseldorf GmbH*)

Compared with other aspects of aviation, the airports have not been well served by writers, other than in a general way. There have been books on individual airports and even airports of an area, but few attempts at documenting the main airports at any particular period. Exceptions were *Grosser Luftverkehrs-Atlas von Europa*, published in Berlin in 1927, which provided limited descriptions, simple plans and photographs of European airports; and *Guide Aéronautique International*, published in Paris in 1932, which included short descriptions and layout plans of airports in many parts of the world. The latter book has proved of great value in researching the history of some of the airports in this book.

Notes on this book

Authority: This term is used to denote either the owner or operating authority.

Runway dimensions, elevations and other measurements: These are given in both metric and imperial units and the unit of the country concerned is the authoritative figure except where countries, such as Australia and the United Kingdom, have changed their standards. In these instances the authoritative figure is the one in use at the time of construction.

Conversions have been rounded to the nearest unit except where the metric and imperial figures are both published by the relevant authority, in which case there are sometimes slight discrepancies. For example, the official Japanese pavement loading figures show some variation— Kumamoto and Nagasaki show isolated single wheel loadings of 24,000 kg converted as 52,800 lb, Miyazaki shows the conversion as 53,000 lb, while Matsuyama publishes the figures as 23,950 kg and 52,800 lb. Where no official conversion is quoted I have shown 24,000 kg as 52,911 lb.

In the case of airport elevations, these are mostly shown converted to the nearest full figure, but some airports, mostly in Japan, show elevations taken to one or even two decimal points.

Distances from cities are normally from the central or business area.

Displaced thresholds, stopways and clearways: These have not been given throughout.

Pavement strength: LCN (Load Classification Number). This system is widely used and is based on a combination of wheel loading in pounds and tyre pressure in psi (lb/sq inch). For example, LCN 85 can be derived from a wheel loading of 65,000 lb with 170 psi tyre pressure or 75,000 lb and 135 psi. LCN 100 is derived from 80,000 lb and 170 psi.

LCG (Load Classification Group). This system is used in the United Kingdom. The LCG figure represents the safe loading level below maximum that the pavement will carry, so it is possible at the discretion of the airport authority to allow occasional and infrequent use of the pavement by aircraft one group above that published.

LCG I	= LCN 101–120	LCG V	= LCN 16–30
LCG II	= LCN 76–100	LCG VI	= LCN 11–15
LCG III	= LCN 51–75	LCG VII	= LCN 10 and under
LCG IV	= LCN 31–50		

Aerobridges, also known as air bridges, air jetties and loading bridges, at Edinburgh Airport; a Plane-Mate mobile lounge at John F Kennedy International Airport, New York; and the Airtrans system at Dallas/Fort Worth Regional Airport. (*Scottish Airports, Port Authority of New York & New Jersey, and Dallas/Fort Worth Regional Airport Board*)

Examples are:

Four-wheel bogie

Concorde (184 psi tyre pressure) 76,657 kg, LCN 37, LCG IV; 108,866 kg, LCN 51, LCG III; 174,636 kg, LCN 85, LCG II; 176,450 kg, LCN 85, LCG II.
Boeing 747B (185 psi) 168,000 kg, LCN 35, LCG IV; 254,000 kg, LCN 54, LCG III; 353,000 kg, LCN 74, LCG III.
Douglas DC-8-63 (198 psi) 66,271 kg, LCN 31, LCG IV; 115,210 kg, LCN 55, LCG III; 158,760 kg, LCN 76, LCG II.

Four wheels in line on each main undercarriage unit

Trident 1E (150 psi) 32,100 kg, LCN 24, LCG V; 49,000 kg, LCN 40, LCG IV; 61,200 kg, LCN 50, LCG IV.
Trident 3B (170 psi) 38,690 kg, LCN 33, LCG IV; 57,150 kg, LCN 49, LCG IV; 68,040 kg, LCN 59, LCG III.

Single wheel on each main unit

Douglas DC-3 (45 psi) 8,300 kg, LCN 7, LCG VII; 11,400 kg, LCN 10, LCG VII.
DHC Twin Otter 300 (38 psi) 2,860 kg, LCN 2, LCG VII; 5,670 kg, LCN 4, LCG VII.

Twin wheel main undercarriage

Airbus A300 (130 psi) 67,950 kg, LCN 32, LCG IV; 108,000 kg, LCN 51, LCG III; 120,000 kg, LCN 57, LCG III; 137,250 kg (147 psi), LCN 66, LCG III.
Boeing 727-200 (135 psi) 42,500 kg, LCN 34, LCG IV; 67,100 kg, LCN 53, LCG III; 76,600 kg, LCN 61, LCG III.
Fokker F.27 200/400 (80 psi) 10,840 kg, LCN 9, LCG VII; 18,150 kg, LCN 16, LCG V; 19,730 kg, LCN 18, LCG V.

Other systems. Many airports quote pavement strength in terms of isolated single wheel loading (ISWL) while in the United States the figures are normally maximum weights depending on undercarriage configuration. In this book 1 represents single wheel, 2 dual wheels, 3 bogie or dual tandem and 4 double bogie. In Hawaii the figures are quoted for maximum landing weight.

Unless specifically stated the pavement strength figures may apply only to the strongest runway.

Lighting: Runway and approach lighting has been described as fully as available information allows because of its enormous importance for safe operation. United Kingdom and United States systems are in widescale use. The United States and Australian standards are set out as introductions to these sections of the book.

United Kingdom standards are laid down as requirements and shown on the next page as they appear in the *Civil Air Pilot*.

	HI C/L and 5 bar App System	Supplementary App inner 300 m	HI App 1 bar (simple system)	LI App 1 bar (simple system)	VASIS	AVASIS	AAIs	HI runway edge	LI runway edge	HI runway centreline	Touchdown zone	HI threshold and end lights	LI threshold and end lights	Taxiway edge	Taxiway centreline	Light beacon	Obstruction lights	Secondary power supply
L1 Precision App CAT III	X	X	X					X		X	X	X			X	X	X	X
L2 Precision App CAT II	X	X	X					X		X	X	X			X	X	X	X
L3 Precision App CAT I	X		X					X			O	X		X	O	X	X	X
L4 Instrument App			X		X	X		X				X		X	O	X	X	O
L5 Instrument App			O		X	X		X				X		X	O	X	X	O
L6 Non-instrument App				O		O	X		X		O		X	X	O	X	X	O
L7 Non-instrument App						O	X		X				X	X		X	X	

X = Requirement O = Operationally desirable HI = High intensity LI = Low intensity
VASIS = Visual Approach Slope Indicator System AAI = Angle of Approach Indicator

Scales L1, 2 and 3 relate to runways served by ILS or PAR.

Scale L4 relates to runways served by SRA procedures terminating at ½ nm from touchdown.

Scale L5 relates to runways served by NDB, TVOR or VDF procedures, and SRA procedures if the latter terminate at 2 nm or more from touchdown.

Scale L6 is the minimum to be used at night by public transport aeroplanes carrying passengers on scheduled journeys, or by public transport aeroplanes carrying passengers on other than scheduled journeys whose maximum total weight authorized exceeds 12,500 lb and will apply only where the approach procedure is not aligned with a runway. The AAIs for this scale shall be LITAS (Low Intensity Two Colour Approach System slope indicators).

Scale L7 will normally apply to grass runways. LITAS should be provided to meet the AAI requirement for this scale.

The standard approach lighting for CAT I operation is the Calvert centreline and crossbar system. This comprises 'a coded line of white lights, 910 m (3,000 ft) long, on the extended centreline of the runway together with additional rows of white lights arranged symmetrically at 150 m (500 ft) intervals and at right angles to the centreline to form five horizontal crossbars. The bars decrease in width towards the runway threshold, with the outer ends of the bars contained by two straight lines that converge to meet the runway centreline 300 m (1,000 ft) from the threshold.'

The coding consists of triple lights on the outer third of the centreline, double lights on the centre third, and single lights on the inner section.

For CAT II and III operations the system is modified. Over the inner 300 m (1,000 ft) the centreline consists of white barrettes instead of single lights, except that the single line may be retained if the threshold is displaced by 300 m (1,000 ft) or more—centreline white barrettes consist of five lights spaced 1.2 m (3 ft 9 in) apart. In addition, red barrettes (four lights spaced 1.5 m/5 ft apart) are placed either side of each centreline

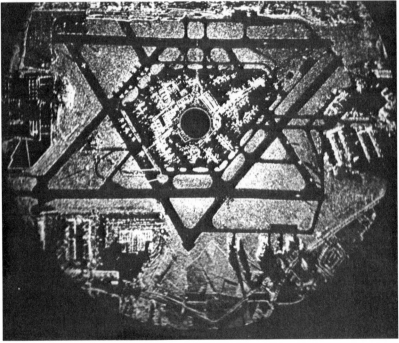

Following the Tenerife collision between two Boeing 747s on the runway in March 1977, considerable publicity was given to the Airport Surface Movement Indication system (ASMI). These photographs show London Airport Heathrow and the returns by the Decca ASMI. Aircraft can clearly be seen on taxiways and near the threshold of 28L. (*British Airports Authority and Decca Radar Ltd*)

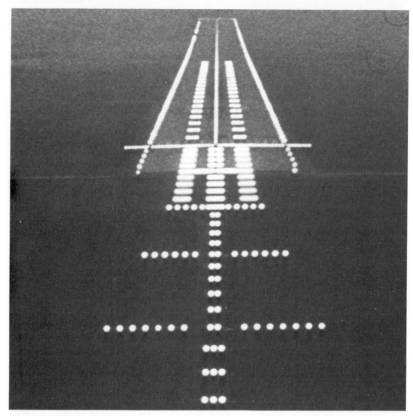

Category III lighting at Basle - Mulhouse Airport. This shows the approach centreline and crossbars, inner section supplementary barrettes, threshold lights, runway edge and centreline lights and narrow-gauge touchdown zone lights. This installation by Erni & Co (Switzerland) had to have about three times the ICAO recommended intensity because of local meteorological conditions.

barrette over the inner 270 m (900 ft) of the approach lighting system. The lateral spacing of the red barrettes is equal to that of the touchdown zone lighting. +

+ In this section the CAA metric and imperial figures have been used.

The United States does not favour the Calvert system with its extremely useful crossbars but places more reliance on sequenced flashing lights.

In this book, other than in the United States section, high-intensity, medium-intensity and low-intensity lights are indicated by the ICAO abbreviations LIH, LIM and LIL.

The letters A, R and T have been used to denote approach, runway and threshold lighting at the airports which are only briefly described. These lighting descriptions apply to the airport and not to a particular runway.

Runway layout drawings: Many of the runway layout drawings were supplied by the individual airport authorities and therefore vary in style. Others were kindly supplied by the CAA Aeronautical Information Service, International Aeradio, British Airways Aerad, Alitalia, Deutsche Lufthansa, SAS and Swissair. A few maps were specially drawn.

Their main purpose is to show the runway layouts; therefore in some cases, parts of the originals have been excluded, and on some, details, such as spot heights, have been deleted for clarity. Displaced thresholds are not always shown.

One of Hong Kong's problems. Crossbar No. 3 of the approach lights leading to runway 13 had to be erected on a street corner. (*The General Electric Co*)

Acknowledgements

Writing a book of this complexity would not have been possible without the assistance and co-operation of many people and organizations throughout the world. I am grateful to all of them. Regrettably, numbers of civil aviation and airport authorities did not reply to repeated requests for information and this made even more valuable the generous and unlimited help which I received from:

Klaus Vomhof, *ABC World Airways Guide*; John Green and Norman Clark and their staff, Aeronautical Information Service, CAA; Gilson Campos, ARSA Aeroportos do Rio de Janeiro SA; Theana Y.Kastens, Airport Operators Council International; Jeffrey S.Bacall, Alitalia; Department of Transport, Commonwealth of Australia; R.P.Ollerenshaw, British Airways Aerad; Brian W.Smith, UK Civil Aviation Authority; Horst W.Burgsmüller, Deutsche Lufthansa; L.J.N.Steijn, Fokker-VFW International b.v; Federal Aviation Administration, US Department of Transportation; Owen Miyamoto, State of Hawaii, Department of Transportation, Airports Division; E.Sochor and Mrs E.Zay, International Civil Aviation Organization; Yukihiko Komada, Deputy Director of Aerodromes, Japan Civil Aviation Bureau; Civil Aviation Division, Ministry of Transport, New Zealand; Max Virchaux, then of Swissair; Transport Canada; and, as always, my wife Patricia.

I am no less grateful to the following of whom I asked much less:
Individuals
Norman A.Barfield, Jerzy Cynk, Professor Laura Crowell, M.A.S.Dalal, R.E.G.Davies, David Dorrell, Günter Endres, Dr René J. Francillon, Arthur Gibson, A.G.Heape, Justus L.Hellmuth, Gottfried Hilscher, Michael J.Hooks, Donald Kirk, Søren Liby, Haruya Miura, Lilian and Jacques Noetinger, Masatoshi Ohtsuka, John Paleocrassas, Leonardo Pinzauti, Dr Ace C.Powers, Joan Rieck, Guy Roberty, Eiichiro Sekigawa, Anthony Vandyk, Eric Warburg, Clem Watson, Gordon S.Williams, David Woolley, E.A.'Chris' Wren.
Airlines
Air France, Air Niugini, Alitalia, All Nippon Airways, Braathens SAFE Air Transport, British Airways, Delta Air Lines, Deutsche Lufthansa, Interflug, LOT, Sabena, SAS, South African Airways, Swissair, TAP, United Airlines, Varig.
Other Companies
Boeing Commercial Airplane Company, British Aerospace-Aircraft Group, Decca Radar, Douglas Aircraft Company, Erni & Co (Switzerland), Image in Industry, International Aeradio, Tata Ltd.
Organizations
Aviation Society of Africa, GIFAS.
Publications
Airline Executive, Air Pictorial, Airport Forum, Airports International, British Airways News, Esso Air World, Flight International.

Airport and Civil Aviation Authorities
State of Alaska, Division of Aviation; Albany County Airport; City of Albuquerque; County of Allegheny Department of Aviation; City of Atlanta; Bundesministerium für Verkehr, Austria.

Civil Aviation Directorate, State of Bahrain; Aéroport Bâle-Mulhouse; Department of Civil Aviation, People's Republic of Bangladesh; Civil Aviation Division, Barbados; Régie des Voies Aériennes, Belgium; Berliner Flughafen-Gesellschaft mbH; Department of Civil Aviation, Bermuda; Birmingham Airport (UK); Department of Aviation, City of Birmingham, Alabama; Flughafen Bremen GmbH; Bristol Airport; British Airports Authority.

Direction de l'Aéronautique Civile, République Unie du Cameroun; City of Chicago Department of Aviation; Dirección General de Aeronautica Civil, Chile; Kenton County Aviation Board, Cincinnati; City of Cleveland; Division of Airports, City of Columbus; State of Connecticut, Department of Transportation; Copenhagen Airports Authority; Director of Civil Aviation, Cyprus.

Metropolitan Dade County Aviation Department; Dallas/Fort Worth Regional Airport Board; Department of Aviation, City of Dayton; Stapleton International Airport, Denver; Directorate of Civil Aviation, Denmark; City of Des Moines Department of Aviation; Dirección General de Aeronautica, Dominican Republic; Flughafen Düsseldorf GmbH.

Director General of Civil Aviation, East African Community; East Midlands Airport; Edinburgh Airport; El Paso International Airport & Mass Transit Board.

National Board of Aviation, Finland; Broward County Aviation Division, Fort Lauderdale; Direction des Bases Aériennes, Direction Générale de l'Aviation Civile, France; Flughafen Frankfurt/Main AG.

Aéroport de Genève (Cointrin); Civil Aviation Authority, Greece; States Airport, Guernsey.

Hakodate Airport; Flughafen Hamburg GmbH; Flughafen Hannover GmbH; Hong Kong Government Information Services; City of Houston Department of Aviation; LRI (Air Traffic and Airport Administration), Hungary.

Deputy Director General of Civil Aviation, India; Indianapolis Airport Authority; Directorate General of Air Communications, Republic of Indonesia; Department General of Civil Aviation, Iran; Aer Rianta-Irish Airports; Isle of Man Airports Board; Ministero dei Trasporti, Italy.

Jacksonville Port Authority; Civil Aviation Department, Jamaica; Ports of Jersey.

Kagoshima Airport; Air Commerce Division, Aviation Department, Kansas City International Airport; Flughafen Köln/Bonn GmbH; Kushiro Airport.

Clark County Department of Aviation, Las Vegas; Leeds Bradford Airport; Liverpool Airport; City of Los Angeles Department of Airports; Louisville and Jefferson County Air Board; Luton Airport; Service Aéronautique, Ministère des Transports, Luxembourg; Aéroport International de Lyon.

Chief Civil Aviation Officer, Malawi; Civil Aviation Department, Malaysia; Department of Civil Aviation, Malta GC; Manchester International Airport Authority; Aéroport International de Marseille-Marignane; Maryland Department of Transportation, State Aviation Administration; Massachusetts Port Authority (Massport); Matsuyama Airport; Memphis-Shelby County Airport Authority; Società Esercizi Aeroportuali-SEA, Milan; Department of Public Works, Airport Division, Milwaukee County; Minneapolis-Saint Paul Metropolitan Airports Commission; Miyako Airport; Ministère des Travaux Publics et des Communications, Direction de l'Air, Morocco; Flughafen München.

Naha Airport; Nashville Metropolitan Airport Authority; Netherlands Department of Civil Aviation; Newcastle Airport; New Orleans Aviation Board; The Port Authority of New York and New Jersey; Niagara Frontier Transportation Authority; Chambre de Commerce et d'Industrie de Nice et des Alpes-Maritimes; Niigata Airport; Norfolk Port and Industrial Authority; Northern Ireland Airports Ltd; Luftfartsdirektoratet, Norway; Flughafen Nürnberg GmbH.

Board of Port Commissioners, City of Oakland; Oita Airport; Department of Airports, City of Oklahoma City; Omaha Airport Authority; Directorate General of Civil Aviation, Sultinate of Oman; Greater Orlando Aviation Authority.

Department of Civil Aviation, Pakistan; Aeropuerto de Palma de Mallorca; Dirección de Aeronautica Civil, Panamá; Aéroport de Paris; Division of Aviation, Department of Commerce, City of Philadelphia; Phoenix Sky Harbor International Airport; Port of Portland, Oregon; Direcção-Geral da Aeronáutica Civil, Portugal; Ports Authority, Commonwealth of Puerto Rico.

Civil Aviation Department, State of Qatar.

Raleigh-Durham Airport Authority; City of Reno Department of Airports; Director, Reykjavík Airport; Department of Civil Aviation, Rhodesia; County of Monroe, Department of Public Works, Rochester; Aeroporti di Roma.

Salt Lake City Airport Authority; Flughafen Salzburg; San Diego Unified Port Authority; Airports Commission San Francisco; NV Luchthaven Schiphol; Port of Seattle Sea-Tac International Airport; Sendai Airport; Division Aéronautique Civile, Ministère des Travaux Publics de l'Urbanisme et des Transports, République du Sénégal; Department of Civil Aviation, Republic of Singapore; Department of Transport, Republic of South Africa; Southampton Airport; City of St Louis Airport Authority; Flughafen Stuttgart GmbH; City of Syracuse Department of Aviation; Director General of Civil Aviation, Syrian Arab Republic.

Civil Aeronautics Administration, Taiwan, ROC; Hillsborough County Aviation Authority, Tampa; New Tokyo International Airport Authority; Tucson Airport Authority; Tulsa Airport Authority.

Virgin Islands Port Authority.

Board of Wayne County Road Commissioners; Flughafen Wien Betriebsgesellschaft mbH.

Régie des Voies Aériennes, République du Zaïre; Civil Aviation Department of the Canton of Zürich.

JOHN STROUD
Nairn
November 1979

Airline changes

The following changes have occurred since the book went to the printer: Air UK formed by merger of Air Anglia, Air Wales, Air West and British Island Airways; Allegheny Airlines renamed USAir; British Cargo Airlines formed by merger of IAS Cargo Airlines and Transmeridian Air Cargo; Jersey European Airways formed by merger of Express Air Services and Intra Airways: National Airlines now a subsidiary of Pan American World Airways; North Central Airlines and Southern Airways merged to form Republic Airlines; TAP renamed Air Portugal; Transair merged with Pacific Western Airlines; Trans International Airlines (TIA) renamed Transamerica Airlines.

Abbreviations

A	Approach lighting (at airports with under 1 mn passengers)
AAI	Angle of Approach Indicator
ACR	Aerodrome Control Radar
ADF	Automatic Direction Finder
AGNIS	Aircraft Guidance Nose-In System
AIP	Aeronautical Information Publication
ALS	Approach Lighting System
ALSF	High intensity Approach Lighting System with Sequenced Flashers
App	Approach
ARSR	Air Route Surveillance Radar
ARTS	Automatic Radar Terminal Service
ASDE	Airport Surface Detection Equipment (radar)
ASMI	Airport Surface Movement Indication (radar)
ASR	Airport Surveillance Radar
ATC	Air Traffic Control
auw	all-up weight
AVASIS	Abbreviated VASIS
DME	Distance Measuring Equipment
DVORTAC	Doppler VORTAC
GCA	Ground Controlled Approach
HIRL	High Intensity Runway Lights
IATA	International Air Transport Association
ICAO	International Civil Aviation Organization
ILS	Instrument Landing System
ISWL	Isolated Single Wheel Loading
KGSP	Soviet ILS
L	Locator
LCG	Load Classification Group
LCN	Load Classification Number
LDA	Landing Distance Available
LIH	Light Intensity High (ICAO code)
LIL	Light Intensity Low (ICAO code)
LIM	Light Intensity Medium (ICAO code)
LITAS	Low Intensity Two-colour Approach System
LLWSAS	Low Level Wind Shear Alert System
LOM	Compass Locator (ILS Outer Marker)
m	metres
MALS	Medium intensity Approach Lighting System
MALSF	MALS with Sequenced Flashers
MALSR	MALS with RAIL
MIRL	Medium Intensity Runway Lights

NDB	Non-Directional radio Beacon
nm	nautical miles
PAR	Precision Approach Radar
psi	pounds per square inch
PSP	Perforated Steel Plate
R	Runway lighting (at airports with under 1 mn passengers)
RAD	Radar (unspecified)
RAIL	Runway Alignment Indicator Lights
Ref temp	Reference temperature
REIL	Runway End Identifier Lights
RIL	Runway Identification Lighting (Canadian)
RSR	En-Route Surveillance Radar
RVR	Runway Visual Range (measuring equipment)
RVV	Runway Visibility Values (measuring equipment)
R/W	Runway
SALS	Short Approach Lighting System (high intensity)
SRE	Surveillance Radar Element of GCA
SSALF	Simplified SALS with Sequenced Flashers
SSALR	Simplified SALS with RAIL
SSALS	Simplified SALS (high intensity)
SSR	Secondary Surveillance Radar
STOL	Short Take Off and Landing
T	Threshold lighting (at airports with under 1 mn passengers)
TAC	TACAN
TACAN	UHF Tactical Air Navigation facility
TAR	Terminal Area surveillance Radar
TDZ	Touchdown Zone lighting
Thr	Threshold
TODA	Take-Off Distance Available
TORA	Take-Off Run Available
T-VASIS	Australian adaptation of VASIS
TVOR	Low-power Terminal VOR
Twr	Control Tower
Txy	Taxiway
UDF	Ultra-high frequency Direction Finding station
UHF	Ultra-High Frequency (300 to 3,000 MHz)
VAR	Visual—Aural Radio Range
VASI(S)	Visual Approach Slope Indicator (System)
VDF	Very-high frequency Direction Finding station
VFR	Visual Flight Rules
VOR	VHF Omni-directional Radio Range
VORTAC	Combined VOR and TACAN
VTOL	Vertical Take Off and Landing
1*	Single wheel
2*	Dual wheels
3*	Dual tandem/bogie
4*	Double bogie

*Used only in relation to pavement strength.

Algeria (Algérie)

Algiers (El Djezair) (Alger)   Aéroport d'Alger/Dar El Beida

36° 41′ 40″ N   03° 13′ 04″ E   9.11 nm (16.87 km) ESE of city
ICAO: DAAG   IATA code: ALG   Time zone: GMT
Authority: Department of Civil Aviation
Elevation: 82 ft (25 m)   Ref temp: 26.7 deg C
Runways: 06/24   3,500 × 60 m (11,483 × 197 ft) concrete
         10/28   2,350 × 45 m (7,710 × 148 ft) concrete
         R/W 10 landings only, R/W 28 take-offs only
         There is an emergency strip alongside and north of 10/28
Pavement strength: 50,000 kg (110,231 lb) ISWL
Landing category: ICAO CAT I
Lighting:
    R/W   LIH and LIL white edge, red stopway
    App   R/W 24   LIH and LIL white coded centreline with
           crossbars
    Thr   LIH green
    Txy   blue edge
Aids: VOR/DME, NDB, VDF, L, ILS CAT I 24
Twr frequency: 118.7/119.7   App frequency: 121.4
Terminal: Passenger terminal on northern side of airport, with 14 aircraft
         stands

Algiers Airport - Dar El Beida. (*Fokker–VFW*)

1

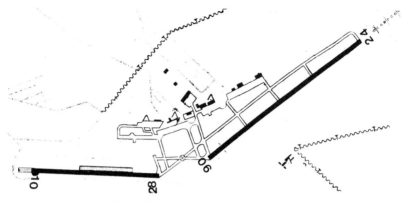

Algiers/Dar El Beida Airport. (*Swissair*)

Scheduled services 1978: 21 airlines
Main base: Air Algérie

Traffic:	1970	1975	1976	1977
Passengers*	915,488	1,795,938	1,964,097	2,396,127
Cargo (tonnes)	5,868	14,494	19,556	29,092
Aircraft movements	70,580	56,141	50,829	—
Transport movements	23,524	31,610	32,321	38,001

*Transit passengers excluded

Algiers airport Dar El Beida is the French Maison Blanche which in prewar years served as a civil airport and military base. After being under Vichy control the aerodrome was captured by a United States combat team a few hours after the Allied landings at Algiers on 8 November, 1942. Eighteen Hurricanes of No. 43 Squadron, RAF, landed there by 09.00 hr that day, and thereafter, in spite of Luftwaffe attacks, Maison Blanche became an important Allied base. After the war it served as Algeria's principal civil airport and considerable development has taken place. Work began on terminal extension in 1979 and runway 10/28 is being extended and will be equipped with ILS.

Annaba (formerly Bône)   Aéroport d'Annaba

ICAO: DABB   IATA: AAE

36° 49′ 18″ N   07° 48′ 36″ E   Elevation: 16 ft (5 m)
Longest runway: 01/19   3,000 m (9,842 ft)   RT   VASI 01
Aids: VOR, NDB, L

	1971	1975	1976	1977
Passengers	120,672	253,615*	308,797	393,485
Transport movements	2,459	4,459	5,074	6,069

*Transit passengers excluded
Scheduled services 1978: Air Algérie, Air France and Swissair

Constantine   Aéroport de Constantine/Ain el Bey

ICAO: DABC   IATA: CZL

36° 17' 12" N   06° 37' 18" E   Elevation: 2,303 ft (702 m)
Runway: 14/32   2,400 m (7,874 ft)   RT   VASI 14/32
Aids: VOR, NDB, VDF, ILS CAT I 32

	1970	1975	1976	1977
Passengers	111,148	347,717	406,817	494,848
Transport movements	2,772	5,545	5,508	6,628

Scheduled services 1978: Air Algérie and Air France

Oran   Aéroport d'Oran/Es Sénia

ICAO: DAOO   IATA: ORN

35° 37' 40" N   00° 36' 33" E   Elevation: 295 ft (90 m)
Longest runway: 07/25   3,000 m (9,842 ft)   ART
Aids: VOR, NDB, VDF, L, ILS 25

	1970	1975	1976	1977
Passengers	150,181	457,143*	533,392	696,025
Transport movements	4,486	8,499	8,365	8,592

*Transit passengers excluded

Scheduled services 1978: Air Algérie, Air France and Swissair

Angola

Luanda   Luanda Airport

ICAO: FNLU   IATA: LAD

08° 51' 15" S   13° 14' 12" E   Elevation: 243 ft (74 m)
Longest runway: 06/24   3,700 m (12,139 ft)   ART   VASI 06/24
Aids: VOR/DME, NDB, VDF, L

	1970	1976	1977*
Passengers	443,731	288,937	169,949
Transport movements	19,573	9,952	5,475

Scheduled services 1978: 10 airlines
Main base: Angola Airlines

*January—June only

Argentina

Buenos Aires   Aeropuerto Ezeiza

34° 49′ 40″ S   58° 32′ 27″ W   11.88 nm (22 km) SSW of city
ICAO: SAEZ   IATA code: EZE   Time zone: GMT −3
Authority: Comando de Regiones Aéreas
Elevation: 66 ft (20 m)   Ref temp. 25.7 deg C
Runways: 05/23   2,199 × 70 m   (7,214 × 230 ft) asphaltic concrete
      11/29   3,300 × 80 m (10,827 × 262 ft) asphaltic concrete
      17/35   2,805 × 70 m   (9,203 × 230 ft) asphaltic concrete
Pavement strength: R/W 11/29   155,000 kg (341,716 lb) 1, 200,000 kg
   (440,924 lb) 2, 320,000 kg (705,479 lb) 3, 450,000 kg (992,080 lb) 4.
   Other runways of reduced strength.
Landing category: ICAO CAT II
Lighting:
   R/W   11/29   LIH and LIL edge, and end lights. 05/23 and
         17/35 LIL edge
   App   R/W 11   Calvert LIH coded centreline with four
         crossbars
         R/W 35   LIL short coded centreline with two crossbars
   Thr   LIH green R/W 11,   LIL green other runways
   Txy   lights on short taxiways but not on taxiway to threshold 11
Aids: VOR/DME, NDB, L, ILS CAT II 11, ILS CAT I 35
Twr frequency: 119.1/121.5   App frequency: 119.9/121.5
Terminal: Passenger terminal with nine close-in aircraft stands
Scheduled services 1978: 22 airlines

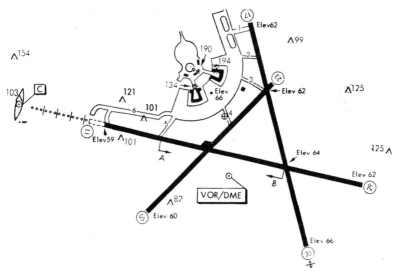

Ezeiza Airport, Buenos Aires. (*Swissair*)

4

Aerolineas Argentinas Douglas DC-6 LV-ADU *Gral. Belgrano* at Ezeiza Airport, Buenos Aires, in the late 1950s or early 1960s.

Main base: Aerolineas Argentinas and Aerotransportes Entre Rios SRL

Traffic:	1970	1975	1976	1977
Passengers (total)	830,848	1,411,824	1,219,753	1,470,270
Cargo (tonnes)	23,170	31,792	36,374	50,373
Aircraft movements	33,248	31,288	28,077	30,404
Transport movements	16,581	18,812	19,324	21,048

During the 1940s the Argentine Government adopted a five-year plan for the construction of a national network of airports and aerodromes. Ezeiza was planned as the major airport to serve Buenos Aires and the design called for a tangential runway system with three pairs of parallel runways and a central terminal area. However, the plan was modified and only three runways were constructed: 04/22, now 05/23; 10/28 originally 2,500 m (8,202 ft) in length and now 11/29 of 3,300 m (10,827 ft); and 16/34 originally 2,100 m (6,890 ft) long and now 17/35 of 2,805 m (9,203 ft).

The northern 04/22 was presumably intended for take-offs only and no parallel taxiway was planned, but this runway was not constructed and neither were the western 16/34 or northern 10/28.

Ezeiza was opened in October 1949, as Aeropuerto Ministro Pistarini, and replaced Morón which had served postwar operations.

Buenos Aires

Aeroparque de la Ciudad de Buenos Aires (Jorge Newbery)

34° 33′ 36″ S   58° 24′ 50″ W   Adjacent to NE of city
ICAO: SABE   IATA code: AEP   Time zone: GMT −3
Authority: Comando de Regiones Aéreas
Elevation: 20 ft (6 m)   Ref. temp: 25.7 deg C
Runway: 13/31   2,100 × 40 m (6,889 × 131 ft) asphalt
Pavement strength: 60,000 kg (132,277 lb) 1, 93,000 kg (205,030 lb) 2, 160,000 kg (352,740 lb) 3
Landing category: ICAO CAT I
Lighting:
     R/W   edge and end
     App   R/W 13 Calvert centreline with crossbars. VASIS 13
     Thr   green

Aids: VOR, NDB, L, ILS CAT I 13
Twr frequency: 118.3   App frequency: 119.5
Terminal: No information available
Scheduled services 1978: Aerolineas Argentinas, Austral, LADE and Pluna

Traffic:	1970	1975	1976	1977
Passengers (total)	1,538,423	3,004,579	2,967,773	3,420,664
Cargo (tonnes)	10,776	19,262	22,233	22,825
Aircraft movements	93,125	100,375	98,993	84,560
Transport movements	44,264	50,002	53,766	58,329

Aeroparque de la Ciudad de Buenos Aires was also built under the Argentine Government five-year plan for airports and was intended to give the City of Buenos Aires extremely convenient access to air transport, being sited near the Palermo gardens on the bank of the Rio de la Plata (River Plate) and only a few minutes' drive from the city centre. It was also situated close to the then busy marine air terminal from which some domestic and cross-river flying-boat services operated.

Domestic services are believed to have begun operating from the new airport on 8 January, 1947, and it was planned that there would be three or four runways. Work on at least the second and third runways was begun but it is not known whether these were completed. Today the airport has a single asphalt runway.

Córdoba   Aeropuerto Córdoba

ICAO: SACO   IATA: COR

31° 18' 46" S   64° 12' 14" W   Elevation: 1,604 ft (489 m)
Longest runway: 18/36   3,200 m (10,499 ft)   RT
Aids: VOR/DME, NDB, L, ILS 18

	1970	1975	1976	1977
Passengers	282,091	438,300	365,029	565,004
Transport movements	8,423	10,364	10,935	10,976

Scheduled services 1978: Aero Chaco, Aerolineas Argentinas and Austral

Mendoza   Aeropuerto El Plumerillo

ICAO: SAME   IATA: MDZ

32° 50' 00" S   68° 47' 44" W   Elevation: 2,312 ft (705 m)
Runway: 17/35   3,013 m (9,885 ft)   ART
Aids: VOR/DME, NDB

	1970	1975	1976
Passengers	140,512	244,446	269,912
Transport movements	5,187	4,312	4,238

Scheduled services 1978: Aerolineas Argentinas, Austral and LAN-Chile

San Carlos de Bariloche   Aeropuerto San Carlos de Bariloche

ICAO: SAZS   IATA: BRC

41° 09′ 09″ S   71° 09′ 43″ W   Elevation: 2,772 ft (845 m)
Runway: 10/28   2,348 m (7,703 ft)   RT
Aids: VOR, NDB, L

	1970	1975	1976	1977
Passengers	84,843	294,074	314,590	314,558
Transport movements	2,763	5,198	5,516	5,399

Scheduled services 1978: Aerolineas Argentinas, Austral, Cruzeiro, LADE and LAN-Chile

Australia

Airport Lighting

Australia operates a multi-stage intensity approach and runway lighting system. Precision approach runway lighting has five or six stages of intensity; and other multi-stage systems, three stages.

The initial intensities are normally selected by the tower controller in accordance with the table for approach and runway lighting, and variations of these intensities are made in accordance with a pilot's requests—normally an initial high intensity with lower intensities as the aircraft nears the runway.

Visibility	Stages—	Day	Night
Not more than 2,000 m		6	4
More than 2,000 m but not more than 4,000 m		5	3
More than 4,000 m but not more than 6 km		4	2
More than 6 km		—	1

Threshold lights—Green and located in a straight line at right angles to the runway centreline and comprise two groups of two lights on either side of the runway with a line of lights across the runway between the two groups. When the threshold is displaced down the runway the threshold lights consist of only two groups—one on each side of the runway.
Fixed distance lights—On selected runways a line of 11 white lights is installed on each side of the runway—1.2 m outside the runway edge lights—adjacent to and over the length of the fixed distance markings.
Stopway lights—Side and end red lights when stopway is longer than 180 m and the associated runway less than 1,500 m.
Taxiway lights—Blue edge lights or green centreline. Where there is an extensive system of taxiways, the lights at the entrance from the runway or apron are flashing lights of the same colour as the taxiway lights.
Approach lights—Throughout Australia the Calvert centreline and crossbar system is used with coded white centreline and normally five crossbars.

The high intensity T-VASIS is the standard installation for day and night use.

7

Adelaide, South Australia   Adelaide Airport

34° 56′ 48″ S   138° 31′ 54″ E   3.25 nm (6 km) W of city
ICAO: AAAD   IATA code: ADL   Time zone: GMT plus 9½
Authority: Department of Transport
Area: 762 hectares (1,883 acres)
Elevation: 12 ft (4 m)   Ref temp: 24.4 deg C
Runways: 05/23   2,438 × 45 m (8,000 × 148 ft) asphalt
　　　　 12/30   1,652 × 45 m (5,420 × 148 ft) asphalt
Pavement strength: LCN 90
Landing category: ICAO CAT I
Lighting:
　R/W   05/23 and 12/30   edge and end
　App   R/W 23   Calvert LIH white precision approach.
　　　　 T-VASIS 05, 12/30
　Thr   green
　Txy   green centreline, blue edge
Aids: VOR/DME, NDB, ILS CAT I 23
Twr frequency: 120.5   App frequency: 118.1/124.2/255.4
Terminal: Domestic terminal with ground-floor finger development with
　four departure-gate/arrival channels

Adelaide Airport. Threshold 05 is in the bottom left corner and the terminal area is
at the top between the 12 and 23 thresholds.

8

Adelaide Airport in December 1964. The Vickers Vimy G-EAOU can be seen in its memorial hall. (*John Stroud*)

Scheduled services 1978: Ansett Airlines of Australia, Ansett Airlines of South Australia, Murray Valley Airlines, Opal Air Pty, PEGAS Airlines, TAA and Williams Airlines
Main base: Ansett Airlines of South Australia, Opal Air and PEGAS

Traffic:	1970	1975	1976
Passengers (total)	1,023,171	1,506,317	1,538,332
Cargo (tonnes)	15,976	16,640	18,061
Transport movements	21,818	25,020	24,071

Adelaide Airport, beside the Gulf of St Vincent, was constructed on an area of clay swamp and sandhills and opened in 1955.

A memorial hall near the terminal building houses the Vickers Vimy G-EAOU in which Ross Smith, Keith Smith, J.M.Bennett and W.H.Shiers made the first flight from the United Kingdom (or anywhere else) to Australia in November–December 1919.

Brisbane, Queensland   Brisbane Eagle Farm Airport

27° 25′ 24″ S   153° 05′ 13″ E   3.25 nm (6 km) NE of city
ICAO: ABBN   IATA code: BNE   Time zone: GMT plus 10
Authority: Department of Transport
Area: 1,865 hectares (4,608 acres)
Elevation: 7 ft (2 m)   Ref temp: 26.7 deg C
Runways: 04/22   2,365 × 60 m   (7,760 × 197 ft) asphalt
              13/31   1,539 × 30 m* (5,049 × 98 ft)   sealed
              *R/W 13/31 has 7 m (23 ft) sealed shoulders
Pavement strength: 04/22 LCN 100,   13/31 LCN 11
Landing category: ICAO CAT I

9

Brisbane Eagle Farm Airport in November 1974.

Lighting:

R/W   04/22 and 13/31   edge

App   R/W 22   Calvert LIH white precision approach.

            T-VASIS 04/22

Thr   green

Txy   green centreline, blue edge

Aids: VOR/DME, NDB, ILS CAT I 22

Twr frequency: 120.5/335.6   App frequency: 124.7/269.3

Terminals: Three separate terminal complexes—Ansett single-level with two departure/arrival channels; TAA single-level with five departure gate lounges and one arrival gate; international single-level with three gate lounges

Scheduled services 1978: 17 airlines

Traffic:	1970	1975	1976	1977
Passengers (total)	1,330,119	2,441,745	2,342,726	2,421,109*
Cargo (tonnes)	22,011	28,851	26,876	25,856
Aircraft movements	60,455	82,396	80,011	84,184
Transport movements	33,851	47,636	46,589	37,769

* Excludes transit passengers

Brisbane Airport, then known as Eagle Farm, was first used in the 1920s, and it was there that, on 9 June, 1928, Charles Kingsford Smith and his crew landed in the Fokker F.VII-3m *Southern Cross* to complete the first air crossing of the Pacific, from Oakland, California, via Hawaii and Fiji. The *Southern Cross* is now preserved at Brisbane Airport in a special memorial hall.

Eagle Farm is on swampy ground but during the 1939–45 war the United States Air Force constructed three paved runways and in 1946 the aerodrome was taken over as the Brisbane Airport, as successor to Archerfield Aerodrome. With the introduction of DC-6s the runways rapidly deteriorated and major reconstruction became necessary. Using layers of crushed coral and rock as a foundation, a new 04/22 runway was built 7 ft (2 m) above the original runway. New taxiways were constructed as well as dykes and floodgates to protect the airport from flooding.

Wartime igloo-type hangars served for many years as passenger terminals, but Ansett's was extensively remodelled and expanded in 1971, and TAA's new terminal was completed in 1972. The new international terminal came into operation in December 1975. Major redevelopment of Brisbane Airport was planned to begin early in 1980.

Cairns, Queensland   Cairns Airport

ICAO: ATCS   IATA: CNS

16° 53′ 14″ S   145° 45′ 26″ E   Elevation 6 ft (2m)
Runway: 15/33   2,011 m (6,600 ft)   ART, T-VASI 15/33
Aids: VOR/DME, NDB, L, ILS CAT I 15

	1970	1975	1976	1977
Passengers	146,576	281,044	298,529	305,539
Aircraft movements	6,199	8,631	7,241	8,175

Scheduled services 1978: Ansett Airlines of Australia, Bush Pilots Airways and TAA
Main base: BPA. Base for Royal Flying Doctor Service and the Cairns aerial ambulance

Canberra, Australian Capital Territory   Canberra Airport

ICAO: ASCB   IATA: CBR

35° 18′ 31″ S   149° 11′ 38″ E   Elevation: 1,873 ft (571 m)
Longest runway: 17/35   2,683 m (8,802 ft)   ART, T-VASI 17
Aids: VOR/DME, NDB, L, ILS CAT I 35

	1970	1975	1976
Passengers	577,918	981,888	871,338
Aircraft movements	18,227	19,857	16,898

Scheduled services 1978: Ansett Airlines of Australia, Hazelton Air Services, Kendell Airlines, Masling Commuter Services, Southbank Aviation and TAA

Coolangatta, Queensland   Coolangatta Airport

ICAO: ABCG   IATA: OOL

28° 09′ 58″ S   153° 30′ 13″ E   Elevation: 18 ft (5 m)
Longest runway: 14/32   2,042 m (6,700 ft)   ART, T-VASI 14/32
Aids: VOR/DME, NDB

Coolangatta Airport on Queensland's Pacific coast in February 1975, seen from 6,000 ft (1,829 m). The main 14/32 runway runs from right to left, the 609 m (1,998 ft) 18/36 is just left of centre and the terminal area near the base of the photograph. (*Department of Transport*)

	1970	1975	1976
Passengers	152,356	321,799	308,503
Aircraft movements	3,860	6,001	5,512

Scheduled services 1978: Ansett Airlines of Australia, East-West Airlines, New England Airways, North Coast Airlines, TAA and Tricon International Airlines

The airport is located on the borders of Queensland and NSW

Darwin, Northern Territory   Darwin Airport

ICAO: ADDN   IATA: DRW

12° 25' 01" S   130° 52' 28" E   Elevation: 94 ft (29 m)
Longest runway: 11/29   3,352 m (10,997 ft)   ART, T-VASI 11/29
Aids: VORTAC, NDB, VDF, GCA, ILS CAT I 29

	1970	1975	1976	1977
Passengers	126,646	252,358	220,649	235,308
Aircraft movements	7,940	8,716	6,858	7,905

Scheduled services 1978: Ansett Airlines of Australia, Connair, Mac.Robertson Miller Airline Services, Merpati Nusantara Airlines, Qantas and TAA

Hobart, Tasmania   Hobart Airport

ICAO: ALHB   IATA: HBA

42° 50′ 17″ S   147° 30′ 35″ E   Elevation: 8 ft (2 m)
Runway: 12/30   1,981 m (6,500 ft)   ART, T-VASI 30
Aids: DME, NDB, VAR, ILS CAT I 12

	1970	1975	1976
Passengers	209,368	378,489	399,172
Aircraft movements	6,301	7,848	7,543

Scheduled services 1978: Air Tasmania, Ansett Airlines of Australia,
    Business Jets Pty, Geelong Air Travel and TAA
Main base: Air Tasmania

Launceston, Tasmania   Launceston Airport

ICAO: ALLT   IATA: LST

41° 32′ 49″ S   147° 12′ 49″ E   Elevation: 546 ft (166 m)
Runway: 14/32   1,981 m (6,500 ft)   ART, T-VASI 14
Aids: VOR/DME, NDB, L, ILS CAT I 32

	1970	1975	1976
Passengers	186,312	296,065	299,136
Aircraft movements	10,463	10,358	9,532

Scheduled services 1978: Air Tasmania, Ansett Airlines of Australia,
    Executive Airlines (Australia) and TAA
Launceston Airport was formerly known as Western Junction

Mackay, Queensland   Mackay Airport

ICAO: ATMK   IATA: MKY

21° 10′ 23″ S   149° 10′ 43″ E   Elevation: 14 ft (4 m)
Longest runway: 14/32   1,981 m (6,500 ft)   RT, T-VASI 14/32
Aids: VOR/DME, NDB

	1970	1975	1976
Passengers	105,638	246,832	250,805
Aircraft movements	7,225	10,309	10,749

Scheduled services 1978: Ansett Airlines of Australia, Bush Pilots Airways
    and TAA

Melbourne, Victoria   Melbourne Airport (Tullamarine)

37° 40′ 30″ S   144° 50′ 32″ E   10.26 nm (19 km) NW of city centre
ICAO: AMML   IATA code: MEL   Time zone: GMT plus 11
Authority: Department of Transport
Area: 2,120 hectares (5,238 acres)
Elevation: 392 ft (119 m)   Ref temp: 21.7 deg C

Runways: 09/27   2,286 × 45 m   (7,500 × 148 ft) asphalt
          16/34   3,657 × 45 m (11,998 × 148 ft) asphalt, concrete ends
Pavement strength: LCN 165
Landing category: ICAO CAT I
Lighting:
    R/W   09/27 and 16/34   edge and end. Centreline and TDZ 16
            and 27
    App   R/W 16 and 27   Calvert LIH white precision approach.
            T-VASIS 09 and 34
    Thr   green
    Txy   green centreline, blue edge
Aids: VOR/DME, NDB, ILS CAT I 16 and 27
Twr frequency: 120.5/322.4   App frequency: 124.7/269.3
Terminals: Combined domestic/international in three sections with three
    traffic fingers—Ansett Airlines of Australia (south), two-level with 10
    gates and five aerobridges; TAA (east), two-level with 10 gates and five
    aerobridges; international (centre), three-level with five gates and four
    aerobridges. Ansett, Qantas and TAA cargo terminals.
Scheduled services 1978: 18 airlines
Main base: Ansett Airlines of Australia and TAA

Traffic:	1970	1975	1976	1977	1978
Passengers (total)	2,799,433*	4,688,964	4,795,708	5,025,047	5,388,145
Cargo (tonnes)	56,358*	67,552	75,448	79,013	98,879
Aircraft movements	63,101†	95,994	92,697	97,709	98,389
Transport movements	59,050†	81,305	78,896	74,746	——

* 1970 figures cover Melbourne (Tullamarine) and Essendon
† Figures for Essendon Airport

Melbourne Airport (Tullamarine). The Ansett (south) pier is in the centre of the
picture with, to the left, the international and TAA (east) piers. Five Boeing 747s
and a DC-10 are visible. (*Department of Transport*)

14

Melbourne Airport (Tullamarine) in 1972. The main 16/34 runway runs across the photograph and threshold 09 is at bottom left.

For many years Melbourne was served by Essendon Airport but by the late 1950s it was realized that it could not be developed to meet the city's future air transport needs—the Comet was the only jet transport allowed to use the airport and the Lockheed Electra was the heaviest aircraft permitted. A site, on grazing land at Tullamarine, was selected for a new airport and in May 1959 Government approval was given to the purchase of 2,120 hectares (5,238 acres) for airport development.

The new airport was originally planned to take aircraft of up to 500,000 lb (226,796 kg) with twin bogie undercarriages, with its runways allowing Boeing 707s to fly nonstop to Darwin, Fiji and Perth and the Qantas 707-138Bs to fly nonstop to Manila and Singapore. Later it was decided to extend runway 16/34 from its original 2,591 m (8,500 ft) to 3,657 m (11,998 ft) to enable Boeing 747s to fly nonstop to Honolulu.

There is adequate space to extend runway 09/27 to the west and, if required, a set of runways can be constructed on the southern part of the airport to give two sets of parallel runways although this could involve extensive taxi-ing.

Melbourne-Tullamarine was officially opened for international operations on 1 July, 1970, and domestic operations were transferred from Essendon in June 1971. Essendon now handles cargo, charters and general aviation.

15

Perth, Western Australia   Perth Airport

ICAO: APPH   IATA: PER

31° 56′ 29″ S   115° 57′ 55″ E   Elevation: 53 ft (16 m)
Longest runway: 02/20   3,144 m (10,315 ft)   ART, T-VASI 02/20 and 06
Aids: VOR/DME, NDB, L, ILS CAT I 24

	1970	1975	1976	1977
Passengers	536,704	846,762	874,990	955,645
Aircraft movements	13,362	15,492	10,854	14,834

Scheduled services 1978: 13 airlines
Main base: Mac.Robertson Miller Airline Services (MMA)

Sydney, New South Wales   Sydney (Kingsford Smith) Airport

33° 56′ 28″ S   151° 10′ 21″ E   4.32 nm (8 km) S of city
ICAO: ASSY   IATA code: SYD   Time zone: GMT plus 11
Authority: Department of Transport
Area: 635 hectares (1,569 acres)
Elevation: 6 ft (2 m)   Ref temp: 23.3 deg C
Runways: 07/25   2,530 × 45 m   (8,300 × 148 ft) asphalt
         16/34   3,962 × 45 m (13,000 × 148 ft) asphalt
Pavement strength: 07/25 LCN 100,   16/34 LCN 70
Landing category: ICAO CAT I
Lighting:
    R/W   07 white LIH edge, and end; 16 white LIH edge and centreline, end and TDZ; 25 and 34 white LIM edge, and end
    App   07 Calvert LIH white; 16 Calvert LIH white with barrettes on inner 305 m (1,000 ft). T-VASIS 16/34 and 25
    Thr   green
    Txy   green centreline, blue edge
Aids: VOR/DME, NDB, ILS CAT I 07 and 16/34
Twr frequency: 120.5/279.5   App frequency: 119.4/307.8
Terminals: Three separate terminal complexes—TAA curved lineal design with seven departure gates/arrival channels each with aerobridge; Ansett finger complex with six departure gates/arrival channels with five aerobridges; international three-level finger complex with 11 arrival gates and seven aerobridges and 11 departure gates with access to arrival aerobridges
Scheduled services 1978: 29 airlines
Main base: Ansett Airlines of New South Wales and Qantas

Traffic:	1970	1975	1976	1977	1978
Passengers (total)	4,358,194	6,589,397	6,548,856	6,778,809*	7,474,107
Cargo (tonnes)	76,323	96,886	101,607	104,257	129,404
Aircraft movements	125,480	156,801	156,136	161,807	169,005
Transport movements	97,358	126,658	121,285	105,459	127,746

*Excludes transit passengers

16

Sydney (Kingsford Smith) Airport seen from 18,000 ft in April 1975. The 16/34 extension into Botany Bay is clearly seen.

Sydney's Kingsford Smith Airport began as a 160 acre (65 hectare) grass aerodrome in the suburb of Mascot from which it took its original name. It served the pioneer Australian airlines and was gradually expanded until it was a three-runway airport sited within a loop of the Cooks River at the point where it enters Botany Bay.

To meet the needs of postwar air traffic, reconstruction began in 1946 and this involved diverting the river into a new course 1¼ miles (2 km) long and 500 ft (152 m) wide. The old river course was filled with more than 6,000,000 cubic yards of earth, sand and rock, and two new runways were constructed, 07/25 of 7,900 ft (2,408 m) and 16/34 of 5,500 ft (1,676 m). A new terminal and hangar blocks were erected and the airport equipped with ILS and GCA.

Runway 07/25 was extended to 8,300 ft (2,530 m) and was the main runway when jet aircraft were introduced, but the decision was taken to extend runway 16/34 to 9,100 ft (2,774 m) by reclaiming land from Botany Bay and sinking the six-lane General Holmes Drive motorway to pass beneath the runway. Subsequently the runway was further extended to 13,000 ft (3,962 m).

As is customary in Australia, there were separate terminals for the two major domestic airlines and an international terminal. These were all sited in the northeast part of the airport close to the Qantas maintenance base.

17

Sydney (Kingsford Smith) Airport, showing the international terminal, with runway 16/34 on the left and 07/25 running from left to right. The Cooks River is on the right, and General Holmes Drive can be seen near the shore of Botany Bay at the top of the picture. (*Department of Transport*)

But in May 1970 a completely new international terminal came into operation in the northwest area of the airport—it was officially opened in 1971. In 1974 TAA's new terminal was officially opened and in 1977 Ansett's terminal was being remodelled and extended. Future plans call for the construction of new domestic terminals flanking the international terminal.

*   *   *

From July 1938 Australia's international services were operated by flying-boats, these took-off from Sydney Harbour and used the terminal at Rose Bay, as did Tasman Empire Airways' trans-Tasman flying-boat services. Rose Bay remained in operation until the withdrawal of Ansett's Sydney—Lord Howe Island flying-boat services in 1974.

Townsville, Queensland   Townsville Airport

ICAO: ATTL   IATA: TSV

19° 15′ 10″ S   146°45′ 56″ E   Elevation: 11 ft (3 m)
Longest runway: 01/19   2,438 m (8,000 ft)   RT, T-VASI 01/19
Aids: VORTAC, DME, NDB, GCA

	1970	1975	1976
Passengers	200,886	332,360	330,409
Aircraft movements	10,203	13,290	12,948

Scheduled services 1978: Ansett Airlines of Australia, Bush Pilots Airways and TAA

Austria (Österreich)

Salzburg   Flughafen Salzburg

ICAO: LOWS   IATA: SZG
47° 47′ 42″ N   13° 00′ 14″ E   Elevation: 1,410 ft (430 m)
Runway: 16/34   2,200 m (7,218 ft)   ART
Aids: VOR/DME, NDB, VDF, ILS 16

	1970	1975	1976
Passengers	142,117	243,936	255,669

Scheduled services 1978: Austrian Airlines and Swissair.
The runway is to be extended to 2,500 m (8,202 ft)

Vienna (Wien)   Flughafen Wien - Schwechat

48° 06′ 39″ N   16° 34′ 15″ E   9 nm (16.6 km) SE of city
ICAO: LOWW   IATA code: VIE   Time zone: GMT plus 1
Authority: Flughafen Wien Betriebsgesellschaft mbH (Vienna Airport
    Authority)
Area: 960 hectares (2,375 acres)
Elevation: 600 ft (183 m)   Ref temp: 25.1 deg C
Runways: 12/30   3,000 × 45 m (9,842 × 148 ft) bitumen, grooved
         16/34   3,600 × 45 m (11,811 × 148 ft) bitumen
Pavement strength: R/W 12/30 auw 63,000 kg (138,891 lb) 1, 82,000 kg
    (180,779 lb) 2, 200,000 kg (440,924 lb) 3; R/W 16/34 LCN 100
Landing category: ICAO CAT II
Lighting:
    R/W   12/30   LIH white edge with last 600 m (1,968 ft) yellow,
    and LIL white edge. LIH red end lights
           16/34   LIH and LIL white edge, and LIH white
    centreline with last 300 m (984 ft) red and previous 600 m
    (1,968 ft) red/white. TDZ 16

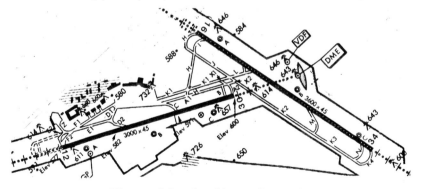

Vienna - Schwechat Airport. (*Swissair*)

19

App   R/W 12   Calvert LIH white precision approach with three crossbars.

R/W 30   CAT I LIH white bar centreline with crossbar and sequenced flashers.

R/W 16/34   LIH white bar centreline with crossbar and sequenced flashers. Red barrette supplementary lights on inner 300 m (984 ft) R/W 16.

T-VASIS 16/34

Thr   green

Txy   blue edge

Aids: VOR/DME, NDB, VDF, L, PAR, SRE, RVR, ILS CAT II 16, ILS CAT I 12/30 and 34

Twr frequency: 118.1   App frequency: 119.4

Terminal: Two-level passenger terminal and 21 aircraft stands. Separate cargo building

Scheduled services 1978: 33 airlines

Main base: Austrian Airlines

Traffic:	1970	1975	1976	1977	1978
Passengers (total)	1,469,130	2,185,716	2,445,902	2,578,620	2,777,532
Cargo (tonnes)	22,062	28,602	28,551	30,276	30,698
Aircraft movements	53,351	62,733	66,353	72,206	79,709
Transport movements	34,886	43,487	46,331	47,138	49,231

In 1976 DC-9s accounted for 60.35 per cent of all transport movements.

In 1938 Heinkel, the German aircraft manufacturer, began construction of a works aerodrome on the site now occupied by Vienna Airport. During the war the facilities suffered considerable damage but the British occupation forces partly restored the aerodrome to serve as the Vienna airport as successor to the· prewar Aspern which had been the customs airport since the early 1920s. BEA operated the first postwar services to and from Vienna in 1946.

Vienna Airport Authority took over administration and operation on 1 January, 1954, and immediately began restoration. In 1954–55 the runway was extended from 1,500 m (4,921 ft) to 2,000 m (6,562 ft) and

Vienna Airport terminal area with runway 12/30 on the right and 16/34 under construction in the distance. (*Flughafen Wien*)

20

taxiways were constructed. Following preparation of a master plan, construction of a concrete and glass terminal was begun in 1956 and the runway was further extended to 3,000 m (9,842 ft).

The terminal was opened on 17 June, 1960. It was built as a two-level complex for separated arrivals and departures but traffic at that time did not warrant two-level use. The hangar which had previously served as the terminal was restored to its normal function.

Further terminal improvements took place and in 1970 the terminal was extended and two-level operation introduced.

A second runway, 16/34, was approved by the Austrian Government in January 1973 and was commissioned, for CAT II operations, in autumn 1977. A high-speed rail link with Vienna has been provided, and by 1980 a terminal satellite is to be constructed with underground connection to the existing terminal. A second terminal (Terminal East) with further satellites is planned for some time after 1985.

Bahamas

Freeport, Grand Bahama Island   Freeport International Airport

	ICAO: MYGF	IATA: FPO	
26° 33′ 24″ N	78° 41′ 58″ W		Elevation: 8 ft (2 m)
Runway: 06/24	3,353 m (11,000 ft)	RT	VASI 06/24

Aids: VOR/DME, NDB, ILS CAT I 06

	1970	1976	1977
Passengers	742,640	711,258*	687,127*
Aircraft movements	86,755	—	44,289
Transport movements	—	16,955	13,758

* Excluding transit

Scheduled services 1978: Air Canada, Bahamasair, British Airways, Delta Air Lines, Eastern Air Lines and Mackey International Airlines

Nassau, New Providence Island   Nassau International Airport

25° 02′ 51″ N   77° 27′ 52″ W   7.5 nm (14 km) WSW of city
ICAO: MYNN   IATA code: NAS   Time zone: GMT −4
Authority: Ministry of Transport
Elevation: 7 ft (2 m)   Ref temp: 31.7 deg C
Runways: 05/23   1,562 × 46 m   (5,126 × 150 ft) asphalt*†
            09/27   2,580 × 46 m   (8,463 × 150 ft) asphalt**†
            14/32   3,353 × 46 m   (11,000 × 150 ft) asphalt†

*Last 114 m (375 ft) of 05 and first 114 m (375 ft) of 23 not available at night
**Last 56 m (185 ft) of 09 not available at night and first 56 m (185 ft) of 27 not available at night or for daytime landings
†Runways 09, 23 and 27 have 61 m (200 ft) stopways of graded coral, 05 has a similar stopway of 152 m (500 ft) and 14/32 has 61 m (200 ft) paved stopways

Pavement strength: Boeing 747s accepted
Landing category: No ILS
Lighting:
R/W   LIL white edge
App   R/W 05 and 09 LIL white centreline, 14 LIL white centreline with one crossbar, 23 and 32 LIH white centreline. VASIS 09/27 and 14/32
Thr   green threshold or displaced threshold
Txy   blue edge some taxiways
Aids: VOR/DME, NDB
Twr frequency: 119.5   App frequency: 121.0
Terminal: Passenger terminal with three piers and 14 aircraft stands. Separate cargo apron
Scheduled services 1978: 10 airlines
Main base: Bahamasair and International Air Bahama

Traffic: It has not proved possible to obtain traffic figures but total passengers are known to exceed 1 mn annually. In 1970 there were 85,516 aircraft movements and 42,287 transport movements.

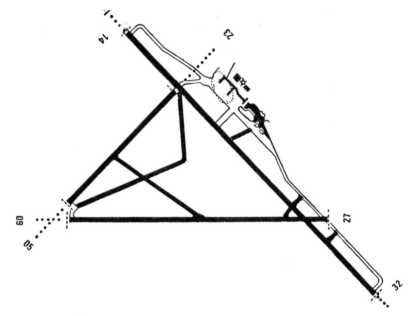

Nassau International Airport. (*British Airways Aerad*)

On 2 January, 1929, Pan American Airways inaugurated the first air service to Nassau when one of its Sikorsky S-38 amphibians flew from Miami with one passenger and 80 lb (36 kg) of mail, and in 1937 Bahamas Airways began inter-island flying-boat services. In early 1939 the United Kingdom Government began construction of an airport 1¾ miles (2.8 km) south of Nassau but in December 1939 the uncompleted airport was sold to

22

Sir Henry Oakes, co-founder of Bahamas Airways, on the understanding that he would complete the project and maintain it solely for flying.

Two runways were completed in January 1940 and from April Pan American Airways operated to and from Nassau with DC-3s in place of flying-boats.

Largescale development of the airport took place during the Second World War, and in June 1946, as Oakes Field, the aerodrome passed to the Bahamas Government and work began to convert it to a civil airport. Three runways were constructed; by 1949 09/27 was 6,000 ft (1,829 m) long and 03/21 and 12/30 were 5,000 ft (1,524 m) and all were 150 ft (46 m) wide.

During the war Windsor Field, a Royal Air Force training aerodrome, was prepared just west of Lake Killarney and about 5 nm (9.25 km) west of Oakes Field, and in the early 1960s this became the Nassau airport, with three runways in the standard RAF triangular pattern. In 1969 runway 14/32 was lengthened from 7,100 ft (2,164 m) to its present 11,000 ft (3,353 m). The terminal building has also been expanded, with three piers and 14 aircraft stands.

In 1977–78 plans were in hand to install CAT II ILS on R/W 14 and improve the approach lighting to CAT II standard. Radar is to be installed and centreline lighting on the taxiways to runways 05 and 09.

Nassau International Airport in 1969, after the extension of runway 14/32 to 11,000 ft (3,353 m). (*Bahama Islands Tourist Office, courtesy Airports International*)

23

Bahrain International Airport with a British Airways Concorde and two Gulf Air BAC One-Elevens on the apron. (*British Aerospace*)

State of Bahrain

Bahrain   Bahrain International Airport

26° 16′ 11″ N   50° 38′ 03″ E   3.45 nm (6.4 km) N of capital
ICAO: OBBI   IATA code: BAH   Time zone: GMT plus 3
Authority: Civil Aviation Directorate, Bahrain Government
Elevation: 6 ft (2 m)   Ref temp: 35 deg C
Runway: 12/30   3,962 × 61 m (13,000 × 200 ft) concrete with asphalt
        surface and 304 m (997 ft) concrete ends
Pavement strength: LCN 100
Landing category: ICAO CAT I
Lighting:
    R/W   LIH and LIL white edge
    App   R/W 12   426 m (1,398 ft) white and red centreline with
        LIH white and red crossbar 305 m (1,000 ft) before
        threshold.
        R/W 30   915 m (3,002 ft) centreline with single white and
        red lights over inner 305 m (1,000 ft), double white lights
        over centre 305 m and triple white over outer 305 m. Five
        white crossbars with additional red lights 305 m before
        threshold. Red runway edge lights over 305 m (1,000 ft) from
        end to landing threshold. VASIS 12/30

Thr	green with green wing bars
Txy	green centreline and red stop bars. Two runway—taxiway links have twin coloured centreline lights, showing green leading off runway and red leading to runway. Blue edge lights on international apron

Aids: VOR/DME, NDB, L, ILS CAT I 30

Twr frequency: 118.5   App frequency: 119.5

Terminals: Passenger terminal and apron with five gates, 17 aircraft stands and four aerobridges. Nose-in parking and push-back mandatory. Planned extension to terminal with fifth aerobridge. Cargo terminal and apron with five aircraft bays and separate domestic apron

Scheduled services 1978: 27 airlines

Main base: Gulf Air

Traffic:	1970	1975	1976	1977
Passengers (total)	329,701	1,055,336	1,626,461	1,887,673
Cargo (tonnes)	4,471	7,769	16,774	18,986
Transport movements	16,098	28,918	35,714	19,863

Bahrain has occupied an important position on the world's air routes since October 1932 when Imperial Airways switched the routing of its United Kingdom–India services from the Persian to the Arabian side of the Gulf. An aerodrome was prepared on Muharraq Island which is connected to the main island by a causeway.

During the war a PSP runway of nearly 7,000 ft (2,134 m) was laid and there was a 18/36 sand runway of 2,900 ft (884 m). The PSP runway was replaced by a 7,500 ft (2,286 m) 12/30 tarmac runway, and a new terminal area was built with the apron occupying part of the area previously covered by the PSP runway.

A new terminal was opened in December 1962 and the rebuilt runway extended to 13,000 ft (3,962 m). The present terminal was brought into partial operation in 1971 and full operation in 1972. A new cargo terminal is to be built. By 1978 primary and secondary radar had been ordered.

On 21 January, 1976, Bahrain became the first airport to receive a British supersonic service, when British Airways Concorde G-BOAA arrived on the inaugural flight from London.

People's Republic of Bangladesh

Dacca	Tejgaon Airport	ICAO: VGDC	IATA: DAC

23° 46′ 10″ N	90° 23′ 20″ E	Elevation: 25 ft (8 m)	
Runway: 17/35	2,743 m (9,000 ft)	RT	VASI 17/35

Aids: VOR, NDB, L, ILS CAT I 17

	1970	1975	1976	1977
Passengers	672,779	349,391	476,765	501,625*
Transport movements	18,641	38,288	38,194	17,453

* Excludes transit passengers

Scheduled services 1978: Aeroflot, Air-India, Bangladesh Biman, British
Airways, Indian Airlines, PIA and Thai Airways
Main base: Bangladesh Biman

New Dacca International Airport, Kurmitola, with 3,048 m (10,000 ft)
runway, is under construction 3 nm (5.5 km) NE of Tejgaon

Barbados

Bridgetown　　　Grantley Adams International Airport

13° 04′ 24″ N　　　59° 29′ 18″ W　　　8.5 nm (15.74 km) E of city
ICAO: MKPB　　　IATA code: BGI　　　Time zone: GMT −4
Authority: Department of Civil Aviation
Elevation: 170 ft (52 m)　　　　　　　　Ref temp: 28.3 deg C
Runway: 09/27　　　3,353 × 46 m (11,000 × 150 ft) asphalt
Pavement strength: LCN 100
Landing category: ICAO CAT I
Lighting:
　　R/W　　LIH white edge
　　App　　R/W 09　　Variable intensity 3,000 ft (914 m) red
　　　　　　centreline with one crossbar 1,000 ft (305 m) from threshold,
　　　　　　and T-VASIS
　　　　　　R/W 27　　VASIS
　　Thr　　LIL green
　　Txy　　blue edge, green centreline on main taxiways
Aids: VOR/DME, NDB, SRE, ILS CAT I 09
Twr frequency: 118.7/121.5　　　　　　App frequency: 119.7
Terminal: Passenger terminal north of runway with 13 aircraft stands,
　　three capable of taking wide-bodied aircraft
Scheduled services 1978: 11 airlines
Main base: Caribbean Airways

Traffic:	1970	1975	1976	1977
Passengers (total)	681,649	907,381	940,660	1,059,960
Cargo (tonnes)	5,490	7,658	9,025	10,999
Aircraft movements	26,099	27,766	26,874	26,934
Transport movements	11,831	20,011	20,660	22,426

Grantley Adams International Airport is situated on the south coast
of the island, the 27 runway threshold being only a few metres from the
shore. It was originally a grass aerodrome providing a maximum distance
of 3,000 ft (914 m) from east to west and northeast to southwest, with runs
of 2,700 ft (823 m) from north to south and 2,400 ft (732 m) from northwest
to southeast.

Opened on 19 October, 1938, as Seawell Airport and used from that
day by KLM, and later named Seawell International, the present name
was adopted in June 1976. The first use of the airport by British West
Indian Airways (BWIA) was on 27 November, 1940, when it inaugurated a

daily Trinidad–Barbados service with the Lockheed Lodestar VP-TAE.

The airport was initially under the managing authority of the Barbados Harbour and Shipping Master, with BWIA in temporary control of landings. By 1947 there was a 5,200 ft (1,585 m) paved 09/27 runway, a 220 by 100 ft (67 by 30 m) apron to the north of the runway, and a terminal building.

A new terminal was opened in 1968, the runway has been extended on a number of occasions, and further development was undertaken in the mid-1970s with the aid of a $10 mn Canadian loan. Among these last developments was an increase in apron area and two additional links between the runway and the parallel taxiway which connects the terminal area with the 09 threshold.

Belgium (Belgique/België)

Brussels (Bruxelles/Brussel)　　　Brussels National Airport
　　(Aéroport Bruxelles - National/Luchthaven Brussel - Nationaal)

50° 54′ 08″ N　　　04° 29′ 09″ E　　　6.5 nm (12 km) NE of city
ICAO: EBBR　　　IATA code: BRU　　　Time zone: GMT plus 1
Authority: Régie des Voies Aériennes
Area: 1,100 hectares (2,718 acres)
Elevation: 180 ft (55 m)　　　　　　　　　Ref temp: 23.8 deg C
Runways:　02/20　　　2,819 × 50 m　(9,249 × 164 ft) concrete
　　　　　07L/25R　　3,638 × 45 m　(11,936 × 148 ft) concrete
　　　　　07R/25L　　3,211 × 45 m　(10,535 × 148 ft) concrete
　　　　　There is a 1,900 × 100 m (6,233 × 328 ft) grass crash landing strip
　　　　　alongside 07L/25R
Pavement strength: 02/20 and 07L/25R　　all up weight 90 tonnes
　　(198,416 lb) 1, 120 tonnes (264,555 lb) 2, 200 tonnes (440,924 lb) 3, 380
　　tonnes (837,756 lb) 4.　　07R/25L 70 tonnes (154,324 lb) 1, 90 tonnes
　　(198,416 lb) 2, 160 tonnes (352,740 lb) 3, 325 tonnes (716,502 lb) 4
Landing category: ICAO CAT II
Lighting:
　　R/W　　02/20 and 07L/25R　　LIH distance coded edge, and red
　　　　　　end lights.
　　　　　　07R/25L　　LIH white centreline, LIH white edge, and red
　　　　　　end lights. LIH white TDZ 25L
　　App　　R/W 07L, 07R and 20 simple sodium centreline with two
　　　　　　crossbars; 25R simple LIH centreline with three crossbars;
　　　　　　02 LIH precision CAT I with five crossbars; 25L LIH
　　　　　　precision CAT II with white centreline barrettes, red side
　　　　　　row barrettes, white and red crossbars and 20 sequenced
　　　　　　flashing lights. VASIS all runways
　　Thr　　LIH green
　　Txy　　blue edge
Aids: VOR/DME, NDB, VDF, SSR, RSR, SRE, TAR, ILS CAT I 02 and
25R, ILS CAT II 25L

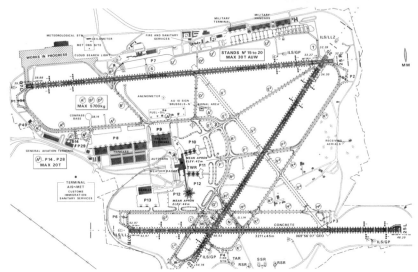

Brussels National Airport.

Twr frequency: 118.6   App frequency: 118.25

Terminals: Multi-storey passenger terminal with three traffic piers and one
    circular satellite. Aerobridges at piers and satellite. Separate general
    aviation and cargo terminals

Scheduled services 1978: 39 airlines

Main base: European Air Transport, Sabena, Sobelair and Trans
    European Airways

Traffic:	1970	1975	1976	1977	1978
Passengers (total)	2,816,286	4,105,757	4,301,505	4,549,496	4,844,921
Cargo (tonnes)	115,080	119,382	127,912	127,840	143,022
Aircraft movements	92,879	97,070	102,094	104,702	111,085
Transport movements	67,185	70,653	74,422	75,175	—

In 1976 Boeing 737s accounted for 37.23 per cent of transport movements, DC-9s for
11.54 per cent and Boeing 707s for 9 per cent.

From the start of civil air services Brussels was served by the 1914–18
war aerodrome known by the alternative names Evère and Haren, and
when air services were resumed after the Second World War Sabena was
still based at the old airport. However, during the German occupation a
Luftwaffe base was constructed close by at Melsbroeck and this had three
concrete runways which measured 1,600 m (5,249 ft), 1,650 m (5,413 ft) and
1,800 m (5,905 ft).

It was soon realized that Evère/Haren could not continue as the
Brussels airport and after a short time traffic was transferred to Melsbroeck
where the ex-Luftwaffe officers' mess, rather like a large farmhouse, served
as the passenger terminal. For some time Sabena aircraft operated from
Melsbroeck but taxied to and from Evère/Haren for maintenance.

Two runways were soon lengthened and became 02/20 of 2,000 m
(6,562 ft) and 06/24 of 2,050 m (6,726 ft) while 12/30 remained 1,650 m
(5,413 ft) in length.

28

Brussels National Airport in 1973, with the main terminal on the right and Satellite A in the centre. (*Inbel*)

During the first decade after the war all traffic handling took place on the north side of the airport between the main east–west runway and the main road to Brussels. But in 1956 a major rebuilding programme began and a new terminal was built near the centre of the airport. The new Brussels National terminal was opened in 1958 as well as the direct railway link to the city.

The multi-storey terminal now has three traffic piers, two short piers projecting onto the apron in front of the building and a long pier extending from the southeast corner to a circular satellite (Satellite A). Satellites B and C are to be added to the short piers. New arrival and departure halls opened in June 1976 should bring the annual passenger capacity to 10 mn, with a peak-hour capacity of 5,500.

The main runways are now the parallel 07L/25R and 07R/25L. Runway 02/20 has been lengthened to 2,819 m (9,249 ft) and runway 12/30 was extended to 2,510 m (8,235 ft) but is now only part of the taxiway system.

The north side of the airport is now occupied by a military terminal and hangars, and a number of private companies, and a large cargo terminal complex is under construction near the west end of runway 07L/25R.

Bermuda

Bermuda
  US Naval Air Station Kindley Field/Bermuda Air Terminal

32° 21′ 54″ N   64° 41′ 18″ W   6 nm (11 km) NE of Hamilton
ICAO: MXKF   IATA code: BDA   Time zone: GMT −4
Authority (civil): Bermuda Government
Elevation: 11 ft (3 m)   Ref temp: 28 deg C

Runways: 08/26   1,712 × 46 m (5,617 × 150 ft) asphalt/concrete*
12/30   2,944 × 46 m (9,660 × 150 ft) concrete/asphalt

* Available for emergency landings only

Pavement strength: 27,000 kg (59,525 lb) 1, 58,000 kg (127,868 lb) 2,
78,000 kg (171,960 lb) 3
Landing category: ICAO CAT I
Lighting:
R/W   LIH white edge
App   R/W 12/30   LIH white centreline with crossbars and
sequenced flashers
Thr   LIH green with strobes
Txy   lights on some taxiways
Aids: VORTAC, NDB, ASR, PAR, ILS CAT I 30
Twr frequency: 118.1/291.0   App frequency: 121.9/335.8
Terminal: Civil terminal to south of west end of 08/26 with south apron.
North apron for refuelling except for Boeing 747s. Ten aircraft stands
Scheduled services 1978: Air Canada, American Airlines, British Airways,
Delta Air Lines and Eastern Air Lines

Traffic:	1970	1976
Passengers (total)	785,553	1,034,923
Cargo (tonnes)	8,366	7,594
Aircraft movements	11,366	10,972
Transport movements	10,616	—

In 1976 Boeing 707s accounted for 38 per cent of movements, Boeing 727s and Lockheed
TriStars 16 per cent each, and Boeing 747s and Douglas DC-8s 14 per cent each.

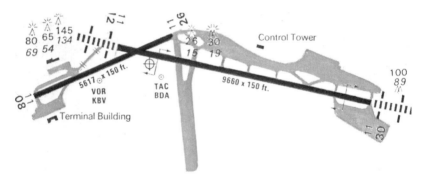

US Naval Air Station Kindley Field, with Bermuda Air Terminal on the left.
(*British Airways Aerad*)

Bermuda's first air services began on 16 June, 1937, when the Imperial
Airways Short C class flying-boat G-ADUU *Cavalier* and Pan American
Airways Sikorsky S-42 NC16735 *Bermuda Clipper* began operation of
Bermuda–New York services. The Bermuda terminus was Darrell's Island
Marine Airport which was formally opened on 12 June, 1937, and
consisted of a large hangar, apron and slipway.

In 1941 the United Kingdom leased, for 99 years, a site on St David's Island at the east end of the chain, for construction of a base as part of an exchange agreement granting the United Kingdom use of 50 United States destroyers. On this site was constructed the US military aerodrome known as Kindley Field, which had four runways—01/19 of 5,080 ft (1,548 m), 05/23 of 3,010 ft (917 m), 08/26 of 5,870 ft (1,789 m) and 12/30 of 7,490 ft (2,283 m). All runways were 150 ft (46 m) wide.

After the Second World War a temporary agreement opened the base to United Kingdom and United States commercial aircraft, and a civil terminal was built at the western end of the base near the 08 threshold. The short 05/23 runway was closed and became part of the taxiway system and, more recently, runway 01/19 has been withdrawn from use. Runway 12/30 has been extended to 9,660 ft (2,944 m), and 08/26, which is now only available for emergency landings, has been reduced to 5,617 ft (1,712 m) but with paved stopways at each end.

The airport is correctly known as United States Naval Air Station Kindley Field and the civil section is called Bermuda Air Terminal.

Bermuda Air Terminal. The civil terminal is in the foreground. The closed 05/23 and emergency 08/26 runways are beyond the terminal. The western end of 12/30 can be seen. In the foreground is the causeway to Bermuda (Main) Island and in the distance can be seen St George. (*Bermuda News Bureau*)

Lufthansa's McDonnell Douglas DC-10-30 D-ADCO *Frankfurt* at La Paz. The terminal bears the title Aeropuerto 'El Alto' La Paz. (*Deutsche Lufthansa*)

Bolivia

La Paz   Aeropuerto Internacional J. F. Kennedy*

ICAO: SLLP   IATA: LPB
16° 31′ S   68° 11′ W   Elevation: 13,355 ft (4,070.6 m)**
Longest runway: 09R/27L   4,000 m (13,123 ft)   RT   VASI 09
Aids: VOR, NDB, L

	1970	1975	1976	1977
Passengers	127,529	332,000 =	467,390	533,453
Transport movements	9,014	12,600 =	13,086	14,434

= Rounded figures
Scheduled services 1978: Aerolineas Argentinas, Braniff International, Cruzeiro, LAB, LAN-Chile and Lufthansa

* The airport is also known as Aeropuerto El Alto
** This is the official elevation shown in the Bolivian AIP but for many years there has been a notice at the airport which reads '13,358 ft (4,071 m) The highest Commercial Airport in The World'

Santa Cruz   Aeropuerto El Trompillo

ICAO: SLCZ   IATA: SRZ
17° 48′ S   63° 11″ W   Elevation: 1,433 ft (437 m)
Runway: 15/33   2,780 m (9,121 ft)   RT
Aids: VOR, NDB

	1971	1975	1976	1977
Passengers	103,400*	224,874*	368,216	417,532
Transport movements	3,960	6,668	6,986	8,292

* Excluding transit passengers

Scheduled services 1978: Aerolineas Argentinas, Cruzeiro, LAB and
    Líneas Aéreas Paraguayas

Brazil (Brasíl)

Belém, Pará   Aeroporto de Val de-Cáes

ICAO: SBBE   IATA: BEL
01° 22′ 55″ S   48° 28′ 44″ W   Elevation: 52 ft (16 m)
Longest runway: 06/24   2,526 m (8,287 ft)   ART   VASI 06
Aids: VOR/DME, NDB, VDF, ILS CAT I 06

	1970	1975	1976	1977
Passengers	240,516	435,846	518,571	569,852
Aircraft movements	13,850	16,570	17,706	21,619

Scheduled services 1978: Cruzeiro, TABA, Transbrasil, Varig, VASP and
    Votec
Main base: TABA - Transportes Aéreos de Bacia Amazonica

Belo Horizonte, Minas Gerais   Aeroporto da Pampulha

19° 51′ S   43° 57′ W   2.7 nm (5 km) N of city
ICAO: SBBH   IATA code: BHZ   Time zone: GMT −3
Authority: DEPAC (Civil Aviation Authority, Department of Civil
    Aviation)
Elevation: 2,582 ft (787 m)   Ref temp: 25.9 deg C
Runway: 13/31   2,535 × 45 m (8,317 × 148 ft) concrete
Pavement strength: all up weight 73,480 kg (161,996 lb)
Lighting:
    R/W   white edge, last 610 m (2,000 ft) yellow/white. Red end lights
    App   VASIS 13
    Thr   green
    Txy   blue edge
Aids: VOR/DME, NDB
Twr frequency: 118.7   App frequency: 120.7
Terminal: Passenger terminal to south of runway, linked to runway by
    three taxiways

Scheduled services 1978: Cruzeiro, Transbrasíl, Varig, VASP and Votec

Traffic:	1970	1975	1976	1977
Passengers (total)	289,789	1,229,898	963,676	1,112,061
Cargo (tonnes)	1,990	10,728	3,070	3,338
Aircraft movements	26,948	34,895	41,866	48,770

Belo Horizonte, the capital of Minas Gerais State, is situated on a plateau about 360 km (some 225 miles) north of Rio de Janeiro. It was founded at the turn of the century and was Brazil's first planned city.

Regrettably, the history of the airport's development has not been traced although in the late 1940s and early 1950s it was reported to have a single runway of 900 m (2,953 ft).

Brasília, Distrito Federal   Aeroporto Internacional de Brasília

15° 51′ 45″ S   47° 54′ 32″ W   5.9 nm (11 km) S of city
ICAO: SBBR   IATA code: BSB   Time zone: GMT − 3
Authority: DEPAC (Civil Aviation Authority, Department of Civil Aviation)
Elevation: 3,478 ft (1,060 m)   Ref temp: 26.6 deg C
Runway: 10/28   3,184 × 45 m (10,446 × 148 ft) concrete-asphalt
Pavement strength: all up weight 123,830 kg (272,998 lb)
Landing category: ICAO CAT I
Lighting:
    R/W   white edge, last 540 m (1,772 ft) yellow/white. Red end lights
    App   R/W 10   precision approach LIH white bar centreline
               and crossbar. VASIS 10
    Thr   green
    Txy   blue edge
Aids: VOR/DME, NDB, SRE, ILS CAT I 10
Twr frequency: 118.1/121.5/121.9   App frequency: 119.2/120.0
Terminal: Passenger terminal with wing buildings south of runway and
    towards western end of airport. Ten gates and seven close-in stands for
    Boeing 707 category aircraft plus seven remote stands
Scheduled services 1978: Cruzeiro, Pan American, Transbrasíl, Varig,
    VASP and Votec
Main base: Transbrasíl

Traffic:	1970	1975	1976	1977
Passengers (total)	343,538	806,741	1,390,115	1,572,773
Cargo (tonnes)	5,020	4,920	21,675	20,974
Aircraft movements	18,999	43,877	47,550	49,245

Brasília, the capital of Brazil since 1960, is on rolling country at an elevation of about 1,000 m (3,281 ft), a little over 900 km (more than 560 miles) northwest of Rio de Janeiro. Development of the city began in the mid-1950s and it is laid out in the form of an aeroplane with the wings stretching for more than 10 km (6¼ miles).

The airport has a single runway with parallel taxiway and three high-speed exits, but provision has been made for a second runway and when this is constructed the terminal will occupy a central position between them. The dual connecting taxiways have already been built between the

Brasília International Airport terminal and cantilevered control tower. (*Varig*)

main taxiway and a point south of the terminal apron.

The glass-faced terminal building, designed by Tercio Fontana Pacheco, comprises a main block measuring about 150 by 70 m (492 by 230 ft) and two wing buildings which give a total length of about 350 m (1,148 ft). The terminal and apron cost $10 mn, were designed to handle 2 mn passengers annually, and were completed in the early 1970s. *Airport Forum* described the terminal as 'The Jewel of Brasilia.'

Campinas, São Paulo   Aeroporto Internacional de Viracopos

              ICAO: SBKP   IATA: VCP
23° 00′ 23″ S   47° 08′ 02″ W   Elevation: 2,169 ft (661 m)
Runway: 14/32   3,240 m (10,630 ft)   RT   VASI 14/32
Aids: VOR/DME, NDB, SRE, ILS CAT I 14

	1970	1975	1976	1977
Passengers	245,658	499,716	473,264	217,625
Aircraft movements	11,320	21,379	20,839	13,014

Scheduled services 1978: 19 airlines

Viracopos is the international airport serving the City of São Paulo

Curitiba, Paraná   Aeroporto Afonso Pena

              ICAO: SBCT   IATA: CWB
25° 31′ 39″ S   49° 10′ 23″ W   Elevation: 2,989 ft (911 m)
Longest runway: 15/33   2,215 m (7,267 ft)   RT   VASI 10 and 15
Aids: VOR/DME, NDB, ILS 15

	1970	1975	1976	1977
Passengers	148,886	523,920	626,850	720,878
Aircraft movements	8,399	17,388	19,910	23,078

Scheduled services 1978: Cruzeiro, Rio-Sul, Transbrasíl, Varig and VASP

Fortaleza, Ceará   Aeroporto Pinto Martins

ICAO: SBFZ   IATA: FOR
03° 47′ S   38° 32′ W   Elevation: 82 ft (25 m)
Longest runway: 13/31   2,545 m (8,350 ft)   RT   VASI
Aids: VOR, NDB, VDF

	1970	1975	1976	1977
Passengers	158,590	289,422	353,690	401,844
Aircraft movements	8,578	10,252	13,490	12,746

Scheduled services 1978: Cruzeiro, Transbrasíl, Varig and VASP

Foz do Iguaçu (Iguaçu Falls), Paraná   Aeroporto Cataratas

ICAO: SBFI   IATA: IGU
25° 35′ 48″ S   54° 29′ 16″ W   Elevation: 776 ft (237 m)
Runway: 14/32   2,200 m (7,218 ft)   RT
Aids: VOR, NDB

	1970	1975	1976	1977
Passengers	34,443	142,928	210,230	263,524
Aircraft movements	3,641	7,655	9,682	10,398

Scheduled services 1978: Cruzeiro, Transbrasíl, Varig and VASP

Manáus, Amazonas   Aeroporto Internacional Eduardo Gomes

ICAO: SBEG   IATA: MAO
03° 02′ 21″ S   60° 02′ 49″ W   Elevation: 279 ft (85 m)
Runway: 10/28   2,700 m (8,858 ft)   ART   VASI 10/28

Eduardo Gomes International Airport, Manáus, showing the curved terminal, car parks, part of the runway and the curved taxiway leading to the 28 threshold.
(*Varig*)

36

Aids: VOR/DME, NDB, VDF, ILS 10

	1970	1975	1976	1977
Passengers	160,666	444,034	496,691	507,983
Aircraft movements	9,160	20,144	22,258	21,410

Scheduled services 1978: Air France, Cruzeiro, Surinam Airways, Transbrasíl, Varig and VASP

This airport is believed to have opened in 1975, replacing Ponta Pelada for which the 1970 traffic figures apply

Pôrto Alegre, Rio Grande do Sul   Aeroporto Salgado Filho

ICAO: SBPA   IATA: POA
29° 59′ 35″ S   51° 10′ 16″ W   Elevation: 10 ft (3 m)
Runway: 10/28   2,280 m (7,480 ft)   ART   VASI 10/28
Aids: VOR/DME, NDB, VDF, L, ILS CAT I 10

	1970	1975	1976	1977
Passengers	298,568	762,845	839,031	867,332
Aircraft movements	29,889	39,044	40,155	35,320

Scheduled services 1978: Aerolineas Argentinas, Cruzeiro, Pluna, Rio-Sul, Transbrasíl, Varig and VASP
Base: Rio-Sul

It is planned to extend the runway to 3,000 m (9,842 ft)

Recife, Pernambuco   Aeroporto dos Guararapes

ICAO: SBRF   IATA: REC
08° 07′ 33″ S   34° 55′ 33″ W   Elevation: 36 ft (11 m)
Runway: 18/36   2,444 m (8,018 ft)   ART   VASI 18
Aids: VOR/DME, NDB, ILS CAT I 18

	1970	1975	1976	1977
Passengers	346,031	653,688	762,884	834,149
Aircraft movements	18,151	19,936	24,041	23,477

Scheduled services 1978: British Caledonian Airways, Cruzeiro, TAP, Transbrasíl, Varig and VASP

Rio de Janeiro, Guanabara
        Aeroporto Internacional do Rio de Janeiro

22° 47′ 48″ S   43° 14′ 11″ W   7 nm (13 km) NNW of city
ICAO: SBGL   IATA code: GIG   Time zone: GMT − 3
Authority: Aeroportos do Rio de Janeiro (ARSA)
Area: 1,578 hectares (3,899 acres)
Elevation: 29 ft (9 m)   Ref temp: 30.4 deg C
Runways: 09/27   4,000 × 45 m (13,123 × 148 ft) concrete
        14/32   3,300 × 47 m (10,827 × 154 ft) concrete

37

Rio de Janeiro International Airport. Running diagonally across the photograph is the new 09/27 runway, opened in January 1979. In the distance is 14/32 with the old Galeão terminal area on the left and the new terminal at the right. Near the centre the new Varig maintenance base can be seen under construction.

(Aeroportos do Rio de Janeiro SA)

Pavement strength: 46,000 kg (101,413 lb) 1, 95,000 kg (209,440 lb) 2, 196,000 kg (432,106 lb) 3, 366,000 kg (806,892 lb) 4

Landing category: ICAO CAT II

Lighting:

R/W	09/27	LIH white edge, yellow/white last sections, and centreline. Red end lights. TDZ 09/27
	14/32	LIH white edge, last sections yellow/white. Red end lights 32
App	R/W 09	ALSF-2 and VASIS
	R/W 14	LIH white bar centreline and crossbar. VASIS
	R/W 27 and 32	VASIS
Thr	green	
Txy	blue edge, green centreline on high-speed exits 09/27	

Aids: VOR/DME, NDB, VDF, ASR, SRE, PAR, GCA, L, ILS CAT II 09, ILS CAT I 14

Twr frequency: 118.0   App frequency: 119.0

Terminals: Semi-circular four-storey terminal with 12 aircraft stands and 19 aerobridges. Separate cargo facilities in old terminal area

Scheduled services 1978: 23 airlines

Main base: Cruzeiro and Varig

Traffic:	1970	1975	1976	1977
Passengers (total)	1,333,731	3,997,649	4,305,291	4,611,231
Cargo (tonnes)	20,763	79,767	87,133	90,637
Aircraft movements	30,967	75,677	80,280	86,752
Transport movements	30,952	75,353	79,633	82,928

Rio de Janeiro International Airport occupies a large part of Ilha do Governador (Governor's Island) in Guanabara Bay. A naval aviation base was established on the island during the 1920s and there is still an air force base.

Until 1947 Santos Dumont was Rio de Janeiro's airport and it was used by Douglas DC-4s and Lockheed Constellations, but its limited size and proximity to the city made it necessary to transfer international operations to the military aerodrome which became Aeroporto do Galeão and, later Galeão International Airport.

There was a 14/32 runway parallel with the southwest shore, this measured 2,500 m (8,202 ft) and has been extended to 3,300 m (10,827 ft). The terminal area was developed near the 32 threshold and although extended from time to time, and provided with a temporary domestic terminal, overcrowding earned the airport a bad reputation.

A detailed study of Brazil's airport needs began in 1967 and in 1969 work began on the task of developing Galeão into a very large modern airport capable of meeting Rio de Janeiro's air traffic requirements into the next century.

The master plan comprised a two-runway system with four passenger terminals by 1990, new cargo terminals, and large maintenance areas.

The nature of Governor's Island made the construction of the modernized airport a monumental task. The island is a rock embankment comprised of intensely fractured gneiss overlaid with soils of many different origins. The rock level is of such diversity that both deep and shallow foundations were required only 20 m (65.6 ft) apart making it necessary to test bore for almost every pile. Nearly half of the new 09/27 runway and much of the terminal area is built on fill, and there was a marshy area running from the terminal area to the sea over which the runway and taxiways had to be laid. Some land had to be reclaimed from the sea, and site preparation involved moving 30 mn cubic metres of earth, 3 mn cubic metres of mud and 1½ mn cubic metres of rock. Construction of the runway, taxiways, aprons and buildings took 382,000 cu m of concrete, 40,000 cu m of asphalt and 27,000 tonnes of steel.

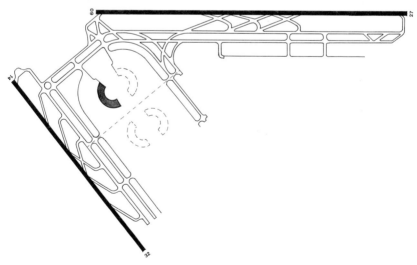

Rio de Janeiro International Airport. (*Clem Watson*)

39

The airport is being developed in phases and the first phase included one passenger terminal, the 09/27 runway, an administration building and control tower. The new runway is parallel to the north shore of the island and the terminal area is being developed to the east of runway 14/32, giving it an approximately central position between the two runways.

The layout chosen for the terminal area is similar to that at Dallas/Fort Worth, with semi-circular units arranged in pairs on each side of a spine road. The first unit, Terminal 1, is the southerly one of the northwest pair. It is a multi-level fully air-conditioned building with 69 check-in counters on the third-level departure floor. Arrivals are handled on the second level, and on the fourth level are a hotel, shops, other passenger amenities and a long curved observation promenade. The building has 200,000 sq m (2,152,800 sq ft) floor space, is 760 m (2,493 ft) long and designed to handle 5 mn passengers a year with 3,500 in a peak hour. The apron covers 280,000 sq m (3,013,920 sq ft) and there are 12 nose-in aircraft stands with 19 aerobridges (seven stands and 14 aerobridges for wide-bodied aircraft) and 19 remote stands. Tall lighting towers are positioned along the apron face of the building and on the outer edge of the apron and make apron centreline taxi-ing lights unnecessary. The terminal contains 32 escalators and, on the road side, parking space for 1,400 cars.

The interior of the terminal is divided into three sections. Section A handles domestic flights and B and C international. When the second terminal, opposite, is completed it will handle domestic services and the present terminal will be used solely for international flights.

Rio de Janeiro International Airport. The first terminal unit, control tower and apron. The curved area beyond the control tower is the site of the second terminal. Runway 09/27 is under construction in the background. (*Varig*)

The 56 m (183.7 ft) high control tower is centred between the two first terminals, and the administration building is between Terminal 1 and the projected Terminal 3.

The new terminal area was dedicated by President Ernesto Geisel on 20 January, 1977, and the first service from the new terminal was the 06.00 to Belo Horizonte and Brasília on 1 February, operated by VASP's Boeing 737 PP-SMY. The old Galeão temporary domestic terminal was then closed.

International operations began on 20 April, 1977, with the arrival at 05.55 of British Caledonian Airways Boeing 707 G-ATZC *Loch Katrine* from London. After that the old Galeão terminal was used for cargo, charter flights and executive aircraft.

During the first nearly two years of the new terminal all operations were from the 14/32 runway but on 20 January, 1979, runway 09/27 and its associated taxiways came into use, the first take off from 09/27 being by an air force Bandeirante at 00.01 with the Brazilian Air Minister on board.

Runway 09/27 has CAT II ILS and lighting on the 09 approach but will later be CAT II in both directions. It has a fire station 1 km (3,281 ft) from each end and also a marine rescue station. With the opening of 09/27 it became possible to modernize 14/32.

A large area south of runway 09/27 has been allocated for aircraft maintenance and cargo terminals. Known as the Varig Industrial Maintenance Complex, the airline's technical centre will include two hangars, engine overhaul shops, a turbine test unit, equipment store and administration building on a 90,000 sq m (968,760 sq ft) site. The two hangars will each have an area of 14,960 sq m (161,029 sq ft) and be capable of housing three DC-10s and two Boeing 707s. The hangars will have a door opening of 136 m (446 ft), the widest free span in South America, a depth of 110 m (361 ft) and a height of 30 m (98 ft).

The cargo terminal is to have 120,000 tonnes annual capacity in phase 1 and eventually double this.

The proposed development of the passenger terminal area was scheduled to provide Terminal 2 and its apron in 1980, Terminal 3 in 1985, and Terminal 4 in 1990, to give the airport an annual capacity of 30 mn passengers, and an apron area of 1 mn sq m (10.764 mn sq ft); but the actual programme will depend on the rate of traffic growth. Even with completion of the four-unit terminal complex there is space to bring the total to eight units by the year 2000 if needed. There is also the possibility that a 14L/32R runway may be constructed.

Fuel for the airport is delivered via a 15 km (9.3 mile) pipeline direct from the Duque de Caxias refinery.

In addition to providing first-class passenger and operational facilities, the mixed-economy Aeroportos do Rio de Janeiro, founded in 1973 to administer and operate the Rio de Janeiro airports, has paid a lot of attention to landscaping, some 400,000 sq m (4.3 mn sq ft) having been sown with grass and hundreds of trees planted.

In place of the overcrowded Galeão, Rio de Janeiro has now built the most modern airport in South America, one that meets the world's best standards and will be adequate well into the 21st century. Perhaps the least satisfactory aspect is access, but there are plans to link the terminal area with the mainland by a new expressway.

Santos Dumont Airport, Rio de Janeiro, in 1975, showing the closely spaced runways, the extensive aircraft parking area, the terminal on the left and the proximity of the city. The Brazilian Navy School occupies the island on the right.
(*Aeroportos do Rio de Janeiro SA*)

Rio de Janeiro, Guanabara   Aeroporto Santos Dumont

22° 54′ 35″ S   43° 09′ 44″ W   Adjoining city
ICAO: SBRJ   IATA code: SDU   Time zone: GMT −3
Authority: Aeroportos do Rio de Janeiro (ARSA)
Elevation: 10 ft (3 m)   Ref temp: 29.7 deg C
Runways: 02L/20R   1,260 × 30 m (4,134 × 98 ft)   concrete
          02R/20L   1,323 × 42 m (4,341 × 138 ft) asphalt
Pavement strength: auw 47,600 kg (104,940 lb)
Landing category: uncategorized
Lighting:
     R/W   white edge with last 540 m (1,772 ft) yellow/white
     App   R/W 20L VASIS
     Thr   green
     Txy   blue edge
Aids: NDB
Twr frequency: 118.7
Terminal: Passenger terminal with 18 close-in aircraft stands and numerous remote stands
Scheduled services 1978: Cruzeiro, Rio-Sul, Transbrasíl, Varig, VASP and Votec

Airline bases: Varig and VASP
Main base: Rio-Sul and Votec

Traffic:	1970	1975	1976	1977
Passengers (total)	1,134,504	1,085,011	1,272,251	1,431,421
Cargo (tonnes)	10,474	5,650	2,261	3,271
Aircraft movements	61,638	45,117	45,431	50,807

Rio de Janeiro's Santos Dumont Airport is hard against the high buildings of the city's central area and has the waters of Guanabara Bay on three sides. There is a Brazilian report that a short runway was opened on the site in 1932 but this may not be true. In March 1934 the City signed a contract for the levelling of ground on the Ponta do Calabouço, a point of land jutting into the Bay and measuring about 900 by 500 m (2,953 by 1,640 ft), for the construction of a municipal land and marine airport. The contract also covered construction of a sea wall and some land reclamation. It was proposed that the Ponta do Calabouço should be joined to the island of Villegagnon about 500 m (1,640 ft) offshore in order to allow construction of a 1,400 m (4,593 ft) main runway. Initially a period of only 18 months was allowed for the work.

The airport, named Santos Dumont and officially opened by the President of Brazil on 1 November, 1938, was almost square and near its northwest corner had a large hangar and flying-boat slipway. When the original 02/20 runway was built it was a little under 1,000 m (3,281 ft) in length and 45 m (148 ft) wide.

Since the Second World War considerable development has taken place. Further land was reclaimed at the south, the runway was extended and a second, parallel, runway (02R/20L) built about 40 m (131 ft) to the east. A new terminal was built on the west, and on some of the additional reclaimed land Varig and VASP maintenance bases were constructed. Almost the entire area between the 02L/20R runway and the apron and inner taxiway is occupied by hard standings, 24 for aircraft of up to 5,700 kg (12,566 lb) and 45 for DC-3s and larger aircraft.

The apron in front of the 200 m (656 ft) long terminal is divided into four areas—A with eight stands for aircraft up to Bandeirante type, B and C each with two stands for twin-engined aircraft and two Air Bridge Lockheed Electras, and D with two stands for twin-engined types.

The airport is severely restricted and cannot be enlarged. The 407.3 m (1,336 ft) high Pão de Açúcar, better known as the Sugar Loaf, is almost in line with the runways and only 3½ km (2 miles) from the 02 thresholds, and the proximity of the city imposes strict noise abatement control. Jet aircraft are not allowed to use Santos Dumont—the only exception having been some very successful demonstrations by a Fokker F.28 in 1978.

However, in spite of its limitations Santos Dumont is very convenient for its users, and it is between Santos Dumont and São Paulo's Congonhas Airport that Cruzeiro, Transbrasil, Varig and VASP operate the Ponte Aérea (Air Bridge) services with Lockheed Electras flying the 367 km (228 miles) sector 187 times a week in both directions, with departures from Santos Dumont from 06.00 to 20.50 and in the reverse direction from 06.50 to 21.50.*

* Based on May 1979 schedules.

43

Salvador, Bahia Aeroporto Dois de Julho

12° 54′ 48″ S   38° 20′ 19″ W   9.9 nm (18.3 km) E of city
ICAO: SBSV   IATA code: SSA   Time zone: GMT −3
Authority: INFRAERO
Elevation: 62 ft (19 m)   Ref temp: 31.1 deg C
Runways: 10/28   3,007 × 45 m (9,865 × 148 ft) asphalt
         17/35   1,528 × 45 m (5,013 × 148 ft) asphalt
Pavement strength: 10/28 maximum auw 366,000 kg (806,892 lb); 17/35
    181,600 kg (400,359 lb) dual tandem
Landing category: ICAO CAT I
Lighting:
    R/W   LIH white edge, last 525 m (1,722 ft) 17/35 and last 960 m
          (3,150 ft) 10/28 yellow/white, and red end lights
    App   R/W 10   VASIS
    Thr   green
    Txy   blue edge
Aids: VOR/DME, NDB, L, ILS CAT I 10
Twr frequency: 118.1/121.5/126.3   App frequency: 119.1
Terminal: Passenger terminal with three piers situated between 10 and 35
    thresholds
Scheduled services 1978: Cruzeiro, Nordeste, Transbrasil, Varig and VASP
Main base: Nordeste

Traffic:	1970	1975	1976	1977
Passengers (total)	320,255	705,072	889,748	1,006,736
Cargo (tonnes)	6,699	6,447	16,927	17,836
Aircraft movements	20,596	26,031	55,975	58,280

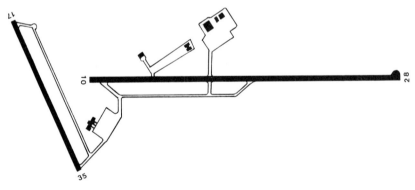

Dois de Julho Airport, Salvador.

Salvador, formerly named Bahia, and the capital of Bahia State, is on
a peninsula between Todos Santos Bay and the Atlantic. It is about
1,200 km (745 miles) north-northeast of Rio de Janeiro and until 1763 was
the capital of Brazil.
    The airport is close to the Atlantic coast and east of the city. It has not
been possible to trace the airport's history but it appears that the almost
level runway 17/35 was the original and that the 10/28 instrument runway

was built for jet operations. The 10 threshold is at an elevation of 8.5 m (28 ft) and the 28 threshold at 19 m (62 ft). Most of the slope is on the eastern half.

São Paulo   Aeroporto de Congonhas

23° 37′ 36″ S   46° 39′ 21″ W   3.8 nm (7 km) S of city
ICAO: SBSP   IATA code: CGH   Time zone: GMT − 3
Authority: DEPAC (Civil Aviation Authority, Department of Civil Aviation)
Elevation: 2,631 ft (802 m)   Ref temp: 24.6 deg C
Runways: 16L/34R   1,445 × 49 m (4,741 × 161 ft) concrete
         16R/34L   1,738 × 49 m (5,702 × 161 ft) concrete
Pavement strength: auw 16L/34R 43,540 kg (95,989 lb); 16R/34L 87,091 kg (192,003 lb)
Landing category: ICAO CAT I
Lighting:
    R/W   16R/34L   LIL white edge, last 430 m (1,411 ft) 16R and 485 m (1,591 ft) 34L yellow/white, and red end lights
    App   R/W 16R   LIH white bar centreline with crossbars, and VASIS
    Thr   16R   LIL green wing bars beside stopway,
             34L   LIL green
    Txy   blue edge
Aids: VOR/DME, NDB, GCA, PAR, L, ILS CAT I 16R
Twr frequency: 118.1   App frequency: 119.1/119.8/120.4
Terminal: Passenger terminal with two lateral piers. Separate building with VIP lounge
Scheduled services 1978: 11 airlines
Main base: Transportes Aéreos Regionals Mariloia (TAM) and VASP

Traffic:	1970	1975	1976	1977
Passengers (total)	1,569,406	3,425,132	4,341,419	4,512,000
Cargo (tonnes)	15,643	41,725	43,458	53,366
Aircraft movements	72,581	100,722	111,044	115,797
Transport movements	45,951	79,247	78,056	88,906

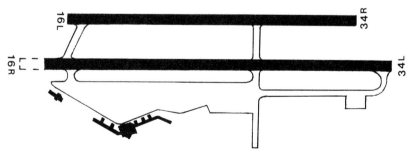

Congonhas Airport, São Paulo.

Congonhas Airport, São Paulo, with a Fokker F.28 and a Varig Boeing 737.
(*Fokker–VFW*)

São Paulo, the capital of São Paulo State, is situated on a plateau at an elevation of about 800 m (2,625 ft). It is South America's leading industrial centre and among the world's fastest growing cities.

In the mid-1930s Syndicato Condor was operating Junkers landplanes to São Paulo, using an airport with small wooden hangar to which was attached a small office, probably used as an administration building. It has not been possible to establish whether this aerodrome was Congonhas. By the late 1930s Pan American Airways DC-3s were using Congonhas which then had a small single-storey terminal.

Ten years later Congonhas had a northwest–southeast runway of 1,326 m (4,350 ft) and its published width of 146 m (480 ft) suggests that it may have been grass. The present 16L/34R was probably developed on the site of that runway.

The present terminal building had been constructed by the mid-1950s although it has since been extended.

Increasing traffic combined with restrictions at Congonhas led to a feasibility study, completed in 1975, for a new airport at Cumbica to be ready by 1980–81.

Bulgaria

Sofia   Vrajdebna Airport

42° 42′ 21″ N   23° 25′ 00″ E   2.7 nm (5 km) E of city
ICAO: LBSF   IATA code: SOF   Time zone: GMT plus 2
Authority: Bulgarian Civil Aviation - Balkan
Elevation: 1,742 ft (531 m)   Ref temp: 19 deg C
Runway: 10/28   2,800 × 60 m (9,186 × 197 ft) concrete and asphalt.
The main concrete section has a width of 80 m (262 ft). There is a
1,800 × 100 m (5,906 × 328 ft) grass runway alongside the
northern edge of the main runway
Pavement strength: LCN 60
Landing category: ICAO CAT I
Lighting:
R/W   LIH white edge, last 600 m (1,968 ft) yellow. Touchdown
wing bars 300 m (984 ft) from thresholds
App   R/W 10   LIL red centreline with crossbars,
R/W 28   Calvert LIH white and LIL red centreline with
crossbars. VASIS 10/28
Thr   green
Txy   blue edge
Aids: VOR/DME, VDF, L, PAR, SRE, ILS CAT I 28
Twr frequency: 118.1   App frequency: 125.5
Terminal: Passenger terminal to south of runway with 31 aircraft stands.
Ten stands take large jet aircraft and seven are used for An-24s and
Yak-40s

A British Airways Trident 2 at Vrajdebna Airport, Sofia. (*British Airways*)

47

Scheduled services 1978: 16 airlines
Main base: Balkan
Traffic: No figures are available

At the beginning of 1939 the new airport was being built near the village of Vrajdebna to replace the Bojourichte Airport, but it is doubtful whether this was completed before the war. The history of the airport's development is not known.

Burma

Rangoon   Mingaladon Airport   ICAO: VBRR   IATA: RGN

16° 54′ 15″ N   96° 08′ 30″ E   Elevation: 109 ft (33 m)
Runway: 03/21   2,652 m (8,700 ft)   ART   VASI 03/21
Aids: VOR, NDB, L, ILS CAT I 21
Scheduled services 1978: Aeroflot, Burma Airways, CAAC, KLM and
    Thai Airways International
Main base: Burma Airways
    No traffic figures are available.
    The runway is to be lengthened to 3,048 m (10,000 ft)

Cameroon (République Unie du Cameroun)

Douala   Douala Airport   ICAO: FKKK   IATA: DLA

04° 00′ 48″ N   09° 42′ 35″ E   Elevation: 33 ft (10 m)
Longest runway: 12/30   2,850 m (9,350 ft)   ART
Aids: VOR, NDB, VDF, ILS 30

	1970	1975	1976	1977
Passengers	231,293	295,825	341,855	447,450
Transport movements	10,556	11,170	13,892	14,971

Scheduled services 1978: 11 airlines
Main base: Cameroon Airlines

48

Canada

This section covers all Canadian airports handling 250,000 or more passengers in 1976. These airports are all operated by Transport Canada (Department of Transport).

Pavement load ratings of 12 or 12 plus can take the Concorde, Boeing 747-200, Douglas DC-8-63, DC-10-30/40 and Lockheed TriStar. Pavement load rating 11 can take the Airbus A300B, Boeing 707, 727 and 747-100, SP and SR, Douglas DC-8 except the -63 version, and DC-10-10, Ilyushin Il-62, and Vickers VC10. The load ratings quoted are for maximum weight. Overloading by 1 or 2 groups is normally allowed.

Tyre pressure, where indicated, is the maximum permissible main unit pressure but special permission may be given to allow excess tyre pressure.

This section is accurate to February 1978 and has been agreed with Transport Canada.

The abbreviation RIL is used for Runway Identification Lighting, equivalent to the United States RAIL and REIL.

Calgary, Alberta   Calgary International Airport

51° 06′ 50″ N   114° 01′ 09″ W   6 nm (11 km) NNE of city
ICAO: CYYC   IATA code: YYC   Time zone: GMT −7 (−6 DT).
Area: 1,983 hectares (4,900 acres)
Elevation: 3,557 ft (1,084 m)   Ref temp: 18.83 deg C
Runways: 07/25   1,890 × 46 m   (6,200 × 150 ft) asphalt concrete
         10/28   2,438 × 61 m   (8,000 × 200 ft) asphalt concrete
         16/34   3,863 × 61 m (12,675 × 200 ft) asphalt concrete

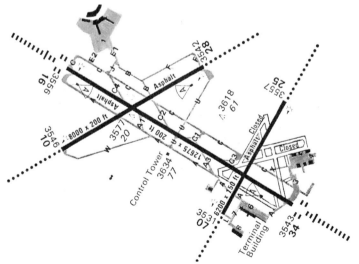

Calgary International Airport. (*British Airways Aerad*)

49

Pavement load rating: 07/25 9, 10/28 11 (200 psi), 16/34 12 plus
Landing category: ICAO CAT I
Lighting:
R/W   07/25   LIL white edge, 10/28   LIM white edge, 16/34   LIH white edge. RIL 10, 16 and 28

App   R/W 07   LIL yellow centreline and pre-threshold bar
R/W 25   LIL yellow lefthand line and pre-threshold bar
R/W 16/34   LIH CAT I white bar centreline with two crossbars and pre-threshold wing bars. VASIS 16 and 28, AVASI 10.

Thr   green
Txy   blue

Aids: VORTAC, NDB, ILS CAT I 16/34 and 28
Twr frequency: 118.7   App frequency: 119.3
Terminal: Three-level terminal with two piers, adjoining North Wing, and total of 22 aircraft stands
Scheduled services 1978: Air Canada, CP Air, Hughes Airwest, Pacific Western Airlines, Time Air and Western Airlines

Traffic:	1970	1975	1976	1978
Passengers (total)	1,243,162	2,283,064	2,345,292	2,926,100
Cargo (tonnes)	8,700	15,500	18,500	19,451
Aircraft movements	198,815	176,639	199,774	—
Transport movements	—	—	54,204	46,032

In 1976 DC-8-60s accounted for 29.6 per cent of international service movements, Boeing 747s for 27.5 per cent and Boeing 737s for 13.1 per cent. DC-9s accounted for 20.2 per cent of transborder service movements, Boeing 727s for 14.2 per cent and Boeing 737s for 13 per cent. Boeing 737s accounted for 12.1 per cent of domestic service movements and DC-9s for 10.8 per cent.

In June 1928 Calgary purchased 251 acres (101.5 hectares) of land from the Canadian Pacific Railway on a site $1\frac{1}{2}$ miles (2.4 km) from the centre of the city and a year later began construction of Calgary Municipal Airport. In its first year the airport handled 441 passengers and 3,400 lb (1,542 kg) of freight. TCA's demand for runway improvement and the increasing use of DC-3s forced Calgary to decide whether to improve the airport or seek a new site. The latter course was chosen and in May 1938 the decision was taken to build a new airport on a 640 acre (259 hectare) site on the McLeod Trail. A permanent licence was issued for the new Calgary Municipal Airport on 25 September, 1939.

During the war the Department of Transport leased the airport and made various improvements. In 1949 runway 07/25 was lengthened to 6,200 ft (1,890 m) and 16/34 to 6,400 ft (1,950 m). At about the same time terminal facilities were provided by converting former USAF buildings on the airport's west side. A new terminal was built in 1956.

On 15 February, 1956, extension of runway 16/34 to 8,600 ft (2,621 m) was completed and four days later Calgary informed the Department that Calgary Municipal Airport would have the alternate name McCall Field— McCall having been a First World War Canadian fighter pilot.

In 1964 an economic and traffic survey was made to determine future requirements and recommended that a new terminal be built between the eastern ends of runways 07/25 and 10/28. The recommendation was

The new terminal at Calgary International Airport. Beyond the curved upper level and to the right of the control tower is the North Wing. (*Transport Canada*)

followed by long discussions, mainly over finance and airport ownership, between the City of Calgary and the Federal Government. Treasury approval for the new terminal was sought in 1972 but in 1975 a major redesign was undertaken because of changed conditions, which included an agreement for US airlines to serve Calgary and Canadian carriers to open new routes to the United States; a dramatic increase in transborder traffic; the purchase by CP Air of four Boeing 747s, and an increase in Air Canada's Boeing 747 fleet. The necessary redesign work delayed the opening of the new terminal from early 1976 until the autumn of 1977.

The Central Terminal is a curved structure handling arrivals on the ground floor, departures on the first floor, and with the top floor housing concessions and restaurants. Total floor area is 55,740 sq m (599,985 sq ft). Projecting from the southeast corner of the building is a pier handling domestic flights, while at the opposite end of the building is a pier for international and domestic services and flights to and from the USA. To the north of the terminal is the separate curved North Wing which is used by Pacific Western Airlines for its 'Airbus' operations.

The terminals have capacity for some 3 mn passengers a year and are expected to prove adequate up to about 1982. Provision has been made for three phases of expansion up to the year 2000 when the terminal buildings will form a semi-circle and have 30 main ramp aircraft stands.

51

53° 18′ 35″ N   113° 34′ 43″ W   15.66 nm (29 km) SSW of city
ICAO: CYEG   IATA code: YEG   Time zone: GMT −7 (−6 DT)
Area: 2,914 hectares (7,200 acres)
Elevation: 2,373 ft (723 m)   Ref temp: 18.4 deg C
Runways: 01/19   3,353 × 61 m (11,000 × 200 ft) concrete
         11/29   3,109 × 61 m (10,200 × 200 ft) concrete
Pavement load rating: 11
Landing category: ICAO CAT I
Lighting:
     R/W   LIH edge
     App   R/W 01 and 11 LIH and LIL CAT I centreline and two
           crossbars
           R/W 19 and 29 LIL centreline and pre-threshold bar. VASIS
           19 and 29
     Thr   green
     Txy   blue
Aids: VORTAC, NDB, ASR, ILS CAT I 01 and 11
Twr frequency: 118.3   App frequency: 119.5
Terminal: Three-storey passenger terminal (built 1962) with 33,444 sq m
     (360,000 sq ft) gross area, four aerobridges and three remote areas
     capable of taking up to nine aircraft with mobile lounge access.
Scheduled services 1978: Air Canada, CP Air, Hughes Airwest, Northwest
     Orient Airlines, Pacific Western Airlines and Western Airlines

Traffic:	1970	1975	1976	1978
Passengers (total)	632,953	1,441,762	1,485,130	1,751,955
Cargo (tonnes)	7,600	19,000	20,200	24,807
Aircraft movements	58,979	106,861	99,504	—
Transport movements	—	—	33,468	30,337

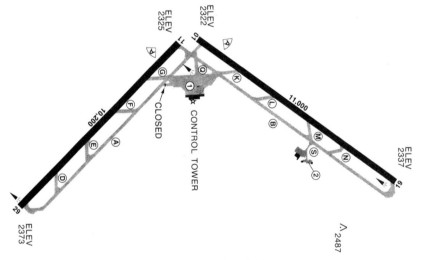

Edmonton International Airport.

Edmonton International Airport. On the apron are Pacific Western Airlines Boeing 737 C-GAPW, a Western Airlines Boeing 727, a Wardair Boeing 747 and a mobile lounge. (*Transport Canada*)

In 1976 DC-8s accounted for 32.2 per cent of international service movements, Boeing 707s for 29.6 per cent and Boeing 747s for 24 per cent. Boeing 727s accounted for 39.6 per cent of transborder service movements and DC-9s for 21 per cent. Boeing 737s accounted for 21.7 per cent of domestic service movements and Boeing 727s and DC-9s for 10 per cent each.

During the 1950s the City of Edmonton and the Department of Transport foresaw capacity problems at Edmonton Municipal Airport, and in December 1954 the Department announced plans for a new major international airport for which it would be fully responsible. Construction of the Edmonton International Airport began in 1958 with two runways and a temporary terminal. The airport was officially opened in December 1960 and a permanent terminal in February 1964. Air Canada and CP Air transferred operations to the new airport in 1960 but Pacific Western Airlines decided to continue its operations from the old site, Edmonton Industrial Airport*, which is nearer to the city. Further terminal expansion is planned at Edmonton International.

*This reverted to its old title Edmonton Municipal in 1979.

Halifax, Nova Scotia   Halifax International Airport

44° 52′ 51″ N   63° 30′ 33″ W   23 nm (42.5 km) NNE of city
ICAO: CYHZ   IATA code: YHZ   Time zone: GMT−4 (−3 DT)
Area: 931 hectares (2,300 acres)
Elevation: 477 ft (145 m)   Ref temp: 19.7 deg C
Runways: 06/24   2,682 × 61 m (8,800 × 200 ft) concrete
         15/33   2,347 × 61 m (7,700 × 200 ft) asphalt concrete
Pavement load rating: 11
Landing category: ICAO CAT II

Lighting:
R/W   LIH edge both runways. Centreline 06/24. TDZ 24
App   R/W 06 and 33 LIL centreline and pre-threshold bar, 24
        LIH and LIL CAT II centreline and three crossbars with
        supplementary inner section, 15 LIH and LIL CAT I
        centreline with two crossbars and pre-threshold wing bars.
        VASIS 06 and 33
Thr   green
Txy   blue
Aids: VOR/DME, NDB, PAR, ASR, ILS CAT II 24, ILS CAT I 15
Twr frequency: 118.4   App frequency: 119.2
Terminal: Passenger terminal of 25,288 sq m (272,200 sq ft) with 12 aircraft
        stands
Scheduled services 1978: Air Canada and Eastern Provincial Airways
Airline bases: Air Canada and Eastern Provincial Airways

Traffic:	1970	1975	1976	1978
Passengers (total)	686,308	1,212,445	1,257,136	1,350,872
Cargo (tonnes)	7,500	12,400	11,300	12,445
Aircraft movements	71,336	78,550	73,166	—
Transport movements	—	—	24,039	24,532

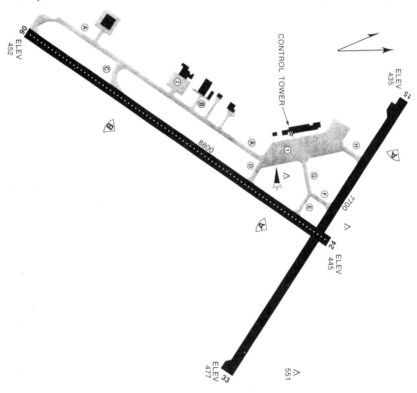

Halifax International Airport.

In 1976 DC-8s accounted for 68 per cent of international service movements and Boeing 737s for 10.1 per cent. DC-9s accounted for 49 per cent of transborder service movements. On domestic services DC-9s accounted for 23.5 per cent of movements, Piper Cherokees for 16.3 per cent and Boeing 747s for 12.8 per cent.

Construction of the first Halifax airport began at Bluebell Farm on 16 June, 1930, with landing strips measuring 1,800 ft (549 m) by 600 ft (183 m) and 2,000 ft (610 m) by 600 ft (183 m). A temporary public airport licence was issued on 9 January, 1931. In the autumn of 1938 both runways were extended by about 200 ft (61 m) and runway drainage was improved.

Following development studies in 1938–39 it was decided that the RCAF aerodrome at Dartmouth would be used as the Halifax airport.

Surveys for yet another airport were undertaken from 1945, and many sites were examined but proved unsuitable. In 1952 TCA suggested an area north of Waverley near Kelly Lake and, after two years of weather observations, construction of 8,000 ft (2,438 m) 06/24 and 6,200 ft (1,890 m) 15/33 runways began in November 1955.

A temporary licence for VFR operations only was issued in June 1960 and a full licence on 1 July, 1960. The terminal was officially opened on 10 September, 1960, and the runways extended to their present length in the same year.

Montreal, Quebec Province
Montreal (Dorval) International Airport

45° 28′ 05″ N   73° 44′ 30″ W   11.29 nm (20.92 km) SW of city
ICAO: CYUL   IATA code: YUL   Time zone: GMT −5 (−4 DT)
Area: 1,457 hectares (3,600 acres)
Elevation: 117 ft (36 m)   Ref temp: 22.8 deg C
Runways: 06L/24R   3,353 × 61 m (11,000 × 200 ft) concrete and
                                       asphalt concrete
        06R/24L   2,926 × 61 m (9,600 × 200 ft) concrete
          10/28   2,134 × 61 m (7,000 × 200 ft) asphalt concrete
Pavement load rating: 11
Landing category: ICAO CAT II
Lighting:
    R/W   LIH edge all runways. Centreline 06L/24R. TDZ 06L. RIL
             24L, 24R and 28
    App   R/W 06L   LIH and LIL CAT II centreline with
             crossbars and supplementary inner section.
             R/W 10   LIH and LIL CAT I centreline with crossbar
             and pre-threshold wing bars. All other approaches LIL
             centreline and pre-threshold bar. VASIS 06R and 28
    Thr   green
    Txy   blue
Aids: VORTAC, DME, NDB, PAR, ASR, VHF/DF, ILS CAT II 06L,
    ILS CAT I 10, 24L and 24R
Twr frequency: 119.9   App frequency: 118.9
Terminals: Passenger terminal with 101,855 sq m (1,096,368 sq ft) gross
    area. Ground floor arrival level and first floor departure level. Total of

eight floors including control tower. Satellite building connected to main terminal by tunnels. Twenty-eight aerobridges and 45 aircraft stands. Separate cargo terminal.

Scheduled services 1978: 12 airlines

Main base: Air Canada, Nordair and Quebecair

Traffic:	1970	1975	1976	1977	1978
Passengers (total)	4,606,216	6,704,866	5,260,203	5,857,421	6,495,590
Cargo (tonnes)	104,300	116,100	46,900	46,125	42,942
Aircraft movements	250,915	192,657	160,178	159,366	—
Transport movements	109,714	128,828	93,584	92,263	75,498

In 1976 DC-8s accounted for 34.3 per cent of international service movements and TriStars for 9.6 per cent. Boeing 727s accounted for 25.5 per cent of transborder service movements, DC-9s for 14 per cent and BAC One-Elevens for 9.6 per cent. DC-9s accounted for 19.3 per cent of domestic service movements and Boeing 727s for 13.3 per cent.

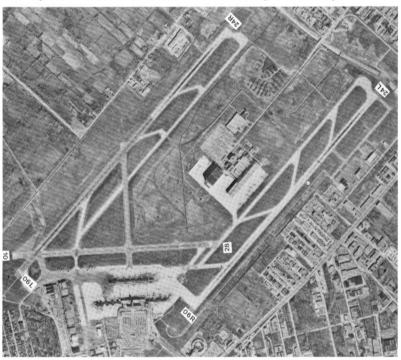

Montreal (Dorval) International Airport in 1975.

The airport was originally built as a base from which military aircraft could be ferried across the North Atlantic to the European war theatre and became the North American headquarters of RAF Ferry Command.

In 1940 the Canadian Department of Transport had acquired 1,500 acres (607 hectares) of land at the Dorval racecourse and by that October three paved 4,000 ft (1,219 m) by 200 ft (61 m) runways were under construction with completion planned for August 1941. Sufficient land had been acquired to extend the runways to 5,000 ft (1,524 m).

Montreal (Dorval) International Airport, showing main and satellite terminals and in the background runway 06R/24L. Runway 10/28 is beyond the satellite apron.
(*Transport Canada*)

By September 1941 two runways had been completed to 5,000 ft (1,524 m) and the north–south runway was 5,270 ft (1,606 m) in length. During that month all airline operations were transferred to Dorval from the old St Hubert Airport across the St Lawrence to the southeast of the city.

A small terminal building was completed on 25 February, 1942. This was of attractive design with curved frontage and resembled the original Washington National terminal. In February 1946 the Department of Transport took over the RAF facilities and a permanent airport licence was issued on 11 December, 1946. Transatlantic passengers were handled at a small single-storey prefabricated terminal.

By January 1952 the airport had two 7,000 ft (2,134 m) runways and the original north–south runway. Subsequently the original southwest–northeast runway was lengthened to 11,000 ft (3,353 m), the parallel 06R/24L and runway 10/28 were built and the north–south runway was withdrawn from use.

Construction of the present terminal began on 8 May, 1956, and when completed it was claimed as 'the largest international air terminal in the world housing under one roof all the passenger and baggage handling facilities of all the airlines using the airport.' The building is 2,131 ft (649 m) in length and is a steel structure, with curtain wall exterior, surmounted by the control tower, and with extension arrival and departure areas at each end. A parallel satellite building is reached via two tunnels beneath the apron.

Following studies of Montreal's future airport requirements it was decided that Dorval would need new terminal facilities and that by 1985 there would have to be extensive and costly land purchase for additions to the runway network. By the time the studies were made Dorval was already in a highly urbanized area and aircraft noise was also a major problem. The decision was taken to build a new Montreal international airport, and it is anticipated that by 1985 Dorval traffic will be cut back to about 3 mn passengers a year.

Montreal, Quebec Province
Montreal (Mirabel) International Airport

45° 41′ N   74° 02′ W   29.5 nm (54.7 km) NW of city
ICAO: CYMX   IATA code: YMX   Time zone: GMT − 5 (− 4 DT)
Area: 35,612 hectares (88,000 acres); 6,879 hectares (17,000 acres)
    operational area; 2,104 hectares (5,200 acres) Phase I
Elevation: 270 ft (82 m)   Ref temp: 26.3 deg C
Runways: 06/24   3,658 × 61 m (12,000 × 200 ft) concrete
         11/29   3,658 × 61 m (12,000 × 200 ft) concrete
Pavement load rating: 12 plus (up to 1,000,000 lb–543,592 kg)
Landing category: ICAO CAT II
Lighting:
    R/W   06/24   LIH edge and centreline. TDZ 06
            11/29   LIH edge.
    App   LIH and LIL centreline and crossbars all approaches, with
            supplementary inner section on 06 and 11 and pre-threshold
            wing bars 24 and 29. VASIS 29
    Thr   green
    Txy   blue
Aids: VOR/DME, NDB, ASR/SSR, ILS CAT II 06, ILS CAT I 11 and 24
Twr frequency: 119.1   App frequency: 125.15
Terminals: Four-storey rectangular passenger terminal with glazed
    exterior walls, connected to parallel aeroquay building with boarding
    gates, four aerobridges and six aircraft stands. Gross area of terminal
    87,326 sq m (940,000 sq ft). Four satellite cluster buildings with 18
    aircraft stands. Fourteen passenger transfer vehicles (PTV) link
    terminal and cluster buildings. Two cargo terminals with four aircraft
    stands.

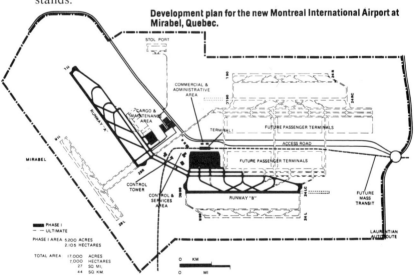

Montreal (Mirabel) International Airport master plan.

Montreal (Mirabel) International Airport—Phase I. The 24 threshold is in the foreground, with the terminal and runway 11/29 in the distance. Runways 06/24 and 11/29 will later become 06RC/24LC and 11L/29R. (*Transport Canada*)

Scheduled services 1978: 25 airlines

Traffic:	1975*	1976	1977	1978
Passengers (total)	93,756	1,428,060	2,061,284	1,189,810
Cargo (tonnes)	4,800	66,100	62,162	67,977
Aircraft movements	3,935	49,101	50,526	—
Transport movements	3,031	31,895	32,935	22,431

*Airport opened to traffic 29 November, 1975

In 1976 Boeing 707s accounted for 27.9 per cent of international service movements, Boeing 747s for 26.5 per cent and DC-8s for 26.3 per cent. Boeing 707s accounted for 36.7 per cent of transborder service movements, Boeing 747s for 25.4 per cent and DC-8s for 12.8 per cent. DC-8s accounted for 14.6 per cent of domestic service movements and Piper Aztecs and Apaches for 10 per cent.

Because Montreal's Dorval Airport was expected to reach its maximum capacity by 1985 the decision was taken to build an entirely new airport at Ste-Scholastique, some 34 miles (55 km) northwest of the city and 32 miles (51 km) northwest of Dorval.

In planning the airport very great care was taken to safeguard the new airport from uncontrolled building which would inhibit the airport's expansion and continued use well into the 21st century. Regulation of land use in the area has been ensured as well as a large buffer zone to avoid nuisance from aircraft noise.

The master plan calls for completion of the airport next century, with a design capacity of 630,000 aircraft movements a year. In a bold step the Government acquired 88,000 acres (35,612 hectares) of land on which to construct an airport of 17,000 acres (6,879 hectares), the remaining area being subject to strict land use zoning regulations.

The Mirabel terminal and aeroquay building. (*Transport Canada*)

Operations began at the new airport on 29 November, 1975, with the official opening on 4 October, 1975. Phase I, occupying 5,200 acres (2,104 hectares), is being implemented over the period up to 1979. In it there are two 12,000 ft (3,658 m) runways with associated taxiways; passenger terminal with parallel aeroquay with boarding gates, four aerobridges and six aircraft stands, and large apron (1,016 by 617 m–3,335 by 2,025 ft) with four satellite buildings—transfer from terminal to the 18 aircraft stands being by 150-passenger PTVs (14 being required initially and 21 or 22 by 1980); administration building; 215 ft (65.5 m) high control tower; two 7,896 sq m (85,000 sq ft) floor area cargo terminals each with 250,000 tons annual capacity and apron of 32,515 sq m (350,000 sq ft) with four aircraft stands; maintenance area; hotel; parking for 6,000 vehicles; and access roads. A unique feature of Mirabel is its aircraft de-icing station capable of handling two aircraft. De-icing fluid is recycled and cannot enter the drainage system.

In later phases there will be new runways parallel to the existing runways and on the opposite side of the access road another parallel pair of runways. When construction is complete there will be four 06/24 runways and two 11/29. Provision has been made for five more passenger terminals, each bigger than the present terminal, further cargo terminals and maintenance buildings, a general aviation area and a STOLport.

Completion date for the six-runway six-terminal airport is 2025 when there will be 150 aircraft parking positions and terminal capacity for more than 50 mn passengers a year.

At present Mirabel handles international flights (other than Canada–USA) and has capacity for 6–10 mn passengers and 600,000 tons of cargo annually. Transborder and long-distance domestic services are expected to be transferred from Dorval early in the 1980s, and it is expected that by 1985 Mirabel will be handling 17 mn passengers and 730,000 tons of air freight.

Mirabel is a bold concept but at present has two disadvantages—distance from the city and the problems for passengers changing from international to domestic flights; to overcome these, high-speed electric trains will be introduced in the early 1980s to link the airports with each other and with the city.

Ottawa, Ontario   Ottawa International Airport

45° 19′ 21″ N   75° 40′ 10″ W   6.9 nm (12.8 km) S of city
ICAO: CYOW   IATA code: YOW   Time zone: GMT −5 (−4 DT)
Area: 2,064 hectares (5,100 acres)
Elevation: 374 ft (114 m)   Ref temp: 22.6 deg C
Runways: 04/22   1,006 × 61 m   (3,300 × 200 ft) asphalt concrete
         07/25   2,438 × 61 m   (8,000 × 200 ft) asphalt concrete
         14/32   3,048 × 61 m (10,000 × 200 ft) asphalt concrete
         17/35   1,250 × 61 m   (4,100 × 200 ft) asphalt concrete
Pavement load rating: 04/22 and 17/35   6 (60 psi), 07/25 and 14/32
    10 (200 psi)
Landing category: ICAO CAT I
Lighting:
    R/W   07/25 and 14/32   LIH edge. RIL 14 and 25
    App   R/W 07   LIH and LIL CAT I centreline with two
             crossbars and pre-threshold wing bars, 32 LIH and LIL
             centreline with five crossbars, 25 LIL centreline and pre-
             threshold bar. VASIS 14 and 25
    Thr   green
    Txy   blue
Aids: VORTAC, NDB, DME, ASR, GCA, ILS CAT I 07
Twr frequency: 118.3   App frequency: 120.8
Terminal: Five-storey passenger terminal with 19,483 sq m (209,715 sq ft)
    gross area and five aircraft stands.
Scheduled services 1978: Air Canada, CP Air, Eastern Air Lines, First Air,
    Great Lakes Airlines, Nordair and Otonabee Airways

Ottawa International Airport in 1975.

Ottawa International Airport. In the foreground are runways 04/22 (running across the picture) and 17/35 (right). The main 14/32 runway is parallel with the military apron in the centre and 07/25 is beyond the civil terminal. (*Transport Canada*)

Traffic:	1970	1975	1976	1978
Passengers (total)	887,254	1,510,049	1,493,498	1,646,638
Cargo (tonnes)	3,900	6,500	6,500	5,382
Aircraft movements	201,266	207,440	194,979	—
Transport movements	—	—	37,994	32,942

In 1976 Boeing 707s accounted for 55.6 per cent of international service movements, Boeing 727s accounted for 12.8 per cent of transborder service movements and DC-9s accounted for 32.8 per cent of domestic service movements.

The airport site was first leased by the Ottawa Flying Club from private owners in 1928. Laurentian Air Services bought the aerodrome in 1936 and sold it to the Department of Transport in 1938. The Department constructed two runways, a 3,000 ft (914 m) east–west runway now disused and the 3,300 ft (1,006 m) 04/22.

The airport was formally opened and licensed on 20 August, 1938. It was designated for military use in December 1939 and at it the RCAF established its first Service Flying Training School. A permanent licence was issued on 23 April, 1940, after installation of lighting and in the same year the 4,100 ft (1,250 m) runway 17/35 was constructed.

In 1951 two new runways were constructed south of the then existing system. These were 07/25 of 6,000 ft (1,829 m) and 14/32 of 8,800 ft (2,682 m). Both were 200 ft (61 m) wide.

On 15 July, 1954, Ottawa Airport was designated a North Atlantic alternate. The new terminal was completed in June 1960 and in the following year work began on extending runway 14/32 to 10,000 ft (3,048 m) and 07/25 to 8,000 ft (2,438 m).

The official name was changed to Ottawa International Airport on 24 August, 1964. The original name of the airport was Uplands.

62

Quebec, Quebec Province   Quebec Airport

ICAO: CYQB   IATA: YQB
46° 48′ N   71° 24′ W   Elevation: 239 ft (73 m)
Longest runway: 06/24   2,286 m (7,500 ft)   App lights 06/24
Aids: VORTAC, NDB, VDF, ILS 06

	1970	1975	1976	1978
Passengers	276,047	538,322	555,771	595,705
Aircraft movements	109,676	158,316	132,285	—

Scheduled services 1978: Air Canada, Bar Harbor Airlines, Nordair and
    Quebecair

Regina, Saskatchewan   Regina Airport

ICAO: CYQR   IATA: YQR
50° 26′ N   104° 40′ W   Elevation: 1,894 ft (577 m)
Longest runway: 12/30   2,408 m (7,900 ft)   App lights 12/30
Aids: VORTAC, NDB, ILS 12

	1970	1975	1976	1978
Passengers	273,029	498,655	484,776	419,345
Aircraft movements	86,804	137,540	138,614	—

Scheduled services 1978: Air Canada and Norcanair

A study is being made to assess the merits of an additional parallel
major runway versus relocation of the airport

St John's, Newfoundland   St John's (Torbay) Airport

ICAO: CYYT   IATA: YYT
47° 37′ 07″ N   52° 45′ 11″ W   Elevation: 461 ft (140 m)
Longest runway: 11/29   2,591 m (8,500 ft)   App lights 11/29
Aids: VOR/DME, GCA, ILS 17

	1970	1975	1976	1978
Passengers	224,913	387,285	415,327	478,721
Aircraft movements	29,854	28,319	38,644	—

Scheduled services 1978: Air Canada and Eastern Provincial Airways

Saskatoon, Saskatchewan   Saskatoon Airport

ICAO: CYXE   IATA: YXE
52° 10′ N   106° 42′ W   Elevation: 1,653 ft (504 m)
Longest runway: 08/26   2,530 m (8,300 ft)   App lights 08/26
Aids: VORTAC, NDB, VDF, ILS 08 and 32

	1970	1975	1976	1978
Passengers	226,658	427,391	483,118	424,547
Aircraft movements	69,213	141,310	143,333	—

Scheduled services 1978: Air Canada and Norcanair
    Runway extension is planned

Thunder Bay, Ontario   Thunder Bay Airport

ICAO: CYQT   IATA: YQT
48° 22′ N   89° 19′ W   Elevation: 653 ft (199 m)
Longest runway: 07/25   1,890 m (6,200 ft)   App lights 07/25
Aids: VORTAC, NDB, VDF, ILS 07

	1970	1975	1976
Passengers	187,868	331,627	341,540
Aircraft movements	46,129	90,482	87,432

Scheduled services 1978: Air Canada, Norontair, North Central Airlines
    and Transair
    Formerly Lakehead Airport. The terminal building was extended in
1977–78

Toronto, Ontario   Toronto International Airport (Malton)

43° 40′ 38″ N   79° 37′ 51″ W   14.7 nm (27.35 km) W of city
ICAO: CYYZ   IATA code: YYZ   Time zone: GMT −5 (−4 DT)
Area: 5,787 hectares (14,300 acres)
Elevation: 569 ft (173 m)   Ref temp: 22.83 deg C
Runways: 05L/23R   3,200 × 61 m (10,500 × 200 ft) asphalt concrete
             05R/23L   2,896 × 61 m (9,500 × 200 ft) concrete
             10/28   2,195 × 61 m (7,200 × 200 ft) asphalt concrete
             14/32   3,368 × 61 m (11,050 × 200 ft) asphalt concrete
Pavement load rating: 12—all runways

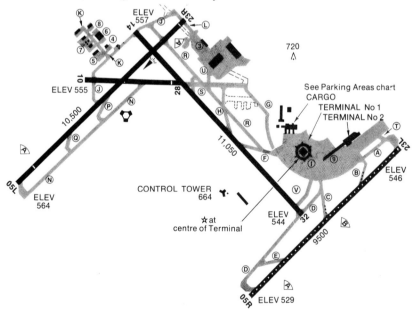

Toronto International Airport.

Landing category: ICAO CAT II
Lighting:
R/W   LIH edge all runways. Centreline 05R/23L. TDZ 05R.
          RIL 23L, 23R and 32
App   R/W 05R   LIH and LIL CAT II centreline with three
          crossbars and supplementary inner section.
          R/W 05L and 14   LIH and LIL CAT I centreline with
          two crossbars and pre-threshold wing bars.
          R/W 10, 23L, 23R and 32   LIL centreline and
          pre-threshold bar, VASIS 23L and 23R
Thr   green
Txy   blue
Aids: VORTAC, NDB, PAR, ASR, VHF/DF, ASDE, ILS CAT II 05R,
ILS CAT I 05L and 14
Twr frequency: 118.0   App frequency: 119.2
Terminals: Terminal 1 of 83,401 sq m (897,728 sq ft) gross area with six
traffic piers, 23 aerobridges and 53 aircraft stands. Associated eight-
level car parking garage.
      Terminal 2 of 62,171 sq m (669,209 sq ft) gross area with 22
aerobridges and 19 aircraft stands. Separate cargo terminal with three
aircraft stands.
Scheduled services 1978: 20 airlines
Airline bases: Air Canada and CP Air

Traffic:	1970	1975	1976	1977	1978
Passengers (total)	6,414,796	10,513,413	10,782,224	11,953,942	11,216,067
Cargo (tonnes)	93,400	142,300	160,600	152,494	161,892
Aircraft movements	220,996	238,197	244,849	243,182	—
Transport movements	125,710	157,455	152,742	161,598	126,872

In 1976 DC-8-60s accounted for 32.2 per cent of international service movements, Boeing
707s for 21 per cent and Boeing 747s for 18.6 per cent. DC-9s accounted for 24.4 per cent of
transborder service movements and Boeing 727s for 19 per cent. On domestic services DC-9s
accounted for 20.7 per cent of movements and Boeing 727s for 12 per cent.

In the early days of aviation Toronto was served by five small grass
aerodromes but the implementation of the transcontinental airway system
made provision of a major airport vital. Throughout the winter of 1936–37
the Department of Transport and the Toronto Harbour Commission
considered a number of possible sites and on 27 April, 1937, a 1,400 acre
(567 hectare) site at Malton, 17 miles (27 km) from the city centre was
recommended. Three 3,000 ft (914 m) runways were constructed, two of
them paved, and lighting installed by 30 September, 1938. TCA began
scheduled services through the airport on 18 October, 1938, and a
permanent licence for the airport was issued on 24 January, 1939, the
airport being leased to the Department of Transport by the City of
Toronto.
    Initially a converted farmhouse served as terminal and weather centre
but a permanent terminal was built in July 1939. The first ILS was
commissioned in May 1948 and a new single-storey brick terminal was
completed in 1949. In 1957 the Department of Transport took over the
airport and runway 14/32 was extended to 11,050 ft (3,368 m).
    On 28 November, 1960, the airport was renamed Toronto
International Airport (Malton) and on 21 November, 1962, the new

Toronto International Airport. Terminal 1 is on the right, Terminal 2 is the long low building on the left, and the cargo terminal is at the base of the photograph. Runway 05R/23L is in the background. (*Transport Canada*)

9,500 ft (2,896 m) 05R/23L runway was completed. In 1963 the Terminal 1 complex was completed. This has separate arrival and departure levels with departure ring concourse, is a steel and concrete structure primarily enclosed with glass, and was designed to handle 3.4 mn passengers a year but has been modified several times to provide for more than 5 mn passengers annually and further development is planned. The terminal is surmounted by eight-level car parking.

In September 1969 work began on the first stage of Terminal 2. This is a linear building comprising a number of two-level modules, each being a separate terminal unit. Completion of stage three in 1978 with 10 modules brought total airport capacity to 12.5 mn passengers. All Air Canada services use Terminal 2. The two terminals are connected by a tunnel with moving pavements and there are inter-terminal buses.

Runway 05L/23R was extended to 10,500 ft (3,200 m) in 1970.

In 1968 long-term planning required the additional acquisition of about 3,000 acres (1,214 hectares) so that extra runways could be provided up to the year 2000; but opposition to the purchase of extra land forced the expansion programme to remain within the existing airport boundaries. The 1972–74 plan for a new airport at Pickering has been abandoned.

Vancouver, British Columbia   Vancouver International Airport

49° 11′ 20″ N   123° 10′ 45″ W   5.4 nm (10 km) SW of city
ICAO: CYVR   IATA code: YVR   Time zone: GMT −8 (−7 DT)
Area: 1,457 hectares (3,600 acres)
Elevation: 8 ft (2 m)   Ref temp: 17.9 deg C

Runwrays: 08/26   3,353 × 61 m (11,000 × 200 ft) concrete and asphalt
                                                              concrete
         12/30   2,225 × 61 m (7,300 × 200 ft) concrete
Pavement load rating: 12
Landing category: ICAO CAT II
Lighting:
    R/W   08/26   LIH edge and centreline. TDZ 08
           12/30   LIM edge. RIL 12/30 and 26
    App   R/W 08   LIH and LIL CAT II centreline with crossbars
           and supplementary inner section,
           R/W 26   LIH and LIL centreline with crossbar and pre-
           threshold wing bar,
           R/W 12/30   LIL centreline and pre-threshold bars.
           VASIS 12/30 and 26
    Thr   green
    Txy   blue
Aids: VORTAC, DME, NDB, PAR, ASR, ILS CAT II 08, ILS CAT I 26
Twr frequency: 124.0   App frequency: 120.8
Terminals: Four-storey passenger terminal with 62,763 sq m (675,581 sq ft)
    gross area, four traffic piers, 17 aerobridges and 22 aircraft stands.
    117 ft (35.6 m) high control tower integral with terminal. A cargo
    terminal was constructed in 1965–68.
Scheduled services 1978: Air Canada, Airwest Airlines, CP Air, Japan Air
    Lines, Pacific Coastal Airlines, Pacific Western Airlines, Qantas,
    United Airlines and Western Airlines
Airline base: Air Canada

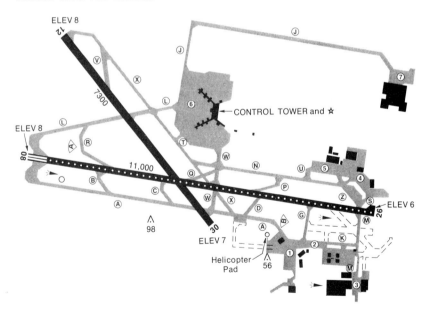

Vancouver International Airport.

67

Main base: CP Air, Okanagan Helicopters and Pacific Western Airlines. The airport also has seaplane facilities.

Traffic:	1970	1975	1976	1977	1978
Passengers (total)	2,591,356	4,677,075	4,762,572	5,287,486	5,415,585
Cargo (tonnes)	36,300	62,100	71,600*	59,990	61,825
Aircraft movements	149,521	203,253	216,622	234,498	—
Transport movements	61,462	84,140	74,205	89,664	60,695

* 1976 cargo could be understated due to reporting errors.

In 1976 on international flights Boeing 747s accounted for 43.9 per cent of movements, Boeing 707s for 17 per cent and DC-8-60s for 14.2 per cent. On transborder services Boeing 727s accounted for 30 per cent of movements and Boeing 737s for 20 per cent. No single type accounted for 10 per cent of domestic service movements.

Vancouver International Airport, situated on an island at the mouth of the Fraser River, was once known as Sea Island Airport and for many years was a main base for scheduled services by flying-boats and seaplanes as well as landplanes.

The airport was opened on 22 July, 1931, and consisted of a 475 acre (192 hectare) site with a single 2,400 ft (732 m) by 100 ft (30 m) runway, a small administrative building and two hangars.

In the period 1936–38 two paved 3,000 ft (914 m) runways were constructed, together with taxiways, and lighting installed. The first scheduled services began when TCA opened its first route, to Seattle, on 1 September, 1937, using Lockheed 10 Electras.

From 1931 until 1962 the airport was administered by the City of Vancouver, apart from the period from August 1940 to October 1947 when

Vancouver International Airport in 1968. The terminal building and control tower, with an Air Canada DC-8 and two DC-9s at the southwest pier, and a Canadian Pacific DC-6B at the northwest pier. (*Transport Canada*)

68

it was operated by National Defense. During the war the runways were lengthened and strengthened and other improvements made. The original administration building was destroyed by fire early in 1949 and a temporary replacement was completed in March 1950. In the summer of 1952 the terminal was modified and expanded—it is now known as the North Terminal.

In the spring of 1953 runway 08/26 was constructed to replace the original 07/25 and in the summer of 1961 the new 12/30 runway was built.

A West Terminal was opened in July 1957 and expanded in 1963, by which time the airport had come under the ownership and operation of the Department of Transport. A completely new central area terminal was built in 1966–68 and opened to traffic in September 1968.

In 1972 proposals were made for the construction of a second east–west runway but this led to great public controversy and no final conclusion on future airport development had been reached by the end of 1977, although modifications to the main terminal are projected.

Victoria, British Columbia   Victoria International Airport

ICAO: CYYJ   IATA: YYJ
48° 39′ N   123° 25′ W   Elevation: 63 ft (19 m)
Longest runway: 08/26   2,134 m (7,000 ft)   App lights 08/26
Aids: VOR, NDB, VDF, ILS 08 and 26

	1970	1975	1976	1978
Passengers	265,803	444,298	387,537	517,883
Aircraft movements	107,686	185,478	186,176	—

Scheduled services 1978: Air Canada, Airwest Airlines and Pacific Western Airlines

Windsor, Ontario   Windsor Airport

ICAO: CYQG   IATA: YQG
42° 16′ 29″ N   82° 57′ 30″ W   Elevation: 622 ft (190 m)
Longest runway: 07/25   2,408 m (7,900 ft)   App lights 07/25
Aids: VOR, NDB, VDF, ILS 25

	1970	1975	1976
Passengers	234,282	333,622	302,630
Aircraft movements	77,304	82,370	92,757

Scheduled services 1978: Air Canada and Nordair
    The airport will be expanded or relocated

Winnipeg, Manitoba   Winnipeg International Airport

49° 54′ 32″ N   97° 14′ 04″ W   3.47 nm (6.43 km) W of city
ICAO: CYWG   IATA code: YWG   Time zone GMT −6 (−5 DT)
Area: 1,538 hectares (3,800 acres)
Elevation: 783 ft (239 m)   Ref temp: 21.7 deg C

Winnipeg International Airport.

Runways: 07/25   2,134 × 61 m (7,000 × 200 ft) asphalt concrete and concrete
        13/31   2,652 × 61 m (8,700 × 200 ft) asphalt concrete
        18/36   3,353 × 61 m (11,000 × 200 ft) asphalt concrete and concrete

Pavement load rating: 07/25 8, 13/31 and 18/36 12
Landing category: ICAO CAT II
Lighting:
    R/W   07/25   LIM edge
             13/31   LIH edge
             18/36   LIH edge and centreline. TDZ 36.
             RIL 18 and 31
    App   R/W 13   LIH and LIL CAT I centreline, crossbar and pre-threshold wing bar
             R/W 36   LIH and LIL CAT II centreline with crossbars and supplementary inner section
             R/W 07/25, 18 and 31   LIL centreline and pre-threshold bar. VASIS 13
    Thr   green
    Txy   blue and amber
Aids: VORTAC, NDB, ASR, ILS CAT II 36, ILS CAT I 13
Twr frequency: 118.3   App frequency: 119.5
Terminal: Two-storey passenger terminal of 29,803 sq m (320,799 sq ft) gross area with five aerobridges and 13 aircraft stands.
Scheduled services 1978: Air Canada, CP Air, Frontier Airlines, North Central Airlines, Northwest Orient Airlines, Onair and Transair
Airline base: Air Canada

Main base: Transair

Traffic:	1970	1975	1976	1978
Passengers (total)	1,255,017	1,977,359	1,915,429	1,994,039
Cargo (tonnes)	18,900	23,600	23,700	23,140
Aircraft movements	158,358	148,503	150,748	—
Transport movements	—	—	40,972	36,605

In 1976 Boeing 707s accounted for 37.5 per cent of international service movements, DC-8-60s for 30.4 per cent and Boeing 747s for 17.2 per cent. Boeing 727s accounted for 19.1 per cent of transborder service movements and Boeing 737s for 13 per cent. DC-9s accounted for 14.4 per cent of domestic service movements, and Cessna 150s for 10.4 per cent.

The airport came into being in 1929 as Stevenson Field when the Winnipeg Flying Club leased 160 acres (65 hectares) of land from the Municipality of St James. Expansion took place and by 1937 the aerodrome had been extended to 620 acres (251 hectares). The City of Winnipeg joined with St James in establishing an Airport Commission which operated the airport until it was taken over by the Federal Government during the Second World War.

After the war further development took place and during the mid-1950s runway 07/25 was constructed. In that period the title Winnipeg International Airport was adopted. A new terminal, administration building and control tower was built during 1960–63 and in the same period runway 13/31 was rebuilt and 18/36 was extended to its present 11,000 ft (3,353 m).

Winnipeg International represents an important part of the Canadian civil airport system and also includes a 630 acre (255 hectare) Canadian Forces base—in 1974 military aircraft movements exceeded those at any other Canadian non-military aerodrome.

Winnipeg International Airport terminal and control tower. Three baggage trains are serving the Air Canada Lockheed TriStar at Stand 9. (*Transport Canada*)

71

Cape Verde (Cabo Verde)

Sal Island   Amilcar Cabral International Airport

ICAO: GVAC   IATA: SID
16° 44′ 37″ N   22° 57′ 01″ W   Elevation: 177 ft (54 m)
Longest runway: 02/20   3,270 m (10,729 ft)   ART   VASI 02/20
Aids: VOR, NDB, ILS 02

	1976	1977
Passengers	275,812*	250,831
Transport movements	4,655	4,432

*Includes 203,555 transit passengers

Scheduled services 1978: South African Airways, TAP and Transportes
    Aéreos de Cabo Verde (Cape Verde Airlines)

Chile

Punta Arenas   Aeropuerto Presidente Carlos Ibañez del Campo

ICAO: SCCI   IATA: PUQ
53° 00′ 17″ S   70° 51′ 02″ W   Elevation: 130 ft (40 m)
Longest runway: 07/25   2,245 m (7,365 ft)   RT
Aids: VOR, NDB, L

	1970
Passengers	103,031
Transport movements	4.214

Scheduled services 1978: LAN-Chile

Santiago   Aeropuerto Internacional de Pudahuel

ICAO: SCEL   IATA: SCL
33° 23′ 24″ S   70° 47′ 06″ W   Elevation: 1,554 ft (474 m)
Runway: 17/35   3,200 m (10,499 ft)   ART
Aids: VOR, NDB, ILS CAT I 17

	1970	1975	1976	1977
Passengers	789,012	614,836	639,226	894,628
Transport movements	19,711	11,444	13,568	11,514

Scheduled services 1978: 17 airlines
Main base: Ladeco

China (People's Republic)

Although the Chinese airline CAAC has an extensive domestic route network, little is known about Chinese airports, the Chinese AIP only giving brief details of airports used for regular international services and alternates for these designated airports. The controlling authority for these airports is the Civil Aviation Administration of China (CAAC). Standard time is GMT plus 8 hr. No traffic statistics are available.

The abbreviation SA is used for simple approach lights.

Canton (Guangzhou), Kwantung Paiyun Airport

23° 11′ N	113° 16′ E	3.78 nm (7 km) NNE of city
	ICAO: ZGGG	IATA code: CAN

Elevation: 43 ft (13 m) Ref temp: 32.7 deg C
Runway: 03/21 3,380 × 60 m (11,089 × 197 ft) concrete
Pavement strength: 180,000 kg (396,832 lb) auw
  There is a parallel taxiway
Lighting:
  R/W LIH white edge
  App R/W 03 LIH white and LIL red centreline and four crossbars
    R/W 21 LIH white and LIL red centreline and three crossbars
  Thr LIH
  Txy no details
Aids: NDB, ILS CAT I 03
Twr frequency: 118.1/119.7
Terminal: On west of airport with 360 × 153 m (1,181 × 502 ft) concrete apron
Scheduled services 1978: CAAC only

Paiyun Airport, Canton. Road-side view of terminal.
(*Courtesy Airports International*)

73

Hangchow (Hangzhou), Chekiang   Chienchiao Airport

30° 20′ N   120° 51′ E   ICAO: ZSHC   IATA code: HGH
Elevation: 16 ft (5 m)
Longest runway: 07/25   3,200 m (10,500 ft)   ART
Pavement strength: 148,000 kg (326,284 lb) auw
Scheduled services 1978: CAAC only

Nanning, Kwangsi-Chuang AR   Wuyu Airport

22° 37′ N   108° 11′ E   ICAO: ZGNN   IATA code: NNG
Elevation: 420 ft (128 m)
Longest runway: 05/23   2,400 m (7,874 ft)   SA 05/23 R
Pavement strength: 80,000 kg (176,370 lb) auw
Scheduled services 1978: CAAC only

Peking's new terminal and control tower for 1980.

Peking (Beijing), Hopei
     Capital International Airport (formerly Central Airport)

40° 05′ N   116° 36′ E   13.5 nm (25 km) NE of city centre
          ICAO: ZBAA   IATA code: PEK
Elevation: 105 ft (32 m)   Ref temp: 30.2 deg C
Runway: 18/36   3,200 × 80 m (10,500 × 262 ft) concrete with 60 m
          (197 ft) asphalt overrun each end
Pavement strength: 150,000 kg (330,693 lb) auw
Landing category: ICAO CAT I
Lighting:
     R/W   LIL white edge, and end lights
     App   R/W 18   LIH red centreline and one crossbar
          R/W 36   LIH red centreline and three crossbars. VASIS
               18/36
     Txy   edge

74

Aids: NDB, ILS CAT I 36
Twr frequency: 118.1
Terminals: Old terminal, and three-storey terminal with two satellite
    buildings to be opened in 1980. 16 aircraft docking positions at new
    terminal.
Scheduled services 1978: Aeroflot, Air France, CAAC, Ethiopian Airlines,
    International Air Cargo, Iran Air, Japan Air Lines, PIA, Swissair and
    Tarom
Main base: CAAC
    A parallel runway 1.1 nm (2,000 m) west of R/W 18/36 was under
    construction in 1979.

Shanghai, Kiangsu   Hungchiao Airport

31° 12′ N   121° 20′ E   7 nm (13 km) WSW of city centre
                 ICAO: ZSSS   IATA code: SHA
Elevation: 14 ft (4.4 m)   Ref temp: 32 deg C
Runway: 18/36   3,200 × 58 m (10,500 × 190 ft) concrete with 200 m
    (656 ft) macadam overrun each end
Pavement strength: 200,000 kg (440,924 lb) auw
    There is a parallel taxiway
Landing category: ICAO CAT I
Lighting:
    R/W   LIH and LIL white edge
    App   R/W 18   LIH white and LIL red centreline and one
             crossbar
             R/W 36   LIH white and LIL red centreline and four
             crossbars
    Thr   LIH and LIL
    Txy   edge
Aids: NDB, ILS CAT I 18/36
Twr frequency: 118.1
Terminal: On east side of airport with 330 × 130 m (1,083 × 426 ft) concrete
    apron. There is a railway siding at the airport
Scheduled services 1978: CAAC and Japan Air Lines

Hungchiao Airport, Shanghai, on the occasion of the first arrival by Ethiopian
Airlines. (*Courtesy Airports International*)

Taiyuan, Shansi   Wusu Airport

37° 45′ N   112° 37′ E   ICAO: ZBYN   IATA code: TYN
Elevation: 2,556 ft (779 m)
Longest runway: 13/31   2,500 m (8,202 ft)
Scheduled services 1978: CAAC only

Urumchi (Urumqi), Sinkiang-Uighur AR   Aweitan Airport

43° 57′ N   87° 05′ E   ICAO: ZWWW   IATA code: URC
Elevation: 2,418 ft (737 m)
Longest runway: 11/29   3,200 m (10,500 ft)
Scheduled services 1978: CAAC only

Colombia

Barranquilla   Aeropuerto Ernesto Cortissoz

	ICAO: MCBQ	IATA: BAQ	
10° 53′ 36″ N	74° 47′ 00″ W	Elevation: 94 ft (28.7 m)	
Runway: 04/22	3,000 m (9,842 ft)	RT	VASI 04

Aids: VOR/DME, NDB, ILS 04

	1971	1975	1976	1977
Passengers (terminal)	568,207	684,748	710,053	762,923
Transport movements	32,069	30,574	30,676	32,209

Scheduled services 1978: Aerocondor, ALM, Avianca, COPA, LACSA
and Sociedad Aeronáutica de Medellín

Bogotá   Aeropuerto de El Dorado

04° 42′ 22″ N   74° 08′ 32″ W   5.4 nm (10 km) NNW of city
ICAO: MCBO   IATA code: BOG   Time zone: GMT −5
Authority: Departamento Administrativo de Aeronáutica
Elevation: 8,355 ft (2,547 m)   Ref temp: 18.6 deg C
Runway: 12/30   3,800 × 48 m (12,467 × 157 ft) asphalt
Pavement strength: 273,000 kg (601,862 lb) auw
Landing category: uncategorized
Lighting:
          R/W   LIH white edge
          App   VASIS 12/30
          Thr   green
          Txy   blue edge
Aids: VOR/DME, NDB, L, ILS 12
Twr frequency: 118.1   App frequency: 119.7

El Dorado Airport, Bogotá, with BOAC's Super VC10 G-ASGJ on the apron.
(*British Airways*)

Terminal: Five-level passenger terminal with two two-level piers with 18
  gates. Separate cargo terminal and general aviation area
Scheduled services 1978: 15 airlines
Main base: Aeropesca Colombia, Avianca, Satena and TANA

Traffic:	1971	1975	1976	1977
Passengers (terminal)	1,982,144	2,695,643	3,094,523	3,362,274
Cargo and mail (tonnes)	76,202	80,631	86,898	102,017
Aircraft movements	78,646	70,496	78,482	—
Transport movements	60,804	52,869	58,567	61,494

Colombia can claim some of the earliest airline operations in South
America, SCADTA having been founded in 1919 and regular services
starting in 1921. Because of the difficult terrain the SCADTA services were
operated by Junkers-F 13 floatplanes over the Magdalena River route,
linking the port of Barranquilla with Girardot, the railhead for Bogotá.

Later Bogotá was served by landplanes, its Techo Airport serving until
the end of 1959. This airport had numerous shortcomings and could not be
brought up to the required standards. The decision to build a new airport
was made and work on clearing the site at Fontinbon-Engativa began in
July 1955. This work involved the moving of more than $1\frac{1}{2}$ mn cu m (53 mn
cu ft) of earth. By July 1957 the runway and taxiways had been completed
and construction of the terminal was in hand. The official opening was on
11 December, 1959.

The runway had a length of 3,800 m (12,467 ft), and a parallel taxiway
was provided, with three connecting taxiways near the terminal area. The
terminal, with two traffic piers and apron, occupied an area of 220,000 sq m
(2,368,080 sq ft). One pier is used for international services and the other
for domestic flights. A cargo terminal was constructed to the east of the
passenger terminal and a four-lane highway was built to link the airport
and city.

Provision has been made for a second runway, of 3,500 m (11,483 ft),
but no date has been given for its construction.

Cali   Aeropuerto Palmaseca   ICAO: MCCL   IATA: CLO

03° 32′ 46″ N   76° 23′ 06″ W   Elevation: 3,162 ft (964 m)
Runway: 01/19   3,000 m (9,842 ft)   ART   VASI 01/19
Aids: VOR/DME, NDB

	1971	1975	1976	1977
Passengers (terminal)	653,161	774,400	890,634	940,069
Transport movements	21,591	17,560	20,763	21,427

Scheduled services 1978: Aerocondor, Avianca, Braniff, Ecuatoriana,
   LAN-Chile, Sociedad Aeronáutica de Medellín and VIASA.
   The airport was opened in July 1971

Cartagena   Aeropuerto Crespo - Cartagena

               ICAO: MCCG   IATA: CTG
10° 27′ N   75° 31′ W   Elevation: 7 ft (2.13 m)
Runway: 18/36   2,200 m (7,218 ft)   RT   VASI 18/36
Aids: NDB

	1970	1975	1976	1977
Passengers (terminal)	174,294	329,413	384,267	401,743
Transport movements	—	14,859	12,824	13,331

Scheduled services 1978: Aerocondor, Avianca, LACSA and Sociedad
   Aeronáutica de Medellín.
   The runway is to be extended.

Medellín   Aeropuerto Olaya Herrera

06° 13′ 15″ N   75° 35′ 35″ W   1.6 nm (2.96 km) SSW of city
ICAO: MCMD   IATA code: MDE   Time zone: GMT −5
Authority: Departamento Administrativo de Aeronáutica
Elevation: 4,941 ft (1,506 m)   Ref temp: 28.7 deg C

Olaya Herrera Airport, Medellín, with Avianca Boeing 727-24C HK-1271
Almirante Padilla in the foreground.

Runway: 01/19   2,507 × 50 m (8,225 × 164 ft) asphalt/concrete
Pavement strength: auw 111,400 kg (245,595 lb) bogie
Lighting: none
Aids: VOR/DME, NDB
Twr frequency: 118.1   App frequency: 121.1
Terminal: Multi-storey passenger terminal with integral control tower and
    open aircraft parking
Scheduled services 1978: ACES - Aerolineas Centrales de Colombia,
    Aerocondor, ALM, Avianca, COPA and Sociedad Aeronáutica de
    Medellín.
Main base: ACES and SAM

Traffic:	1972	1975	1976	1977
Passengers (terminal)	986,734	1,057,628	1,197,771	1,255,830
Cargo (tonnes)	16,897*	15,770	16,778	19,404
Aircraft movements	62,926	49,918	50,902	—
Transport movements	47,392	34,042	33,530	34,209

* Includes mail

A new airport is to be built to serve Medellín

San Andrés (Islas)   Aeropuerto Sesquicentenario

            ICAO: MCSP   IATA: ADZ
12° 35′ N   81° 42′ W   Elevation: 19 ft (5.81 m)
Runway: 06/24   2,380 m (7,808 ft)   RT   VASI 06
Aids: VOR, NDB

	1970	1975	1976	1977
Passengers (terminal)	169,805	293,039	291,894	300,648
Transport movements	—	5,408	5,309	5,467

Scheduled services 1978: Aerocondor, Avianca, LACSA, SAHSA and
    Sociedad Aeronáutica de Medellín

Costa Rica

San José   Aeropuerto Internacional de El Coco*

            ICAO: MROC   IATA: SJO
09° 59′ 58″ N   84° 12′ 20″ W   Elevation: 3,021 ft (921 m)
Runway: 07/25   3,012 m (9,882 ft)   RT
Aids: VOR/DME, NDB

	1970	1975	1976	1977
Passengers	381,278	759,098	771,407	634,886=
Transport movements	8,360	—	—	22,725

Scheduled services 1978: 9 airlines
Main base: LACSA

*Also known as Juan Santamaría   = Excludes transit passengers

79

Cuba

Havana (La Habana)   Aeropuerto Internacional José Martí

	ICAO: MUHA	IATA: HAV	
22° 59′ 26″ N	82° 24′ 23″ W	Elevation: 210 ft (64 m)	
Runway: 05/23	4,000 m (13,123 ft)	ART	VASI 05

Aids: VOR/DME, NDB, L

	1971	1975	1976	1977
Passengers (terminal)	619,369	552,511	596,600*	740,786*
Transport movements	9,573	9,238	10,500*	13,371*

* ICAO estimates

Scheduled services 1978: Aeroflot, Air Canada, Angola Airlines, ČSA,
    Cubana, Iberia, Interflug and Méxicana
Main base: Cubana

Cyprus (Kypros)

Larnaca   Larnaca Airport   ICAO: LCLK   IATA: LCA

34° 52′ 44″ N	33° 37′ 49″ E		Elevation: 6 ft (2 m)
Runway: 04/22	2,530 m (8,300 ft)	RT	VASI

Aids: VOR/DME, NDB

	1975	1976	1977
Passengers	178,671	391,356	533,148
Transport movements	5,053	8,308	11,126

Scheduled services 1978: 16 airlines
Main base: Cyprus Airways
    The airport was opened in February 1975

Czechoslovakia (Československo)

Bratislava   Ivánka Airport   ICAO: LKIB   IATA: BTS

48° 10′ 14″ N	17° 12′ 52″ E		Elevation: 436 ft (133 m)
Longest runway: 04/22	2,900 m (9,514 ft)	ART	VASI 22

Aids: VOR, NDB, PAR, SRE, ILS CAT I 22 and 31

	1970	1975	1976	1977
Passengers	360,282	599,816	584,084	598,943
Transport movements	13,752	18,620	19,117	19,371

Scheduled services 1978: Aeroflot, Balkan, ČSA, Interflug and Slov-Air
Main base: Slov-Air

Prague (Praha)   Ruzyně Airport

50° 06′ 06″ N   14° 15′ 43″ E   5.94 nm (11 km) W of city
ICAO: LKPR   IATA code: PRG   Time zone: GMT plus 1
Authority: Czechoslovak Civil Aerodromes Administration
Area: 819.3 hectares (2,024 acres)
Elevation: 1,247 ft (380 m)   Ref temp: 19 deg C
Runways: 04/22   2,000 × 60 m   (6,562 × 197 ft) concrete and asphalt
         07/25   3,100 × 45 m (10,170 × 148 ft) concrete
         08/26   1,670 × 40 m   (5,479 × 131 ft) concrete and asphalt
         13/31   3,250 × 45 m (10,663 × 148 ft) concrete
         There is a 2,000 × 100 m (6,562 × 328 ft) emergency strip
         alongside 07/25 and another alongside 13/31 between taxiway
         6D and the west end of 08/26
Pavement strength: 04/22 and 08/26 LCN 28, 07/25 LCN 120, 13/31 LCN
         80
Landing category: ICAO CAT II
Lighting:
   R/W   04/22 LIL white edge, last 300 m (984 ft) red; 07 LIL white
           edge, last 600 m (1,968 ft) yellow; 25 LIH and LIL white
           edge, last 600 m (1,968 ft) yellow; 13 LIL white edge, last
           600 m (1,968 ft) yellow; 31 LIH and LIL white edge, last
           1,000 m (3,281 ft) yellow, and centreline white from
           threshold to 1,995 m (6,545 ft), red/white 2,009–2,954 m
           (6,591–9,691 ft), red 2,954 m (9,691 ft) to end.
           TDZ 900 m (2,953 ft) LIH white 25 and 31. Red end lights
           13/31 and 07/25. REIL 25 and 31
   App   R/W 07 LIL white 930 m (3,051 ft) centreline with two
           crossbars
           R/W 25 LIH white 1,000 m (3,281 ft) Calvert centreline
           with six crossbars and flashers and LIL white centreline
           with two crossbars
           R/W 31 LIH white 900 m (2,953 ft) barrette centreline with
           two crossbars and flashers.
           VASIS 25 and 31
   Thr   R/W 07, 13 and 22 LIL green, 25 LIH and LIL green
           flashing lights and green wing bars, 31 LIH and LIL green
   Txy   blue edge, some sections with centreline
Aids: VOR/DME, NDB, VDF, L, PAR, SRE, RVR 25 and 31, ILS CAT II
   31, ILS CAT I 25
Twr frequency: 118.1   App frequency: 121.4
Terminals: Widely separated north and south terminals. North,
   international, terminal with 14 close-in aircraft stands and nine
   remote; South (domestic) terminal with six close-in and 13 remote
   aircraft stands.
Scheduled services 1978: 21 airlines
Main base: ČSA

Traffic:	1970	1975	1976	1977
Passengers (total)	1,618,617	2,131,796	2,028,343	2,029,457
Cargo (tonnes)	12,038	13,379	11,521	10,667
Aircraft movements	45,321	59,476	60,423	57,685
Transport movements	40,334	49,674	49,140	50,008

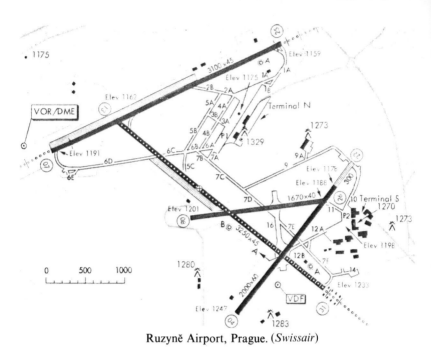

Ruzyně Airport, Prague. (*Swissair*)

In 1976 Tupolev Tu-134s accounted for 28 per cent of transport movements, Yak-40s for 19 per cent, Ilyushin Il-18s for 15 per cent and DC-9s for 5.77 per cent.

In the spring of 1934 work began on the preparation of a new Prague airport to replace Kbely. The site chosen was northwest of Ruzyně and had an area of 108 hectares (267 acres). The well-drained grass surface provided a maximum take-off distance of 1,200 m (3,937 ft), from northeast to southwest. The east–west measurement was 1,000 m (3,281 ft) and north–south 900 m (2,953 ft). Full lighting was installed, including landing

Ruzyně Airport, Prague. The north passenger terminal.
(*Courtesy Airports International*)

direction lights for poor visibility. A passenger terminal, with separate domestic and international arrival and departure gates, was built near the mid-point of the eastern boundary. Three hangars and the control tower were sited in the southeast corner of the airport. The 140 by 110 m (459 by 361 ft) apron was of rolled clinker. The airport was opened on 1 March, 1937, and the master plan allowed for subsequent extension.

A pattern of tarmac runways was constructed, probably during the war, and by 1951 these were: 04/22 1,800 m (5,905 ft), 09/27 1,318 m (4,324 ft), 13/31 1,020 m (3,346 ft) plus 500 m (1,640 ft) grass at the southeast, and 17/35 950 m (3,117 ft) plus 500 m (1,640 ft) grass at the south end. A tarmac taxiway connected the intersection of all but the 09/27 runway with the terminal area and there was a taxiway between the terminal and 27 threshold. There were six sodium lights on the 22 approach.

Subsequently 04/22 was lengthened to 2,000 m (6,562 ft) with a 300 m (984 ft) stopway at the northeast end; 09/27 was renumbered 08/26 and extended westward to its present 1,670 m (5,479 ft); 13/31 became the main runway with a length of 3,250 m (10,663 ft) thus extending the airport considerably to the northwest. Runway 17/35 was abandoned and a completely new 3,100 m (10,170 ft) 07/25 runway was built to the north of the airport. An international terminal was constructed in the angle between runways 07/25 and 13/31, together with an extensive system of taxiways.

Denmark (Danmark)

Ålborg (Aalborg)   Lufthavn Aalborg

                    ICAO: EKYT   IATA: AAL
57° 05′ 35″ N   09° 51′ 00″ E   Elevation: 10 ft (3 m)
Longest runway: 09L/27R   2,650 m (8,695 ft)   ART   VASI 09L/27R
Aids: VORTAC, L-DME, VDF, GCA, ILS 27

	1970	1975	1976	1978
Passengers	313,204	401,159	460,309	426,247
Aircraft movements	45,989	56,384	55,846	49,543

Scheduled services 1978: SAS only

Billund   Lufthavn Billund   ICAO: EKBI   IATA: BLL

55° 44′ 25″ N   09° 09′ 10″ E   Elevation: 247 ft (75 m)
Runway: 09/27   3,100 m (10,170 ft)   ART   VASI 09
Aids: NDB, TAR, ILS 09/27

	1970	1975	1976	1978
Passengers	320,164	582,511	618,855	678,400
Aircraft movements	55,207	54,487	53,440	57,635

Scheduled services 1978: Danair only

Copenhagen (København)   Københavns Lufthavn Kastrup

55° 37' 05" N   12° 39' 28" E   4.4 nm (8.14 km) SSE of city
ICAO: EKCH   IATA code: CPH   Time zone: GMT plus 1
Authority: Københavns Lufthavnsvæsen (Copenhagen Airport Authority)
Area: 1,100 hectares (2,718 acres)
Elevation: 17 ft (5 m)   Ref temp: 18.8 deg C
Runways: 04/22   650 × 30 m (2,133 × 98 ft) grass
          04L/22R   3,600 × 46 m (11,811 × 151 ft) concrete and
                                                    asphalt
          04R/22L   3,300 × 46 m (10,827 × 151 ft) concrete and
                                                    asphalt
          09/27   1,800 × 46 m (5,905 × 151 ft) concrete and
                                                    asphalt
          12/30   3,070 × 46 m (10,072 × 151 ft) concrete and
                                                    asphalt
       R/W 04L landing and take-off last 2,000 ft (610 m) not available, R/W
       22R landing first 2,000 ft (610 m) not available, R/W 12/30 landing first
       886 ft (270 m) and take-off last 886 ft (270 m) not available
Pavement strength: 04R/22L 190,000 kg (418,878 lb) 3; 09/27 45,000 kg
       (99,208 lb) 2, 90,000 kg (198,416 lb) 3; 12/30 153,000 kg (337,307 lb) 3
Landing category: ICAO CAT II
Lighting:
       R/W   04L   LIH and LIL edge—white 2,400 m (7,874 ft),
       clearway yellow 600 m (1,968 ft), stopway red 600 m (1,968

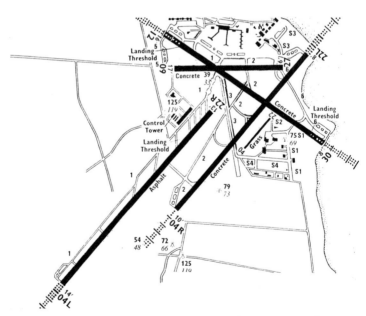

Kastrup Airport, Copenhagen. (*British Airways Aerad*)

ft). LIH and LIL white centreline 3,000 m (9,842 ft). Red end lights at Thr 22R. White TDZ

22R   LIH and LIL edge—red 600 m (1,968 ft), white 2,400 m (7,874 ft), clearway yellow 600 m (1,968 ft). LIH and LIL white centreline 3,000 m (9,842 ft). Red end lights 04R/22L LIH and LIL white edge 3,300 m (10,827 ft), LIM white centreline. LIL white TDZ 22L. Red end lights

09/27   LIH and LIL white edge. Red end lights

12/30   LIH and LIL edge—red 270 m (886 ft), white 1,930 m (6,332 ft), clearway yellow 600 m (1,968 ft), stopway red 270 m (886 ft). LIL white TDZ. Red end wing bars

App   R/W 04L and 22L   900 m (2,953 ft) LIH and LIL Calvert CAT II

          R/W 04R   690 m (2,264 ft) LIH white Calvert

          R/W 12/30   900 m (2,953 ft) LIH and LIL white Calvert VASIS 12/30 and 22R

Thr   green

Txy   blue and yellow edge, green centreline

Aids: VOR/DME, NDB, VDF, SRE, ILS CAT II 04L and 22L, ILS CAT I 04R and 12

Twr frequency: 118.1   App frequency: 119.8

Terminals: International terminal with one 315 m (1,033 ft) traffic pier and two 300 m (984 ft) piers, one 282 m (925 ft) cross finger and domestic terminal with 36 international and seven domestic aircraft stands. Cargo area with eight stands

Scheduled services 1978: 42 airlines

Main base: Danair A/S, Maersk Air, SAS and Sterling Airways

Traffic:	1970	1975	1976	1977	1978
Passengers (total)	6,790,569	8,492,036	8,948,971	8,897,872	9,593,616
Cargo (tonnes)	112,873	129,615	144,452	156,313	182,569
Aircraft movements	156,809	163,033	163,731	163,843	—
Transport movements	146,086	148,363	147,654	147,170	156,342

In 1976 DC-9s accounted for 56.52 per cent of transport movements and Caravelles for 6.83 per cent.

When DDL (Det Danske Luftfartselskab) began operation on 7 August, 1920, over the Copenhagen–Warnemünde route the airline used a Friedrichshafen FF 49 seaplane, but subsequent landplane operations were based on Kløvermarksvej military aerodrome. However, as early as 1920 plans had been made for a Copenhagen airport at Kastrup, beside Öresund, and construction began in 1923.

A grass landing area was prepared, a two-storey houselike administration building and a hangar were erected, and the airport opened for traffic on 20 April, 1925. There were facilities for seaplanes and flying-boats, and the attractive gunpowder magazine, built in 1781 and surrounded by a moat, served as the airport restaurant.

Kastrup has been a major European airport for well over half a century and its history has been one of continuing expansion and development. A fine terminal and administration building, with large concrete apron, was completed in 1939. German invasion forces occupied Kastrup on 10 April, 1940, and during the war the Germans constructed

85

Kastrup Airport, Copenhagen. The terminal area and runways, looking south-southeast. (*Civil Aviation Administration*)

four concrete runways—04/22 1,800 m (5,905 ft), 09/27 1,600 m (5,249 ft), 12/30 1,200 m (3,937 ft) and 17/35 1,200 m (3,937 ft).

Limited airline operations continued at Kastrup during the war and when the British forces liberated Denmark a variety of German aircraft were found at Kastrup. On 1 April, 1946, the Royal Air Force handed over the airport to the Danish authorities and the airport returned to full civil status.

Runway 04/22 is now 04R/22L with a length of 3,300 m (10,827 ft); 09/27 has only been lengthened by 200 m (656 ft); 12/30 is now 3,070 m (10,072 ft); and 17/35 is now part of the taxiway system.

A completely new runway, 04L/22R of 3,600 m (11,811 ft) was commissioned in the early 1970s and this was cleared for CAT II operations on 16 February, 1976.

A new passenger terminal was opened in 1960, with a separate domestic terminal being commissioned in 1969. Expansion of the cargo terminal has taken place, with every effort being made to provide adequate capacity without the expense of a new terminal.

The limited area of Kastrup and closeness of shipping lanes to the eastern boundary inhibit continued expansion of the airport, and for many years it had been planned to build a completely new airport on Saltholm between Copenhagen and Malmö but this project was abandoned in 1979.

Some relief for Kastrup came with the opening, on 1 April, 1973, of a second Copenhagen aerodrome, at Roskilde. In 1975 this aerodrome handled 89,509 aircraft movements and 25,019 passengers.

Tirstrup (Århus)　　　Lufthavn Tirstrup

ICAO: EKAH　　　　IATA: AAR
56° 18′ 01″ N　　　10° 37′ 15″ E　　　　Elevation: 82 ft (25 m)
Longest runway: 10/28　　2,708 m (8,884 ft)　　ART
Aids: TACAN, NDB, PAR, SRE, ILS 28

	1970	1975	1976	1978
Passengers*	262,856	331,777	361,861	425,825
Aircraft movements	8,600	8,425	8,930	10,075

* Scheduled traffic only

Scheduled services 1978: SAS only

Dominican Republic (República Dominicana)

Santo Domingo　　　Aeropuerto Internacional de Las Américas

ICAO: MDSD　　　　IATA: SDQ
18° 25′ 57″ N　　　69° 40′ 14″ W　　　　Elevation: 57 ft (17 m)
Runway: 17/35　　3,353 m (11,000 ft)　　RT
Aids: VOR/DME, NDB

	1970	1975	1976	1977
Passengers	409,445	758,721	830,365	960,588*
Transport movements	13,822	17,941	20,483	19,783

* Excludes transit passengers

Scheduled services 1978: 10 airlines
Main base: Aerovias Quisqueyana and Dominicana

Ecuador

Guayaquil　　　Aeropuerto Simón Bolívar

ICAO: SEGU　　　　IATA: GYE
02° 09′ 12″ S　　　79° 53′ 00″ W　　　　Elevation: 13 ft (4 m)
Runway: 03/21　　2,440 m (8,004 ft)　　ART　　VASI 21
Aids: VOR/DME, NDB, L, ILS CAT I 21

	1970	1975	1976
Passengers	433,250	290,741*	260,302*
Transport movements	31,771	—	—

* International only

Scheduled services 1978: 12 airlines
Main base: ANDES Airlines

Quito valley, looking north, in November 1974, with Mariscal Sucre Airport and its 17/35 runway in the centre. (*René J. Francillon*)

Quito   Aeropuerto Mariscal Sucre

ICAO: SEQU	IATA: UIO
00° 08′ 20″ S 78° 29′ 06″ W	Elevation: 9,226 ft (2,812 m)
Runway: 17/35 3,120 m (10,236 ft)	ART VASI 35

Aids: VOR/DME, NDB

	1970	1975	1976
Passengers	374,626	251,921*	288,722*
Transport movements	17,414	—	—

*International only

Scheduled services 1978: 10 airlines
Main base: Ecuatoriana, SAETA and TAME
    A new airport is to be built at Puembo about 30 km (18½ miles) from the city.

88

Arab Republic of Egypt

Cairo (El Qahira)   Cairo International Airport

30° 06′ 15″ N   31° 24′ 29″ E   13 nm (24 km) ENE of Central Stn
ICAO: HECA   IATA code: CAI   Time zone: GMT plus 2
Authority: Cairo Airport Authority
Area: 1,200 hectares (2,965 acres)
Elevation: 381 ft (116 m)   Ref temp: 30.6 deg C
Runways: 05L/23R   3,300 × 60 m (10,827 × 197 ft) asphalt
         05R/23L   4,000 × 45 m (13,123 × 148 ft) concrete
         16/34   3,150 × 60 m (10,335 × 197 ft) asphalt
Pavement strength: LCN 131
Landing category: ICAO CAT II
Lighting:
  R/W   LIH white edge, last 600 m (1,968 ft) yellow. White
          centreline 05R/23L. TDZ 05R. Red end lights
  App   R/W 05L Calvert CAT I
          R/W 23R Calvert CAT II
          R/W 05R Precision approach CAT II
          R/W 23L Precision approach CAT I
          R/W 34 LIH white centreline and crossbar
          VASIS all runways

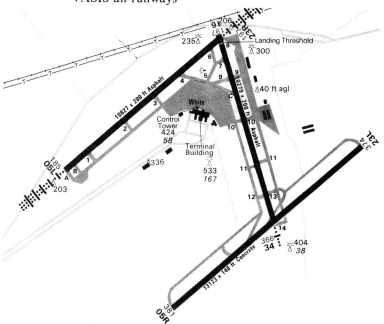

Cairo International Airport. Approach lighting for 05R/23L not shown.
(*British Airways Aerad*)

89

Thr   green, with wing bars on 16/34
Txy   blue edge. Centreline on 05R/23L exits
Aids: VOR/DME, NDB, L, SRE, ILS CAT I 23R, ILS CAT II 05R
Twr frequency: 118.1   App frequency: 119.1
Terminal: Multi-storey terminal in angle of 05L/23R and 16/34 runways.
    Two aprons with 27 aircraft stands
Scheduled services 1978: 46 airlines
Main base: Egyptair

Traffic:	1970	1975	1976	1977
Passengers (total)	1,221,559	2,562,581*	3,373,435	3,487,954
Cargo (tonnes)	13,717	24,428	29,741	38,074
Aircraft movements	31,264	43,299	50,859	52,948
Transport movements	27,824	40,068	49,833	50,496

*Excluding transit passengers

When the Royal Air Force began operation of the Desert Air Mail Route, between Cairo and Baghdad, on 23 June, 1921, the RAF aerodrome at Heliopolis served as the Cairo base, and Heliopolis continued to serve as Cairo's airport when Imperial Airways opened its Cairo–Baghdad–Basra service in January 1927. In 1932 a civil airport was opened at Almaza, just beyond Heliopolis and on the edge of the desert.

Almaza Airport continued in operation into the 1950s and had three runways, the longest, 18/36, measuring 6,309 ft (1,923 m). Heliopolis has long been closed and Almaza is now a military aerodrome.

During the Second World War the United States Government constructed an aerodrome in the desert beyond Almaza. This was known as Payne Field, and was transferred to the Egyptian Government on 16 December, 1946. It was destined to become the main Cairo airport and named Farouk.

Farouk Airport had three asphalt runways—02/20 of 6,000 ft (1,829 m) and 13/31 and 16/34 each of 6,990 ft (2,130 m). A terminal building was constructed on the east side of the airport.

In the early 1950s the 05/23 asphalt runway of 9,350 ft (2,850 m) was built—later being extended at its southwest end to give a length of 10,827 ft (3,300 m). Runways 02/20 and 13/31 were abandoned and 16/34 was lengthened southward to provide 10,279 ft (3,133 m).

Cairo International Airport, landside view of the terminal in 1960. (*John Stroud*)

In 1963 the terminal area was transferred westward to be sited in the angle formed by runways 05/23 and 16/34. A national contest was held for the design of the terminal building and this appeared as a multi-storey structure with 75,000 sq m (807,300 sq ft) total floor area. The terminal was built in less than five years, cost £E 6 mn and was opened by President Nasser on 18 May, 1963.

The new 4,000 m (13,123 ft) 05R/23L instrument runway with parallel taxiway and high-speed exits was brought into operation on 2 July, 1979.

Further developments include a second terminal to bring the airport's capacity to 10 mn passengers a year by 1981. It was reported in mid-1978 that planning had begun for a new airport to serve both Cairo and Alexandria.

El Salvador

San Salvador   Aeropuerto Internacional Ilopango

ICAO: MSSS   IATA: SAL
13° 42′ 04″ N   89° 07′ 18″ W   Elevation: 2,047 ft (624 m)
Longest runway: 15/33   2,240 m (7,349 ft)   RT   VASI 15/33
Aids: VOR/DME, NDB

	1970	1975	1976	1977
Passengers	235,189	296,957	343,363	382,146
Transport movements	9,850	10,201	11,453	11,899

Scheduled services 1978: nine airlines
Main base: TACA International Airlines

A new airport has been constructed at Cuscatlán, with 3,200 m (10,500 ft) instrument runway.

Fiji

Nadi   Nadi International Airport

17° 45′ 16″ S   177° 26′ 50″ E   12.96 nm (24 km) S of Lautoka
ICAO: NFFN   IATA code: NAN   Time zone: GMT plus 12
Authority: Department of Civil Aviation
Area: 483 hectares (1,193 acres)
Elevation: 63 ft (19 m)   Ref temp: 28.1 deg C
Runways: 03/21   3,200 × 46 m (10,500 × 150 ft) concrete
         09/27   2,134 × 46 m   (7,000 × 150 ft) bitumen
Pavement strength: 03/21 LCN 70, 09/27 LCN 25
Landing category: ICAO CAT I

Lighting:
R/W   03/21   LIH white edge, last 2,000 ft (610 m) yellow
           09/27   LIM white edge
App   R/W 03   LIH white and LIL red centreline with crossbars
           R/W 09   LIL red centreline and crossbar. VASIS 09 and
                         03/21
Thr   R/W 03 LIH green with wing bars, R/W 09 LIL green
           with wing bars, R/W 21 LIH green, R/W 27 LIL green
Txy   blue

There is a red flashing beacon beyond R/W 03 to warn of turning point to
    clear Sambeto mountains 2.5 nm (4.63 km) to the north
Aids: VOR/DME, NDB, L, ILS CAT I 03
Twr frequency: 119.1
Terminal: Passenger terminal in angle of 21 and 27 runways, with 14
    aircraft stands on three connected aprons
Scheduled services 1978: 10 airlines

Traffic:	1970
Passengers (total)	439,220
Aircraft movements	12,432

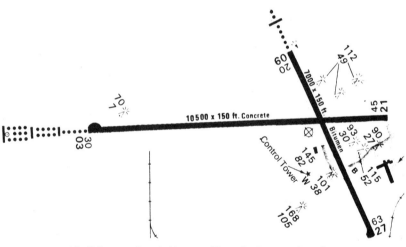

Nadi International Airport. (*British Airways Aerad*)

The airport was built during the Second World War as a staging post
for Allied military aircraft. The site on the west coast of Viti Levu was
chosen because it has better weather than the Suva area in the east.
    The first commercial service to use Nadi was the inaugural
Sydney–San Francisco–Vancouver flight of Australian National Airways
on 15 September, 1946. The service was operated on behalf of British
Commonwealth Pacific Air Lines and the first flight made by the DC-4
VH-ANC *Warana* which also called at Canton Island and Honolulu.

Nadi International Airport, Fiji. The approach to runway 03, photographed at the end of 1964. (*John Stroud*)

In spite of increased aircraft range, Nadi is still a vital part of Pacific communications. Feeder services connect Nadi with the Suva Airport of Nausori—an air stage of 66 nautical miles (122 km) but a very much longer road journey.

Administration of the airport was transferred from New Zealand to the Fiji Department of Civil Aviation on 1 July, 1957.

The name of the airport is frequently wrongly spelled as Nandi which is the pronunciation of Nadi.

Finland (Suomi)

Helsinki   Helsinki - Vantaa Airport

60° 19′ 01″ N   24° 57′ 59″ E   9.2 nm (17 km) NNE of city
ICAO: EFHK   IATA code: HEL   Time zone: GMT plus 2
Authority: National Board of Aviation
Area: 1,170 hectares (2,891 acres)
Elevation: 167 ft (51 m)   Ref temp: 17.9 deg C
Runways: 04/22   3,200 × 60 m (10,500 × 197 ft) asphalt/concrete
         15/33   2,900 × 60 m (9,514 × 197 ft) asphalt/concrete
Pavement strength: 04/22 LCN 80, 15/33 LCN 85
Landing category: ICAO CAT II
Lighting:
     R/W   LIH and LIL white edge, last 600 m (1,968 ft) yellow; white
             centreline, last 300 m (984 ft) red, previous 600 m (1,968 ft)
             red/white. TDZ 22

App   R/W 04   LIH white and LIL red centreline with three crossbars
           R/W 15   LIH white and LIL red centreline with five crossbars
           R/W 22   LIH white and LIL red centreline with five crossbars and red barrettes on inner 300 m (984 ft)
           R/W 33   LIH white and LIL red centreline with one crossbar
           VASIS all runways
Thr   LIH and LIL green
Txy   blue edge

Aids: VOR/DME, NDB, VDF, SRE, L, ILS CAT II 22, ILS CAT I 15
Twr frequency: 118.6   App frequency: 119.1
Terminal: International and domestic terminal with 10 close-in aircraft stands and seven outer stands. Two aerobridges. Separate Finnair cargo terminal with five aircraft stands
Scheduled services 1978: 13 airlines
Main base: Finnair and Kar-Air

Traffic:	1970	1975	1976	1977
Passengers (total)	1,395,582	2,812,668	2,840,812	2,711,000
Cargo (tonnes)	14,346	18,626	20,810	21,497
Aircraft movements	51,411	86,076	83,820	78,962
Transport movements	31,930	52,610	52,368	48,498

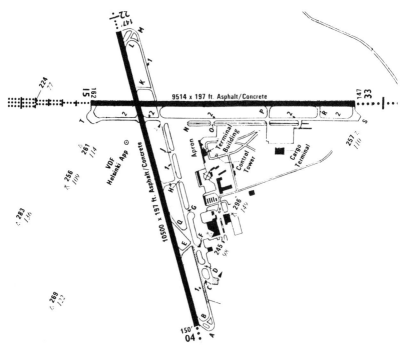

Helsinki - Vantaa Airport. (*British Airways Aerad*)

Helsinki - Vantaa Airport in 1977. Terminal area with Finnair DC-9s and Caravelle and a Tupolev Tu-134 on the apron.

Finland's early air services were all worked by seaplanes but in 1932 plans were made for the construction of an airport at Malmi, 11 km (7 miles) northeast of Helsinki. This airport, which had four paved runways, a circular terminal building with two wings, and a hangar, was sufficiently advanced for traffic on the Helsinki–Turku–Stockholm route to use it from December 1936. Helsinki - Malmi was officially opened on 15 May, 1938.

After the war Malmi continued as the Helsinki airport but plans were prepared for a new and larger airport and work was expedited to get it operational before the 1952 Olympic Games. This was achieved and the airport opened for traffic on 6 July, 1952, with the official opening on 26 October that year. The first commercial flight to serve the new airport was operated by the SAS DC-6B OY-KMA *Torkil Viking*.

When the airport opened there was a single runway, 04/22 of 2,000 m (6,562 ft), and a single-storey prefabricated terminal building.

In order to study the requirements and try to produce the best possible terminal, construction of a permanent building was delayed but finally opened in 1969. The terminal, with cantilevered roof and glass airside face, is to be extended to the southwest to enlarge the international arrivals section and this work is due for completion in 1981. Four more aerobridges are to be added.

Oulu   Oulu Airport   ICAO: EFOU   IATA: OUL

64° 55′ 44″ N   25° 21′ 34″ E   Elevation: 47 ft (14 m)
Longest runway: 12/30   2,500 m (8,202 ft)   ART   VASI 12/30
Aids: VOR/DME, NDB, VDF, RVR, L, ILS CAT I 12

	1970	1975	1976	1977
Passengers	200,340	319,881	323,256	250,858
Transport movements	6,352	11,330	9,944	6,616

Scheduled services 1978: Finnair only

Turku Turku Airport   ICAO: EFTU   IATA: TKU

60° 30′ 53″ N 22° 15′ 54″ E   Elevation: 161 ft (49 m)
Runway: 08/26 2,000 m (6,562 ft) ART   VASI 08
Aids: VOR/DME, NDB, VDF, L, ILS CAT I 26

	1970	1975	1976	1977
Passengers	168,266	272,334	303,849	240,853
Transport movements	6,298	8,152	8,100	7,882

Scheduled services 1978: Finnair only

The airport opened on 23 April, 1955

France

Ajaccio, Corsica (Corse)   Aéroport d'Ajaccio - Campo-Dell 'Oro

     ICAO: LFKJ   IATA: AJA
41° 55′ 27″ N   08° 48′ 11″ E   Elevation: 16 ft (5 m)
Longest runway: 03/21 2,125 m (6,972 ft) RT VASI 21
Aids: NDB, ILS 03

	1970	1975	1976	1977	1978
Passengers	316,971	484,653	475,210	472,834	547,770
Transport movements*	8,580	10,551	11,244	10,625	10,474

*Includes all categories of aerial work

Scheduled services 1978: Air France, Air Inter and Air Littoral

Bastia, Corsica (Corse)   Aéroport de Bastia - Poretta

     ICAO: LFKB   IATA: BIA
42° 32′ 57″ N   09° 29′ 10″ E   Elevation: 26 ft (8 m)
Runway: 16/34 2,320 m (7,611 ft) RT
Aids: VOR, VDF, ILS 34

	1970	1975	1976	1977
Passengers	324,170	490,489	478,113	494,057
Transport movements*	7,828	9,471	8,825	8,080

*Includes all categories of aerial work

Scheduled services 1978: Air France, Air Inter and Royal Air Maroc

Bordeaux   Aéroport International de Bordeaux - Mérignac

ICAO: LFBD   IATA: BOD
44° 49′ 44″ N   00° 42′ 54″ W   Elevation: 161 ft (49 m)
Longest runway: 05/23   3,100 m (10,170 ft)   ART   TDZ 23
Aids: VORTAC, NDB, VDF, PAR, ILS CAT III 23

	1970	1975	1976	1977	1978
Passengers	355,311	599,241	679,882	953,627	984,840
Transport movements*	15,449	19,008	20,961	20,313	20,424

* Includes all categories of aerial work

Scheduled services 1978: 13 airlines

Lille   Aéroport de Lille - Lesquin

ICAO: LFQQ   IATA: LIL
50° 33′ 46″ N   03° 05′ 15″ E   Elevation: 157 ft (48 m)
Longest runway: 08/26   2,400 m (7,874 ft)   ART   TDZ 26
Aids: VDF, ILS CAT II 26

	1970	1975	1976	1977
Passengers	113,295	196,419	238,498	293,710
Transport movements*	14,567	11,419	8,891	—

* Includes all categories of aerial work

Scheduled services 1978: Air Algérie, Air France, Air Inter, KLM, Royal Air Maroc, Sabena and Touraine Air Transport

Lyon   Aéroport International de Lyon - Satolas

45° 43′ 32″ N   05° 04′ 54″ E   11 nm (20.37 km) ESE of city
ICAO: LFLL   IATA code: LYS   Time zone: GMT plus 1
Authority: Lyon Chamber of Commerce
Area: 1,100 hectares (2,718 acres)
Elevation: 814 ft (248 m)   Ref temp: 25.7 deg C
Runway: 18/36   4,000 × 45 m (13,123 × 148 ft) hydrocarbon
Pavement strength: 25,000 kg (55,115 lb) 1, 36,000 kg (79,366 lb) 2,
     70,000 kg (154,324 lb) 3.
Landing category: ICAO CAT IIIa
Lighting:
   R/W   LIH and LIL white edge and LIH and LIL colour-coded
            centreline. Red end lights. TDZ 36
   App   R/W 18   LIL yellow 600 m (1,968 ft) centreline with one
            crossbar
            R/W 36   LIH and LIL white 900 m (2,953 ft) centreline
            with five crossbars and LIL yellow 600 m (1,968 ft)
            centreline with orange crossbar and inner red barrettes.
            VASIS 18
   Thr   LIH and LIL green
   Txy   LIL blue edge, some LIH green centreline

Aids: TACAN, VOR/DME, NDB, VDF, L, RAD, ILS CAT IIIa 36
Twr frequency: 120.0/128.0   App frequency: 125.8/128.5
Terminals: Central building with two adjoining semi-circular wing buildings. The southern wing building has four blocks, three serving international flights and one serving Paris flights. The northern wing has three blocks, two used by Air Inter (except Paris) and one used by third-level airlines. Nose-in aircraft stand for each block and aerobridge. There is a separate 12,000 sq m (129,168 sq ft) cargo terminal and a mail terminal.

Scheduled services 1978: 22 airlines

Traffic:	1970*	1975	1976	1977
Passengers (total)	870,563	1,624,722	1,864,683	2,066,764
Cargo (tonnes)	6,814	9,280	27,023	41,579
Aircraft movements	—	100,532	104,180	100,473
Transport movements	28,663	39,952	43,461	45,342
Night mail movements	3,775	4,063	4,107	—

*Figures for Lyon - Bron

During 1977 Caravelles accounted for 19.54 per cent of transport movements, Fokker F.27s for 17.01 per cent, Boeing 727s for 7.74 per cent, Dassault Mercures for 6.88 per cent, Fokker F.28s for 5.97 per cent and Corvettes for 4.82 per cent.

From the earliest days of French air transport Lyon played an important role. The short-range aircraft then in service refuelled there on flights between Paris and the Mediterranean coast and it was also the junction for flights to Geneva. The airport, with small grass landing area, was Lyon - Bron, situated beside the Lyon–Chambéry road, 6 km (3¾ miles) ESE of Lyon and 1½ km (1,640 yards) from the village of Bron, and, much improved and enlarged, it continued to serve the city after the Second World War and now has an 1,820 m (5,971 ft) runway. By the 1950s, however, it was becoming saturated and the closeness of urban development prevented runway extension.

The Lyon area is economically and industrially second only to Paris, there is a population of about 5 mn, and most of the Rhône-Alpes cities are within an hour's drive. It was therefore essential that Lyon should have a new airport, one capable of expansion, and one that should not be restricted by noise abatement requirements.

Planning began in 1960 and a site was chosen about 20 km (12½ miles) east–southeast of the city and close to the A43 Lyon–Chambéry toll motorway. The area is generally level and uninhabited. Land purchase began in 1969 for an airport occupying 1,100 hectares (2,718 acres) but with eventual expansion to 3,000 hectares (7,413 acres). Construction began in 1970.

There were to have been two parallel 18/36 runways available when the airport opened but financial restrictions led to postponement of construction of one of these.

The terminal area is at the south of the airport and west of the runway. The terminal building consists of a central block flanked by two curved arrival and departure buildings—the south building being the international wing with four blocks, three serving international flights and one services to and from Paris; the north building has three blocks, two being used by Air Inter for domestic services other than those to Paris and one by third-level airlines. Each block has a nose-in stand and aerobridge boarding.

Lyon - Satolas Airport in April 1976. The central terminal and wing buildings. An Air France Concorde is on the apron. (*Courtesy Lyon Chamber of Commerce*)

Eventually the two wing buildings will be extended to form semi-circles with 100 m (328 ft) inside radius, each will have an annual passenger capacity of 3 mn and each will have 16 aerobridges.

The runway is served by a parallel taxiway and there are cargo and mail terminals south of the passenger terminal.

Lyon - Satolas was opened on 12 April, 1975, and Lyon - Bron is now used for general aviation activities.

The master plan for Satolas envisages extensive development as traffic demand grows. First, expansion of runway, terminal and maintenance facilities would be on the present site with a 18L/36R runway of 3,000 m (9,842 ft) situated parallel to the existing runway with 350 m (1,148 ft) separation between their centrelines. Additional taxiways and high-speed exits are planned for the existing runway.

North of the present terminal area it is planned that there should be two more semi-circular terminals. Provision has also been made for expansion of cargo and maintenance facilities and at the north end of the airport a general aviation area, close to which land has been allocated for a 600 by 90 m (1,968 by 295 ft) STOL runway and a 120 by 90 m (394 by 295 ft) VTOL pad—there being provision for a second VTOL pad at the south of the airport.

Looking much further ahead, the entrance road to the airport would become a spine separating east and west areas, the western area to have a 18/36 runway and associated taxiways, passenger, cargo, maintenance and general aviation areas. The two separate areas would be linked by dual taxiways at central and southern positions. It is also planned that there should be a railway link between Lyon and the airport terminal area.

The Lyon - Satolas Airport was built on time, for less than its forecast cost, and its passenger terminals have been praised for their pleasant atmosphere, human scale and imaginative use of colour. Airport landscaping includes the planting of about 10,000 trees.

Marseilles - Marignane Airport in May 1978. View from over Étang de Berre showing the extension to runway 14L in the foreground. The terminal area is on the left and in the distance can be seen the Mediterranean and the city of Marseilles.
(Marseilles Airport Authority)

Marseilles (Marseille)　　　Aéroport de Marseille - Marignane

43° 26′ 12″ N　　　05° 12′ 56″ E　　　14.6 nm (27 km) NW of city
ICAO: LFML　　　IATA code: MRS　　　Time zone: GMT plus 1
Authority: Marseilles Airport Authority
Area: 500 hectares (1,235 acres) approximately
Elevation: 66 ft (20 m)　　　　　　　　Ref temp: 29 deg C
Runways: 14L/32R　　3,500 × 45 m (11,483 × 148 ft) concrete
　　　　　14R/32L　　2,370 × 45 m　(7,775 × 148 ft) concrete
　　　　　There is a 1,650 by 35 m (5,413 by 115 ft) grass runway for
　　　　　emergency wheels-up landings between the main runways.
Pavement strength: 14L/32R 35,000 kg (77,162 lb) 1, 40,000 kg (88,185 lb)
　　2, 80,000 kg (176,370 lb) 3; 14R/32L 25,000 kg (55,115 lb) 1, 31,000 kg
　　(68,343 lb) 2, 52,000 kg (114,640 lb) 3.
Landing category: ICAO CAT I
Lighting:
　　R/W　　14L/32R　　LIH and LIL white edge, red end lights, red
　　　　　　edge lights in 14L undershoot area before displaced
　　　　　　threshold, red lights on end of runway before 14L
　　　　　　undershoot area. TDZ wing bars 32R
　　　　　　14R/32L　　LIL white edge, red end lights
　　App　　Nil
　　Thr　　LIH and LIL green wing bars 14L/32R and 14R, LIL green
　　　　　　wing bars 32L
　　Txy　　blue edge

Aids: TVOR, NDB, VDF, SRE, L, ILS CAT I 14L
Twr frequency: 118.1   App frequency: 120.2
Terminals: Passenger terminal to northeast of runways, with three aircraft
    aprons and 24 stands. Extensions in progress 1979. Separate cargo
    terminal and general aviation area
Scheduled services 1978: 20 airlines

Traffic:	1970	1975	1976	1977	1978
Passengers (total)	1,659,051	2,468,789	3,077,402	3,411,786	3,605,662
Cargo (tonnes)	10,530	15,727	20,964	22,735	23,690
Aircraft movements	48,072	83,790	86,153	84,564	—
Transport movements	29,410	41,981	44,517	43,559	45,207

During 1977 Boeing 727s accounted for 24.96 per cent of transport movements by
aircraft of over 20 tonnes, Caravelles for 24.75 per cent, Mercures for 6.95 per cent, Airbus
A300s for 5.4 per cent, Boeing 707s for 4.06 per cent and DC-8s for 2.62 per cent.

In 1920 the site of the present Marseilles airport at Marignane was
chosen for development as a naval airship base. France was due to receive
three German Zeppelins under the terms of the Treaty of Versailles. The
L72 was delivered on 13 July, 1920, and became the *Dixmude*, LZ 113 was
received on 9 October that year, and on 13 June, 1921, the ex-Delag
Nordstern arrived at St Cyr near Paris. The *Dixmude* and the *Nordstern*,
renamed *Méditerranée*, were based at Cuers near Toulon; the LZ 113 was
never flown. None of the airships was based at Marignane and in 1922 the
aerodrome was taken over from the Navy by the civil authorities, and in the
following year it was decided to develop Marignane as a major combined
land and marine airport, for which its situation on the shore of the Étang de
Berre made it eminently suitable.

Trans-Mediterranean flying-boat services had been started as early as
1921, to Ajaccio, and these were operated from Antibes, but on 16 May,
1923, Cia Aero-Marítima Mallorquina began flying-boat services from

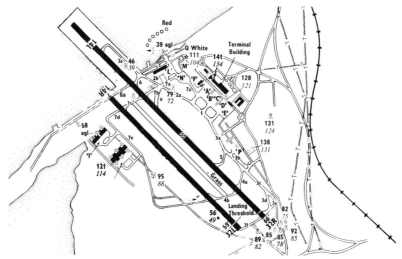

Marseilles - Marignane Airport. (*British Airways Aerad*)

101

Marignane to Algiers. In the same year Latécoère began operating landplane services from Marignane and during the year the airport recorded 413 aircraft movements and a grand total of 57 passengers. At that time the airport had a grass landing area of 250 hectares (618 acres), an administration building and a number of hangars.

The land terminal was established on the east side of the airport, and the marine terminal, with slipways, hangars and a 10-tonne crane, on the north. For many years Marignane was more important as a flying-boat base than as a land airport and up to 1939 major development of the marine terminal took place. New hangars were built, a 30-tonne crane installed and there was an offshore protective breakwater. The designated alighting area measured 5,000 m (16,404 ft) by 5,000 m. At that time the landing ground was roughly square with 1,000 m (3,281 ft) sides. It was soft after heavy rain and dangerous parts had to be marked by red pennants.

From 1933 Marignane was the main base for Air France's flying-boat services, Imperial Airways' Australia and Africa services staged through after the introduction of the Short C class flying-boats in 1937, Ala Littoria's Genoa–Barcelona flying-boat and seaplane services used Marignane, and on 29 June, 1939, Pan American Airways' Boeing 314 *Dixie Clipper* arrived at Marignane from New York to complete the first North Atlantic passenger service by a heavier-than-air craft.*

The war caused a drastic reduction in operations but in spite of this many improvements were made. A 1,650 m (5,413 ft) 14/32 concrete runway was laid, a new 80 by 50 m (262 by 164 ft) hangar was built and also a provisional terminal. These were all destroyed by German occupation forces in 1944.

At the end of 1945 work began on removing the debris and rehabilitating the airport. The runway was repaired and lengthened to 2,000 m (6,562 ft), a temporary terminal was built as well as four hangars— two of them concrete structures 100 by 60 m (328 by 197 ft). The work was completed in 1946 and the airport reopened for traffic.

A permanent 3-mn passenger annual capacity terminal was opened in June 1960 and in 1961 the airport handled 1 mn passengers for the first time. A new runway, 14L/32R, of 3,000 m (9,842 ft) was commissioned on 2 April, 1963, in 1967 the earlier runway (14R/32L) was refurbished and in 1972 was extended to its present length. On 3 June, 1964, the 36,000 tonnes annual capacity cargo terminal was opened.

During the 1960s Marignane's main function was handling traffic to and from Africa (62 per cent of its total traffic with 55 per cent on routes to North Africa) but in the following decade 56 per cent of Marignane's traffic was domestic, with only 36 per cent African.

In 1969 the Marseilles Airport Authority studied the long-term planning needs to enable the airport to play its important role in the development of the area and continue as the gateway to the Mediterranean coast and North Africa. The decision was taken to extend the main runway to 3,500 m (11,483 ft) to make possible transatlantic operations with full

---

* The last use of the marine terminal was by Aquila Airways' Short Solents which operated Southampton–Marignane–Capri services for a short time, beginning on 3 June, 1954.

payload. This work involved building a platform over Étang de Berre and was planned in two stages, the main structural work being completed by 1978 although the runway was not opened to its full length until the end of 1979.

The terminal is being developed to have 8 mn passengers annual capacity by the building of six two-level units between the terminal and the apron. Each unit has arrival and departure lounges and aerobridge loading for two aircraft other than Boeing 747s of which only one can be handled. Sheltered passageways link the units with the main terminal. The first unit built, No. 5, is for domestic use, has one single and one double aerobridge and was commissioned in October 1972; No. 4, for domestic and international services with one single and two double aerobridges was opened in January 1976; and No. 3 was completed at the end of 1979. The other units will be built as traffic demands.

In 1971 the apron was enlarged to take 14 aircraft and by 1985 it is expected that there will be 24–30 stands. There is also the possibility that a seven-gate satellite, of about 80 m (262 ft) diameter, may be built on the apron with a 170 m (558 ft) tunnel link to the main terminal. The cargo terminal can be greatly enlarged when required, and a new 49 m (161 ft) high control tower is due to be commissioned early in 1980.

There is a large general aviation area, near the old flying-boat base, and in 1969 a general aviation hangar of 200 by 30 m (656 by 98 ft) was opened.

Nantes   Aéroport de Nantes - Château-Bougon

ICAO: LFRS   IATA: NTE
47° 09′ 26″ N   01° 36′ 26″ W   Elevation: 89 ft (27 m)
Longest runway: 03/21   2,900 m (9,514 ft)   ART   TDZ 03
Aids: VOR/DME, NDB, ILS CAT II 03

	1970	1975	1976	1977	1978
Passengers	143,240	225,154	285,835	339,958	367,399
Transport movements*	7,100	9,152	11,243	11,061	11,043

* Includes all aerial work

Scheduled services 1978: Air France, Air Inter, Air Rhuys, Nantes Aviation and Touraine Air Transport

Nice   Aéroport de Nice - Côte d'Azur

43° 39′ 55″ N   07° 12′ 54″ E   3.24 nm (6 km) W of Nice
ICAO: LFMN   IATA code: NCE   Time zone: GMT plus 1
Authority: Chambre de Commerce et d'Industrie de Nice et des Alpes-Maritimes
Area: 200 hectares (494 acres)
Elevation: 13 ft (4 m)   Ref temp: 26.5 deg C

Runways: 04/22   1,700 × 45 m (5,577 × 148 ft) bituminous concrete
05/23   3,000 × 60 m (9,842 × 197 ft) bituminous concrete
(05/23 carry the designations 05L/23R)
Pavement strength: 45,000 kg (99,208 lb) ISWL
Landing category: ICAO CAT I
Lighting:
R/W   05   LIH white edge (yellow last 600 m/1,968 ft), yellow distance bars and red end lights.
23   LIL white edge and red end lights.
04/22   LIL white edge (red 300 m/984 ft threshold to displaced threshold 04).
App   red bar before thresholds 05/23
Thr   green wing bars
Txy   blue edge
Aids: VOR/DME, NDB, VDF, SRE, L, ILS CAT I 05
Twr frequency: 118.7/121.7   App frequency: 119.7/120.25
Terminals: Passenger terminal with domestic and international areas. Ground area 12,000 sq m (129,168 sq ft), floor area 30,000 sq m (322,920 sq ft). Twelve gates. Separate cargo building.
Scheduled services 1978: 20 airlines

Traffic:	1970	1975	1976	1977	1978
Passengers (total)	1,678,345	2,450,427	2,620,194	2,578,331	3,270,072
Cargo (tonnes)	11,122	9,566	10,025	10,986	11,110
Aircraft movements	36,547	56,888	59,041	59,865	—
Transport movements	35,140	38,341	41,289	43,029	45,673

During 1977 Caravelles accounted for 18.82 per cent of transport movements, Boeing 727s for 12.88 per cent, DC-9s for 10.49 per cent, Mercures for 9.39 per cent, Transalls for 4.99 per cent, Fokker F.27s for 4.78 per cent and Airbus A300s for 4.74 per cent.

In September 1902 Ferdinand Ferber flew his No. 5 glider from the stony field beside the Mediterranean and alongside the mouth of the Var River, and in December he conducted experiments there with a powered biplane suspended from the cross arm of an 18 m (59 ft) high steel pylon. The next aeronautical event held on this piece of land was the flying meeting of April 1910 organized by the town of Nice. Some 3,000 people attended and during the meeting Hubert Latham, with his Antoinette monoplane, set a speed record of 83.82 km/h (52.08 mph) and an altitude record of 656 m (2,152 ft).

In 1920 this historic area became the Californie aerodrome with a grass strip of 700 m (2,297 ft). It was the private landing ground of the Aero Club of Nice and the Côte d'Azur and was limited to aircraft weighing less than 2,000 kg (4,409 lb). In 1936 Potez Aéro-Service began a Nice–Toulouse–Bordeaux service and there were plans for the preparation of three runways, but this project was frustrated by the war.

In 1944 Allied military forces constructed the 05/23 runway to a length of 1,350 m (4,429 ft), later extended to 1,700 m (5,577 ft), and in 1946 the site was opened to commercial air traffic under the title Aéroport de Nice - le Var. At that time the airport occupied 163 hectares (403 acres).

The Chamber of Commerce and Industry of Nice and Alpes-Maritimes obtained a 50-year concession to operate the airport in 1956 and began construction of a new 1 mn passenger capacity terminal and a 2,200 m

Nice - Côte d'Azur Airport from the southwest, with Nice beyond the bay. The terminal area is on the left beyond the mouth of the Var River. (*Chamber of Commerce and Industry of Nice and Alpes - Maritimes*)

(7,218 ft) 05/23 runway. Both facilities were commissioned in 1957 and the original runway was then redesignated 04/22. In 1961 the main runway was extended eastward to give it a length of 2,685 m (8,809 ft) and this involved reclaiming 5 hectares (12.35 acres) from the sea.

Nice Airport handled 1 mn passengers for the first time in 1964 and in the same year studies were made for extension of the terminal, work beginning in 1967.

During 1972 the airport handled 2 mn passengers and the estimated traffic for 1980 was 100,000 aircraft movements and about 5 mn passengers, an indication that saturation was approaching. Consideration was therefore given to expansion of the airport to the south and when, in 1973, the 05/23 runway was lengthened to 3,000 m (9,842 ft) by reclaiming 24 hectares (59.3 acres) from the Var and the sea to the west of the airport, a tunnel was made beneath the runway to make possible the development of a southward extension of the airport.

As early as August 1969 a study group had been set up to examine the problems posed by the air transport requirements of the area. The present airport site is the only possible one in the region and by 1972–73 the various responsible authorities had accepted the fact that southward extension of the airport was the only acceptable solution—mountains blocked northward expansion, the Var prevented expansion to the west and Nice and its environs prohibited eastward development. On 24 December, 1974, the French Government authorized southward development and the cost was to be shared 35 per cent by the State, 17½ per cent each by the Department of Alpes-Maritimes and Nice, and 30 per cent by the Chamber of Commerce of Nice and Alpes-Maritimes.

A survey showed that there was an alluvial plateau at a depth of 10–15 m (33–49 ft) which permitted reclamation of about 300 hectares (741 acres) of which two-thirds could be used to satisfy airport needs, bringing the total airport area to about 400 hectares (988 acres). Some 30 mn tonnes of fill was required and this was excavated from hills about 11 km (6.8 miles) north of the site and at an elevation of up to 230 m (755 ft). A road was built between the site and the airport, the hills being excavated and material transported at the rate of 60,000 tonnes a day.

Actual construction of embankments began in late 1975 and the programme called for commissioning of Phase 1 developments by 1979. This first phase consists of a new 3,200 m (10,500 ft) runway to the south of the existing 05/23 with the centrelines separated by 480 m (1,575 ft). The new runway is 700 m (2,297 ft) further west and will reduce noise nuisance in the Nice area.

The commissioning of the new south runway will make possible the withdrawal from use of the existing 05/23, and a new 05/23 runway of 3,000 by 45 m (9,842 by 148 ft) will be built 130 m (426 ft) to the south so that ultimately there will be a parallel pair of runways separated by 350 m (1,148 ft).

This second phase will allow extension of the apron area, the construction of a second terminal building, a cargo terminal and a general aviation area. Nose-in parking could be provided for at least 20 aircraft with three additional stands at the cargo terminal. The master plan also shows two satellite buildings on the south side of the apron, each with five aircraft stands.

Nice - Côte d'Azur Airport master plan. (*Aéroport de Paris*)

The master plan covering the period up to 1985 shows future aprons, hangars, general aviation, third-level airline and helicopter facilities parallel to and south of the south runway, with a railway serving the area. Even further south there is provision for a commercial seaport which would handle car ferries and relieve the port of Nice, leaving it free for leisure use. A site has also been reserved south of the port for eventual provision of a 600 by 45 m (1,968 by 148 ft) east–west STOL and VTOL runway.

Both main 05 runways are to be equipped with ILS.

When the new runways and terminal facilities are in full operation the airport will be capable of handling 10 mn passengers a year.

Paris   Aéroport de Paris - Le Bourget

48° 58′ 10″ N   02° 26′ 32″ E   6.5 nm (12 km) NNE of city
ICAO: LFPB   IATA code: LBG   Time zone: GMT plus 1
Authority: Aéroport de Paris
Area: 570 hectares (1,408 acres)
Elevation: 217 ft (66 m)   Ref temp: 24 deg C
Runways: 03/21   2,665 × 60 m (8,743 × 197 ft) tarmac*
         07/25   3,000 × 45 m (9,842 × 148 ft) concrete

* 150 m (492 ft) concrete at 21 threshold.

Pavement strength: 03/21   30,000 kg (66,139 lb) 1, 35,000 kg (77,162 lb) 2, 60,000 kg (132,277 lb) 3;   07/25 35,000 kg (77,162 lb) 1,40,000 kg (88,185 lb) 2, 70,000 kg (154,324 lb) 3.
Landing category: ICAO CAT II
Lighting:
    R/W   03/21   LIL white edge with LIL white distance wing bar at 300 m (984 ft). Red end lights.
             07   LIL white edge, last 600 m (1,968 ft) yellow, with LIL white distance wing bar at 300 m (984 ft) and LIL yellow distance wing bar at 2,700 m (8,858 ft). Red end lights.
             25   LIH and LIL white edge, last 600 m (1,968 ft) yellow, with LIH and LIL white distance wing bar at 300 m (984 ft) and yellow distance wing bar at 2,700 m (8,858 ft), and LIH white centreline (last 300 m/984 ft red, previous 600 m/1,968 ft red/white). LIH white 900 m (2,953 ft) TDZ. Red end lights.
    App   R/W 03   LIL yellow centreline with yellow crossbar and two LIL red pre-threshold bars.
             R/W 21   two LIL red pre-threshold bars.
             R/W 07   flashing runway alignment indicator lights at 135 m (443 ft) and 60 m (197 ft) before threshold.
             R/W 25   LIH and LIL white 900 m (2,953 ft) centreline with crossbars and sequenced flashers. Red barrettes on inner 300 m (984 ft).
    Thr   03/21 LIL green, 07 LIL green wing bars with strobes, 25   LIH and LIL green with LIL green wing bars.
    Txy   blue edge, white centreline on high-speed exits from 25.

107

Aids: TVOR, L, Charles de Gaulle radar, ILS CAT II 25
Twr frequency: 119.1　　　　　　　　　App frequency: 118.15/119.85
Terminal: 230 m (755 ft) long terminal with 17 aircraft stands on adjacent
　　apron and seven on remote apron.
Scheduled services 1978: Air Alpes, Air Alsace, Air Anjou Transports and
　　Air Westward

Traffic:	1970	1975	1976	1977	1978
Passengers (total)	2,150,422	1,493,303	1,562,272	465,910	254,185
Cargo (tonnes)	52,571	16,315	14,467	3,411	454
Aircraft movements	86,124	85,046	89,422	68,731	—
Transport movements	44,424	39,993	37,898	20,727	15,212

One of Europe's truly historic airports, Le Bourget was established as
a military aerodrome in 1917 and played its part in the air defence of Paris.
Following the armistice Le Bourget became the Paris airport and was the
terminal for many pioneer air services. It was also the destination of
Charles Lindbergh who landed there in the dark on 21 May, 1927, at the
conclusion of the first solo crossing of the North Atlantic and the first
nonstop flight between the continents of North America and Europe; some
300,000 people were on the airport to greet him.

The airport was roughly triangular, with the civil installations
alongside the southwest–northeast aligned Route Nationale No. 2, military
installations on the western side, and the north of the landing area bounded
by the old course of the River Morée. The longest run available, roughly
north–south, was 1,800 m (5,905 ft) and at the northern end the distance
available, west-northwest–east-southeast, was 1,200 m (3,937 ft), but some
of the ground at the northern end was poor.

For most of the prewar period there was a small terminal building,
flanked by hangars, but on 12 November, 1937, President Lebrun opened a
new 200 by 30 m (656 by 98 ft) terminal, which was at that time almost
certainly the best in Europe, if not the world. The area of the airport was

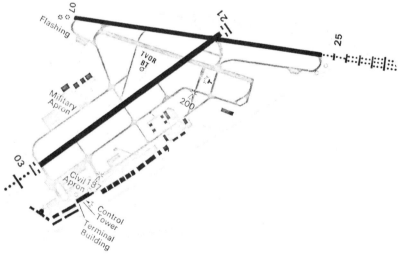

Le Bourget Airport, Paris. (*British Airways Aerad*)

Paris - Le Bourget Airport. The terminal building which was opened in November 1937. Imperial Airways Handley Page H.P.42 *Hanno*, a Swissair DC-3 and a British Airways Lockheed Electra are on the apron. The fog line can be seen in the bottom right hand corner.

also enlarged. An unusual feature of Le Bourget was its very advanced lighting. In addition to boundary lights, obstruction lights, beacons, floodlights and illuminated wind direction indicators, the northern boundary had green threshold lights, there was a distance-coded line of landing lights running NNE–SSW and a 4,000 m (13,123 ft) line of sodium approach lights with groups of high intensity sodiums short of the northern threshold.

In 1932 Le Bourget handled 9,285 aircraft movements, 66,691 passengers and 1,492 tonnes of cargo. By 1936 traffic had increased to 16,626 movements, 102,065 passengers and 2,141 tonnes of cargo, but although continuing to serve essential transport needs in the early months of the war, the airport was badly damaged by both German and Allied bombing.

French airlines returned to Le Bourget in November 1944 and in 1946 the airport returned to civil status. Rebuilding of hangars and workshops was completed in 1949, and a new control tower was commissioned on 1 February, 1953. After the war there were two tarmac runways, 03/21 of 2,100 m (6,890 ft) and 08/26 (later designated 09/27) of 1,600 m (5,249 ft). 03/21 was extended to 2,400 m (7,874 ft) and eventually 2,665 m (8,743 ft); 09/27 was lengthened to 1,960 m (6,432 ft) before being replaced on 18 August, 1960, by the new 3,000 m (9,842 ft) 07/25, when the old runway became a taxiway.

A new cargo terminal was opened in August 1962, the main terminal had been modified and extended by March 1963, and on 1 July, 1967, a separate charter terminal was opened. In 1970 runway and apron modifications were made in order to accept Boeing 747s.

In 1973 Le Bourget was handling 16.1 per cent of Paris passenger traffic and 21.4 per cent of air cargo.

It was at the end of the 1950s that it had become clear that by the mid-1970s Le Bourget and Orly would be operating to maximum capacity, and in 1959 it was decided to go ahead with construction of a new major airport at Roissy en France only 12 km (7½ miles) northeast of Le Bourget.

On 30 March, 1977, all major carrier operations were transferred to the new airport and to Orly, and Le Bourget was then restricted to operations by third-level airlines, general aviation and military communications flights.

It had been intended that Le Bourget should be closed but it was subsequently decided that the airport could play an important role as a business airport. However, further restrictions will be imposed on Le Bourget when Charles de Gaulle Airport's runway 10/28 is extended to its full length and becomes fully operational in 1981. The existing Le Bourget runways will be withdrawn from use (07/25 closing in 1981) and the old 08/26 (long known as 09/27) is to be repaired and reopened. The present maintenance and military areas will be retained although the latter may be reduced in size to form part of the parkland ordered by the government. New general aviation and STOL facilities will be provided at the north of the airport while much of the southern area will become an exhibition site. The Salon de l'Aéronautique, first staged at Le Bourget in 1953, will continue to be held there. The Musée de l'Air has for some time had part of its magnificent collection on view in a number of hangars and it is to take over the hangars formerly used as a cargo terminal and also the south wing of the passenger terminal.

Paris   Aéroport de Paris - Roissy-Charles de Gaulle

49° 00′ 35″ N   02° 32′ 55″ E   13.5 nm (25 km) NE of city
ICAO: LFPG   IATA code: CDG   Time zone: GMT plus 1
Authority: Aéroport de Paris
Area: 3,104 hectares (7,670 acres)
Elevation: 387 ft (118 m)   Ref temp: 20.9 deg C
Runways: 09/27   3,600 × 60 m (11,811 × 197 ft) concrete*
              10/28   2,865 × 45 m   (9,400 × 148 ft) concrete

* 60 m (197 ft) concrete stopways 09/27 and 10, 100 m (328 ft) 28.

Pavement strength: 28,000 kg (61,729 lb) 1, 45,000 kg (99,208 lb) 2, 100,000 kg (220,462 lb) 3.
Landing category: ICAO CAT IIIa
Lighting:
      R/W   LIH and LIL white edge, LIH white centreline (last 300 m/984 ft red, previous 600 m/1,968 ft red/white), TDZ 900 m (2,953 ft) white, red end lights.
      App   R/W 09/27 and 28   LIH white centreline with five cross-bars and sequenced flashers and red side barrettes on inner 600 m (1,968 ft). LIL centreline with crossbar 09/27 only. Turboclair on R/W 09.
      Thr   LIH and LIL green
      Txy   blue edge, green centreline and red stop bars.
Aids: VOR, L, RAD, ASDE, ILS CAT III 09/27
Twr frequency: 119.25   App frequency: 118.15/119.85/121.15/124.35
Terminals: Circular No. 1 terminal with seven satellites, 35 gates and 58 aircraft stands. Linear No. 2 terminal under construction. Separate cargo terminals.
Scheduled services 1978: 29 airlines
Main base: Air France and UTA

110

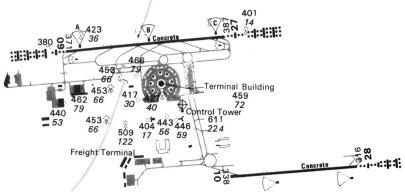

Roissy - Charles de Gaulle Airport, Paris. (*British Airways Aerad*)

Traffic:	1975	1976	1977	1978
Passengers (total)	6,009,057	7,751,684	8,605,297	9,279,660
Cargo (tonnes)	220,244	253,470	283,961	335,820
Aircraft movements	85,800	95,567	99,925	—
Transport movements	83,506	92,530	97,115	103,403

During 1977 Caravelles accounted for 22.94 per cent of transport movements, Boeing 727s for 14.55 per cent, Boeing 707s for 11.44 per cent, Boeing 747s for 8.75 per cent, Airbus A300s for 6.08 per cent and DC-8s also 6.08 per cent. Concorde movements represented 0.89 per cent.

Traffic projections having shown that Le Bourget and Orly would reach their maximum capacity in the mid-1970s, and urban development having made expansion of Le Bourget impossible, the search was begun in 1957 for a site for a major Paris airport.

By the end of 1959 it had been decided to build the new airport on the plateau between the Seine and the Marne, astride the A1 Paris–Lille–Brussels motorway near the village of Roissy en France in the Île de France region northeast of Paris and about 12 km (7½ miles) northeast of Le Bourget. The area was flat farmland and sparsely inhabited—only one house had to be demolished. Official approval was given by the French Government on 16 June, 1964, and work on the site began on 1 December, 1966.

Land was acquired for an airport of 3,104 hectares (7,670 acres); the first phase, comprising a 3,600 m (11,811 ft) east–west runway, terminal building, air traffic control building, hangars, cargo terminal and other essential buildings, was due for completion during 1972, and it was envisaged that the entire airport would be completed sometime after 1985 when it would have an annual capacity of 50 mn passengers and 2 mn tonnes of cargo. In the early stages the airport was referred to as Paris-Nord; it soon became known as Roissy en France but on 24 October, 1973, was officially renamed Charles de Gaulle.

The master plan included two sets of 3,600 m (11,811 ft) parallel runways (aligned east–west), a 3,600 m crosswind runway, and a shorter east–west runway for general aviation. It was anticipated that by 1990 two runways would be used for take offs and two for landings and that this should make possible 150 movements an hour. Provision was made to extend all main runways to 5,000 m (16,404 ft).

111

Roissy - Charles de Gaulle Airport, Paris. The No. 1 terminal and satellite buildings with the 09/27 runway on the right. (*Air France*)

The runways were to be Nos. 1 and 1bis at the north of the site, Nos. 2 and 2bis and the short runway at the south, and the transverse runway at the east. Cargo and maintenance areas were to be located at the west. The biggest part of the remaining area within the runway pattern was to be occupied by three side-by-side circular terminals to the north and a pair to the south—each terminal to have five groups of satellite docks with aerobridges serving up to five or six aircraft, but this plan was abandoned.

Work on bridging the motorway began in April 1968 and was completed at the end of 1970. Work on the first runway, 09/27, and its associated taxiways started on 1 August, 1969, and this was also completed by the end of 1970.

The first terminal, No. 1, consists of a circular central building, 192 m (630 ft) in diameter and 52.7 m (173 ft) high, served by a ring of seven satellites, with 35 gates with aerobridges. The central building has eleven storeys plus four car park levels and was designed to provide minimum walking distances. The links between departure, transfer and arrival levels are moving pavements enclosed in glazed tubes which cross the central void of the building, and underground moving pavements link the terminal with the satellites. Terminal construction began in September 1968 and work on the satellites started late in 1970. Annual capacity is about 10 mn passengers.

By September 1973 the runway, taxiways and buildings had been constructed and a few aircraft had landed—some by mistake. Also built during Phase 1 were Air France and UTA hangars, and a pooled cargo terminal with an annual capacity of 400,000 tonnes.

The new airport was officially opened on 8 March, 1974, by President Pompidou and came into operation on 13 March. On 21 January, 1976, Charles de Gaulle Airport and London Heathrow became the first airports ever to despatch a supersonic passenger service when Air France's Concorde F-BVFA and British Airways G-BOAA took off simultaneously, respectively bound for Rio de Janeiro via Dakar, and Bahrain.

Charles de Gaulle and Orly airports were the first to be equipped with Turboclair fog disposal system (FDS), becoming operational in November 1974, and at Charles de Gaulle this system is installed on runway 09. The operating conditions specified are: aircraft must be approved for FDS use; aircraft equipment must be at least CAT II; all main engines must be operating; all operating crew members must be qualified for CAT II; mid-point RVR must be at least 150 m (200 m for Boeing 747s and Concorde); and all FDS units must be operating.

An example of Turboclair's capability is that recorded for 28 February, 1976, at Charles de Gaulle—at 07.50 RVR was 150 m with no identifiable ceiling and by 07.52 with Turboclair, at normal operating speed, visibility had risen to 800 m.

During 1977 Air France opened its cargo terminal in two phases. First to come into use was the 190 by 48.6 m (623 by 159 ft) dock building which has a covered area of 9,500 sq m (102,258 sq ft), three aircraft nose-in

The Turboclair installation on runway 09 at Roissy - Charles de Gaulle Airport. (*Aéroport de Paris*)

113

stands, and is used for large shipments. The second phase was the commissioning of the main 216 by 108 m (709 by 354 ft) warehouse with 29,150 sq m (313,771 sq ft) floor area. The entire unit covers 33 hectares (81.5 acres), has 250,000 tonnes annual capacity and can be greatly enlarged.

To provide rapid transport between Paris and Charles de Gaulle, Aéroport de Paris and SNCF (French Railways) built a railway link between the Gare du Nord and the airport. This involved 13.4 km (8.32 miles) of new track and a four-track airport underground station. Known as Roissy Rail, this link was opened on 30 May, 1976. There is a projected Metro link due for completion in 1982.

Phase 2 of the airport construction was begun with work on terminal No. 2 and partial building of the second runway. Even before the airport was opened it had been decided not to build more circular terminals. Instead the southern terminal had been designed as a linear modular complex with eight curved terminals arranged in pairs separated by a spinal road. Each module is to have 12,000 sq m (129,168 sq ft) ground area and be capable of handling 5 mn passengers a year. There are to be six aerobridges per module, and as now proposed this terminal unit will stretch for 1.5 km (1,640 yards) and require some form of transport system. Work began in the spring of 1973 but was interrupted early in 1975 as a result of the oil crisis, recession and traffic stagnation. Instead of being completed in 1978 the first unit is due to be ready in time for 1981 summer schedules.

The second runway was built 2,900 m (9,514 ft) south of the first runway and like the first aligned 085/265 but designated 10/28. This runway has only been completed to 2,865 m (9,400 ft) and, although it has full approach lights on the 28 approach, is only available when 09/27 is unserviceable and on ATC instructions.

There is still provision for the lengthening of 10/28, the building of the other planned runways and a third terminal.

Paris   Aéroport de Paris - Orly

48° 43′ 24″ N   02° 22′ 49″ E   7.5 nm (13.9 km) S of city
ICAO: LFPO   IATA code: ORY   Time zone: GMT plus 1
Authority: Aéroport de Paris
Area: 1,536 hectares (3,795 acres)
Elevation: 292 ft (89 m)   Ref temp: 21 deg C
Runways: 02L/20R   2,400 × 60 m   (7,874 × 197 ft) concrete
              02R/20L   1,850 × 60 m   (6,069 × 197 ft) concrete
              06/24   500 × 30 m   (1,640 × 98 ft) grass*
              07/25   3,650 × 45 m (11,975 × 148 ft) concrete
              08/26   3,320 × 45 m (10,892 × 148 ft) concrete

* 06/24 is for light and low-powered aircraft only.

Pavement strength: 07/25 and 08/26   40,000 kg (88,184 lb) 1, 45,000 kg (99,208 lb) 2, 90,000 kg (198,416 lb) 3; 02L/20R   35,000 kg (77,162 lb) 1, 40,000 kg (88,184 lb) 2, 75,000 kg (165,347 lb) 3; 02R/20L   10,000 kg (22,046 lb) 1, 15,000 kg (33,070 lb) 2, 25,000 kg (55,115 lb) 3.

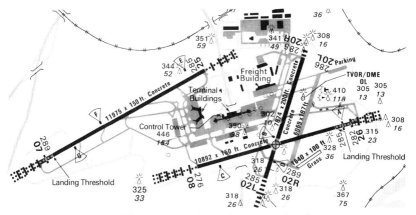

Orly Airport, Paris. (*British Airways Aerad*)

Landing category: ICAO CAT IIIa
Lighting:
   R/W   O2L/20R   LIH and LIL white edge with LIH and LIL white distance wing bars at 300 m (984 ft). Red end lights.
            02R/20L   LIL white edge. Red end lights.
            07/25   LIH and LIL white edge, last 900 m (2,953 ft) yellow, with LIH white distance wing bar at 300 m (984 ft) and yellow at 300 m (984 ft) from end. LIH white centreline, last 300 m (984 ft) red and previous 600 m (1,968 ft) red/white. Red end lights. TDZ 07.
            08/26   LIH and LIL white edge, last 600 m (1,968 ft) yellow, with LIH and LIL white distance wing bar at 300 m (984 ft) and yellow at 300 m (984 ft) from end. LIH white centreline, last 300 m (984 ft) red and previous 600 m (1,968 ft) red/white. Red end lights. TDZ 26.
   App   R/W 02L   LIH and LIL white centreline and crossbar.
            R/W 20R   Two red LIL crossbars before threshold.
            R/W 02R/20L   nil.
            R/W 07   LIH white centreline with crossbars and sequenced flashers. Red barrettes on inner 300 m (984 ft). LIH and LIL yellow centreline and crossbar.
            R/W 25 and 08/26   LIH white centreline with crossbars and sequenced flashers, and yellow LIL centreline with crossbars. VASIS 26.
   Thr   02L, 25 and 08/26   LIH and LIL green.
            20R   LIL green
            02R/20L   nil.
            07   LIH and LIL green wing bars.
   Txy   blue edge all taxiways, green centreline on high-speed exits and some taxiways.
Aids: TVOR/DME, SRE, ASDE, ILS CAT III 07, ILS CAT II 26, ILS CAT I 02L and 25
Twr frequency: 118.7   App frequency: 120.85/124.45

Terminals: Orly South and Orly West terminals with 116 gates and 108
aircraft stands. Separate cargo terminal
Scheduled services 1978: 63 airlines
Main base: Air France (joint with Charles de Gaulle) and Air Inter

Traffic:	1970	1975	1976	1977	1978
Passengers (total)	10,381,885	10,611,422	10,988,137	12,867,316	13,999,436
Cargo (tonnes)	176,285	119,870	140,491	162,934	166,042
Aircraft movements	183,268	150,088	151,904	170,568	—
Transport movements	161,017	142,969	144,502	161,867	171,348

During 1977 Caravelles accounted for 19.2 per cent of transport movements, Boeing 727s
for 17.58 per cent, Fokker F.27s for 13 per cent, DC-9s for 9.05 per cent, Boeing 707s for 7.83
per cent and Boeing 737s for 4.28 per cent.

Orly was established by the United States as a military aerodrome
towards the end of the 1914–18 war and in 1918 housed a unit of the US
Army Air Service. The western boundary was formed by the road to
Corbeil, now Route Nationale No. 7. The aerodrome was on a plateau
close to the villages of Orly, Paray-Vieille-Poste and la Ferme-Champagne,
and the landing area occupied 280 hectares (692 acres).

After the war the aerodrome became a centre for aviation meetings
and in 1920 the wellknown pilot, Charles Nungesser, established a flying
school there. Some time later two large concrete airship sheds, 70 m (230 ft)
in height, were erected to the south of the landing area which measured 900

Paris - Orly Airport. The South terminal and control tower, with the cargo terminal
at top right. (*Aéroport de Paris*)

116

by 750 m (2,953 by 2,461 ft). L'Aéronavale established a base between the airship sheds and the road. Orly also became a test centre.

During the Second World War Orly was badly bombed, all its installations being completely destroyed. As late as September 1949 large pieces of concrete from the airship sheds were still to be seen. These great sheds occupied the area which now lies between the cargo terminal and the maintenance area, and Route Nationale No. 7 has been sunk to pass beneath Orly's central terminal area and runway 08/26.

In 1946 the first studies were made to convert Orly into a civil airport and a temporary terminal was provided. The 2,100 m (6,890 ft) runway 08/26 was in service by the end of 1947 and it may have been preceded by the 1,806 m (5,925 ft) 03/21 (later 02R/20L and extended to 1,850 m/ 6,069 ft). The plan was to have two east–west primary runways and two north–south secondary runways. These were all built, 08L/26R having a length of 1,560 m (5,118 ft) and 03L/21R, opened in 1953, was 2,400 m (7,874 ft) long. The 03/21 runways were later redesignated 02/20. Eventually 08L/26R was abandoned but on 1 September, 1965, the 3,650 m (11,975 ft) 07/25 runway was completed—thus greatly increasing Orly's extension to the west.

A second temporary north terminal was opened in May 1948 and on 14 August, 1954, a much more ambitious south terminal was commissioned—this was constructed in only nine months and served until the opening of the very large permanent terminal on which work began at the end of 1956. The main block of the new permanent multi-storey terminal (now known as Orly - Sud) was about 400 m (1,312 ft) in length—it was officially opened by President de Gaulle on 24 February, 1961, and became operational on 8 March.

Orly - Sud had been designed to handle up to 6 mn passengers a year but it soon became obvious that further capacity was required. Increased capacity was obtained by internal rearrangement of the check-in and baggage handling areas and by the construction of aerobridge-equipped satellites at each end of the building—both capable of handling Boeing 747s. These satellites were commissioned in the winter of 1969–70 and increased the terminal capacity to 9 mn passengers.

In order to bring overall annual passenger capacity to 15 mn a completely new terminal, Orly - Ouest, was built about 300 m (984 ft) west of the Orly - Sud western satellite. The completely self-contained Orly - Ouest terminal consists of a central building with two projecting halls, each with 10 aerobridges. Hall No. 2 (north) handles domestic flights and Hall No. 3 (south) domestic and short-haul European services. Construction of Orly - Ouest began in October 1967 and the terminal was brought into service on 7 March, 1971.

Experiments in fog dispersal were first undertaken at Orly in December 1958 and in November 1974 the Turboclair fog dispersal system was commissioned on runway 07. Runway 07 was cleared for CAT IIIa operations in 1973.

The preferential take off runways are 08 and 25, and landing runways 07 and 26. The first 300 m (984 ft) of 07 and first 435 m (1,426 ft) of 26 are not available for landings.

117

Strasbourg   Aéroport de Strasbourg - Entzheim

ICAO: LFST   IATA: SXB
48° 32′ 27″ N   07° 37′ 58″ E   Elevation: 502 ft (153 m)
Runway: 05/23   2,400 m (7,874 ft)   ART   VASI 05/23
Aids: VORTAC, NDB, SRE, PAR, ILS CAT II 23

	1970	1975	1976	1977
Passengers	132,517	285,744	334,578	389,498
Transport movements*	4,980	9,851	9,749	10,961

*Includes all aerial work

Scheduled services 1978: Air France, Air Inter, Dan-Air Services, Royal
   Air Maroc and Tunis Air

Tarbes   Aéroport de Tarbes - Ossun-Lourdes

ICAO: LFBT   IATA: LDE
43° 11′ 10″ N   00° 00′ 10″ E   Elevation: 1,243 ft (379 m)
Runway: 03/21   2,400 m (7,874 ft)   ART
Aids: VOR, NDB, VDF, ILS CAT I 21

	1970	1975	1976	1977
Passengers	164,589	287,709	302,783	389,497
Transport movements*	3,927	4,407	4,266	3,879

*Includes all aerial work

Scheduled services 1978: Air Inter and Aer Lingus

Toulouse   Aéroport de Toulouse - Blagnac

ICAO: LFBO   IATA: TLS
43° 37′ 22″ N   01° 22′ 51″ E   Elevation: 499 ft (152 m)
Longest runway: 15R/33L   3,500 m (11,483 ft)   ART   TDZ 15R
Aids: VOR/DME, NDB, VDF, SRE, ILS CAT III 15R, ILS CAT II 15L
   and 33L

	1970	1975	1976	1977
Passengers	417,664	689,194	775,555	921,352
Transport movements*	13,606	22,246	24,413	18,889

*Includes all aerial work

Scheduled services 1978: Air Algérie, Air France, Air Inter, Air Rouergue,
   Iberia, Royal Air Maroc, TAT and Tunis Air

Basle - Mulhouse Airport in 1977. The main runway has since been lengthened.
(*Flughafen Basel - Mulhouse*)

France/Switzerland

Basle (Bâle/Basel) Aéroport de Bâle-Mulhouse

ICAO: LFSB IATA: BSL*
47° 35′ 24″ N 07° 31′ 48″ E Elevation: 883 ft (269 m)
Longest runway: 16/34 3,900 m (12,795 ft) ART
Aids: VOR, ILS CAT III 16

	1970	1975	1976	1977	1978
Passengers	727,633	831,579	857,801	794,741	906,790
Transport movements	20,952	22,458	23,083	20,062	24,612

Scheduled services 1978: 11 airlines
Main base: Balair

* The airport is on French territory and has a Customs road into Switzerland. The IATA code for French domestic flights is MLH

French Antilles (Antilles Françaises)

Fort-de-France, Martinique Aéroport de Fort-de-France - Le Lamentin

ICAO: MFFF IATA: FDF
14° 35′ 26″ N 60° 59′ 59″ W Elevation: 16 ft (5 m)
Runway: 09/27 3,300 m (10,827 ft) ART VASI 09
Aids: VOR/DME, NDB, VDF, ILS 09

	1970	1975	1976	1977
Passengers	232,313	476,691	538,705	700,248
Transport movements*	18,913	12,768	16,833	17,314

* Includes all aerial work

Scheduled services 1978: Air Antilles, Air Canada, Air France, Air Martinique (SATAIR), American Airlines, Caribbean Air Services, Eastern Air Lines and LIAT
Main base: Air Martinique

Pointe-à-Pitre, Guadeloupe   Aéroport de Pointe-à-Pitre - Le Raizet

ICAO: MFFR   IATA: PTP
16° 16′ 00″ N   61° 31′ 18″ W   Elevation: 36 ft (11 m)
Runway: 11/29   3,505 m (11,499 ft)   ART
Aids: VOR/DME, NDB, VDF, ILS 11

	1970	1975	1976
Passengers	292,964	653,290	741,664
Transport movements*	18,913	33,928	39,333

*Includes all aerial work

Scheduled services 1978: Air Antilles, Air Canada, Air France, Air
    Guadeloupe, American Airlines, Caribbean Air Services, Eastern Air
    Lines, LIAT and Puerto Rico International Airlines
Main base: Air Antilles and Air Guadeloupe

Gabon (République Gabonaise)

Libreville   Aéroport de Libreville - Léon M'Ba

ICAO: FOOO   IATA: LBV
00° 27′ 28″ N   09° 24′ 50″ E   Elevation: 39 ft (12 m)
Runway: 16/34   3,000 m (9,842 ft)   ART
Aids: VOR, DME, NDB, VDF, L, ILS 16

	1970	1975	1976	1977
Passengers	132,222	388,316	493,037	505,005
Transport movements	13,062	25,952	32,432	30,016

Scheduled services 1978: 10 airlines
Main base: Air Gabon

German Democratic Republic (Deutsche Demokratische Republik)

Berlin   Flughafen Berlin - Schönefeld

52° 22′ 48″ N   13° 31′ 20″ E   9.72 nm (18 km) SE of city
ICAO: ETBS   IATA code: SXF   Time zone: GMT plus 1
Authority: Interflug
Elevation: 154 ft (47 m)   Ref temp: 19.3 deg C
Runways: 07L/25R   2,700 × 60 m (8,858 × 197 ft) concrete
         07R/25L   3,000 × 60 m (9,842 × 197 ft) concrete
         There is an emergency 1,800 × 100 m (5,905 × 328 ft) grass strip
         to the south of and immediately alongside 07R/25L

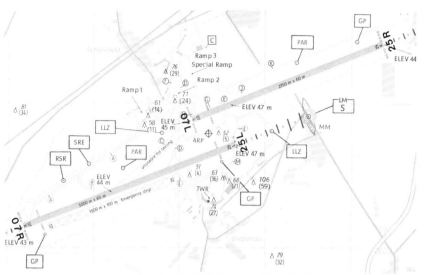

Berlin - Schönefeld Airport. (*Interflug*)

Pavement strength: 45,000 kg (99,208 lb) ISWL
Landing category: ICAO CAT II
Lighting:

R/W   07L/25R   LIH and LIL white edge, LIH white centreline, distance lights 600 m (1,968 ft) from each end. Touchdown point and LIH white landing mat 25R. LIL red stopway outline each end.

        07R/25L   LIH and LIL white edge and distance lights

App   R/W 07R/25L and 25R   LIH and LIL white Calvert centreline with six crossbars

Thr   LIH and LIL green

Txy   LIL blue edge. Green centreline on some runway exits

Aids: PAR, SRE, RVR, ILS CAT I 07R/25L and 25R, SP-70 CAT II laser landing system.

Twr frequency: 119.7/121.3   App frequency: 119.5/119.7

Terminals: Separate international and domestic passenger terminals and cargo terminal. Three aircraft parking ramps, with eight or nine stands (according to aircraft size) at international terminal. Total aircraft stands believed to exceed 50

Scheduled services 1978: 16 airlines

Main base: Interflug

Traffic:	1970	1975	1976	1977
Passengers (total)	1,146,987	1,606,685	1,642,184	1,736,540
Cargo (tonnes)	8,617	12,287	12,446	12,379
Aircraft movements	19,721	29,446	30,445	25,219
Transport movements	—	16,674	15,134	15,634

In 1976 Tupolev Tu-134s accounted for 43.14 per cent of transport movements, Ilyushin Il-18s for 31.78 per cent, Tu-154s for 8.03 per cent and Il-62s for 5.08 per cent.

There are plans to build an underground railway link to the city.

Berlin - Schönefeld Airport. The international terminal which was opened on 1 June, 1976. (*Interflug*)

In December 1978 a Soviet SP-70 Glissada laser landing system was installed, the first outside the USSR, allowing CAT II operation.

Dresden   Flughafen Dresden   ICAO: ETDN   IATA: DRS

51° 08′ 02″ N   13° 46′ 08″ E   Elevation: 755 ft (230 m)
Runway: 04/22   2,500 m (8,202 ft)   ART
Aids: NDB, GCA, L, RVR, KGSP 04/22
Scheduled services 1978: Aeroflot, Interflug and Malév
No traffic figures are available

Leipzig   Flughafen Leipzig   ICAO: ETLS   IATA: LEJ

51° 24′ 55″ N   12° 13′ 45″ E   Elevation: 466 ft (142 m)
Runway: 11/29   2,500 m (8,202 ft)   ART   TDZ
Aids: VOR, TAR/PAR, NDB, SRE, L, ILS
Scheduled services 1978: Aeroflot, British Airways, Finnair, Interflug,
     KLM, Malév, SAS and Swissair
No traffic figures available

122

German Federal Republic
(Deutsche Bundesrepublik)

Berlin   Flughafen Berlin - Tegel

52° 33′ 40″ N   13° 17′ 22″ E   4.3 nm (8 km) NW of Berlin zoo
ICAO: EDBT   IATA code: TXL   Time zone: GMT plus 1
Authority: Berliner Flughafen - Gesellschaft mbH
Area: 460 hectares (1,137 acres)
Elevation: 121 ft (37 m)   Ref temp: 23 deg C
Runways: 08L/26R   3,021 × 46 m (9,911 × 150 ft) asphalt
             08R/26L   2,421 × 61 m (7,943 × 200 ft) concrete/asphalt
Pavement strength: 08L/26R   35,000 kg (77,162 lb) 1, 50,000 kg
     (110,231 lb) 2, 90,000 kg (198,416 lb) 3; 08R/26L   17,000 kg
     (37,478 lb) 1, 25,000 kg (55,116 lb) 2, 50,000 kg (110,231 lb) 3
Landing category: ICAO CAT IIIa
Lighting:
     R/W   LIH white edge, and LIH white centreline with last 300 m
             (984 ft) red and previous 600 m (1,968 ft) red/white. TDZ
             26L and 26R
     App   R/W 08L and 08R   LIH white bar centreline with
             crossbar and sequenced flashers. Supplementary lights on
             inner section 08L
             R/W 26L and 26R   LIH white bar centreline with
             crossbar and sequenced flashers, red LIH crossbars and red
             barrettes on inner 300 m (984 ft). VASIS 08L/26R and
             08R/26L
     Thr   LIH green, with strobes on 08L, 08R and 26L
     Txy   LIL blue edge, LIH and LIL green centreline on high-speed
             exits
Aids: DVORTAC, NDB, ILS CAT III 08L, ILS CAT II 26L and 26R, ILS
     CAT I 08R

Berlin - Tegel Airport in March 1974. The terminal building and control tower.
(Berliner Flughafen-Gesellschaft mbH)

123

Twr frequency: 118.7/119.7 App frequency: 120.95/125.8

Terminals: Hexagonal passenger terminal with 15 gates, 14 with aerobridges. Separate cargo terminal. Total of 32 aircraft stands

Scheduled services 1978: Air Alsace, Air France, British Airways, KLM and Pan American

Airline bases: Air France, British Airways, Dan-Air Service, Laker Airways and Pan American

Traffic:	1970*	1975	1976	1977	1978
Passengers (total)	5,538,885	1,806,860	3,985,064	4,042,292	4,029,360
Cargo (tonnes)	26,658	4,541	12,794	11,570	11,316
Aircraft movements	77,571	23,192	53,069	53,892	—
Transport movements	77,128	22,686	52,446	52,648	53,315

*Figures for Tempelhof

During 1977 Boeing 727s accounted for 51.71 per cent of transport movements, BAC One-Elevens for 44.98 per cent and Boeing 720s for 2.37 per cent.

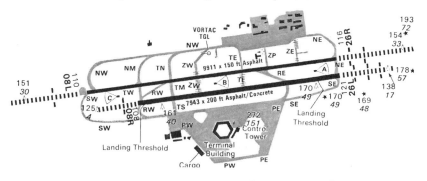

Berlin - Tegel Airport (*British Airways Aerad*)

For most of the period between the First and Second World Wars Berlin was the hub of European air transport and Tempelhof was the city's airport. The site at Tempelhof, only a tram ride from the city, was used for demonstration flights by the Wright brothers in 1908 and during the 1914–18 war was a military aerodrome. It was officially opened as Berlin Airport on 8 October, 1923.* In prewar days Tempelhof's landing area measured 1,350 by 1,000 m (4,429 by 3,281 ft) and in 1934 construction began of a very large terminal with capacity for 300,000 passengers a year. The terminal, which in plan view resembled an eagle with wings spread, included a curved structure occupying the entire northwest corner of the airport, and the straight-line distance between the two ends exceeded 1,000 m (3,281 ft). On the apron side the building had a continuous cantilever roof beneath which aircraft were parked to give weather protection to boarding and disembarking passengers.

Tempelhof continued to serve Berlin after the war and was one of the airlift terminals in 1948–49. There are now two almost parallel runways, 09L/27R of 2,093 m (6,867 ft) and 09R/27L of 2,116 m (6,942 ft), but the

*Johannisthal, established in 1909 and later both an aerodrome and airship station, served as the Berlin Airport until the opening of Tempelhof.

airport is completely surrounded by built-up areas and approaches are made *beside* high blocks of flats.

Although used by jet transports, mainly BEA/British Airways BAC One-Elevens and Pan American Boeing 727s, Tempelhof had become unacceptable as the city's airport and the decision was made in 1964 to develop Tegel, to the northwest.

Tegel, in the French sector of the city, was opened in 1948 at the time of the airlift and had two 2,400 m (7,874 ft) 08/26 runways, and a single-storey terminal was constructed on the north side—limited civil operations beginning in 1960—the airport being the Berlin terminal for Air France.

In 1965 a design competition was held for a $7\frac{1}{2}$ mn annual passenger capacity terminal for the south side of the airport, and Air France and charter operators moved to the new terminal on 1 November, 1974, following the opening ceremony on 23 October. The runways had been extended to 3,021 m (9,911 ft), 08L/26R, and 2,421 m (7,943 ft), 08R/26L, and ILS and lighting upgraded to CAT II. British Airways and Pan American began operating from Tegel on 1 April, 1975, and on 1 September, 1975, all commercial traffic was transferred, after which Tempelhof handled only US military aircraft and civil diversions. In 1976 Tegel was cleared for CAT III operations—the fourth in Europe after Heathrow, Paris - Orly and Paris - Charles de Gaulle.

There is provision in the master plan for a second, identical, terminal immediately to the east of the present terminal but there are no plans at present for its construction, nor for any further runway development.

Bremen	Flughafen Bremen	ICAO: EDDW		IATA: BRE

53° 02' 56" N   08° 47' 16" E   Elevation: 11 ft (3 m)
Runway: 09/27   2,034 m (6,673 ft)   ART   VASI 09
Aids: VOR, NDB, VDF, SRE, ILS CAT I 27

	1970	1975	1976	1977	1978
Passengers	534,333	554,091	622,245	636,180	647,330
Transport movements	18,107	12,793	14,243	14,649	15,373

Bremen Airport. A view showing its proximity to the city. The old runways are still visible. A new 2,500 m (8,202 ft) runway is to be built parallel to and south of the present 09/27. The extension will be to the west. (*Flughafen Bremen GmbH*)

Scheduled services 1978: British Airways, DLT, KLM, Lufthansa and NLM
The airport has been in operation since 1919. A new 2,500 m (8,202 ft) 09R/27L runway is planned

Cologne/Bonn (Köln/Bonn)   Flughafen Köln/Bonn (Wahn)

50° 52′ 02″ N   07° 08′ 37″ E   8 nm (14.8 km) SE of Cologne
ICAO: EDDK   IATA code: CGN   Time zone: GMT plus 1
Authority: Flughafen Köln/Bonn GmbH
Area: 1,000 hectares (2,471 acres)
Elevation: 300 ft (91 m)   Ref temp: 19.4 deg C
Runways: 07/25   2,459 × 46 m   (8,067 × 150 ft) concrete, grooved
            14L/32R   3,800 × 60 m   (12,467 × 197 ft) prestressed-
                                            concrete
            14R/32L   1,866 × 50 m   (6,122 × 164 ft) concrete-tarmac
Pavement strength: 07/25 LCN 63, 14L/32R LCN 100, 14R/32L LCN 53
Landing category: ICAO CAT II
Lighting:
    R/W   07   LIH and LIL white edge, white LIH centreline over
                first 1,859 m (6,134 ft); 25 LIH and LIL white edge, LIH
                centreline over final 1,859 m (6,134 ft) - 600—1,800 m white
                1,800—2,100 m red/white, 2,100—2,459 m red.
            14L/32R   LIH and LIL white edge, white LIH centreline
                with last 300 m red and previous 600 m red/white. TDZ wing
                bars.
            14R/32L   LIH white edge
    App   R/W 07   LIH and LIL white bar centreline and cross-
                bars.
            R/W 25   LIH and LIL white bar centreline with cross-
                bars and sequenced flashers.
            R/W 14L   LIH and LIL white distance-coded centreline
                and crossbars.
            R/W 32R   LIH and LIL white bar centreline with cross-
                bars and sequenced flashers. Red barrettes on inner 300 m.
            R/W 14R/32L   LIH and LIL white bar centreline and
                crossbars
    Thr   LIH and LIL green/red
    Txy   blue edge, green centreline on exits from 14L/32R and some
                other sections
Aids: DVORTAC, NDB, VDF, ASR, SRE, PAR, L, ILS CAT II 32R, ILS
    CAT I 14L and 25
Twr frequency: 118.9   App frequency: 118.75/120.25
Terminals: 150 m (492 ft) long central terminal with two wing buildings and
    two pier-connected satellites each with six aerobridges. Thirty aircraft
    stands. Separate cargo terminal with three aircraft stands and general
    aviation area with eight stands

Scheduled services 1978: 10 airlines (19 non-scheduled airlines)

Traffic:	1970	1975	1976	1977	1978
Passengers (total)	1,404,640	1,883,526	1,960,252	1,927,363	2,198,564
Cargo (tonnes)	17,711	19,538	30,842	70,093	79,003
Aircraft movements	55,533	69,041	69,059	76,564	88,181
Transport movements	32,292	33,677	34,149	36,433	37,121

During 1977 Boeing 737s accounted for 27.28 per cent of transport movements, Boeing 727s for 24.42 per cent, BAC One-Elevens for 12.57 per cent, DC-9s for 9.05 per cent and Boeing 707s for 3.9 per cent.

In 1909–10 an airship station, with large hangar, was established at Bickendorf, between Ossendorf and Bocklemünd on the northwestern edge of the city, and in 1922 Bickendorf served as Cologne's airport when Instone Air Line inaugurated its London–Brussels–Cologne service—the first arrival being the Vickers Vimy Commercial G-EASI *City of London* on 2 October, bad weather having enforced a night stop at Brussels.

However, the airport which was destined to serve the city for most of the between-wars period was Butzweilerhof. The City of Cologne had first planned an aerodrome as early as 1911 and on 15 September, 1912, leased land at Butzweilerhof, 6 km (3¾ miles) northwest of the city and 2 km (1¼ miles) north of Bickendorf, to the army administration and a landing ground was prepared and buildings erected.

By 1914 three hangars had been built at Butzweilerhof and the site served as a military aerodrome during the 1914–18 war. From the armistice the aerodrome was occupied by British forces but after their departure on 1 January, 1926, Butzweilerhof became Cologne's city-owned airport, measured 1,200 by 1,100 m (3,937 by 3,609 ft), was accessible by tram, and served into the Second World War. Ground was broken on 23 April, 1935, for an attractive modern terminal building and hangar and these were commissioned in July 1936.

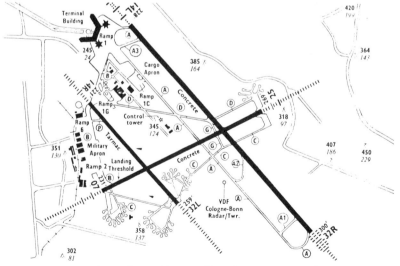

Cologne/Bonn Airport. (*British Airways Aerad*)

127

Cologne/Bonn Airport. Lufthansa's Boeing 707-330B D-ABUB *Stuttgart* refuelling at Gate B3. (*Deutsche Lufthansa*)

Although aviation has long since disappeared from the northwest suburbs of Cologne the area's association with early flying is recalled by such street names as Bleriotstrasse and Von-Hünefeld-Strasse.

In 1938 the Luftwaffe built an aerodrome on the artillery range on Wahner Heide (Wahn Heath) to the east of the Rhine and almost equidistant from Cologne and the postwar capital, Bonn. In 1945 the Royal Air Force took over Wahn aerodrome, and its first runway was 14/32 of 1,860 m (6,122 ft), now 14R/32L. A second runway, 07/25 of 2,460 m (8,071 ft)* was constructed, a small terminal built, and Wahn opened as a civil airport on 13 November, 1950. BEA began operating London–Wahn services with DC-3s. The airport was handed over to the civil authorities on 1 February, 1951, but taken back by the RAF from 1952 until 1957, with civil operations restricted to eight movements a day.

Construction of the 3,800 m (12,467 ft) 14L/32R runway began in 1959 and this was commissioned for nonstop intercontinental flights in 1961.

In 1966 work began on a completely new decentralized terminal with central block, two wing buildings each with six-gate satellite with aerobridges, and the new terminal was opened by the German President, Gustav Heinemann, on 20 March, 1970. Provision has been made for the southeastward extension of runway 14R/32L to 2,400 m (7,874 ft) and on a 652 hectare (1,611 acre) area to the northeast a 3,600 m (11,811 ft) 14LL/32RR runway.

*Flughafen Köln/Bonn state that runway 07/25 was 2,460 m (8,071 ft) long, 1953 charts show it as 8,000 ft (2,438 m), and AIP Germany gives its present length as 2,459 m (8,067 ft).

128

Düsseldorf   Flughafen Düsseldorf

51° 16′ 56″ N   06° 45′ 29″ E   5.4 nm (10 km) NW of city
ICAO: EDDL   IATA code: DUS   Time zone: GMT plus 1
Authority: Flughafen Düsseldorf GmbH
Area: 550 hectares (1,359 acres)
Elevation: 147 ft (45 m)   Ref temp: 19.2 deg C
Runways: 06/24   3,000 × 45 m (9,842 × 148 ft) asphalt/concrete
         16/34   1,630 × 50 m (5,348 × 164 ft) asphalt/concrete
Pavement strength: LCN 100
Landing category: ICAO CAT IIIa
Lighting:
    R/W   06/24   LIH and LIL white edge, and centreline with last
            300 m (984 ft) red and previous 600 m (1,968 ft) red/white.
            TDZ LIH white 24.
            16/34   LIH and LIL white edge.
    App   R/W 06   LIH white bar centreline with crossbars.
            R/W 24   LIH white CAT III centreline with crossbars
            and supplementary lights on inner 300 m (984 ft).
            R/W 16/34   LIL red Calvert centreline with crossbars.
            VASIS 06/24 and 16/34
    Thr   06/24 LIH green, 16/34   LIL green
    Txy   LIL blue edge with LIL green centreline on main taxiway
            and turn-offs
Aids: VOR, NDB, ASR, RVR, ILS CAT III 24, ILS CAT I 06
Twr frequency: 118.3   App frequency: 119.4
Terminals: Terminal 1 (old terminal) handles charter flights and some
    scheduled services and has 24 gates. Terminal 2 with two traffic piers,
    170,000 sq m (1,829,880 sq ft) floor area and 20 aircraft stands. There
    are 14 remote stands. Terminal 3 is the cargo terminal with 50,000
    tonnes annual capacity.

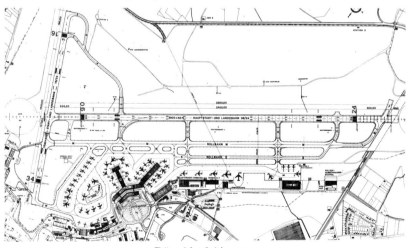

Düsseldorf Airport.

129

Scheduled services 1978: 23 airlines
Main base: LTU (Lufttransport-Unternehmen)

Traffic:	1970	1975	1976	1977	1978
Passengers (total)	3,600,613	5,218,429	5,280,027	5,809,218	6,360,320
Cargo (tonnes)	32,288	27,081	34,748	34,711	39,601
Aircraft movements	108,502	112,379	108,217	111,035	113,234
Transport movements	64,686	74,925	76,351	80,420	84,034

During 1977 Boeing 727s accounted for 22.7 per cent of transport movements, Boeing 737s for 20.46 per cent, DC-9s for 12.9 per cent and BAC One-Elevens for 10.49 per cent.

In 1909 the City of Düsseldorf built an airship hangar on Golzheimer Heide (Golzheimer Heath) near Lohausen on the east bank of the Rhine. On 19 September, 1909, the Zeppelin Z.I (formerly LZ 3) visited Düsseldorf and was housed in the hangar and an estimated 10,000 people went to see it. The hangar was a wooden structure with curtain 'doors' and from 1910 was leased to Delag. From that hangar, on 28 June, 1910, the Delag Zeppelin LZ 7 *Deutschland** set out on the first-ever cruise by an aircraft carrying passengers. Unfortunately the *Deutschland* was wrecked but subsequent Delag Zeppelins operated from Düsseldorf. When the Düsseldorf shed was built there were only two others in Germany, at Friedrichshafen and Baden-Oos. After a time the shed was given more imposing doors above which appeared the title Luftschiffhalle Düsseldorf.

In 1910 an aeroplane landing ground was prepared to the east of the airship shed. During the 1914–18 war the Golzheimer site was a military airship station with three large Zeppelin sheds and served as a military aerodrome. All four airship sheds were dismantled during 1919.

The Treaty of Versailles imposed severe restrictions on German aviation, and the consequent 50-km (31-mile) demilitarized zone on the east bank of the Rhine prevented any operation of the aerodrome at Düsseldorf. However, the Paris Agreement of 22 May, 1926, eased some of the restrictions and enabled Düsseldorf to create its civil airport. A 60 hectare (148 acre) grass landing ground was prepared during the winter of 1926–27, and the terminal area, with three wooden hangars, occupied the site of the Zeppelin station and incorporated the old barracks, mess and gasworks buildings. On 19 April, 1927, the airport handled its first services when Luft Hansa opened a Düsseldorf–Berlin service with Junkers-F 13s. The present general aviation area is on the old terminal site and the Zeppelin sheds stood immediately west of the present main taxiway.

During the Second World War the Luftwaffe established a base on the south of the airport. By the war's end most of the airport's installations had been destroyed or badly damaged, but when British occupation forces decided to reopen the airport they rebuilt the Luftwaffe administration building as the first postwar terminal.

The Luftwaffe had constructed three short black-top runways which formed an incomplete triangle—the runways being aligned approximately 06/24, 10/28 and 17/35. German workers under British supervision laid a PSP and tarmac 17/35 runway of 4,500 ft (1,372 m) which was ready for use in 1949 and on 4 April that year BEA began London–Düsseldorf–Hamburg Viking services, to be followed next day by SAS Copenhagen–Düsseldorf–Stuttgart DC-3 services.

*The Zeppelin *Deutschland* was the first aircraft built to carry passengers.

Düsseldorf Airport in May 1977. The two-pier Terminal 2 is in the centre with Terminal 1 in the left foreground. The cargo terminal is on the right edge of the photograph. Runway 06/24 is at the top. (*Courtesy Flughafen Düsseldorf GmbH*)

In July 1949 work began on construction of the main 06/24 concrete and tarmac runway to a length of 3,300 ft (1,006 m) but this was not connected to 17/35. By August 1950 the 06/24 runway was 1,128 m (3,700 ft) long. During this period there were extensions to the apron and buildings and new taxiways.

In 1951 a new 16/34 tarmac runway of 1,450 m (4,757 ft) replaced the 17/35 runway, and 06/24 was lengthened to 1,850 m (6,070 ft). A major development took place in 1952 when 06/24 was extended southwestward to connect with 16/34 and have a length of 2,475 m (8,120 ft). Since then both runways have been lengthened again and there is a plan for an 06L/24R runway.

Since the airport was reopened there has been almost continuous expansion of aprons and terminal buildings and a new terminal area was planned as early as 1952. Eventually it was decided that the new terminal should be alongside the already existing facilities and have a rail link to the Düsseldorf–Duisburg railway.

Development plans were based on the use of parallel runways separated by 503 m (1,650 ft) with capacity for 40–45 movements an hour under IFR conditions and an annual passenger capacity of about 11 mn. The existing buildings could handle 3–4 mn passengers annually and the capacity of the new building was set at 8–9 mn. Having settled on the site and the capacity it was decided to design a terminal providing the maximum number of gates in the area available. The new terminal (Terminal 2) was built with two piers and 20 aircraft stands and will later have a southwest pier. The control tower is at the outer end of the central pier. The new terminal with its central pier was officially opened on 30 March, 1973, with introduction into service on 7 April; Pier C came into use in 1974; and the railway link was opened on 24 October, 1975. Completion of the third phase with Pier A is scheduled for 1980.

Frankfurt am Main   Flughafen Frankfurt Main

50° 02′ 04″ N   08° 34′ 17″ E   6.5 nm (12 km) SW of city
ICAO: EDDF   IATA code: FRA   Time zone: GMT plus 1
Authority: Flughafen Frankfurt Main AG
Area: 1,203 hectares (2,973 acres)
Elevation: 368 ft (112 m)   Ref temp: 24 deg C
Runways: 07L/25R   3,900 × 60 m (12,795 × 197 ft) concrete
         07R/25L   3,750 × 45 m (12,303 × 148 ft) concrete
Pavement strength: LCN 100
Landing category: ICAO CAT I
Lighting:
    R/W   07L/25R   LIH and LIL white edge, 07R/25L   LIH and
        LIL white edge and LIH white centreline
    App   R/W 07L/25R   LIH and LIL white coded centreline with
        crossbars and sequenced flashers.
        R/W 07R   LIH white bar centreline and crossbar.
        R/W 25L   LIH and LIL white coded centreline with
        crossbars.
        VASIS all runways
    Thr   LIH and LIL green on all runways
    Txy   LIL blue edge with LIL red on two taxiways on north side
Aids: VORTAC, DME, NDB, VDF, ASR, SRE, SSR, PAR, ASDE, ILS
    CAT I 07L/25R and 25L
Twr frequency: 119.5   App frequency: 120.8
Terminals: Terminal Mitte (middle) with four functional levels, two wing
    piers and central Y pier. Pier A handles Lufthansa flights, Pier B
    international airlines and Berlin flights and Pier C charter flights.
    There are 54 gates, 36 with aerobridges, and 79 aircraft stands. There
    are separate cargo terminals and there is a military area on the south
    side of the airport.
Scheduled services 1978: 68 airlines

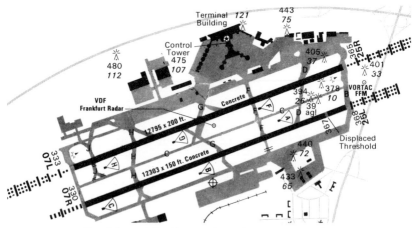

Frankfurt Main Airport. (*British Airways Aerad*)

Airline bases: Bavaria Germanair and Pan American
Main base: Condor, DLT, German Cargo Services, and Lufthansa

Traffic:	1970	1975	1976	1977	1978
Passengers (total)	9,365,465	11,938,943	14,214,345	14,968,377	15,883,148
Cargo (tonnes)	288,455	402,518	552,702	541,056	627,838
Aircraft movements	194,368	206,497	212,208	212,101	216,522
Transport movements	175,788	191,232	200,560	201,765	207,506

During 1977 Boeing 727s accounted for 30.86 per cent of transport movements, Boeing 737s for 13.93 per cent, DC-9s for 11.87 per cent, Boeing 747s for 7.65 per cent, Boeing 707s for 7.64 per cent and Airbus A300s for 4.58 per cent.

From 1924 Frankfurt am Main's airport was the 1,100 by 750 m (3,609 by 2,461 ft) Flughafen Rebstock, a few kilometres west of the city. In the early 1930s Frankfurt was anxious to become the German terminal for the transatlantic Zeppelin services and, because the Rebstock airport was too small for the larger aircraft being developed, it was decided early in 1934 to build a combined airport and airship station on a wooded site to the southwest of the city.

On 29 November, 1934, Südwestdeutsche Flugbetriebs-AG Rhein-Main (SWF), successor of the 1924 Südwestdeutsche Luftverkehrs-AG and predecessor of the present Flughafen Frankfurt Main AG, signed an agreement with Luftschiff Zeppelin GmbH to develop an airport and in 1935 work began on a 640 hectare (1,581 acre) airport and airship station. The airship station with, initially, one large hangar was on the south side of the airport.

The *Graf Zeppelin* made the first landing at Frankfurt on 11 May, 1936. On 6 May that year the *Hindenburg* left Friedrichshafen to inaugurate the first North Atlantic air services, and on its return flight it landed at Frankfurt where it was then based; but there was only the one hangar and the *Graf Zeppelin* had to be based at Friedrichshafen and shuttle to and from Frankfurt to operate the South Atlantic services.

The *Hindenburg* left Frankfurt for the last time on 3 May, 1937, to open the season's North Atlantic services but was destroyed by fire as it was landing at Lakehurst, New Jersey. The *Graf Zeppelin* was then withdrawn from service and on 19 June, 1937, made its last flight, to Frankfurt where it was put on public view. A second Frankfurt hangar was built and this enabled the LZ 130 *Graf Zeppelin II* to be housed there, but both Zeppelins were dismantled early in 1940 and on 6 May, 1940, on Göring's orders the hangars were dynamited.

The Frankfurt Zeppelin base had been officially opened by General Milch on 8 July, 1936, and it was on that day that the first aeroplane landed at the airport—Lufthansa's Junkers-Ju 52/3m D-AQUQ *Adolf v. Tutschek*. The landing area was grass surfaced and there was a pleasant terminal of the kind that became standard at German airports in the mid-1930s.

With the start of the Second World War Frankfurt's airport was taken over by the Luftwaffe and in 1943 a 1,500 m (4,921 ft) 07/25 runway was constructed, with the soil stabilized to a depth of 15 cm (6 in). This was the first stage of the building of the present 07R/25L.

The airport was extensively damaged during the war and was captured by United States forces. US troops and German prisoners began reconstruction on 22 May, 1945, and the runway was rebuilt in concrete and lengthened to 1,800 m (5,905 ft). In May 1946 American Overseas Airlines began Frankfurt–New York services with DC-4s.

During the course of the 1948–49 Berlin Airlift, Frankfurt had very heavy traffic, at some periods a take off every three minutes, and the runway suffered severe damage. As a result, in the spring of 1949, construction began of the parallel 07L/25R runway. It was initially 2,100 m (6,890 ft) long and became operational on 22 December, 1949. Frankfurt brought ILS into operation in 1952, 07L/25R was extended to 3,000 m (9,842 ft) in 1957 and later to 3,900 m (12,795 ft), the terminal was expanded in 1958 and in 1963 a new arrivals building was commissioned. In 1962 and 1964, runway 07R/25L was lengthened to bring it finally to 3,750 m (12,303 ft).

Frankfurt had become Germany's busiest and most important airport and in terms of passenger volume ranked second to Heathrow. Largescale terminal development was essential and on 16 June, 1965, the foundation stone was laid for a terminal with 30 mn annual passengers capacity. The east pier (C) was opened on 6 January, 1970; the central terminal with its Y-shaped pier (B) on 14 March and the west pier (A) on 1 April. On 14 March, 1972, the completed terminal was brought into full operation and by that time the direct railway link to the city was in operation.

The terminal area, with maintenance buildings, cargo centre, offices and general aviation area occupy the entire airport area north of the runways and this section of the airport is divided into three zones, West, Mitte (centre) and Ost (east), with the passenger complex being known as Terminal Mitte. South of the runways is Zone South with the United States Air Force base and Germanair maintenance facilities.

Frankfurt is an extremely important cargo centre. Cargo Terminal II used by Lufthansa has 360,000 tonnes annual capacity, Terminal III has an area of 12,500 sq m (134,550 sq ft) and serves Pan American and Seaboard

Terminal Mitte at Frankfurt Main Airport, showing the main building and concourse B and B west ramp. The building in the foreground at the extremity of B west ramp houses gates B34–38. (*Deutsche Lufthansa*)

Lufthansa's Frankfurt Main 'wide-bodied' hangar. (*Deutsche Lufthansa*)

World Airlines, and Terminal I with an area of 33,000 sq m (355,212 sq ft) serves the other airlines. In course of phased development is the new Frankfurt Cargo Centre which will ultimately have an area of 1,100,000 sq m (11,840,400 sq ft), 750,000 tonnes annual capacity, and 25 aircraft stands including 13 for Boeing 747 freighters. Lufthansa's terminal will form one unit of the Centre.

When built in the 1970s Lufthansa's Boeing 747 hangar at Frankfurt was the largest in the world and had the biggest cable roof span—130 m (426 ft). It is a stressed-ribbon structure, and 10 anchor weights, each of 1,000 tonnes, carry a framework at each side of the hangar to resist tension. Straight cables stiffen the roof and sagging cables support the precast concrete roof.

There have long been plans to extend both runways at their western ends because the proximity of the eastern thresholds to an eight-lane autobahn prevents upgrading the airport for CAT II operations and the installation of ILS on 07R. A third (approximately north–south) runway is also considered desirable but a Higher Hessian Administration Court decision, upheld by a Federal Court decision, prevented these developments until the end of 1978 when westward extension of 07R/25L began.

Hamburg   Flughafen Hamburg (Fuhlsbüttel)

53° 37′ 55″ N   09° 59′ 22″ E   4.6 nm (8.5 km) N of city
ICAO: EDDH   IATA code: HAM   Time zone: GMT plus 1
Authority: Flughafen Hamburg GmbH
Area: 526 hectares (1,300 acres)
Elevation: 53 ft (16 m)   Ref temp: 18.4 deg C
Runways: 05/23   3,095 × 45.8 m (10,154 × 150 ft) concrete/bitumen
         16/34   3,220 × 45.8 m (10,564 × 150 ft) bitumen, concrete
                                                                     ends
            There is also a 1,200 × 50 m (3,937 × 164 ft) 05/23 grass
            emergency strip
Pavement strength: LCN 100 for paved runways
Landing category: ICAO CAT II

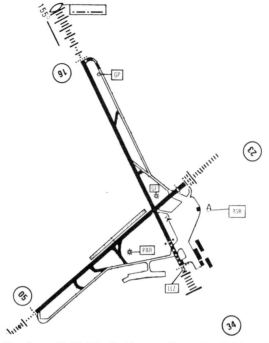

Hamburg (Fuhlsbüttel) Airport. (*Deutsche Lufthansa*)

Lighting:
R/W   LIH and LIL white edge and LIH white centreline with last 300 m (984 ft) red and previous 600 m (1,968 ft) red/white. LIH and LIL TDZ 23
App   R/W 05   LIH white and LIL red coded centreline with three crossbars, and sequenced flashers
R/W 23   CAT II precision approach with LIH red supplementary inner section, and sequenced flashers
R/W 16/34   LIH and LIL white coded centreline with six crossbars (16) and four crossbars (34), and sequenced flashers
VASIS 05/23 and 16/34
Thr   LIH green 05/23 and 34, LIH and LIL green 16
Txy   LIL blue edge, LIL green centreline on some sections
Aids: DVORTAC, NDB, VDF, PAR, ASR, ILS CAT II 23, ILS CAT I 16
Twr frequency: 118.1   App frequency: 120.6
Terminals: Central terminal building handles international services and flights to and from Berlin, southern wing handles domestic services and northern wing charter traffic. Construction of a new domestic terminal began in mid-1978, for service in summer 1979. Separate cargo terminal. About 27 aircraft stands, according to aircraft size.
Scheduled services 1978: 16 airlines
Airline base: Lufthansa

Traffic:	1970	1975	1976	1977	1978
Passengers (total)	3,130,039	3,503,725	3,647,938	3,955,055	4,159,255
Cargo (tonnes)	30,239	24,830	28,932	26,395	24,805
Aircraft movements	89,205	95,644	94,709	92,534	94,945
Transport movements	64,353	61,813	60,991	63,142	63,386

During 1977 Boeing 737s accounted for 29.05 per cent of transport movements, Boeing 727s for 29.02 per cent, DC-9s for 12.15 per cent, Caravelles for 5.36 per cent and Airbus A300s for 3.27 per cent.

Hamburg's airport at Fuhlsbüttel is among the world's oldest established airports. The city first considered preparation of an aerodrome in 1908, Hamburger Luftschiffhallen GmbH was founded on 10 January, 1911, and by 1912 a double airship-shed of 160 by 45 m (525 by 148 ft) had been erected. During that year the Delag passenger Zeppelins *Hansa* and *Viktoria Luise* were based at Fuhlsbüttel, and Navy crew training began on the *Viktoria Luise* at Hamburg on 1 July, 1912. Subsequently Fuhlsbüttel became a naval airship base. Aeroplanes were flying from Fuhlsbüttel by 1913 and there was then a flying school.

Following the 1914–18 war Fuhlsbüttel became the Hamburg airport and by the early 1930s the airport provided a maximum take off and landing run of 900 m (2,953 ft). During its early years there was a large hangar and a few small huts but in the 1930s a large terminal building was erected and this still forms the central core of the terminal complex although it has been much modified. The early airship associations are recalled by Zeppelin Strasse, the road which passes the terminal and over which approaches to runway 23 are made.

In the Second World War the airport was taken over by the Luftwaffe. At the war's end the airport came under the Royal Air Force but was handed back to the German authorities on 1 October, 1950.

Hamburg Airport terminal area, showing largescale extension to the prewar terminal. (*Flughafen Hamburg*)

137

Civil operations began with an 05/23 PSP runway of 4,800 ft (1,463 m) but a concrete runway of 5,913 ft (1,802 m) was soon built to the northwest of and parallel with the PSP strip. The main runway was soon lengthened to 6,169 ft (1,880 m) and a 4,818 ft (1,468 m) 16/34 concrete runway was built. Subsequently 05/23 was brought to its present standard mainly by extension to the southwest, and 16/34 was extended at its northern end.

Considerable development of the terminal took place as traffic developed. A southern wing was added to handle domestic traffic and a northern wing for charter flights. A pier, with aerobridges, was built for Boeing 747s and a large cargo terminal was constructed.

In spite of all the major developments it became obvious that the Fuhlsbüttel site would not be able to handle the area's total traffic indefinitely—aircraft movements increased from 18,424 to 99,052 in the period 1951–71—and as early as 1960 the Hamburg parliament requested the setting up of a commission to study the area's air transport needs. A site to the west of Kaltenkirchen in Schleswig-Holstein and 35 km (21¾ miles) north of Hamburg was selected by 1961. Early in 1962 the governments of Hamburg and Schleswig-Holstein agreed to acquire the necessary land and purchase began for a 2,900 hectare (7,166 acre) airport.

In the spring of 1968 the planning committee for what had become known as Projekt Kaltenkirchen commissioned three groups of engineers and architects to each produce two plans for the airport on the assumption that final capacity would be 100–120 aircraft movements an hour with 25–30 mn annual passengers and that there should be space for 90 close-in

Model of two of the terminal units for the projected Hamburg - Kaltenkirchen Airport. (*Flughafen Hamburg GmbH*)

aircraft stands. Seven designs were actually produced and the chosen one consisted of a central linear terminal area flanked by two 4,000 m (13,123 ft) runways, each with two parallel taxiways. Provision was made for runway extension to 5,880 m (19,291 ft) and for two outer runways to give a layout comprising two parallel pairs.

The terminals are to be two-level semi-circular structures arranged in pairs as at Dallas / Fort Worth. The outer radius of each terminal is specified as 140 m (459 ft), there would be 10–15 aircraft stands at each terminal and annual passenger capacity of 4 mn. The first stage calls for construction of one terminal and the southerly main runway, but the overall plan allows for six semi-circular terminals with space for an additional pair. The western end of the central area would be reserved for maintenance facilities and a very large cargo terminal complex.

After considerable delays approval was finally given by the Federal Ministry of Transport in 1977, and it is anticipated that when the new airport comes into operation Fuhlsbüttel will continue to serve European and domestic services.

Hanover (Hannover) Flughafen Hannover (Langenhagen)

52° 27′ 42″ N 09° 41′ 05″ E 6 nm (11 km) N of city
ICAO: EDVV IATA code: HAJ Time zone: GMT plus 1
Authority: Flughafen Hannover-Langenhagen GmbH
Elevation: 183 ft (56 m) Ref temp: 18.6 deg C
Runways: 09L/27R 2,700 × 45 m (8,858 × 148 ft) concrete*
09R/27L 2,340 × 45 m (7,677 × 148 ft) concrete*
09C/27C 780 × 22.5 m (2,559 × 74 ft) asphalt

*Centre portion marked with touchdown points for light aircraft

Pavement strength: Main runways LCN 100, 09C/27C limited to aircraft up to 5,700 kg (12,566 lb) all-up weight
Landing category: ICAO CAT IIIa
Lighting:
R/W LIH and LIL white edge 09L/27R with LIH white centreline on 27R with last 300 m (984 ft) red and previous 600 m (1,968 ft) red/white. TDZ LIH white each end
09R/27L LIH white edge and LIL white centreline
App R/W 09L/27R LIH and LIL white centreline with crossbar and sequenced flashers. Red barrettes on inner 300 m (984 ft). VASIS 27R
R/W 09R LIH white bar centreline with crossbar and sequenced flashers, LIL red centreline with crossbar
R/W 27L LIH and LIL white bar centreline with crossbar and sequenced flashers
Thr LIH and LIL green with strobes
Txy LIL blue edge, white centreline on high-speed exit from 27R
Aids: TVOR, NDB, VDF, PAR, ASR, L, ILS CAT IIIa 27R, ILS CAT I 09L and 27L
Twr frequency: 118.9 (north), 123.55 (south) App frequency: 118.05

Terminals: Terminal with rectangular centre section and two triangular boarding areas, with 12 close-in aircraft stands with aerobridges (four for Boeing 747s) and 12 remote stands. Cargo terminal with one aircraft stand.

Scheduled services 1978: nine airlines

Airline base: Hapag Lloyd-Flug

Traffic:	1970	1975	1976	1977	1978
Passengers (total)	2,398,788	1,734,162	1,752,481	2,050,929	2,097,860
Cargo (tonnes)	11,392	8,844	11,844	13,125	12,341
Aircraft movements	84,063	69,579	70,340	70,042	76,584
Transport movements	39,959	32,241	33,161	35,429	36,579

During 1977 Boeing 737s accounted for 24.82 per cent of transport movements, BAC One-Elevens for 20.22 per cent, Boeing 727s for 23.6 per cent, DC-9s for 5.62 per cent and Airbus A300s for 2.78 per cent.

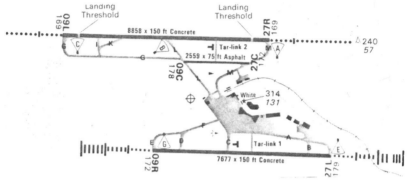

Hanover (Langenhagen) Airport. (*British Airways Aerad*)

Hanover has had a very long association with flying, Karl Jatho having 'flown' an aeroplane of his own design a distance of 18 m (59 ft) on 18 August, 1903, on Vahrenwalder Heide (Vahrenwalde Heath) north of the city. It was also from the heath that Delag operated the passenger Zeppelin *Hansa* in 1912. Later an aerodrome was established in the same area.

During the 1914–18 war Hannoversche Waggonfabrik, manufacturer of railway rolling stock, was required by the government to build aircraft. A factory and test aerodrome were established at Linden, west of Hanover, and some 47,000 aeroplanes were built including more than a thousand of the biplane-tailed Hannover two-seat biplanes. It was the Linden aerodrome that was used when Deutsche Luft-Reederei began Berlin–Brunswick–Hanover–Gelsenkirchen services on 15 April, 1919.

On 23 October, 1923, Flughafen Vahrenwald was established, 5 km (3 miles) north of the city, and this remained the Hanover airport until taken over by the Luftwaffe at the start of the Second World War.

The present airport had its beginnings in the Langenhagen-Evershorst base established by the Luftwaffe in 1935. During the war much of its northern area was occupied by hardstandings and taxiways, and an RAF reconnaissance photograph shows these mostly occupied by Heinkel He 111s and Junkers Ju 88s.

140

When civil operations began after the Second World War RAF Station Bückeburg was used and it was between Northolt and Bückeburg that on 15 August, 1951, BEA operated the first cargo service ever flown by a turbine-powered aircraft—the Dart-powered DC-3 G-ALXN RMA *Sir Henry Royce*.

In July 1950 the first plans were made to convert Langenhagen-Evershorst into the Hanover airport. On 26 November, 1951, construction began of a concrete 1,680 m (5,512 ft) runway—originally designated 10/28 but now part of 09R/27L. The Luftwaffe base had been badly damaged in Allied attacks but among the few surviving buildings were two hangars and one of these was converted to serve as the passenger terminal. The runway and terminal apron were connected by a single 500 m (1,640 ft) taxiway.

The airport was officially opened on 26 April, 1952, and on that day the BEA DC-3 G-ALYF RMA *Pionair* arrived from Berlin and SAS also began DC-3 services.

By the following year the runway was lengthened to 1,980 m (6,496 ft) with additional taxiways to serve each end and in 1959 it was again lengthened to bring it to its present 2,340 m (7,677 ft). Development then started north of the original aerodrome area, with two grass runways being brought into use in 1960 and then, in 1963, a 780 m (2,559 ft) asphalt runway with associated taxiways. This short runway is now 09C/27C.

Further development of the northern area was undertaken in 1965–66 with the construction of the concrete runway 09L/27R and a parallel taxiway. The original length, when opened on 26 April, 1966, was 2,400 m (7,874 ft), but in 1969 it was extended to 2,700 m (8,858 ft) by which time it had been cleared for CAT II approaches from the east. The northeast–southwest crosswind runway proposed in the 1951 plans was never built.

Hanover - Langenhagen Airport. View from the southeast showing the parallel 09/27 runways and central terminal. (*Flughafen Hannover - Langenhagen GmbH*)

Hanover's traffic grew rapidly from 323,026 terminal passengers and 17,086 aircraft movements in 1953, the first full year, to 1,034,734 passengers and 48,331 movements in 1965. Cargo and mail, in the same period, increased from 1,486 and 373 tonnes to 5,543 and 2,158 tonnes. In addition, the Hanover Trade Fair added a considerable volume of traffic over a short period. So by 1965 it seemed advisable to begin planning a new terminal.

Detailed planning began in 1967 for a terminal which would initially have a capacity of 4 mn passengers a year and the ability to handle the peak 20,000 a day during the Trade Fair. The design chosen was based on decentralized handling and comprised two six-gate triangular units with aerobridge loading and a linking building containing various passenger amenities. The foundation stone was laid on 23 March, 1971, the opening ceremony took place on 6 April, 1973, and the terminal became operational on 9 April. The cargo terminal was opened on 23 October, 1976.

The Hanover air show, first held in 1958, staged at the airport has now become a regular feature of the European aeronautical calendar.

Munich (München)   Flughafen München (Riem)

48° 07′ 54″ N   11° 41′ 57″ E   5.4 nm (10 km) E of city centre
ICAO: EDDM   IATA code: MUC   Time zone: GMT plus 1
Authority: Flughafen München GmbH
Area: 400 hectares (988 acres) approximately
Elevation: 1,737 ft (529 m)   Ref temp: 19.1 deg C
Runway: 07/25   2,804 × 60 m (9,200 × 197 ft) asphalt-concrete
There is an 800 × 30 m (2,625 × 98.5 ft) 07/25 grass runway to the north of the paved runway, but only 650 m (2,132 ft) is available
Pavement strength: Main runway LCN 100, grass runway 35,000 kg (77,162 lb) ISWL
Landing category: ICAO CAT III
Lighting:
R/W   LIH and LIL white edge, and LIH white centreline with last 304 m (997 ft) red and previous 600 m (1,968 ft) red/white. Red end lights. LIH white TDZ 25
App   R/W 07   LIH and LIL white bar centreline with crossbar and sequenced flashers. VASIS
R/W 25   LIH and LIL white bar centreline with crossbar, sequenced flashers, and on inner 300 m (984 ft) LIH red side barrettes
Thr   LIH green with strobes
Txy   LIL blue edge, LIH green centreline on high-speed exit from 25. Yellow holding point indicators
Aids: VORTAC, NDB, VDF, ASR, PAR, SRE, L, ILS CAT III 25, ILS CAT I 07
Twr frequency: 118.7   App frequency: 124.05
Terminal: International and domestic terminal with 33 gates, six aerobridges and 30 aircraft stands

Scheduled services 1978: 22 airlines
Main base: Bavaria Germanair

Traffic:	1970	1975	1976	1977	1978
Passengers (total)	3,550,929	4,543,138	4,608,723	5,299,122	5,617,990
Cargo (tonnes)	23,729	25,506	28,704	30,342	32,664
Aircraft movements	102,907	116,668	119,332	123,403	130,783
Transport movements	72,381	74,533	73,417	77,662	81,963

During 1977 Boeing 727s accounted for 35.72 per cent of transport movements, Boeing 737s for 27.51 per cent, DC-9s for 13.78 per cent, BAC One-Elevens for 8.01 per cent and wide-bodied aircraft for 4.2 per cent.

On 1 April, 1909, one of the early Zeppelins landed on the Oberwiesenfeld army parade ground about 5 km (3 miles) north of Munich, and in 1910–11 the area was being used for training military aeroplane pilots; but this activity ceased after a number of troops had been injured by aircraft making forced landings, and flying was transferred to Schleissheim about 10 km (6 miles) further north.

After the 1914–18 war Oberwiesenfeld became the Munich airport and in 1919 or 1920 (the date is disputed) Rumpler-Luftverkehr began operating services from Oberwiesenfeld with Rumpler single-engined biplanes. Initially some of the army buildings served the needs of the airport but a new terminal was opened in 1930. The landing area was circular with a diameter of about 1,000 m (3,281 ft).

Although improvements had taken place, it had become obvious by 1936 that a new Munich airport would be required and a site was selected near Riem village to the east of the city. Oberwiesenfeld was destined to become the site for the 1972 Olympic Games.

The new Munich - Riem Airport was roughly oval in shape, had a grass landing area providing a maximum length of nearly 2,000 m (6,562 ft) and

Munich Airport. View of the terminal area in March 1973.
(*Luftbildverlag Hans Bertram GmbH*)

143

in the northwestern area a modern terminal building. The opening of the new airport, on 1 September, 1939, coincided with the start of the Second World War and all civil aviation was banned, but after a short period Lufthansa was allowed to resume operations and on 25 October began operating from Munich - Riem. Even during the last stages of the war in Europe Lufthansa was operating its Berlin–Madrid–Lisbon services through Munich.

On 9 April, 1945, the airport was severely damaged by Allied bombing, some 70 per cent of the buildings being destroyed. The airport came under the control of United States forces and these began essential rehabilitation, erected temporary buildings and laid a PSP runway.

Civil operation at Munich - Riem was allowed again in 1948 and on 6 April a Pan American DC-3 made the first postwar landing by a civil aircraft.

Work was begun on the construction of a 1,900 m (6,234 ft) concrete 07/25 runway and this was opened with due ceremony on 22 November, 1949. The extension to 2,600 m (8,530 ft) was opened on 29 October, 1958, and on that day an Air France Caravelle became the first jet transport to land at Munich. The runway was finally extended to its present 2,804 m (9,200 ft) in a brilliant operation which took place from 11 to 31 August, 1969, when the entire runway was reconditioned.

In 1962 Riem handled a million passengers for the first time, more than 2 mn were handled in 1967, over $3\frac{1}{2}$ mn in 1970 and in excess of 4 mn in 1971. To keep pace with this rapid traffic growth buildings were altered and extended and new ones constructed so that by the time of the Olympic Games in 1972 the airport's capacity was $6\frac{1}{2}$ mn passengers a year.

However, further development at Riem was strictly limited. Noise had become a serious problem and there was no space for a second runway. Because of its elevation and proximity to the Alps, Riem suffers heavier snowfalls than most European airports and its single runway causes flights to be delayed, diverted or cancelled during snow clearance. The airport was approved for CAT IIIa on 2 November, 1978.

As early as 8 March, 1963, the Munich Airport Site Commission (Die Kommission 'Standort Grossflughafen München') was founded and the Commission submitted its report in October 1964. The 2,300 hectare (5,683 acre) site finally chosen for a new airport was between Erding and Freising, 28 km (17.4 miles) northeast of the city.

The new airport, known as München II, is to be financed by the State of Bavaria (51 per cent), the Federal Republic (26 per cent), and the City of Munich (23 per cent), and the estimated cost at March 1978 was DM 2,400 mn.

Following a long series of hearings and an architectural competition for the terminal area, actual construction was scheduled to begin during 1979 and the new airport is intended to replace Riem from May 1985, when the old airport will be closed.

Munich II will have a central terminal area sited between a pair of parallel 4,000 by 60 m (13,123 by 197 ft) runways, 09L/27R to the south of the terminal and 08R/26L to the north. Each runway will have two parallel taxiways with multiple high-speed exits. Land has been acquired to provide for two more runways of 2,500 by 45 m (8,202 by 148 ft). These would be 09R/27L on the south of the site for use as a reserve runway and 08L/26R to

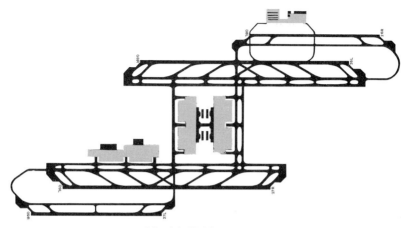

Munich II Airport plan.

the north to serve general aviation. These secondary runways would each have a parallel taxiway and the north runway would serve a special general aviation area.

The terminal will be H-shaped with a central building served by underground railway and two parallel 600-m (1,968-ft) long terminals each consisting of five modules with 2 mn passengers a year capacity. Each module will have two nose-in aircraft stands and aerobridge loading. Initially it is expected that six modules will be constructed but the site allows for extension of both terminal blocks in excess of the 10 planned modules. A parallel pair of taxiways will link the runways with each terminal apron. The space between the two terminal blocks will contain car parks.

To the west of the terminal area will be the cargo terminal with 70,000 sq m (753,480 sq ft) apron and five aircraft stands and the maintenance area with 98,000 sq m (1,054,872 sq ft) apron and six stands. The general aviation apron will have an area of about 73,000 sq m (785,772 sq ft) and covered positions for 156 small aircraft. In the terminal area there will be 16 remote stands.

The airport is being planned for CAT IIIa operations and great attention is being given to landscaping and the avoidance of any kind of pollution.

Nuremberg (Nürnberg)   Flughafen Nürnberg

ICAO: EDDN   IATA: NUE
49° 29′ 59″ N   11° 04′ 45″ E   Elevation: 1,045 ft (318 m)
Runway: 10/28   2,700 m (8,858 ft)   ART
Aids: TVOR, NDB, VDF, ILS CAT II 28, ILS CAT I 10

	1970	1975	1976	1977	1978
Passengers	516,689	717,307	778,419	777,191	765,949
Transport movements	11,489	14,063	13,344	12,735	12,677

145

Nuremberg Airport in 1977. (*Flughafen Nürnberg GmbH*)

Scheduled services 1978: KLM, Lufthansa and Pan American
The airport was opened on 6 April, 1955. Previously Nuremberg had been served by Fürth/Atzenhof (1920–33), Nürnberg - Marienberg (1933–45) and Industrieflughafen Fürth (1950–55).

Stuttgart   Flughafen Stuttgart

48° 41′ 19″ N   09° 12′ 39″ E   7 nm (13 km) S of city
ICAO: EDDS   IATA code: STR   Time zone: GMT plus 1
Authority: Flughafen Stuttgart GmbH
Area: 278 hectares (687 acres)
Elevation: 1,300 ft (396 m)   Ref temp: 19.4 deg C
Runway: 08/26   2,550 × 50 m (8,366 × 164 ft) concrete
Pavement strength: LCN 75
Landing category: ICAO CAT I
Lighting:
    R/W   LIH and LIL white edge, and LIH white centreline with last
            300 m (984 ft) red and previous 600 m (1,968 ft) red/white.
            TDZ wing bars 26
    App   R/W 08   Calvert centreline and crossbar
            R/W 26   LIH white coded centreline with five crossbars
            and sequenced flashers. VASIS 08/26
    Thr   LIH and LIL green wing bars with strobes
    Txy   edge and centreline
Aids: NDB, VDF, ASR, SRE, ILS CAT I 26
Twr frequency: 118.8/122.7   App frequency: 119.2/125.05

Terminals: Passenger terminal with 26 gates and 19 aircraft stands. Separate general aviation and cargo terminals. Seven aircraft stands for general aviation and three for local flying

Scheduled services 1978: 12 airlines

Traffic:	1970	1975	1976	1977	1978
Passengers (total)	1,662,176	2,201,633	2,422,971	2,337,198	2,635,858
Cargo (tonnes)	25,960	17,630	21,124	19,637	20,878
Aircraft movements	85,188	95,040	89,199	76,406	—
Transport movements	46,636	47,924	47,150	42,460	49,203

During 1977 Boeing 727s accounted for 29.96 per cent of transport movements, Boeing 737s for 19.55 per cent, DC-9s for 10.71 per cent, BAC One-Elevens for 8.97 per cent and Airbus A300s for 2.38 per cent.

Although the present Stuttgart Airport is simply called Flughafen Stuttgart, it was conceived in 1936 as Flughafen Stuttgart - Echterdingen, Stuttgart being the city served and Echterdingen a village which has given its name to aviation history.

Count Ferdinand von Zeppelin set out to make a 24-hour flight with his fourth rigid airship, LZ 4, leaving the floating shed at Manzell on Lake Constance (Bodensee) at 06.22 on 4 August, 1908. Following engine trouble the Count decided to have the engine repaired by Daimler at Stuttgart and at 07.51 on 5 August the Zeppelin alighted near Echterdingen—the first Zeppelin landing on ground instead of water. That afternoon a storm began and the Zeppelin broke its moorings, hit some trees and was destroyed by fire. This disaster produced enormous sympathy and support for Zeppelin, made future construction possible and became known as the 'miracle of Echterdingen'. A memorial now marks the landing site which is about 1.6 km (1 mile) southwest of the present airport.

Stuttgart Airport after the extension of the runway in 1961.
(*Flughafen Stuttgart GmbH*)

But when air transport first served Stuttgart the airport was 1 km west–northwest of Böblingen and 19 km (12 miles) southwest of Stuttgart. The first service through Stuttgart - Böblingen was on 20 April, 1925, when Deutscher Aero-Lloyd opened its Frankfurt–Stuttgart–Zürich service.

Böblingen provided a take-off distance of about 1,000 m (3,281 ft) and could not easily be extended, and the decision was taken to build a new airport near Echterdingen. Work began in 1937 and the airport, occupying 278 hectares (687 acres), was completed in 1939.

Stuttgart - Echterdingen was reopened as the civil airport in 1948, the first arrival being a Pan American aircraft on 3 October. The single 08/26 runway measured 1,400 m (4,593 ft) and the terminal area was on the north side of the airport. In 1951 the runway was lengthened to 1,800 m (5,905 ft) and this brought the 26 threshold almost up to the road linking Plieningen, to the north, and Bernhausen, to the south. It was necessary to attach triangular red and white daylight markings to the approach light crossbar to warn pilots on the approach of heavy road traffic immediately beyond the crossbar.

In 1959 work began on extending the runway eastward to its present length of 2,550 m (8,366 ft) and to make this possible the north–south road had to be sunk beneath the runway. The entire project took 20 months and the full length of the runway was opened on 21 April, 1961.

Traffic growth has necessitated considerable terminal development. The apron area was increased to 40,000 sq m (430,560 sq ft) in 1959 and then more than doubled in 1964, the year in which work began on a separate arrivals building. The area of the terminal complex was doubled in 1966, a new control tower was opened in May 1970, a new cargo terminal was commissioned in 1977, and further runway extension has been planned.

Ghana

Accra   Kotoka International Airport

ICAO: DGAA   IATA: ACC
05° 35′ 47″ N   00° 10′ 12″ W   Elevation: 205 ft (62 m)
Runway: 03/21   2,987 m (9,800 ft)   ART   VASI 21
Aids: VOR, SRE, L, ILS CAT I 21

	1970	1975	1976
Passengers	290,963	334,327	325,693
Transport movements	8,466	7,847	7,743

Scheduled services 1978: 16 airlines
Main base: Ghana Airways

Athens Airport. The East Terminal with Transavia Holland Boeing 737, Libyan Arab Airlines Boeing 727, KLM DC-8-63 *Vasco da Gama* and Swissair DC-9 on the apron. (*Greek Government*)

Greece (Hellas)

Athens (Athinai)   Athens Airport

37° 53′ 45″ N   23° 43′ 40″ E   4.5 nm (8.33 km) S of Acropolis
ICAO: LGAT   IATA code: ATH   Time zone: GMT plus 2
Authority: Civil Aviation Authority
Elevation: 90 ft (27 m)   Ref temp: 32 deg C
Runways: 03/21   1,810 × 60 m   (5,938 × 197 ft)* asphalt
            15L/33R   3,500 × 60 m (11,483 × 197 ft) asphalt, concrete
                                                          ends
            15R/33L   3,350 × 45 m (10,990 × 148 ft) asphalt

* Thr 03 displaced 965 m (3,166 ft) and 21 displaced 80 m (262 ft)

Pavement strength: 03/21 LCN 70–100, 15L/33R and 15R/33L LCN 100
Landing category: ICAO CAT I
Lighting:
   R/W   03/21   LIH white edge between displaced thresholds.
               End lights 21
               15L/33R   LIH white edge and centreline. End lights.
               TDZ 33R
               15R/33L   LIH white edge. End lights
   App   R/W 33R   LIH white barrette centreline. VASIS
               15L/33R and 15R/33L

Thr green all runways except 03
Txy blue edge
Aids: VOR, NDB, SRE, ILS CAT I 33R
Twr frequency: 118.1   App frequency: 119.1/121.4
Terminals: West Terminal (Olympic Airways) with 35 aircraft stands and
 East Terminal (other airlines) with seven gates and 36 stands
Scheduled services 1978: 45 airlines
Main base: Olympic Airways

Traffic:	1970	1975	1976	1977
Passengers (total)	3,631,760	6,137,845	7,451,465	8,295,863
Cargo (tonnes)	24,963	32,583	44,927	49,809
Aircraft movements	101,514	97,140	106,410	104,810
Transport movements	72,834	84,873	93,619	99,719

Athens Airport, formerly known as Hellinikon, was opened in 1948, replacing Hassani and the prewar Tatoi which was renamed Dekelia in 1936. The airport is situated on a narrow strip of land between the sea and a range of hills and beside the coastal road running south from the city.

The tarmac runways were originally 5,900 ft (1,798 m) long. The northwest–southeast runway, then known as 16/34, was lengthened to 7,382 ft (2,250 m) and now, as 15L/33R, is 11,483 ft (3,500 m) long. The parallel taxiway to the west of the main runway was developed as a second 15/33 runway but is now mainly used as a taxiway.

The early terminal area was near the coast road and is now known as the West Terminal, used only by Olympic Airways. All other carriers use the East Terminal which was designed by Eero Saarinen and opened on 29 June, 1969. It comprises a main building with 20,225 sq m (217,702 sq ft) of floor area, an arrivals building of 3,444 sq m (37,140 sq ft) and charter building of 3,400 sq m (36,666 sq ft).

It is planned that by 1985 a new Athens International Airport will be constructed 20 nautical miles (37 km) east of the present airport. The new airport has been designed by Aéroport de Paris, Flughafen Frankfurt Main AG and the Greek consulting engineers ADK. The plan envisages a pair of 4,000 m (13,123 ft) staggered parallel runways, with a central terminal spine having three circular terminals each with four piers and satellite buildings. There are to be separate cargo and general aviation areas.

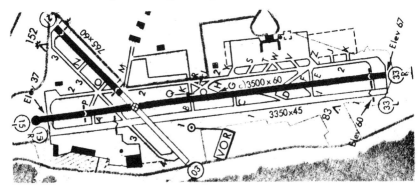

Athens Airport. (*Swissair*)

150

Corfu (Kerkyra)   Kerkyra Airport

	ICAO: LGKR	IATA: CFU

39° 36′ 24″ N   19° 54′ 32″ E   Elevation: 6 ft (2 m)
Runway: 17/35   2,400 m (7,874 ft)   RT   VASI 17/35
Aids: VOR/DME, NDB, L

	1970	1975	1976
Passengers	168,383	388,530	521,600
Transport movements	3,061	4,267	5,776

Scheduled services 1978: British Airways and Olympic Airways

Heraklion (Iraklion), Crete (Kriti)   Iraklion Airport

	ICAO: LGIR	IATA: HER

35° 20′ 17″ N   25° 10′ 39″ E   Elevation: 121 ft (36 m)
Longest runway: 09/27   2,680 m (8,792 ft)   RT   VASI 27
Aids: TACAN, TVOR, NDB

	1970	1975	1976
Passengers	178,549	506,745	686,127
Transport movements	3,126	5,236	7,132

Scheduled services 1978: Olympic Airways only

Rhodes (Rhodos)   Paradisi Airport

36° 24′ 20″ N   28° 05′ 13″ E   8 nm (14.8 km) WSW of harbour
ICAO: LGRP   IATA code: RHO   Time zone: GMT plus 2
Authority: Civil Aviation Authority
Elevation: 14 ft (4 m)   Ref temp: 33 deg C
Runway: 07/25   3,260 × 45 m (10,696 × 148 ft) asphalt, concrete ends
Pavement strength: LCN 80
Landing category: ICAO CAT II lighting
Lighting:
    R/W   LIH white edge and centreline. Red end lights. TDZ 07/25
    App   R/W 07   LIH white centreline with crossbar
           R/W 25   LIH white centreline with crossbar and sequenced flashers. Red barrettes over inner 305 m (1,000 ft). VASIS 07/25
    Thr   LIH green
    Txy   blue edge with green centreline on exits
Aids: VORTAC, TVOR, DME, NDB
Twr frequency: 120.85   App frequency: 120.6
Terminal: To south of runway. Three-storey building with ground floor area of 7,200 sq m (77,500 sq ft), four gates and nine aircraft stands
Scheduled services 1978: El Al and Olympic Airways

Traffic:*	1970	1975	1976
Passengers (total)	378,036	756,580	1,039,113
Cargo (tonnes)	726	1,540	2,229
Transport movements	6,048	7,585	10,460

* Figures are for Rhodes - Maritsa

Paradisi Airport, Rhodes. The terminal and control tower, with, between it and the sea, the runway. (*Greek Government*)

For many years Rhodes was served by Maritsa Airport which is situated at an elevation of 204 ft (62 m). The airport is surrounded by hills, landings and take-offs had to be made with great care, and the airport was severely criticized by pilots.

The new Paradisi Airport, although close to Maritsa, is beside the sea at an elevation of only 14 ft (4 m). It was opened on 28 June, 1977, and is now the main Rhodes airport, but Maritsa is still in use. Paradisi has a parallel taxiway but this does not extend the full length of the runway and thus enforces some backtracking on the runway.

Salonica (Thessaloniki)   Thessaloniki Airport

ICAO: LGTS   IATA: SKG
40° 31′ 10″ N   22° 58′ 25″ E   Elevation: 26 ft (8 m)
Longest runway: 10/28   2,440 m (8,005 ft)   ART   VASI 17 and 28
Aids: VORTAC, NDB, SRE, PAR, ILS CAT I 17

	1970	1975	1976
Passengers	314,451	821,453	942,491
Transport movements	5,360	9,400	11,684

Scheduled services 1978: Austrian Airlines, British Airways, Cyprus Airways, KLM, Lufthansa and Olympic Airways
Runway 17/35 is 2,400 m (7,874 ft) long

Guatemala

Guatemala City Aeropuerto Internacional La Aurora

ICAO: MGGT		IATA: GUA	
14° 34′ 55″ N 90° 31′ 39″ W		Elevation: 4,941 ft (1,506 m)	
Runway: 01/19 2,987 m (9,800 ft)		RT AVASI 01	
Aids: VOR/DME, NDB, Radar			

	1971	1975	1976	1977
Passengers	304,946	596,782	564,322	504,490
Transport movements	—	12,423	14,483	14,922

Scheduled services 1978: 11 airlines
Main base: Aerolineas de Guatemala - Aviateca

La Aurora Airport, Guatemala, with Aviateca BAC One-Eleven in the foreground and the Agua volcano in the background.

153

Hong Kong

Hong Kong   Hong Kong International Airport (Kai Tak)

22° 19′ 07″ N   114° 12′ 00″ E
               2.33 nm (4.33 km) NE of Star Ferry Pier, Kowloon
ICAO: VHHH   IATA code: HKG   Time zone: GMT plus 8
Owner: Hong Kong Government
Area: 222 hectares (549 acres)
Elevation: 15 ft (5 m)   Ref temp: 31.9 deg C
Runway: 13/31   3,329 × 61 m (10,930 × 200 ft) asphalt, grooved
         (R/W 31 is 2,890 m (9,490 ft) plus 500 m (1,640 ft) stopway)
Pavement strength: LCN 104
Landing category: ICAO CAT I
Lighting:
    R/W   LIH and LIL white edge
    App   R/W 13   LIH white and LIL red 1,925 m (6,315 ft)
             curved centreline with five crossbars and sequenced strobe
             lights
             R/W 31   LIH white and LIL red 594 m (1,950 ft)
             centreline with one crossbar. Three white strobe lights, one
             either side of threshold and one at centreline approach light
             immediately NW of crossbar. VASIS 31, VASGS (Visual
             Approach Slope Guidance System) 13 after passing middle
             marker
    Thr   LIH 13/31
    Txy   blue edge
Aids: VOR/DME, NDB, ASR, SSR, L, PAR, GCA, RVR 13/31,
ILS CAT I 31
Twr frequency: 118.7   App frequency: 119.1
Terminals: Passenger terminal with 5,000 passengers/hr capacity and 35
    aircraft stands. Cargo complex with main building having 38,000 sq m
    (409,032 sq ft) floor area and 500,000 tonnes annual capacity
Scheduled services 1978: 27 airlines
Main base: Cathay Pacific Airways

Traffic:	1970	1975	1976	1977
Passengers (total)	2,324,900	3,596,000	4,162,380	5,441,393
Cargo (tonnes)	55,507	141,620	163,235	173,953
Aircraft movements	87,013	83,191	77,887	84,374
Transport movements	46,841	51,094	50,194	50,320

More than 5 mn passengers were handled in the financial year 1977–78

In 1920 Dr Ho Kai and Mr Au Tak founded a company to reclaim
land from Kowloon Bay, with part set aside for an aerodrome. This was
opened as RAF Station Kai Tak on 10 March, 1927, and was the RAF's
first base in the Far East. Kai Tak was situated beside Kowloon Bay, had a
grass landing area, and on its landward side was extremely close to high
hills. The Hong Kong Flying Club began operation in June 1930 but the
first air service to use Kai Tak was the Imperial Airways Penang–Hong

Kong branch from the United Kingdom–Australia route, which opened in March 1936 with the D.H.86 *Dorado* making the first departure from Hong Kong on 27 March. Before the Pacific war Kai Tak had become quite busy with landplane services of Air France, CNAC, Eurasia Aviation Corporation and Imperial Airways/BOAC and trans-Pacific flying-boat services of Pan American Airways.

After the surrender to the Japanese on Christmas Day 1941, Allied prisoners were forced to build two concrete runways. In expanding the airport the Japanese are known to have removed a sacred hill in Kowloon which was surmounted by a boulder bearing the characters Sung Wong Toi (Sung Emperor Stone).

The original runways were 07/25 and 13/31 which in the immediate postwar period measured 4,730 ft (1,442 m) and 4,580 ft (1,396 m) respectively. Runway 13/31 was later extended to 5,418 ft (1,651 m).

It was obvious that the airport was unsuitable for growing traffic and larger aircraft, for landing minima were already high because of the difficult approaches. Numerous sites were examined for suitability for a new airport but eventually it was decided to develop Kai Tak and build a new runway stretching out into Kowloon Bay.

It was initially decided to build a 13/31 runway measuring 7,200 × 200 ft (2,195 × 61 m) with turning or holding loops at the mid-point and seaward end, and construct a new terminal area.

Hong Kong's runway which was built on land reclaimed from Kowloon Bay. This view shows the displaced 31 threshold.
(*Hong Kong Government Information Services*)

Hong Kong International Airport. The terminal area, in the winter of 1973–74, with further extension work in progress. The runway can be seen projecting into Kowloon Bay. (*Hong Kong Government Information Services*)

A revised plan extended the runway to 8,350 ft (2,545 m) and this was built almost entirely on an 800 ft (244 m) wide promontory reclaimed from the bay. 163 acres (66 hectares) were reclaimed in an average depth of 24 ft (7 m), enclosed by 3½ miles (5.6 km) of sea wall. Two hills at the landward end were levelled, providing stone for the sea wall and spoil for reclamation, and dredging and hill levelling involved moving more than 20 mn tons. A 75 ft (23 m) wide taxiway was constructed parallel to the runway, and lighting was installed, including a curved approach system built on pylons among blocks of tenements. This work formed Stage 1 of the redevelopment plan and was formally opened by HE The Governor of Hong Kong, Sir Robert Black, on 12 September, 1958. Stage 2 covered construction of a new apron and temporary terminal and Stage 3 the permanent terminal.

In 1968 a further development plan was begun with runway extension to its present length, further increase in apron area and enlargement of passenger and cargo facilities. But by 1974–75 the passenger terminal was handling up to 3,000 passengers an hour, against a design capacity of 2,300, and further extension had to be undertaken to increase capacity to 5,000 passengers/hr.

Hong Kong International plays a vital part in the Colony's economy—about 25 per cent of domestic exports and 30 per cent of re-exports (by value) left Hong Kong by air in 1975–76—and a cargo complex with 500,000 tonnes annual capacity was officially opened on 12 May, 1976. Floor area of the main building is 38,000 sq m (409,032 sq ft).

Due to physical limits on the further expansion of the airport, the Hong Kong Government has been considering the feasibility of building a new international airport and a site has been proposed on Chek Lap Kok Island about 15 km (9.3 miles) west of the city.

156

Hungary (Magyarország)

Budapest   Budapest/Ferihegy Airport

47° 26' 18" N   19° 14' 27" E   8.6 nm (16 km) ESE of city
ICAO: LHBP   IATA code: BUD   Time zone: GMT plus 1
Authority: LRI-KPM Légiforgalmi és Repülőteri Igazgatóság (Air
    Traffic and Airport Administration)
Area: 675 hectares (1,668 acres)
Elevation: 449 ft (137 m)   Ref temp: 22 deg C
Runway: 13/31   3,010 × 60 m (9,875 × 197 ft) concrete
    There is a grass landing area to the northeast of the paved
    runway. This provides 800 m (2,625 ft) 01/19 and 900 m (2,953 ft)
    09/27. There is also an emergency strip, 1,800 × 60 m
    (5,905 × 197 ft) to the northeast of and parallel with the paved
    runway
Pavement strength: LCN 76 over centre 1,610 m (5,283 ft), LCN 72 over
    northwest 700 m (2,296 ft) and LCN 81 over southeast 700 m (2,296 ft)
Landing category: ICAO CAT II
Lighting:
    R/W   LIH and LIL white edge, last 550 m (1,804 ft) both ends
            orange
    App   R/W 13   LIH CAT II centreline and two crossbars with
            first 600 m (1,968 ft) of centreline flashing.
            R/W 31   LIH Calvert centreline with six crossbars.
            VASIS 13/31
    Thr   LIH green and red
    Txy   LIL blue edge
            There is a warning that a brilliantly lit highway to the left of
            R/W 31 can be mistaken for the runway

A Malév Tupolev Tu-154 at Budapest/Ferihegy Airport in 1974, with the terminal
in the background. (*Malév*)

Aids: SSR, SRE, PAR, RVR, ILS CAT II 13, ILS CAT I 31
Twr frequency: 118.1   App frequency: 121.1
Terminals: Passenger terminal with eight gates and 20 aircraft stands.
    Separate cargo terminal
Scheduled services 1978: 20 airlines
Main base: Malév

Traffic:	1970	1975	1976	1977
Passengers (total)	804,577	1,042,702	1,347,055	1,301,522
Cargo (tonnes)	13,013	13,740	19,142	19,015
Aircraft movements	22,643	27,064	30,913	34,435
Transport movements	19,569	24,302	25,726	28,431

During 1976 Ilyushin Il-18s, Tupolev Tu-134s and Tu-154s accounted for the biggest percentage of movements.

For many years Budapest's air transport requirements were served by Mátyásföld but in the summer of 1937 the new Budaörs Airport was opened; but, with hills on three sides, the airport had disadvantages and it was decided to build another new airport east-southeast of the city. It was planned that traffic should be transferred to the new Ferihegy Airport at the end of 1939, with completion of buildings in 1940.

During the war the new airport was virtually destroyed and Budaörs had to be brought back into service. Reconstruction of Ferihegy was undertaken and the airport reopened in 1950. The 2,500 m (8,202 ft) 13/31 runway was brought into service in 1952 and in 1958 was extended to 3,010 m (9,875 ft). The original terminal has also been extended, and the apron was enlarged in 1964 and again in 1972 so that it can provide stands for 15 large aircraft. ILS and Calvert approach lighting were installed in the late 1950s.

In spite of the various extensions and impovements the airport was nearing its capacity in the mid-1970s and a major modernization plan was agreed for the period 1976–80. A new 3,700 m (12,139 ft) ILS-equipped runway is to be built to replace the existing runway. This requires major engineering work including relocation of the Ecser–Vacses trunk road and the renewal of gas mains. Completion is scheduled for 1980, at which time it is planned to complete the extension of the underground railway link between city and airport.

A new terminal with 6 mn passengers a year capacity is to be constructed. This will consist of seven straight segments arranged to form a semi-circle, have four triangular gate modules each with six aircraft stands and aerobridge boarding. There will be a two-level road system. By 1983 it is expected that Ferihegy will be handling 4 mn passengers a year.

Iceland (Ísland)

Keflavík   Keflavík Airport   ICAO: BIKF   IATA: KEF

63° 59′ 29″ N   22° 37′ 10″ W   Elevation: 169 ft (52 m)
Longest runway: 12/30   3,052 m (10,014 ft)   ART   T-VASI
  03 and 07/25
Aids: VORTAC, DME, NDB, L, GCA, ILS CAT II 21, ILS CAT I 12

	1970	1975	1976	1977
Passengers	436,797	473,343	505,693	529,826
Transport movements	6,588	6,536	6,562	8,094

Scheduled services 1978: Icelandair, Loftleiðir and SAS

Reykjavík   Reykjavík Airport   ICAO: BIRK   IATA: REK

64° 07′ 44″ N   21° 56′ 33″ W   Elevation: 45 ft (14 m)
Longest runway: 02/20   1,670 m (5,479 ft)   ART   VASI
  02/20   AVASI 14
Aids: NDB, L, SRE, ILS CAT I 20

	1970	1975	1976	1977
Passengers	128,859	248,818	257,580	279,631
Transport movements	15,056	24,108	24,168	20,368

Scheduled services 1978: Íscargo HF, Icelandair and Vaengir
Main base: Íscargo HF and Icelandair

A Flugfélag Íslands (Icelandair) Boeing 727 landing at Reykjavík Airport—
emphasizing the airport's proximity to the city.
(Icelandic Photo & Press Service, courtesy Director, Reykjavík Airport)

Bombay Airport terminal after several extensions.
(*Courtesy Deputy Director General of Civil Aviation*)

India (Bharat)

Bombay   Bombay Airport (formerly Santacruz)

19° 05′ 27″ N   72° 52′ 00″ E   7.8 nm (14.4 km) NE of city
ICAO: VABB   IATA code: BOM   Time zone: GMT plus 5½
Authority: International Airport Authority of India
Area: 1,000 hectares (2,471 acres)
Elevation: 27 ft (8 m)   Ref temp: 31.3 deg C
Runways: 09/27   3,492 × 46 m (11,455 × 150 ft)* asphalt/concrete
         14/32   2,730 × 46 m (8,956 × 150 ft)* asphalt/concrete
Pavement strength: 09/27 LCN 100, 14/32 LCN 60
Landing category: ICAO CAT I†
Lighting:
    R/W   09   LIM white edge, last 610 m (2,000 ft) yellow
           27   LIH and LIM white edge, last 610 m (2,000 ft) yellow
           14/32   LIM white edge, last 10 pairs yellow
    App   R/W 09 and 14   LIH white centreline. VASIS
           R/W 27   LIH white centreline and one crossbar. VASIS
    Thr   green
    Txy   blue edge
Aids: VOR/DME, NDB, VDF, ARSR, SRE, L, PAR, GCA, ILS CAT I 27
Twr frequency: 118.1   App frequency: 127.9
Terminal: Main terminal severely damaged by fire in 1979. Interim
    international terminal for departures opened October 1979.
    New international terminal scheduled for mid-1980.
Scheduled services 1978: 31 airlines
Base: Regional base Indian Airlines
Main base; Air-India and Airworks India

* R/W 09 first 137 m (450 ft) not available, R/W 27 first 538 m (1,765 ft) not
available for landing. R/W 14/32 only available to Boeing 747s when 09/27 is
closed. R/W 09/27 is being extended by 457 m (1,499 ft).
† R/W 09/27 is to be upgraded for CAT II operations.

160

Traffic:	1970	1975	1976	1977–78
Passengers (total)	1,818,216	2,308,670	2,617,978	4,100,094
Cargo (tonnes)	17,002	50,009	59,889	70,434
Aircraft movements	47,164	45,611	50,053	—
Transport movements	34,560	41,320	44,380	—

Juhu, opened in 1932, was the first Bombay airport, a grass aerodrome near the coast, and it was the base for Tata's operations when the Karachi–Bombay–Madras mail service was begun in October 1932. East–west and north-northwest–south-southeast bitumen runways were built in 1936–37 but during the monsoons operations were transferred to Poona. By the end of 1938 there were two all-weather concrete runways and a third runway was begun in 1939.

Throughout the war Juhu remained the Bombay airport but the site could not be developed and traffic was transferred to the larger Santacruz, a little further inland. The proximity of the two airports was the cause of embarrassment on at least two occasions. On one a BOAC Comet was landed at Juhu in error but after being stripped of all non-essentials was successfully flown out. The second incident involved a Japanese DC-8 but that was seriously damaged.

The early Santacruz terminal area was on the southern side of the airport, now occupied by Air-India and Indian Airlines' bases, but a permanent terminal was built to the west. It was enlarged several times before the fire in 1979. A new Gulf terminal was opened in October 1979 as an interim international departures building.

Runway 09/27 has been lengthened several times and is now more than double its original length. As the runway was extended at its eastern end it became necessary to remove the hills in the approach area—fortunately these hills were of earth and not of rock as had at first been thought.

Aéroport de Paris has designed a new international terminal for Bombay Airport and as planned would comprise three adjoining modules forming a continuous shallow curve, with arrivals and departures being handled on the first floor via 12 short traffic piers. This terminal is due to open in 1980.

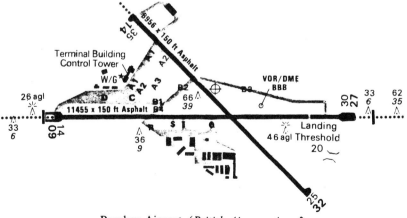

Bombay Airport. (*British Airways Aerad*)

161

Sultanate of Oman Air Force BAC One-Eleven at Calcutta Airport.
(*British Aerospace*)

Calcutta   Calcutta Airport (formerly Dum Dum)

22° 39′ 11″ N   88° 26′ 57″ E   8 nm (14.8 km) NE of Howrah Stn.
ICAO: VECC   IATA code: CCU   Time zone: GMT plus 5½
Authority: International Airport Authority of India
Elevation: 17.5 ft (5 m)   Ref temp: 31.8 deg C
Runways: 01L/19R   2,347 × 46 m   (7,700 × 150 ft) asphalt
         01R/19L   3,627 × 46 m (11,900 × 150 ft)* asphalt, concrete
                                                            ends
         07/25   1,524 × 46 m   (5,000 × 150 ft)**

* R/W 01R first 610 m (2,000 ft) not available, R/W 19L first 427 m (1,400 ft) not available
** Not used for commercial operations

Pavement strength: 01L/19R LCN 30,   01R/19L LCN 70
Landing category: ICAO CAT I
Lighting:
    R/W   01L/19R   LIM white edge, last 610 m (2,000 ft) yellow.
           End lights
           01R/19L   LIH white edge, last 610 m (2,000 ft) yellow.
           End lights
    App   R/W 19L   LIH red at edges of displaced threshold from
           61 m (200 ft) to 427 m (1,400 ft) with one crossbar. Lead-in
           lights to R/W 01L/19R. VASIS 01R/19L
    Thr   R/W 01L/19R   LIM green, R/W 01R LIH green, R/W 19L
           LIH green wing bars
    Txy   blue edge

Aids: VOR/DME, NDB, VDF, PAR, GCA/SRE, ILS CAT I 19L
Twr frequency: 118.1   App frequency: 119.3/127.9
Terminal: Passenger terminal with 18 aircraft stands—1–3 up to Boeing
    727 and DC-9, 4–10 international, 11–14 domestic up to Boeing 737,
    15–17 domestic up to Boeing 727 and DC-9, 18 VIP
Scheduled services 1978: Aeroflot, Air-India, Bangladesh Biman, British
    Airways, Burma Airways, Indian Airlines, Royal Nepal Airlines, SAS
    and Thai Airways International
Base: Regional base Indian Airlines
Main base: Jamair

Traffic:	1970	1975	1976	1977
Passengers (total)	880,912	957,430	1,029,946	1,136,301
Cargo (tonnes)	16,800	11,238	13,244	14,122
Aircraft movements	37,376	28,628	26,935	25,495
Transport movements	29,546	23,814	22,681	20,504

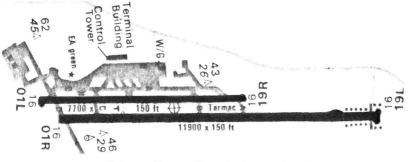

Calcutta Airport. (*British Airways Aerad*)

The preparation of a grass aerodrome at Dum Dum resulted from a
March 1927 Government vote for a supplementary grant of Rs 996,000
(then £74,700) which was passed by the Legislative Assembly in Delhi for
purchases of aerodromes at Bombay, Calcutta and Rangoon. In its early
days as a grass surfaced airport Dum Dum was subject to flooding during
monsoons, although in 1929–30 it was stated that it had been made fit for
year-round use at a cost of £23,500.

Dum Dum became the eastern terminal of the United Kingdom–India
air service in July 1933 when the route was extended from Delhi. The first
service to Calcutta left Karachi on 7 July and was flown by Indian Trans-
Continental Airways Armstrong Whitworth XV *Arethusa*. The early Far
East services of KLM and French companies staged through Dum Dum.

A northwest–southeast experimental fog line was provided in winter
1936–37 and three unpaved runways had been completed by the autumn of
1938.

During the war paved runways were constructed and these have since
been lengthened to meet the increasing demands of heavier aircraft.

The main terminal, for international traffic, was opened in 1970 but
domestic services continued to be handled in an old wartime building. In
August 1974 domestic traffic was transferred to the new terminal after it
had been modified. It was the first Indian terminal with nose-in aircraft
parking.

163

Delhi   Delhi Airport (Palam)

28° 34′ 07″ N   77° 06′ 48″ E   8 nm (14.8 km) SW of city
ICAO: VIDP   IATA code: DEL   Time zone: GMT plus 5½
Authority: International Airport Authority of India
Area: 410 hectares (1,013 acres)
Elevation: 744 ft (227 m)   Ref temp: 36.8 deg C
Runways: 09/27   2,292 × 46 m (7,520 × 150 ft) asphalt, concrete ends
          10/28   3,810 × 46 m (12,500 × 150 ft)* asphalt, concrete ends
          15/33   2,057 × 46 m (6,750 × 150 ft) asphalt
          R/W 09/27 is for daylight operation only and R/W 15/33 is used
          only for night parking

* R/W 10 first 152 m (500 ft) and R/W 28 first 305 m (1,000 ft) not available for
landing

Pavement strength: 09/27 LCN 40, 10/28 LCN 95
Landing category: ICAO CAT I
Lighting:
      R/W   09/27   LIM white edge, last 610 m (2,000 ft) yellow. End
              lights
              10/28   LIH white edge, last 610 m (2,000 ft) yellow, and
              red before displaced thresholds
      App   R/W 10   white centreline and crossbar. VASIS
              R/W 27   LIH white and LIH red centreline and crossbar
              R/W 28   LIH white centreline and crossbars with last
              152 m (500 ft) red. VASIS
      Thr   R/W 09/27 and 10/28   green wing bars
      Txy   edge lights on all taxiways
Aids: VOR/DME, NDB, VDF, ARSR, SRE, PAR, GCA, ILS CAT I 28
Twr frequency: 118.1   App frequency: 118.1

Delhi Airport terminal with the domestic section on the right.
(*Courtesy Deputy Director General of Civil Aviation*)

164

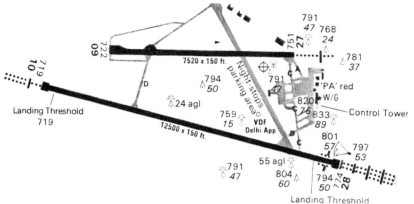

Delhi Airport (Palam). (*British Airways Aerad*)

Terminal: Terminal building with international and domestic wings (renovated in mid-1970s) with 18 aircraft stands, five for aircraft up to Boeing 747

Scheduled services 1978: 19 airlines

Main base: Indian Airlines

Traffic:	1970	1975	1976	1977
Passengers (total)	1,226,977	1,637,944	1,849,361	2,571,414
Cargo (tonnes)	11,445	27,783	31,303	37,353
Aircraft movements	34,009	52,831	54,350	53,672
Transport movements	26,056	28,921	29,241	29,798

On 22 February, 1936, HE The Viceroy of India opened the Willingdon Airport, to the south of Delhi and close beside Safdarjang's tomb. The terminal set the style for other British overseas airports including that at Karachi. After India became an independent sovereign State the airport was renamed Safdarjang and continued as the base for Indian domestic services operated by aircraft up to DC-3 category.

The international airport was established at the wartime Palam further to the west in more open country, the southern part of New Delhi having virtually surrounded Safdarjang.

The terminal has been enlarged and completely refurbished and in 1971–72 Aéroport de Paris produced three alternative master plans for the Delhi Airport terminal area. One of these was for a series of terminals which would ultimately form a large circle except for the segment occupied by the approach road system. These terminals would be multi-level and have aerobridge boarding.

It is expected that the new international terminal will be completed in 1984 and the present 3.3 mn passenger capacity building will then be used for domestic services until completion of a new domestic building by 1987. The airport is planned to be capable of handling 40 mn passengers and 70,000 tonnes of cargo annually into the 21st century.

Runway 10/28 is to be brought to CAT II standard.

165

Hyderabad   Hyderabad Airport (Begumpet)

ICAO: VOHY   IATA: HYD
17° 27' 09" N   78° 27' 50" E   Elevation: 1,741 ft (530.5 m)
Longest runway: 09/27   2,768 m (9,080 ft)   ART   VASI 09/27
Aids: VOR/NDB, VDF, L

	1975	1976
Passengers	252,088	283,955
Transport movements	7,976	6,618

Scheduled services 1978: Indian Airlines only

Indian Airlines Boeing 737 VT-EAI on the apron at Madras Airport.
(*Courtesy Deputy Director General of Civil Aviation*)

Madras   Madras Airport*   ICAO: VOMM   IATA: MAA

12° 59' 36" N   80° 10' 37" E   Elevation: 34 ft (10.5 m)
Longest runway: 07/25   3,063 m (10,050 ft)   ART   VASI 07/25
Aids: VOR/DME, NDB, VDF, ARSR, ILS CAT I 07

	1970	1975	1976	1977
Passengers	369,644	533,043	657,359	759,791
Transport movements	10,050	12,381	13,128	12,774

Scheduled services 1978: Air Ceylon, Air-India, Indian Airlines, Malaysian
   Airline System and Singapore Airlines

* Formerly St Thomas's Mount and Meenambakkan

Sepinggan Airport, Balikpapan, in 1973, with the nose of Garuda Indonesian Airways Fokker F.28 *Bogowonto*. (*Fokker-VFW*)

Indonesia (Republik Indonesia)

Balikpapan, Kalimantan (Borneo)   Balikpapan - Sepinggan Airport

ICAO: WRBL   IATA: BPN
01° 16′ S   116° 54′ E   Elevation: 10 ft (3 m)
Runway: 07/25   1,800 m (5,905 ft)   RT
Aids: NDB, L

	1975	1976
Passengers	416,290	481,198

Scheduled services 1978: Bouraq Indonesia Airlines, Garuda Indonesian Airways and Merpati Nusantara Airlines
Main base: Bouraq Indonesia Airlines

Denpasar, Bali   Denpasar - Bali International Airport (Ngurah Rai)

ICAO: WRDD   IATA: DPS
08° 45′ 09″ S   115° 10′ 00″ E   Elevation: 10 ft (3 m)
Runway: 09/27   2,700 m (8,858 ft)   RT   VASI 09/27
Aids: VOR, NDB, ILS CAT I 27

	1970	1975	1976
Passengers	138,015	412,439	562,830

Scheduled services 1978: Garuda Indonesian Airways, Merpati Nusantara Airlines, Qantas and Thai Airways International

167

Jakarta, Java
Jakarta International Airport Halim Perdanakusuma

06° 16′ 01″ S   106° 53′ 39″ E   6 nm (11 km) SE of city
ICAO: WIIH   IATA code: HLP   Time zone: GMT plus 7
Owner: Directorate of Civil Aviation, managed by Perum Angkasa Pura
Elevation: 84 ft (26 m)   Ref temp: 31 deg C
Runway: 06/24   3,000 × 45 m (9,842 × 148 ft) asphaltic concrete
Pavement strength: LCN 110
Landing category: ICAO CAT I
Lighting:
R/W	06	LIH white edge and REIL
	24	LIH white edge, last 305 m (1,000 ft) yellow
App	R/W 24	LIH white bar centreline and crossbar with sequenced flashers. VASIS 06/24
Thr	R/W 06 green with strobes, R/W 24 green wing bars	
Txy	blue edge	

Aids: VOR/DME, NDB, L, ILS CAT I 24
Twr frequency: 118.3   App frequency: 119.7
Terminals: One departure and two arrival buildings, one for Hadj traffic.
Scheduled services 1978: 15 airlines

Traffic:	1975*	1976	1977
Passengers (total)	2,635,025	1,361,161	1,570,838
Cargo (tonnes)	31,814	16,901	18,109
Aircraft movements	102,887	29,825	36,649
Transport movements	69,262	22,219	23,575

* Combined totals for Halim Perdanakusuma and Kemayoran. Figures, other than passenger totals, are from ICAO

In January 1974 a completely new international airport*—Halim Perdanakusuma—was opened to handle Jakarta's international traffic and services to Bali, the old Kemayoran Airport having long been criticized for its congestion and lack of adequate facilities. The new airport has a two-level concrete and glass terminal with white and brownish-yellow exterior.

* The airport was previously a military base.

The terminal building at Jakarta International Airport Halim.

168

Indonesian air traffic approximately trebled in volume during the period 1970–75 and growth is likely to continue. It has therefore been decided to build a new international airport at Cengkareng, 45 km (28 miles) west of Jakarta. A 1,000 hectare (2,471 acre) site has been acquired and construction is to begin in 1980 on Phase 1 which will include one runway and three terminals with 21 gates, completion being scheduled for about 1984. Stage 2 envisages doubling the area and the addition of a second runway and three more terminals.

Jakarta's Kemayoran Airport in 1973 bearing the title international before the opening of Halim. The Fokker F.27-600 Friendship is Garuda Indonesian Airways PK-GFG *Merapi*. (*Fokker-VFW*)

Jakarta, Java   Jakarta - Kemayoran Airport

06° 08′ 35″ S   106° 50′ 51″ E   1 nm (1.85 km) NE of city
ICAO: WIII   IATA code: JKT   Time zone: GMT plus 7
Owner: Directorate of Civil Aviation, managed by Perum Angkasa Pura
Area: 410 hectares (1,013 acres)
Elevation: 20 ft (6 m)   Ref temp: 26.6 deg C
Runways: 08/26   1,900 × 45 m (6,233 × 148 ft)*
      17/35   2,475 × 60 m (8,120 × 197 ft) asphalt

* R/W 08 first 260 m (853 ft) and R/W 26 last 260 m (853 ft) not available for landing

Pavement strength: 08/26   36,000 kg (79,366 lb) 1, 50,000 kg (110,231 lb) 2; 17/35   72,000 kg (158,733 lb) 1, 90,000 kg (198,416 lb) 2, 127,000 kg (279,987 lb) 3
Landing category: ICAO CAT I

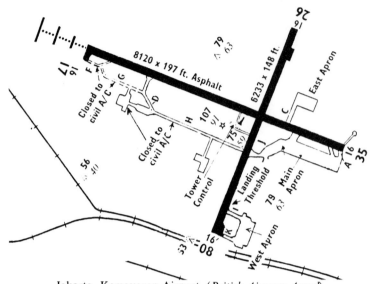

Jakarta - Kemayoran Airport. (*British Airways Aerad*)

Lighting:
R/W   08/26   LIL white edge, 17/35 LIH white edge
App   R/W 17   LIH white centreline with crossbars. VASIS
                  17/35
Thr   green
Txy   edge
Aids: VOR, NDB, L, ILS CAT I 17
Twr frequency: 119.7   App frequency: 119.7
Terminals: Three terminal buildings with main apron at south of airport.
   Also west and east aprons
Scheduled services 1978: Bouraq Indonesia Airlines, Garuda Indonesian
   Airways and Merpati Nusantara Airlines
Base: Merpati Nusantara Airlines
Main base: Garuda Indonesian Airways

Traffic:	1970	1975*	1976	1977
Passengers (total)	839,510	2,635,025	1,686,202	2,027,050
Cargo (tonnes)	26,383	31,814	18,902	24,126
Aircraft movements	40,827	102,887	74,049	78,205
Transport movements	24,370	69,262	50,647	53,935

* Combined totals for Kemayoran and Halim Perdanakusuma. Figures, other than
passenger totals, are from ICAO

Jakarta's postwar airport, Kemayoran, is situated a few miles
southwest of the prewar Batavia airport Tjililitan. Kemayoran was subject
to frequent criticism by pilots and passengers, but in 1974 congestion was
eased by the opening of Halim Perdanakusuma as the international airport
and Kemayoran is now used mainly for domestic operations.

170

A warning to pilots using Kemayoran states that 'Small paper kites may be encountered at heights up to approximately 300 ft' on the approaches to R/W 08 and 35.

Medan, Sumatra   Medan - Polonia International Airport

ICAO: WIPM   IATA: MES
03° 34′ S   98° 41′ E   Elevation: 89 ft (27 m)
Runway: 05/23   2,450 m (8,038 ft)   AR*   VASI 05/23
Aids: VOR/DME

	1970	1975	1976
Passengers	119,973	341,958	423,394

Scheduled services 1978: Garuda Indonesian Airways, Malaysian Airline System, Merpati Nusantara Airlines and Singapore Airlines

* Runway lights available on request

Surabaya, Java   Surabaya - Juanda Airport

ICAO: WRRD   IATA: SUB
07° 22′ S   112° 46′ E   Elevation: 10 ft (3 m)
Runway: 10/28   3,000 m (9,842 ft)   ART
Aids: VOR, NDB

	1970	1975	1976
Passengers	166,692	601,320	711,905

Scheduled services 1978: Bouraq Indonesia Airlines, Garuda Indonesian Airways and Merpati Nusantara Airlines

Ujung-Pandang, Sulawesi (Celebes)
              Ujung-Pandang - Hasanuddin Airport

ICAO: WRMM   IATA: UPG
05° 04′ S   119° 33′ E   Elevation: 105 ft (32 m)
Runway: 08/26   1,550 m (5,085 ft)   ART
Aids: VOR, NDB

	1970	1975	1976
Passengers	62,147	233,632	292,100

Scheduled services 1978: Bouraq Indonesia Airlines, Garuda Indonesian Airways and Merpati Nusantara Airlines

Iran

Abadan   Abadan International Airport

ICAO: OIAA   IATA: ABD
30° 22′ 00″ N   48° 14′ 00″ E   Elevation: 10 ft (3 m)
Longest runway: 14R/32L 3,100 m (10,170 ft)   ART   VASI all R/Ws
Aids: NDB, VDF, L, ILS CAT I 32L

	1970	1975	1976	1977
Passengers*	229,329	403,153	502,310	575,465
Transport movements	13,329	12,738	15,049	15,335

* Transit passengers excluded

Scheduled services 1978: Iran Air, KLM and Kuwait Airways

Teheran (Tehran)   Tehran/Mehrabad International Airport

35° 41′ 21″ N   51° 18′ 49″ E   3 nm (5.5 km) W of city
ICAO: OIII   IATA code: THR   Time zone: GMT plus 3½
Authority: Civil Aviation Organization
Elevation: 3,963 ft (1,208 m)   Ref temp: 32.3 deg C
Runways: 11L/29R   4,000 × 45 m (13,123 × 148 ft) asphalt
　　　　11R/29L   3,999 × 60 m (13,120 × 197 ft) asphalt
　　　　There are military jet barriers on all runways except 11L, that on
　　　　29L is on the stopway before the Kan River
Pavement strength: LCN 100
Landing category: ICAO CAT I

Teheran's Mehrabad International Airport in the early 1950s, with the terminal
under construction. The aircraft is BOAC's Canadair Four Argonaut class *Astra*.
(*British Airways*)

172

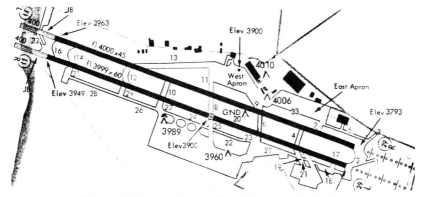

Teheran/Mehrabad International Airport. (*Swissair*)

Lighting:

R/W	11L LIL white edge, 11R/29L and 29R LIH and LIL white edge. Fixed distance bars 244 m (800 ft) from thresholds 29L and 29R
App	R/W 29L LIH white and LIL red Calvert centreline with five crossbars. VASIS
	R/W 29R LIH white Calvert centreline with five crossbars and LIL red centreline with one crossbar
Thr	R/W 11R/29L and 29R LIH and LIL green
	R/W 11L goosenecks
Txy	edge lights

Aids: VORTAC, DME, NDB, L, SRE, PAR, RVR 29L and 29R, ILS CAT I 29L

Twr frequency: 118.1   App frequency: 119.7

Terminals: Passenger terminal with east and west aprons and separate Hadj pilgrim terminal

Scheduled services 1978: 25 airlines

Main base: Iran Air and Pars Air

Traffic:	1970	1975	1976	1977
Passengers (total)	901,611	2,291,633*	3,020,917	3,455,815
Cargo (tonnes)	13,513	58,626	100,414	122,476
Aircraft movements	85,006	137,052	143,233	152,915
Transport movements	28,732	48,089	54,703	59,952

*Excludes transit passengers

Teheran, situated in a mountainous area and at an elevation of nearly 4,000 ft (1,219 m), was of little aeronautical significance before the Second World War although some services to and from the city were for a time operated by Junkers-Luftverkehr Persien. When Imperial Airways extended its Cairo–Basra services to Karachi in 1929 the route followed the Gulf coast of Iran.

During and just after the war Teheran was served by Doshan Tappeh Airport but a new airport was constructed about 7½ miles (12 km) further west. Known as Mehrabad, the new airport had 11/29 and 18/36 runways of approximately 6,000 ft (1,829 m) and what was then a large terminal.

173

Mehrabad became an important airport and home base of Iran Air, which was one of the fastest growing airlines. Runway 18/36 is now a taxiway, 11/29 was extended to 3,000 m (9,842 ft) and then to its present length forming 11R/29L of the parallel pair. The terminal was also extended but unfortunately, on 5 December, 1974, part of the structure collapsed under the weight of a heavy snowfall with fatal results and it was suggested that the collapse was, at least in part, due to the additions which had been made.

In 1978 work was in progress to increase Mehrabad's capacity to 5 mn passengers a year, and there were plans to build the Aryamehr Airport, some 40 km (25 miles) from the city, for operation in 1982–83. The new international airport was to have two sets of 4,420 m (14,500 ft) parallel runways and 10 terminals but as a result of the 1979 revolution this project is likely to be cancelled.

The projected Aryamehr International Airport, Teheran, with linear terminal complex and parallel pairs of runways.

Iraq (Al Jumhouriya al 'Iraqia)

Baghdad   Baghdad International Airport

33° 14′ 27″ N   44° 14′ 02″ E   10 nm (18.5 km) SW of city
ICAO: ORBB   IATA code: BGW   Time zone: GMT plus 4
Authority: The State Organization of Iraqi Civil Aviation
Elevation: 113 ft (34 m)   Ref temp: 43.1 deg C
Runway: 15/33   3,300 × 45 m (10,827 × 148 ft) concrete
Pavement strength: LCN 100
Landing category: ICAO CAT I
Lighting:
    R/W   LIH white edge, last 610 m (2,000 ft) yellow, LIH white
      centreline and TDZ
    App   R/W 15   LIL red centreline with crossbars
      R/W 33   LIH white CAT I centreline with crossbars
      and LIL red centreline with crossbars. VASIS 33
    Thr   LIH green
    Txy   green centreline and some blue edge lights
Aids: VOR/DME, NDB, L, SRE, ILS CAT I 33
Twr frequency: 118.7/121.5   App frequency: 119.4
Terminal: On east side of airport with eight aircraft stands
Scheduled services 1978: 26 airlines
Main base: Iraqi Airways

Traffic:	1970	1975	1976	1977
Passengers (terminal)	200,998	605,052	822,951	1,007,000*
Cargo (tonnes)	3,457	17,750	14,124	15,568
Transport movements	6,402	10,674	14,739	14,505

*Rounded figure

When the Royal Air Force began the Cairo–Baghdad Desert Air Mail service on 23 June, 1921, the Iraqi terminal was Baghdad West but soon after the terminal was transferred to RAF Station Hinaidi which later became the Iraq Air Force Station Rashid. Hinaidi also served as the Baghdad Airport when Imperial Airways opened its Cairo–Baghdad–Basra section of the United Kingdom–India service on 7 January, 1927.

The decision was taken to develop Baghdad West as the civil airport and, with a fine passenger terminal, it was opened on 5 April, 1933. It served as Baghdad's airport, with its original terminal and the addition of paved runways, until the present Baghdad International Airport was opened in January 1970.

In 1974 the 1975–79 five-year plan was approved for airport development in Iraq and proposals for Baghdad International included construction of a CAT III 4,000 m (13,123 ft) runway parallel to the existing 15/33 runway, and construction of a new passenger terminal and control tower.

The new terminal is to be a three-storey building with capacity for 7 mn passengers a year.

Ireland (Eire)

Cork (Corcaigh)   Cork Airport   ICAO: EICK   IATA: ORK

51° 50′ 27″ N   08° 29′ 20″ W   Elevation: 502 ft (153 m)
Longest runway: 17/35   1,829 m (6,000 ft)   ART   VASI 17/35 and 25
Aids: VOR/DME, PAR, ILS CAT I 17

	1970	1975	1976
Passengers	198,585	255,595	272,676
Transport movements	4,439	5,586	5,473

Scheduled services 1978: Aer Lingus, British Airways, Brymon Airways, Dan-Air Services and Touraine Air Transport

The airport was opened by the Irish Prime Minister Sean Lemass on 16 October, 1961.

Dublin (Baile Átha Cliath)   Dublin Airport

53° 25′ 52″ N   06° 15′ 12″ W   5.3 nm (9.8 km) N of city
ICAO: EIDW   IATA code: DUB   Time zone: GMT
Authority: Department of Transport and Power
Area: 303 hectares (750 acres)
Elevation: 222 ft (68 m)   Ref temp: 18.6 deg C
Runways: 06/24   2,286 × 61 m (7,500 × 200 ft) concrete-asphalt
       12/30   1,356 × 61 m (4,450 × 200 ft) concrete
       17/35   2,073 × 61 m (6,800 × 200 ft) concrete-asphalt
Pavement strength: Maximum landing weight all runways—23,000 kg (50,706 lb) 1, 30,000 kg (66,138 lb) 2, 60,000 kg (132,277 lb) 3
Landing category: Partially ICAO CAT II.   R/W 06/24 ILS, RVR and runway lighting CAT II, but approach lighting CAT I. R/W 12/30 and 17/35 CAT I

Dublin Airport, showing the terminal, pier and satellite pavilion opened in 1972. The original terminal is on the right. (*Courtesy Aer Lingus*)

176

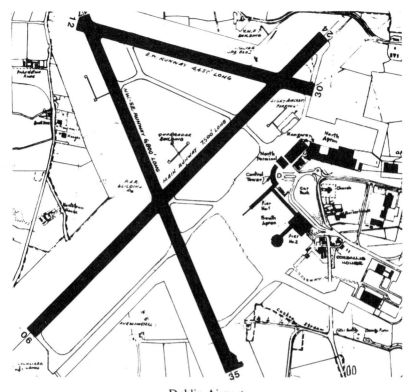

Dublin Airport.

Lighting:
R/W   06/24   LIH white edge with yellow over last 600 m (1,968 ft), LIH colour-coded centreline. White TDZ R/W 24
            12/30   LIH white edge with fixed distance bars on 12
            17/35   LIH white edge. Red end lights all runways
App   R/W 06   455 m (1,493 ft) LIL centreline with one crossbar
            R/W 24   744 m (2,441 ft) LIH centreline with five crossbars and 472 m (1,548 ft) LIL centreline with one crossbar
            R/W 17   910 m (2,985 ft) LIH centreline with six crossbars and 610 m (2,000 ft) LIL centreline with one crossbar
            R/W 35   488 m (1,600 ft) LIL centreline with one crossbar
            R/W 12/30   455 m (1,493 ft) LIL centreline with one crossbar.
All approach lights white. VASIS 06/24, 17/35 and 30

177

Thr   R/W 06, 12/30 and 35   LIH green
        R/W 17 and 24   LIH green with green wing bars
Txy   blue edge, some with green centreline
Aids: VOR/DME, NDB, SRE, PAR, RVR, ILS CAT II 06/24, ILS CAT I
    12/30 and 17/35
Twr frequency: 118.6   App frequency: 121.1
Terminals: Passenger terminal, pier and satellite with 15 gates, 22 aircraft
    stands and aerobridges. Cargo terminal with two stands.
Scheduled services 1978: Aer Arann, Aer Lingus, British Airways, British
    Island Airways, British Midland Airways, Iberia, Lufthansa and
    TWA
Base: Irish Helicopters
Main base: Aer Lingus and Aer Turas

Traffic:	1970	1975	1976	1977
Passengers (total)	1,897,917	2,195,688	2,208,882	2,267,057
Cargo and mail (tonnes)	39,805	44,731	46,637	45,734
Aircraft movements	65,199	79,416	80,622	85,036
Transport movements	35,540	35,470	35,848	35,724

In 1976 Boeing 737s accounted for 20 per cent of movements, BAC One-Elevens for 12 per cent and general aviation for 55 per cent.

When Midland and Scottish Air Ferries began its short-lived Hooton–Liverpool–Dublin service in September 1933 and Aer Lingus began its Dublin–Bristol service, with the Dragon EI-ABI *Iolar*, on 27 May, 1936, the Dublin terminal was the Baldonnel military aerodrome. But about 700 acres (283 hectares) of land was acquired for a permanent Dublin airport north of the city, and some 300 acres (121 hectares) was allocated for the initial stage which comprised a roughly triangular grass landing area providing a maximum length of 5,288 ft (1,612 m), a passenger terminal and two hangars with door openings of 200 ft (61 m) and 150 ft (46 m).

Construction began in 1937 and the airport, known as Collinstown, was opened to commercial traffic on 19 January, 1940. The approaches were good but the landing area was rather uneven and subject to water logging. The 400 ft (122 m) long terminal on the eastern boundary was one of the best in Europe when it was opened and it was surmounted by a control tower 65 ft (20 m) above ground level. The airport was adequately equipped for night operation and Lorenz 'blind landing' system was installed for approaches from northeast.

In 1947 construction of three concrete runways was begun— 06/24 4,280 ft (1,305 m), 12/30 4,450 ft (1,356 m) and 17/35 4,500 ft (1,372 m). Runways 06/24 and 17/35 were later extended.

The new North Terminal for arrivals was opened in July 1959, a new catering building in 1969 and cargo terminal in 1970. The present passenger terminal, with pier and satellite pavilion, was opened in May 1972.

Land has been acquired for two new 11/29 runways. No date has yet been decided for construction but this is likely to start in the early 1980s.

Shannon Airport terminal. (*Aer Rianta*)

Limerick Shannon Airport

52° 42′ 04″ N   08° 55′ 15″ W   10.8 nm (20 km) WNW of Limerick
ICAO: EINN   IATA code: SNN   Time zone: GMT
Authority: Department of Transport and Power
Area: 384 hectares (950 acres)
Elevation: 47 ft (14 m)   Ref temp: 19.1 deg C
Runways: 06/24   3,200 × 46 m (10,500 × 150 ft) concrete-asphalt
         14/32   1,720 × 46 m (5,643 × 150 ft) concrete
Pavement strength: Max landing weight 06/24 32,000 kg (70,548 lb) 1,
    42,000 kg (92,594 lb) 2, 84,000 kg (185,188 lb) 3, 14/32
    16,000 kg (35,274 lb) 1, 23,000 kg (50,706 lb) 2.
Landing category: ICAO CAT I lighting but CAT II ILS R/W 24
Lighting:
    R/W   06/24   LIH and LIL white edge with LIH showing
             yellow over last 600 m (1.968 ft)
             14/32   LIL white edge. Red end lights all runways
    App   R/W 06   470 m (1,542 ft) LIL white centreline with one
             crossbar
             R/W 24   898 m (2,946 ft) LIH white centreline with five
             crossbars and 598 m (1,962 ft) LIL white centreline with one
             crossbar
             R/W 14/32   455 m (1,493 ft) LIL red centreline with one
             crossbar. VASIS 06/24 and 32
    Thr   R/W 06   LIH and LIL green
             R/W 24   LIH green with green wing bars
             R/W 14/32   LIL green
    Txy   blue edge
Aids: VOR/DME, NDB, SSR, SRE, PAR, RVR, ILS CAT II 24
Twr frequency: 118.7   App frequency: 121.4
Terminals: Passenger terminal with 10 gates, 14 aircraft stands and six
    aerobridges. Separate cargo terminal
Scheduled services 1978: Aer Lingus, Air Canada, British Airways,
    Gennair and TWA

179

Traffic:	1970	1975	1976	1977
Passengers (total)	833,378	1,031,876	1,100,977	1,165,870
Cargo and mail (tonnes)	9,702	17,397	12,952	14,984
Aircraft movements	52,320	34,440	32,962	40,582
Transport movements	17,457	20,654	21,122	15,650

In 1976 Boeing 707s accounted for 24 per cent of movements, DC-8s for 13 per cent and general aviation 26 per cent.

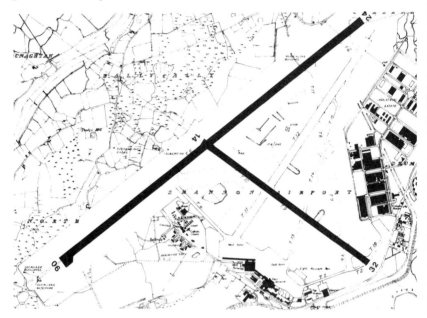

Shannon Airport.

The west coast of Ireland, being the nearest point in Europe to North America, played an important part in the development of North Atlantic air services and a flying-boat base was established at Foynes on the Shannon in County Clare. It was from Foynes, on 5 July, 1937, that Imperial Airways Short C class flying-boat *Caledonia* set out on the first North Atlantic commercial survey flight and on the following day Pan American Airways Sikorsky S-42 *Clipper III* alighted there at the end of the reciprocal flight.

In the same year construction of a grass aerodrome—known as Rineanna—was begun some distance to the northeast on a point extending into the Shannon and when on 5 August, 1939, Imperial Airways began experimental transatlantic mail services between Southampton and Montreal and New York, the flying-boats were refuelled in flight from a Harrow tanker based at Rineanna.

During the war four concrete runways were constructed—05/23 7,027 ft (2,142 m) 09/27 5,628 ft (1,715 m), 14/32 5,640 ft (1,719 m) and 18/36 5,274 ft (1,608 m). Since that time runways 05/23 and 18/36 have become taxiways, 09/27 has been abandoned and the new 06/24 has been built.

After being requisitioned by the Irish Government during the war the airport was opened to civil traffic late in 1945 and on 24 October an American Export Airlines DC-4 operated the first transatlantic service through the airport*. The name Shannon Airport was adopted in 1947.

For more than a decade the airport played an important part in North Atlantic operations, it achieved fame in 1951 by becoming the first Customs-free airport in Europe and by 1960 had become the biggest centre of employment on the west coast of Ireland.

The introduction of long-range aircraft seriously threatened the airport's wellbeing and the Irish Government set out to attract industry and tourism in order to bring traffic to Shannon. A duty-free industrial area was established with success and cargo traffic was dramatically increased—the cargo terminal being opened in 1961. In addition low traffic density and lack of fog induced a number of airlines to transfer their flying training to Shannon.

The present passenger terminal was opened on 6 May, 1971, and in 1977 Eurocontrol commissioned its upper airspace air traffic control centre. Because of the proximity of the river and the tidal mud flats, Shannon's rescue equipment includes amphibious vehicles.

*BOAC had operated some Bristol–Rineanna services with Frobisher class de Havilland Albatrosses from 21 February, 1942, and Aer Lingus operated Dublin–Rineanna services from 12 August until 30 October, 1942.

Israel

Tel Aviv   Ben Gurion International Airport

32° 00′ 38″ N   34° 52′ 38″ E   9.72 nm (18 km) ESE of city
ICAO: LLBG   IATA code: TLV   Time zone: GMT plus 2
Authority: Ben Gurion Airport Authority
Area: About 906 hectares (2,240 acres)
Elevation: 135 ft (41 m)   Ref temp: 26 deg C
Runways: 03/21   1,770 × 45 m   (5,807 × 148 ft) asphalt
         08/26   3,657 × 45 m (11,998 × 148 ft) asphalt
         12/30   3,040 × 45 m   (9,974 × 148 ft) asphalt
Pavement strength: R/W 03/21 and 08/26 LCN 110, R/W 12/30 LCN 90
Landing category: ICAO CAT II
Lighting:
    R/W   03/21   LIL edge and centreline
             08/26   LIH edge and centreline. TDZ 26
             12/30   LIH edge

App	R/W 12	LIH white bar centreline with crossbar

App   R/W 12   LIH white bar centreline with crossbar
        R/W 30   LIH white bar centreline with crossbar and
        sequenced flashers
        R/W 26   LIH white bar centreline with crossbar, red
        barrettes on inner 1,000 ft (305 m). VASIS 12/30 and 26
Thr   green all thresholds, with wing bars 12/30
Txy   edge on all taxiways
Aids: VOR/DME, NDB, VDF, L, SRE, RVR 12/30, ILS CAT II 26, ILS
    CAT I 12
Twr frequency: 118.3   App frequency: 120.5
Terminals: Separate international and domestic terminals with 31 aircraft
    stands. Separate general aviation apron
Scheduled services 1978: 16 airlines
Main base: Arkia Israel Inland Airlines and El Al

Traffic:	1970	1975	1976	1977
Passengers (total)	1,110,444	1,533,274	1,944,043	2,308,247
Cargo (tonnes)	30,740	44,138	58,968	107,468
Aircraft movements	19,952	16,340	18,685	20,173
Transport movements	17,573	15,811*	18,116	18,961

*International only

    Early in 1934 the Palestine Government decided to build an airport near Lydda (Lod), its terminal area being sited immediately adjacent to Lydda racecourse with its football and polo grounds and polo school ground. The subsoil was a form of wind-blown clay and the area had been used for the growing of corn. By the autumn of 1934 two unpaved runways were in use and Misr Airwork was operating to and from the aerodrome.
    The overall plan called for four runways each of 1,200 by 100 m (3,937 by 328 ft), a terminal 'house' and two hangar and workshop blocks. Lighting was planned from the start, including an experimental runway floodlight and illuminated sighting targets for night take-offs.

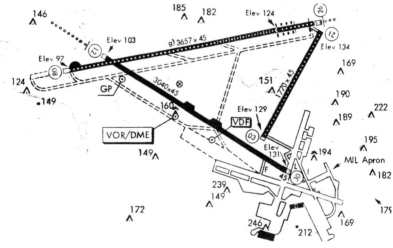

Ben Gurion International Airport. (*Swissair*)

An El Al Boeing 747 landing at Ben Gurion International Airport, Tel Aviv.

The runways were 01/19, 06/24, 10/28 and 14/32, and in the early postwar period these had respective lengths of 5,100 ft (1,554 m), 3,600 ft (1,097 m), 6,300 ft (1,920 m) and 4,200 ft (1,280 m). Later, 10/28 was extended to 6,562 ft (2,000 m) and 06/24 and 14/32 were withdrawn from use.

The present three-runway pattern is to the northwest of the original airport. Future plans include lengthening runway 08/26 and the construction of more taxiways including parallel taxiways for both main runways and high-speed exits.

With the creation of the State of Israel the airport was known as Lod but was renamed Ben Gurion International Airport in 1974.

Italy (Italia)

Bologna   Aeroporto Bologna/Borgo Panigale

	ICAO: LIPE	IATA: BLQ	
44° 31′ 50″ N	11° 17′ 33″ E		Elevation: 125 ft (38 m)
Runway: 12/30	2,150 m (7,054 ft)	ART	T-VASI

Aids: VOR/DME, NDB, VDF, ILS CAT I 12

	1970	1975	1976	1977
Passengers	46,887	476,321	462,953	454,428
Transport movements	3,244	14,901	15,106	12,255

Scheduled services 1978: Air France, Alisarda, Alitalia, ATI and Itavia

The runway is to be extended to 2,600 m (8,530 ft).

183

Cagliari, Sardinia (Sardegna)   Aeroporto Cagliari Elmas

ICAO: LIEE   IATA: CAG
39° 14′ 47″ N   09° 03′ 27″ E   Elevation: 12 ft (3.66 m)
Runway: 14/32   2,078 m (6,817 ft)   ART
Aids: VOR/DME, NDB, VDF, L, ILS CAT I 32.

	1970	1975	1976	1977
Passengers	447,606	717,474	744,562	786,820
Transport movements	10,541	14,300	14,386	13,618

Scheduled services 1978: Alisarda, Alitalia, ATI and Itavia

The runway is to be lengthened to 2,213 m (7,260 ft).

Catania, Sicily (Sicilia)   Aeroporto Catania/Fontanarossa

ICAO: LICC   IATA: CTA
37° 27′ 56″ N   15° 03′ 50″ E   Elevation: 43 ft (13.1 m)
Runway: 08/26   2,340 m (7,677 ft)   RT   VASI 08/26
Aids: VOR/DME, NDB, VDF

	1970	1975	1976	1977
Passengers	624,356	770,458	815,811	893,128
Transport movements	13,715	14,703	15,428	13,425

Scheduled services 1978: Alitalia, ATI and Itavia.

Genoa (Genova)   Aeroporto Sestri (Cristoforo Colombo)

ICAO: LIMJ   IATA: GOA
44° 24′ 47″ N   08° 50′ 16″ E   Elevation: 10 ft (3 m)
Runway: 11/29   2,930 m (9,613 ft)   RT   VASI 11/29
Aids: VOR/DME, NDB, VDF, SRE, ILS CAT I 29

	1970	1975	1976	1977
Passengers	570,504	492,029	515,815	535,689
Transport movements	15,081	11,044	10,791	10,001

Scheduled services 1978: Alisarda, Alitalia, ATI, British Caledonian
Airways, Lufthansa and Swissair.

Milan (Milano)   Aeroporto Milano/Linate

45° 26′ 30″ N   09° 16′ 40″ E   4.32 nm (7.96 km) ESE of city
ICAO: LIMM   IATA code: LIN   Time zone: GMT plus 1
Authority: Società Esercizi Aeroportuali (SEA)
Elevation: 352 ft (107 m)   Ref temp: 25.3 deg C
Runways: 18L/36R   2,440 × 60 m (8,005 × 197 ft) bitumen
         18R/36L   620 × 32 m (2,034 × 105 ft) bitumen
Pavement strength: R/W 18L/36R 30,000 kg (66,140 lb) ISWL, R/W 18R/36L
    7,000 kg (15,432 lb) ISWL
Landing category: ICAO CAT II

Lighting (R/W 18L/36R only):

R/W   LIH white and yellow coded edge, centreline and end lights. TDZ 36R

App   R/W 18L   150 m (492 ft) LIH lead-in

          R/W 36R   LIH white Calvert and supplementary inner, with flashers. VASIS 36R

Thr   LIH green, with supplementary lights each side of Thr 18L

Txy   blue

Aids: NDB, VDF, L, PAR, GCA, SRE, ASMI, RVR 18L/36R, ILS CAT II 36R

Twr frequency: 118.1   App frequency: 118.8

Terminal: Terminal at north end of airport with 23 aircraft stands on 125,892 sq m (1,355,101 sq ft) apron. Cargo terminal with four aircraft stands. General aviation area to the west with 30,000 sq m (322,920 sq ft) apron

Scheduled services 1978: 25 airlines

Traffic:	1970	1975	1976	1977	1978
Passengers (total)	2,947,519	4,163,895	4,373,320	4,407,783	4,996,820
Cargo (tonnes)	51,536	52,043	49,583	53,902	55,839
Aircraft movements	74,632	91,366	96,172	96,521	—
Transport movements	62,888	73,284	78,234	79,433	78,076

In 1975 DC-9s accounted for 68.48 per cent of transport movements, Caravelles for 7.88 per cent, Boeing 727s for 7.04 per cent and Boeing 737s for 4.07 per cent.

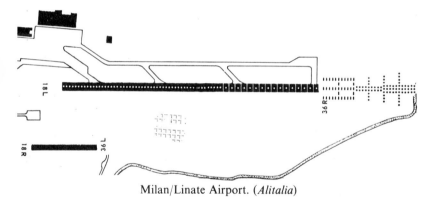

Milan/Linate Airport. (*Alitalia*)

Milan's Linate Airport was constructed in the 1930s as Aeroporto E. Forlanini and is believed to have been completed in 1938. The site chosen was just outside the city's southeastern suburbs and immediately alongside an artificial lake which served as a seaplane alighting area providing a maximum length of 2,500 m (8,202 ft). The River Lambro formed the western boundary of the new airport and the village of Linate was immediately to the south.

The original grass landing ground had an area of 300 hectares (741 acres) and provided a maximum length of 2,400 m (7,874 ft), from northwest to southeast. In the northeast corner, close to the large modern terminal and hangar, was a paved WNW–ESE runway which measured

The terminal area at Milan's Linate Airport. In the background is the artificial lake which used to be used for marine aircraft operations. (*Società Esercizi Aeroportuali*)

600 by 60 m (1,968 by 197 ft). The terminal, with a covered ramp leading to the apron, and the hangar were sited to serve both the landplane and marine aircraft traffic.

Later a 18/36 bitumen-surfaced runway was built within the confines of the original airport and this had a length of 620 m (2,034 ft), but it could not be extended because of the proximity of Linate village and a new 18/36 runway was built to bypass Linate on its eastern side. These runways are now known respectively as 18R/36L and 18L/36R. A new terminal area has been constructed partly on the site occupied by the original 1938 hangar.

Milan (Milano)   Aeroporto Milano/Malpensa

45° 37′ 58″ N   08° 43′ 56″ E   21.58 nm (40 km) NW of city
ICAO: LIMC   IATA code: MXP   Time zone: GMT plus 1
Authority: Società Esercizi Aeroportuali (SEA)
Area: 666 hectares (1,645 acres)
Elevation: 767 ft (234 m)   Ref temp: 24.2 deg C
Runways: 17L/35R   3,915 × 60 m (12,844 × 197 ft) bitumen, concrete
                                                            ends
            17R/35L   2,625 × 60 m   (8,612 × 197 ft) bitumen, concrete
                                                            ends

Pavement strength: 45,000 kg (99,208 lb) ISWL both runways
Landing category: ICAO CAT II (to be upgraded to CAT III)
Lighting:
R/W	17L/35R	LIH and LIL white edge and centreline. TDZ 35R
	17R/35L	LIL white edge
App	R/W 35L	LIH Calvert white CAT I with flashers
	R/W 35R	LIH Calvert white CAT II with LIH flashers and inner supplementary lights. VASIS 35R
Thr	green	
Txy	blue	

Aids: NDB, VDF, UDF, L, SRE, PAR 35R, ASMI, RVR 17L/35R, ILS CAT II 35R

Twr frequency: 120.9/121.6   App frequency: 118.8

Terminals: Terminal area at northern end of airport between ends of the parallel runways, with 26 aircraft stands. Separate cargo terminal

Scheduled services 1978: Aeroflot, Alitalia, CP Air, Egyptair, LOT, Saudi Arabian Airlines, Seaboard World Airlines, TWA and VIASA

Airline bases: Alitalia and TWA

Traffic:	1970	1975	1976	1977	1978
Passengers (total)	634,493	1,004,130	976,614	1,229,952	1,058,192
Cargo (tonnes)	22,555	35,724	33,290	41,076	41,511
Aircraft movements	18,440	22,845	20,761	20,077	—
Transport movements	13,614	16,302	14,770	14,254	14,118

In 1976 DC-9s accounted for 14.44 per cent of transport movements, Boeing 707s for 12.5 per cent, DC-8s for 12.43 per cent, Boeing 747s for 10.43 per cent, DC-10s for 8.24 per cent and BAC One-Elevens for 7.77 per cent.

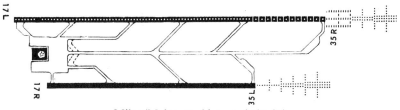

Milan/Malpensa Airport. (*Alitalia*)

Malpensa was a First World War grass aerodrome used by the Italian Air Force. It was still a military aerodrome during the Second World War, and it was then that the 2,024 m (6,640 ft) 17/35 runway was constructed. After the war the aerodrome was acquired by a group of local businessmen who formed Società p.A Aeroporto di Busto (the name being changed to the present Società Esercizi Aeroportuali—SEA in 1955).

Airline operations to and from Malpensa began in the early 1950s although the aerodrome had few facilities other than its single runway, perimeter track, wooden customs building and small café. It found favour with pilots because in winter some clearance of fog occurred there on days when it persisted all day at Linate Airport. The airlines preferred Linate because it is closer to the city.

Malpensa Airport, Milan. View looking southeast across the terminal area to runway 17L/35R. (*Società Esercizi Aeroportuali*)

SEA expanded the airport and in 1958 began construction of a new runway—17R/35L, and subsequently the old runway, redesignated 17L/35R, was lengthened.

In 1965 Malpensa was designated Milan's international and intercontinental airport, with Linate handling domestic services but this division of operations has not survived.

It is realized that Malpensa requires largescale development to meet future traffic demands and in 1972 the Italian Government approved the first stage of the master development plan. This calls for a new seven-storey terminal of 650 by 100 m (2,132 by 328 ft) with four satellites. Annual design capacity is 12 mn passengers, with peak hour capacity for 7,500. There are to be about 20 nose-in aircraft stands served by aerobridges, plus remote parking. There is also to be a new cargo terminal. These developments are to take place on the southwest part of the airport.

Naples (Napoli)   Aeroporto Napoli/Capodichino

40° 53′ 00″ N   14° 17′ 20″ E   3.24 nm (6 km) NNE of city
ICAO: LIRN   IATA code: NAP   Time zone: GMT plus 1
Authority: Italian Air Force
Elevation: 289 ft (88 m)   Ref temp: 26.5 deg C
Runway: 06/24   2,195 × 45 m (7,202 × 148 ft)* Macadam
Pavement strength: 28,000 kg (61,729 lb) ISWL
Landing category: uncategorized
Lighting:
    R/W   LIH white edge, last 2,000 ft (610 m) orange
    App   nil
    Thr   green
    Txy   blue edge
Aids: VOR/DME, TACAN, NDB, VDF, GCA (PAR and SRA), SRE, ILS 24

*Runway 06 landing threshold is displaced 215 m (706 ft) and take-off threshold is displaced 95 m (312 ft). Jet barriers are installed

Twr frequency: 118.5/122.1/123.5   App frequency: 120.95
Terminal: Passenger terminal at southwest corner of airport, with nine
    aircraft stands
Scheduled services 1978: Alitalia, ATI, British Airways and Lufthansa
Main base: Aerotrasporti Italiani (ATI)

Traffic:	1970	1975	1976	1977
Passengers (total)	674,118	887,388	873,096	1,010,899
Cargo (tonnes)	5,307*	6,109*	6,111*	3,857
Transport movements	21,203	15,797	14,678	15,154

* Includes mail

Capodichino was a 1914–18 war military base which remained in
operation and became a customs aerodrome, known as Aeroporto Ugo
Niutta. The irregular-shaped landing area measured 670 by 660 m (2,198 by
2,165 ft) and the eastern part was unsuitable for flying operations. For
night flying there were landing floodlights and a beacon.

Following the Allied landings in southern Italy the aerodrome was
used by British and United States forces. When civil flying was resumed
there was a single 06/24 runway of 1,798 m (5,900 ft), 1,036 m (3,400 ft)
being asphalt and the remainder pressed steel plating (PSP).

Although the runway has been lengthened to 2,195 m (7,202 ft) and
has a Macadam surface, the airport, which is a joint military and civil
facility, still suffers from flooding, and severe operating restrictions are also
imposed by the proximity of high ground. Vesuvius, 1,281 m (4,203 ft), is
only 6 nm (11 km) southeast of the airport and there is high ground about
10 nm (18.5 km) to the east.

Alitalia prohibits night landings on runway 06 and DC-8 landings are
prohibited in heavy rain or when the runway is flooded.

Alitalia's DC-9-32 *Isola di Caprera* and an ATI Fokker F.27 at Capodichino, the
Naples Airport. (*Alitalia*)

189

Palermo, Sicily (Sicilia)   Aeroporto Palermo/Punta Raisi

ICAO: LICJ   IATA: PMO
38° 10′ 47″ N   13° 06′ 13″ E   Elevation: 71 ft (21.5 m)
Longest runway: 07R/25L   3,000 m (9,842 ft)   ART   T-VASI 03/21
   and 07R/25L
Aids: VOR/DME, NDB, VDF, L, SRE, ILS 25

	1970	1975	1976	1977
Passengers	643,534	778,467	801,274	927,310
Transport movements	13,191	15,615	14,554	14,597

Scheduled services 1978: Alitalia, ATI and Itavia.

Pisa   Aeroporto Pisa/San Giusto (Galileo Galilei)

ICAO: LIRP   IATA: PSA
43° 40′ 50″ N   10° 23′ 34″ E   Elevation: 8 ft (2.44 m)
Longest runway: 04R/22L   2,587 m (8,488 ft)   ART
Aids: VOR/DME, VDF, L, GCA, ILS 04R

	1970	1975	1976	1977
Passengers	276,951	369,945	379,497	447,843
Transport movements	9,834	11,769	11,334	12,066

Scheduled services 1978: Air France, Alisarda, Alitalia, ATI, British
   Airways and Itavia
Runway 04R/22L is to be extended by 400 m (1,312 ft).

Rimini   Aeroporto Rimini/Miramare

ICAO: LIPR   IATA: RMI
44° 01′ 15″ N   12° 36′ 44″ E   Elevation: 39 ft (11.88 m)
Runway: 13/31   2,373 m (7,785 ft)   ART
Aids: VOR/DME, NDB, VDF, ARTS II, GCA

	1970	1975	1976	1977
Passengers	441,079	369,597	362,625	300,757
Transport movements	7,093	4,107	4,188	3,512

Scheduled services 1978: Alitalia only

Rome (Roma)   Aeroporto Roma/Ciampino

IACO: LIRA   IATA: CIA
41° 47′ 58″ N   12° 35′ 36″ E   Elevation: 423 ft (129 m)
Runways: 15L/33R and 15R/33L   2,200 m (7,218 ft)   ART
   non-std VASI
Aids: VOR/DME, NDB, VDF, SRE, GCA, ILS 15R

	1970	1975	1976	1977	1978
Passengers	450,409	822,516	753,711	898,537	911,629
Transport movements	12,307	15,830	14,658	16,040	13,966

Scheduled services 1978: Itavia only

Rome's Fiumicino Airport. A view across the terminal area to runway 16R/34L and the Mediterranean. (*Aeroporti di Roma*)

Rome (Roma)   Aeroporto Roma/Fiumicino (Leonardo da Vinci)

41° 48′ 40″ N   12° 15′ 09″ E   18.9 nm (35 km) WSW of city
ICAO: LIRF   IATA code: FCO   Time zone: GMT plus 1
Authority: Aeroporti di Roma
Area: 1,430 hectares (3,534 acres)
Elevation: 14 ft (4.26 m)   Ref temp: 25.4 deg C
Runways: 07/25   3,295 × 60 m (10,810 × 197 ft)* bitumen, concrete
                                                    ends
          16L/34R   3,900 × 60 m (12,795 × 197 ft)* bitumen,concrete
                                                    ends
          16R/34L   3,900 × 60 m (12,795 × 197 ft) bitumen

*Threshold 07 is displaced 405 m (1,329 ft), threshold 16L 700 m (2,297 ft) and threshold 34R 300 m (984 ft)

Pavement strength: 16L/34R LCN 100,   07/25 and 16R/34L 45,000 kg
   (99,210 lb) ISWL
Landing category: ICAO CAT II
Lighting:
   R/W   LIH white edge. LIH centreline 16L/34R. TDZ 16L/34R
            and nonstandard TDZ 16R. Red edge lights to displaced
            thresholds 25 and 34R, and red centreline 34R

191

App   R/W 07   LIH reduced Calvert displaced 450 m (1,476 ft) from thr
R/W 25   LIH CAT II Calvert centreline with three crossbars, supplementary inner lights and integrated sequenced flashers
R/W 16L/34R   LIH CAT II Calvert centreline with three crossbars, supplementary inner lights and integrated sequenced flashers
R/W 16R   LIH CAT I Calvert centreline with five crossbars and integrated sequenced flashers
R/W 34L   LIH reduced Calvert (450 m/1,476 ft). VASIS

Thr   LIH green
Txy   blue centreline

Aids: VOR/DME, NDB, SSR, ASR, SRE, L, VDF, PAR, ASMI, RVR 16R/34L and 25, ILS CAT II 16L/34R, ILS CAT I 16R

Twr frequency: 118.7   App frequency: 119.2

Terminals: International and domestic passenger terminals, with 59 aircraft stands, including seven for wide-bodied aircraft, and three aerobridges. Separate airport authority and Alitalia cargo terminals

Scheduled services 1978: 70 airlines

Traffic:	1970	1975	1976	1977	1978
Passengers (total)	7,030,817	9,235,740	9,431,588	10,472,687	11,027,346
Cargo (tonnes)	149,215*	130,422	138,337	153,574	158,457
Aircraft movements	144,734	142,847	144,586	144,346	144,375
Transport movements	—	140,820	142,145	142,095	143,006

*Includes mail

During 1977 DC-9s accounted for 56.9 per cent of aircraft movements, Boeing 727s for 10.1 per cent, Boeing 707s for 9 per cent, Boeing 747s for 5.3 per cent, DC-8s for 4.4 per cent and DC-10s for 3.7 per cent.

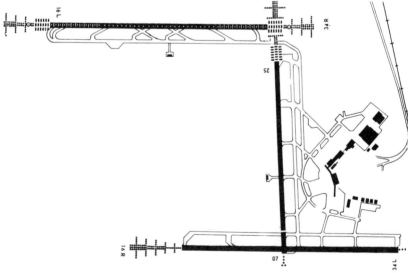

Rome/Fiumicino (Leonardo da Vinci) Airport. (*Alitalia*)

In the period between the world wars Rome was served by both landplanes and marine aircraft. Flying-boats and seaplanes operated from the mouth of the Tiber, near Ostia, the base on the south shore being known as Aeroporto del Prete. From January 1937 Imperial Airways Short C class flying-boats operated from Lago di Bracciano (Lake Bracciano) about 26 km (16 miles) northwest of Rome, where a new marine terminal was opened on 9 July, 1938. Landplane services operated from the Littorio airport, also known as Urbe, situated within a loop of the Tiber just north of the city.

During the 1914–18 war an airship station had been established at Ciampino to the south of Rome and subsequently an aerodrome was established on the site. It was known as Ciampino Nord and as Aeroporto Giovanni Battista Pastine. Ciampino, with a single PSP runway, became the post Second War Rome airport and quickly became established as one of Europe's most important junction airports. But the space available for expansion at Ciampino was strictly limited and it was realized that a new major airport would be required.

The Roman Emperors Claudius and Trajan built a port for Rome at the mouth of the Tiber. The six-sided inner harbour was Porto Traiano* and the outer harbour Porto Claudio. Over the centuries storms and silt from the Tiber obliterated these ports and claimed land from the sea thus producing a spacious flat area which was to provide an ideal site for Rome's new airport.

Work began on the site in 1951 and the new Fiumicino International Airport (later to be named Leonardo da Vinci) was opened on 16 January, 1961, by which time there was a large terminal building and two runways, the instrument runway 16/34 of 3,900 m (12,795 ft) and 07/25 of 2,653 m (8,704 ft). It was planned that there should later be two sets of parallel runways, but the third runway, 16L/34R of 3,900 m (12,795 ft) was not opened until 13 August, 1974. This runway was closed twice because of aircrew objections and finally opened with full aids on 10 November, 1975. Runway 07/25 was extended to 3,295 m (10,810 ft) in 1973.

Fiumicino was expected to handle 2,200,000 passengers a year by 1970, but this number was exceeded during the first year of operation. Terminal congestion has long been a problem and as long ago as 1967 the suggestion was made that a completely new terminal area should be constructed to the north of the east–west runway. Considerable development has taken place at the original terminal and two-level handling of international traffic was introduced on 29 July, 1973. A separate domestic terminal was built to the southeast of the international terminal and this has since been doubled in size.

The international terminal is to be further extended, with a Y-shaped traffic pier extending onto the apron and having 17 gates, but the major development is envisaged as a completely new terminal complex between the pair of north–south runways. A second east–west runway is also planned. At the end of 1979 Fiumicino's development plans were still awaiting government approval.

_____

* Reconstructed as the ornamental Lago Traiano

The Alitalia DC-9-32 *Isola di Tavolaria* at Turin/Caselle Airport. (*Alitalia*)

Turin (Torino)   Aeroporto Torino/Caselle

ICAO: LIMF   IATA: TRN
45° 12′ 04″ N   07° 39′ 00″ E   Elevation: 989 ft (301.4 m)
Runway: 18/36   3,000 m (9,842 ft)   ART   VASI 36
Aids: VOR/DME, NDB, VDF, L, PAR, ILS CAT II 36

	1970	1975	1976	1977
Passengers	418,811	495,134	507,998	545,215
Transport movements	12,725	11,552	11,240	10,622

Scheduled services 1978: Air France, Alitalia, ATI, British Airways, Itavia
and Lufthansa

Venice (Venezia)   Aeroporto Venezia/Tesséra (Marco Polo)

ICAO: LIPZ   IATA: VCE
45° 30′ 00″ N   12° 21′ 00″ E   Elevation: 7 ft (2 m)
Runway: 04/22   3,300 m (10,827 ft)   ART
Aids: VOR/DME, NDB, VDF, L, SRA, PAR, ILS CAT II 04*

	1970	1975	1976	1977
Passengers	639,685	557,643	634,998	785,796
Transport movements	14,475	9,748	11,013	11,969

Scheduled services 1978: Air France, Alitalia, ATI and British Airways

* To be upgraded to CAT III

Ivory Coast (République de Côte d'Ivoire)

Abidjan   Aéroport d'Abidjan - Port-Bouet

ICAO: DIII   IATA: ABJ
05° 15′ 06″ N   03° 55′ 49″ W   Elevation: 20 ft (6 m)
Runway: 03/21   2,700 m (8,858 ft)   ART
Aids: VOR, NDB, L, ILS CAT I 21

	1970	1975	1976	1977
Passengers	228,537	488,671	546,727	655,873
Transport movements	7,037	11,814	12,990	14,105

Scheduled services 1978: 19 airlines
Main base: Air Ivoire

A new parallel 4,000 m (13,123 ft) CAT II runway is to be built and a master plan envisages a second, parallel, runway and four circular terminal buildings.

Jamaica

Kingston Norman Manley International Airport

	ICAO: MKJP	IATA: KIN	
17° 55′ 59″ N	76° 47′ 20″ W		Elevation: 10 ft (3 m)
Runway: 11/29	2,480 m (8,135 ft)	ART	VASI 11/29
Aids: VOR/DME, NDB			

	1970	1975	1976	1977
Passengers	527,132	712,913	704,770	627,875
Transport movements	20,209	15,507	13,952	11,062

Scheduled services 1978: 10 airlines
Main base: Air Jamaica

The runway is being extended to 2,678 m (8,785 ft)

Formerly Palisadoes International Airport, it was renamed in 1972.

The terminal and control tower at Norman Manley International Airport, Kingston.

Montego Bay   Sangster International Airport

ICAO: MKJS   IATA: MBJ
18° 30′ 01″ N   77° 54′ 57″ W   Elevation: 4 ft (1 m)
Runway: 07/25   2,591 m (8,500 ft)   ART   VASI 07/25
Aids: NDB

	1970	1975	1976	1977
Passengers	641,595	757,970	622,708	695,507
Transport movements	26,685	27,098	26,714	19,689

Scheduled services 1978: Air Canada, Air Jamaica, American Airlines, Eastern Air Lines and Trans-Jamaican Airlines
Main base: Trans-Jamaican Airlines

Japan

Amami, Amami-Oshima, Ryuku Islands   Amami Airport

ICAO: RJKA   IATA: ASJ
28° 24′ 55″ N   129° 41′ 55″ E   Elevation: 59 ft (17.9 m)
Runway: 02/20   1,240 m (4,070 ft)   Thr identification and VASI
Aids: NDB

	1970	1975	1976	1977
Passengers*	175,000	369,000	416,000	424,000
Transport movements	4,826	10,183	10,049	10,586

Scheduled services 1978: All Nippon Airways and TOA Domestic Airlines

*Rounded figures

Chitose, Hokkaido   Chitose Airport

42° 47′ 43″ N   141° 40′ 11″ E   1.7 nm (3.14 km) SSE of Chitose
21 nm (38.89 km) SE of Sapporo
ICAO: RJCC   IATA code: CTS   Time zone: GMT plus 9
Authority: Japan Self Defense Agency and Civil Aviation Bureau, Ministry of Transport
Elevation: 82 ft (25 m)   Ref temp: 25.5 deg C
Runways: 18L/36R   3,000 × 60 m (9,842 × 197 ft) concrete
18R/36L   2,700 × 45 m (8,860 × 148 ft) asphalt concrete
Pavement strength: 18L/36R   41,000 kg (90,300 lb) 1, 69,500 kg (153,000 lb) 2, 123,000 kg (271,000 lb) 3; 18R/36L   20,000 kg (44,000 lb) 1, 25,000 kg (55,000 lb) 2.
Landing category: ICAO CAT I
Lighting:
R/W   LIH white edge, last 600 m (1,968 ft) yellow. Take off aiming light 154 m (505 ft) off extended centreline 36L

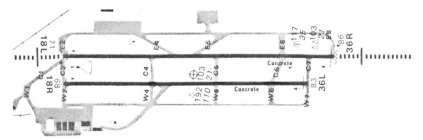

Chitose Airport. (*British Airways Aerad*)

App   R/W 18L/36R   LIH white bar centreline and crossbar.
        VASIS 36R
Thr   LIH green
Txy   East taxiway green centreline, other taxiways blue edge
Aids: VOR/DME, TACAN, NDB, ASR, SRE/PAR, ASDE, VDF, ILS
    CAT I 36R
Twr frequency: 121.5/126.2   App frequency: 120.1/121.5/124.7/125.3
Terminal: Civil terminal and apron to east of northern section 18L/36R
    with 10 aircraft stands. Second civil apron with two stands. Military
    apron at northwest corner of airport.
Scheduled services 1978: All Nippon, Japan Air Lines and TOA Domestic

Traffic:	1970	1975	1976	1977
Passengers (total)*	2,290,000	4,774,000	5,558,000	6,253,000
Cargo (tonnes)	18,336	34,057	38,618	47,178
Aircraft movements†	23,972	36,988	40,848	73,858
Transport movements	22,842	36,244	40,124	43,145

* Rounded figures
† Excludes movements by Japan Self Defense Force and US Army

View of Chitose Airport looking southeast. (*All Nippon Airways*)

197

Chitose Airport, which serves Sapporo, is shared with the Japan Self Defense Force and came into operation on 25 October, 1951. It is situated within a generally level wooded area, and was an alternate airport for Tokyo from the time that the Europe–Japan Polar route opened. Runway 18R/36L was completed to its present length on 20 December, 1961, and 18L/36R on 2 November, 1973.

There are parallel taxiways for both runways with high-speed exits leading to the civil area.

In 1977 TOA Domestic Airlines commissioned two 90-passenger mobile lounges at Chitose.

Chitose has been designated as an airport to be developed to handle international services to help relieve the Tokyo airports.

Fukuoka, Kyushu   Fukuoka International Airport

33° 34′ 52″ N   130° 27′ 14″ E   1.6 nm (2.96 km) E of Hakata Stn
ICAO: RJFF   IATA code: FUK   Time zone: GMT plus 9
Authority: Civil Aviation Bureau, Ministry of Transport
Elevation: 30 ft (9.1 m)   Ref temp: 33.4 deg C
Runway: 16/34   2,819 × 60 m (9,250 × 197 ft) asphalt concrete
Pavement strength: 28,200 kg (62,040 lb) ISWL
Landing category: ICAO CAT I
Lighting:
R/W   LIH white edge and LIH white centreline, last 300 m (984 ft) red and previous 600 m (1,968 ft) red/white. TDZ 16
App   R/W 16   LIH white bar centreline with crossbar and sequenced flashers
          R/W 34   LIH white bar centreline with crossbar
          VASIS 16/34
Thr   LIH green wing bars. Strobes on 34
Txy   blue edge, centreline lights on high-speed exits and some taxiways
Aids: VORTAC, TACAN, NDB, ASR, SSR, SRE, GCA, RVR, ILS CAT I 16
Twr frequency: 118.4/126.2   App frequency: 119.1/119.7/120.7/127.9
Terminals: Civil terminal at northeast of airport with 25 aircraft stands, 11 on remote east apron. Separate cargo building
Scheduled services 1978: All Nippon, Cathay Pacific, China Airlines, Japan Air Lines, Korean Air Lines and TOA Domestic.

Traffic:	1970	1975	1976	1977
Passengers (total)*	3,016,000	4,609,000	5,012,000	6,637,000
Cargo (tonnes)	15,621	38,714	42,681	49,441
Aircraft movements	45,728†	54,286	55,928	62,206
Transport movements	39,437	44,624	45,381	51,157

* Rounded figures
† Excludes JSDF and US Army movements

Fukuoka International Airport, view looking northwest. (*All Nippon Airways*)

Fukuoka International Airport was originally a USAAF base but was handed over to Japan on 1 April, 1972. The airport is south of Hakata Bay and close to built-up areas.

The terminal building, a mix of three- and four-storeys, was constructed in two stages, work began in November 1967, the northern half was opened in 1968 and the remainder in 1969.

Hachijo-Jima, Ko Shima   Hachijo-Jima Airport

	ICAO: RJTH	IATA: HAC
33° 06′ 43″ N	139° 47′ 26″ E	Elevation: 299 ft (91 m)
Runway: 08/26	1,500 m (4,921 ft)	RT and App guidance lights.
VASI 08/26		
Aids: NDB		

	1970	1975	1976
Passengers	217,880	204,567	220,653

Scheduled services 1978: All Nippon Airways YS-11As

Hakodate, Hokkaido   Hakodate Airport

	ICAO: RJCH	IATA: HKD
41° 46′ 08″ N	140° 49′ 11″ E	Elevation: 102 ft (31 m)
Runway: 12/30	2,000 m (6,562 ft)	ART VASI 12/30
Aids: VOR/DME, NDB, ILS 12		

	1970	1975	1976
Passengers	226,135	501,286	582,678

Scheduled services 1978: All Nippon Airways, Nihon Kinkyori Airways
   and TOA Domestic Airlines

Hakodate Airport terminal in 1977, with TOA Domestic DC-9 on the apron.

Ishigaki, Ishigaki Island, Ryuku Islands   Ishigaki Airport

	ICAO: ROIG	IATA: ISG
24° 20′ 21″ N	124° 11′ 12″ E	Elevation: 86 ft (26.2 m)
Runway: 04/22	1,500 m (4,921 ft)	RT VASI
Aids: NDB		

	1970	1975	1976	1977
Passengers*	135,000	330,000	375,000	453,000
Transport movements	2,684	7,613	9,430	11,105

Scheduled services 1978: Southwest Airlines

* Rounded figures

Kagoshima Airport with threshold 34 in the foreground and the terminal area beyond. (*All Nippon Airways*)

Kagoshima, Kyushu   Kagoshima Airport

31° 48′ 07″ N   130° 43′ 13″ E
      15.7 nm (29 km) NE of Nishi-Kagoshima railway station
ICAO: RJFK   IATA code: KOJ   Time zone: GMT plus 9
Authority: Civil Aviation Bureau, Ministry of Transport
Area: 143.64 hectares (355 acres)
Elevation: 891 ft (271.6 m)   Ref temp: 29.7 deg C
Runway: 16/34   2,500 × 45 m (8,202 × 148 ft) asphalt concrete
Pavement strength: 24,000 kg (52,800 lb) ISWL
Landing category: ICAO CAT I
Lighting:
    R/W   LIH white and yellow edge and LIH white centreline. LIH white TDZ 34. Red overrun lights each end*
    App   R/W 16   approach light beacons, amber sodium approach guidance lights and 420 m (1,378 ft) ALPA-type approach lights
            R/W 34   900 m (2,953 ft) centreline with sequenced flashers. VASIS 16/34
    Thr   LIH green
    Txy   blue edge and centreline
Aids: VOR/DME, NDB, RVR, ILS CAT I 34
Twr frequency: 118.2   App frequency: 120.5
Terminals: Passenger terminal with 20,152 sq m (216,916 sq ft) area, five gates, four aerobridges and 15 aircraft stands. Separate cargo terminal
Scheduled services 1978: Air Nauru, Air Niugini, All Nippon Airways, Japan Air Lines and TOA Domestic Airlines
Airline bases: All Nippon Airways and TOA Domestic Airlines

Traffic:	1970	1975	1976
Passengers (total)	1,178,753	2,446,770	2,734,911
Cargo (tonnes)	1,617	6,308	6,833
Aircraft movements	37,862	36,386	37,798
Transport movements	20,440	28,698	29,498

* Runway distance marker lights available

The present Kagoshima Airport was opened on 1 April, 1972, and replaced the old Kagoshima City Airport. The airport is situated in hilly country, and there are amber sodium approach guidance lights, obstruction lights and hazard beacons to ensure safe approaches to runway 16. The active volcano Sakurajima is close to the airport at 31° 35′ N, 130° 40′ E.

The runway, which is to be extended to 3,000 m (9,842 ft) in 1980, slopes from north to south with the 16 threshold at 275.5 m (903.9 ft) and the 34 threshold at 264.9 m (869.1 ft). The highest point, near the 16 threshold, is 276.3 m (906.5 ft).

Kochi, Shikoku   Kochi Airport

	ICAO: RJOK	IATA: KCZ	
33° 32′ 28″ N	133° 40′ 37″ E		Elevation: 20 ft (6 m)
Runway: 14/32	1,500 m (4,921 ft)	RT	VASI 14/32
Aids: VOR, NDB			

	1970	1975	1976	1977
Passengers*	560,000	710,000	854,000	969,000
Transport movements	10,797	13,389	12,970	17,359

* Rounded figures

Scheduled services 1978: All Nippon and TOA Domestic
The airport was opened on 1 April, 1960

Kumamoto, Kyushu   Kumamoto Airport

32° 49′ 55″ N   130° 51′ 09″ E   8 nm (14.8 km) NE of city
ICAO: RJFT   IATA code: KMJ   Time zone: GMT plus 9
Authority: Civil Aviation Bureau, Ministry of Transport
Elevation: 633 ft (193 m)   Ref temp: 32.3 deg C
Runway: 07/25   2,500 × 45 m (8,202 × 148 ft) asphalt-concrete
Pavement strength: 24,000 kg (52,800 lb) ISWL
Landing category: ICAO CAT I
Lighting:
    R/W   white edge and centreline, distance marker lights, overrun and take off aiming lights. TDZ 07
    App   R/W 07   900 m (2,953 ft) bar centreline with crossbar
            R/W 25   420 m (1,378 ft) centreline with crossbar and approach guidance beacons 600 m (1,968 ft) and 900 m (2,953 ft) from threshold
            VASIS 07/25
    Thr   green and threshold identification lights
    Txy   blue edge, with centreline on exit taxiways
Aids: VOR/DME, NDB, ASR, TAR, SSR, RVR, ILS CAT I 07
Twr frequency: 118.7/126.2   App frequency: 119.0/126.5
Terminal: South of runway with five aircraft stands and helicopter pad
    JSDF apron to west of terminal

Kumamoto Airport viewed from the approach to runway 07. (*All Nippon Airways*)

Scheduled services 1978: All Nippon Airways only

Traffic:	1970*	1975	1976	1977
Passengers (total)†	221,000	810,000	977,000	1,215,000
Cargo (tonnes)	729	2,760	4,188	4,607
Aircraft movements	41,484	25,362	27,488	24,632
Transport movements	6,269	7,656	8,508	8,509

* Figures for old airport Kumamoto City
† Rounded figures

Kumamoto, situated a short distance from the eastern shore of Kaiwan (Kai Bay) and to the west of Kyushu's mountain spine, was from 1 April, 1960, served by the airport at Kumamoto City, which had a 1,200 m (3,937 ft) runway.

The present airport at Kikuyoh town was opened on 15 August, 1971. It is in an attractive parklike setting of agricultural land and woods, with an impressive mountain background to the east.

The 2,500 m (8,202 ft) runway, served by a parallel taxiway with six taxiway–runway links, is to be extended to 3,000 m (9,842 ft) with completion scheduled for April 1980.

The airport achieved international status with the opening of Japan Air Lines' Kumamoto - Seoul service on 26 September, 1979.

Kushiro, Hokkaido   Kushiro Airport

	ICAO: RJCK	IATA: KUH	
43° 02′ 14″ N	144° 11′ 51″ E		Elevation: 307 ft (93.64 m)
Runway: 17/35	1,800 m (5,906 ft)	ART	

Aids: VOR/DME, NDB, ILS 17

	1970	1975	1976
Passengers	81,168	391,614	489,246
Transport movements	2,255	4,510	4,966

Scheduled services 1978: All Nippon Airways and TOA Domestic Airlines

Matsuyama Airport, looking approximately north and showing the proximity of densely built-up areas. (*All Nippon Airways*)

Matsuyama, Shikoku   Matsuyama Airport

33° 49′ 20″ N   132° 42′ 15″ E   2.7 nm (5 km) W of city
ICAO: RJOM   IATA code: MYJ   Time zone: GMT plus 9
Authority: Civil Aviation Bureau, Ministry of Transport
Area: 1,028.435 hectares (2,541.25 acres)
Elevation: 13 ft (3.88 m)   Ref temp: 15.4 deg C
Runway: 14/32   2,000 × 45 m (6,562 × 148 ft) asphalt
Pavement strength: 23,950 kg (52,800 lb) ISWL
Landing category: ICAO CAT I
Lighting:
    R/W   edge, centreline and distance markers
    App   R/W 32   approach lights with approach light beacons
           936 m (3,070 ft) and 593 m (1,945 ft) from threshold.
           VASIS 14/32
    Thr   threshold and threshold identification lights
    Txy   edge, centreline and guidance lights
Aids: VOR/DME, NDB, ILS CAT I 14
Twr frequency: 118.5/126.2   App frequency: 128.7/134.1
Terminals: Passenger and cargo terminals to northeast of runway. Seven
    aircraft stands
Scheduled services 1978: All Nippon Airways and TOA Domestic Airlines

Traffic:	1971	1975	1976	1977
Passengers (total)	530,358	941,616	1,061,201	1,198,000*
Cargo (tonnes)	1,306	3,137	3,586	3,249
Aircraft movements	7,410	7,270	7,068	14,776
Transport movements	4,686	5,041	5,055	9,713

* Rounded figure

The airport is situated on the northwest coast of Shikoku, and the northwest end of the runway and parallel taxiway has been built on land reclaimed from the sea. The airport was opened on 10 October, 1960, with the runway measuring 1,200 m (3,937 ft), and the runway lengthened to 2,000 m (6,562 ft) came into operation on 16 April, 1972. Noise restrictions are in operation and whenever possible take offs are made from runway 32 and landings on 14, ensuring that approaches and departures are made over water.

Miyako, Sakishima, Ryuku Islands   Miyako Airport

	ICAO: ROMY		IATA: MMY	
24° 46′ 52″ N	125° 17′ 53″ E		Elevation: 146 ft (44.45 m)	
Runway: 04/22	1,500 m (4,921 ft)		RT	
Aids: VORTAC, NDB				

	1970	1975	1976	1977*
Passengers	164,455	313,693	352,217	161,966
Transport movements	1,634	2,961	3,902	1,774

* January–May
Scheduled services 1978: Southwest Airlines only

Miyazaki, Kyushu   Miyazaki Airport

31° 52′ 28″ N	131° 26′ 44″ E	2 nm (3.7 km) SE of city
ICAO: RJFM	IATA code: KMI	Time zone: GMT plus 9
Authority: Civil Aviation Bureau, Ministry of Transport		
Elevation: 20 ft (6 m)		Ref temp: 31 deg C
Runways: 09/27	1,800 × 45 m (5,800 × 148 ft) asphalt/concrete*	
13/31	1,340 × 30 m (4,396 × 98 ft) concrete	

* 60 m (197 ft) overrun each end.

Pavement strength: 09/27 24,000 kg (53,000 lb) ISWL;   13/31 3,000 kg (6,000 lb) ISWL

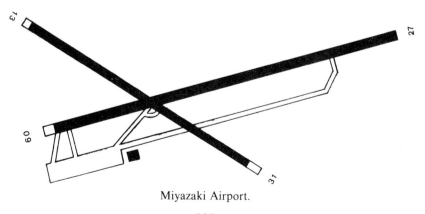

Miyazaki Airport.

205

Lighting:
R/W   09/27   edge and centreline, distance marker lights, overrun and take off aiming lights
App   VASIS 09/27
Thr   R/W 09/27   green and threshold identification lights
Txy   blue edge
Aids: VOR/DME, NDB, ASR, PAR
Twr frequency: 118.3/126.2   App frequency: 120.1/126.2
Terminal: At southwest corner of airport with 420 by 80 m (1,378 by 262 ft) apron and seven aircraft stands.
Scheduled services 1978: All Nippon Airways and TOA Domestic Airlines

Traffic:	1970	1975	1976	1977
Passengers (total)*	834,000	1,328,000	1,525,000	1,774,000
Cargo (tonnes)	1,034	2,107	2,569	2,853
Aircraft movements	95,908	37,714	34,538	35,476
Transport movements	10,988	18,514	19,567	21,526

* Rounded figures

    Miyazaki is on the east coast of Kyushu and its airport is situated on the narrow strip between the main road to the south and the Pacific. Opened on 1 April, 1957, the airport is served by Boeing 737s and Douglas DC-9s, but as far back as 1973 it was planned to extend runway 09/27 into the sea to give it a length of 2,500 m (8,202 ft) and make it suitable for Lockheed TriStars. Such runway extension is a largescale undertaking and it was finally decided on limited extension to 1,900 m (6,234 ft)—this work being scheduled for completion in April 1979.

Nagasaki, Kyushu   Nagasaki Airport

32° 54′ 43″ N   129° 55′ 03″ E   10.4 nm (19.26 km) NE of city
ICAO: RJFU   IATA: code: NGS   Time zone: GMT plus 9
Authority: Civil Aviation Bureau, Ministry of Transport
Elevation: 8 ft (2.31) m)   Ref temp: 29.6 deg C
Runways: 14/32   2,500 × 60 m (8,202 × 197 ft) asphalt concrete. Area B
        18/36   1,200 × 30 m (3,940 × 98 ft) asphalt concrete. Area A
Pavement strength: 14/32 24,000 kg (52,800 lb) ISWL;   18/36 8,500 kg (18,740 lb) ISWL
Landing category: ICAO CAT I
Lighting:
R/W   14/32   LIH white edge and centreline, distance marker lights and overrun lights
        18/36   white edge and take off aiming point
App   R/W 14/32   bar centreline (420 m/1,378 ft 14, 900 m /2,953 ft 32) and crossbar. VASIS 14/32 and 18/36
Thr   green all runways and threshold identification lights 18/36
Txy   blue edge
Aids: VOR/DME, NDB, TAR, SSR, ASR, ILS CAT I 32
Twr frequency: 118.5/122.7/126.2   App frequency: 120.2/121.0

Terminals: Separate terminals at Area A (mainland site) and Area B (island
    site), the latter with 275 by 100 m (902 by 328 ft) apron, six aircraft
    stands and two aerobridges
Scheduled services 1978: All Nippon and TOA Domestic

Traffic:	1970	1975	1976	1977
Passengers (total)*	260,000	612,000	898,000	1,317,000
Cargo (tonnes)	731	2,271	3,403	4,281
Aircraft movements	16.556	19,886	19,672	24,052
Transport movements	6,834	8,147	9,455	11,328

* Rounded figures

The Nagasaki area is mountainous and offers little scope for the siting
of airports and this has led to a very interesting airport layout. The airport,
originally a Navy aerodrome, was constructed on a narrow strip of land
between the built-up area of Omura and the east shore of Omura Wan
(Omura Bay or Gulf), an almost entirely land-locked lake about 20 miles
(32 km) long and averaging about 8 miles (13 km) in width. It was opened to
civil traffic on 1 April, 1960.

On this narrow strip of land is the 1,200 m (3,940 ft) 18/36 runway with
a parallel taxiway on each side. This part is known as Area A.

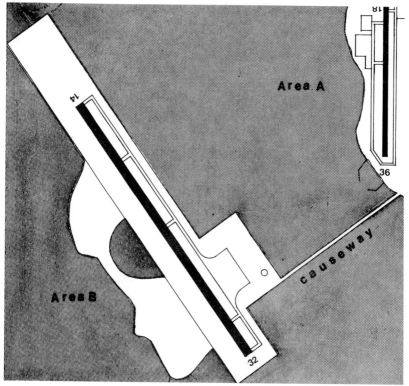

Nagasaki Airport. (*Clem Watson*)

Nagasaki Airport with the 14/32 runway and terminal (Area B) on reclaimed land.
On the mainland immediately to the left of the causeway is the original airport
(Area A) with its 18/36 runway. (*Courtesy Airports International*)

In order to cater for jet aircraft a new runway was required and a most
ingenious solution was found to overcome the shortage of land. Just
offshore to the southwest are what might be regarded as two islands joined
by a very narrow neck of land. A new 14/32 runway of 2,500 m (8,202 ft)
was constructed across these 'islands' and on land reclaimed from the lake
with fill from the 'islands'. Sufficient land was reclaimed to extend the
runway northwest for at least another 500 m (1,640 ft) if required. A
parallel taxiway runs the whole length of the runway and has three
intermediate exits, there is a new terminal building and a control tower.
Facing the terminal, on the other side of the runway, the name Nagasaki
appears in large capital letters on a piece of inclined ground.

The new 'airport' was opened on 1 May, 1975, and is connected to the
shore by a causeway approximately a kilometre in length, this meets the
shore about 400 m (1,312 ft) south of the 36 threshold of the old airport.
This island site is known as Nagasaki Airport Area B.

Nagasaki Airport is to be further developed to handle international
traffic to help relieve the Tokyo airports.

Terminal area at Nagasaki Airport with causeway to the mainland on the left.

208

Nagoya, Honshu   Nagoya International Airport

35° 15′ 06″ N   136° 55′ 39″ E   5.4 nm (10 km) NNE of city
ICAO: RJNN   IATA code: NGO   Time zone: GMT plus 9
Authority: Civil Aviation Bureau, Ministry of Transport
Elevation: 46 ft (14 m)   Ref temp: 31.4 deg C
Runway: 16/34   2,740 × 45 m (8,989 × 148 ft) asphalt concrete*

* 60 m (197 ft) concrete overrun each end.

Pavement strength: 35,000 kg (77,000 lb) ISWL
Landing category: ICAO CAT I
Lighting:
    R/W   LIH white edge, last 600 m (1,968 ft) yellow. Distance
            marker lights and red end lights
    App   R/W 16   LIH white 480 m (1,575 ft) centreline with
            crossbar
            R/W 34   LIH white 450 m (1,476 ft) centreline with
            crossbar and sequenced flashers. Approach guidance
            beacons 550 and 1,230 m (1,804 and 4,035 ft) from 34
            threshold on extended centreline
            VASIS 16/34
    Thr   LIH green
    Txy   blue edge, green centreline on some sections
Aids: VOR/TACAN, DME, NDB, PAR, ASR/SSR, SRE, RVR, ILS
    CAT I 34
Twr ·frequency: 118.7/121.5/122.7/126.2   App frequency: 120.3/121.5
Terminal: Two-level terminal to west of runway, with 13 nose-in aircraft
    stands and light aircraft apron. JSDF apron on east side.
Scheduled services 1978: All Nippon, Japan Air Lines, Korean Air Lines
    and TOA Domestic

Traffic:	1970	1975	1976	1977
Passengers (total)*	308,000	1,244,000	1,329,000	1,962,000
Cargo (tonnes)	2,248	5,023	6,546	7,147
Aircraft movements	68,590	59,826	60,786	67,950
Transport movements	6,815	15,888	15,797	20,432

* Rounded figures.

    Nagoya International Airport came into operation on 1 May, 1965,
and like many other Japanese airports is shared with the Japan Self Defense
Force. To the west of the runway is a parallel taxiway serving the civil
apron and terminal and on the east is a second parallel taxiway which
serves the JSDF base. There is also a police helicopter unit on the east side.
    There is extensive military jet flying in the area as well as flying by
military rescue helicopters.
    At the northern end of the airport the runway and east taxiway are
carried over the Oyama River and the 16 threshold has been temporarily
displaced by 379 m (1,243 ft) in this area, only aircraft of 50,000 kg (110,000 lb)
or less being allowed to use the extreme north end of the runway because of
bearing strength limitations.

The terminal area at Nagoya International Airport. An All Nippon Airways Boeing 737 is on the apron and the Miles Marathon can be seen on the near end of the terminal roof. (*All Nippon Airways*)

There is arresting gear 236 m (774 ft) inside the normal 16 threshold and at the 34 threshold and there are overrun barriers 9 m (29 ft 6 in) outside the normal 16 threshold and 37 m (121 ft) outward of the arresting gear at the 34 threshold.

As at a number of Japanese airports there are aircraft on public display on the terminal roof—at Nagoya they are a Miles Marathon and a North American F-86 Sabre.

Naha, Okinawa   Naha Airport

26° 11′ 37″ N   127° 38′ 52″ E   2.16 nm (4 km) W of Naha City
ICAO: ROAH   IATA code: OKA   Time zone: GMT plus 9
Authority: Civil Aviation Bureau, Ministry of Transport
Area: 279 hectares (689 acres)
Elevation: 13 ft (4 m)   Ref temp: 29.4 deg C
Runway: 18/36   2,700 × 45 m (8,858 × 148 ft) asphalt concrete
        Arresting gear 625 m (2,050 ft) from 36 threshold and 345 m
        (1,132 ft) from 18 threshold. Jet barriers on both overruns
Pavement strength: 35,000 kg (77,000 lb) ISWL
Landing category: ICAO CAT I
Lighting:
    R/W   edge and centreline. TDZ 36
    App   R/W 18   LIH 450 m (1,476 ft) centreline with crossbar
           R/W 36   LIH 900 m (2,953 ft) centreline with sequenced
           flashers and crossbar. VASIS 18/36
    Thr   lights on both thresholds
    Txy   edge lights, centreline lights on runway exits

210

Aids: VOR/TACAN, NDB, ASR, SSR, PAR/GCA, RVR, ILS CAT I 36
Twr frequency: 126.2   App frequency: 119.1
Terminals: Two-storey domestic terminal (between Okinawa and mainland) with 14,780 sq m (159,092 sq ft) area, three aerobridges and five stands capable of handling Boeing 747s; 1,163 sq m (12,518 sq ft) inter-island terminal; and 6,283 sq m (67,630 sq ft) two-storey international terminal with stands for three Boeing 747s and five YS-11s. Total apron area 297,832 sq m (3,205,586 sq ft). Separate 3,100 sq m (33,368 sq ft) cargo terminal
Scheduled services 1978: Air Nauru, All Nippon, Flying Tiger, Japan Air Lines, Northwest Orient, Pan American and Southwest Airlines
Airline bases: All Nippon and Japan Air Lines. Also Japanese Air Force, Army and Navy
Main base: Southwest Airlines

Traffic:	1973	1975*	1976	1977
Passengers (total)	2,125,166	3,916,484	2,744,383	3,426,004
Cargo (tonnes)	20,752	30,016	29,884	33,050
Aircraft movements	58,134	64,012	55,960	59,044
Transport movements	24,280	37,446	33,686	35,136

* Expo 75 held in Okinawa increased 1975 traffic

Situated near the southern end of Okinawa, Naha Airport was constructed in 1933 as a Japanese Navy base, with an area of 10 hectares (24.7 acres). In 1936 the aerodrome was enlarged to serve as a civil airport for flights linking the Japanese mainland and Formosa (Taiwan).

In 1942 the airport was taken over to serve again as a Japanese naval air base. After the capture of Okinawa in June 1945 the aerodrome came under the control of the US Air Force and was not returned to the Japanese Government until 14 May, 1972. Construction then began of a domestic

Naha Airport, showing the new terminal area on reclaimed land in the foreground.
(*Naha Airport*)

passenger terminal building and in the first full year of commercial operation the airport handled more than 2 mn passengers and more than 50,000 aircraft movements.

Both approaches are over the sea and airport extensions have been made on reclaimed land at the northern end of the airport. There are taxiways on each side of the runway and the military area occupies the southern half of the area to the east.

Niigata, Honshu   Niigata Airport

ICAO: RJSN   IATA: KIJ
37° 57′ 08″ N   139° 07′ 09″ E   Elevation: 3 ft (1 m)
Longest runway: 10/28 1,900 m (6,230 ft)   ART   VASI 10/28 and 22
Aids: VORTAC, NDB, L, ILS CAT I 28

	1970	1975	1976
Passengers	72,209	246,986	314,748
Transport movements	2,975	3,140	1,976

Scheduled services 1978: Aeroflot, All Nippon Airways, Japan Air Lines, Nihon Kinkyori Airways and TOA Domestic Airlines

新潟空港

Looking along runway 10/28 towards the east at Niigata Airport. The terminal is on the right with runway 04/22 beyond. (*All Nippon Airways*)

Oita, Kyushu   Oita Airport   ICAO: RJFO   IATA: OIT

33° 28′ 34″ N   131° 44′ 23″ E   Elevation: 16 ft (4.9 m)
Runway: 01/19   2,000 m (6,562 ft)   ART   VASI 01/19
Aids: VOR/DME, NDB, SSR, RVR, ILS CAT I 01

212

Oita Airport, view looking north. The terminal is to the west of the runway.
(*Oita Airport*)

	1970	1975	1976
Passengers	461,704	735,846	788,974
Transport movements	19,678	13,150	13,053

Scheduled services 1978: All Nippon Airways and TOA Domestic Airlines
The airport was opened on 16 October, 1971

The runway is to be extended to 3,000 m (9,842 ft)

Osaka, Honshu Osaka International Airport

34° 46′ 52″ N 135° 26′ 31″ E 8.64 nm (16 km) NW of Osaka
ICAO: RJOO IATA code: OSA Time zone: GMT plus 9
Authority: Civil Aviation Bureau, Ministry of Transport
Area: 317 hectares (783 acres)
Elevation: 39 ft (12 m)   Ref temp: 29.7 deg C
Runways: 14L/32R 1,828 × 45 m (5,997 × 148 ft) asphalt-concrete
    14R/32L 3,000 × 60 m (9,842 × 197 ft) concrete
Pavement strength: 14L/32R 22,000 kg (48,502 lb) ISWL;
  14R/32L 35,000 kg (77,162 lb) ISWL
Landing category: ICAO CAT I

Lighting:
R/W   LIH white edge, last 600 m (1,968 ft) yellow, and centreline (14R/32L   last 300 m (984 ft) red, previous 600 m (1,968 ft) red/white). TDZ 32L and 32R

App   R/W 14L   LIH white bar centreline with sequenced flashers and one crossbar. Yellow approach guidance lights on extended centreline
R/W 14R   short neon centreline of white bars
R/W 32L   LIH white bar centreline with one crossbar and sequenced flashing barrettes on inner section
R/W 32R   LIH white bar centreline with one crossbar and sequenced flashing barrettes. Alignment beacon 1,000 m from threshold
Pre-threshold wing bars on all runways except 14R

Thr   LIH green. Strobes on 14L and 14R
Txy   edge

Aids: VOR/DME, NDB, ASR, SSR, SRE, GCA, PAR, ASDE, RVR, ILS CAT I 32L

Twr frequency: 118.1/126.2/127.5   App frequency: 124.7/126.2

Terminals: Passenger terminal with four piers and aerobridges. Separate domestic and international aprons. Cargo terminal with four aircraft stands

Scheduled services 1978: 17 airlines

Traffic:	1970	1975	1976	1977	1978
Passengers (total)	8,966,995	10,898,870	11,510,992	13,934,931	15,314,181
Cargo (tonnes)	74,917	119,487	132,969	126,333	168,618
Aircraft movements	166,018	133,556	131,556	130,878	126,681
Transport movements	150,730	128,124	131,150	126,002	—

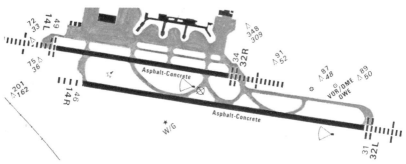

Osaka International Airport. (*British Airways Aerad*)

Osaka International Airport, Japan's second busiest, is surrounded by industrial zones and housing. It is in a mountainous area, those to the west are only 4 km (2.5 miles) distant and a 945 m (3,100 ft) mountain rises due west of the runways. Left turns must be made as soon as possible after take offs from the 14 runways because of the proximity of the mountains. Houses come to within 100 m (328 ft) of the taxiway serving runway 32L, and it is estimated that 1.7 mn people are seriously affected by aircraft noise, therefore strict noise abatement rules are enforced.

Looking southwest across Osaka International Airport, with the terminal area in the foreground, the 32R threshold at the left and runway 14R/32L beyond.
(*Courtesy Airport Forum*)

Short-range jet aircraft and propeller-driven types use 32R and heavy aircraft and long-range jets use 32L for landings; 96 per cent of take offs are from 32L and 4 per cent from 14R. Whenever possible rolling starts have to be made from 32L with take-off power only applied on reaching the upwind VASI units. Adding to the airport's difficulties is the separation of only 260 m (853 ft) between the runways.

The airport has a number of noise suppression structures. One is a cement wall 293 m (961 ft) long and 6 m (19.7 ft) high and another is a 15 m (49 ft) high 240 m (787 ft) long double fence with earth fill and grass top. Trees have also been planted to reduce noise.

The Osaka airport was opened on 17 March, 1958, with a single 14/32 runway (now 14L/32R) of 1,828 m (5,997 ft), and the second runway, 14R/32L of 3,000 m (9,842 ft) was completed on 5 February, 1970; but for many years a site has been sought for a new airport and in 1971 there was a plan to build on land reclaimed from Osaka Bay and providing four 4,000 m (13,123 ft) and four 3,200 m (10,500 ft) runways.

The present airport is situated in the City of Toyonaka but is known locally as Itami Airport and in March 1973 the Itami City Assembly passed a resolution demanding closure of the airport; far from achieving closure, in the spring of 1978 the Ministry of Transport announced that the airport was open for 80 movements a week by wide-bodied aircraft operating international services—eight of these movements being by Japan Air Lines aircraft operating to and from Honolulu.

No decision is known to have been taken on the site for a new airport, but in 1977 the Japanese shipbuilding industry, at the government's request, submitted to the Ministry of Transport a project for an offshore airport comprising three floating structures in Osaka Bay some 5 km (3 miles) southwest of the city. One structure, 3,500 m (11,483 ft) long and 450 m (1,476 ft) wide, would contain the terminal area and be linked to the shore by a bridge. The second structure, alongside the first and parallel with the shore, would provide a 4,000 m (13,123 ft) runway. The third structure, positioned to the north and further from the shore, would have an area of 164 hectares (405 acres) and provide a runway of 3,200 m (10,500 ft) at an angle of 45 degrees to the main runway. A bridge between the runways would carry a taxiway. The entire three-structure system would have an area of 576 hectares (1,423 acres), use 5½ mn tonnes of steel, and be floated on 24,000 very large buoys. It is claimed that such an airport would be cheaper to build than one on reclaimed land, would eliminate noise problems, help the shipbuilding industry survive the economic recession and serve Osaka for 60 years.

Sendai Airport. Looking along runway 12/30 with 09/27 running diagonally across the picture. The terminal is in the foreground between the runways. (*All Nippon Airways*)

Sendai, Honshu   Sendai Airport   ICAO: RJSS   IATA: SDJ

38° 08′ 11″ N   140° 55′ 31″ E   Elevation: 5.7 ft (1.73 m)
Longest runway: 09/27   2,000 m (6,562 ft)   ART   VASI
Aids: VOR/DME, NDB, TAR, ILS 27

	1970	1975	1976	1977
Passengers	195,203	535,136	630,412	809,339
Transport movements	4,506	4,756	5,650	7,584

Scheduled services 1978: All Nippon Airways and TOA Domestic Airlines

Takamatsu, Shikoku   Takamatsu Airport

                ICAO: RJOT   IATA: TAK
34° 17′ 25″ N   134° 04′ 19″ E   Elevation: 66 ft (20 m)
Runway: 09/27   1,200 m (3,940 ft)   RT   VASI
Aids: VOR/DME, NDB, TAR

	1970	1975	1976	1977
Passengers*	443,000	464,000	494,000	529,000
Transport movements	11,413	9,648	9,284	9,033

* Rounded figures

Scheduled services 1978: All Nippon Airways and TOA Domestic Airlines

Tokushima, Shikoku   Tokushima Airport

ICAO: RJOS   IATA: TKS
34° 07′ 49″ N   134° 36′ 02″ E   Elevation: 5 ft (1.5 m)
Runway: 11/29   1,500 m (4,921 ft)   RT
Aids: TACAN, NDB, ASR, SSR, SRE/PAR

	1970	1975	1976	1977
Passengers*	337,000	413,000	471,000	495,000
Transport movements	7,744	8,235	8,810	8,852

* Rounded figures

Scheduled services 1978: TOA Domestic Airlines only

Tokyo, Honshu   Tokyo International Airport - Haneda

35° 32′ 53″ N   139° 46′ 13″ E   7.6 nm (14 km) S of Tokyo Station
ICAO: RJTT   IATA code: HND   Time zone: GMT plus 9
Authority: Civil Aviation Bureau, Ministry of Transport
Area: 427 hectares (1,055 acres)
Elevation: 8 ft (2.5 m)   Ref temp: 31.1 deg C
Runways: 04/22   2,500 × 45 m   (8,202 × 148 ft) asphalt-concrete
     15L/33R   3,150 × 60 m (10,335 × 197 ft) asphalt-concrete
Pavement strength: LCN 100
Landing category: ICAO CAT I
Lighting:
    R/W   LIH white edge, last 600 m (1,968 ft) yellow, and white centreline, last 300 m (984 ft) red and previous 600 m (1,968 ft) red/white. TDZ LIH white 22 and 33R. Red overrun end lights 04/22 and 15L/33R
    App   R/W 15L   LIH white bar centreline (double yellow row on first 500 m (1,640 ft)) and crossbar
    R/W 33R   LIH white bar centreline with sequenced flashers on first 750 m (2,461 ft) and one crossbar
    R/W 04   beacon lights 710 m (2,329 ft) and 1,010 m (3,314 ft) from threshold
    R/W 22   LIH white bar centreline with sequenced flashers and one crossbar. Red barrettes on inner 300 m (984 ft)
    VASIS 04/22 and 15L/33R. Circling guidance amber sodium lights for 15L and fixed and flashing guidance lights at Shinagawa for 22
    Thr   LIH green
    Txy   blue edge and green centreline
Aids: VOR/DME, NDB, ASR, SRE, GCA/PAR, ASDE, RVR (except 04), ILS CAT I 22 and 33R
Twr frequency: 118.1/118.8/121.5/126.2
App frequency: 119.1/121.5/126.5
Terminals: Adjoining domestic and international terminals with 22 aircraft stands and about 50 remote stands. Separate cargo terminal

Scheduled services 1978: 36 airlines before international carriers, except
   China Airlines and Japan Asia Airways, moved to Narita
Main base: All Nippon Airways, Japan Air Lines (domestic operations),
   Japan Asia Airways, Nihon Kinkyori Airways and TOA Domestic
   Airlines

Traffic:	1970	1975	1976	1977	1978
Passengers (total)	10,362,226	18,218,933	20,000,778	23,641,455	20,794,899
Cargo (tonnes)	181,465	363,648	425,798	444,779	303,116
Aircraft movements	172,716	164,426	168,442	168,500	141,750
Transport movements	163,622	150,446	165,832	165,816	—

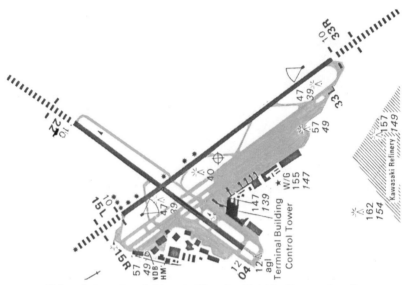

Tokyo International Airport - Haneda. (*British Airways Aerad*)

Situated on the west side of Tokyo Bay between Tokyo and
Yokohama, Haneda Airport was established in 1931 with an available
take-off distance of 300 m (984 ft). There was a paved apron and small
terminal building and by 1939 the airport measured 600 by 600 m (1,968 by
1,968 ft). During the period 1938–40 further expansion took place and two
800 m (2,625 ft) runways were provided. Most of the airport's development
has involved land reclamation.

United States occupation forces more than doubled the size of the
airport during 1945–52 and constructed a main and subsidiary runway.
These were, respectively, 15/33 of 2,134 m (7,000 ft), and 04/22 of 1,570 m
(5,150 ft), later increased to 1,676 m (5,500 ft). In July 1952 the airport was
handed over to the Japanese Ministry of Transport, reopened for public
use, and renamed Tokyo International Airport.

A new terminal building was opened in 1955 and in 1964 the 3,150 m
(10,335 ft) runway 15L/33R was opened, the original primary runway
becoming 15R/33L, increased to 3,000 m (9,842 ft) in length, but later used
as a taxiway.

218

Tokyo's traffic grew rapidly, averaging about 30 per cent annually through the 1960s and into the 1970s and this enforced almost continuous development of facilities on what was a very restricted site. The terminal was expanded and remodelled, with two-way vertical flow for international services, and a domestic arrival building was constructed. An international cargo terminal was opened in 1966, a domestic cargo terminal was completed in 1968 and in the same year the domestic departure lobby was doubled in size.

Further development was necessary to handle Boeing 747s. By May 1970 the international terminal had been expanded and remodelled yet again and it became the departure building. In the following month the new international arrivals building was opened, with two-storey concourse and three piers for Boeing 747s. In 1971 runway 04/22 was extended to 2,500 m (8,202 ft).

By the mid-1970s, when the new airport at Narita should have been in service, capacity was set at 460 aircraft movements a day, 167,900 a year, 86 for any 3-hr period or 34 per hour. These daily movements were allocated as 148 international, 292 domestic and the remaining 20 for non-scheduled operations, check flights and other contingencies such as VIP flights. In fact these figures were exceeded in 1976.

Because of its proximity to densely inhabited areas the airport imposes severe noise-abatement rules. No jet aircraft are allowed to operate between 14.00 and 21.00 GMT (23.00/06.00 LT), preferential runways are 04 and 15L for take off and 22 and 33R for landing.

Tokyo International Airport is linked to the city by a monorail which runs every seven minutes, takes 15 minutes for the journey and carries about 75 per cent of terminating domestic passengers.

A strange aspect of Haneda operation comes to light in Notams which warn of a 30 m (98 ft) high ship which passes the approaches to 15L and 22 and requires 20 minutes' holding for take offs from 04 and 33R and landings on 15L and 22.

Some relief for Haneda finally came on 21 May, 1978, when international operations were transferred to Narita, except for those of China Airlines and Japan Asia Airways.

The second prototype BAC/Aérospatiale Concorde at Tokyo International Airport - Haneda. (*Arthur Gibson, Image in Industry*)

The New Tokyo International Airport (Narita) before it was opened to traffic. This view is looking south and shows the cargo terminal area in the foreground with the airport expressway on the left, the passenger terminal in the centre, the maintenance area in the distance, and runway 16R/34L. (*Courtesy Airports International*)

Tokyo, Honshu   New Tokyo International Airport (Narita)

35° 45′ 50″ N   140° 23′ 28″ E   32.4 nm (60 km) NE of city
ICAO: RJAA   IATA code: NRT   Time zone: GMT plus 9
Authority: New Tokyo International Airport Authority
Area: Phase 1: 550 hectares (1,359 acres), Phase 2: 1,065 hectares (2,632 acres)
Elevation: 135 ft (41 m)   Ref temp: 31.5 deg C
Runway: 16R/34L   4,000 × 60 m (13,123 × 197 ft)* asphalt-concrete

*There is a concrete stopway each end, and threshold 34 is displaced 750 m (2,461 ft)

Pavement strength: auw 50,000 kg (110,231 lb) 1, 80,000 kg (176,370 lb) 2, 160,000 kg (352,740 lb) 4
Landing category: ICAO CAT II
Lighting:
    R/W   LIH white edge, last 600 m (1,968 ft) yellow and red before displaced 34 threshold. Colour-coded centreline. TDZ 16R/34L
    App   R/W 16R   CAT II LIH white centreline with crossbars. Sequenced flashers end 100 m (328 ft) from threshold
              R/W 34L   CAT II LIH white centreline barrettes before threshold and wing bar lights alongside runway to displaced threshold (not in accordance with ICAO requirements). VASIS 16R/34L
    Thr   LIH green
    Txy   no details
Aids: VOR/DME, NDB, ASR, SSR, SRE, ASDE, ILS CAT II 16R/34L

Twr frequency: 118.2/122.7/126.2   App frequency: 121.5/124.4/125.8
Terminals: Five-storey passenger terminal with 160,000 sq m (1,722,240 sq ft)
    floor area. South wing for foreign airlines and North wing for Japan
    Air Lines and companies handled by JAL. Four satellite buildings
    each with gates for five Boeing 747s and two DC-8-60s or three Boeing
    747s and five DC-8-60s. Plus 42 remote stands. Original design
    capacity 5,400,000 annual passengers, ultimate capacity 16 mn.
    Cargo terminal comprising 30,000 sq m (322,920 sq ft) JAL
    building, two other cargo buildings, common import warehouse,
    cargo agents building and customs and quarantine office. Original
    annual design capacity 410,000 tonnes, ultimate capacity 1,400,000
    tonnes. Fourteen cargo aircraft stands.
    Phase 1 apron area is 1,334,100 sq m (14,360,252 sq ft).
Scheduled services 1978: All international airlines serving Tokyo except
    China Airlines and Japan Asia Airways
Main base: Japan Air Lines (international operations)

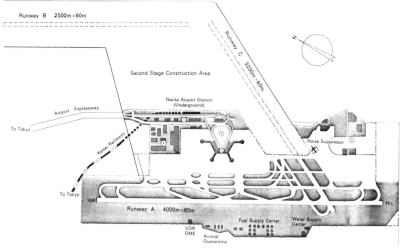

New Tokyo International Airport (Narita)

Tokyo's Haneda airport has long suffered severe limitations due to its
proximity to the city, its limited area and the rapid growth of traffic. To
overcome these problems the Japanese Government decided in 1966 that a
new airport should be built in the Narita area about 60 km (37 miles)
northeast of the city. There was much criticism of this choice, which it has
been claimed was made without consulting the airlines or the people in the
Narita area, but work began on Phase 1 which occupies about 550 hectares
(1,359 acres) of the 1,065 hectares (2,632 acres) allocated to the final layout.
    The decision to build Narita, now New Tokyo International Airport,
was taken in March 1967 and Phase 1, comprising runway 16R/34L, a
parallel taxiway, terminal building, cargo terminal and maintenance area,
was completed in April 1973, but it was to be six years before the airport
could become operational.

221

Model showing Narita terminal area after completion of Phase 2.

Numerous dates for the opening were set but opponents of the airport used every device to prevent its use. Steel towers were erected in the approach area and the continuing riots cost at least five lives and several thousand injured. The Government was determined that Narita should be brought into operation and everything was set for 30 March, 1978, but rioters managed to get into the control tower and did so much damage that operation was impossible. Although riots continued the airport was officially opened, amid security precautions involving thousands of police, on 20 May, 1978, and on the following day a Japan Air Lines cargo flight from San Francisco was the first arrival, followed by a JAL DC-8 passenger service from Frankfurt.

Japan Air Lines' Narita No. 1 hangar, built in 1972, had at the time the sixth largest roof span anywhere, 190 by 90 m (623 by 295 ft), it weighs 4,536 tonnes and was lifted 20 m (66 ft) from nine temporary towers by means of jacks, at that time the world's eleventh heaviest lift.

The planned second stage of Narita development, which is still violently opposed, is due to begin by the end of 1979 and includes construction of runways 16L/34R—2,500 by 60 m (8,202 by 197 ft), and 03/21, 3,200 by 60 m (10,500 by 197 ft); a second terminal, with three traffic piers; and a large northeast apron.

When Phase 2 construction is complete the apron area will be 2,552,200 sq m (27,471,880 sq ft), there will be 96 gate positions and 116 remote stands for passenger aircraft and 18 stands for cargo aircraft. Design annual passenger capacity is 16 mn.

Narita has been severely criticized because of the time required to reach it both from the city, and from the old airport when international/domestic transfers are involved. There is a proposal to build the Tokyo Bay Shore Highway which would link the city and airports; Keisei Electric Railways is to provide a link to the airport; and Japan Air Lines is developing its own HSST (High Speed Surface Transport) project.

The supply of fuel to Narita has also been a source of serious trouble. Twin pipelines are to be laid over a distance of 44 km (27 miles) from Chiba port but this has been delayed and vigorous opposition to surface transport of fuel has limited its availability with consequent limitations of both scheduled and non-scheduled operations.

In its first year of operation the airport handled 61,480 transport movements, 7,481,000 passengers and 379,300 tonnes of cargo.

Hashemite Kingdom of Jordan

Amman   Amman Airport   ICAO: OJAM   IATA: AMM

31° 58′ 11″ N   35° 59′ 05″ E   Elevation: 2,548 ft (777 m)
Runway: 06/24   3,282 m (10,768 ft)   ART   VASI 06/24
Aids: VOR/DME, NDB, L, ILS 24

	1970	1975	1976	1977
Passengers	227,456	601,550	786,167	976,191
Transport movements	6,379	8,835	11,844	13,944

Scheduled services 1978: 17 airlines
Main base: Alia Royal Jordanian Airline, Arab Wings and Jordanian
    World Airlines

The New Queen Alia International Airport under construction at Jiza
(Ziza), 25 km (13.5 miles) south of the city, is due for commissioning in the
winter 1979–80. There are to be staggered parallel 08/26 3,660 m (12,007 ft)
runways 1,525 m (5,003 ft) apart, with a central terminal area and, initially,
two five-gate terminals. The first runway and associated taxiways were
completed in July 1978 and work then started on the apron and second
runway. Ultimate planned capacity is four terminals with 28 gates serving
6 mn to 8 mn passengers annually by the year 2000.

Kenya

Mombasa   Mombasa Airport

ICAO: HKMO   IATA: MBA
04° 01′ 30″ S   39° 35′ 50″ E   Elevation: 186 ft (57 m)
Longest runway: 03/21   3,350 m (10,991 ft)   ART   VASI 03
Aids: VOR/DME, NDB, VDF, L, ILS

	1970
Passengers	180,707
Aircraft movements	18,375

Scheduled services 1978: Air Comores and Kenya Airways

Nairobi   Jomo Kenyatta International Airport

01° 19′ 07″ S   36° 55′ 33″ E   6.3 nm (11.66 km) ESE of city
ICAO: HKNA   IATA code: NBO   Time zone: GMT plus 3
Authority: Kenya Government
Elevation: 5,327 ft (1,624 m)   Ref temp: 23.4 deg C
Runway: 06/24   4,117 × 46 m (13,507 × 150 ft) asphalt
Pavement strength: LCN 100

Landing category: ICAO CAT I
Lighting:
R/W   edge lights and stopway (06 LIH, 24 LIL)
App   R/W 06   LIH white precision approach, R/W 24
       LIL red simple (328 m/1,076 ft). VASIS 06/24
Thr   06   LIH,   24   LIL
Txy   edge
Aids: VOR/DME, NDB, VDF, L, SRE, RVR 06, ILS CAT I 06
Twr frequency: 118.7   App frequency: 119.7
Terminals: International and domestic passenger terminal south of
    runway, with 23 aircraft stands. Separate cargo terminal
Scheduled services 1978: 26 airlines
Main base: Kenya Airways

Traffic:	1970	1975	1976	1977
Passengers (total)	861,800	1,378,438	1,488,631	1,321,939
Cargo (tonnes)	15,230	35,311	35,111	32,994
Aircraft movements	39,042	34,646	32,998	26,027
Transport movements	20,165	24,906	23,995	19,164

Jomo Kenyatta International Airport, Nairobi, with the terminal opened in
March 1978 and in the foreground a British Airways Boeing 747 taking off on
runway 06. (*Azhar Chaudhry, courtesy British Airways*)

When Wilson Airways operated its East African regional services
during the 1930s and Imperial Airways its United Kingdom–South Africa
landplane route, Nairobi West was Kenya's main airport. Later, heavier
long-distance aircraft used RAF Station Eastleigh. Both airports remained
in operation after the Second World War.
    The Kenya Government realized that the capital would require a
modern airport and the decision was taken to build an international airport
on the Athi Plains at Embakasi, close to the Nairobi National Park game
reserve.

224

Nairobi's high elevation and temperatures made necessary the provision of a 10,000 ft (3,048 m) runway, and its construction involved removal of some 600,000 tons of black cotton soil, of an average depth of 2 ft 6 in (76 cm), which lay on a floor of ancient lava. In order to provide a flat and level bed for the runway foundation about 400,000 tons of lava had to be removed before the rock fill foundations could be laid. Work began in August 1953 and excavation took most of 1954. At that time Kenya was fighting the Mau Mau campaign and the finance available for the airport was limited. To cut costs Mau Mau prisoners undertook much of the work which would normally have been done by machines.

The runway had an asphalt surface, there was a parallel taxiway at its southwest end and a turning loop at the other end. The apron measured 1,100 by 900 ft (335 by 274 m) and was to the north of the runway. There was a simple and attractive terminal which had an indoor garden, and the airport facilities were designed to handle 18 peak-hour movements. There were 10 aircraft stands.

The new airport was opened by HM Queen Elizabeth, the Queen Mother, on 9 March, 1958. Nairobi West Airport was then renamed Wilson Airport in honour of Mrs F. K. Wilson (founder of Wilson Airways), and Eastleigh was closed to civil traffic.

Later the runway was increased in length to 13,507 ft (4,117 m) and in October 1969 planning began for a new terminal to meet traffic growth. The new terminal complex was constructed on the south side of the runway and comprises a central arrivals and administrative building nearly enclosed by a circular two-level departure and transit building. Check-in facilities are at ground level in two international units and a domestic unit. Transit and departure lounges are on the upper level with aerobridge access to the aircraft which are parked nose-in. Design capacity is 1,250 arriving, 1,250 departing and 500 transit passengers an hour.

The World Bank assisted in financing the new Nairobi terminal, which was opened on 14 March, 1978, the airport being closed for five hours while the transfer was made from the old to the new terminal.

A new taxiway was commissioned south of and parallel to the western half of the runway, and there is a new cargo terminal with cold room storage for handling fruit and vegetable exports.

On 8 December, 1978, the name of the airport was changed from Nairobi Airport (Embakasi) to Jomo Kenyatta International Airport in honour of Kenya's first president who had died earlier in the year.

Republic of Korea

Seoul   Kimpo International Airport

37° 33′ 15″ N	126° 47′ 59″ E	14 nm (26 km) W of city
ICAO: RKSS	IATA code: SEL	Time zone: GMT plus 9
Authority: Civil Aviation Authority		
Elevation: 58 ft (18 m)		Ref temp: 25.5 deg C
Runway: 14/32	3,200 × 46 m (10,500 × 150 ft) asphalt	

Drawing of the international terminal being built at Kimpo International Airport, Seoul. The existing terminal is in the distance on the right.

Pavement strength: 29,000 kg (63,934 lb) 1, 59,000 kg (130,073 lb) 2, 118,000 kg (260,145 lb) 3
Landing category: ICAO CAT I
Lighting:
R/W   LIH white edge
App   R/W 14   LIH CAT I centreline with crossbars. VASIS 32
Thr   green, with strobes on 14
Txy   blue edge
Aids: VOR/DME, L, ILS CAT I 14
Twr frequency: 118.1/121.5/126.2   App frequency: 119.1/121.5
Terminal: Combined international and domestic terminal with triangular apron and 22 aircraft stands
Scheduled services 1978: Air France, Cathay Pacific, China Airlines, Flying Tiger, Japan Air Lines, Korean Air Lines, Northwest Orient, Singapore Airlines and Thai Airways International
Main base: Korean Air Lines

Traffic:	1975	1976	1977
Passengers (total)	1,713,749	2,305,923	2,845,856
Cargo (tonnes)	64,693	96,169	111,668
Transport movements	23,558	29,699	32,694

Kimpo International Airport, formerly Kimpo Airfield, is situated on the narrow coastal plain between Seoul, the Korean capital, and its port at Inchon. Kimpo has served as the Seoul airport since the end of the Korean War.

A new international terminal and apron are due to come into use in 1980 when the existing terminal will be used for domestic operations.

State of Kuwait

Kuwait   Kuwait International Airport

29° 13′ 12″ N   47° 58′ 05″ E   8 nm (14.8 km) S of city
ICAO: OKBK   IATA code: KWI   Time zone: GMT plus 3
Authority: Kuwait Government
Area: 2,200 hectares (5,436 acres)
Elevation: 189 ft (58 m)   Ref temp: 39.1 deg C
Runways: 15L/33R   3,205 × 46 m (10,518 × 150 ft) asphalt
          15R/33L   3,399 × 46 m (11,152 × 150 ft) concrete
Pavement strength: 15L/33R LCN 25, 15R/33L LCN 100
Landing category: ICAO CAT I*

* Two sets of CAT II ILS have been ordered.

Lighting:
    R/W   15L/33R   LIL edge, stopway and wing bar
              15R/33L   LIH edge and centreline, end lights, TDZ 33L
    App   R/W 15L/33R   LIL red centreline with three crossbars
              R/W 15R   LIH white centreline with one crossbar
              R/W 33L   LIH CAT II barrettes and sequenced
              flashers. VASIS 15R/33L
    Thr   15L/33R   LIL,   15R/33L   LIH
    Txy   Western taxiway centreline, Eastern taxiway edge.

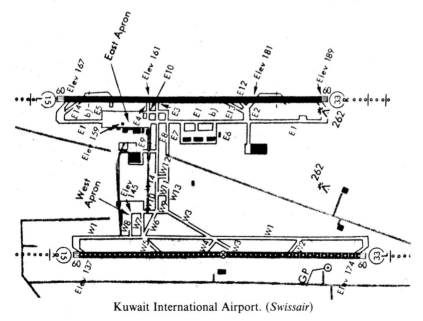

Kuwait International Airport. (*Swissair*)

227

A British Airways Concorde at Kuwait. (*British Aerospace*)

Aids: VOR/DME, VDF, L, SRE, RVR 33L, ILS CAT I 33L
Twr frequency: 118.3   App frequency: 121.3
Terminal: To west of 15L/33R with 17 aircraft stands. Also small west apron.
Scheduled airlines 1978: 34 airlines
Main base: Kuwait Airways

Traffic:	1970	1975	1976	1977
Passengers (total)	636,236	1,267,328	1,545,482	1,843,731
Cargo (tonnes)	10,061	16,546	28,008	35,479
Aircraft movements	24,232	30,111	35,084	38,264
Transport movements	13,720	18,238	21,434	26,413

Kuwait first appeared on the air route map in 1932 when Imperial Airways switched its England–India route from the Persian to the Arabian side of the Gulf. Handley Page 42s were used, and regular landings at Kuwait are believed to have begun on 22 December, 1932. The desert landing ground was just outside the town wall.

When civil operations were resumed at Kuwait after the war another desert aerodrome was used, somewhat further from town. This had a stony surface and a very primitive terminal which was in use until at least the late 1950s.

Since that time Kuwait has experienced largescale traffic growth and its own national airline has an all-jet fleet. Its international airport, with parallel runways, is to have a new terminal building capable of handling 2.2 mn passengers a year. This is a three-storey concrete building with 58,000 sq m (624,312 sq ft) floor area with the ground floor designed to handle arrivals and the top floor departures. There will be 13 air-conditioned telescopic loading jetties to link the aircraft with the arrival and departure lounges.

Work on the terminal began in 1975 and the new facilities are due to open late in 1980. The master plan allows for construction of a second terminal when required.

228

Lebanon (Liban)

Beirut   Beirut International Airport

33° 49' 14" N   35° 29' 21" E   4 nm (7.4 km) S of city
ICAO: OLBA   IATA code: BEY   Time zone: GMT plus 2
Authority: Directorate of Civil Aviation
Area: About 350 hectares (865 acres)
Elevation: 85 ft (26 m)   Ref temp: 28 deg C
Runways: 03/21   3,180 × 61 m (10,433 × 200 ft) concrete
        18/36   3,250 × 61 m (10,663 × 200 ft) concrete

Runways 21 and 36 are normally used for take-offs and 03 and 18 for landings.

Pavement strength: 67,000 kg (147,710 lb) ISWL
Landing category: ICAO CAT I
Lighting:
R/W   LIH white edge, last 850 m (2,789 ft) of 18/36 and 450 m (1,746 ft) of 03 red
App   R/W 18   LIH white 900 m (2,953 ft) centreline and three crossbars
           VASIS 03/21 and 18. Runway alignment beacon 3.9 nm (7.2 km) from 18 threshold
Thr   LIH green 18/36, LIL green 03/21
Txy   blue
Aids: VOR, NDB, L, SRE, ILS CAT I 18
Twr frequency: 118.9   App frequency: 120.3
Terminal: Multi-storey passenger terminal with handling on two levels. Apron with parking space for about 50 large aircraft, with 22 refuelling positions
Scheduled services 1978: 28 airlines
Main base: MEA and TMA

Traffic:	1970	1975	1976	1977
Passengers (total)	1,551,375	1,949,872	390,000*	581,000*
Cargo (tonnes)	52,104	—	7,486	6,947
Aircraft movements	41,553	43,815	—	13,021
Transport movements	37,345	—	—	9,646

*Rounded figures. The traffic statistics are not representative of normal operations. The airport reopened on 19 November, 1976, after being closed for more than a year because of political troubles and there has since been further disruption of operations. The 1978 passenger figure has been reported as 1,292,000.

The first air services to Beirut were those operated by Air Union–Lignes d'Orient using CAMS 53 flying-boats which alighted in St George's Bay. It was difficult to find a suitable site for a land airport because the ground was uneven or covered with olive trees, but finally a site was selected at Khalde on the edge of the city on an area of sand dunes, and a large volume of sand was removed and taken to the harbour where improvements were taking place.

229

Beirut International Airport terminal. (*British Airways*)

Three runways, one 825 m (2,707 ft) long and two 845 m (2,772 ft), were constructed together with terminal, control tower and hangar, and the airport was brought into operation late in 1938. One of the runways was extended to 1,139 m (3,720 ft) but the airport could not be developed to meet postwar requirements and a new airport was constructed beside the Mediterranean to the south of the city.

The new Beirut International Airport was opened on 1 September, 1950, at which time one runway had been completed to a length of 1,800 m (5,905 ft). By 1954 two 2,400 m (7,874 ft) runways were in use and the permanent terminal had been completed, the airport becoming an important junction for the region and a transit stop for services to and from the East and Australia.

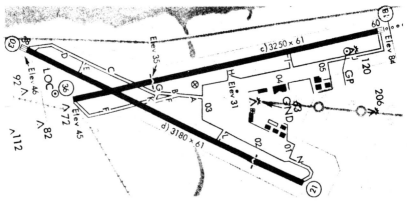

Beirut International Airport. (*Swissair*)

At the start of the jet era the runways were extended to their present length, the terminal was doubled in size, the apron extended, and a new increased-capacity hydrant refuelling system installed.

Due to the fighting in Lebanon the airport was shut for more than a year during 1975–76 and subsequent troubles have seriously restricted its normally rapid traffic growth.

In 1974 Aéroport de Paris was commissioned to design extensions to the terminal and runways and plan a new terminal area. It is proposed that runway 03/21 should be lengthened with its southwest end extended offshore. The terminal extensions envisaged comprise wings at each end of the present terminal building and two traffic piers onto the present apron, with aerobridge boarding.

Libyan Arab Jamahiriya

Benghazi   Benina Airport   ICAO: HLLB   IATA: BEN

32° 05′ 59″ N   20° 16′ 02″ E   Elevation: 433 ft (132 m)
Longest runway: 15L/33R   3,600 m (11,811 ft) ART VASI 15L/33R
Aids: VOR, NDB, L

	1970	1975	1976	1977
Passengers	205,825*	396,129*	508,441	626,276
Transport movements	9,296	9,663	8,279	9,549

* Excluding transit

Scheduled services 1978: nine airlines

Tripoli   Tripoli International Airport

32° 40′ 10″ N   13° 09′ 24″ E   11.88 nm (22 km) S of city
ICAO: HLLT   IATA code: TIP   Time zone: GMT plus 2
Authority: Libyan Government
Elevation: 263 ft (80 m)   Ref temp: 31 deg C
Runway: 09/27   3,600 × 46 m (11,811 × 150 ft) asphalt*

* 360 m (1,181 ft) concrete each end

Pavement strength: LCN 100
Landing category: ICAO CAT I
Lighting:
   R/W   LIH white edge and centreline, last 600 m (1,968 ft) yellow.
            TDZ 27
   App   R/W 09   LIH white and LIL red Calvert centreline and
            crossbars
            R/W 27   LIH white and LIL red Calvert centreline with
            crossbars and red barrettes on inner 300 m (984 ft). VASIS
            09/27

Thr   green wing bars
Txy   green centreline
Aids: TVOR/DME, NDB, VDF, L, ILS CAT I 27
Twr and app frequencies: 118.1/120.1/121.5/124.0
Terminal: Passenger terminal in central position to north of runway and
    west of old aprons
Scheduled services 1978: 26 airlines

Traffic:	1971	1975	1976	1977
Passengers (total)	352,766*	893,760	1,369,653	1,151,549
Cargo (tonnes)	12,791	27,989	29,743	22,848
Aircraft movements	—	—	26,525†	36,675
Transport movements	16,929	22,643	25,077	25,238

* Excludes transit passengers   † ICAO estimate

Tripoli International Airport. (*British Airways Aerad*)

In November 1928 SA Navigazione Aerea (SANA) inaugurated *La
Freccia Rossa* (*The Red Arrow*) service between Rome and Tripoli, using
Dornier Wal flying-boats. The flying-boats operated from Tripoli harbour
where there was an alighting area measuring 2,000 by 1,800 m (6,562 by
5,905 ft). The air station was alongside the inner end of the east breakwater.

Services between Tripoli and Benghazi were begun in the early 1930s
by Società Nord-Africa Aviazione with Caproni Ca 101 three-engined
landplanes and these worked from a small grass aerodrome at Mellaha
near the coast and 11 km (6.8 miles) east of Tripoli.

The present airport, built on a generally level sandy plain and
surrounded mostly by agricultural land reclaimed from the desert, was
originally the Italian Air Force base Castel Benito. There were hangars and
administration buildings along the western boundary but no runways.

The Eighth Army entered Tripoli in the early hours of 23 January,
1943, and on 26 January BOAC's Lockheed 14 G-AFKE *Lothair* made the
first 'postwar' landing at Castel Benito by a civil aircraft. The Royal
Engineers built three runways in 1943. These were north–south (18/36),
southwest–northeast (05/23) and west-northwest–east-southeast (11/29).
They consisted of 4-in bitumen-grouted crushed stone on 6–8 in of sand
and crushed stone, and pronounced unevenness and surface disintegration
made it necessary to resurface them in 1945. It is believed that each runway

Tripoli International Airport terminal which was opened in 1978.
(*Courtesy Libyan Arab Airlines*)

was originally 4,950 ft (1,509 m) long. Subsequently, 18/36 was lengthened to 7,316 ft (2,230 m) and 05/23 was abandoned.

Runways, taxiways and aprons continued to cause trouble and major work was done on both runways in 1945. Runway 18/36 was again resurfaced in 1965 but its condition was poor by the following year, 11/29 was generally bad and collected a considerable amount of water after rain, as did the apron. Some taxiways had to be abandoned because of their poor condition.

Plans for a triangular terminal were made during the early 1960s but this was never built and a war-scarred hangar continued to serve as the terminal.

Because of the unsatisfactory state of the airport, the Government decided in 1966 to build a new east–west runway. Revolution delayed the work but eventually the 3,600 m (11,811 ft) 09/27 runway was constructed—18/36 is now part of the taxiway system but may be used by light aircraft. Preliminary design of the new terminal began in 1972 and the terminal was in use in 1977 and officially opened on 28 July, 1978.

Following the creation of the Libyan State in 1951 the airport's name was changed from Castel Benito to Idris el Awal (Idris 1st) but when the monarchy was overthrown in 1969 the name was changed to Tripoli International Airport.

Luxembourg (Grand Duchy of Luxembourg)

Luxembourg   Aéroport de Luxembourg

ICAO: ELLX   IATA: LUX
49° 37′ 24″ N   06° 12′ 18″ E   Elevation: 1,240 ft (378 m)
Longest runway: 06/24   2,830 m (9,285 ft)   ART
Aids: VOR, NDB, VDF, L, ILS CAT I 24

	1970	1975	1976	1977
Passengers	471,410	637,328	705,716	714,988
Transport movements	11,861	15,422	17,162	13,828

Scheduled services 1978: 11 airlines
Main base: Cargolux Airlines International and Luxair

Malawi

Blantyre   Chileka Airport   ICAO: FWCL   IATA: BLZ

15° 40′ 43″ S   34° 58′ 06″ E   Elevation: 2,555 ft (779 m)
Longest runway: 10/28   2,325 m (7,628 ft)   ART
Aids: VOR/DME, NDB, VDF

	1970	1975	1976	1977
Passengers	157,612	280,636	171,325	176,885
Transport movements	6,684	9,217	7,091	6,857

Scheduled services 1978: Air Malawi, British Airways, Royal Swazi, South
    African Airways and Zambia Airways
Main base: Air Malawi

Malaysia

Kota Kinabalu (formerly Jesselton), Sabah
                Kota Kinabalu Airport

ICAO: WBKK   IATA: BKI
05° 56′ 27″ N   116° 02′ 58″ E   Elevation: 10 ft (3 m)
Runway: 02/20   2,987 m (9,800 ft)   RT   VASI 02
Aids: VOR/DME, NDB, L, ILS (on test 1978)

	1970	1972
Passengers	290,575	355,259
Aircraft movements	21,372	29,615

Scheduled services 1978: Cathay Pacific Airways, Malaysian Airline
    System and Royal Brunei Airlines

Kuala Lumpur International Airport in 1967. (*British Airways*)

Kuala Lumpur   Kuala Lumpur International Airport (Subang)

03° 07′ 49″ N   101° 33′ 05″ E   8 nm (14.8 km) W of KL station
ICAO: WMKK   IATA code: KUL   Time zone: GMT plus 7½
Authority: Civil Aviation Department, Peninsular Malaysia
Area: 388 hectares (959 acres)
Elevation: 89 ft (27 m)   Ref temp: 32.7 deg C
Runway: 15/33   3,474 × 45 m (11,397 × 148 ft) flexible pavement,
                                            tarmac surface
    There is a 1,524 × 46 m (5,000 × 150 ft) parallel crash strip
Pavement strength: LCN 100
Landing category: ICAO CAT I
Lighting:
    R/W   LIH white edge, alternating white/amber last 610 m (2,000 ft)
    App   R/W 15/33   LIH white 914 m (2,998 ft) centreline with
                two crossbars. T-VASIS 15/33
    Thr   green wing bars
    Txy   blue edge and green centreline. White centreline on high-
                speed exits
    There are green and white visual circling guidance lights facing west

235

Aids: VOR/DME, NDB, L, ASR, ILS CAT I 33
Twr frequency: 125.1   App frequency: 125.1
Terminals: Passenger terminal with two piers and 12 aircraft stands.
   Separate cargo building.
Scheduled services 1978: 20 airlines
Main base: Malaysian Airline System

Traffic:	1970	1975	1976	1977
Passengers (total)	703,245	1,228,395	1,524,415	1,983,076
Cargo (tonnes)	2,671	11,666	16,310	22,959
Aircraft movements	28,858	43,448	49,560	51,304
Transport movements	22,798	33,848	38,548	40,450

In 1976 Boeing 737s accounted for more than 25 per cent of aircraft movements.

The first landing area at Kuala Lumpur was the polo ground about 1 mile (1.6 km) east of the city; but an aerodrome was prepared close to the southern edge of the city and was used by the Kuala Lumpur Flying Club from 1931 and by Imperial Airways and Indian Trans-Continental Airways from 1933. This site became known as Simpang Airport and is now used by the Royal Malaysian Air Force.

In the early 1950s Simpang was given a 1,890 m (6,200 ft) runway but it was soon realized that the airport would require considerable improvement or have to be replaced, and as it was considered that Simpang was too close to the city, work began on a new site, at Subang, in 1960.

At Subang the aprons were completed in March 1964, the 3,480 m (11,417 ft) runway in June and the taxiway in August. The terminal building and 41 m (135 ft) high control tower were finished in the following year, the opening ceremony took place on 30 August, 1965, and operations began in September. VOR/DME was installed in 1969, a hangar and ancillary buildings were completed in 1971 and in the following year the cargo building was enlarged.

The terminal is a three-level structure with separate international and domestic arrival and departure sections. Ramps lead from the terminal to the apron and there are two covered piers.

Penang   Penang Airport (Bayan Lepas)

              ICAO: WMKP   IATA: PEN
05° 17′ 51″ N   100° 16′ 41″ E   Elevation: 12 ft (4 m)
Runway: 04/22   3,353 m (11,000 ft)   ART   T-VASI 04/22
Aids: TVOR/DME, L, ILS ordered 1978

	1970	1975	1976	1977
Passengers	198,661	560,631	588,577	714,484
Transport movements	8,018	12,372	13,274	13,692

Scheduled services 1978: Cathay Pacific Airways, Malaysian Airline System, Merpati Nusantara Airlines, Thai Airways and Thai Airways International

Malta, G.C.

Valletta   Luqa Airport   ICAO: LMML   IATA: MLA

35° 51′ 31″ N   14° 28′ 41″ E   Elevation: 300 ft (91 m)
Longest runway: 14/32   3,550 m (11,647 ft)   ART
    VASI 06/24 and 14/32
Aids: VORTAC, DME, NDB, VDF, PAR, radar, ILS 24 and 32

	1970	1975	1976	1977
Passengers	401,172	761,761	745,674	798,830
Transport movements	7,981	10,023	9,818	—

Scheduled services 1978: Air Malta, Alitalia, British Airways, JAT, Libyan
    Arab Airlines and UTA
Main base: Air Malta

Mauritius

Port Louis   Plaisance Airport

                    ICAO: FIMP   IATA: MRU
20° 25′ 40″ S   57° 40′ 31″ E   Elevation: 186 ft (57 m)
Runway: 13/31   2,600 m (8,530 ft)   ART   VASI 13/31
Aids: VOR/DME, NDB, L, ILS CAT I 13

	1970	1975	1976	1977
Passengers	118,598	266,536	303,628	323,494
Transport movements	1,820	4,794	5,333	4,948

Scheduled services 1978: 10 airlines
Main base: Air Mauritius

A new airport is to be built at Plaine des Roches in the north of the
island

Acapulco International Airport terminal building. (*Enrique Puente*)

México

Acapulco, Guerrero

Aeropuerto Internacional General Juan N. Alvarez

16° 45′ 05″ N   99° 45′ 27″ W   10.8 nm (20 km) SE of city
ICAO: MMAA   IATA code: ACA   Time zone: GMT −6
Authority: Aeropuertos y Servicios Auxiliares
Elevation: 18 ft (5 m)   Ref temp: 29 deg C
Runways: 06/24   1,700 × 35 m   (5,577 × 115 ft) concrete
              10/28   3,300 × 45 m (10,827 × 148 ft) concrete
Pavement strength: 06/24 LCN 100; 10/28 auw 54,000 kg (119,000 lb) 1,
     90,000 kg (198,000 lb) 2, 150,000 kg (331,000 lb) 3, 310,000 kg
     (683,000 lb) 4
Landing category: ICAO CAT I
Lighting:
     R/W   LIH white edge 10/28
     App   R/W 10/28   LIH white bar centreline with crossbar.
              VASIS 06/24 and 10/28
     Thr   R/W 10   strobes,   R/W 28   LIH green
     Txy   edge lights
Aids: VOR/DME, NDB, VDF, TAR, SRE, ILS CAT I 28
Twr frequency: 118.5   App frequency: 119.9
Terminal: Passenger terminal on north side of airport with twin pier. Eight
     aircraft stands, four capable of taking Boeing 747s

Scheduled services 1978: Aeroméxico, American Airlines, Braniff, Eastern
Air Lines, Méxicana and Western Airlines

Traffic:	1970	1975	1977	1978
Passengers (total)	809,399	1,510,479*	1,734,731	1,977,250
Cargo (tonnes)	942	2,320	3,250	14,957
Aircraft movements	23,897	28,581	31,963	32,178
Transport movements	17,505	21,282	23,400	—

* Excludes transit passengers

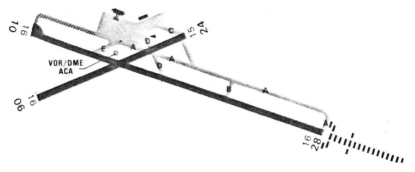

General Juan N. Alvarez International Airport, Acapulco.
(*British Airways Aerad*)

Situated on the narrow coastal strip between the Pacific and the
mountains, to the southeast of the city, Acapulco Airport was opened on 14
January, 1954, as Aeropuerto Internacional Plan de los Amates. There was
a single, 10/28, runway of 3,100 m (10,171 ft) with a 61 m (200 ft) overrun at
the western end and a 45 m (148 ft) overrun at the eastern end. Taxiways
only served the centre part of the runway.

Jet services through Acapulco began in November 1964 when Qantas
inaugurated   Sydney–Fiji–Tahiti–Acapulco–Mexico   City–Nassau–
Bermuda–London services with Boeing 707s.

Since that time the main runway has been lengthened and is served by
a parallel taxiway and the 06/24 runway has been completed.

Guadalajara, Jalisco
Aeropuerto Internacional Don Miguel Hidalgo y Castilla

20° 31′ 12″ N   103° 18′ 57″ W   9.7 nm (18 km) SSE of city
ICAO: MMGL .   IATA code: GDL   Time zone: GMT −6
Authority: Aeropuertos y Servicios Auxiliares
Elevation: 5,010 ft (1,527 m)   Ref temp: 9 deg C
Runways: 02/20   1,769 × 35 m (5,806 × 115 ft) concrete
         10/28   3,999 × 60 m (13,120 × 197 ft) concrete
Pavement strength: 54,000 kg (119,000 lb) 1, 90,000 kg (198,000 lb) 2,
    146,000 kg (322,000 lb) 3, 310,000 kg (683,000 lb) 4
Landing category: ICAO CAT I
Lighting:
    R/W   02/20   LIL white edge,   10/28   LIH white edge

239

App   R/W 28   LIH white bar centreline with crossbar.
            VASIS 10/28
Thr   R/W 10   strobes,   R/W 28 greeen
Txy   edge lights
Aids: VOR/DME, NDB, ILS CAT I 28
Twr frequency: 118.1/121.5   App frequency: 120.8
Terminal: To north of main runway
Scheduled services 1978: Aeroméxico, Hughes Airwest and Méxicana

Traffic:	1970	1975	1977	1978
Passengers (total)	652,632	1,193,521*	1,837,231	2,326,866
Cargo (tonnes)	4,112	7,850	11,335	33,381
Aircraft movements	40,653	49,720	101,075	—
Transport movements	21,051	31,039	38,313	68,075

*Excludes transit passengers

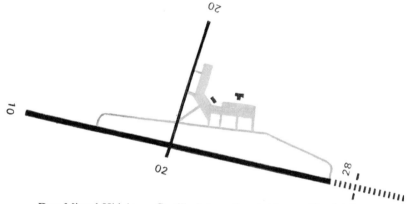

Don Miguel Hidalgo y Castilla International Airport, Guadalajara.
(*British Airways Aerad*)

    Guadalajara, on the central plateau, is México's second largest city. It is an important commercial, industrial and communications centre and the seat of two universities—one established in 1792.
    The present airport was opened on 20 March, 1951, and achieved international status on 20 October, 1958. In 1976 the airport had the longest runway in México but México City's 05R/23L is now 23 m (76 ft) longer.

La Paz, Baja California
    Aeropuerto Internacional General Manuel Marquez de León

             ICAO: MMLP   IATA: LAP
24° 07′ 55″ N   110° 27′ 52″ W   Elevation: 69 ft (21 m)
Runway: 18/36   2,500 m (8,202 ft)   RT   VASI 36
Aids: VOR/DME, NDB

	1970	1978
Passengers	200,441	513,620
Transport movements	10,073	26,508

Scheduled services 1978: Aeroméxico and Hughes Airwest

The airport was opened on 17 June, 1952, and achieved international status on 20 August, 1958.

Mazatlán, Sinaloa
Aeropuerto Internacional General Rafael Buelna

ICAO: MMMZ		IATA: MZT	
23° 09' 27" N	106° 15' 21" W		Elevation: 33 ft (10 m)
Runway: 08/26	2,700 m (8,858 ft)	RT	VASI 08/26
Aids: VOR/DME, NDB			

	1970	1978
Passengers	219,290	669,290
Transport movements	7,702	21,424

Scheduled services 1978: Aeroméxico, Hughes Airwest and Méxicana

Mérida, Yucatán
Aeropuerto Internacional Manuel Crescencio Rejón

ICAO: MMMD	IATA: MID	
20° 56' 21" N	89° 39' 18" W	Elevation: 30 ft (9 m)

Longest runway: 10/28 2,700 m (8,858 ft) R VASI 10/28 and 17/35
Aids: VOR/DME, NDB, ILS ordered in 1978

	1970	1975	1977	1978
Passengers	302,007	524,947	693,083	815,006
Transport movements	9,963	12,294	12,928	23,789

Scheduled services 1978: Aeroméxico, Aviateca, Lufthansa, Méxicana, Pan American and TACA International

The airport was built by Méxicana and achieved international status on 16 June, 1943.

México City, Distrito Federal
Aeropuerto Internacional Benito Juárez

19° 26' 13" N   99° 04' 10" W   2.7 nm (5 km) E of city
ICAO: MMMX   IATA code: MEX   Time zone: GMT −6
Authority: Aeropuertos y Servicios Auxiliares
Elevation: 7,341 ft (2,237 m)   Ref temp: 22 deg C
Runways: 05L/23R   3,100 × 40 m (10,171 × 131 ft) asphalt
         05R/23L   4,022 × 45 m (13,196 × 148 ft) asphalt
         13/31   2,300 × 40 m   (7,546 × 131 ft) asphalt
Pavement strength: auw 40,000 kg (88,000 lb) 1, 68,000 kg (149,000 lb) 2, 162,000 kg (356,000 lb) 3, 359,000 kg (792,000 lb) 4

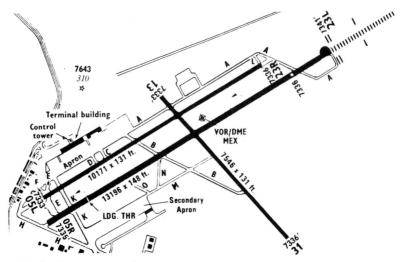

Benito Juárez International Airport, México City. (*British Airways Aerad*)

Landing category: ICAO CAT I
Lighting:
    R/W   LIH white edge and REIL
    App   R/W23L   LIH white bar centreline with crossbar, others nil
               VASIS 05L/23R and 05R/23L, AVASI 13
    Thr   green, with strobes on 05L, 05R and 13
    Txy   edge lights
Aids: VOR/DME, NDB, L, SRE, ILS CAT I 05R/23L
Twr frequency: 118.1   App frequency: 121.2
Terminals: Passenger terminal in northwest corner of airport, with
    domestic and international aprons, four piers and 23 aircraft stands.
    There is a secondary apron in the southwest corner of the airport.
    Plane-Mates serve remote stands
Scheduled services 1978: 31 airlines
Main base: Aeroméxico and Méxicana

Traffic:	1970	1975	1977	1978
Passengers (total)	3,360,532	6,560,600*	8,026,076	9,428,505
Cargo (tonnes)	42,306	69,520	85,896	213,438
Aircraft movements	123,843	153,630	221,809	206,972
Transport movements	69,058	98,235	107,253	—

* Excludes transit passengers

    The first commercial flights at México City used the Balbuena military
aerodrome but in 1929 Puerto Central Aéreo de la ciudad de México
(México Central Airport) was opened on the present site. There was
originally an 800 m (2,625 ft) north–south runway and later the 10/28
crosswind runway was added. Sometime after 1930 the north–south
runway was realigned and this has been developed into the present
05L/23R.

242

Work was begun on a terminal building which was linked by a bridge to the control tower, but while under construction an earth tremor caused the terminal to collapse and its construction was never completed. The first terminal to be completed was opened in 1938 and it incorporated the airport's first radio-equipped control tower. The airport achieved international status on 16 June, 1943.

In the immediate postwar years the airport had parallel 05/23 runways of 1,433 m (4,700 ft) and 2,469 m (8,100 ft), 10/28 of 1,524 m (5,000 ft) and 14/32 of 1,615 m (5,300 ft). By the mid-1960s runway 10/28 had been withdrawn from use—it is now part of the apron area—05L/23R had been lengthened to 3,134 m (10,283 ft) with a 225 m (738 ft) overrun at its southwest end, 05R/23L was 3,300 m (10,824 ft) with a 200 m (656 ft) overrun at its southwest end, 14/32 had been reduced to 990 m (3,247 ft) with a 41 m (135 ft) overrun at its southern end, and a new runway, 13/31, had been built with a length of 2,300 m (7,546 ft). Subsequently 05R/23L was lengthened, and 14/32 was closed and integrated with the taxiway system.

The present terminal building was opened on 1 June, 1954, and has since been enlarged and equipped with aerobridges, 13 of which were ordered in 1974. To meet the increasing traffic demands consideration was given to the construction of long traffic piers but it was decided instead to use 150-passenger Plane-Mates to serve remote stands and three were ordered in 1974. Approval for the construction of a new international airport northeast of the city was given in 1979.

An Air France Concorde in front of the terminal at Mexico City's Benito Juárez International Airport. (*Felipe Martinez, courtesy Air France*)

243

Monterrey, Nuevo León
Aeropuerto Internacional General Mariano Escobedo

ICAO: MMMY   IATA: MTY
25° 46′ 24″ N   100° 06′ 06″ W   Elevation: 1,270 ft (387 m)
Longest runway: 11/29   3,000 m (9,842 ft)   ART   VASI 11
Aids: VOR/DME, L, SRE/TAR

	1970	1975	1977	1978
Passengers	148,086	644,314*	786,670	969,049
Transport movements	3,774	13,116	12,442	27,435

Scheduled services 1978: Aeroméxico, Iberia, Méxicana and Texas
    International
The airport was built by American Airlines and achieved international
status on 24 October, 1942.

* Excludes transit passengers

Puerto Vallarta, Jalisco
Aeropuerto Internacional Lic Gustavo Díaz Ordaz

ICAO: MMPR   IATA: PVR
20° 41′ 03″ N   105° 15′ 30″ W   Elevation: 20 ft (6 m)
Runway: 04/22   2,750 m (9,020 ft)   RT   VASI 04/22
Aids: VOR/DME, ILS CAT I 04

	1970	1978
Passengers	235,697	636,139
Transport movements	5,875	21,077

Scheduled services 1978: Aeroméxico, Hughes Airwest and Méxicana

Tijuana, Baja California
Aeropuerto Internacional Abelardo L. Rodríguez

ICAO: MMTJ   IATA: TIJ
32° 32′ 44″ N   116° 58′ 57″ W   Elevation: 499 ft (152 m)
Longest runway: 09/27   2,500 m (8,202 ft)   ART   AVASI 09/27
Aids: VOR/DME, NDB

	1970	1978
Passengers	140,847	606,521
Transport movements	3,720	26,190

Scheduled services 1978: Aeroméxico only

The airport was opened on 1 May, 1951.

Morocco (Royaume du Maroc)

Agadir   Aéroport Inezgane   ICAO: GMAA   IATA: AGA

30° 23′ N   09° 33′ W   Elevation: 82 ft (25 m)
Longest runway: 11/29   2,910 m (9,547 ft)   RT
Aids: VOR/DME, ILS CAT I 29

	1970	1975	1976	1977
Passengers	88,372	309,225	323,739	383,161
Aircraft movements	4,514	9,073	10,628	10,976

Scheduled services 1978: Air France, Royal Air Inter and Royal Air Maroc

Casablanca   Aéroport de Casablanca - Nouasser*

33° 21′ 58″ N   07° 34′ 58″ W   16.19 nm (30 km) S of city
ICAO: GMMN   IATA code: CMN   Time zone: GMT
Authority: Ministère des Travaux Publics et des Communications–
    Direction de l'Air
Elevation: 656 ft (200 m)   Ref temp: 26 deg C
Runway: 17/35   3,720 × 45 m (12,205 × 148 ft) asphalt**
Pavement strength: 32,000 kg (70,548 lb) 1, 58,000 kg (127,868 lb) 2, 100,000 kg
    (220,462 lb) 3
Landing category: ICAO CAT II
Lighting:
  R/W   LIH white edge and centreline and red end lights. TDZ 35
  App   R/W 35   LIH Calvert coded centreline with five
           crossbars and red and white barrettes on inner 300 m (984
           ft). VASIS 17
  Thr   LIH green with wing bars
  Txy   blue edge
  Aids: VOR/DME, ILS CAT II 35
Twr frequency: 118.5/119.9   App frequency: 121.3
Terminals: Temporary terminal to east of runway with up to 16 aircraft
    stands. New passenger terminal and cargo terminal with three aircraft
    stands under construction
Scheduled services 1978: 21 airlines
Main base: Royal Air Inter and Royal Air Maroc

Traffic:	1970	1975	1976	1977
Passengers (total)	436,427	753,973	844,129	1,092,812
Cargo (tonnes)	7,729	13,785	16,004	16,716
Aircraft movements	13,910	17,636	17,212	19,545
Transport movements	11,219	14,795	16,177	17,056

* Formerly spelled Nouasseur

** First 350 m (1,148 ft) of 35 is concrete. Jet barrier each end

View of Casablanca - Nouasser looking south-southeast, with the control tower in the foreground and, beyond, the temporary passenger terminal.
(*Ministère des Travaux Publics et des Communications - Direction de l'Air*)

Casablanca's prewar airport was Cazes, 6 km (3.7 miles) southwest of the city beside the Casablanca–Mazagan road. It had a landing area of 1,200 m (3,937 ft) by 800 m (2,625 ft) but its surface was soft after heavy rain. After the war the airport continued to serve the city, was given a 1,826 m (5,990 ft) 03/21 asphalt runway and later named Casablanca - Anfa. However, Anfa could not be expanded to handle the growing traffic and new generations of jet aircraft, and in 1961 the Ministry of Public Works and Communications gave the Aéroport de Paris a contract to select a site for a new Moroccan international airport.

The USAF base south of the city was chosen for development. The 4,500 hectare (11,119 acre) site was handed over to the Moroccan Government in December 1963 and in 1965 planning began for a civil airport occupying about a third of it. Work began in 1967 with US financial assistance and included fencing the site, construction of administration, technical, passenger and cargo buildings, improvement of lighting and installation of ILS. The temporary terminal was designed to have an annual capacity of 600,000 passengers.

The new airport, Casablanca - Nouasser, was opened to traffic on 5 December, 1969, and Casablanca - Anfa was closed. During 1969–70 a maintenance base was built for Royal Air Maroc and in 1970 design work began on a permanent terminal building.

The temporary terminal had to be expanded to cope with the continuing traffic increase, and the apron was enlarged to provide stands for 10 Boeing 747s or 14 Boeing 707s or 16 Caravelles.

246

Casablanca's new terminal, which is scheduled to come into use in 1980, is a three-level curved building with a total area of 24,000 sq m (258,336 sq ft). It will be served by an elevated road, have its passenger handling area on the second level and provide boarding via five double aerobridges. The new terminal is sited 300 m (984 ft) north of the temporary terminal and has been designed to handle 3 mn passengers a year by 1985 and 4 mn in 1990.

Casablanca - Anfa was reopened in April 1970 to handle domestic services of the newly formed Royal Air Inter.

Rabat   Aéroport Salé   ICAO: GMME   IATA: RBA

34° 03′ 00″ N   06° 45′ 25″ W   Elevation: 276 ft (84 m)
Longest runway: 04/22   3,500 m (11,483 ft)   ART
Aids: VOR, ILS CAT I 04

	1970	1975	1976
Passengers	187,483	283,814	265,084
Aircraft movements	47,350	37,526	28,532

Scheduled services 1978: Aeroflot, Air France, Royal Air Inter and Royal Air Maroc

Tangier (Tanger)   Aéroport Boukhalf

ICAO: GMTT   IATA: TNG
35° 43′ 24″ N   05° 54′ 34″ W   Elevation: 62 ft (19 m)
Longest runway: 10/28   3,500 m (11,483 ft)   RT   VASI 10
Aids: VOR/DME, ILS 28

	1970	1975	1976	1977
Passengers	249,337	377,772	364,628	417,994
Aircraft movements	7,994	11,603	9,937	9,276

Scheduled services 1978: Air France, Gibraltar Airways, Iberia, Royal Air Inter, Royal Air Maroc and Sabena

Mozambique (Moçambique)

Beira   Aeroporto da Beira   ICAO: FQBR   IATA: BEW

19° 47′ 40″ S   34° 54′ 32″ E   Elevation: 33 ft (10 m)
Longest runway: 12/30   2,400 m (7,874 ft)   ART   VASI 12/30
Aids: VOR, NDB, ILS CAT I 12

	1970	1975	1976
Passengers	228,974	273,802	221,814
Transport movements	21,345	15,724	12,817

Scheduled services 1978: Air Malawi and DETA

Maputo (formerly Lourenço Marques)   Aeroporto Mavalane

ICAO: FQMA   IATA: LUM
25° 55′ 06″ S   32° 34′ 24″ E   Elevation: 131 ft (40 m)
Longest runway: 05/23   2,700 m (8,858 ft)   ART   VASI 05/23
Aids: VOR, NDB, ILS 23

	1970	1975	1976
Passengers	164,229	255,826	263,410
Transport movements	9,584	8,764	10,022

Scheduled services 1978: Aeroflot, DETA, South African Airways, TAP
  and Zambia Airways
Main base: DETA Mozambique Airlines

Nepal

Kathmandu   Kathmandu Airport (Tribhuvan)

ICAO: VNKT   IATA: KTM
27° 42′ 02″ N   85° 21′ 47″ E   Elevation: 4,386 ft (1,337 m)
Runway: 02/20   2,012 m (6,600 ft)   R   VASI 02
Aids: VOR, DME, L

	1976	1977
Passengers (terminal)	434,872	468,165
Transport movements	14,976	17,609

Scheduled services 1978: Bangladesh Biman, Burma Airways, Indian
  Airlines, Royal Nepal Airlines and Thai Airways International
Main base: Royal Nepal Airlines

Tribhuvan Airport, Kathmandu, with four of Royal Nepal Airlines' DC-3s. The
Asian Development Bank is financing a $20 mn improvement programme including
an international terminal and new control tower, scheduled for completion in 1983.
(*A. K. Tarafdar*)

The Netherlands (Nederland)

Amsterdam   Schiphol Airport (Luchthaven Schiphol)

52° 18′ 40″ N   04° 47′ 28″ E   4 nm (7.4 km) SW of city
ICAO: EHAM   IATA code: AMS   Time zone: GMT plus 1
Authority: Schiphol Airport Authority (NV Luchthaven Schiphol)
Area: 1,750 hectares (4,324 acres)
Elevation: −13 ft (−4 m)   Ref temp: 20 deg C
Runways: 01L/19R   3,300 × 45 m (10,827 × 148 ft) asphalt/concrete
         01R/19L   3,400 × 45 m (11,155 × 148 ft) asphalt/concrete
         06/24   3,250 × 45 m (10,663 × 148 ft) asphalt/concrete
         09/27   3,453 × 45 m (11,330 × 148 ft) asphalt/concrete
         Take offs only on 01L, 09, 19L and 24
         Landings only on 01R, 06, 19R and 27
Pavement strength: auw 350,000 kg (771,618 lb)
Landing category: ICAO CAT II*
Lighting:
    R/W   All runways—LIH white edge, last 600 m (1,968 ft) yellow,
            and white centreline, last 300 m (984 ft) red, previous 600 m
            (1,968 ft) red/white. TDZ 01R, 06, 19R and 27
    App   R/W 01R, 06, 19R and 27   LIH white bar centreline with
            two crossbars and flashers. Red barrettes on inner 270 m
            (886 ft)
    Thr   green
    Txy   blue edge, green centreline on high-speed exits and some
            taxiways
Aids: VORTAC, DME, NDB, VDF, SRE, TAR, ASDE, L, ILS CAT II
    01R, 06, 19R and 27
Twr frequency: 118.1   App frequency: 121.2
Terminals: Central passenger terminal with four traffic piers and 46–48
    aircraft stands with aerobridges. Separate cargo terminals. Space
    exists for second terminal with two piers
Scheduled services 1978: 61 airlines
Main base: KLM, Martinair and Transavia

Traffic:	1970	1975	1976	1977	1978
Passengers (total)	5,171,934	7,534,257	8,254,699	8,931,985	9,468,302
Cargo (tonnes)	172,323	226,324	256,464	274,397	269,960
Aircraft movements	135,520	173,267	176,423	183,834	187,960
Transport movements	105,466	129,543	132,216	136,329	143,156

During 1977 Douglas DC-9s accounted for 30.87 per cent of transport movements and DC-8s took second place with 7.8 per cent.

Although a small nation, the Netherlands has long held an outstanding reputation in three spheres of aviation: airline operation by KLM, aircraft manufacture by Fokker, and Amsterdam's Schiphol Airport.

* R/W 19R is to be upgraded to CAT III

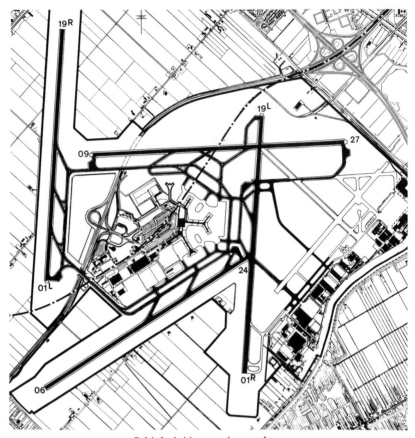

Schiphol Airport, Amsterdam.

The airport, only 4½ miles (7½ km) southwest of the city, is 13 ft (4 m) below sea level and built on land reclaimed from the Haarlemmermeer (Haarlem Lake) which used to cover about 18,200 hectares (some 45,000 acres). On 26 May, 1573, a naval battle between the Netherlands and Spain was fought on this lake. The extreme northeastern part of the lake was funnel shaped and during southwest gales it became so dangerous to shipping that it became known as Schipshol—a ship's hole or grave.

The lake was reclaimed in 1852 and turned into fertile polderland. After the reclamation, where Schipshol had been, a fort was built on a piece of land jutting into the ringvaart (ring canal) and was named Schiphol. In 1917 a military aerodrome was prepared, immediately west of the fort, an almost square field of 76 hectares (187 acres), and it had six wooden hangars in a row near the fort. It continued to bear the name Schiphol.

On 17 May, 1920, H. 'Jerry' Shaw landed Aircraft Transport & Travel's D.H.16 G-EALU at Schiphol, inaugurating a joint AT & T—KLM service over the London–Amsterdam route. From that time

Schiphol was developed as the Amsterdam airport, and it became the main base of KLM and Fokker's flight-test aerodrome.

A three-bay KLM hangar was built to the southwest of the six military hangars and later, at right angles to it, Fokker's hangar. On 1 April, 1926, operation of the airport was taken over by the City of Amsterdam and put under the management of the Municipal Sea and Airport Authority. The airport then took the name Gemeente Luchthaven Amsterdam (Amsterdam Municipal Airport) but has always been known more simply as Schiphol. Initially the passenger terminal was a small wooden hut beside the KLM hangar and when the Authority took over it laid a concrete apron in front of the hangar. By 1931 the apron area had been greatly enlarged and by 1935 there was a modern terminal.

Work then began on enlarging the airport to 210 hectares (519 acres) and the construction of concrete runways. The airport's landing area then measured 1,500 m (4,921 ft) from southeast to northwest and 1,200 m (3,937 ft) from southwest to northeast. By 1937 sections of two of the runways were completed and part of the taxiway system. Strangely, the runway thresholds and taxiways bore numbers which were painted on, underlined and followed by a full point. In the completed layout, the runway ends bore the numbers 1 to 8 and taxiways bore numbers with an A suffix.

The terminal area at Schiphol Airport, Amsterdam. The traffic piers are, left to right, C, B, A and D. The cargo terminal and apron are on the left, runway 01L/19R is in the distance and the 09 threshold is on the right. (*Aerophoto-Schiphol B.V.*)

251

Schiphol was the second European airport, after Bromma, to have paved runways and they were: 05/23 of 1,020 m (3,346 ft), 09/27 of 775 m (2,543 ft), 14/32 of 750 m (2,461 ft) and 18/36 of 850 m (2,789 ft). All runways were 40 m (131 ft) wide. The airport was equipped with radio and D/F stations, lighting including eight floodlights, and two approach lights near the 23 threshold.

In its last period before the German attack on 10 May, 1940, Schiphol was considered to be one of the world's best-equipped airports.

During the war the Germans extended runway 05/23 to 1,625 m (5,331 ft), 09/27 to 1,400 m (4,593 ft) and 14/32 to 1,275 m (4,183 ft), and built the southwest extension of 05/23 to a width of 80 m (262 ft). Taxiways were also constructed to connect the ends of the runways.

Repeated Allied air attacks did much damage but in September 1944, the German forces, before they retreated, destroyed all Schiphol's facilities. High priority was given to restoring the airport, the Municipality was assisted by the Royal Air Force, the Royal Engineers and US Air Transport Command and the first transport aircraft landed on 28 July, 1945. By that November all runways were serviceable again and from July operations had been conducted from a group of wooden barracks known as Liberty Street.

Runway 05/23 was extended to 2,150 m (7,054 ft), the extension being 60 m (197 ft) wide, and 09/27 was extended to 1,730 m (5,676 ft). A new 1,800 m (5,905 ft) 14/32 runway was built 410 m (1,345 ft) southwest of the original and opened in October 1948, the old 14/32 becoming a taxiway. In the autumn of 1948 work began on a 1,550 m (5,085 ft) 01/19 runway, this was opened in 1949 and soon extended to 1,800 m (5,905 ft).

A semi-permanent terminal was built, mainly single-storey but with three-storey central section. This was to undergo numerous extensions before it was finally replaced. A programme of large hangar building was put in hand and these were given names of aviation pioneers including Louis Blériot, Santos Dumont, Kingsford Smith, Orville and Wilbur Wright, Alcock and Brown and Jan Olieslagers. The Fokker hangar was named Anthony Fokker.

A government resolution of 8 October, 1945, had designated Schiphol as Netherlands World Airport and work began on planning its future development. The recommendations were published in February 1949. The aim in planning was to provide a pair of runways for each main wind direction, with one for take offs and one for landings. A number of layouts were produced including Plan 3T with four sets of parallel runways on one side of the terminal area and Plan 11B with four sets of parallel runways arranged around a central terminal complex. Both plans allowed for a ninth runway to the northwest of the Amsterdam–The Hague highway. These plans were found to have serious disadvantages and therefore a tangential layout was proposed with six runways of 1,800 m (5,905 ft) and later extension to 2,550 m (8,366 ft). It was also envisaged that there might ultimately be 10 runways.

The new 14/32 of 1948 represented the first of the tangential runways, followed by 01/19 (now 01R/19L). The existing 05/23 and 09/27 were to be abandoned eventually. 06/24 of 3,250 m (10,663 ft) was opened in April 1960, a new 09/27 of 3,453 m (11,330 ft) was opened in 1967, and 01L/19R of 3,300 m (10,827 ft) was opened in 1968, thus completing the modified tangential layout which was finally agreed. These developments increased the airport to its present size.

The design of the central terminal area called for a passenger terminal with 6 mn passengers a year capacity, and with space for a second when required; control tower; crew centre; catering buildings; cargo terminals; bonded warehouses; a hotel; line service facilities; car parks; and the national aviation museum. The whole complex to be surrounded by dual taxiways and served by an Amsterdam–Schiphol–The Hague railway. The plans necessitated diversion of the Amsterdam–The Hague National Highway No. 4, taking it beneath runway 09/27 in an 800 by 50 m (2,625 by 164 ft) tunnel.

Construction of the 274 hectares (677 acres) Central Terminal Area began on 15 June, 1963, the new terminal was officially opened by HM Queen Juliana on 26 April, 1967, and became operational that May.

The passenger terminal as originally built had an apron facade measuring 107 m (351 ft) and a depth of 100 m (328 ft). The ground floor was designed for arriving traffic and the first floor for departures. There were three piers with 25 aircraft positions each served by an aerobridge. Only the centre pier (B) was completed in 1967; it was Y-shaped and measured 255 m (837 ft) from the terminal to the Y junction and each branch was 115 m (377 ft) long. The south pier (C) was completed to a length of 270 m (886 ft) and the north pier (A) was 275 m (902 ft).

On 7 July, 1969, work began on extending pier C by 125 m (410 ft) and this was commissioned on 8 April, 1971, adding five stands for Boeing 747s. In August 1970 work began on expansion of the main terminal by extending its facade 17 m (56 ft) forward on the land side and the increased area came into use on 8 April, 1971. Work on northward extension of the terminal and construction of a northwest pier (D) with eight wide-bodied stands began in 1971/72, with completion in April 1975, bringing the number of gates to 42 and terminal capacity to 18 mn passengers annually. It is planned to extend pier A. Work on the railway connection began in 1974 and the Schiphol–Amsterdam South section was opened on 20 December, 1978.

It is expected that the second terminal, connected to the existing one, will be required by 1989 and this would bring capacity to about 35 mn passengers. Looking further ahead space has been provided for a second terminal area to the west of runway 01L/19R and it is also expected that a third north–south runway will be required. This would be built to the west and designated 01LL/19RR. It was originally thought that the fifth runway would be required by 1977 and that the second terminal area would be needed by about 1988 but the expected traffic growth did not materialize.

There had also been a suggestion that the Netherlands would require a second major international airport but a study completed early in 1979 has confirmed that Schiphol will have sufficient capacity to handle the country's international traffic for many years although the fifth runway may be required.

Rotterdam   Luchthaven Rotterdam

ICAO: EHRD   IATA: RTM
51° 57′ 25″ N   04° 26′ 14″ E   Elevation: −15 ft (−4.5 m)
Longest runway: 06/24 1,800 m (5,906 ft)   ART*   VASI 06/24
Aids: VOR/DME, NDB, VDF, L, ILS CAT I 24

	1970	1975	1976	1977
Passengers	489,525	326,887	315,856	287,526
Transport movements	12,487	7,654	8,043	8,639

Scheduled services 1978: Air France, British Air Ferries, British
    Caledonian Airways, British Island Airways, Íscargo HF, KLM,
    NLM and Sabena

*CAT II approach lights R/W 24

The Netherlands Antilles (Nederlandse Antillen)

Oranjestad, Aruba   Luchthaven Prinses Beatrix

ICAO: MACA   IATA: AUA
12° 30′ 15″ N   70° 00′ 44″ W   Elevation: 60 ft (18 m)
Runway: 11/29 2,743 m (9,000 ft)   RT   VASI 11, AVASI 29
Aids: VOR

	1970	1975
Passengers	282,063	524,688
Transport movements	10,815	9,702

Scheduled services 1978: Aerocondor, Aeropostal, ALM, American
    Airlines and KLM

Willemstad, Curaçao   Luchthaven Dr Albert Plesman

ICAO: MACC   IATA: CUR
12° 11′ 31″ N   68° 57′ 25″ W   Elevation: 27 ft (8 m)
Runway: 11/29 3,410 m (11,188 ft)   ART   VASI 11, AVASI 29
Aids: VOR/DME, NDB, SRE, ILS 11

	1970	1975	1976	1977
Passengers	469,500*	729,802	736,442	815,493
Transport movements	17,570	17,934	16,292	18,670

*Estimated

Scheduled services 1978: Aerocondor, Aeropostal, ALM, American
    Airlines, KLM, Surinam Airways and VIASA
Main base: ALM Antillean Airlines

Philipsburg, St Maarten   Luchthaven Prinses Juliana

	ICAO: MACM	IATA: SXM	
18° 02′ 23″ N	63° 06′ 43″ W		Elevation: 13 ft (4 m)
Runway: 09/27	2,150 m (7,054 ft)	RT*	VASI 09

* Lead-in lights R/W 27, take-off path lights R/W 09

Aids: NDB

	1970	1975	1976	1977
Passengers	203,999	359,424	437,791	423,301
Transport movements	26,210	19,458	23,510	25,812

Scheduled services 1978: Aero Virgin Islands, Air France, ALM, Caribbean Air Services, Eastern Air Lines, KLM, LIAT, Puerto Rico International Airlines and Windward Islands Airways
Main base: Windward Islands Airways International

New Zealand

Auckland, North Island   Auckland International Airport (Mangere)

37° 00′ 36″ S	174° 47′ 29″ E	9.5 nm (17.6 km) S of city
ICAO: NZAA	IATA code: AKL	Time zone: GMT plus 12/13

Owner: Auckland Regional Authority
Area: 547 hectares (1,352 acres)
Elevation: 23 ft (7 m)   Ref temp: 23.8 deg C
Runway: 05/23   3,292 × 46 m (10,800 × 150 ft) concrete
              The grass R/W 14/32 is no longer in use
Pavement strength: LCN 110
Landing category: ICAO CAT I
Lighting:
     R/W   LIH white edge and white variable intensity centreline
     App   LIH white coded centreline with five crossbars and LIL red centreline with two crossbars. T-VASIS 05/23
     Thr   green with wing bars
     Txy   blue edge, green centreline and green centreline on high-speed exits
Aids: VOR/DME, NDB, SRE, ILS CAT I 05/23
Twr frequency: 118.7   App frequency: 123.9/124.3
Terminals: Interim domestic and new international passenger terminals. Separate cargo area.
Scheduled services 1978: 10 airlines
Airline bases: Air New Zealand, and Pan American cargo facility
Main base: Air New Zealand (international operations)

Traffic:	1970	1975	1976–7	1978
Passengers (total)	708,565	1,812,648	1,772,330	2,279,059
Cargo (tonnes)	10,868	—	46,366	40,477
Aircraft movements	35,345	68,000	76,066	77,583
Transport movements	17,988	39,302	48,528	45,042

255

Auckland International Airport with the Air New Zealand base in the foreground and the terminal beyond.

Mangere was a 234 acre (95 hectare) grass aerodrome beside Manukau Harbour and its limitations caused the transfer of operations to the military aerodrome at Whenuapai in September 1947—many of New Zealand's long-distance services at that time being operated by flying-boats based at Mechanics Bay. But the Whenuapai site could not be developed to handle jet aircraft and in February 1961 work began on reconstruction of Mangere to international standards with an 8,500 ft (2,591 m) paved runway and the necessary lighting and navigational aids. The airport was reopened on 24 November, 1965, and officially opened by the Governor-General on 29 January, 1966.

The runway was extended to its present 10,800 ft (3,292 m) in 1973, a satellite crash/rescue station near the western end of the runway was completed in 1976, and a new international terminal was completed at the end of 1977. A unique feature of Auckland International Airport's rescue service is its SR N6 hovercraft, purchased in May 1969.

There are plans for a new domestic terminal when needed and for a new cargo terminal area to the west of the international terminal. Land has been protected for a second, parallel, runway.

Christchurch, South Island   Christchurch International Airport

43° 29′ 20″ S   172° 32′ 00″ E   5 nm (9.26 km) WNW of city
ICAO: NZCH   IATA code: CHC   Time zone: GMT plus 12/13
Owner: Christchurch Airport Authority
Area: 424 hectares (1,047 acres)
Elevation: 123 ft (37 m)   Ref temp: 22 deg C
Runways: 02/20   2,442 × 46 m (8,014 × 150 ft) bitumen
         11/29   1,737 × 46 m (5,700 × 150 ft) bitumen
Pavement strength: R/W 02/20 LCN 80; R/W 11/29 LCN 65
Landing category: ICAO CAT I
Lighting:
  R/W   02/20   LIH white edge
  App   R/W 02/20   LIH white centreline with five crossbars and
          LIL red centreline with two crossbars.
          R/W 11/29   LIL red centreline with one crossbar.
          T-VASIS 02/20 and 11/29
  Thr   02/20   green
  Txy   blue edge
Aids: VOR/DME, NDB, TAC, SRE, ILS CAT I 02/20
Twr frequency: 118.3   App frequency: 120.9/124.1
Terminal: Combined domestic and international terminal with nine
  domestic and two international aircraft stands. Separate hard-
  standings for light aircraft and aircraft supporting US Antarctic
  operations. There are two cargo terminals.

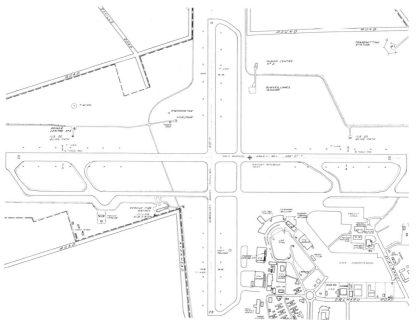

Christchurch International Airport.

257

Christchurch International Airport with the city in the distance.

Scheduled services 1978: Air New Zealand, Capital Air Services, Mount
  Cook Airlines and Qantas
Main base: Air New Zealand (domestic operations, formerly New Zealand
  National Airways Corporation) and Mount Cook Airlines

Traffic:	1970	1975	1976–7	1978
Passengers (total)	1,016,447	1,180,754	1,190,003	1,694,778
Cargo (tonnes)	24,982	25,000*	16,822	18,728
Aircraft movements	133,938	98,628	118,536	110,121
Transport movements	22,760	26,703	28,607	30,675

* Rounded figure

Before the Second World War Christchurch was served by the military
aerodrome at Wigram. A municipal airport had been planned at Harewood
and was completed in 1940 but taken over for the duration of the war by the
RNZAF.

The new airport was relatively small and grass surfaced but adequate
for DC-3s which operated most of the postwar New Zealand domestic air
services. Sealed runways and taxiways were completed in 1951 to permit
international operations by DC-4s and, later, DC-6s and Electras. In 1965
the main runway, 02/20, was lengthened from its original 6,614 ft (2,016 m)
to its present 8,014 ft (2,442 m) and strengthened to take Boeing 707s and
Douglas DC-8s. At the same time lighting and navigational aids were
improved.

It is planned that runway 02/20 will be extended to 3,660 m (12,008 ft),
the 20-year old terminal can be expanded to cope with increased traffic and
an extension is planned to handle international traffic.

Wellington North Island   Wellington International Airport

41° 19' 44" S   174° 48' 18" E   3 nm (5.5 km) SE of city centre
ICAO: NZWN   IATA code: WLG   Time zone: GMT plus 12/13
Owner: Wellington Airport Authority
Area: 88.6 hectares (219 acres)
Elevation: 40 ft (12 m)   Ref temp: 21.1 deg C
Runway: 16/34   1,935 × 46 m (6,350 × 150 ft) bitumen
              There is a parallel taxiway with numerous exits
Pavement strength: LCN 60
Landing category: ICAO CAT I
Lighting:
      R/W   LIH white edge, with TDZ each end
      App   T-VASIS and REIL each end
      Thr   green with wing bars
      Txy   blue edge, green centreline
Aids: VOR/DME, NDB, PAR, SRE, bi-directional CAT I ILS for offset
      approach to 16 and straight-in for 34
Twr frequency: 118.7/255.4   App frequency: 119.3/120.3
Terminal: Combined domestic and international terminal with covered
      walkways to 10 domestic and two international aircraft stands.
      Separate cargo areas.
Scheduled services 1978: Air New Zealand, Capital Air Services and
      Qantas
Airline bases: Air New Zealand (cargo and catering) and Safeair (cargo
      facility)

Traffic:	1970	1975	1976–7
Passengers (total)	1,239,371	1,360,504	1,295,005
Cargo (tonnes)	59,379	2,631*	11,049
Aircraft movements	73,354	106,578	84,753
Transport movements	46,101	50,521	53,330

* International only

View of Wellington International Airport from the 16 approach. The
name Wellington Airport appears in capital letters just short of the threshold.
(*Wellington Evening Post*)

259

A small grass aerodrome was built at Rongatai on the edge of the city in 1929. With some development this aerodrome was suitable for the aircraft in use up to the Second World War, but it was unsuitable for DC-3s and in September 1947 most services were transferred to the military aerodrome at Paraparaumu, some 30 miles (48 km) to the north of the city. As a result there was public demand for an airport closer to the city and it was decided to develop Rongatai by reclaiming land from the sea. The aerodrome was closed for reconstruction from 1 August, 1957, and a 5,750 ft (1,752 m) 16/34 runway was constructed, together with taxiways and hardstandings. A factory was converted to serve as the terminal and, with additions and alterations, this is still in service.

The reconstructed airport was officially opened on 20 July, 1959, and is essentially the same now except that in 1972 the runway was extended by 600 ft (183 m) to the south to enable Air New Zealand to replace its Electras with DC-8s.

The deep water of Cook Strait, just off the 34 threshold, and Evans Bay, just before the 16 threshold, makes it impossible to install approach lighting. In spite of terrain problems ILS localizer performance was found to be satisfactory and was brought into operation in 1972.

A new multi-level terminal is due for completion in 1982 and one of the two-level piers is to be used as an international terminal to relieve congestion at the existing building. This decision has increased construction costs and therefore international traffic will not be transferred from the North West Pier to the new terminal until additional space is required.

Further development of the airport is hampered by lack of available land, particularly in the terminal area. Contrary to expectations ILS glide path facilities have proved possible and will be provided on both approaches. Marker beacons cannot be sited but DME can serve as a substitute. Consideration is being given to lengthening the runway.

Nicaragua

Managua   Aeropuerto Internacional Agusto Cesar Sandino

ICAO: MNMG		IATA: MGA	
12° 08′ 30″ N	86° 10′ 24″ W		Elevation: 195 ft (59 m)
Runway: 09/27	2,438 m (8,000 ft)	RT	VASI 09
Aids: VOR/DME, NDB			

	1970	1975	1976
Passengers	174,157	269,635	232,500*
Transport movements	9,785	10,819	12,000*

* Estimated

Scheduled services 1978: Aviateca, COPA, Iberia, LANICA, Pan
American, SAHSA, Sociedad Aeronáutica de Medellín and TACA
International
Main base: LANICA
The name was changed from Aeropuerto de Las Mercedes in 1979

Nigeria

Kano   Kano Airport   ICAO: DNKK   IATA: KAN

12° 02′ 57″ N   08° 31′ 30″ E   Elevation: 1,565 ft (477 m)
Longest runway: 06/24   3,300 m (10,827 ft)   ART   VASI 05/23
Aids: VOR/DME, NDB, VDF, L, ILS CAT I 05

	1970
Passengers	182,233
Transport movements	7,059

Scheduled services 1978: Aeroflot, British Caledonian Airways, Egyptair,
KLM, Nigeria Airways, Sabena, Sudan Airways and UTA.

Runway 06/24 became operational on 17 October, 1978, for daylight
VMC only. For the 06 direction there are LIH white runway edge lights,
green threshold lights, and LIH white coded-centreline and crossbar
approach lights.

Lagos   Murtala Mohammed Airport

            ICAO: DNLL   IATA: LOS
06° 35′ 26″ N   03° 19′ 46″ E   Elevation: 135 ft (41 m)
Runway: 01/19   2,743 m (9,000 ft)   ART
Aids: VOR/DME, NDB, L, ILS 01

	1970
Passengers	379,288
Transport movements	1,720

Scheduled services 1978: 25 airlines
Main base: Nigeria Airways

Formerly Ijeka International, the airport was renamed in 1976. A new
3,900 m (12,795 ft) 01/19 runway is planned and the existing runway is to be
extended to 3,650 m (11,975 ft)

Norway (Norge)

Ålesund   Vigra Lufthavn   ICAO: ENAL   IATA: AES

62° 33′ 40″ N   06° 06′ 51″ E   Elevation: 71 ft (22 m)
Runway: 07/25   1,600 m (5,249 ft)   ART   VASI 25
Aids: VOR/DME, NDB, VDF, ILS 25

	1970	1975	1976
Passengers	586,700*	754,200*	836,400*
Transport movements	8,143	11,324	11,906

* Rounded figures

Scheduled services 1978: Braathens SAFE and Widerøe's Flyveselskap

Bergen   Flesland Lufthavn

60° 17′ 38″ N   05° 13′ 11″ E   6.5 nm (12 km) SW of city
ICAO: ENBR   IATA code: BGO   Time zone: GMT plus 1
Authority: Civil Aviation Administration (Luftfartsverket)
Elevation: 165 ft (50 m)   Ref temp: 16.3 deg C
Runway: 18/36   2,450 × 45 m (8,038 × 148 ft)* asphalt
Pavement strength: LCN 118
Landing category: ICAO CAT I
Lighting:
    R/W   LIH white edge. Red end lights. Edge lights and wing bars
            on stopways
    App   R/W 18   LIH white centreline with three crossbars.
            R/W 36   LIH short centreline and crossbar. VASIS
                  18/36
    Thr   green
    Txy   blue edge
Aids: VORTAC, NDB, VDF, RVR, ILS CAT I 18
Twr frequency: 119.1/122.1   App frequency: 121.0
Terminal: Small passenger terminal to east of parallel taxiway, with 10
    aircraft stands. Nose-in parking with AGNIS at seven positions
Scheduled services 1978: Air Anglia, Braathens SAFE, Danair, Dan-Air
    Services, SAS and Widerøe's Flyveselskap

Traffic:	1970	1975	1976	1977
Passengers (total)	716,019	848,543	991,800	1,076,200
Cargo (tonnes)	2,542	3,517	3,827	4,029
Aircraft movements	31,448	37,148	41,220	45,736
Transport movements	17,183	21,506	22,988	25,103

* Braking wires on south end on stopway 11 m (36 ft) and 46 m (151 ft) south of
threshold

From the early days of Norwegian air transport Bergen was served by
seaplanes and flying-boats operating from the picturesque Sandviken base,
within a short walk of Bergen's tramway system. The surrounding terrain

made provision of a land airport apparently impossible, and this was NATO's conclusion after studying the area; but Norwegians do not easily give up and eventually it was decided to build an airport to the southwest of the city.

The site chosen at Flesland consisted of a mixture of rocks, hillocks, swamp and forest. Trees were felled, valleys filled and rocks blasted—some 16 mn cu ft of rock and more than 9 mn cu ft of earth being moved. A runway was constructed, considerably higher than the terrain immediately to the west and in 1955 the airport was opened for traffic, after which scheduled flying-boat services ceased.

The airport is on a difficult site with hills to the east rising to 843 m (2,765 ft) at just over 10 nm (18.5 km) and an island nearly 366 m (1,200 ft) high immediately to the west. There is a 137 m (450 ft) hill between the ILS outer and middle markers.

Turbulence is common in moderate winds, there are severe down-draughts on the final approach to 18 during crosswinds and some of the worst icing conditions in Europe can exist in the climb and descent area to the east of the airport.

Although the runway is a masterpiece of engineering and has proved suitable for aircraft up to DC-8 category, it is far from level. The 270 m (886 ft) stopway before the 18 threshold slopes down towards the threshold at 1.5 per cent. The runway continues this drop from 165 ft (50 m) at the threshold to its lowest point of 139 ft (42 m) in a distance of 880 m (2,887 ft). It then climbs to 152 ft (46 m) in 605 m (1,985 ft), reaches 154 ft (47 m) in another 360 m (1,181 ft) from where it descends to 150 ft (46 m) in 380 m (1,247 ft) and 225 m (738 ft) further on has an elevation of 147 ft (45 m) at the 36 threshold beyond which the stopway drops at 0.5 per cent over 130 m (426 ft) before climbing at 1.5 per cent over the remaining 140 m (459 ft). There is also an up slope on the taxiway to the apron and on the apron.

In spite of its terrain and its weather, Flesland has an admirable safety record, and Bergen now has a place in the world air transport system which it could never have achieved with marine aircraft.

Flesland Airport, Bergen, during construction. (*John Stroud*)

263

Bodø   Bodø Lufthavn   ICAO: ENBO   IATA: BOO

67° 16′ 09″ N   14° 22′ 20″ E   Elevation: 42 ft (13 m)
Runway: 08/26   2,793 m (9,163 ft)   ART   VASI 26
Aids: VOR/DME, VDF, SRE, PAR, GCA, ILS CAT I 08

	1970	1975	1976	1978
Passengers	119,900*	214,700*	225,900*	515,906
Transport movements	10,681	18,387	19,813	—

* Rounded figures

Scheduled services 1978: Braathens SAFE, SAS and Widerøe's Flyveselskap

Kristiansand   Kjevik Lufthavn   ICAO: ENCN   IATA: KRS

58° 12′ 22″ N   08° 05′ 19″ E   Elevation: 57 ft (17 m)
Runway: 04/22   1,900 m (6,234 ft)   ART   VASI 04/22
Aids: VOR/DME, NDB, VDF, ILS CAT I 04

	1970	1975	1976	1978
Passengers	143,200*	301,400*	226,900*	378,495
Transport movements	9,672	10,634	10,448	—

* Rounded figures

Scheduled services 1978: Braathens SAFE, Dan-Air Services and SAS

Oslo   Fornebu Lufthavn

59° 53′ 46″ N   10° 37′ 07″ E   4.3 nm (8 km) SW of city
ICAO: ENFB   IATA code: OSL   Time zone: GMT plus 1
Authority: Civil Aviation Administration (Luftfartsverket)
Elevation: 54 ft (16 m)   Ref temp: 19.6 deg C
Runways: 01/19   1,750 × 50 m (5,741 × 164 ft) asphalt
       06/24   2,200 × 50 m (7,218 × 164 ft) asphalt
Pavement strength: LCN 90
Landing category: ICAO CAT I
Lighting:
  R/W   01   LIH and LIL white edge; 19   LIL white edge;
      06/24   LIH and LIL edge and centreline, colour-coded first 1,300 m (4,265 ft) white, 600 m (1,968 ft) white/red and last 300 m (984 ft) red
  App   R/W 01   LIH and LIL centreline with four crossbars
      R/W 19   LIL centreline with two crossbars
      R/W 06   LIH and LIL centreline with three crossbars on Torvöya, and a fourth bar on mainland
      R/W 24   LIH and LIL centreline with three crossbars. VASIS 01 and 06/24
  Thr   green wing bars all thresholds
  Txy   blue edge lights, yellow on turns
      There are circling lights NNE of threshold 19

Aids: VOR/DME, NDB, L, VDF, TAR, ILS 01 and 06
Twr frequency: 118.1   App frequency: 120.8
Terminal: On east side of airport with three remote gates and 20 aircraft
  stands
Scheduled services 1978: 11 airlines
Airline bases: Braathens SAFE Air Transport, Helikopter Service A/S,
  SAS and Steller Airfreighter

Traffic:	1970	1975	1976	1977	1978
Passengers (total)	2,096,847	2,678,558	2,991,819	3,221,233	3,487,915
Cargo (tonnes)	16,381	23,481	24,298	26,448	26,031
Aircraft movements	91,370	80,664	89,066	93,972	—
Transport movements	53,871	50,525	52,518	55,770	38,927

In 1975 DC-9s accounted for 56.66 per cent of transport movements, Boeing 737s for
17.91 per cent, Fokker F.28s for 10.33 per cent and Caravelles for 3.2 per cent.

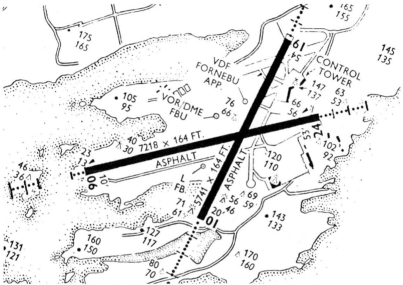

Fornebu Airport, Oslo. (*British Airways Aerad*)

Norway's terrain made the construction of land airports both difficult
and costly, and so most early Norwegian air services were operated by
seaplanes. The need for an airport for the Norwegian capital was
recognized as early as 1919 but it was not until 1934 that the City Council
decided to build one at Fornebu, adjacent to the seaplane station.

Work on Oslo Airport began in October 1934 and 8,700,000 cu m
(307,237,890 cu ft) of rock had to be removed from the airport area and a
further 50,000 cu m (1,765,735 cu ft) removed to provide adequate
approaches. The plan called for three runways in the initial phase—
north–south and northeast–southwest each of 800 m (2,625 ft) and
northwest–southeast of 700 m (2,296 ft). In the final stage a fourth runway
was to be constructed and all runways were to be at least 1,000 m (3,281 ft)
long. Work on the runways began in October 1937 and a start was made on
erecting a terminal and hangar.

265

Fornebu Airport, Oslo, in the early 1950s. The aircraft on the apron is an SAS Saab Scandia. (*SAS*)

On 1 June, 1939, Fornebu was opened for traffic but it was to see less than a year's operation before the Luftwaffe's Junkers-Ju 52/3ms landed there as part of the German invasion forces. After the war the airport resumed its civil role although for several years DNL's Oslo–Tromsø services were worked by Short Sandringham flying-boats operating from the adjacent seaplane base—this was dictated by the lack of airports north of Trondheim.

By skilful engineering Fornebu has been enlarged to an almost unbelievable extent and still serves as the Oslo Airport; the second airport, Gardermoen, being used for diversions, charters and general aviation.

Oslo   Gardermoen Lufthavn   ICAO: ENGM   IATA: GEN

60° 12′ 10″ N   11° 05′ 08″ E   Elevation: 670 ft (204 m)
Runway: 01/19   2,553 m (8,376 ft)   ART
Aids: NDB, VDF, PAR, ILS CAT I 19

	1975	1976	1977	1978
Passengers	316,517	348,143	410,451	451,558
Transport movements	3,942	3,988	5,499	—

No scheduled services

Stavanger   Sola Lufthavn

58° 52′ 52″ N   05° 37′ 52″ E   6 nm (11 km) SW of city
ICAO: ENZV   IATA code: SVG   Time zone: GMT plus 1
Authority: Civil Aviation Administration (Luftfartsverket)
Elevation: 29 ft (9 m)   Ref temp: 15.6 deg C
Runways: 11/29   2,200 × 45 m (7,218 × 148 ft) asphalt*
     18/36   2,550 × 60 m (8,366 × 197 ft) asphalt

* R/W 11 first 500 m (1,640 ft) concrete

Pavement strength: 11/29 LCN 60; 18/36 LCN 80
Landing category: ICAO CAT I
Lighting:

R/W   11/29   LIH white edge; 18/36 LIH and LIL white edge

App   R/W 11   LIH and LIL white centreline and crossbar

R/W 29   LIH and LIL white centreline with three crossbars

R/W 18   LIH and LIL white centreline with two crossbars and sequenced flashers

R/W 36   LIH and LIL white centreline with three crossbars

VASIS 11/29 and 18/36

Thr   LIH green

Txy   edge lights

Aids: VORTAC, DME, NDB, VDF, UDF, L, TAR, SRE, PAR, GCA 11 and 18/36, ILS CAT I 11 and 18

Twr frequency: 118.1/118.35/122.1   App frequency: 119.4/119.6

Terminal: Passenger terminal at north of airport, west of R/W 18/36

Scheduled services 1978: Air Anglia, Braathens SAFE, British Airways, Dan-Air Services, KLM and SAS

Traffic:	1970	1975	1976	1977
Passengers (total)	484,787	766,978	773,164	1,007,388
Cargo (tonnes)	1,180	2,438	3,085	4,372
Aircraft movements	35,322	59,789	66,979	78,908
Transport movements	15,809	18,843	22,681	23,845

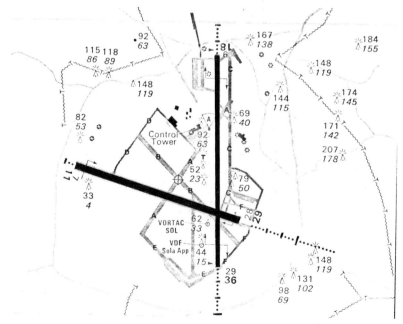

Sola Airport, Stavanger. (*British Airways Aerad*)

Construction of Stavanger's Sola Airport began early in 1936 on 60 hectares (148 acres) of land immediately south of Hafrsfjord and east of Sola Bay, and another 25 hectares (61 acres) was reserved for future development. Two concrete runways, northeast–southwest (04/22) of 870 m (2,854 ft) and northwest–southeast (14/32) of 995 m (3,264 ft), were built as well as a hangar, workshops and terminal, and there were obstruction lights, boundary lights, runway edge and threshold lights and landing area floodlights. Lorenz instrument landing system was planned as an early installation. A seaplane base was built at the southern end of Hafrsfjord and connected to the airport terminal by a 900 m (2,953 ft) road.

It was planned that Sola should be opened in time for Allied Airways (Gandar Dower) to open its Newcastle–Stavanger service on 19 April, 1937, but there was a slight delay and the inaugural service was flown on 12 July by the D.H.86B G-AETM *The Norseman*.

Sola was among the first European airports with paved runways, but it was to see less than three years' civil operation before being occupied by German forces on 9 April, 1940. The airport became an important Luftwaffe base and was severely bombed by the Royal Air Force. Luftflotte 5 and X Fliegerkorps had their headquarters at Sola and on Adler Tag (Eagle Day), 13 August, 1940, KG 26 with Heinkel He 111s and ZG 76 with Messerschmitt Bf 110s were based at Sola, JG 77 had some of its Bf 109Es there, and there were several reconnaissance units with Do 17Ps, Do 215s, He 111s and Ju 88s. Coastal Group 506 had its Heinkel He 115 seaplanes on Hafrsfjord. Later, Sola was to be a base for Focke-Wulf Fw 200 Condors operating against Atlantic shipping.

Details of wartime and immediate postwar development have not

Sola Airport, Stavanger, with a Braathens SAFE Boeing 737.
(*Braathens SAFE Air Transport*)

268

been discovered, but by 1947 runway 04/22 had been extended to 2,000 m (6,562 ft), 14/32 to 1,800 m (5,905 ft), and the 1,700 m (5,577 ft) 11/29 runway had been built. By the end of 1949 the new 01/19 (now 18/36) runway had been built, with a length of 2,550 m (8,366 ft), and 11/29 had been extended to 2,420 m (7,940 ft). All runways then had edge lighting, and there was approach lighting to all runways except 11, the threshold of which was only about 100 m (328 ft) from the shore of Sola Bay.

Runway 11/29 was known as the Atlantic Runway and it was thought that Stavanger would play an important role in North Atlantic air transport, but the importance of Copenhagen's Kastrup as the Scandinavian junction airport combined with increased aircraft range deprived Sola of its opportunity. However, in recent years Sola has experienced a traffic boom as a result of the discovery and exploitation of North Sea oil and gas. Sola is also an important NATO base.

Sola's seaplane base is no longer used by scheduled services, but until the opening of Bergen Airport in 1955 VLS operated Short Sealand flying-boats over the Sola–Haugesund–Bergen route.

Runways 04/22 and 14/32 have been withdrawn from use and form part of the taxiway system. Strict noise abatement rules are in force and runway 11 is the preferential runway for landings after 22.00 hr. There is arrester gear inset from each threshold.

Tromsø   Langnes Lufthavn   ICAO: ENTC   IATA: TOS

69° 40′ 53″ N   18° 55′ 10″ E   Elevation: 29 ft (9 m)
Runway: 01/19   2,000 m (6,562 ft)   ART   VASI 01/19
Aids: VOR, DME, NDB, VDF, ILS 19

	1970	1975	1976	1978
Passengers	87,800*	214,100*	242,200*	439,351
Transport movements	4,884	10,724	11,373	—

* Rounded figures

Scheduled services 1978: Braathens SAFE, SAS and Widerøe's Flyveselskap
The airport was opened on 4 September, 1964.

Trondheim   Vaernes Lufthavn   ICAO: ENVA   IATA: TRD

63° 27′ 29″ N   10° 55′ 33″ E   Elevation: 55 ft (17 m)
Longest runway: 09/27   2,365 m (7,759 ft)   ART   VASI 27
Aids: NDB, DME, VDF

	1970	1975	1976	1978
Passengers	322,300*	448,600*	491,500*	633,220
Transport movements	13,846	15,907	14,947	—

* Rounded figures

Scheduled services 1978: Braathens SAFE, SAS and Widerøe's Flyveselskap

Sultanate of Oman

Muscat   Seeb International Airport

ICAO: OOMS   IATA: MCT
23° 35′ 30″ N   58° 16′ 45″ E   Elevation: 43 ft (13 m)
Longest runway: 08/26   3,050 m (10,000 ft)   ART   VASI 08/26
Aids: VOR/DME, NDB, ILS CAT I 26

	1975	1976	1977
Passengers	264,378	323,704	498,541
Transport movements	8,573	9,420	9,963

Scheduled services 1978: 15 airlines
     The airport opened for commercial traffic in September 1972 and was officially opened on 23 December, 1973

Pakistan

Islamabad   Islamabad Airport (formerly Rawalpindi - Chaklala)

ICAO: OPRN   IATA: RWP
33° 37′ 02″ N   73° 05′ 57″ E   Elevation: 1,665 ft (507 m)
Runway: 12/30   2,743 m (9,000 ft)   ART
Aids: VOR, NDB, ILS CAT I 30

	1970–71	1974–5	1975–6	1977
Passengers	268,205	468,536	608,442	784,593
Transport movements	6,596	10,607	13,275	16,859

Scheduled services 1978: British Airways and PIA

Karachi   Karachi Airport

24° 54′ 05″ N   67° 09′ 00″ E   8.64 nm (16 km) ENE of city
ICAO: OPKC   IATA code: KHI   Time zone: GMT plus 5
Authority: Department of Civil Aviation
Area: 518 hectares (1,280 acres)
Elevation: 100 ft (30 m)   Ref temp: 34.8 deg C
Runways: 07L/25R   3,200 × 46 m (10,500 × 150 ft) concrete
          07R/25L   2,286 × 46 m (7,500 × 150 ft) bitumen
Pavement strength: 07L/25R LCN 83; 07R/25L 7 tons/sq ft (76.5 tonnes/
     sq m)
Landing category: ICAO CAT I

Lighting:
R/W   07L/25R   white edge
App   R/W 25R   LIH white centreline with crossbars
Thr   R/W 07L/25R   green
Txy   edge
Aids: VOR/DME, NDB, ASR, ILS CAT I 25R
Twr frequency: 118.3   App frequency: 121.3/123.7
Terminals: Passenger terminal with single-level handling and 17 aircraft
    bays (10 remote) and Gulf terminal
Scheduled services 1978: 29 airlines
Main base: Pakistan International Airlines

Traffic:	1970–71	1974–75	1975–76	1977
Passengers (total)	862,942	1,434,670	1,762,568	2,422,349
Cargo (tonnes)	13,236	31,487	37,415	45,428
Aircraft movements	48,044	49,357	70,703	—
Transport movements	20,995	23,496	27,194	30,388

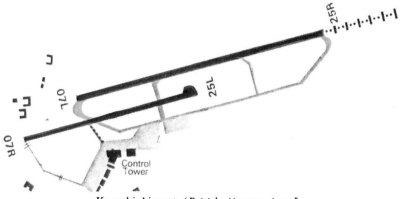

Karachi Airport. (*British Airways Aerad*)

Karachi, then in India, was the terminus for the England–India air
service when it was inaugurated with the first departure from Croydon on
30 March, 1929. It is believed that initially Imperial Airways used the RAF
station at Drigh Road, but by 1929 preparations were in hand, on a site
further east, to build the Karachi Airship Base. A 201 ft (61 m) high airship
shed was built just north of the main road and railway, and about 2,400 ft
(731 m) further north a 203 ft (62 m) high mooring mast was erected.

The large hangar and the mast were ready to receive the R101 at the
end of its flight from Cardington in October 1930, but the airship crashed in
France and no airship service was operated. The mast was never used but
the hangar served Imperial Airways Handley Page 42s and A.W.XV
Atalantas and was only dismantled, because it was dangerous, in 1961.

A landing ground for aeroplanes was prepared slightly north of the
airship base and this measured 2,700 ft (823 m) by 2,700 ft. Hangars were
erected and there was a small Customs building. The landing ground was
subsequently extended and on 5 December, 1938, the Governor of Sind
opened a permanent terminal building which had a circular central hall and

Karachi Airport terminal, with the PIA maintenance base on the right. (*Boeing*)

two wing sections. With modifications, this building is still in use after 40 years.

The airport was still further expanded to the east and a paved runway laid. Its date of construction and original length have not been traced but during the 1950s it had a length of 7,500 ft (2,286 m). This 07/25 runway was inadequate for heavy jet aircraft and in 1960 or 1961 a parallel 10,500 ft (3,200 m) runway was constructed to its north.

In 1965 the Department of Civil Aviation and PIA produced a master plan for a new terminal but action is still awaited and in 1978, to ease congestion, PIA constructed Terminal Two to handle Gulf traffic. Situated southeast of the 1938 terminal, it is a single-storey prefabricated structure 427 ft (130 m) in length. It has two departure lounges, one for 577 passengers and the other for 50 first class passengers, can serve four wide-bodied aircraft simultaneously, cost Rs 10 mn, and has been built to last 60 years.

The preliminary design for the new main terminal is a two-storey building with two traffic piers and 17 aircraft stands, passenger handling to be on the upper level.

Lahore	Lahore Airport	ICAO: OPLA	IATA: LHE

31° 31′ 17″ N   74° 24′ 09″ E   Elevation: 700 ft (213 m)
Runway: 18/36   2,743 m (9,000 ft)   ART   VASI 18/36
Aids: VOR, NDB, ILS CAT I 36

	1970–71	1974–75	1975–76	1977
Passengers	373,548	478,365	581,471	698,464
Transport movements	7,374	8,437	10,234	11,893

Scheduled services 1978: Indian Airlines and Pakistan International Airlines

República de Panamá

Panamá City   Aeropuerto Internacional de Tocumen

09° 04' 55" N   79° 22' 52" W   8 nm (14.8 km) NE of city
ICAO: MPTO   IATA code: PTY   Time zone: GMT −5
Authority: Dirección de Aeronáutica Civil
Elevation: 135 ft (41 m)   Ref temp: 28 deg C
Runways: 03L/21R   2,682 × 61 m   (8,800 × 200 ft) concrete
         03R/21L   3,050 × 45 m (10,006 × 148 ft) concrete
Pavement strength: 03L/21R LCN 44;   03R/21L LCN 100
Landing category: ICAO CAT I
Lighting:
   R/W   LIH white edge, last 600 m (1,968 ft) yellow. End lights.
           REIL 21R
   App   R/W 03L and 03R   LIH white bar centreline with
           crossbar
           VASIS 03L/21R and 03R/21L
   Thr   green
   Txy   blue edge
Aids: VOR/DME, NDB, L, SRE, ILS CAT I 03R
Twr frequency: 118.1   App frequency: 119.7/120.8
Terminals: International terminal with two piers and satellite buildings and
   12 aircraft stands. Separate domestic terminal. Cargo complex at
   north of airport.
Scheduled services 1978: 21 airlines
Main base: Air Panamá International, COPA and Inair

Traffic:	1970	1975	1976	1977
Passengers (total)	745,253	900,059	973,488	1,094,369
Cargo (tonnes)	27,400*	29,977	42,134	41,311
Aircraft movements	——	29,938	32,749	32,633
Transport movements	24,943	21,243	22,418	23,014

* Rounded figure

Tocumen International Airport, which serves Panamá City and
Balboa, is close to the south coast and in a mountainous area, and it came
into operation in the early 1950s as the replacement for the prewar Paitilla
Airport which was nearer to the city.

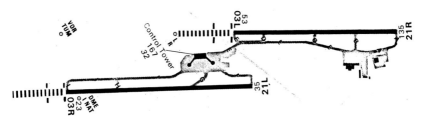

Tocumen International Airport, Panamá City. (*British Airways Aerad*)

The new runway and terminal at Tocumen International Airport, Panamá City.
(*Dirección de Aeronáutica Civil*)

The new airport had a single 03/21 runway of 2,134 m (7,000 ft). This was subsequently lengthened to 2,682 m (8,800 ft) and had a parallel taxiway leading to the passenger terminal and cargo zone at the northeast end of the airport.

Panamá occupies an important position on air routes between North and South America, and to meet traffic demands a feasibility study for the airport's expansion was prepared in 1969. The decision was taken to build a second runway and new terminal complex which virtually amounted to building a new airport adjacent to the original one. The project was financed with the help of the World Bank, and the first construction work began on 10 October, 1971. Tenders for the passenger terminal were invited in the second half of 1974.

The 'new airport' was completed on 15 August, 1978, the new terminal and 3,050 m (10,006 ft) 03R/21L runway came into service on 5 September, 1978, and the old runway was redesignated 03L/21R.

The new international terminal is a three-storey building built on the hyperbolic paraboloid principle. The elevated entrance road is covered for most of the length of the terminal and resembles a large arcade. From the apron-side corners of the building, traffic fingers project to two circular satellite buildings, with five aerobridges at Satellite A (south) and three at Satellite B (north). There are three gates with aerobridges in the apron face of the building. Close to the southern end of the main terminal is a small domestic terminal.

The old terminal at the north of the airport is now a cargo centre.

Papua New Guinea

Lae   Nadzab Airport   ICAO: AYNZ   IATA: LAE

06° 43′ 02″ S   146° 43′ 29″ E   Elevation: 230 ft (70 m)
Runway: 09/27   2,438 m (7,998 ft)   R   T-VASI 09/27
Aids: VOR, DME, L

	1970	1972
Passengers*	180,360	216,794
Transport movements*	10,659	12,406

* Traffic figures for the original Lae Airport

Scheduled services 1978: Air Niugini, Douglas Airways, Panga Airways
    and Talair

An Air Niugini Fokker F.28 at Nadzab Airport, Lae, at the end of 1977.
(Air Niugini)

Port Moresby   Jacksons Airport   ICAO: AYPY   IATA: POM

09° 26′ 38″ S   147° 12′ 57″ E   Elevation: 126 ft (38 m)
Longest runway: 14L/32R   2,745 m (9,006 ft)   ART VASI 14L/32R
Aids: VOR, DME, NDB, L, ILS 32L and 32R

	1973	1975
Passengers*	388,490	402,248
Transport movements	26,677	25,504

* Transit passengers excluded

Scheduled services 1978: Air Niugini, Air Pacific, Douglas Airways,
    Philippine Air Lines, Qantas and Talair
    Runway 14L/32R is to be extended to 2,900 m (9,514 ft)

Paraguay

Asunción   Aerodromo Internacional Presidente General Stroessner

ICAO: SGAS   IATA: ASU
25° 14′ 21″ S   57° 31′ 09″ W   Elevation: 292 ft (89 m)
Runway: 02/20   3,353 m (11,000 ft)   RT   AVASI 20
Aids: VOR, NDB, L

	1970	1975	1976
Passengers	143,000	235,400*	215,800*
Transport movements	27,386	13,900*	13,600*

* Estimated figures excluding transit passengers

Scheduled services 1978: 10 airlines
Main base: Líneas Aéreas Paraguayas

Perú

Lima - Callão   Aeropuerto Internacional Jorge Chávez

12° 01′ 06″ S   77° 06′ 44″ W   8.6 nm (16 km) NW of city
ICAO: SPIM   IATA code: LIM   Time zone: GMT −5
Authority: CORPAC
Elevation: 105 ft (32 m)   Ref temp: 23.3 deg C
Runway: 15/33   3,507 × 45 m (11,506 × 148 ft) concrete
Pavement strength: auw 160,000 kg (352,740 lb)
Landing category: ICAO CAT I
Lighting:
    R/W   LIH white edge (last 600 m/1,968 ft yellow) and centreline.
            TDZ 15
    App   R/W 15   LIH white bar centreline and crossbar
    Thr   15 green, 33 green with strobes
    Txy   blue edge
Aids: VOR/DME, NDB, L, ILS CAT I 15
Twr frequency: 118.3   App frequency: 118.1
Terminal: Passenger terminal with two traffic piers and 13 aircraft stands
Scheduled services 1978: 20 airlines
Main base: Aeronaves del Perú, AeroPerú and Cia de Aviación Faucett

Traffic:	1970	1975	1976	1977
Passengers (total)	1,168,319	2,174,457	2,423,663	1,973,364
Cargo (tonnes)	17,406	34,944	27,026	31,773
Aircraft movements	29,688	42,770	44,265	43,731
Transport movements	25,046	35,100	36,635	35,196

Jorge Chávez International Airport is situated by the coast close to Callão, the seaport for Lima. Only a few miles to the east are the foothills of

The terminal, administration block and control tower at Jorge Chávez International Airport, Lima. On the apron are two of AeroPerú's DC-8-50s. (*Courtesy Günter Endres*)

the Andes. The airport's single runway has a full-length parallel taxiway with three high-speed exits, there is a large apron to the east and a passenger terminal with two traffic fingers. Take offs from runway 15 are restricted between 24.00 and 12.00 unless the wind component exceeds 10 kt (18.5 km/h) from the south.

The previous Lima airport was Lima - Tambo situated about 7 miles (11 km) to the southeast and at an elevation of 445 ft (136 m). In the late 1940s and early 1950s Tambo had a north-northeast–south-southwest runway of 1,982 m (6,504 ft) and north-northwest–south-southeast runway of 1,796 m (5,894 ft). It is now used for general aviation.

Republic of the Philippines

Lapu-Lapu, Cebu   Mactan International Airport

10° 18′ 48″ N   123° 58′ 58″ E   4.3 nm (8 km) from city
ICAO: RPMT   IATA code: NOP   Time zone: GMT plus 8
Authority: Civil Aeronautics Administration
Elevation: 34 ft (10 m)   Ref temp: 29.6 deg C
Runway: 04/22   2,591 × 45 m (8,500 × 148 ft) concrete
Pavement strength: all up weight 45,000 kg (99,208 lb) single wheel, 84,000 kg (185,188 lb) dual wheel, 159,000 kg (350,535 lb) bogie
Landing category: ICAO CAT I

Lighting:
- R/W   white and yellow edge, and end lights
- App   R/W 04   LIH white bar centreline with crossbar. AVASIS 04/22
- Thr   green
- Txy   edge lights

Aids: VOR/DME, TAC, NDB, GCA, ILS CAT I 04
Twr frequency: 118.1   App frequency: 120.0/126.2
Terminal: Terminal and large apron to west of runway
Scheduled services 1978: Philippine Air Lines only

Traffic:	1970	1972
Passengers (total)	827,247	949,353
Aircraft movements	31,275	28,934

Up to date traffic figures are not available but the 1972 total of 949,353 passengers suggests that the airport is now handling well over 1 mn passengers annually. There is a taxiway parallel to the entire length of the runway, with three connecting taxiways.

No information on the airport's history is available.

Manila   Manila International Airport

14° 30′ 41″ N   121° 00′ 57″ E   4.8 nm (9 km) SE of city
ICAO: RPMM   IATA code: MNL   Time zone: GMT plus 8
Authority: Civil Aeronautics Administration
Elevation: 74 ft (23 m)   Ref temp: 34.6 deg C
Runways: 06/24   3,354 × 61 m (11,004 × 200 ft) asphaltic-concrete centre, cement-concrete ends
          13/31   2,425 × 30 m   (7,956 × 100 ft) asphaltic-concrete
Pavement strength: 06/24 all up weight 40,455 kg (88,188 lb) single wheel, 90,900 kg (200,400 lb) dual wheel, 163,636 kg (360,755 lb) dual tandem;   13/31 34,090 kg (75,155 lb) single wheel, 50,000 kg (110,231 lb) dual wheel, 75,000 kg (165,347 lb) dual tandem
Landing category: ICAO CAT I
Lighting:
- R/W   06/24 LIH and LIL white edge; 13/31 LIH white edge
- App   R/W 24   LIH white bar centreline with LIH red wing bars on inner 150 m (492 ft). VASIS 06/24 and 13
- Thr   green all runways
- Txy   blue edge all taxiways

Aids: VOR/DME, NDB, L, SSR, ILS CAT I 24
Twr frequency: 118.1   App frequency: 119.7
Terminal: Curved terminal in intersection of runways, with pier and 12 aircraft stands. Apron areas: domestic terminal 24,195 sq m (260,435 sq ft), international terminal 98,455 sq m (1,059,770 sq ft), former international terminal 34,195 sq m (368,075 sq ft)
Scheduled services 1978: 25 airlines

Runway thresholds 06 and 24 are displaced 150 m (492 ft) and 13 and 31 are displaced 160 m (525 ft).

278

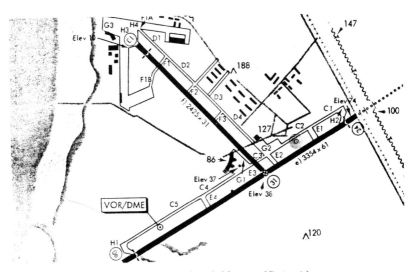

Manila International Airport. (*Swissair*)

Main base: Air Manila, Philippine Air Lines and Sterling Philippine
  Airways

Traffic:	1977	1978
Passengers (total)	3,438,313	4,003,415
Cargo (tonnes)	—	26,635
Transport movements	50,746	56,640

Before the Pacific war Manila was served by Nielson Airport,
immediately south of San Pedro Makati and only about 1½ miles (some
2 km) from Manila's southern outskirts. In 1939 this airport provided east-
northeast–west-southwest and northwest–southeast take-off distances of
870 m (2,854 ft) on strips, possibly paved, 30 m (100 ft) wide.
  Known after the war as Makati Airport the site was used until

An Air France Concorde at Manila International Airport. (*British Aerospace*)

279

1948, the Government having decided in 1947 to convert Nichols Field into the Manila International Airport. Philippine Air Lines began moving from Makati on 31 January, 1948, and completed its transfer on 28 June.

Following the destruction of the international terminal by fire on 22 January, 1972, a new air-conditioned international terminal with 3.4 mn passenger annual capacity was opened on 11 September, 1973. Present plans call for further development to provide capacity for 8 mn passengers a year by 1992. A study is being made for a new Manila airport.

Poland (Polska)

Warsaw (Warszawa)   Okęcie Airport

52° 09′ 58″ N   20° 58′ 08″ E   5.4 nm (10 km) SW of city
ICAO: EPWA   IATA code: WAW   Time zone: GMT plus 1
Authority: Air Traffic and Airports Administration
Area: 300 hectares (741 acres)
Elevation: 361 ft (110 m)   Ref temp: 20.6 deg C
Runways: 11/29   2,300 × 50 m (7,546 × 164 ft) asphalt/concrete
       15/33   3,003 × 60 m (9,852 × 197 ft) asphalt/concrete
Pavement strength: 11/29 LCN 86; 15/33 LCN 99
Landing category: ICAO CAT I*
Lighting:
  R/W   11/29   LIL white edge and LIL red end lights
        15/33   LIH and LIL white edge, last 600 m (1,968 ft) yellow, LIH and LIL red end lights. TDZ 15/33
  App   R/W 11   LIL 900 m (2,953 ft) red centreline (double row on inner section) and one crossbar
      R/W 15   LIM 550 m (1,804 ft) red centreline with one crossbar and LIH red crossbar 60 m (197 ft) from threshold
      R/W 29   LIL 750 m (2,461 ft) red centreline with LIM red crossbar 300 m (984 ft) from threshold
      R/W 33   LIH 1,000 m (3,281 ft) Calvert white centreline with seven crossbars—1 to 4 yellow, 5 white, 6 yellow and 7 red—and LIM red centreline with three crossbars
  Thr   11/29   LIL green,   15/33   LIH and LIL green
  Txy   blue edge
Aids: VOR, NDB, L, PAR, SRE, RVR 11/29 and 15/33, ILS CAT I 33
Twr frequency: 119.0   App frequency: 128.8
Terminals: International terminal on east of airport and domestic terminal at north end. Three aircraft aprons.

* CAT II ILS is reported to have been ordered.

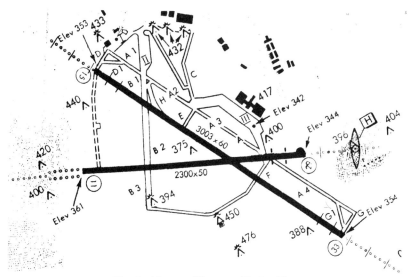

Okęcie Airport, Warsaw. (*Swissair*)

Scheduled services 1978: 21 airlines
Main base: LOT

Traffic:	1970	1975	1976	1977
Passengers (total)	980,654	1,755,523	1,892,717	2,092,493
Cargo (tonnes)	9,751	12,674	12,775	12,840
Aircraft movements	32,676	44,202	49,691	49,625
Transport movements	30,297	41,999	47,166	47,395

In 1910 the Warsaw Aviation Society 'Aviata' prepared Poland's first aerodrome. This was on military ground at Mokotów, 2.5 km (1½ miles)

Polskie Linie Lotnicze LOT's Ilyushin Il-62 SP-LAB at Okęcie Airport, Warsaw. (*ZAIKS, courtesy LOT*)

281

south of the city's central railway station, and it was served by a tram route. This aerodrome, which measured 1,400 by 600 m (4,593 by 1,968 ft), was to serve as a military base, factory aerodrome and civil airport until the 1930s.

Inevitably, in view of its situation, Mokotów was becoming hemmed in by built-up areas and blocking city development, so the present airport at Okęcie was planned in the early 1920s as a military aerodrome to accommodate two air regiments. The plan was approved and instructions for compulsory purchase of land were issued by the Ministry of Military Matters on 7 April, 1924, and construction was scheduled to be completed in 1927; but due to an economic crisis in 1926–27 most work on the project was stopped although some earth-moving work was given to the unemployed.

In 1929 work was resumed to provide a civil airport, radio was installed in 1930, and airline operations were transferred from Mokotów to Okęcie on 1 November, 1933.

The new airport, situated 10 km (6.2 miles) southwest of Warsaw, was roughly elliptical and had a grass landing area measuring 1,470 m (4,824 ft) east–west and 1,270 m (4,167 ft) north–south. There was a small terminal building, and some hangars, and the P.Z.L. aircraft factory had been transferred to the new aerodrome.

During the occupation of Warsaw, German forces laid paved runways but when the Germans retreated in 1944 they destroyed all the facilities including the runways and the P.Z.L. factory.

After the war three runways were constructed—02/20 of 1,700 m (5,577 ft), 11/29 of 1,800 m (5,905 ft) and 15/33 of 2,000 m (6,562 ft). A modest terminal building was erected. The 02/20 runway was later abandoned and is now taxiway B2 and B3 with its widened northern end serving as apron No. 2. Runways 11/29 and 15/33 have been considerably lengthened and 11/29 has a full-length parallel taxiway. A new international terminal was constructed on the east side of the airport and the old northern terminal is now used for domestic services.

There are plans for an entirely new Warsaw airport.

Polynesia (Polynésie)

Papeete, Tahiti   Aéroport de Tahiti - Faaa

ICAO: NTTT   IATA: PPT
17° 33′ 28″ S   149° 36′ 41″ W   Elevation: 6 ft (2 m)
Runway: 04/22   3,416 m (11,207 ft)
RT and approach alignment lights. VASI 22
Aids: VOR/DME, NDB, VDF, ILS CAT I 04

	1970	1975	1976	1977
Passengers	321,487	530,115	591,141	720,229
Transport movements*	27,513	37,855	33,110	32,727

* Includes all aerial work

Tahiti Airport - Faaa. Flying-boats operated from the lagoon within the reef.
(*John Stroud*)

Scheduled services 1978: Air New Zealand, Air Polynésie, LAN-Chile, Pan American, Qantas and UTA
Main base: Air Polynésie

The airport was officially opened on 16 October, 1960, and the first arrival was the TAI DC-7C F-BIAQ.

Portugal

Santa Maria, Azores (Açores)   Aeroporto de Santa Maria

ICAO: LPAZ   IATA: SMA
36° 58′ 22″ N   25° 10′ 17″ W   Elevation: 305 ft (93 m)
Longest runway: 01/19   3,048 m (10,000 ft)   ART   VASI 01/19
Aids: VOR, NDB, VDF, ILS CAT I 19

	1970	1975
Passengers	245,295	130,977*
Transport movements	5,456	4,544

* Excluding transit

Scheduled services 1978: Air France, KLM, SATA, Surinam Airways, TAP and TWA

Faro   Aeroporto de Faro   ICAO: LPFR   IATA: FAO

37° 00′ 46″ N   07° 57′ 53″ W   Elevation: 23 ft (7 m)
Runway: 11/29   2,400 m (7,874 ft)   RT   VASI 11/29
Aids: VOR, NDB

	1970	1975	1976	1977
Passengers	337,002	274,674*	367,990	687,907
Transport movements	5,361	4,640	6,276	8,152

* Excluding transit

Scheduled services 1978: British Airways, Lufthansa and TAP

Funchal, Madeira (Ilha de Madeira)   Aeroporto de Santa Catarina

          ICAO: LPFU   IATA: FNC
32° 41′ 26″ N   16° 46′ 27″ W   Elevation: 190 ft (58 m)
Runway: 06/24   1,600 m (5,249 ft)   RT*   VASI 06/24
Aids: NDB

	1970	1975	1976	1977
Passengers	174,644	392,260	561,649	665,695
Transport movements	2,730	5,019	7,808	8,750

Scheduled services 1978: TAP only

* There is a curved line of sodiums from displaced threshold 06 with three crossbars. 06 and 24 have green aiming point lights 300 m (984 ft) from displaced thresholds, available on request

Lisbon (Lisboa)   Aeroporto de Portela de Sacavém

38° 46′ 22″ N   09° 07′ 58″ W   4.5 nm (8.3 km) N of city
ICAO: LPPT   IATA code: LIS   Time zone: GMT
Authority: Direcção-Geral da Aeronáutica Civil
Area: 516 hectares (1,275 acres)
Elevation: 374 ft (114 m)   Ref temp: 24.2 deg C
Runways: 03/21   3,805 × 45 m (12,483 × 148 ft) bituminous asphalt
              18/36   2,400 × 45 m   (7,874 × 148 ft) bituminous asphalt
Pavement strength: 03/21 LCN 80; 18/36 35,000 kg (77,162 lb) ISWL
Landing category: ICAO CAT I
Lighting:
      R/W   03/21   white edge, last 600 m (1,968 ft) yellow, LIH white
                  centreline. LIH white TDZ 21. Green end lights
                  18/36   white edge, last 600 m (1,968 ft) yellow. 18 red end
                  lights, 36 green end lights
      App   R/W 03 and 36   LIH red centreline with one crossbar
                  R/W 21   LIH Calvert white centreline with five crossbars
                  and red side barrettes, and LIL red centreline with two
                  crossbars
                  AVASI 18, VASIS 03/21 and 36

Thr   green
Txy   blue edge with green centreline on some sections
Aids: VOR, NDB, VDF, L, approach radar, ILS CAT I 21
Twr frequency: 118.1   App frequency: 119.1
Terminal: Passenger terminal with three domestic and 12 international
    gates and 28 aircraft stands
Scheduled services 1978: 24 airlines
Main base: TAP

Traffic:	1970	1975	1976	1977	1978
Passengers (total)	2,239,288	2,792,434	2,684,640	2,992,543	3,196,435
Cargo (tonnes)	17,828	35,960	36,767	41,813	50,845
Aircraft movements	42,996	44,981	43,545	45,975	—
Transport movements	34,392	38,081	35,775	37,443	38,880

During 1976 Boeing 727s accounted for 40.29 per cent of aircraft movements, Boeing 707s for 30.12 per cent, Boeing 747s for 4.64 per cent, DC-10s for 4.63 per cent, DC-9s for 4.57 per cent and DC-8s for 3.51 per cent.

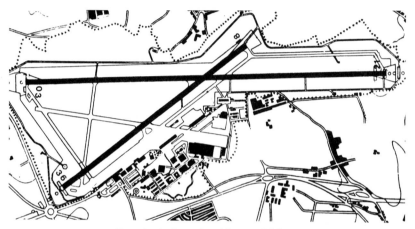

Portela de Sacavém Airport, Lisbon.

Portela de Sacavém came into operation as Lisbon's airport in October 1942 when all airline operations were transferred from the military aerodrome at Sintra (Cintra). The new Lisbon airport originally had four runways measuring 1,023 m (3,356 ft), 1,171 m (3,842 ft), 1,202 m (3,944 ft) and 1,350 m (4,429 ft). Of these 18/36 has been lengthened to 2,400 m (7,874 ft) and the others serve as taxiways, a new main runway, 03/21, of 3,805 m (12,483 ft) having been constructed.
    A simple terminal building had been completed by 1943 and a road link was constructed between the new airport and the Lisbon flying-boat base.
    In spite of development, the airport is expected to reach saturation point in about 1980. It cannot be further expanded and its proximity to the city causes noise problems. It was therefore decided to build a new airport, and surveys of a site at Rio Frio, about 32 km (20 miles) east of the city but on the other side of the Tagus, began in 1969.

285

A British United Airways BAC One-Eleven at Portela de Sacavém, Lisbon.
Considerable terminal expansion has taken place since this photograph was taken.
(*British Aerospace*)

The new Lisbon airport (Novo Aeroporto de Lisboa) will initially
occupy about 3,200 hectares (7,907 acres), will have one 3,750 m (12,303 ft)
runway, one terminal and a cargo centre, but is not expected to come into
operation before 1990. Planned capacity for about 1995 is 40 mn
passengers by which time there should be four parallel runways, each of
3,750 m (12,303 ft). The pairs of runways will be 760 m (2,493 ft) apart and
the two sets separated by 2,320 m (7,611 ft). Provision is being made for
runway extension to 4,250 m (13,943 ft).

Oporto (Pôrto)   Aeroporto de Pedras Rubras

ICAO: LPPR   IATA: OPO
41° 14′ 02″ N   08° 40′ 36″ W   Elevation: 249 ft (76 m)
Longest runway: 18/36   3,480 m (11,417 ft)   ART   AVASI 18, VASI 36
Aids: VOR, VDF, L, ILS CAT I 18

	1970	1972
Passengers	244,751	330,280
Aircraft movements	14,491	14,999

Scheduled services 1978: Air France, British Airways, Swissair and TAP

Commonwealth of Puerto Rico

San Juan Puerto Rico International Airport
(Aeropuerto Internacional de Isla Verde)

18° 26′ 28″ N   66° 00′ 04″ W   3 nm (5.5 km) SE of city
ICAO: MJSJ   IATA code: SJU   Time zone: GMT −4
Authority: Puerto Rico Ports Authority
Area: 640 hectares (1,581 acres)
Elevation: 9 ft (3 m)   Ref temp 30.8 deg C
Runways: 07/25   3,048 × 61 m (10,000 × 200 ft) concrete/asphalt
        10/28   2,438 × 46 m (8,000 × 150 ft) concrete/asphalt
                There is an arrester cable on 25
Pavement strength: 100,000 lb (45,359 kg) 1, 200,000 lb (90,718 kg) 2,
    350,000 lb (158,757 kg) 3.
Landing category: ICAO CAT II
Lighting:
    R/W   LIH white edge (HIRL).
    App   R/W 07   LIH white bar centreline with crossbar and
            sequenced flashers (ALSF-1)
            R/W 10   LIM white bar centreline with crossbar.
            Flashing centreline 1,400–3,000 ft (427–914 m) from
            threshold (SSALR)
            R/W 25   REIL
            VASIS all runways
    Thr   R/W 25   green with strobes
    Txy   blue edge
Aids: VORTAC, VDF, SRE, ILS CAT II 07, ILS CAT I 10
Twr frequency: 118.3   App frequency: 119.4/124.6

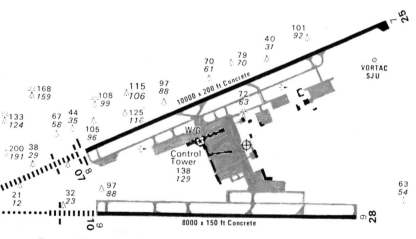

Puerto Rico International Airport, San Juan. (*British Airways Aerad*)

287

Part of Prinair's Heron fleet, a Convair-Liner and an Iberia DC-8 at Puerto Rico International Airport, San Juan.

Terminals: Passenger terminal with piers and 26 gates. Cargo terminal with 11 aircraft stands. Inter-island terminal planned.
Scheduled services 1978: 22 airlines
Main base: Prinair

Traffic:	1970	1975	1976	1977	1978
Passengers (total)	4,496,183	5,239,460	5,037,634	5,296,042	5,703,357
Cargo (tonnes)	79,646	105,918	122,854	158,011	57,930
Aircraft movements	167,061	197,251	195,314	194,961	196,142
Transport movements	129,561	136,322	51,034	142,000	153,838

Puerto Rico International Airport, also known as Aeropuerto Internacional de Isla Verde, is situated on the north coast of the island, to the east of San Juan and between Laguna Los Corozos, to the west, and Laguna La Torrecilla, to the east.

The airport was opened on 24 May, 1955, replacing Aeropuerto de Isla Grande, alongside US Naval Station San Juan and projecting into San Juan Bay. The old airport had two runways, 05/23 of 3,100 ft (945 m) and 09/27 of 5,630 ft (1,716 m), but could not be expanded without largescale reclamation. Flying still takes place at Isla Grande and care has to be taken to avoid conflict between the circuits of the two airports—Vieques Air Link, a commuter airline, flies Britten-Norman Islanders on the high-frequency half-hour flights between Isla Grande and Vieques.

288

State of Qatar

Doha   Doha International Airport

ICAO: OTBD   IATA: DOH
25° 15′ 37″ N   51° 33′ 57″ E   Elevation: 35 ft (11 m)
Runway: 16/34   4,572 m (15,000 ft)   ART
Aids: VOR/DME, NDB, ILS 34

	1970	1975	1976	1977
Passengers	106,214	455,300	624,875	733,814
Transport movements	6,724	13,802	15,080	15,765

Scheduled services 1978: 18 airlines

A 4,100 m (13,451 ft) parallel runway is planned for 1985, and a new airport is under construction.

Réunion

Saint-Denis   Aéroport de Saint-Denis - Gillot

ICAO: FMEE   IATA: RUN
20° 52′ 39″ S   55° 31′ 20″ E   Elevation: 66 ft (20 m)
Runway: 13/31   2,670 m (8,760 ft)   RT   VASI 13
Aids: VOR/DME, NDB, VDF, ILS 13

	1975	1976	1977
Passengers	211,435	256,487	295,659
Transport movements	3,982	3,908	4,221

Scheduled services 1978: Air France, Air Madagascar, Air Mauritius, Réunion Air Service and South African Airways
Main base: Réunion Air Service

Romania

Bucharest (Bucureşti)   Bucureşti - Otopeni Airport

44° 33′ 59″ N   26° 06′ 02″ E   9 nm (16.8 km) N of city
ICAO: LROP   IATA code: BUH   Time zone: GMT plus 2
Authority: Ministerul Apărării Nationale Comandamentul Aviatieci Civile
Elevation: 312 ft (95 m)   Ref temp: 24.9 deg C

289

The terminal and control tower at Otopeni Airport, Bucharest.
(*Courtesy M. J. Hooks*)

Runway: 08/26   3,500 × 45 m (11,483 × 148 ft) concrete*
Pavement strength: 45,000 kg (99,208 lb) ISWL
Landing category: ICAO CAT I
Lighting:
 R/W LIH and LIL white edge, last 600 m (1,968 ft) yellow, and white centreline. White TDZ 08. Optimum landing point indicated by five lights each side of runway 300 m (984 ft) from thresholds and red critical distance lights 300 m (984 ft) short of far threshold
 App R/W 08 LIH white Calvert 900 m (2,953 ft) centreline with five LIH yellow crossbars and LIL centreline with two white crossbars. LIH red lights both sides of centreline on inner 300 m (984 ft)
     R/W 26 LIL white simplified Calvert 900 m (2,953 ft) centreline with two white crossbars
 Thr LIH and LIL green
 Txy blue edge lights on all taxiways
Aids: NDB, VDF, L, SRE, PAR, RVR 08, ILS CAT I 08/26
Twr frequency: 120.9   App frequency: 120.6
Terminals: Spacious multi-level terminal at west end of airport. Separate cargo terminal and apron to north of runway
Scheduled services 1978: 20 airlines
Base: Liniile Aeriene Romane (LAR) and Tarom
Traffic: No figures available

From the early days of air transport Bucharest was served by Băneasa Airport, 8 km (5 miles) north of the city. In 1932 Băneasa's landing area measured 700 by 550 m (2,297 by 1,804 ft) and was soft after heavy rain. Băneasa continued to meet the city's air traffic requirements after the Second World War and remains the domestic airport although operations are limited by a night curfew.

* There is a 30 × 30 m (98.4 × 98.4 ft) helicopter landing area on taxiway 7 with pavement strength of 17 tonnes (37,478 lb) ISWL.

A government drive to attract tourists, particularly to Black Sea resorts, was successful and this, combined with the envisaged saturation of Băneasa, made it necessary to construct a more suitable international airport. A site was chosen, still north of the city but at twice the distance, and the new Bucharest - Otopeni Airport was opened in 1965.

No precise traffic figures are available but it is believed that Otopeni handled 1½ mn passengers in 1975 and is expected to handle 2 mn passengers in 1980.

In 1965 the Romanian Civil Aviation Department commissioned Aéroport de Paris to produce a master plan for the development of Otopeni and design the terminal area and terminal building to handle a traffic peak of 2,000 passengers an hour. When the new terminal is in operation it is expected that the existing building will be used to handle domestic traffic.

Construction of a second runway is due to begin in 1980.

Kingdom of Saudi Arabia

Dhahran   Dhahran International Airport

26° 12′ 21″ N   50° 10′ 05″ E   2 nm (3.7 km) WSW of Al-Khobar
ICAO: OEDR   IATA code: DHA   Time zone: GMT plus 3
Authority: Director General of Civil Aviation
Elevation: 71 ft (22 m)   Ref temp: 38 deg C
Runways: 06/24   1,835 × 46 m   (6,020 × 150 ft) asphalt
           16L/34R   3,050 × 45 m (10,006 × 148 ft) asphalt*
           16R/34L   3,659 × 45 m (12,006 × 148 ft) asphalt with
                                                      concrete ends**
Pavement strength: 16L/34R and 16R/34L LCN 80; 06/24 LCN 40
Landing category: ICAO CAT I
Lighting:
    R/W   LIH white edge, and end lights
    App   R/W 34R   LIH white precision CAT I centreline and
             crossbars
             R/W 16L/34R   VASIS for military use only
    Thr   green on all runways
    Txy   edge
Aids: VORTAC, NDB, ILS CAT I 34R
Twr frequency: 118.7   App frequency: 120.7/121.5
Terminals: Separate international and domestic terminals with 19 aircraft
    stands
Scheduled services 1978: 24 airlines

* R/W 16L/34R has Safeland barriers at each end, lit when raised
** R/W 16R/34L is restricted to military aircraft making low approaches

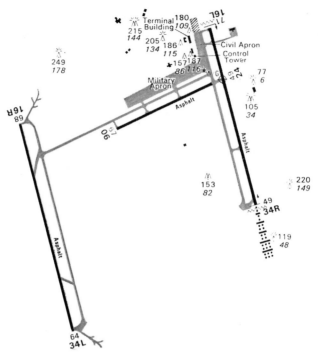

Dhahran International Airport. (*British Airways Aerad*)

Traffic:	1976	1977
Passengers (total)	1,393,712	1,862,000*
Cargo (tonnes)	19,966	27,753
Aircraft movements	73,854	87,960
Transport movements	21,510	30,028

* Rounded figure

Dhahran International Airport was originally a military aerodrome and is still a Royal Saudi Arabian Air Force base, but in the 1950s it began to play an important part in commercial air transport. Minoru Yamasaki was commissioned to design a civil terminal building and photographs of a model of the building were first published early in 1960.

The building, of precast concrete, appears to consist of rows of stylized palm trees linked by wall panels which are ribbed to resemble Arabic grille work. When completed during the 1960s the Dhahran terminal was one of the most beautiful airport structures and won an award from the International Society of Architecture.

Development plans call for terminal extensions, a new cargo building, and extensions to runways, taxiways and aprons. A second main runway is also planned.

A new Eastern Province International Airport is to be built near Dhahran. Boeing Aerosystems International is the consultant and

The second prototype Concorde in front of the beautiful Dhahran International Airport terminal. (*Arthur Gibson, Image in Industry*)

architectural responsibility has been given to Minoru Yamasaki Associates. The layout chosen has two 4,000 m (13,123 ft) parallel runways, each with parallel taxiways; a central terminal area with an apron each side; two satellites per terminal each with eight or nine aircraft stands; and high-speed exits leading to the terminal.

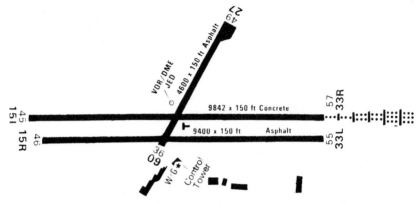

Jeddah International Airport. (*British Airways Aerad*)

Jeddah   Jeddah International Airport

21° 30′ 12″ N   39° 12′ 06″ E   1.29 nm (2.4 km) ENE of city
ICAO: OEJD   IATA code: JED   Time zone: GMT plus 3
Authority: Director General of Civil Aviation
Elevation: 57 ft (17 m)   Ref temp: 33 deg C
Runways: 15L/33R   3,000 × 46 m (9,842 × 150 ft) concrete
        15R/33L   2,865 × 46 m (9,400 × 150 ft) asphalt
        There is also an 09/27   1,402 m (4,600 ft) asphalt runway
        which is only available to local light training aircraft
Pavement strength: LCN 90
Landing category: ICAO CAT I
Lighting:
    R/W   LIH white edge, and end lights
    App   R/W 33R   LIH white precision CAT I centreline with
        crossbars.
        VASIS 15L/33R and 33L
    Thr   LIH green
    Txy   edge
Aids: VOR/DME, TVOR, NDB, RVR, ILS CAT I 33R
Twr frequency: 118.1   App frequency: 124.0
Terminals: Passenger and cargo terminals and accommodation for
pilgrims
Scheduled services 1978: 36 airlines
Main base: Saudi Arabian Airlines (Saudia)

Traffic:	1970	1975	1976
Passengers (total)	713,278	2,538,674*	3,261,422*
Cargo (tonnes)	6,730	13,681	16,395
Aircraft movements	23,032	58,957	69,802
Transport movements	21,187	47,690	56,612

* Excluding transit passengers

Jeddah International Airport, although officially stated to be 2.4 km
east-northeast of the city, is in fact part of the city—some main offices being

294

only a road-width from the terminal. The airport was originally without runways and the landing ground measured 1,006 by 1,006 m (3,300 by 3,300 ft).

Jeddah is the main Saudi Arabian port and its airport and seaport handle a very large number of Hadj pilgrims travelling to and from Mecca. This traffic is concentrated into a very short period, with inward and outward flow within less than two months, and produces about 40 per cent of the total annual passenger traffic. A new airport terminal was opened in the spring of 1978 and much of the old terminal was allocated to the handling and accommodation of pilgrims.

It was obviously impossible to develop the existing airport, and a site for a new airport was selected 25 km (15½ miles) north of the city. The first contracts were placed in 1974 and work on the site began in 1975.

Traffic growth in the area has been so rapid that the plans had to be modified even after work began, and the airport is now said to be the world's biggest, being 1½ times the size of Dallas/Fort Worth. Forecast traffic is 7 mn passengers a year by 1990 with 10 mn during the 1990s.

Initially, the new airport will have a staggered pair of 16/34 runways measuring 3,810 m (12,500 ft) and 3,300 m (10,827 ft) in length and they are to be equipped to CAT III standard. Later there will be an eastern 16/34 runway associated with the planned air force base. The runways will have parallel taxiways and there will be dual links between the runways at both north and south.

To the west of the 16C/34C runway will be the main two-level air-conditioned terminal designed to handle 16,000 passengers a day. To the north of this terminal and between 16C/34C and the southern end of 16R/34L will be three parallel aprons—10 West German-built 150-passenger mobile lounges having been ordered to link the terminal and aprons.

North of the aprons is Terminal 2, originally intended as the Hadj terminal but later considered too small, and further north the 42 hectare (105 acre) Hadj terminal comprising two vast buildings, divided by access

Jeddah International Airport terminal and pilgrim accommodation.

roads, and each with its own apron. This terminal will have a Teflon-coated glass fibre tent-like roof supported on 440 tapering pylons. Design capacity is 100,000 passengers a day and boarding will be via 30 aerobridges. It is planned that this terminal will be ready for the 1980 pilgrimage.

On the west of the airport will be the Royal pavilion and apron and at the northeast the Saudi Arabian Airlines maintenance base including a hangar measuring 216 by 122 m (708.6 by 400 ft).

The cargo terminal is planned to have capacity for 46,000 tonnes at one time.

Full operation of the new Jeddah airport is scheduled for 1982.

Riyadh   Riyadh International Airport

24° 42′ 04″ N   46° 43′ 40″ E   On northern edge of city
ICAO: OERY   IATA code: RUH   Time zone: GMT plus 3
Authority: Director General of Civil Aviation
Elevation: 2,052 ft (625 m)   Ref temp: 37 deg C
Runways: 01/19   3,101 × 46 m (10,174 × 150 ft) asphalt
           11L/29R   2,998 × 46 m   (9,836 × 150 ft) concrete
           11R/29L   1,676 × 46 m   (5,500 × 150 ft)
Pavement strength: LCN 85
Landing category: ICAO CAT II

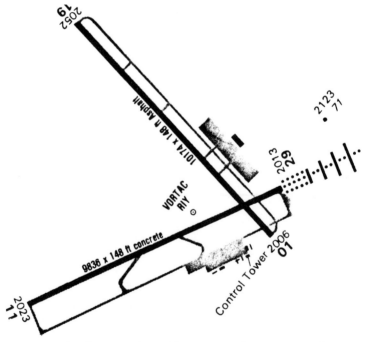

Riyadh International Airport. (*British Airways Aerad*)

The terminal and control tower at Riyadh International Airport in November 1968.
(*John Stroud*)

Lighting:
R/W	01/19	LIM white edge, and end lights
	11L/29R	LIH white edge and centreline, and end lights.
	TDZ 29	
App	R/W 29R	LIH white precision CAT II centreline with crossbars, and barrettes on inner 305 m (1,000 ft). VASIS 01/19 and 11L/29R
Thr	green	
Txy	edge, with green centreline on taxiways parallel to runways

Aids: VOR/DME, NDB, RVR, ILS CAT II 29
Twr frequency: 118.1   App frequency: 126.0
Terminals: Small terminal of about 240 sq m (2,583 sq ft) mainly used as a
    departure lounge; international arrivals and transit building; and
    Princes' Hall VIP terminal
Scheduled services in 1978: Saudi Arabian Airlines only
Traffic: 1,544,882 passengers in 1976

Riyadh International Airport is immediately adjacent to the northern
part of the city, and in addition to being a civil airport houses the Royal
Saudi Arabian Air Force Academy and has a large military hangar and
apron.
    The site was probably first used as an aerodrome by the DC-3 which
the President of the United States presented to HM The King of Saudi
Arabia shortly after the Second World War. Saudi Arabian Airlines began
scheduled operations to and from Riyadh in 1948. The first runway, 11/29
(now 11R/29L), was built in about 1950 and intended for DC-3 category
aircraft. The second runway, 01/19, was built in about 1956 and intended to
take the Convair CV-340s being acquired by Saudi Arabian Airlines. The
third runway, parallel to the original 11/29, was completed in 1965,
designated 11L/29R, and built for the airline's Boeing 720Bs and 707s.
After completion of 11L/29R, the eastern end of the original 11/29 runway
was abandoned and the runway is now used only by small aircraft.
    In 1974 a site was chosen for a new airport and this is due for
completion in 1983.

297

République du Sénégal

Dakar   Aéroport Dakar - Yoff

	ICAO: GOOO		IATA: DKR	

14° 44′ 41″ N   17° 29′ 59″ W   Elevation: 89 ft (27 m)
Longest runway: 01/19   3,490 m (11,450 ft)   ART   VASI 19
Aids: VOR/DME, L, ILS CAT I 01

	1970	1975	1976	1977
Passengers	323,053	407,612	636,542	757,115
Transport movements	8,724	24,870	13,566	14,500

Scheduled services 1978: 25 airlines
Main base: Sonatra - Air Sénégal

First commercial service to Dakar - Yoff was by a Breguet 14 on 1 June, 1925. On 21 January, 1976, the airport became the first intermediate stop on a supersonic route when Air France began Paris–Dakar–Rio de Janeiro Concorde services.

Republic of Singapore

Singapore   Singapore International Airport (Paya Lebar)

01° 21′ 12″ N   103° 54′ 15″ E   5.9 nm (11 km) NE of city
ICAO: WSSS   IATA code: SIN   Time zone: GMT plus $7\frac{1}{2}$
Authority: Department of Civil Aviation
Area: 283 hectares (700 acres)
Elevation: 65 ft (20 m)   Ref temp: 31.5 deg C
Runway: 02/20 $4,023 \times 61$ m ($13,200 \times 200$ ft) bituminous concrete
Pavement strength: LCN 100
Landing category: ICAO CAT I (both directions)
Lighting:
  R/W   LIH white edge, last 2,000 ft (610 m) yellow. Red end lights
  App   R/W 02/20   LIH white modified Calvert centreline and crossbars and LIL red centreline and crossbars. VASIS 02/20
  Thr   green with wing bars
  Txy   blue edge lights on all taxiways
Aids: VOR/DME, NDB, VDF, ASR, ILS CAT I 02/20
Twr frequency: 118.3   App frequency: 120.3
Terminals: Separate arrival and departure buildings with 37 aircraft stands, and four cargo terminals
Scheduled services 1978: 31 airlines
Airline bases: KLM, Pan American, Qantas and Thai International
Main base: Singapore Airlines

298

Singapore International Airport seen from the 02 approach with the terminal area on the left. (*Courtesy Airports International*)

Traffic:	1970	1975	1976	1977	1978
Passengers (total)	1,688,199	3,324,044	4,495,315	5,130,286	5,697,571
Cargo (tonnes)	21,062	66,087	79,590	88,555	58,093
Aircraft movements	51,508	64,959	65,089	66,950	71,822
Transport movements	34,893	58,820	57,634	59,997	—

In 1976 wide-bodied aircraft accounted for 24 per cent of movements, narrow-bodied four-engined jet aircraft for 33 per cent and narrow-bodied twinjets and trijets for 41 per cent.

When, in December 1933, the London–Singapore service was opened by Imperial Airways and Indian Trans-Continental Airways, the Atalanta monoplanes used the RAF Seletar aerodrome on the island's northeast coast; but on 12 June, 1937, the very fine Singapore Marine and Land Airport, Kallang, was opened on the south coast of the island. Kallang had a circular grass landing area of 3,000 ft (914 m) diameter, a terminal flanked by two hangars, and a flying-boat slipway. The airport remained in use after the Second World War, by which time a paved runway had been constructed, but the site was not suitable for further development as an airport.

A new site was chosen at Paya Lebar and work began in August 1952. Construction involved clearance of 900 acres (365 hectares) of coconut estate, the felling of some 30,000 palm trees and moving about 5 mn tons of earth. The 02/20 runway was initially 8,000 ft (2,438 m) long and land was available to the west for a parallel runway, although this has not been built. Drains were designed to handle 2 in (5 cm) of rain in 20 min. The modified Calvert approach lighting was the first in the Far East.

The first permanent terminal was completed in 1958 and considerable development of passenger and cargo terminal facilities has taken place throughout the past 20 years—a new cargo terminal opened in 1977 is already being quadrupled to provide 160,000 tonnes annual capacity.

The new airport was officially opened on 20 August, 1955, with traffic from 21 August, on which date Kallang was closed. The runway was extended in 1961 and the single arrival and departure terminal was converted into a departure building after the opening of the new arrivals building late in 1977. It is of interest that one of the hangars in use at Paya Lebar is one of the original Kallang structures.

Although development is still in progress, the present Singapore airport is to be replaced by a new airport at Changi on the eastern tip of the island where there is already a military aerodrome with a 2,160 m (7,085 ft) 02/20 runway.

Construction of the new airport began in mid-1978 and it is to be built in two phases. Phase I includes lengthening the existing runway to 4,000 m (13,123 ft), construction of parallel taxiways and four high-speed exits, Terminal Unit 1 with associated apron and 38 aircraft stands (16 remote), control tower, cargo centre with two terminals and four aircraft stands, maintenance area including a hangar for three wide-bodied aircraft and three aircraft stands, access roads, and all necessary operational facilities. This phase is due for completion in 1980.

Phase II will include a parallel 3,355 m (11,007 ft) runway, 02R/20L, with parallel taxiway and four high-speed exits, Terminal Unit 2, and 10 additional aircraft stands, of which two will be for cargo aircraft. Phase II is due to be completed in 1982.

Construction of the new airport, particularly the second runway, has involved largescale reclamation and this was achieved ahead of schedule.

When both runways are in operation 02L and 20L will be equipped to CAT II standard and 02R and 20R to CAT I.

The master plan provides for considerable terminal expansion alongside the central spine road which enters the airport from the south-southwest.

The airport reference point will be 01° 22′ 30″ N and 103° 59′ 24″ E, and its elevation is 10 ft (3 m).

Republic of South Africa
(Republiek van Suid-Afrika)

Cape Town (Kaapstad)   D. F. Malan Airport

33° 58′ 00″ S   18° 36′ 15″ E   7 nm (13 km) SE of city
ICAO: FACT   IATA code: CPT   Time zone: GMT plus 2
Authority: Republic of South Africa
Area: 930 hectares (2,298 acres)
Elevation: 151 ft (46 m)   Ref temp: 22.2 deg C
Runways: 01/19   3,202 × 61 m (10,505 × 200 ft) asphalt
     16/34   1,700 × 46 m   (5,577 × 150 ft) asphalt, concrete ends
Pavement strength: LCN 74
Landing category: ICAO CAT II
Lighting:
     R/W   LIH white edge, last 610 m (2,000 ft) yellow
     App   R/W 01   LIH white bar centreline with crossbar and barrettes on inner 305 m (1,000 ft)
          R/W 19   LIH white centreline with crossbars. VASIS all runways
     Thr   LIH green
     Txy   blue

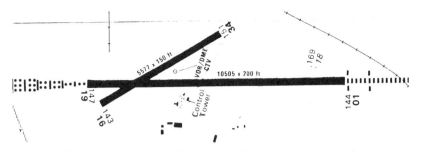

D. F. Malan Airport, Cape Town. (*British Airways Aerad*)

Aids: VOR/DME, NDB, VDF, L, SRE, GCA/PAR, ILS CAT II 01
Twr frequency: 118.1   App frequency: 119.7
Terminals: Simple two-storey terminal with six gates and open apron
   parking. Separate cargo terminal opened 4 July, 1974
Scheduled services 1978: Aerolineas Argentinas, Namakwaland Lugdiens,
   Pan American, South African Airways, Suidwes Lugdiens and Varig
Airline bases: Namakwaland Lugdiens, Rennies Air and South African
   Airways
Main base: Air Cape

Traffic:	1970	1975
Passengers (total)	603,200	1,111,300
Cargo (tonnes)	8,139	14,756
Aircraft movements	41,372	66,274

For many years Wingfield Airport served Cape Town and was the
terminal for the United Kingdom–South Africa services. After the war
South Africa embarked on a programme of airport construction to serve its
major cities and the new Cape Town airport was opened on 26 October,
1955. Before being named D. F. Malan, the airport had borne the names
Bellville and Cape Town National.

The terminal at D. F. Malan Airport, Cape Town.

Durban   Louis Botha Airport

29° 58′ 12″ S   30° 57′ 06″ E   7 nm (13 km) SSW of city
ICAO: FADN   IATA code: DUR   Time zone: GMT plus 2
Authority: Republic of South Africa
Area: 753 hectares (1,860 acres)
Elevation: 25 ft (8 m)   Ref temp: 25.3 deg C
Runway: 05/23   2,443 × 61 m (8,015 × 200 ft) asphalt, first 46 m
          (150 ft) of 23 is concrete
Pavement strength: LCN 74
Landing category: ICAO CAT I
Lighting:
    R/W   LIH and LIL white edge, last third yellow
    App   R/W 05   LIH white simple centreline with one crossbar
           R/W 23   LIH white Calvert centreline with five
           crossbars
           VASIS 05/23
    Thr   green
    Txy   blue
Aids: VOR/DME, NDB, VDF, SRE, ILS CAT I 23
Twr frequency: 118.7   App frequency: 119.1
Terminals: Simple single-storey arrival and departure buildings
Scheduled services 1978: Air Lowveld, AVNA, Commercial Airways,
    Royal Swazi and South African Airways
Airline base: South African Airways

Traffic:	1970	1975	1976	1977
Passengers (total)	619,000	1,114,665	1,107,647	1,087,506
Cargo (tonnes)	6,578	15,796	10,631	10,084
Aircraft movements	24,288	35,942	34,285	42,764
Transport movements	15,934	24,063	22,199	19,284

The airport is situated about a mile from the coast and was opened on
24 November, 1955, replacing Durban's Stamford Hill Airport. Before
being named Louis Botha, the airport had been known as Reunion
Airport, Lamantville Airport and Durban National Airport.

Johannesburg   Jan Smuts Airport

26° 08′ 02″ S   28° 14′ 34″ E   10 nm (18.5 km) ENE of city
ICAO: FAJS   IATA code: JNB   Time zone: GMT plus 2
Authority: Republic of South Africa
Area: 1,842 hectares (4,552 acres)
Elevation: 5,557 ft (1,694 m)   Ref temp: 21.2 deg C
Runways: 03/21   4,418 × 61 m (14,495 × 200 ft) asphalt
          15/33   2,512 × 61 m (8,241 × 200 ft) asphalt
Pavement strength: LCN 74
Landing category: ICAO CAT II

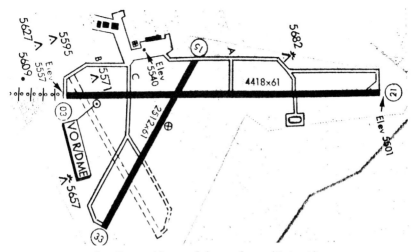

Jan Smuts Airport, Johannesburg. (*Swissair*)

Lighting:
R/W	03/21	LIH white edge, last third yellow	
	15/33	LIL white edge	
App	R/W 03	LIH yellow Calvert centreline with six crossbars.	
	VASIS all runways		
Thr	03/21	LIH green, 15/33	LIL green
Txy	orange all taxiways		

Aids: VOR/DME, NDB, VDF, L, SRE, SSR, ILS CAT II 03
Twr frequency: 118.1   App frequency: 124.5 S sector, 123.7 N sector
Terminals: Domestic and international terminals with nine close-in aircraft stands and 16 remote stands
Scheduled services 1978: 26 airlines
Airline bases: Air Lowveld and Comair
Main base: Safair Freighters, South African Airways and United Air

Traffic:	1970	1975	1976	1977
Passengers (total)	1,729,412	3,252,000	3,362,842*	3,445,258
Cargo (tonnes)	40,300†	81,800†	89,695	86,835
Aircraft movements	—	—	65,487	73,869
Transport movements	47,766	68,684	77,886	65,510

* Excluding transit passengers
† Rounded figure

In prewar years Johannesburg was served by the Rand Airport, Germiston. At one time it was one of the finest airports in Africa, but it only provided a take-off distance of a little over 4,000 ft (1,219 m) which at its elevation of 5,478 ft (1,670 m) was insufficient for heavily loaded aircraft. BOAC used Vaaldam as the terminus for its United Kingdom–South Africa flying-boat services until November 1950, and for postwar landplane operations the South African Government prepared Palmietfontein as a temporary airport.

South African Airways Boeing 727s and 737s in front of the terminal at Jan Smuts Airport, Johannesburg.

For permanent use it was decided to build a new airport with a 10,500 ft (3,200 m) runway on the plateau of the Witwatersrand, about 13 miles (21 km) east-northeast of Johannesburg.

Field Marshal Lord Montgomery named the new airport Jan Smuts, in a ceremony on 7 December, 1947. The airport was built by the South African Railways and Harbour Administration at a cost of about £5½ mn and was transferred to the control of the Department of Transport. The airport was opened on 17 April, 1952, became fully operational on 1 September, 1953, and was officially opened on 3 October that year. Since its opening the main runway has been extended to 14,495 ft (4,418 m), making it one of the longest in Africa. The original airport area was 3,704 acres (1,499 hectares).

The Rand Airport is now a general aviation aerodrome but Palmietfontein is now the site of a township.

Spain (España)

In mid-1978 the Spanish Ministry of Transport and Communications established new classifications for Spanish airports.

The first group (primera especial) comprises Barcelona, Las Palmas. Madrid - Barajas, Palma de Mallorca and Tenerife; the second group (primera) consists of Alicante, Bilbao, Gerona, Ibiza, Lanzarote, Menorca, Santiago de Compostela, Seville and Valencia.

All these airports appear in this section and were the only Spanish airports handling more than 250,000 passengers in 1975 and 1976.

The other categories are second and third class civil airports and military aerodromes open for civil traffic.

304

Alicante   Aeropuerto Alicante

38° 16′ 56″ N   00° 33′ 29″ W   5.9 nm (11 km) SW of city
ICAO: LEAL   IATA code: ALC   Time zone: GMT plus 1
Authority: Subsecretaría de Aviación Civil
Area: 280 hectares (692 acres)
Elevation: 141 ft (43 m)   Ref temp: 27 deg C
Runway: 11/29   2,700 × 45 m (8,858 × 148 ft) concrete
Pavement strength: 28,000 kg (61,729 lb) ISWL
Landing category: ICAO CAT I
Lighting:
    R/W   LIH white edge, last 550 m (1,804 ft) yellow
    App   R/W 11   white precision approach centreline with five
            crossbars.
            VASIS 11/29
    Thr   LIH green with identification light system
    Txy   blue edge
Aids: VOR, NDB, ILS, CAT I 11
Twr frequency: 118.1/121.5   App frequency: 118.8
Terminal: Passenger terminal to northeast of runway with 450 by 160 m
    (1,476 by 525 ft) apron
Scheduled services 1978: Air Algérie, Air France, British Airways and
    Iberia

Traffic:	1970	1975	1976	1977	1978
Passengers (total)	804,045	2,027,556	1,811,620	1,915,250	2,312,221
Cargo (tonnes)	4,210	9,748	10,980	10,052	10,134
Aircraft movements	13,284	24,440	23,425	24,269	—
Transport movements	11,034	20,830	20,312	20,074	22,498

Lignes Aériennes Latécoère, which pioneered the air route from France to South America, opened the Barcelona–Rabat section on 1 September, 1919, and one of the intermediate stops was at Alicante where a small grass aerodrome was prepared close beside the Mediterranean and southwest of the city. Known as l'Alted, this aerodrome passed to Aéropostale and was used by that airline until it became a constituent of Air France. By 1932 the landing area measured 600 by 700 m (1,968 by 2,297 ft) and night facilities had been installed.

    The present airport extends from the site of the old aerodrome in a northwesterly direction and uphill towards the road and railway linking Alicante and Murcia.

Barcelona   Aeropuerto Barcelona - Muntadas

41° 17′ 49″ N   02° 04′ 42″ E   5.4 nm (10 km) SW of city
ICAO: LEBL   IATA code: BCN   Time zone: GMT plus 1
Authority: Subsecretaría de Aviación Civil
Elevation: 13 ft (4 m)   Ref temp: 25 deg C
Runways: 02/20   2,720 × 45 m (8,924 × 148 ft) asphalt*
          07/25   3,353 × 45 m (11,000 × 148 ft) asphalt*

*Threshold 20 is displaced 184 m (604 ft) and threshold 25 is displaced 245 m (805 ft)

Pavement strength: LCN 48
Landing category: ICAO CAT II
Lighting:
    R/W   LIH white edge, last 600 m (1,968 ft) yellow
    App   R/W 07   LIH white Calvert centreline with five crossbars
                and red barrettes on inner 300 m (984 ft) and LIL red
                centreline with two crossbars. VASIS 02 and 07/25
    Thr   green
    Txy   blue edge
    Between thresholds and displaced thresholds on R/Ws 20 and 25 there
    are red and blue edge lights.
Aids: VOR/DME, NDB, VDF, ILS CAT II 07
Twr frequency: 118.1   App frequency: 119.1
Terminals: Passenger and cargo terminals to north of R/W 07/25, with 31
    aircraft stands. There are light aircraft stands at the east end of the
    apron
Scheduled services 1978: 16 airlines

Traffic:	1970	1975	1976	1977	1978
Passengers (total)	2,828,713	4,384,249	4,677,659	5,370,247	6,085,045
Cargo (tonnes)	30,950	40,651	45,700	54,434	61,200
Aircraft movements	61,322	76,751	74,909	79,516	—
Transport movements	57,328	71,878	72,122	75,732	78,848

In 1976 DC-9s accounted for 50.5 per cent of transport movements, Boeing 727s for 34.05 per cent and Caravelles for 5.6 per cent.

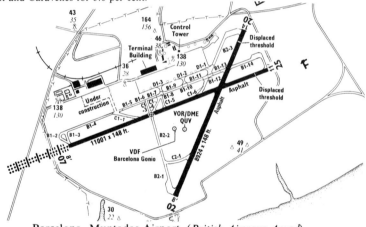

Barcelona - Muntadas Airport. (*British Airways Aerad*)

Situated beside the Mediterranean and southwest of the Rio Llobregat, Barcelona's Muntadas Airport incorporates within its boundaries the small grass aerodrome which in prewar days was owned by Aéropostale and used exclusively by aircraft operating the mail services between Toulouse and West Africa and South America.

After the war a major reconstruction and development plan was undertaken, and a master plan was published which showed three sets of parallel runways, 02/20, 07/25 and 16/34, and a single 13/31 runway. All were to have been of concrete construction.

306

Problems were encountered because of the marshy nature of the ground and flooding occurred but this was overcome by an extensive drainage system. The lengths of the planned runways were: 02L/20R 2,580 m (8,464 ft), 02R/20L 2,150 m (7,054 ft), 07L/25R 3,190 m (10,466 ft), 07R/25L 3,200 m (10,499 ft), 16L/34R and 16R/34L 2,450 m (8,038 ft) and 13/31 1,925 m (6,315 ft). Runway 07L/25R was to be 100 m (328 ft) wide and all others except 13/31 were to have been 60 m (197 ft) wide. The 13/31 runway was regarded as provisional, had a width of 50 m (164 ft) and lower bearing strength.

The provisional runway was completed to a length of 1,385 m (4,544 ft) and came into service in 1946. By early 1950 runways 07L/25R and 16R/34L were well advanced and by 1952 these were in operation as 07/25 of 1,800 m (5,905 ft) and 17/35 of 2,000 m (6,562 ft). As planned the parallel runways would have been only 250 m (820 ft) apart and, wisely, the original plan was abandoned. By 1953 runway 02L/20R was in service as 02/20 with a length of 1,752 m (5,747 ft). The northern part of the projected 16L/34R was built as a taxiway. Runway 07/25 was the instrument runway.

The 07/25 and 02/20 runways have been reconstructed and lengthened to form the present airport and the old 17/35 runway now serves as a taxiway.

Bilbao   Aeropuerto Bilbao   ICAO: LEBB   IATA: BIO

43° 18′ 04″ N   02° 54′ 40″ W   Elevation: 132 ft (40 m)
Runway: 10/28   2,030 m (6,660 ft)   RT
Aids: TVOR, NDB, L

	1975	1976	1977	1978
Passengers	455,322	532,210	593,256	623,334
Transport movements	7,536	8,846	9,659	9,589

Scheduled services 1978: Air France, Aviaco, British Airways and Iberia
A new airport is to be built to serve Bilbao

Gerona   Aeropuerto de Costa Brava

ICAO: LEGE   IATA: GRO
41° 54′ 05″ N   02° 45′ 40″ E   Elevation: 469 ft (143 m)
Runway: 02/20   2,400 m (7,874 ft)   ART   VASI 02/20
Aids: VOR/DME, NDB, ILS CAT I 20

	1970	1975	1976	1977	1978
Passengers	696,804	970,110	793,580	740,503	815,465
Transport movements	8,836	9,582	8,502	7,383	7,892

Scheduled services 1978: Iberia only

Ibiza   Aeropuerto de Ibiza

38° 52' 18" N   01° 22' 10" E   3.7 nm (6.85 km) SW of Ibiza
ICAO: LEIB   IATA code: IBZ   Time zone: GMT plus 1
Authority: Subsecretaría de Aviación Civil
Elevation: 23 ft (7 m)   Ref temp: 26 deg C
Runway: 07/25   2,800 × 45 m (9,186 × 148 ft) concrete
Pavement strength: LCN 105
Landing category: ICAO CAT I
Lighting:
    R/W   LIH white edge, last 600 m (1,968 ft) white/yellow
    App   R/W 25   Calvert LIH white centreline with two crossbars. VASIS 07/25.
    Thr   green wing bars
    Txy   blue edge
Aids: NDB, L, ILS CAT I 25
Twr frequency: 118.5/139.3   App frequency: 119.8
Terminals: Scheduled and charter terminals with single apron
Scheduled services 1978: Aviaco and Iberia

Traffic:	1970	1975	1976	1977	1978
Passengers (total)	878,387	1,514,699	1,514,338	1,637,856	1,898,572
Cargo (tonnes)	2,722	—	6,915	8,493	8,982
Transport movements	13,180	16,478	16,084	16,874	18,120

Ibiza, one of the Balearic Islands off the Spanish east coast, is a popular European tourist resort. Its airport, southwest of the town of Ibiza, in 1978 handled 1,898,572 passengers but less than one-third travelled on Spanish domestic services and 1,174,206 used non-scheduled flights.

A new charter terminal capable of handling 1,800 passengers an hour was opened late in 1971, and it is at the west end of the 750 by 200 m (2,460 by 656 ft) apron on the north side. At the east end of the apron is the older and much smaller scheduled service terminal. There is a full-length parallel taxiway with a high-speed exit for each direction. The 07 threshold is only 400 m (1,312 ft) from the Mediterranean.

Lanzarote, Canary Islands (Islas Canarias)
Aeropuerto de Lanzarote

          ICAO: GCRR   IATA: ACE
28° 56' 15" N   13° 36' 13" W   Elevation: 46 ft (14 m)
Runway: 04/22   2,400 m (7,874 ft)   RT   VASI 04
Aids: VOR/DME, NDB

	1970	1975	1976	1977	1978
Passengers	212,709	560,846	597,570	627,882	737,702
Transport movements	6,340	8,732	8,260	8,532	11,248

Scheduled services 1978: Iberia only

Las Palmas, Canary Islands
Aeropuerto de Las Palmas de Gran Canaria

27° 56′ 00″ N   15° 22′ 45″ W   10.26 nm (19 km) S of Las Palmas
ICAO: GCLP   IATA code: LPA   Time zone: GMT
Authority: Subsecretaría de Aviación Civil
Elevation: 79 ft (24 m)   Ref temp: 25 deg C
Runway: 03/21   3,100 × 45 m (10,170 × 148 ft) asphalt
Pavement strength: LCN 100
Landing category: ICAO CAT I
Lighting:
    R/W   LIH white edge, last 500 m (1,640 ft) white/yellow, and white
                centreline
    App   R/W 03   LIM white coded centreline with crossbars and
                VASIS
                R/W 21   five red bars on left and single red lights on right
                of clearway, and VASIS
    Thr   green wing bars
    Txy   blue edge
Aids: VOR/DME, NDB, VDF, L, ILS CAT I 03
Twr frequency: 118.3/121.5   App frequency: 119.1
Terminal: 100 m (328 ft) long terminal at north of airport. Large apron with
    five INS positions
Scheduled services 1978: 12 airlines
Airline bases: Iberia and Spantax

Traffic:	1970	1975	1976	1977	1978
Passengers (total)	1,742,281	3,717,008	3,814,469	4,362,048	4,482,974
Cargo (tonnes)	14,032	33,960	28,637	36,886	43,605
Aircraft movements	42,252	50,681	50,163	52,783	—
Transport movements	41,207	49,910	48,790	51,258	55,901

During 1976 Douglas DC-9s accounted for 32 per cent of transport movements, Boeing 727s for 13.11 per cent, Fokker F.27s for 9.98 per cent and Douglas DC-8s for 8.43 per cent.

Las Palmas is one of the two main ports in the Canary Islands, and in 1978 more than 2 mn of its air passengers travelled on non-scheduled international flights, emphasizing the scale of the tourist industry.

Earlier known as Gando Airport, in the 1940s and 1950s there was a single 4,000 ft (1,219 m) runway, but as traffic increased considerable development took place and in 1970 money was allocated to enable the airport to handle Boeing 747s.

The airport is beside the shore and its single runway has a parallel taxiway with three high-speed exits. The civil terminal is at the northwest end of the airport, the Spantax maintenance base is at the southwest, and to the east of the runway is a Spanish Air Force base. Air Spain and Iberia have maintenance facilities near the centre of the airport.

Madrid - Barajas Airport on 21 June, 1954. The parallel 05/23 runways and 10/28 (now abandoned) are on the left, 15/33 runs across the picture, and the diagonal runway in the foreground is 01/19. The terminal can be seen under construction near the centre. (*John Stroud*)

Madrid   Aeropuerto Madrid - Barajas

40° 28′ 35″ N   03° 33′ 34″ W   7 nm (13 km) ENE of city
ICAO: LEMD   IATA code: MAD   Time zone: GMT plus 1
Authority: Subsecretaría de Aviación Civil
Elevation: 1,998 ft (609 m)   Ref temp: 28 deg C
Runways: 01/19   3,700 × 45 m (12,139 × 148 ft) concrete
          15/33   4,100 × 45 m (13,451 × 148 ft) concrete
Pavement strength: 01/19   30,000 kg (66,139 lb) ISWL;   15/33
     45,000 kg (99,208 lb) ISWL
Landing category: ICAO CAT I
Lighting:
    R/W   01/19   LIH white edge, last 600 m (1,968 ft) yellow
             15/33   LIH white edge, last 600 m (1,968 ft) yellow, and
             LIH white centreline. Red end lights each runway
    App   R/W 01   LIH white centreline and crossbars
             R/W 15   LIM white centreline with one crossbar
             R/W 33   LIH white centreline with crossbars and
             sequenced flashers. VASIS 01 and 33
    Thr   LIH green
    Txy   blue edge, green centreline on some sections
Aids: VOR/DME, VDF, ASR, L, ILS CAT I 01 and 33
Twr frequency: 118.1/121.5   App frequency: 119.9/120.9
Terminals: National (domestic) terminal with six piers and International (south) terminal with six boarding concourses. Separate cargo terminal.
Scheduled services 1978: 41 airlines

310

Main base: Aviaco, Iberia and Spantax

Traffic:	1970	1975	1976	1977	1978
Passengers (total)	4,518,212	7,959,811	8,417,426	9,378,344	10,530,237
Cargo (tonnes)	53,048	103,437	123,978	147,216	154,255
Aircraft movements	85,912	118,163	121,896	123,610	—
Transport movements	83,650	114,918	117,942	119,914	123,962

During 1976 DC-9s accounted for 33.33 per cent of transport movements and Boeing 727s for 32.6 per cent.

During the 1920s Madrid's customs airport was Getafe, 11 km (6.8 miles) south of the city. This airport, with single asphalt runway, is still in use, but by the early 1930s a new airport had been created southeast of Barajas village and 2 km (1¼ miles) west of the Jarama River.

The new airport, known as Barajas, had a grass landing area measuring 1,400 by 1,200 m (4,593 by 3,937 ft) on which there was a white circle and the name Aeropuerto de Madrid. There was a small terminal building and hangars on the west side of the airport, with three taxiways leading from the apron to the flying area. In describing the airport, the 1932 edition of the *Guide Aéronautique International* stated 'The surrounding fields are cultivated, suitable for forced landings.'

A major development plan was made for Barajas and by 1949 there were two concrete runways, 05/23 of 2,600 m (8,530 ft), and 15/33 of 1,830 m (6,004 ft) with planned extension to 3,050 m (10,006 ft). A 2,600 m (8,530 ft) runway 09/27 had also been planned.

By the spring of 1951 runway 15/33 had been lengthened to 3,060 m

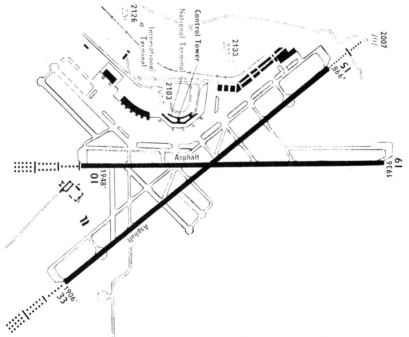

Madrid - Barajas Airport. (*British Airways Aerad*)

311

(10,040 ft), 2,040 m (6,692 ft) of 09/27 had been built, and there was a plan for a 18/36 runway. Runway 09/27 was redesignated 10/28 but the planned extension was never built.

Development continued and by the summer of 1953 the original 05/23 runway had been designated 05L/23R and there was the parallel 05R/23L—both 2,600 m (8,530 ft) long. The planned 18/36 runway had been built as 01/19 with a length of 2,600 m (8,530 ft) and 15/33's length was then given as 3,050 m (10,006 ft). Parallel taxiways had been built for the full length of the 05/23 and 15/33 runways, and the eastward extension of 10/28 and its parallel taxiway was still projected.

Work had also begun on a large multi-level terminal building but its completion was long delayed and it was not opened until the second half of the 1950s.

Since that time runway 01/19 has been extended at its northern end to give an overall length of 3,700 m (12,139 ft) and runway 15/33 has been extended at each end to a length of 4,100 m (13,451 ft). All other runways have been abandoned or incorporated into the taxiway system.

Plans were made for an international terminal, to handle up to 6,000 passengers an hour, for completion by the end of 1972. This is a curved structure, south of the earlier terminal, it has six boarding concourses with aerobridges and was not opened until 1974. Orders and options were placed in 1974 for five Plane-Mates for operation between the terminal and remote stands. The earlier terminal is now used for domestic flights.

Málaga   Aeropuerto de Málaga

36° 40' 30" N   04° 29' 58" W   4.3 nm (7.96 km) SW of city
ICAO: LEMG   IATA code: AGP   Time zone: GMT plus 1
Authority: Subsecretaría de Aviación Civil
Elevation: 52 ft (16 m)   Ref temp: 27 deg C
Runway: 14/32   3,200 × 45 m (10,500 × 148 ft)* asphalt
Pavement strength: 22,000 kg (48,502 lb) ISWL
Landing category: ICAO CAT I
Lighting:
R/W   LIH white edge, last 600 m (1,968 ft) yellow, and centreline
App   R/W 32   LIM white centreline with one crossbar. VASIS 14/32
Thr   green
Txy   blue edge and white centreline
Aids: VOR, NDB, ILS CAT I 32
Twr frequency: 118.1   App frequency: 119.3
Terminals: Separate domestic and international terminals and aprons.
Scheduled services 1978: 11 airlines

Traffic:	1970	1975	1976	1977	1978
Passengers (total)	1,678,392	2,682,003	2,501,553	2,882,432	3,528,957
Cargo (tonnes)	3,495	5,498	6,326	6,446	6,856
Aircraft movements	30,800	40,616	39,283	40,326	—
Transport movements	27,296	35,580	34,284	35,603	38,442

During 1976 Boeing 727s accounted for 26.52 per cent of transport movements, DC-9s for 23.56 per cent and DHC Twin Otters for 13.62 per cent.

* There is a full-length parallel taxiway with high-speed exits.

British Airways BAC One-Eleven 400 G-AWBL at Málaga Airport, with the control tower on the left. (*Austin J. Brown—via Airline Publications and Sales Ltd*)

Málaga in Andalucia first appeared on the air transport map on 1 September, 1919, when Lignes Aériennes Latécoère opened the second stage of the pioneer route from Toulouse to West Africa and ultimately South America. On that day the route was extended from Barcelona to Rabat via Alicante, Málaga and Tangier.

It is almost certain that Latécoère prepared the Málaga aerodrome which passed to its successor, Aéropostale, and then was taken over by the State.

The grass aerodrome, with a landing area measuring 500 by 400 m (1,640 by 1,312 ft) was situated southwest of Málaga, immediately southeast of the village of Churriana, just south of the River Guadalhorce and only a short distance inland from the Mediterranean. By 1932 the landing area had been enlarged to 680 by 550 m (2,231 by 1,804 ft) and at that time the airport was listed as Málaga Churriana but at least as early as 1927 it was known as El Rompedizo and this name was still being used during the early 1950s, when it was still a grass aerodrome with a maximum landing run of about 1,190 m (3,900 ft).

Since that time Spain has attracted an enormous growth of tourism and the Málaga airport, situated mid-way between the city and Torremolinos, was ideally suited to cater for this traffic.

The original site had been so well chosen that it became part of the completely new airport, albeit a very small part, and the present 32 threshold is sited on the old landing ground most of which forms the southeast corner of the present airport.

Menorca (Mahón), Balearic Islands   Aeropuerto de Menorca

	ICAO: LEMH		IATA: MAH	
39° 51′ 47″ N	04° 13′ 02″ E			Elevation: 286 ft (87 m)
Runway: 01/19	2,350 m (7,710 ft)		ART	VASI 01
Aids: VOR, NDB				

	1970	1975	1976	1977	1978
Passengers	238,992	539,861	529,412	513,291	653,100
Transport movements	5,192	7,410	7,572	6,748	7,699

Scheduled services 1978: Aviaco and Iberia

313

Palma de Mallorca Airport from near the 06L threshold, with the terminal area on the right.

Palma de Mallorca, Balearic Islands
Aeropuerto de Palma de Mallorca

39° 33′ 24″ N   02° 43′ 50″ E   4.32 nm (8 km) E of city
ICAO: LEPA   IATA code: PMI   Time zone: GMT plus 1
Authority: Subsecretaría de Aviación Civil
Area: 527 hectares (1,302 acres)
Elevation: 13 ft (4 m)   Ref temp: 26 deg C
Runway: 06L/24R   3,200 × 45 m (10,500 × 148 ft) asphalt, concrete ends
Pavement strength: LCN 120
Landing category: ICAO CAT I
Lighting:
     R/W   LIH white edge, last 600 m (1,968 ft) yellow, and white centreline
     App   R/W 24R   LIH white precision approach centreline with two crossbars. VASIS 06L/24R
     Thr   green
     Txy   blue edge and green centreline
Aids: VOR/DME, TACAN, NDB, ILS CAT I 24R
Twr frequency: 118.3/121.5   App frequency: 119.15/119.4
Terminals: Scheduled service terminal of 18,000 sq m (193,752 sq ft) with 13 departure and six arrival gates; charter terminal of 13,102 sq m (141,030 sq ft) with six departure and six arrival gates; and total of 48 aircraft stands.

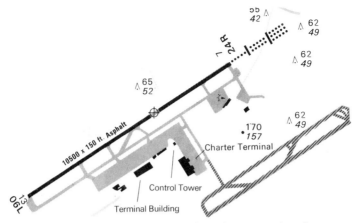

Palma de Mallorca Airport. (*British Airways Aerad*)

Scheduled services 1978: 10 airlines
Main base: Trabajos Aéreos y Enlaces (TAE)

Traffic:	1970	1975	1976	1977	1978
Passengers (total)	4,684,851	6,768,936	6,328,165	7,032,969	7,876,696
Cargo (tonnes)	14,929	22,214	24,541	28,209	30,408
Aircraft movements	67,140	74,132	70,171	75,998	—
Transport movements	63,960	72,868	68,898	74,415	78,991

Majorca (Mallorca) is the largest of the Balearic Islands but it has a population of only a little over a third of a million, yet the airport handles more than 7 mn passengers a year. Most of this traffic consists of holidaymakers who appreciate the island's mild climate and is catered for by largescale charter and inclusive tour operations.

The main hall of the Palma de Mallorca terminal.

315

The island's airport was for many years Son Bonet which had two grass runways—06/24 of 1,493 m (4,900 ft) and 17/35 of 998 m (3,275 ft). Both were approximately 300 m (984 ft) wide. The longest strip was edged with white and yellow lights and had an electric flarepath. The airport had obstruction lights, a flashing beacon and illuminated wind-T, and there were approach lights to 06/24.

This airport was obviously not capable of handling the increasing traffic volume and modern aircraft and the small grass military aerodrome a few miles to the southwest and closer to the coast was developed as the civil airport, although it retains a military area at the northeast end.

The 06/24 runway (now 06L/24R) was built, with full-length parallel taxiway, and in 1966 the scheduled service terminal was opened with its apron facing the runway.

For several years the airport charts have shown the parallel 2,400 m (7,874 ft) 06R/24L runway as under construction but it is not in use. On the southwest side of the taxiway linking the two runways a charter traffic terminal was opened in 1972. The two terminal aprons are joined and form a large L.

Runway 06L/24R's parallel taxiway can be used as an emergency runway, over its full length by day and all but the southwest 500 m (1,640 ft) at night. The taxiway LCN is 91, it has edge and centreline lights and green wing bars near each end.

Puerto del Rosario, Canary Islands   Aeropuerto Fuerteventura

ICAO: GCFV   IATA: FUE
28° 27′ 03″ N   13° 51′ 43″ W   Elevation: 75 ft (23 m)
Runway: 01/19   2,400 m (7,874 ft)   RT   VASI 01
Aids: NDB, VDF, L

	1970	1975	1976	1977	1978
Passengers	68,515	180,650	212,901	275,425	336,597
Transport movements	3,354	4,892	5,482	6,048	5,320

Scheduled services 1978: Iberia only

Santa Cruz de La Palma, Canary Islands   Aeropuerto La Palma

ICAO: GCLA   IATA: SPC
28° 37′ 21″ N   17° 45′ 13″ W   Elevation: 95 ft (29 m)
Runway: 01/19   1,700 m (5,577 ft)   ART   VASI 01
Aids: NDB, L

	1970	1975	1976	1977	1978
Passengers	92,412	201,615	234,829	257,019	320,219
Transport movements	2,978	5,960	6,214	7,384	8,738

Scheduled services 1978: Iberia only

Santiago de Compostela   Aeropuerto de Santiago

ICAO: LEST   IATA: SCQ
42° 53′ 40″ N   08° 24′ 56″ W′   Elevation: 1,214 ft (370 m)
Runway: 18/36   2,550 m (8,366 ft)   ART   VASI 18/36
Aids: VOR/DME, NDB, ILS CAT I 18

	1970	1975	1976	1977	1978
Passengers	89,436	439,389	550,334	638,828	666,782
Transport movements	1,714	5,418	6,590	7,280	7,293

Scheduled services 1978: Air France and Iberia
A crosswind runway is to be constructed

Seville (Sevilla)   Aeropuerto de Sevilla

ICAO: LEZL   IATA: SVQ
37° 25′ 04″ N   05° 53′ 57″ W   Elevation: 112 ft (34 m)
Longest runway: 10/28   3,360 m (11,023 ft)   ART   VASI 10/28
Aids: VOR, NDB, VDF, ILS CAT I 28

	1970	1975	1976	1977
Passengers	425,413	762,719	812,151	921,839
Transport movements	11,506	13,272	14,796	15,752

Scheduled services 1978: Air France, Aviaco and Iberia

Tenerife, Canary Islands
    Aeropuerto de Tenerife - Los Rodeos (Tenerife Norte)

28° 28′ 30″ N   16° 19′ 50″ W   7 nm (13 km) from Santa Cruz
ICAO: GCXO   IATA code: TCI   Time zone: GMT
Authority: Subsecretaría de Aviación Civil
Elevation: 2,073 ft (632 m)   Ref temp: 16 deg C
Runway: 12/30   3,400 × 45 m (11,155 × 148 ft) asphalt*

* First 300 m (984 ft) at threshold 30 is concrete

Pavement strength: 26,000 kg (57,320 lb) ISWL
Landing cateogry: ICAO CAT I
Lighting:
    R/W   white edge, last 500 m (1,640 ft) white/yellow; white
            centreline, first 500 m (1,640 ft) yellow
    App   R/W 30   white centreline with two crossbars. VASIS
            12/30
    Thr   LIH green with strobes
    Txy   blue edge
Aids: VOR/DME, NDB, L, ILS CAT I 30
Twr frequency: 118.7/121.5   App frequency: 119.7

Terminal: Passenger terminal to northeast of runway. Apron approximately 800 by 160 m (2,625 by 525 ft). Passenger handling at first floor level and steps lead to apron loading buses
Scheduled services 1978: Air France, Iberia and Lufthansa

Traffic:	1970	1975	1976	1977
Passengers (total)	1,234,000	2,403,776	2,805,776	2,966,850
Cargo (tonnes)	7,175	17,613	17,480	20,168
Aircraft movements	27,680	37,390	39,624	41,558
Transport movements	27,040	33,990	36,990	38,472

During 1976 DC-9s accounted for 29.4 per cent of transport movements, Fokker F.27s for 27.17 per cent and Boeing 727s for 15.37 per cent.

Tenerife, Canary Islands
Aeropuerto Reina Sofia (Queen Sofia Airport)

28° 02′ 34″ N   16° 34′ 14″ W   32.4 nm (60 km) SSW of Santa Cruz
ICAO: GCTS   IATA code: TFS   Time zone: GMT
Authority: Subsecretaría de Aviación Civil
Elevation: 210 ft (64 m)   Ref temp: 28 deg C
Runway: 08/26   3,200 × 45 m (10,500 × 148 ft) asphalt, concrete ends
Pavement strength: auw 300,000 kg (661,387 lb)
Landing category: ICAO CAT I
Lighting:
  R/W   white edge and centreline
  App   R/W 08   CAT I precision approach. VASIS 08
  Thr   green
  Txy   edge and centreline
Aids: VOR/DME, ILS CAT I 08
Twr frequency: 118.9   App frequency: 120.3
Terminal: Rectangular passenger terminal to north of runway, with 115,640 sq m (1,244,749 sq ft) concrete apron
Scheduled services 1978: Air France, Iberia and Lufthansa*

Traffic: *see* Aeropuerto de Tenerife - Los Rodeos

There is a full-length parallel taxiway with three high-speed exits. According to ICAO the airport is to have CAT II ILS and precision approach lighting and touchdown zone lighting for runway 08.

Tenerife, the largest of the Canary Islands, is part of the Spanish province of Santa Cruz de Tenerife and although only having an area of 2,058 sq km (795 sq miles) its mountains rise to 3,710 m (12,172 ft). For many years the island was served by Los Rodeos Airport in the north of the island and only 8 miles (13 km) from the capital, Santa Cruz.

Tourist traffic from all over Europe has grown enormously in postwar years and total annual passenger arrivals by air are equal to about four times the island's population.

In the early postwar years the single runway, 12/30, was 1,463 m (4,800 ft) long but this has been increased to 3,400 m (11,155 ft) and to its north has a parallel taxiway with high-speed exits. The airport is equipped

* Airlines operating scheduled services to Los Rodeos in summer 1978.

The terminal at Los Rodeos Airport, Tenerife. (*M. J. Hooks*)

with approach lighting and ILS but, being situated at an elevation of 632 m
(2,073 ft) and close to the mountains, is subject to low cloud right down
onto its surface.

Los Rodeos Airport has been described as one of the most dangerous
airports in the world but this is unfair considering that aircraft movements
average around 40,000 a year. However, statistics can be dramatically
changed by a single accident and, on 27 March, 1977, Los Rodeos Airport
was the scene of the worst ever aviation accident. On that day Las Palmas
Airport had suffered a terrorist attack and numerous aircraft were diverted
to Tenerife, where insufficient apron space necessitated some aircraft being
parked on the taxiway. Thus aircraft had to taxi along a section of the
runway before gaining access to the taxiway. Low cloud severely restricted
visibility and a KLM Boeing 747 attempted to take off while a Pan
American Boeing 747 was taxi-ing on the runway. The undercarriage of the
KLM aircraft ploughed through the Pan American aircraft and both were
destroyed by fire. There are contradictory figures for the number killed in
the collision and subsequent fires but these range from 574 to 581. The
report published late in 1978 blamed the KLM crew for taking off without
clearance.

Long before the collision took place the Spanish authorities were
constructing a new airport on the south of the island. The new airport has
the advantage of being at an elevation of only 64 m (210 ft) but is 60 km (37
miles) from Santa Cruz and still relatively close to high ground. Initially
known as Aeropuerto Tenerife Sur (Tenerife South Airport) it came into
operation on 2 November, 1978, and was officially opened on 6 November
by Queen Sofia, whose name the airport has now been given. Design
capacity of the new airport is 8 mn passengers a year and scheduled
completion date was May 1979.

From November 1978 all foreign air services, charter flights of
Spantax and TAE, and 20 per cent of Iberia's scheduled services were
transferred to Queen Sofia Airport. With completion of the airport it is
intended that Los Rodeos, now also referred to as Tenerife Norte (Tenerife
North), will be used as an alternate and for military flights.

319

Valencia   Aeropuerto de Valencia

ICAO: LEVC   IATA: VLC
39° 29' 21" N   00° 28' 54" W   Elevation: 226 ft (69 m)
Longest runway: 12/30   2,696 m (8,845 ft)   ART   VASI 30
Aids: VORTAC, VDF, SRE, PAR, ILS CAT I 30

	1970	1975	1976	1977
Passengers	458,987	813,322	929,493	994,770
Transport movements	11,262	13,148	14,470	14,736

Scheduled services 1978: Air France, Aviaco, British Airways and Iberia.

Sri Lanka (formerly Ceylon)

Colombo   Colombo Airport Katunayake

ICAO: VCBI   IATA: CMB
07° 10' 45" N   79° 52' 59" E   Elevation: 29 ft (9 m)
Runway: 04/22   3,368 m (11,050 ft)   ART   VASI 04/22
Aids: VOR/DME, NDB, ILS CAT I 22

	1970	1975	1976	1977
Passengers	157,531	224,267	203,684	283,446
Transport movements	3,146	7,480	8,587	9,690

Scheduled services 1978: 12 airlines
Main base: Air Lanka

The airport, formerly Bandaranaike International Airport
(Katunayake), was renamed in August 1978.

Sudan

Khartoum   Khartoum Airport   ICAO: HSSS   IATA: KRT

15° 36' 00" N   32° 33' 30" E   Elevation: 1,261 ft (384 m)
Longest runway: 18/36   2,550 m (8,366 ft)   ART   VASI 18/36
Aids: VOR, NDB, VDF, L*

	1976	1977
Passengers	362,872	247,133†
Transport movements	—	4,782†

Scheduled services 1978: 16 airlines
Main base: Sudan Airways

*CAT II ILS was ordered in 1974. †January–September only

SAS's Boeing 747 OY-KHA *Ivar Viking* at Gothenburg Landvetter Airport in November 1977. (*SAS*)

Sweden (Sverige)

Gothenburg (Göteborg)　　　Landvetter Flygplats

57° 39′ 37″ N　　　12° 17′ 37″ E　　　11 nm (20 km) ESE of city
ICAO: ESGG　　　IATA code: GOT　　　Time zone: GMT plus 1
Authority: Board of Civil Aviation
Elevation: 506 ft (154 m)　　　　　　　　Ref temp: 22 deg C
Runway: 03/21　　3,300 × 45 m (10,827 × 148 ft) asphalt
Pavement strength: LCN 115
Landing category: ICAO CAT II*
Lighting:
　　R/W　　LIH and LIL white edge, last 600 m (1,968 ft) yellow; white LIH centreline, last 300 m (984 ft) red, previous 600 m (1,968 ft) red/white. TDZ 03/21. Red end lights
　　App　　R/W 03/21　　LIH and LIL white 900 m (2,953 ft) centreline and crossbars. Red barrettes on inner 300 m (984 ft). VASIS 03/21
　　Thr　　LIH and LIL green
　　Txy　　green centreline with flashing yellow at turning points. Red stop bars
Aids: VOR/DME, VDF/UDF, NDB, SRE, RVR, ILS CAT II 03/21*
Twr frequency: 118.6　　　　　　　App frequency: 124.2
Terminals: Two-level passenger terminal with 13 nose-in and 10 outer stands. Six stands have pneumatic docking system with aerobridges. Two 150-passenger mobile lounges. Separate cargo terminal with three nose-in aircraft stands.

*CAT II not approved by August 1979

Scheduled services 1978: 10 airlines
Airline base: SAS

Traffic:*	1970	1975	1976	1977
Passengers (total)	854,615	1,258,626	1,358,191	1,412,263
Cargo (tonnes)	9,980	13,694	11,710	12,073
Aircraft movements	83,130	98,750	105,104	81,316
Transport movements	26,464	29,186	29,860	29,250

* Göteborg Landvetter came into operation on 3 October, 1977. Figures 1970–76 are for Göteborg Torslanda and 1977 figures cover both airports.

From 1923 until 2 October, 1977, Torslanda served as Gothenburg's airport. It was conveniently situated close to the west of the city, was picturesque but suffered from being surrounded by rocky terrain. In recent years there were noise problems, limitations on operating weight because of runway length, and the land it occupied was regarded as valuable for industrial expansion.

In 1967 it was proposed that there should be a new airport and two years later a site had been selected and financing agreed as a joint venture by the State and local municipalities and county councils.

The area chosen for the new Gothenburg Airport was to the east of the city on a plateau in a rocky wooded area with a number of lakes and peat moors. In order to build the airport some 8 mn cubic metres of rock, earth and peat had to be blasted and excavated but this provided on-site fill for the extensive levelling required and the filling of a number of lakes.

The new airport was officially opened by King Carl XVI Gustaf on 1 October, 1977, an SAS DC-9 on a flight from Torslanda made the first landing, and the airport became operational on 3 October. The single runway, 03L/21R, is served by a full-length parallel taxiway, there are high-speed exits, a second parallel taxiway in the terminal area and a passing link near the 03 threshold. The terminal area is to the east of the runway near its northern end, and it is planned that by 1985 there will be a 2,800 m (9,186 ft) 03R/21L runway 1,600 m (5,249 ft) from the present runway. Runway 03L/21R has CAT II lighting and ILS at each end but initially some limitations had to be imposed because of glidepath irregularities.

The terminal, measuring 300 by 80 m (984 by 262 ft) and clad in stainless steel sheet, was designed to have surplus capacity, about 3 mn passengers annually, on projected traffic of 2.5 mn passengers in 1985. There are six nose-in aircraft stands served by aerobridges, with one capable of handling Boeing 747s and three handling aircraft of DC-10 category. There are also five gates for mobile lounges and two 150-passenger vehicles are already in service. A hot-water snow and ice clearance system is installed in the apron.

The airport has a hangar capable of accommodating two Boeing 747s, and SAS has a cargo terminal which will be capable of handling 40,000 tonnes a year by 1980, 70,000 tonnes by 1985 and 110,000 tonnes by 1990. Passenger forecasts for Gothenburg are 3 mn in 1985, 5 mn in 1995 and 6 mn in 2000.

General aviation including club and school flying is to remain at Torslanda until a new general aviation aerodrome is ready.

Malmö Sturup Airport. (*Courtesy SAS*)

Malmö   Malmö Sturup Flygplats

ICAO: ESMS   IATA: MMA
55° 32′ 54″ N   13° 21′ 34″ E   Elevation: 236 ft (72 m)
Longest runway: 17/35   2,800 m (9,186 ft)   ART
Aids: VOR/DME, NDB, VDF, RVR 17/35, ILS CAT II 17, ILS CAT I 35

	1970*	1975	1976	1977
Passengers	656,277	525,446	676,270	671,643
Transport movements	18,824	13,048	15,796	15,460

*Figures for Malmö Bulltofta

Scheduled services 1978: Linjeflyg and SAS

Bulltofta was the Malmö airport from 1923 until the opening of Malmö Sturup on 1 December, 1972.

Arlanda International Airport, Stockholm, terminal area with a Sterling Airways Caravelle and SAS DC-9 on the apron. (*SAS*)

Stockholm   Arlanda International Airport

59° 39′ 09″ N   17° 55′ 19″ E   20 nm (37 km) N of city
ICAO: ESSA   IATA code: ARN   Time zone: GMT plus 1
Authority: Board of Civil Aviation
Area: 3,116 hectares (7,700 acres)
Elevation: 123 ft (37 m)   Ref temp: 22.2 deg C
Runways: 01/19   3,300 × 45 m (10,827 × 148 ft) concrete cross-grooved
            08/26   2,500 × 45 m (8,202 × 148 ft) concrete cross-grooved
Pavement strength: 01/19 LCN 120; 08/26 LCN 105
Landing category: ICAO CAT II*
Lighting:
    R/W   01/19   LIH and LIL white edge, last 900 m (2,953 ft) yellow, LIH white centreline, last 300 m (984 ft) red, previous 600 m (1,968 ft) red/white. White TDZ 01/19
              08/26   LIH and LIL white edge, last 900 m (2,953 ft) yellow
    App   R/W 01   LIH and LIL white barrette centreline with crossbars and red side barrettes on inner 300 m (984 ft) R/W 19 and 08/26 LIH and LIL white centreline with crossbars. VASIS 08/26
    Thr   LIH green with LIL wing bars.
    Txy   blue edge
Aids: VOR/DME, NDB, VDF, TAR, L, SSR, RVR 01/19, ILS CAT II 01*, ILS CAT I 19 and 26
Twr frequency: 118.5
Terminals: International terminal with two piers and heated apron for 20 nose-in and four remote aircraft stands. Separate domestic terminal with four aircraft stands. Light aircraft apron and additional east and west aprons with 16 aircraft stands
Scheduled services 1978: 20 airlines
Main base: SAS (Sweden)

Traffic:	1970	1975	1976	1977
Passengers (total)	2,600,181	3,743,607	3,941,046	4,126,566
Cargo (tonnes)	36,351	32,178	34,410	34,994
Aircraft movements	74,184	84,910	83,824	88,172
Transport movements	52,984	63,212	66,090	67,314

*CAT II not approved by August 1979

324

Sweden was very early in seeing that its capital city would require a second airport and already by 1947 a site had been chosen. It was not easy to find a suitable area and the site has been criticized for being too far from the city and in the wrong direction.

Initially the new airport site was known as Halmsjön, the closest of the many lakes in the wooded area chosen, and for a long time it was a Swedish joke that work was going ahead—two men with spades doing the actual work. Neither was the first illustration of the project inspiring, for it showed hangars built on one of the runway thresholds.

During the 1950s it was envisaged that Arlanda, as it had become, would handle mostly long-haul international services but soon after its opening in 1959 jet noise at Bromma became a problem. As a result all scheduled international flights were transferred to Arlanda in 1962, international charter flights in 1967–68 and all domestic jet-operated services in 1969.

From its opening Arlanda only had a simple temporary terminal. By the early 1970s the airport was handling more than 3 mn passengers annually and a temporary charter terminal was opened in May 1973 to give some relief to the main temporary terminal.

In December 1962 the airport master plan was completed and this anticipated the need for a parallel main runway sometime in the 1980s and capacity for 15–20 mn annual passengers by the year 2000 or shortly after. To handle this volume of traffic it was decided to build a series of terminal units with a total of 60 aircraft stands—with each apron unit having 6–8 stands.

Design of the first unit was begun in June 1972, construction started in the summer of 1973 and the terminal was opened on 1 November, 1976. The main unit consists of a central roadside four-storey building with two three-storey traffic piers. The central building, served by a two-level road system, is about 200 m (656 ft) long and is really two units—one to serve each pier—with 22 check-in counters in each half.

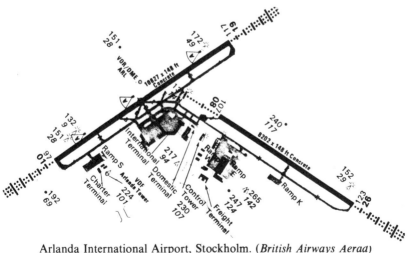

Arlanda International Airport, Stockholm. (*British Airways Aerad*)

325

The piers are 145 m (476 ft) long and each has 10 gate lounges with aerobridges serving 10 nose-in stands. Four stands can take Boeing 747s, 11 can take aircraft of up to DC-10/TriStar/A300 size and five can take aircraft in the Boeing 727/DC-9 category. Some of the gate lounges are too big for present traffic but can handle two loads for such aircraft as the DC-9—one at the gate and one on a remote stand reached by bus. The lefthand pier (B) is mainly used for charters and the righthand pier (A) mainly for scheduled services. Capacity of this first terminal unit is about 4½ mn passengers a year.

No transfer lounge has been provided because only about 2 per cent of Arlanda's total traffic is transit. Attached to this first unit is an SAS operations building. Domestic traffic is handled at a small terminal unit to the east of Pier A.

Each aircraft stand at the international terminal unit has a section with hot-water heating to melt ice and snow.

Although Arlanda was built in open country it now has to impose noise restrictions and take offs on runway 26 are not allowed unless winds are unsuitable for the other runways. As far as possible only idle reverse-thrust is allowed between 21.00 and 05.00 GMT.

Stockholm   Bromma Flygplats

59° 21′ 18″ N   17° 56′ 44″ E   4 nm (7.4 km) WNW of city
ICAO: ESSB   IATA code: BMA   Time zone: GMT plus 1
Authority: Board of Civil Aviation
Area: 270 hectares (667 acres) approximately
Elevation: 48 ft (15 m)   Ref temp: 23 deg C
Runways: 05/23   1,140 × 40 m (3,740 × 131 ft) asphalt
        12/30   1,897 × 45 m (6,224 × 148 ft) asphalt
Pavement strength: 15,000 kg (33,069 lb) ISWL (12/30)
Landing category: ICAO CAT I

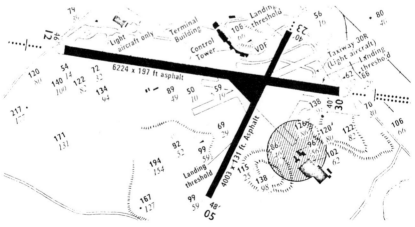

Bromma Airport, Stockholm. (*British Airways Aerad*)

326

Bromma Airport, Stockholm, shortly after its opening in 1936.

Lighting:
R/W	05/23	LIL white edge. Red end lights
	12/30	LIH and LIL white edge, last 600 m (1,968 ft) yellow. Red end lights
App	R/W 23	LIL white centreline with red wing bars
	R/W 12	LIH and LIL white centreline with crossbars. AVASIS
	R/W 30	LIH and LIL white centreline and crossbar and LIH and LIL white/red wing bars. VASIS
Thr	05/23	LIL green, 12/30 LIH and LIL green
Txy	blue edge	

Aids: VOR/DME, NDB, VDF, PAR, TAR, SRE, L, ILS CAT I 12/30
Twr frequency: 118.1
Terminals: Main passenger and charter terminals with 26 aircraft stands plus light aircraft parking area.
Scheduled services 1978: Linjeflyg and Sydaero
Main base: Linjeflyg

Traffic:	1970	1975	1976	1977
Passengers (total)	662,788	826,535	1,036,361	995,222
Cargo (tonnes)	10,773	5,943	5,542	4,895
Aircraft movements	120,626	110,518	107,356	101,886
Transport movements	28,030	26,594	30,360	30,102

When AB Aerotransport (Swedish Air Lines) opened its first service, between Stockholm and Helsinki, on 2 June, 1924, it used Junkers-F 13 floatplanes operating from Lindarängen seaplane base, and for nearly 12 years Swedish air services to the east had to be worked by seaplanes because there was no Stockholm airport. Swedish landplane services to western Europe and foreign airlines' services terminated at Malmö, although some night mail services used the Barkarby military aerodrome near Stockholm.

327

Construction of an airport in the Stockholm area was extremely difficult because of the terrain but in 1933 work began at Bromma and the runways had to be blasted out of rock. In spite of the difficulties a first-class airport was built and it opened on 23 May, 1936. Four paved runways, the first at a European airport, were prepared. These were aligned east–west, approximately north–south, northwest–southeast and southwest–north-east—it is believed that the northwest–southeast runway was 800 m (2,625 ft) long and that the others were each 1,000 m (3,281 ft) in length. There was an attractive terminal building and a large hangar. By July 1938 there was a proposal to build a 1,500 m (4,921 ft) northwest–southeast instrument runway which when built replaced the original shorter runway immediately alongside.

Subsequently some runways were lengthened and others abandoned. In the immediate postwar period the runways were 05/23 of 1,000 m (3,281 ft), 09/27 of 950 m (3,117 ft), 13/31 of 2,000 m (6,562 ft) and 16/34 of 750 m (2,461 ft). Now only two runways remain in use, 05/23 of 1,140 m (3,740 ft) and 12/30 (formerly 13/31) of 1,897 m (6,224 ft). Terminal extensions have been made, partly in the original hangar, and a charter terminal was constructed to the south of the original terminal.

Bromma was always an attractive and convenient airport but it became surrounded by housing and noise became a serious problem. As early as the winter of 1946–47 it had been decided to build a new airport much further from the city. The new airport was eventually opened in 1959 as Arlanda and DC-8 operations were moved from Bromma to the new airport. All Stockholm's scheduled international traffic was transferred to Arlanda in 1962, international charter flights in 1967–68 and domestic jet-operated services in 1969.

The only scheduled jet services using Bromma are those operated by Linjeflyg with Fokker F.28s, the only jet transport to have approval for such operations. There are severe operating restrictions to reduce noise nuisance and the thresholds of 05/23 and 30 are displaced with varying runway length available by day and night. Jet aircraft are prohibited between 21.00 and 05.00 and Linjeflyg's F.28 operations will only be allowed to continue after 1 July, 1981, if their noise level is considerably reduced.

Switzerland (Suisse/Schweiz)

Geneva (Genève)   Aéroport de Genève - Cointrin

46° 14′ 23″ N	06° 06′ 37″ E	2.2 nm (4 km) WNW of city
ICAO: LSGG	IATA code: GVA	Time zone: GMT plus 1

Authority: République et Canton de Genève (State of Geneva)
Area: 320 hectares (791 acres)
Elevation: 1,411 ft (430 m)   Ref temp: 21.5 deg C

The terminal opened in 1968 at Geneva Airport. Three Swissair DC-9s are on the apron. (*State of Geneva*)

Runways: 05/23   3,900 × 50 m (12,795 × 164 ft)* concrete
There is a 675 × 30 m (2,215 × 98 ft) grass general aviation runway parallel to the main runway on its northwest side

*Threshold 05 is displaced 240 m (788 ft)

Pavement strength: LCN 100
Landing category: ICAO CAT II
Lighting:
    R/W   LIH and LIL white edge, LIH white centreline with red/white over last 900–300 m (2,953–984 ft) and red over last 300 m (984 ft). 600 m (1,968 ft) yellow caution zone. Red end lights. 900 m (2,953 ft) LIH white TDZ R/W 23
    App   R/W 05   LIH white 285 m (935 ft) centreline.
           R/W 23   LIH white Calvert centreline with five crossbars, 330 m (1,083 ft) LIL white, and inner 300 m (984 ft) supplementary red CAT II. VASIS 05/23
    Thr   R/W 05   LIH and LIL green wing bars; R/W 23   LIH and LIL CAT II green
    Txy   LIL blue edge, LIH green centreline on high-speed exits
Aids: VOR/DME, NDB, VDF, PAR, SRE, RVR, ILS CAT I 05, ILS CAT II 23
Twr frequency: 118.7   App frequency: 120.3
Terminals: Main passenger terminal with three satellite buildings and 33 aircraft stands. Separate cargo building.
Scheduled services 1978: 35 airlines
Main base: Executive Jet Aviation and SATA

Traffic:	1970	1975	1976	1977	1978
Passengers (total)	2,744,307	5,210,808	4,009,669	4,361,050	4,533,806
Cargo (tonnes)	26,803	35,050	36,660	34,690	36,186
Aircraft movements	112,187	120,951	127,000	130,447	—
Transport movements	59,588	64,389	65,040	68,608	71,535

In 1976 DC-9s accounted for 46.74 per cent of aircraft movements, Caravelles for 8.74 per cent, DC-8s for 7.4 per cent, Boeing 727s for 7.2 per cent, Boeing 707s for 6.06 per cent and Boeing 737s for 5.22 per cent.

Geneva - Cointrin Airport is among Europe's oldest airports. The decision to create an aerodrome at Geneva was taken by the Republic and Canton of Geneva in 1919 and the site between the villages of Meyrin and Cointrin was chosen on 19 June, 1920. Fifty-four hectares (133 acres) of farmland were acquired and a grass aerodrome measuring about 1,000 m (3,281 ft) in length by up to 800 m (2,625 ft) in width was prepared. The Federal Air Office authorized the use of the Aérodrome de Cointrin as a first-class customs airport on 22 September, 1920, and the official inauguration took place on the following day with the landing of Edgar Primault in a Haefeli DH 3 military biplane. An administration building in Swiss chalet style was erected and there were two small wooden hangars by 1 June, 1922, when Ad Astra Aero opened its Geneva–Zürich–Nuremberg service with a Junkers-F 13. On 22 July, 1922, Cie des Grands Express Aériens opened a Paris–Lausanne–Geneva service.

The airport was equipped with radio in 1922, more hangars were erected, the area of the airport was gradually expanded, and in 1937 a southwest–northeast concrete runway was constructed. One of the first in Europe, this was 405 m (1,329 ft) long and 21 m (69 ft) wide. The ends were connected to the apron by 15 m (49 ft) wide bitumen taxiways, the runway and taxiways together having the appearance of a racetrack. Part of this early runway and its taxiway links can still be discerned in the pattern of the apron and taxiways at the southwest end of the present airport.

In 1940 the Federal Air Office accepted the general plan and the Canton of Geneva voted a credit of SFr 5 mn for enlarging the airport, building a 1,065 by 50 m (3,494 by 164 ft) 05/23 runway, installing new lighting, building a new terminal, and other improvements. In 1942 the runway had been constructed to a length of 412 m (1,352 ft) but in 1943 it was decided to enlarge the scale of the development plan to increase the length of the airport to 2,500 m (8,202 ft) and the length of the runway to 2,000 m (6,562 ft). The completed runway was opened in August, 1946 and was the only facility in Switzerland capable of handling Swissair's DC-4s, the first of which arrived at Geneva from Los Angeles on 24 November, 1946. The new terminal, designed to handle 300,000 passengers a year, was opened on 21 October, 1949.

In order to handle the coming turbine-powered aircraft it was decided that the runway should be further extended to the northeast to a length of 3,900 m (12,795 ft). This extension would have taken it into France, so in 1956 Switzerland and France signed an exchange agreement for 42 hectares (104 acres) of territory and the runway was extended to its present length by the summer of 1960.

Rapidly increasing traffic soon showed that the 1949 terminal was too small, in spite of some extensions, and a completely new terminal was constructed between 1962 and 1968. This terminal, opened on 17 May, 1968, is a multi-storey structure 250 m (820 ft) long and 76 m (249 ft) deep. Gates are provided to give direct access to close-parked aircraft while passages, with moving walkways, beneath the apron lead to three satellite buildings. Part of the main terminal is reserved for French customs and immigration and there is a customs road which passes between the terminal and France via a tunnel beneath the runway. Space has been provided for extension of the terminal and apron area and a fourth satellite can be provided to handle wide-bodied aircraft.

Zürich Airport with the terminal area near the centre, the 14/32 runway on the right and part of the Swissair maintenance complex at bottom left. (*Amt für Luftverkehr*)

Zürich   Flughafen Zürich

47° 27′ 34″ N   08° 32′ 57″ E   4.86 nm (9 km) NE of city
ICAO: LSZH   IATA code: ZRH   Time zone: GMT plus 1
Authority: Volkswirtschaftsdirektion des Kantons Zürich (Amt für Luftverkehr)
Area: 724.3 hectares (1,790 acres)
Elevation: 1,416 ft (432 m)   Ref temp: 24 deg C
Runways: 10/28   2,500 × 60 m   (8,202 × 197 ft) concrete
        14/32   3,300 × 60 m (10,827 × 197 ft) concrete*
        16/34   3,700 × 60 m (12,139 × 197 ft) concrete*
Pavement strength: LCN 100 = 125

* For landings the first 150 m (492 ft) of runway 14 and the first 920 m (3,018 ft) of runway 34 are not available. No landings are allowed on runway 32.

Landing category: ICAO CAT IIIa
Lighting:
R/W   10   LIL white edge, last 600 m (1,968 ft) yellow. Red end lights
        28   LIH and LIL white edge, last 600 m yellow. Red end lights
        14/32 and 16/34   LIH and LIL white edge, last 600 m amber. LIH white centreline, last 300 m (984 ft) red, previous 600 m (1,968 ft) red/white. Red end lights. TDZ 14 and 16. Red lights before landing thresholds 14 and 34

331

App   R/W 10/28   LIL white centreline
R/W 14 and 16   LIH white centreline with crossbars and
red barrettes on inner 300 m (984 ft). LIL white 420 m
(1,378 ft) centreline with one crossbar
R/W 32   nil
R/W 34   LIH white centreline
VASIS 10/28 and 34

Thr   10   LIL green; 14   LIH green; 16, 28 and 32   LIH
and LIL green; 34   LIH and LIL green at displaced
threshold

Txy   LIL blue edge, some green centreline

Aids: VOR/DME, NDB, VDF, SRE, ASDE, ILS CAT III 14,
ILS CAT II 16

Twr frequency: 118.1   App frequency: 118.0/118.1/119.7/120.75

Terminals: Passenger terminals A and B, B with nine nose-in dock
positions. Total of 45 aircraft stands. Separate cargo terminal

Scheduled services 1978: 47 airlines

Main base: Swissair

Traffic:	1970	1975	1976	1977	1978
Passengers (total)	4,518,691	5,963,357	6,825,661	7,476,463	7,728,987
Cargo (tonnes)	96,212	113,787	134,508	139,116	153,387
Aircraft movements	130,297	139,011	139,820	145,130	150,456
Transport movements	99,214	104,237	105,084	109,195	98,853

During 1977 DC-9s accounted for 53.24 per cent of transport movements. The next
highest percentage was 7.38 per cent for DC-8s.

The 1914–18 war military aerodrome at Dübendorf served as the
Zürich airport from the start of landplane services until 1948. It had a grass
landing area, small terminal building and was situated 7½ km (4.66 miles)

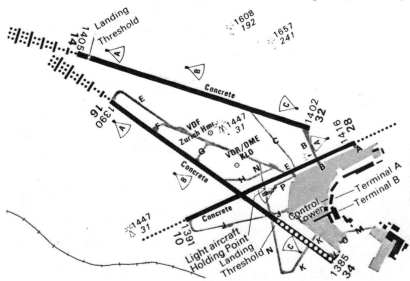

Zürich Airport. (*British Airways Aerad*)

east-northeast of the city. In April 1943, however, the Zürich administration commissioned a feasibility study for a major airport in the vicinity of the city. A site was chosen near Kloten, about 9 km (5.59 miles) northeast of the city, and work on the project began in July 1946, the citizens of Zürich Canton having approved a credit of SFr 36.8 mn for its construction on 5 May that year.

The initial project comprised four runways, with a main 14/36 runway of 2,000 by 60 m (6,562 by 197 ft), a north–south runway of 1,400 m (4,593 ft), a west-northwest—east-southeast runway of 1,650 m (5,413 ft) and a northeast—southwest runway of 1,600 m (5,249 ft)—the three secondary runways to be 45 m (148 ft) wide, and they were to take aircraft of up to 70 tonnes. By 1947 the plan had been modified and three runways were built—10/28 of 1,900 m (6,234 ft) opened on 14 June, 1948, 16/34 of 2,600 m (8,530 ft) opened on 17 November, 1948, as the instrument runway, and 02/20 of 1,535 m (5,096 ft) which was closed after a few years' service, reopened and then finally withdrawn in the early 1970s when it became a taxiway. With the opening of the instrument runway all civil traffic was transferred from Dübendorf to Kloten.

Initially, a village of wooden huts served as the terminal area, but a very impressive—and at that time spacious—terminal and administrative building was completed in 1953 and the airport was officially inaugurated on 29 August. In 1949, its first full year of operation, the airport handled 176,412 passengers and 1,819 tonnes of cargo.

Soon after the terminal's opening it became apparent that the facilities would be inadequate for the anticipated traffic growth and plans were made to extend runway 10/28 to 3,150 m (10,335 ft) and 16/34 to 4,000 m (13,123 ft) as well as building two finger docks and other work; but in Switzerland such work cannot be done without the consent of the population, and on 23 June, 1957, the expansion programme was rejected in a Cantonal referendum. However, on 6 July, 1958, public approval was given to a reduced-scale project which included extending runway 10/28 to 2,500 m (8,202 ft) and 16/34 to 3,700 m (12,129 ft), lengthening and widening the apron, improving airport lighting, and extending the terminal to treble its passenger handling area. On 1 January, 1961, runway 10/28 was opened to its present length and on 15 March that year the lengthened 16/34 was opened to its full length.

In 1970 agreement was reached for the third development stage which included construction of a new 3,300 m (10,827 ft) 14/32 CAT III runway to bring runway capacity to 55 movements an hour, construction of a second terminal for 6 mn passengers a year and thus doubling capacity, and the enlargement of the cargo terminal to provide annual capacity of 250,000 tonnes.

The new terminal, known as Terminal B, was opened on 1 November, 1975. It is a three-storey building with arrival, departure and transit levels, has nine gate lounges for the nine nose-in docking positions with 17 aerobridges, and eight waiting lounges for aircraft parked on remote stands. Terminal B is used for services to Western Europe (except Austria and Germany), intercontinental flights and Swiss domestic services. The terminal is connected to the much modified original terminal, now known as Terminal A, which serves Eastern Europe, Austria, Germany, Israel and charter operations.

The new 14/32 instrument runway was opened on 1 April, 1976, and cleared for CAT III operations on 20 April, 1978.

A railway station has been built beneath Terminal B and it is planned that Zürich Airport will be connected to the Swiss Federal Railways system in May 1980.

The airport master plan calls for continuing development, with four terminal buildings with a total capacity of 25–30 mn passengers by 1990, stands for 90 aircraft, a charter terminal to be built in the existing, but extended, cargo terminal, a new cargo centre with 1 mn tonnes annual capacity, and parking for 12,000 cars. Considerable development of facilities for general aviation is also planned.

Syrian Arab Republic

Damascus (Esh Sham)   Damascus International Airport

33° 24′ 39″ N   36° 30′ 48″ E   12.5 nm (23 km) SE of city
ICAO: OSDI   IATA code: DAM   Time zone: GMT plus 2
Authority: Ministry of Transport
Elevation: 2,020 ft (616 m)   Ref temp: 29.7 deg C
Runways: 05L/23R   2,700 × 45 m   (8,858 × 148 ft) concrete
         05R/23L   3,600 × 45 m (11,811 × 148 ft) concrete
Pavement strength: LCN 110
Landing category: ICAO CAT II
Lighting:
R/W   05L/23R   LIH and LIL white edge, last 900 m (2,953 ft) yellow. Centreline and TDZ R/W 23R
           05R/23L   LIH and LIL white edge, last 1,200 m (3,937 ft) yellow. End lights all runways
App   R/W 05R/23L   LIL 430 m (1,411 ft) simple
           R/W 23R   LIH and LIL Calvert precision CAT II VASIS 05R and 23R
Thr   LIH and LIL green all runways
Txy   blue edge
Aids: VOR/DME, NDB, VDF, L, SRE, RVR 23R, ILS CAT II 23R
Twr frequency: 118.5   App frequency: 120.0
Terminal: Cargo terminal serving as temporary passenger terminal, four aprons and 16 aircraft stands
Scheduled services 1978: 30 airlines
Main base: Syrian Arab Airlines

Traffic:	1970	1975	1976
Passengers (total)	290,551	652,227	1,067,071
Cargo (tonnes)	2,331	5,541	—
Aircraft movements	9,279	—	—
Transport movements	8,839	14,764	18,327

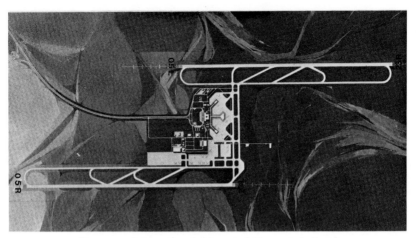

Damascus International Airport. (*Aéroport de Paris*)

Until 1969 Damascus was served by the joint civil/military prewar
aerodrome at Mezzeh, but in 1965 a contract between the Syrian
Government and Aéroport de Paris was signed for studies for a new
airport, and a group of French contractors, France-Technique, was
appointed to build the new airport.

The first phase involved construction of two runways, some taxiways,
cargo terminal, control tower and support buildings. The airport was
opened in 1969, with the cargo terminal being used as the temporary
passenger terminal.

In 1969 it was decided to undertake phase two of the programme
which mainly involved planning and construction of a permanent
passenger terminal with three traffic piers and this was nearing completion
in mid-1978.

Initially, a taxiway linked the 05L and 23L runway thresholds and
there was a short section of taxiway parallel to the northeast end of runway
05R/23L. Ultimately there will be parallel taxiways, with high-speed exits,
for both runways; there will be a second, parallel, link taxiway between the
two runways; and centreline and bar approach lighting is planned for each
approach. A third runway has been planned.

Taiwan, R.O.C.

Taipei   Taipei/Sungshan Airport

25° 04′ 17″ N	121° 33′ E	2.6 nm (4.8 km) NE of city
ICAO: RCSS	IATA code: TAY	Time zone: GMT plus 8

Authority: Civil Aeronautics Administration
Area: 183 hectares (451 acres)
Elevation: 21 ft (6 m)   Ref temp: 30.1 deg C
Runway: 10/28   2,605 × 60 m (8,546 × 197 ft) concrete
Pavement strength: takes Boeing 747s
Landing category: ICAO CAT I
Lighting:
  R/W   LIH white edge, last 600 m (1,968 ft) yellow, white centreline, red end lights. White TDZ 10
  App   R/W 10   CAT II (operation CAT I) 900 m (2,953 ft) white bar centreline with 579 m (1,900 ft) sequenced flashers from outmost unit, 300 m (984 ft) distance marking crossbars and two red wing bars. VASIS 10
  Thr   green
  Txy   blue edge
Aids: VOR, TACAN, DME, NDB, L, ILS CAT I 10
Twr frequency: 118.1/118.7   App frequency: 119.7
Terminals: 493,000 sq m (5,306,652 sq ft) four-storey passenger terminal (opened 20 January, 1964) and 60,000 tonnes-capacity cargo terminal situated side by side on south of airport, with 13 close-in and nine remote aircraft stands
Scheduled services 1978: 14 airlines
Airline bases: China Airlines and Far Eastern Air Transport

Traffic:	1970	1975	1976	1978
Passengers (total)	1,412,243	3,454,154	4,316,820	6,434,039
Cargo (tonnes)	19,117	102,943	116,730	112,804
Aircraft movements	41,662	51,136	58,216	68,957

Taipei   Taipei/Chiang Kai Shek International Airport

25° 05′ 07″ N	121° 13′ 17″ E	16.7 nm (30.9 km) W of city
ICAO: RCTP	IATA code: TPE	Time zone: GMT plus 8

Authority: Civil Aeronautics Administration
Area: 1,200 hectares (2,965 acres)
Elevation: 73 ft (22 m)   Ref temp: 32.1 deg C
Runways: 05L/23R   3,660 × 60 m (12,007 × 197 ft) concrete
         05R/23L   2,719 × 45 m   (8,920 × 148 ft) concrete
Pavement strength: auw 350,000 kg (771,618 lb) for Boeing 747
Landing category: ICAO CAT II (to be upgraded to CAT III)
Lighting:
  R/W   05L/23R   LIH white edge, last 600 m (1,968 ft) yellow, white centreline and red end lights. TDZ 05L/23R
          05R/23L   LIH white edge, and red end lights

App R/W 05L and 23R LIH CAT II 900 m (2,953 ft) white
   bar centreline with crossbars and supplementary red side
   barrettes on inner 300 m (984 ft). VASIS 05L/23R
   R/W 05R/23L REIL
Thr green on all runways
Txy edge and centreline
Aids: VOR/DME, TACAN, NDB, UDF, L, ASR, GCA, RVR 05L/23R,
ILS CAT II 05L and 23R
Twr frequency: 118.7/126.18   App frequency: 119.7/125.1
Terminals: Terminal with two concourses with 22 gates and nose-in aircraft
  stands, 10 for wide-bodied aircraft, and 22 aerobridges. Separate
  cargo terminal with five aircraft stands
Scheduled services 1979: 14 airlines
Main base: Will become main base of China Airlines

Taiwan, earlier known as Formosa, is a mountainous island and its airports can only be sited near the coasts. Taipei, in the north, has been served by Sungshan Airport since 1 March, 1950; its original name Taipei Airport was changed to Taipei International Airport in 1965.

There is a single east–west runway connected to the terminal area by five taxiways. The airport was for many years the main base of CAT - Civil Air Transport.

Taipei's traffic has increased rapidly and it was forecast that the airport's saturation point would be reached in 1976. Because of its environs, including the river which loops round its eastern boundaries, the airport could not be expanded; planning of a new international airport at Taoyuan, to the west of the city, began in 1969, with construction starting in July 1974.

The new airport, near the coast and immediately north of Taoyuan Air Force Base, has been planned in three phases, to be capable of handling 5 mn passengers and 200,000 tonnes of cargo a year up to 1980, 10 mn passengers and 420,000 tonnes of cargo a year during the period 1981–1990, and 19½ mn passengers and 1 mn tonnes of cargo annually during 1991–2000.

The first stage comprises a pair of 05/23 runways, parallel taxiway, terminal with two concourses, control tower, cargo terminal with five aircraft stands, fire station, and China Airlines apron. The two runways,

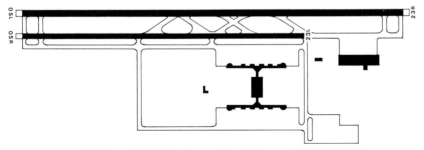

Taipei/Chiang Kai Shek International Airport. (*Clem Watson*)

East face of Chiang Kai Shek passenger terminal. (*CAA*)

both to the northwest of the terminal, are 05L/23R of 3,660 by 60 m (12,007 by 197 ft) and 05R/23L of 2,719 by 45 m (8,920 by 148 ft).

The final terminal area will be of linear design, the northeast of the planned three terminals having been built first. The rectangular terminal is flanked by car parks, and boarding concourses face the aprons to the northwest and southeast of the main terminal. Each boarding concourse has 11 nose-in aircraft positions and there is a total of 22 gates and 22 aerobridges. Ten of the aircraft stands can take wide-bodied aircraft and total apron area is 302,120 sq m (3,252,020 sq ft). Peak-hour capacity of the terminal is 4,000 passengers.

The final plan envisages three terminals, six aprons and six boarding concourses. The additional terminals will be built to the southwest of the first terminal, and the cargo terminal and maintenance areas are at the northeast of the airport. A third 05/23 runway is planned for the southeast side of the airport.

Chiang Kai Shek International Airport* came into operation at 00.01 GMT on 26 February, 1979, from which time the old Taipei airport was renamed Taipei/Sungshan and closed to international operations.

*The original name was Taipei/Taoyuan International Airport but this was changed shortly before the airport opened.

Chiang Kai Shek terminal upper level. (*CAA*)

338

United Republic of Tanzania

Dar-es-Salaam   Dar-es-Salaam Airport   ICAO: HTDA   IATA: DAR
06° 52′ 32″ S   39° 12′ 07″ E   Elevation: 181 ft (55 m)
Longest runway: 05/23   2,378 m (7,802 ft)   ART   VASI 05/23
Aids: VOR/DME, NDB, VDF, SRE, ILS 05

	1970	1975	1976
Passengers	262,500	350,637	314,187*
Transport movements	12,288	12,088	12,200**

* Excluding transit   ** Estimated

Scheduled services 1978: 18 airlines
Main base: Air Tanzania

Dar-es-Salaam Airport on its opening day, 16 October, 1954. (*John Stroud*)

Thailand

Bangkok (Krung Thep)
               Bangkok International Airport (Don Muang)

13° 54′ 52″ N   100° 36′ 30″ E   12 nm (22 km) NNE of city
ICAO: VTBD   IATA code: BKK   Time zone: GMT plus 7
Authority: The Directorate of Civil Aviation
Elevation: 12 ft (4 m)   Ref temp: 35.3 deg C
Runways: 03L/21R   3,550 × 60 m (11,647 × 197 ft) asphaltic-concrete
          03R/21L   3,000 × 45 m (9,842 × 148 ft) concrete
Pavement strength: 34,000 kg (75,000 lb) ISWL
Landing category: ICAO CAT I
Lighting:
    R/W   LIH white edge. Red end lights
    App   R/W 03L and 03R   LIH approach beacons, R/W 21L
              and 21R   thirty-one LIH crossbar lights—centre bars
              white, wing bars red—with 28 condenser discharge lights
              VASIS 21L and 21R
    Thr   green
    Txy   blue
Aids: VOR, TACAN, NDB, L, SRE, ILS CAT I 21R
Twr frequency: 118.1/126.18   App frequency: 119.1
Terminal: Passenger terminal on west side adjacent to highway and
    railway. Jet bay is north apron and Boeing 747 bay is south apron.
    Total civil apron area 70,950 sq m (763,706 sq ft). Royal Thai Air
    Force base on east side of airport
Scheduled services 1978: 36 airlines
Main base: Thai Airways and Thai Airways International

Traffic:	1970	1975	1976	1977
Passengers (total)	1,909,217	3,514,941	3,700,661	4,063,506
Cargo (tonnes)	21,360	52,723	60,081	57,935
Aircraft movements	50,759	56,391	55,816	64,211
Transport movements	40,368	49,063	48,016	47,054

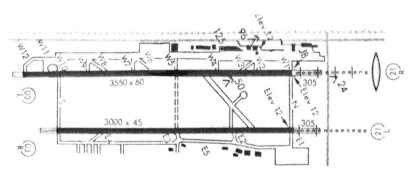

Bangkok International Airport (Don Muang). (*Swissair*)

A Thai Airways Hawker Siddeley 748 at Bangkok International Airport.
(*British Aerospace*)

As early as 1923 Don Muang was listed as an international aerodrome although it had been prepared for military use and was the headquarters of the Siamese Royal Aeronautical Services and an Army Air Service flying school. The grass surface measured about 1,800 by 1,200 m (5,905 by 3,937 ft), but it was swampy and some of the area was unsuitable for flying.

A landing floodlight and a beacon had been installed by 1932 and by 1938 there was a modern terminal building, control tower, rest house and restaurant. Some time during the 1930s two paved runways had been laid. One, apparently of asphalt, was aligned 03/21 and about 1,200 m (3,937 ft) long. Branching from its mid-point was a second runway of similar length. It was aligned approximately east–west and most of its length seems to have been of concrete.

The 03/21 runway was listed as 6,000 ft (1,829 m) in length soon after the Second World War, and by the late 1950s there were parallel runways— 03L/21R of 3,000 m (9,842 ft) and 03R/21L of 2,750 m (9,020 ft). Charts suggest that the old east–west runway became a taxiway linking the parallel runways. Both runways were later increased in length.

There has been a considerable amount of terminal development but increasing traffic led to the planning of a new airport 30 km (18.6 miles) southeast of the city. This project now seems to have been delayed or abandoned, and a largescale development of the existing airport is to take place to provide sufficient capacity for the period up to the late 1980s. The plans include terminal extension with increased apron area and hydrant refuelling, a trebling of cargo capacity and, in the early 1980s, an additional runway.

341

Tunisia (Tunisie)

Jerba (Djerba)   Aéroport de Jerba - Zarzis

           ICAO: DTTJ   IATA: DJE
33° 52′ 25″ N   10° 46′ 40″ E   Elevation: 16 ft (5 m)
Runway: 09/27   3,100 m (10,170 ft)   ART   VASI 09/27
Aids: VOR/DME, VDF, L, ILS 27

	1970	1975	1976	1977
Passengers	112,502	323,825	341,933	330,595
Transport movements	2,549	5,264	5,445	4,586

Scheduled services 1978: Air France and Tunis Air

The airport was opened in 1964.

Monastir   Aéroport de Monastir - Skanès

           ICAO: DTTM   IATA: MIR
35° 45′ 23″ N   10° 45′ 15″ E   Elevation: 7 ft (2 m)
Runway: 08/26   2,950 m (9,679 ft)   ART   VASI 08
Aids: VOR, NDB, L, ILS 08

	1970	1975	1976	1977
Passengers	77,698	547,694	635,874	583,622
Transport movements	1,032	6,024	6,861	6,735

Scheduled services 1978: Air France, Luxair and Tunis Air

The airport was opened on 1 August, 1972.

Tunis   Aéroport International de Tunis - Carthage

36° 50′ 58″ N   10° 13′ 34″ E   4 nm (7.4 km) NE of city
ICAO: DTTA   IATA code: TUN   Time zone: GMT plus 1
Authority: Office des Ports Aériens de Tunisie
Elevation: 20 ft (6 m)   Ref temp: 30.4 deg C
Runway: 01/19   3,200 × 46 m (10,500 × 150 ft) concrete
Pavement strength: LCN 70
Landing category: ICAO CAT I
Lighting:
      R/W   LIH white edge
      App   R/W 19   LIH white bar centreline with crossbar and
               sequenced flashers. VASIS 01
      Thr   LIH green
      Txy   blue edge
Aids: VOR/DME, NDB, VDF, L, ILS CAT I 19
Twr frequency: 118.1   App frequency: 121.2

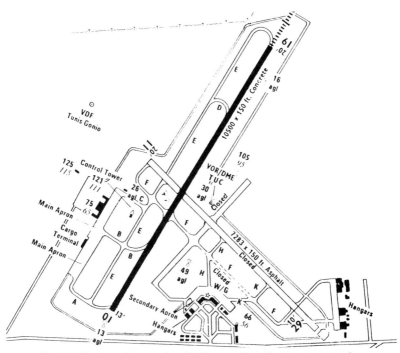

Tunis - Carthage International Airport. (*British Airways Aerad*)

Tunis Air Boeing 727-2H3 TS-JHN at Tunis - Carthage. (*Tunis Air*)

343

Terminal: Passenger terminal to southwest of the south end of runway
01/19, with seven aircraft stands. Separate cargo terminal with six
aircraft stands
Scheduled services 1978: 22 airlines
Main base: Tunis Air and Tunis Avia

Traffic:	1970	1975	1976	1977
Passengers (total)	784,950	1,546,813	1,635,557	1,629,255
Cargo (tonnes)	4,474	7,642	13,613	14,024
Aircraft movements	30,935	27,132	29,850	25,930
Transport movements	15,800	22,077	23,349	22,480

When Tunisia became an independent State in 1956, the capital was
served by the old prewar El Aouina Airport beside El Bahira (Lac de
Tunis). The longest runway was the tarmac 12/30 of 6,000 ft (1,829 m). This
was extended to 7,283 ft (2,220 m) and redesignated 11/29. In 1959 work
began on a master plan for the airport's development and runway 01/19
became the main runway with a length of 10,500 ft (3,200 m). A parallel
taxiway was constructed to its west and a new terminal area built. The
present 22,000 sq m (236,808 sq ft) two-storey terminal was opened on
1 August, 1972, and can handle up to 2,000 passengers an hour. The master
plan called for the retention of runway 11/29, but this was closed at the end
of 1977 and the other earlier runways have been abandoned. The name
Carthage was adopted for the redeveloped airport.

Turkey (Türkiye)

Adana   Adana Civil Airport   ICAO: LTAF   IATA: ADA

36° 59' 01" N   35° 16' 51" E   Elevation: 64 ft (19 m)
Runway: 05/23   2,750 m (9,022 ft)   ART   VASI 05/23
Aids: VOR, NDB

	1970
Passengers	191,351
Transport movements	3,110

Scheduled services 1978: KTHY - Cyprus Turkish Airlines and THY

Ankara   Esenboğa Airport

40° 07' 28" N   32° 59' 35" E   15 nm (28 km) NE of city
ICAO: LTAC   IATA code: ESB   Time zone: GMT plus 2
Authority: General Directorate of State Airports
Area: 760 hectares (1,878 acres)
Elevation: 3,128 ft (953 m)   Ref temp: 25.2 deg C
Runway: 03/21   3,752 × 60 m (12,310 × 197 ft) asphalt
Pavement strength: LCN 58
Landing category: ICAO CAT I

Lighting:
R/W   LIH and LIL edge. End lights
App   R/W 03   LIH white Calvert centreline with five
       crossbars,   R/W 21   LIH white centreline of 510 m
       (1,673 ft) with three crossbars. AVASIS 03/21
Thr   LIH green
Txy   blue edge
Aids: VOR, NDB, DME, TAR, ILS CAT I 03
Twr frequency: 118.1   App frequency: 119.1/119.6/122.1
Terminal: Terminal to east of runway, with two jet aircraft stands and one
    propeller aircraft stand
Scheduled services 1978: Aeroflot, Iran Air, KLM, Lufthansa, MEA, Pan
    American, Swissair, KTHY - Cyprus Turkish Airlines and THY

Traffic:	1970*	1975	1976	1977
Passengers (total)	303,506	993,364	1,373,479	1,584,709
Cargo (tonnes)	2,895	10,103	14,501	16,491
Aircraft movements	10,647	18,648	21,363	23,074
Transport movements	8,319	15,062	17,258	19,248

* Figures for July–December only

    During 1976 DC-9s accounted for 48.26 per cent of transport movements, Fokker F.28s
for 17.98 per cent, Boeing 747s for 17.61 per cent and Boeing 707s for 13.35 per cent.

    The present Esenboğa may have been a military aerodrome but it is
not known when it became Ankara's airport. It certainly existed in 1953 at
which time the civil aerodromes were Ankara Airport, at 39° 57′ N   32°
46′ E*, and Etimesgut, slightly further west at 39° 57′ N   32° 42′ E.
    The old Ankara Airport had three asphalt runways, 06/24 of 1,524 m
(5,000 ft), 09/27 of 1,128 m (3,700 ft) and 18/36 of 808 m (2,650 ft). Its
elevation was 2,700 ft (823 m). Etimesgut had a single paved runway, 11/29
of 2,200 m (7,218 ft) although earlier there had been two other runways.
Elevation was 2,660 ft (811 m). Both of the old airports were in hilly
country but much closer to the city.

* This may have been the prewar military aerodrome, listed as at 40° N 32° 48′ E,
which served the city as an airport during the early 1930s.

Istanbul   Yeşilköy Airport

40° 58′ 36″ N   28° 48′ 55″ E   13 nm (24 km) W of city
ICAO: LTBA   IATA code: IST   Time zone: GMT plus 2
Authority: General Directorate of State Airports
Area: 1,700 hectares (4,201 acres)
Elevation: 157 ft (47.8 m)   Ref temp: 25.1 deg C
Runways: 06/24   2,300 × 60 m (7,546 × 197 ft) concrete
         18/36   3,000 × 45 m (9,842 × 148 ft) concrete
Pavement strength: 06/24 LCN 63; 18/36 LCN 100
Landing category: ICAO CAT I

345

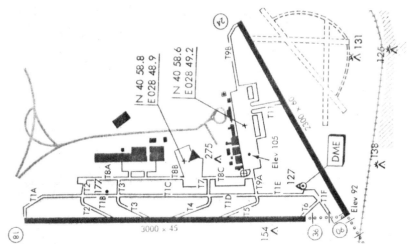

Yeşilköy Airport, Istanbul. (*Swissair*)

Lighting:
R/W	06/24	LIH edge, and end lights
	18/36	LIL edge, and end lights
App	R/W 06	LIH white Calvert centreline with four crossbars
	R/W 36	LIH 420 m (1,378 ft) centreline with two crossbars
	VASIS 24 and 36	
Thr	06/24	LIH green, 18/36 LIL green
Txy	blue edge on all taxiways	

Aids: VOR/DME, NDB, L, RVR 06/24, ILS CAT I 06
Twr frequency: 118.1   App frequency: 121.1 south, 120.5 north
Terminals: International and domestic terminals and separate charter arrival and departure terminals, with 17 aircraft stands
Scheduled services 1978: 30 airlines
Main base: THY

Traffic:	1970	1975	1976	1977
Passengers (total)	1,723,397	2,963,823	3,325,529	3,394,154
Cargo (tonnes)	9,049	16,866	20,571	22,207
Aircraft movements	46,573	49,793	50,619	51,140
Transport movements	38,156	44,298	46,024	46,531

During 1976 DC-9s accounted for 34.73 per cent of aircraft movements, Boeing 727s for 20.54 per cent, Boeing 707s for 14.39 per cent, Fokker F.28s for 6.05 per cent and DC-10s for 4.18 per cent.

Istanbul's Yeşilköy Airport is situated on the north shore of the Sea of Marmara, to the west of the city, and was originally a grass aerodrome measuring 600 by 400 m (1,968 by 1,312 ft) and known as Yeşilköy (San Stefano). It had both landplane and seaplane facilities.

In November 1938 it was reported that concrete or asphalt runways were to be built and in February 1939 that the airport was equipped with lighting and that 800 by 40 m (2,625 by 131 ft) runways would soon be

346

The terminal at Istanbul's Yeşilköy Airport in 1962. (*Qantas*)

completed. In the early postwar years there were three paved runways, 04/22 of 1,367 m (4,485 ft), 09/27 of 1,020 m (3,348 ft) and 18/36 of 1,152 m (3,780 ft). By 1953 a new 2,300 m (7,546 ft) concrete 06/24 runway had been built to the north of the original runways, a new terminal area to the north of the new runway had been planned, runway 09/27 had been closed and the usable length of 18/36 had been restricted.

In 1968 the contract was awarded for a new 18/36 runway, taxiways and apron, which extended the airport considerably to the north. The new runway of 3,000 m (9,842 ft) has a parallel taxiway to its east and there are four high-speed exits. The original three-runway pattern has now been abandoned.

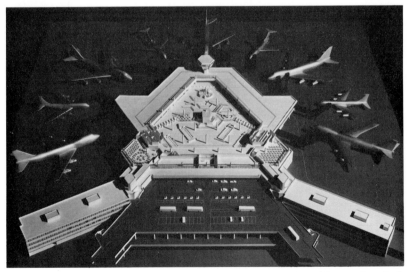

Model of one of the terminal units being constructed at Yeşilköy Airport, Istanbul. (*Courtesy Airport Forum*)

347

Major development of Yeşilköy is taking place, the new 18/36 runway having been the first stage, and it is proposed that this runway should be extended southward to give a length of 3,800 m (12,467 ft). The 06/24 runway can also be extended and there is a plan for a parallel 3,800 m (12,467 ft) runway to the west of the existing 18/36 runway.

The new terminal area will consist of four polygonal units arranged round a circle of 400 m (1,312 ft) diameter within which will be two-level parking for nearly 1,500 vehicles and with the possibility of expansion to quadruple this number. Each three-level terminal unit will contain five concourses each with 390 sq m (4,198 sq ft) waiting lounge area at first-floor level and additional space at apron level. Each unit will be able to handle one Boeing 747 or two smaller aircraft at each concourse—with three aerobridges—to give terminal capacity for up to 20 Boeing 747s or 40 aircraft in the Boeing 707 or Douglas DC-8 category. All aircraft will be parked nose-in to the terminal.

The apron will have an area of 340,000 sq m (3,659,760 sq ft) with room for extension, the control tower is sited in the angle of the runways, and there is to be an underground railway station in the car-parking area. THY's new maintenance facility is to be sited to the northwest of the new terminal area.

Uganda

Entebbe   Entebbe Airport   ICAO: HUEN   IATA: EBB

00° 02′ 11″ N   32° 26′ 16″ E   Elevation: 3,782 ft (1,153 m)
Longest runway: 17/35   3,658 m (12,000 ft)   ART   VASI 17/35
Aids: VOR/DME, NDB, L, SRE, ILS 17

	1970	1975	1976	1977
Passengers	352,100	228,877	265,000*	67,947
Transport movements	11,536	6,303	4,500*	6,401

* Estimated on first nine months

Scheduled services 1978: Aeroflot, Air France, Air Zaïre, Egyptair, Ethiopian Airlines and Sabena

Abu Dhabi International Airport terminal. (*International Aeradio*)

United Arab Emirates

Abu Dhabi Abu Dhabi International Airport

ICAO: OMAD IATA: AUH
24° 25′ 46″ N 54° 27′ 27″ E Elevation: 15 ft (4.5 m)
Runway: 13/31 3,200 m (10,500 ft) ART VASI 13/31
Aids: VOR/DME, NDB, ILS CAT I 31

	1970	1975	1976	1977
Passengers	145,015	616,327	452,000*	627,000*
Transport movements	7,783	20,319	—	23,722

* Rounded figures

Scheduled services 1978: 25 airlines

The airport opened in 1970. A new airport 5.5 nm (10 km) NE of Abu Dhabi is due to be completed in 1980, with a 4,100 m (13,451 ft) runway and a terminal with capacity for 3 mn passengers a year.

Dubai Dubai International Airport

25° 15′ 00″ N 55° 21′ 42″ E 2.5 nm (4.63 km) E of city
ICAO: OMDB IATA code: DXB Time zone: GMT plus 4
Authority: Government of Dubai
Elevation: 25 ft (8 m) Ref temp: 40.1 deg C
Runway: 12/30 3,805 × 46 m (12,483 × 150 ft) concrete/asphalt
Pavement strength: LCN 100
Landing category: ICAO CAT I
Lighting:
    R/W LIH white edge, last 610 m (2,000 ft) yellow, centreline and TDZ

349

App   R/W 12   LIL red centreline with crossbars
R/W 30   LIH white centreline and crossbars with red barrettes on inner 305 m (1,000 ft). VASIS 12/30
Thr   R/W 12   LIH green,   R/W 30   LIH green with wing bars
Txy   green centreline, blue edge at direction changes
Aids: VOR/DME, NDB, RSR, SRE, ILS CAT I 30
Twr frequency: 118.3   App frequency: 124.9
Terminal: Three-storey passenger terminal with four piers, separate VIP suite building, and 14 aircraft stands
Scheduled services 1978: 27 airlines
Bases: UAE Air Force and Dubai Police Air Wing

Traffic:	1970	1975	1976	1977
Passengers (total)	242,361	987,673	1,309,067	1,675,236
Cargo (tonnes)	—	14,958	51,885	34,604
Aircraft movements	11,774	—	—	—

In 1978 Dubai handled 2,066,048 passengers.

The original Dubai Airport was designed by International Aeradio, built by Richard Costain Ltd, and opened in September 1960. The single runway was originally 9,200 ft (2,804 m) long.

The terminal was designed by Page and Broughton and is an elegant three-level structure with passenger handling on the main, or first, floor, operational services at ground level, and public lounges and restaurants on the top floor. The building is 110 m (361 ft) long with a total floor area of 13,400 sq m (144,238 sq ft) and the structure comprises a series of slender columns which at their tops spread to form squares and resemble stylized palm trees. Enclosed within similar but smaller structures are four inclined piers which give access to the apron via helical ramps at their outer ends. At the eastern end of the building is a dome-shaped VIP suite and close to the western end is the cylindrical 28 m (92 ft) high control tower.

The runway was extended to 3,805 m (12,483 ft), and new taxiways and apron constructed. In its reconstructed form the airport was officially opened on 15 May, 1971, by HH Sheikh Rashid Bin Said Al Maktoum, Ruler of Dubai.

It has been decided that Dubai requires a second runway, further terminal extension and yet another terminal, to become operational in 1981.

Terminal and control tower at Dubai International Airport, with a Saudia Boeing 720B on the apron. (*International Aeradio*)

United Kingdom

Aberdeen, Scotland   Aberdeen Airport (Dyce)

57° 12' 15" N   02° 11' 55" W   5.9 nm (11 km) NW of city
ICAO: EGPD   IATA code: ABZ   Time zone: GMT
Authority: British Airports Authority (Scottish Division)
Area: 192 hectares (474 acres)
Elevation: 235 ft (72 m)   Ref temp: 18 deg C
Runway: 17/35   1,829 × 46 m (6,002 × 150 ft) asphalt/concrete
Pavement strength: LCG IV
Landing category: ICAO CAT I
Lighting:
   R/W   Variable intensity white edge
   App   R/W 17   LIH white centreline with two crossbars, LIL
            red centreline with two crossbars
            R/W 35   LIH white Calvert coded centreline with five
            crossbars. VASIS 17/35
   Thr   green with green wing bars
   Txy   blue edge
Aids: VOR/DME, NDB, VDF, ASR, ILS CAT I 17
Twr frequency: 118.1   App frequency: 120.4/121.25*

* Helicopters only

Terminal: Two-storey terminal with single-level handling, four gates and
   10 nose-in aircraft stands. Separate cargo terminal with 7,000 tonnes
   capacity
Scheduled services 1978: Air Anglia, British Airways and Dan-Air Services

The Aberdeen Airport terminal which was opened in June 1977. (*British Airways*)

The new control tower at Aberdeen Airport in November 1978 after completion of the building but before fitting out. (*Studio Morgan, courtesy CAA*)

Bases: British Airways Helicopters and Bristow Helicopters main base for United Kingdom North Sea oil support operations

Traffic:	1970–71	1975–76	1976–77	1977–78	1978–79
Passengers (total)	136,430	692,668	882,007	1,011,008	1,221,952
Cargo (tonnes)	545	4,268	5,580	5,805	6,940
Aircraft movements	24,996	82,007	84,759	93,210	97,926
Transport movements	4,194	37,014	45,897	52,743	58,604

Helicopter movements increased from 4,071 in 1971 to 25,508 in 1975

During 1978–79 Sikorsky S-61N and S-58T helicopters accounted for 32.5 per cent of transport movements (19,038), Fokker F.27s for 9.7 per cent, HS 748s for 18 per cent and Viscounts for 8.6 per cent.

The first commercial flight from the site of Aberdeen Airport seems to have been made on 16 October, 1933, when E. E. Fresson of Highland Airways flew a charter, with three passengers, from Dyce to Kirkwall in the Monospar ST-4 G-ACEW. But the earliest recorded landing was made in March 1931 by Eric Gandar Dower in a Blackburn Bluebird.

Gandar Dower decided to prepare an aerodrome on the site and found an airline—he did both. The grass surfaced aerodrome was officially opened on 28 July, 1934, and on 11 September, that year, Gandar Dower's Aberdeen Airways began Aberdeen–Glasgow services with a Short Scion and a Dragon. Subsequently it was the base for Aberdeen Airways' services to Orkney and Shetland.

During the war Dyce was used by RAF Coastal and Fighter Commands and three concrete runways were laid—01/19 of 3,990 ft (1,216 m), 06/24 of 3,690 ft (1,125 m) and 15/33 of 4,020 ft (1,225 m). After the war the present asphalt 17/35 runway was constructed. A terminal area was situated close to the railway on the eastern boundary.

When oil was discovered in the northern sector of the North Sea, Aberdeen Airport became an important base for oil-related traffic and for several years has had the fastest growing traffic at any mainland United Kingdom airport. The terminal, in spite of a number of extensions, and the apron became extremely congested and a completely new terminal area was developed on the western side of the airport. The British Airports Authority took over ownership and the operation of the airport on 1 January, 1975; the new terminal was opened by HRH Princess Alexandra on 21 June, 1977, and came into operation on 27 June; a new cargo terminal was opened in October 1977 and the new control tower commissioned in 1979. The old terminal area has been converted for general aviation use.

In 1972–73 aircraft movements increased by 45.7 per cent and in 1974–75 the passenger increase over the previous year was 64.5 per cent.

Belfast, Northern Ireland   Aldergrove Airport

54° 39′ 15″ N   06° 13′ 30″ W   11.5 nm (21.3 km) NW of city
ICAO: EGAA   IATA code: BFS   Time zone: GMT
Authority: Northern Ireland Airports Ltd
Elevation: 267 ft (81 m)   Ref temp: 18 deg C
Runways: 08/26   2,777 × 45 m (9,111 × 148 ft) asphalt
        17/35   1,890 × 46 m (6,200 × 150 ft) asphalt
Pavement strength: 08/26 LCG II; 17/35 LCG III
Landing category: ICAO CAT IIIa
Lighting:
    R/W   08/26   LIH white edge, LIH colour-coded centreline, red end lights. TDZ 26
            17/35   LIH and LIL white edge, and red end lights
    App   R/W 08   LIH white centreline with one crossbar
            R/W 26   LIH white coded centreline with five crossbars and red barrettes on inner 288 m (945 ft)
            R/W 17   LIH white centreline with five crossbars
            R/W 35   LIH white centreline with one crossbar
            VASIS all runways
    Thr   R/W 08/26 and 17   LIH green with wing bars
            R/W 35   LIL green
    Txy   blue edge, green centreline on some taxiways
Aids: VORTAC, NDB, VDF, SRE, ILS CAT III 26, ILS CAT I 17

Aldergrove Airport terminal area, view looking southeast to runway 26 threshold, in the early 1960s.

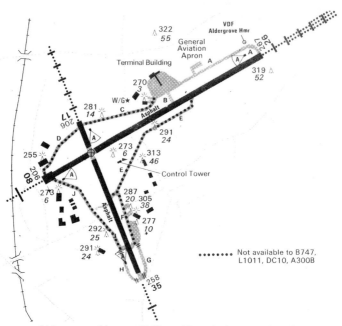

Aldergrove Airport, Belfast. (*British Airways Aerad*)

Twr frequency: 118.3   App frequency: 120.0

Terminal: Passenger terminal with one traffic pier, seven gates and 13
    aircraft stands. Separate general aviation apron

Scheduled services 1978: Aer Lingus, British Airways, British Island
    Airways and British Midland Airways

Traffic:	1970	1975	1976	1977
Passengers (total)	1,117,422	1,184,417	1,082,433	1,039,411
Cargo (tonnes)	22,594	11,159	12,349	14,798
Aircraft movements	47,335	72,985	74,873	75,688
Transport movements	22,559	21,569	21,288	23,909

During the 1914–18 war Handley Page V/1500 four-engined bombers
were built at Belfast by Harland & Wolff and an aerodrome was needed for
flight-testing these large aircraft. Agreement was reached on 28 February,
1918, for a site near Crumlin, County Antrim, and work began on
preparation of an aerodrome, which was originally known as Crumlin.

The first three V/1500s had to be shipped to Cricklewood for flight
tests because the Belfast aerodrome was not ready, and the first to be tested
in Northern Ireland is believed to have flown from Aldergrove (as the
aerodrome was renamed) on 20 December, 1918.

After the war it was decided to retain Aldergrove as a Royal Air Force
station and it was available to civil aircraft in case of emergency.
Aldergrove retained its bomber connection when No. 502 (Ulster)
Squadron was formed there on 15 May, 1925, as a cadre unit of the Special
Reserve. The squadron operated, in turn, Vickers Vimy, Handley Page
Hyderabad and Vickers Virginia night bombers until it was converted to a
day-bomber squadron in October 1935.

354

When Midland & Scottish Air Ferries began a thrice weekly Glasgow–Campbeltown–Belfast service on 1 June, 1933, Aldergrove served as the Belfast airport but, soon after, Newtownards became the Belfast airport. Before the Second World War Sydenham (Harbour Airport) became the Belfast airport, being replaced in turn by Nutts Corner on 16 December, 1946.

On 26 September, 1963, yet another change took place when all services were transferred to Aldergrove. Originally a grass aerodrome, Aldergrove had by 1963 two asphalt runways—08/26 of 6,005 ft (1,830 m) and 17/35 of 6,025 ft (1,836 m). 08/26 was extended to 9,111 ft (2,777 m) in 1973 and CAT II operations on runway 26 were authorized in 1974.

A development programme begun in 1978 brought the airport to CAT III standard and involved improvement in the terminal, car parking, airport entrance and other features.

Birmingham   Birmingham Airport

52° 27′ 12″ N   01° 44′ 47″ W   5.5 nm (10 km) ESE of city
ICAO: EGBB   IATA code: BHX   Time zone: GMT
Authority: West Midlands County Council
Area: 188 hectares (465 acres)
Elevation: 325 ft (99 m)   Ref temp: 21 deg C
Runways: 06/24   1,315 × 46 m (4,314 × 150 ft) tarmac
       15/33   2,255 × 46 m (7,400 × 150 ft) tarmac
Pavement strength: 06/24   LCG IV; 15/33   LCG III
Landing category: ICAO CAT II
Lighting:
   R/W   06/24   LIL white edge, and red end lights
       15/33   LIH and LIL white edge, LIH colour-coded centreline, red end lights, TDZ 33

Birmingham Airport with terminal in foreground, runway 15/33 beyond and the National Exhibition Centre in the background. (*West Midlands County Council*)

App	R/W 06	LIH white centreline with two crossbars and LIL red centreline with one crossbar

App   R/W 06   LIH white centreline with two crossbars and LIL red centreline with one crossbar
R/W 24   LIH white centreline with one crossbar and LIL red centreline with one crossbar
R/W 15   LIH white coded centreline with five crossbars
R/W 33   LIH white coded centreline with five crossbars, LIL red centreline with two crossbars, supplementary lights on inner 300 m (984 ft)
VASIS all runways
Thr   R/W 06/24 green wing bars,   15/33 LIH with green wing bars
Txy   blue edge, green centreline on taxiway between R/Ws 06 and 15. Red stop bars

Aids: NDB, VDF, SRE, ACR, ASR, ILS CAT II 33
Twr frequency: 118.3   App frequency: 120.5
Terminals: Domestic and international terminals with 11 aircraft stands
Scheduled services 1978: Aer Lingus, Air Anglia, British Airways, British Caledonian Airways, British Midland Airways, Dan-Air Services, JAT and NLM
Bases: British Airways and British Midland Airways

Traffic:	1970	1975	1976
Passengers (total)	702,559	1,130,040	1,155,919
Cargo (tonnes)	5,563	2,801	2,629
Aircraft movements	46,328	62,443	66,280
Transport movements	14,344	19,971	21,875

Birmingham's first air services used the old Castle Bromwich aerodrome but as early as 1928 the City Council gave approval to the idea that a municipal airport should be constructed. The project was delayed by the economic depression but eventually a site was chosen at Elmdon alongside the Birmingham–Coventry trunk road and close to the London–Birmingham railway tracks. A total of 750 acres (303 hectares) was purchased and the airport was completed by the end of April 1939, the purchase of land, levelling, draining and construction of terminal building and hangars being achieved for about £360,000.

Railway Air Services transferred its operations from Castle Bromwich to Elmdon on 1 May, 1939, and on the same day Great Western and Southern Air Lines began a Liverpool–Manchester–Birmingham–Bristol–Southampton–Ryde–Shoreham service. Western Airways began a Weston-super-Mare–Bristol–Birmingham–Manchester service on 17 June. On 8 July HRH Princess Marina, Duchess of Kent, officially opened the new Birmingham Airport, and a flying display was staged in spite of bad weather which caused at least one aircraft to become bogged although the large Imperial Airways A.W.27 *Eddystone* landed and took-off without difficulty. An unusual feature of the terminal was the cantilever canopies designed to protect passengers from the weather.

When the airport was opened the grass landing area provided a maximum length of 3,825 ft (1,166 m) from southeast to northwest and a maximum length of 3,075 ft (937 m) north–south.

On 16 September, 1939, the airport was requisitioned by Air Ministry and put under RAF control. During the war it was used for pilot training and flight-testing of Stirling and Lancaster bombers which were built nearby. Additional hangars were erected and two paved runways were laid—06/24 of 4,260 ft (1,298 m) and 15/33 of 4,170 ft (1,271 m).

The airport was transferred to the Ministry of Civil Aviation on 19 June, 1946, but no scheduled operations took place until BEA began a Manchester–Birmingham–Paris DC-3 service on 11 April, 1949. During the 1950s runway 15/33 was extended to 5,006 ft (1,526 m).

On 1 April, 1960, the airport passed to the control of Birmingham City Council, on 1 April, 1961, HRH The Duchess of Kent returned to the airport to open the new international terminal, and in 1962 the original terminal was extended. Major developments took place in 1967 when runway 15/33 was extended to its present 7,400 ft (2,255 m). This involved raising the level of the land in the extension area by up to 21 ft (6.4 m) and this entailed the moving of some million cubic metres of fill. New runway and approach lighting was installed.

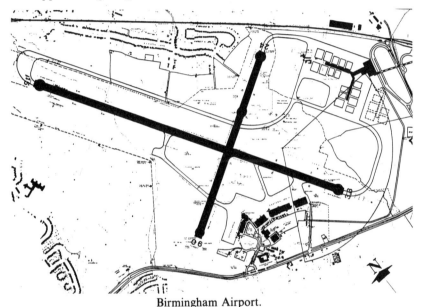

Birmingham Airport.

In 1976 the new National Exhibition Centre was opened on a site just to the east of the airport and beside the railway where a new station (Birmingham International) was provided. Plans have been made to take advantage of these facilities by developing a terminal area in the southeast corner of the airport with direct access to the railway station and exhibition site. The proposed terminal is a two-level building with two traffic piers and 16 close-in aircraft stands. A new system of taxiways is also planned. In 1978 the plans for the new terminal complex had been approved by the West Midlands County Council (responsible for the airport since 1 April, 1974) but Goverment approval was awaited.

357

Bristol   Bristol Airport (Lulsgate)

ICAO: EGGD   IATA: BRS
51° 22′ 57″ N   02° 42′ 47″ W   Elevation: 620 ft (189 m)
Longest runway: 09/27   2,011 m (6,598 ft)   ART   VASI 09/27
  and 16/34
Aids: NDB, VDF, SRE

	1970	1975	1976	1977
Passengers	151,676	252,625	250,855	254,348
Transport movements	6,071	7,083	6,622	6,585

Scheduled services 1978: Aer Lingus, British Airways and Dan-Air Services

Derby   East Midlands Airport

ICAO: EGNX   IATA: EMA
52° 49′ 51″ N   01° 19′ 28″ W   Elevation: 310 ft (94 m)
Longest runway: 10/28   2,280 m (7,480 ft)   ART   VASI 10/28
Aids: VDF, SRE, ILS CAT II 28

	1970	1975	1976	1977
Passengers	312,944	662,490	602,266	607,453
Transport movements	5,996	11,478	12,160	11,590

Scheduled services 1978: Air Bridge Carriers, British Midland Airways and
  Dan-Air Services
Main base: Air Bridge Carriers, Alidair and British Midland Airways.
  The airport was earlier known as Castle Donington.

Edinburgh, Scotland   Edinburgh Airport (Turnhouse)

55° 57′ 09″ N   03° 21′ 41″ W   6 nm (11.26 km) W of city
ICAO: EGPH   IATA code: EDI   Time zone: GMT
Authority: British Airports Authority (Scottish Division)
Area: 364 hectares (901 acres)
Elevation: 135 ft (41 m)   Ref temp: 19 deg C

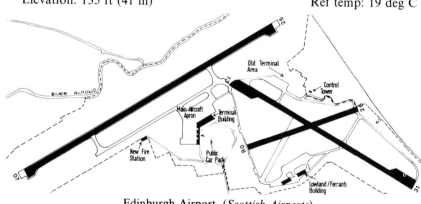

Edinburgh Airport. (*Scottish Airports*)

358

Runways: 07/25   2,560 × 46 m (8,399 × 150 ft) concrete
         08/26   909 × 46 m (2,982 × 150 ft) tarmac
         13/31   1,829 × 46 m (6,000 × 150 ft) tarmac
Pavement strength: 07/25 LCG III; 08/26 LCG V; 13/31 LCG IV
Landing category: ICAO CAT II
Lighting:
    R/W   07/25   LIH white edge and colour-coded centreline, red
            end lights and LIH TDZ
            08/26   LIL white edge, red end lights
            13/31   LIH and LIL white edge, LIH white centreline
            with red last 305 m (1,000 ft), previous 610 m (2,000 ft)
            red/white, and red end lights
    App   R/W 07/25   LIH white coded centreline with five
            crossbars and supplementary lights on inner 300 m (984 ft)
            R/W 08/26   sodium centreline and LITAS
            R/W 13   LIH sodium centreline with one crossbar
            R/W 31   LIH coded centreline with five crossbars
            VASIS 07/25 and 13/31
    Thr   R/W 07/25 and 31 LIH green with wing bars, 08/26 and 13
            LIH green
    Txy   green centreline and red stop bars on taxiway associated
            with R/W 07/25. Blue edge lights other taxiways
Aids: DME, NDB, VDF, SRE, RVR, ILS CAT II 07/25
Twr frequency: 118.7   App frequency: 121.2
Terminal: Multi-level terminal with 13,000 sq m (139,932 sq ft) floor area,
    main concourse and domestic wing, 10 gates, nine aircraft stands and
    three aerobridges
Scheduled services 1978: Aer Lingus, Air Anglia, British Airways, British
    Caledonian Airways, British Island Airways and Loganair

Traffic:	1970–71	1975–76	1976–77	1977–78	1978–79
Passengers (total)	666,329	882,806	1,074,696	1,040,224	1,176,586
Cargo (tonnes)	2,057	2,300	1,602	1,258	1,564
Aircraft movements	55,770	73,691	72,212	62,483	64,604
Transport movements	11,087	18,379	20,496	20,616	22,187

During 1978–79 Tridents accounted for 29 per cent of transport movements, BAC One-Elevens for 24.8 per cent and Fokker F.27s for 18.3 per cent.

Edinburgh Airport was originally established as a Royal Flying Corps aerodrome in 1915 and from 1918 was RAF Station Turnhouse. From 1925 Turnhouse was the home of No. 603 City of Edinburgh Squadron of the Royal Auxiliary Air Force and until the war remained a grass aerodrome with a landing area measuring about 1,650 by 2,250 ft (503 by 686 m). On 15 June, 1928, Imperial Airways Armstrong Whitworth Argosy *City of Glasgow* landed at Turnhouse at the conclusion of its race with the LNER's *Flying Scotsman*; North Eastern Airways extended its Heston–Leeds–Newcastle service to Turnhouse on 27 May, 1935; and on 11 June, that year, Aberdeen Airways opened a short-lived Aberdeen–Turnhouse service to connect with NEA; but there were no sustained air services to Edinburgh until after the Second World War.

The first paved runways were constructed in 1939 and when BEA began its London–Edinburgh–Aberdeen service on 19 May, 1947, there were three tarmac runways—04/22 of 2,100 ft (640 m), 08/26 of 3,510 ft (1,070 m) and 13/31 of 3,990 ft (1,216 m). Subsequently 04/22 was closed and 13/31 was lengthened to 6,000 ft (1,829 m). For many years there was no terminal building and Turnhouse was not handed over to the Ministry of Aviation until 1960, but a civil terminal had by then been constructed and this was later enlarged in an attempt to cope with increasing traffic— the old terminal being in service for more than a year after the introduction of British Airways London–Edinburgh Trident shuttle service on 1 April, 1976.

Edinburgh Airport terminal opened in May 1977.
(*British Airports Authority—Scottish Airports*)

Following protracted negotiations, the airport was taken over by the British Airports Authority on 1 April, 1971, Regularity at Turnhouse had long been poor because of unacceptable crosswinds over the main runway and the conditions of the BAA takeover included a Government grant of 75 per cent of the cost of a new runway. Aligned 07/25 and measuring 2,560 m (8,399 ft), the new runway was brought into operation on 7 April, 1976. Work also began on a completely new terminal on the south side of the airport and this was opened by HM The Queen on 27 May, 1977.

After 30 years as a civil airport Turnhouse had finally been brought to a standard worthy of the Scottish capital, its one remaining shortcoming being the need for aircraft to backtrack on the runway because the parallel taxiway is of insufficient length.

Glasgow, Scotland   Glasgow Airport (Abbotsinch)

55° 52′ 20″ N   04° 25′ 55″ W   6 nm (11 km) W of city
ICAO: EGPF   IATA code: GLA   Time zone: GMT
Authority: British Airports Authority (Scottish Division)
Area: 318 hectares (786 acres)
Elevation: 26 ft (8 m)   Ref temp: 19 deg C
Runways: 06/24   2,566 × 46 m (8,419 × 150 ft) concrete/asphalt with
                                        friction course
         10/28   1,088 × 46 m (3,570 × 150 ft) tarmac
Pavement strength: 06/24 LCG III; 10/28 LCG IV
Landing category: ICAO CAT IIIa
Lighting:
     R/W   06/24   LIH and LIL white edge, LIH colour-coded
                 centreline, TDZ, and red end lights
     App   R/W 06/24   LIH white centreline with five crossbars and
                 red barrettes on inner 300 m (984 ft). VASIS 06/24
     Thr   06/24   LIH green with wing bars
     Txy   green centreline with blue edge on curves
Aids: VOR/DME, NDB, RAD, ILS CAT III 06/24
Twr frequency: 118.8   App frequency: 119.1
Terminals: Passenger terminal with two traffic piers and 28 aircraft stands.
     Cargo terminal with 17,000 tonnes capacity
Scheduled services 1978: 14 airlines
Base: British Airways
Main base: Loganair

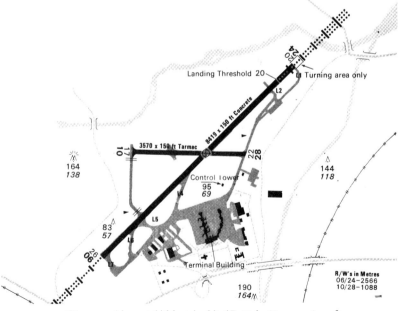

Glasgow Airport (Abbotsinch). (*British Airways Aerad*)

Glasgow Airport with the terminal area at the base of the picture, and the two branches of the River Cart. (*British Airports Authority*)

Traffic:	1970–71	1975–76	1976–77	1977–78	1978–79
Passengers (total)	1,731,065	1,974,704	1,969,804	1,809,116	2,241,468
Cargo (tonnes)	15,560	16,987	17,496	16,788	17,263
Aircraft movements	71,216	76,011	75,697	71,043	81,676
Transport movements	35,457	37,914	36,981	37,314	45,741

During 1978–79 Tridents accounted for 19.4 per cent of transport movements, BAC One-Elevens for 18.5 per cent, Viscounts for 14.7 per cent, HS 748s for 11 per cent, Boeing 737s for 6 per cent and DC-9s for 5.8 per cent.

The present Glasgow Airport at Abbotsinch was originally constructed in 1932 as a military aerodrome. It is situated on the south bank of the Clyde and between the two branches of the River Cart. It was a grass aerodrome and became the headquarters of No. 602 City of Glasgow Royal Auxiliary Air Force Squadron when it was moved from nearby Renfrew in January 1933. In September 1943 the aerodrome was transferred to the Fleet Air Arm as HMS *Sanderling* and some time during the war paved runways were constructed. On 31 October, 1963, HMS *Sanderling* was decommissioned and the site handed over to the Ministry of Aviation.

From the start of Scottish air services in 1933 the old Renfrew aerodrome had served as Glasgow's airport, but it became obvious that Renfrew could not be developed to meet the city's future needs and in November 1960 the Minister of Aviation announced that Abbotsinch would be developed as the Glasgow Airport.

The old Abbotsinch became the new Glasgow Airport on 2 May, 1966, and was officially opened by HM The Queen on 27 June, that year. There were two runways—06/24 of 6,720 ft (2,048 m) and 10/28 of 3,570 ft (1,088 m), and R/W 06/24 had CAT II centreline lighting. There was a large passenger terminal, with 17 aircraft stands, and a cargo building.

For nearly 10 years the airport was owned and operated by Glasgow Corporation but after lengthy negotiations it was taken over by the British Airports Authority on 1 April, 1975, although there were no operations under BAA until 3 April when a prolonged electricians' strike was settled.

362

In its first year of operation Glasgow Airport handled 34,497 aircraft movements and 1,291,388 passengers, and traffic on the London–Glasgow route had increased to such an extent that on 11 January, 1975, British Airways introduced its first shuttle service. The terminal has had to be extended, aerobridges have been installed, and after construction of a new domestic wing the original terminal will be used solely for international operations.

Glasgow Airport was the first in the United Kingdom, after Heathrow, to be equipped and approved for CAT III operations.

Guernsey, Channel Islands   Guernsey Airport

ICAO: EGJB   IATA: GCI
49° 26′ 10″ N   02° 36′ 10″ W   Elevation: 336 ft (102 m)
Runway: 09/27   1,463 m (4,800 ft)   ART   VASI 09/27
Aids: VOR/DME, NDB, SRE, ILS 09/27

	1970	1975	1976
Passengers	390,324	525,254	510,203
Transport movements	30,047	32,068	31,607

Scheduled services 1978: Air Anglia, Air Bridge Carriers, Aurigny Air Services, British Airways, British Island Airways, British Midland Airways, Brymon Airways, Dan-Air Services, Intra Airways and NLM

The airport was opened on 5 May, 1939, and was also known as La Villiaze

Isle of Man   Isle of Man (Ronaldsway) Airport

ICAO: EGNS   IATA: IOM
54° 04′ 55″ N   04° 37′ 37″ W   Elevation: 55 ft (17 m)
Longest runway: 09/27   1,753 m (5,751 ft)   ART   VASI 04/22,
    09/27 and 36
Aids: NDB, VDF, ARI, SRE, ILS CAT I 27

	1970	1975	1976
Passengers	381,309	418,668	366,184
Transport movements*	10,979	10,780	10,405

* Scheduled only

Scheduled services 1978: British Airways, British Island Airways and Dan-Air Services

Jersey, Channel Islands.   Jersey Airport

49° 12′ 30″ N   02° 11′ 45″ W   4 nm (7.4 km) WNW of St Helier
ICAO: EGJJ   IATA code: JER   Time zone: GMT
Authority: States of Jersey
Area: 134 hectares (332 acres)
Elevation: 276 ft (84 m)   Ref temp: 19 deg C
Runway: 09/27   1,706 × 46 m (5,597 × 150 ft) asphalt
Pavement strength: LCG IV
Landing category: ICAO CAT I
Lighting:
    R/W   LIH and LIL white edge
    App   R/W 09   LIH centreline and crossbar
        R/W 27   LIH centreline with two crossbars and LIL
        centreline with two crossbars
        VASIS 09/27
    Thr   green
    Txy   green centreline all taxiways
Aids: NDB, VHF/DF, RAD, ILS uncat 09, ILS CAT I 27
Twr frequency: 119.45   App frequency: 120.3
Terminals: Passenger terminal with one pier and 14 nose-in docking stands.
    Seven other aircraft stands. Separate cargo area and Aurigny Air
    Services terminal
Scheduled services 1978: 12 airlines
Base: British Airways
Main base: Intra Airways

Traffic:	1970	1975	1976	1977
Passengers (total)	1,122,587	1,417,543	1,432,076	1,449,699
Cargo (tonnes)	8,756	10,662	12,985	11,314
Aircraft movements	77,838	94,048	87,866	86,856
Transport movements	48,055	54,864	53,653	53,673

When Jersey Airways began the first regular sustained air services between the mainland and Jersey on 18 December, 1933, the island had no airport and the airline's Dragons used the beach at St Aubins Bay near St Helier. In summer the entire fleet of eight Dragons would fly the route from Portsmouth in a loose formation and all would be parked tail-in to the sea wall. Although the service was maintained with high regularity and nearly

Jersey Airport in 1978. (*Jersey Evening Post*)

20,000 passengers were carried in the first year, the beach was not an acceptable airport and a first-class airport was built on high ground at St Peter.

When opened on 10 March, 1937, the airport occupied 83 acres (33.6 hectares) and its grass surface provided a maximum length of 2,940 ft (896 m) from east to west. There were a terminal building and two hangars, lighting, and an east–west fog line. Cost of constructing the airport was £127,000. The first service to operate from the new airport on 10 March, 1937, was a Jersey Airways flight worked by a D.H.86.

During the war the airport was occupied by German forces. On 26 May, 1945, just over a fortnight after the German surrender, a Jersey Airways and Guernsey Airways operated Dragon Rapide, G-AGLP, landed at Jersey with airline executives in preparation for reopening services and on 21 June regular Croydon–Guernsey–Jersey services were resumed.

On 17 July, 1951, work began on construction of a 4,200 ft (1,280 m) 09/27 asphalt runway. This was completed on 31 May, 1952, at a cost of about £47,000, and exactly one year after work started a flying display was staged to 'mark the construction'. The runway has been lengthened by stages to its present 1,706 m (5,597 ft), taxiways have been built, and terminal area expansion has been an almost continuous process, the latest stage being the addition of a pier to the terminal in 1978.

Constant extension of the runway presented problems because of the proximity of a steep drop to the coast at the west and downward sloping ground to the east. In order to guarantee, as far as possible, its fine safety record, the States of Jersey had installed between the 09 threshold and the adjacent escarpment the soft ground arrester system developed by the Royal Aircraft Establishment. Available ground was insufficient for the full recommended length but an area 100 ft (30 m) long and 30 in (76 cm) deep was filled with rounded shingle from the beach. Installed in 1969, this was the first such airport system and up to mid-1978 one aircraft had run onto it.

Leeds and Bradford   Leeds Bradford Airport (Yeadon)

ICAO: EGNM   IATA: LBA
53° 52′ 00″ N   01° 39′ 10″ W   Elevation: 681 ft (208 m)
Longest runway: 15/33 1,646 m (5,400 ft) ART VASI 15/33 and 28
Aids: NDB, SRE, ILS 33

	1970	1975	1976	1977
Passengers*	253,994	278,144	286,866	282,629
Transport movements	7,890	9,481	10,239	9,867

* Excluding transit

Scheduled services 1978: Aer Lingus, Air Anglia, British Airways, British Island Airways and Dan-Air Services

The airport was opened on 17 October, 1931. Runway extension to 2,250 m (7,380 ft) is planned

Liverpool Liverpool Airport (Speke)

ICAO: EGGP   IATA: LPL
53° 20′ 30″ N   02° 52′ 45″ W   Elevation: 85 ft (26 m)
Longest runway: 09/27   2,286 m (7,500 ft)   ART   VASI 08,
  09/27 and 35
Aids: NDB, SRE, ILS CAT II 27

	1970	1975	1976
Passengers	421,257	437,032	359,083
Transport movements	15,022	12,016	11,085

Scheduled services 1978: Aer Lingus and British Airways
  The airport has full CAT II lighting

London   Gatwick Airport

51° 09′ 10″ N   00° 11′ 24″ W   24.7 nm (46 km) S of city
ICAO: EGKK   IATA code: LGW   Time zone: GMT
Authority: British Airports Authority
Area: 586 hectares (1,448 acres)
Elevation: 202 ft (62 m)   Ref temp: 22 deg C
Runway: 08/26   3,098 × 46 m (10,164 × 150 ft) concrete with friction
                                          course
Pavement strength: LCG II
Landing category: ICAO CAT III

Gatwick Airport with terminal, railway station and car parks in the foreground and
maintenance bases on the left. (*British Airports Authority*)

Lighting:
  R/W   LIH and LIL white edge, LIH colour-coded centreline, red
         end lights. LIH TDZ 08/26
  App   R/W 08/26   LIH coded centreline with five crossbars and
         supplementary lights on inner 300 m (984 ft). VASIS 08/26.
         Red flashing runway alignment beacon 3,307 m (10,850 ft)
         from 08 threshold
  Thr   LIH green with green wing bars
  Txy   blue edge, green centreline main taxiway and high-speed
         exits
Aids: NDB, SRE, ILS CAT I 08, ILS CAT III 26
Twr frequency: 118.1/121.5/121.75   App frequency: 119.6/121.5
Terminals: Departure and International Arrivals Buildings with 92 check-
  in positions and three traffic piers and 55 aircraft stands of which 22
  can handle wide-bodied aircraft. Cargo terminal with 200,000 tonnes
  capacity. General aviation terminal. The passenger terminals are
  directly linked with Gatwick Airport railway station
Scheduled services 1978: 19 airlines
Base: Dan-Air Services
Main base: British Airways Helicopters, British Caledonian Airways,
  British Cargo Airlines and Laker Airways

Traffic:	1970–71	1975–76	1976–77	1977–78	1978–79
Passengers (total)	3,850,387	5,410,565	5,935,753	6,825,776	8,059,953
Cargo (tonnes)	33,557	77,811	83,304	101,302	111,035
Aircraft movements	93,901	106,277	109,342	111,208	129,819
Transport movements	54,603	74,669	81,503	85,929	102,874

During 1978–79 BAC One-Elevens accounted for 38.1 per cent of transport movements,
Boeing 707/720s for 22.8 per cent and Handley Page Heralds for 7.2 per cent.

Gatwick Airport was originally a 1,950 by 1,650 ft (594 by 503 m) grass
aerodrome, situated near Lowfield Heath between the London–Brighton
road to the west and the London–Brighton railway to the east. The
aerodrome was opened on 4 April, 1931, as a private aerodrome of Home
Counties Aircraft Services and used by the Surrey Aero Club. It was only
available to other users in case of emergency.
    Later, Airports Ltd developed Gatwick as a civil airport with terminal
area beside the Southern Railway. There was a circular terminal (originally
referred to as the Martello Tower, it became known as the Beehive) with
surrounding taxiways and two paved strips leading to the grass landing
area. Six telescopic jetties allowed passengers to remain under cover as they
walked to and from the aircraft.
    The Southern Railway built Gatwick Airport Station as close as
possible to the airport terminal to which it was connected by a subway.
    The airport was officially opened by Viscount Swinton, Secretary of
State for Air, on 6 June, 1936, and the ceremony was followed by a flying
display. Being situated south of the Surrey hills it was thought that Gatwick
would find favour because it eliminated a bad weather area between it and
London's terminal airport at Croydon. The original British Airways did
transfer its operations from the Essex Airport, Abridge, to Gatwick, but
the airport became waterlogged in wet weather and on 7 February, 1937,
British Airways moved its operations to Croydon. Some time early in 1937
the Lorenz blind-approach system was installed at Gatwick.

367

After drainage had been improved, the Royal Air Force used Gatwick for training and during the war it became an operational base. At the time of its return to civil use Gatwick had two steel-mesh runways, 05/23 of 4,200 ft (1,280 m) and 09/27 of 3,600 ft (1,097 m) and a 3,150 ft (960 m) grass runway aligned 16/34.

Soon after the war it was decided that a second London airport would be required and, after examination of some 50 possible sites, Gatwick was chosen for development. This amounted to constructing a completely new airport with considerable extension to the west and with the terminal area about a mile further north. The old airport was closed in 1956 and the new airport built at a cost of about £7,800,000.

The London–Brighton road was diverted to run between the new terminal and the railway before turning west to isolate the old terminal area from the new airport. This isolated section is now the main base of British Airways Helicopters, and the Beehive building still stands. An 08/26 concrete runway measuring 7,000 by 150 ft (2,134 by 46 m) was built and to the north of it a parallel taxiway with three high-speed exits. A novel feature of the runway was the use of colour, with dark grey runway and 75 ft (23 m) paved shoulders surfaced with reddish granite chippings. The terminal, at the east side of the airport, and directly connected to a new Gatwick Airport railway station, had a single traffic finger projecting onto the apron which had space for up to 21 aircraft stands, 11 around the pier itself. Calvert approach lighting was installed on both approaches. HM The Queen officially opened the new Gatwick Airport on 9 June, 1958.

Subsequently two further traffic piers were constructed, the terminal enlarged and the runway lengthened to 8,200 ft (2,499 m) and finally to 10,164 ft (3,098 m), the paved shoulders beside the extensions being 25 ft (7.6 m) wide. At one period it was planned to build a parallel runway 3,000 ft (914 m) to the north but approval was never given to this project and in 1978 the Government stated that the proposal should not be revived.

In the summer of 1978 the BAA completed a £100 mn development scheme which included replacement of the original traffic pier, a new terminal to handle arrivals, conversion of the original terminal to a departure building, and new cargo centre.

In 1977 it was decided to prohibit new operations and full-load charters at Heathrow and as a result when Avianca, Braniff and Delta began services to London in 1978 these used Gatwick as the London terminus. Under the Government's 1978 airports policy Gatwick will play a major role as London's second airport and it is to be developed to an annual capacity of 25 mn passengers.

The first stage in this latest development is the addition of 3,500 sq m (37,674 sq ft) to the international arrivals concourse, scheduled for completion in August 1980. The second stage is replacement of the old north pier by an £18 mn satellite. This will be a circular two-storey building with stands for eight wide-bodied aircraft and capacity to handle 1,200 passengers an hour. It will be connected to the main terminal by a Westinghouse fully-automated transit system and is due for completion in 1982.

Planned for 1985 is a second main terminal near the northern boundary of the airport. This would have about 20 aircraft stands. The second terminal is to be the subject of a public inquiry.

BAA is also seeking permission to double the width of the main taxiway over a length of 2,500 m (8,202 ft) for use as an emergency runway in the event of the runway itself being closed by any obstruction—it was closed for this reason for 4 hr 23 min in 1978.

The Gatwick land-use plan also allows for large cargo and maintenance areas north of the runway.

London   Heathrow Airport

51° 28′ 11″ N	00° 27′ 08″ W	12 nm (22 km) W of city
ICAO: EGLL	IATA code: LHR	Time zone: GMT

Authority: British Airports Authority
Area: 1,141 hectares (2,819 acres)
Elevation: 80 ft (24 m)   Ref temp: 22 deg C
Runways: 05/23   2,357 × 91 m (7,734 × 300 ft) concrete
                  10L/28R   3,902 × 91 m (12,802 × 300 ft) concrete with
                                                                              friction course
                  10R/28L   3,658 × 91 m (12,000 × 300 ft) concrete with
                                                                              friction course
    R/W 10L/28R and 10R/28L have 23 m (75 ft) paved shoulders along original length and 7.6 m (25 ft) along 46 m (150 ft) wide western extensions
Pavement strength: LCG II
Landing category: ICAO CAT IIIa
Lighting:
    R/W   05/23   LIH white edge
                  10L/28R and 10R/28L   LIH white edge (first 290 m/951 ft 10L and 10R red); LIH centreline, last 305 m (1,000 ft) red, previous 610 m (2,000 ft) red/white. Elevated amber edge lights for snow. 914 m (3,000 ft) TDZ. Red end lights
    App   R/W 05   LIL red centreline with two crossbars; R/W 23 LIH white coded centreline with four crossbars; R/W 10L/28R and 10R/28L   LIH coded centreline with five crossbars and supplementary lights on inner 300 m (984 ft). VASIS all R/Ws*
    Thr   R/W 05   LIL green, 23   LIH and LIL green, 10L and 10R LIH green with wing bars, 28L and 28R LIH and LIL green with LIH wing bars
    Txy   green centreline, with blue edge to run-up areas. Taxiways divided into numbered blocks and protected by red stop bars
Aids: VOR/DME, NDB, RAD, ASMI, ILS CAT IIIa 10L/28R and 10R/28L, CAT I 23
Twr frequency: 118.7/121.0   App frequency: 119.2/119.5/120.4/127.55

* Early in 1979 PAPI (Precision Approach Path Indicator) was installed on 10L and 28L for evaluation

369

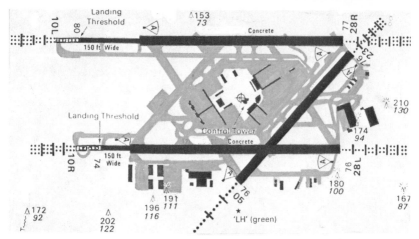

Heathrow Airport, London. (*British Airways Aerad*)

Terminals: Central area with three passenger terminals and seven piers. Terminal 1—domestic and short-haul European traffic, two piers with 20 pier-served aircraft stands and 27 aerobridges; Terminal 2—short- and medium-haul traffic, two piers with 12 pier-served aircraft stands and 14 aerobridges; Terminal 3—long-haul traffic, separate arrival and departure buildings connected by piers. Twenty pier-served aircraft stands and 32 aerobridges. 64.75 hectare (160 acre) cargo terminal complex on south side of airport, with design capacity of one million tonnes/year, with 30 aircraft stands. Total aircraft stands, including cargo area, 152

Scheduled services 1978: 74 passenger and three cargo airlines

Bases: Air-India and Pan American World Airways

Main base: British Airways

Traffic:	1970–71	1975–76	1976–77	1977–78	1978–79
Passengers (total)	15,698,419	21,989,825	24,102,777	23,979,712	26,991,609
Cargo (tonnes)	331,440	394,294	423,858	444,973	478,641
Aircraft movements	270,658	275,454	277,157	267,631	292,968
Transport movements	246,614	253,908	254,768	245,646	269,872

During 1978–79 Tridents accounted for 26.2 per cent of transport movements, Boeing 747s for 10.9 per cent, DC-9s for 10.7 per cent, Boeing 707/720s for 8 per cent, Boeing 737s for 7.8 per cent, Boeing 727s for 5.9 per cent, BAC One-Elevens for 5.2 per cent and Viscounts for 4.5 per cent. The 1,554 Concorde movements represented 0.6 per cent.

When commercial cross-Channel air services began on 25 August, 1919, Aircraft Transport & Travel's D.H.4A and D.H.16 single-engined biplanes operated from the aerodrome on Hounslow Heath, almost under the approach to Heathrow's runway 28L. Hounslow aerodrome closed in March 1920 but three other aerodromes were later opened close to Hounslow.

The first use of part of the site of the present Heathrow came in 1930. Fairey Aviation had used Northolt as its test aerodrome from 1917 but in 1929 was given notice to vacate its premises and cease using the RAF station. Fairey purchased 150 acres (61 hectares) of land between the Bath

370

Road and the Great South West Road and had prepared a private aerodrome with extremely smooth and level grass surface and a large hangar. Flight-testing from the site began in the summer of 1930 and the aerodrome was known by several names—Harmondsworth, Great West Aerodrome and even Heathrow.

In 1944 Fairey's aerodrome was requisitioned by Air Ministry. The area was greatly increased and work begun on constructing the standard RAF triangular pattern of runways. These were to be 10/28 south of and parallel with the Bath Road, and 05/23 and 15/33 which would meet at their southern ends.

The war ended before any of the runways were completed and the decision was taken to develop the site as the major London airport. In September 1945 the London Airport Advisory Layout Panel was established to '... make recommendations as to the best layout for an international airport at Heathrow within a defined area and making maximum use of the three runways being constructed for RAF purposes.' The Panel reported in 1946 and recommended development in three stages. Stage I comprised the three RAF runways, with a parallel taxiway for 10/28, temporary buildings between the taxiway and the Bath Road, and an aircraft maintenance area. Stage II envisaged three additional runways to form an overall pattern of three sets of parallel pairs but with the original 15/33 being replaced by a new runway on this alignment but further west, central area aprons, access tunnel and the first permanent buildings. Stage III consisted of another set of three runways north of the Bath Road, but these were never built. Initially 10/28 was 9,000 ft (2,743 m) long and 05/23 and 15/33 were about 6,000 ft (1,829 m).

On 1 January, 1946, the site was handed over to the Ministry of Civil Aviation and on the same day British South American Airways' Avro

Heathrow Airport in 1978 with runway 10L/28R on the left, 10R/28L on the extreme right and 05/23 beyond the terminal area. The long-haul Terminal 3 is the nearest, with Terminal 1 beyond and Terminal 2 to the right. The British Airways maintenance bases are beyond runway 05/23.
(*British Airports Authority*)

Lancastrian G-AGWG *Starlight* took-off from Heathrow on the first of a series of proving flights to South America. On 28 May, 1946, BOAC began using Heathrow when its Lancastrian G-AGLS left on the joint BOAC/Qantas service to Australia—the first scheduled operation from the new airport. The airport was officially opened on 31 May, 1946, and the first transatlantic services arrived—Constellations of American Overseas Airlines and Pan American Airways. At that time there was a temporary control tower, airline staffs worked from old caravans and a few huts, and passenger accommodation consisted of tents.

Subsequently more permanent structures were built and the North Side terminal area remained in use until the end of March 1962. The first permanent buildings in the central area were the control tower block, the Queen's Building and the short-haul terminal, now known as Terminal 2. London Airport Central became operational on 17 April, 1955, the first departure being a BEA service to Amsterdam operated by Viscount V.701 G-AMOA *George Vancouver*. The long-haul terminal (Terminal 3) came into operation on 16 November, 1961, for BOAC, and for all long-haul carriers on 28 March, 1962. The third terminal (Terminal 1), mainly for use by BEA, was opened by HM The Queen on 17 April, 1969.

Continuous development has taken place at Heathrow over its more than 30 years of service. Its runway pattern has been reduced to a parallel east–west pair and 05/23 but these have all been lengthened. Large cargo and maintenance areas have been established on the southern and eastern boundaries, and on 16 December, 1977, Heathrow Central Underground station was opened, linking the airport with the whole London Underground railway.

The airport was the first to be equipped with Calvert approach lighting and the first in the United Kingdom to be approved for Category III operations. The airport has always had a first class reputation for its operational efficiency, with very high standards of lighting, air traffic control and aids.

In January 1979 work began on the Eastern Satellite Terminal between Terminals 1 and 2 and to be linked to them by moving walkways. On the apron in front of the Queen's Building, the Satellite Terminal will have a waiting area for up to 700 passengers, have four stands for wide-bodied aircraft, and later a fifth, and be used initially to serve the London–Paris Air Bridge operated by Air France and British Airways. It is due to open in August 1980.

In 1978 the Government had decided that BAA's proposals for a fourth main terminal, on the southern side of the airport, should be the subject of a public inquiry. This was held over a period of 96 days and ended in December 1978. If this terminal is built it will increase the airport's capacity to 38 mn passengers.

Heathrow is now the United Kingdom's first port in terms of value of exports and imports handled, £8,791 mn in 1977–78, having overtaken the Port of London.

Heathrow was the first airport anywhere to despatch a jet-operated passenger service (BOAC Comet G-ALYP to Johannesburg on 2 May, 1952) and shared with Paris - Charles de Gaulle the first despatch of a supersonic passenger service (British Airways Concorde G-BOAA to Bahrain on 21 January, 1976).

London   Stansted Airport   ICAO: EGSS   IATA: STN

51° 52′ 58″ N   00° 14′ 02″ E   Elevation: 347 ft (106 m)
Runway: 05/23   3,048 m (10,000 ft)   ART   VASI 05/23
Aids: NDB, SRE, ILS CAT I 23

	1970–71	1975–76	1976–77	1977–78	1978–79
Passengers	528,326	247,452	296,608	296,087	337,707
Transport movements	6,208	3,480	3,879	4,179	4,691

Scheduled services 1978: British Midland Airways and Air Anglia
Base: British Cargo Airlines
    The airport is mainly used for non-scheduled operations, diversions and training, but is to be developed as the fourth major London airport.

Luton   Luton Airport

51° 52′ 34″ N   00° 22′ 05″ W   1.5 nm (2.8 km) E of Luton
ICAO: EGGW   IATA code: LTN   Time zone: GMT
Authority: Luton Corporation
Area: 274 hectares (676 acres)
Elevation: 525 ft (160 m)   Ref temp: 21 deg C
Runways: 06/24   395 × 18 m (1,296 × 59 ft) grass
         08/26   2,160 × 46 m (7,087 × 150 ft) asphalt
         18/36   793 × 46 m (2,602 × 150 ft) grass
Pavement strength: 08/26 LCG III
Landing category: ICAO CAT I
Lighting:
    R/W   08/26   LIH white edge
    App   R/W 08   LIH white and LIL red centreline and crossbar
            R/W 26   LIH white coded centreline with five crossbars and LIL red centreline with crossbar. VASIS 08/26
    Thr   R/W 08   LIH green wing bars. R/W 26 flush unidirectional green with elevated green wing bars
    Txy   green centreline, blue edge in run-up area
Aids: NDB, VDF, SRE, SSR, ILS CAT I 26
Twr frequency: 120.2   App frequency: 129.55
Terminal: Passenger terminal with 17 aircraft stands
Scheduled services 1978: British Midland Airways*
Main base: Britannia Airways, Monarch Airlines and McAlpine Aviation

Traffic:	1970	1975	1976	1977
Passengers (total)	1,971,047	1,881,427	1,815,137	1,951,460
Cargo (tonnes)	1,864	1,777	3,336	6,683
Aircraft movements	52,174	52,488	58,772	61,584
Transport movements	22,354	18,580	18,807	20,808

    During 1976 and 1977 BAC One-Elevens and Boeing 737s accounted for the biggest percentages of transport movements.

* British Midland Airways operates scheduled passenger services and Cyprus Airways scheduled cargo services but most of Luton's traffic comprises inclusive tour and passenger and cargo charter operations.

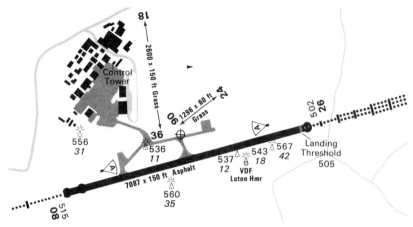

Luton Airport. (*British Airways Aerad*)

The decision to establish a municipal aerodrome at Luton was taken in 1934 and a grass aerodrome of 373 acres (151 hectares) was opened on 16 July, 1938. During the war the aerodrome was requisitioned for government use and several factories established including that of Percival Aircraft. The area of the aerodrome was increased and a number of hangars erected.

From the end of the war until 1959 the aerodrome was mainly used for pleasure flying and flight testing but in 1959 the Borough of Luton constructed a 5,423 ft (1,653 m) 08/26 paved runway and Luton began to play its part as one of the London area's airports. In 1963 the runway was

Luton Airport terminal area with the grass runways beyond the car park and 08/26 in the distance. (*Luton Corporation*)

374

extended to 6,623 ft (2,019 m) and in the winter of 1964–65 a further extension brought the runway to its present length.

The control tower was opened on 24 September, 1952, and the present terminal building was completed in 1966.

Although some seasonal scheduled services are operated to and from Luton Airport, most traffic is carried by non-scheduled airlines engaged in inclusive tour and charter operations.

In HM Government's White Paper *Airports Policy* of February 1978 it was stated 'that Luton Airport should be restricted to the maximum capacity of a single terminal which is estimated at 5 mn passengers a year.'

Manchester   Manchester International Airport

53° 21′ 22″ N	02° 16′ 20″ W	7.5 nm (14 km) SW of city
ICAO: EGCC	IATA code: MAN	Time zone: GMT

Authority: Manchester International Airport Authority
Area: 422 hectares (1,042 acres)
Elevation: 256 ft (78 m)   Ref temp: 21 deg C
Runways: 06/24   2,804 × 46 m (9,200 × 150 ft) concrete/asphalt
           10/28   878 × 46 m (2,880 × 150 ft) asphalt
Pavement strength: 06/24 LCG III; 10/28 LCG V
Landing category: ICAO CAT II
Lighting:
    R/W   06/24   LIH and LIL edge and LIH centreline, white first 1,889 m (6,200 ft), red/white 610 m (2,000 ft) and red last 305 m (1,000 ft). Red end lights. 914 m (3,000 ft) TDZ 24
    App   R/W 06   LIH coded centreline and four crossbars
                 R/W 24   LIH coded centreline with five crossbars and red barrettes on inner 305 m (1,000 ft). VASIS 06/24
    Thr   LIH green with wing bars
    Txy   green centreline with blue edge on sharp curves. Red stop bars at holding positions
Aids: VOR, NDB, VDF, ILS CAT II 24, ILS CAT I 06
Twr frequency: 118.7   App frequency: 119.4

Manchester International Airport.

375

Terminal: Passenger terminal with one domestic and two international piers and 31 aircraft stands
Scheduled services 1978: 15 airlines
Bases: British Airways (BAC One-Elevens) and Dan-Air Services
Main base: Pelican Air Transport

Traffic:	1970	1975	1976	1977
Passengers (total)	1,927,436	2,688,565	2,874,982	2,901,910
Cargo (tonnes)	45,747	37,360	36,395	34,204
Aircraft movements	55,487	68,404	73,920	76,117
Transport movements	39,578	45,981	46,721	46,826

On 24 May, 1919, Avro Civil Aviation Service began operation of the first daily air service in Britain when it started an unsubsidized service between Manchester, Southport and Blackpool. This service was worked for 18 weeks and 194 flights were completed. Then on 23 October, 1922, Daimler Airway started a Manchester–Croydon service with D.H.34s and provided direct connections to Rotterdam, but this operation is believed to have ceased after a fatal accident on 14 September, 1923. Both of these pioneer operations worked to and from the 1914–18 war military aerodrome at Alexandra Park, which was finally closed in 1924.

In 1928 Manchester City Council decided to create an aerodrome on Chat Moss near Eccles and this opened as Barton, or Barton-on-the-Moss, Aerodrome on 1 January, 1930. As an interim measure an aerodrome had been opened on 19 April, 1929, at Rackhouse but there is no evidence that this was ever used by commercial aircraft.

Barton was a small grass aerodrome and, although it was used by transport aircraft for several years, it was unsuitable for aircraft larger than Dragons and Dragon Rapides and the City was forced to construct a better airport. On 28 November, 1935, work began on a 664 acre (269 hectare) site at Ringway and on 25 June, 1938, Ringway Airport was officially opened by Sir Kingsley Wood, the Secretary of State for Air. Railway Air Services transferred its operations from Barton to Ringway on 27 June.

As initially constructed, Ringway was a fine grass-surfaced airport with 230 acres (93 hectares) of landing area and a terminal, administration building and control tower directly attached to a 175 by 120 ft (53 by 36.5 m) hangar with 130 by 22 ft (39.6 by 6.7 m) door opening. At that time Ringway was proposed as the Maybury central junction airport from which air routes would radiate to serve the United Kingdom.

Ringway was not requisitioned during the war but Fairey Aviation had facilities there and the airport was used for largescale paratroop training. During that period three concrete runways were constructed— 02/20 of 3,282 ft (1,000 m), 06/24 of 4,200 ft (1,280 m) and 10/28 of 3,273 ft (998 m).

The airport was reopened for civil operation and a lengthy battle ensued between the City of Manchester and the Government for ownership and finally the City was successful. Railway Air Services introduced an Avro XIX worked Croydon–Manchester–Belfast service on 29 July, 1946, and in the previous month Air France had begun a Paris–Manchester service. In 1953 Sabena began the first transatlantic service to use the airport, in 1955 the name Ringway was dropped in favour of Manchester Airport and on 25 July, 1975, the change was made to Manchester International Airport.

Manchester International Airport, with two Britannia Airways Boeing 737s, a British Airways BAC One-Eleven 510 and KLM's DC-9-15 *City of Brussels*. (*Manchester International Airport Authority*)

06/24 became the main runway and in the early 1950s this was lengthened to 5,900 ft (1,796 m), later it was further increased to 7,500 ft (2,286 m) and in 1969 to 9,200 ft (2,804 m) at which time its width was increased from 150 ft (46 m) to 200 ft (61 m) throughout its length.

A large terminal building with domestic and international piers (A and B) was opened by HRH The Duke of Edinburgh on 28 October, 1962, but rapidly increasing traffic and the impending introduction of Boeing 747s made considerable extension necessary and a plan for terminal development up to 1982 was prepared and submitted to the Airport Committee in 1969. This resulted in expansion of passenger facilities and the building of a second international pier (C) and associated aprons and taxiways which came into operation in March 1974. The new international pier has nose-in parking for seven aircraft, four of which can be wide-bodied with double aerobridge loading.

The original international pier is to be modified for nose-loading, the 06/24 runway is to be strengthened and extended by 800 ft (244 m), a new cargo complex is to be built on the northwest side of the airport and ultimately there will be a second passenger terminal, and a second main runway, parallel to and southeast of the existing 06/24.

377

Newcastle upon Tyne   Newcastle Airport

ICAO: EGNT   IATA: NCL
55° 02′ 14″ N   01° 41′ 24″ W   Elevation: 266 ft (81 m)
Runway: 07/25   2,332 m (7,650 ft)   ART   VASI 07/25
Aids: VOR, NDB, VDF, SRE, ILS CAT I 07

	1970	1975	1976
Passengers	384,416	605,213	687,371
Transport movements	7,131	11,987	13,384

Scheduled services 1978: Air Anglia, British Airways, British Caledonian
   Airways, British Island Airways and Dan-Air Services

Opened as Newcastle Municipal Airport on 26 July, 1935. For many years
   the airport was known as Newcastle-Woolsington.

Prestwick Airport with the terminal in the foreground, the 13/31 runway and in the
distance on the right part of runway 03/21. (*British Airports Authority*)

Prestwick, Scotland   Prestwick Airport

ICAO: EGPK   IATA: PIK
55° 30′ 28″ N   04° 35′ 08″ W   Elevation: 66 ft (20 m)
Longest runway: 13/31 3,139 m (10,300 ft) ART VASI 13/31 and 21
Aids: VOR/DME, NDB, PAR, ILS CAT I 13/31

	1970–71	1975–76	1976–77	1977–78	1978–79
Passengers	508,694	571,311	649,624	605,084	630,855
Transport movements	12,203	9,502	10,172	8,963	8,255

Scheduled services 1978: Air Canada, British Airways, British Caledonian
   Airways, Dan-Air Services, Pan American and SAS

Southampton   Southampton Airport (Eastleigh)

ICAO: EGHI   IATA: SOU
50° 57′ 06″ N   01° 21′ 07″ W   Elevation: 44 ft (13 m)
Runway: 03/21   1,679 m (5,508 ft)   ART   VASI 03/21
Aids: NDB, ACR, VDF, SRE

	1970	1975	1976
Passengers	243,545	318,689	286,159
Transport movements	10,555	11,568	10,967

Scheduled services 1978: Aurigny Air Services, British ·Airways, British
    Island Airways and Brymon Airways
The airport opened in 1932.

Sumburgh, Shetland   Sumburgh Airport

ICAO: EGPB   IATA: LSI
59° 52′ 45″ N   01° 17′ 30″ W   Elevation: 18 ft (5 m)
Longest runway: 15/33 1,426 m (4,680 ft) ART VASI 09/27 and 15
Aids: VOR/DME, NDB, ACR

	1970	1975	1976	1977	1978
Passengers	32,145	176,840	243,230	402,370	686,719
Transport movements	1,882	12,498	15,740	37,662	40,666
Helicopter movements	—	9,577	12,664	18,496	26,823

Scheduled services 1978: British Airways and Loganair

    Sumburgh, opened on 2 June, 1936, is a main base for United
Kingdom North Sea oil operations, with British Airways Helicopters and
Bristow Helicopters bases. The instrument runway is 09/27 of 1,084 m
(3,556 ft).

Sumburgh Airport on the southern tip of the Shetlands is playing a major role in
North Sea oil exploration and production. The longest runway, 15/33, runs from
close to Sumburgh Head, in the background, to the 09/27 instrument runway
running parallel to the Pool of Virkie in the foreground. (*Courtesy CAA*)

United States of America

In this section runway and approach lighting details are listed under their FAA designations. They are:

Runway lights:
HIRL	High Intensity Runway Lights (edge)
MIRL	Medium Intensity Runway Lights (edge)
TDZ	Touchdown Zone Lights

Approach lights:

MALS Medium Intensity Approach Lighting System. 1,400 ft white bar centreline with one crossbar 1,000 ft from threshold.

MALSF Medium Intensity Approach Lighting System with Sequenced Flashers. This is the same as MALS but has sequenced flashers at the three outer bars. Used at locations where approach area identification problems exist.

SALS Short Approach Lighting System. A high intensity system the same as ALSF-1 but with only 400 ft outboard of the 1,000 ft distance marker (crossbar). 70 ft white crossbar 1,000 ft from threshold.

SSALS Simplified Short Approach Lighting System. High intensity system consisting of seven white centreline bars at 200 ft spacing beginning 200 ft from the threshold.

SSALF Simplified Short Approach Lighting System with Sequenced Flashers. This is the same as SSALS but equipped with three sequenced flashers at the outer bars. Used at locations where approach area identification problems exist.

MALSR Medium Intensity Approach Lighting System with Runway Alignment Indicator Lights. An economy type system for precision approaches. 2,400 ft with seven centreline bars on inner 1,400 ft, one crossbar 1,000 ft from threshold, and centreline flashing lights (RAIL) on outer 1,000 ft.

SSALR Simplified Short Approach Lighting System with Runway Alignment Indicator Lights. Has the same use as MALSR but may be installed instead of MALSR where it is anticipated that the system will later be upgraded to ALSF-1 or ALSF-2. Consists of 1,400 ft high intensity white bar centreline and 1,600 ft outer line of flashing lights (RAIL), with 70 ft white crossbar 1,000 ft from threshold.

ALSF-1 Approach Lighting System with Sequenced Flashers CAT I. High intensity system with 22 white centreline bars at 100 ft spacing with 100 ft white crossbar 1,000 ft from threshold (the 1,000 ft distance marker) and 50 ft red terminating bar. Red wing bars before threshold with inner lights in line with runway edge lights. Green threshold lights at 5 ft spacing and extending 35 ft outboard of runway edge lights. Sequenced flashers along centreline. The centreline lights start 300 ft from the threshold and extend to 2,400 ft, or 3,000 ft at international airports.

ALSF-2   Approach Lighting System with Sequenced Flashers CAT II and CAT III. High intensity system with the outer section as ALSF-1 except that it has 30 white centreline bars at 100 ft spacing with 21 flashers. The terminating bar and wing bars of ALSF-1 are replaced with white centreline bars and there are nine red side-row bars on each side of the centreline over the inner 1,000 ft. There is also a white bar between the centreline and red side-bar 500 ft from the threshold (the 500 ft bar).

REIL   Runway End Identifier Lights. Consists of two synchronized flashing lights, one on each side of the runway landing threshold, facing the approach area. Used for identification of runways surrounded by preponderance of other lighting or lacking contrast with the surrounding terrain.

Approach lighting with centreline bars, crossbars, threshold lights, runway edge and centreline lights, narrow gauge touchdown zone lights and high-speed exit centreline lights. (*Port Authority of New York & New Jersey*)

RAIL   Runway Alignment Indicator Lights. A line of flashing lights at 200 ft intervals forming the outer section of the centreline approach lights. These flash in sequence towards the threshold twice a second.

Sequenced Flashers for ALSF-1 and ALSF-2. These emit a bluish-white light and flash in sequence towards the threshold at a rate of twice a second and appear as a ball of light travelling towards the runway threshold at about 4,100 mph (about 6,600 km/h).

The lighting requirements for CAT II and CAT III runways are high intensity approach lights, high intensity runway edge lights, runway centreline lights and touchdown zone lights.

Albany, New York   Albany County Airport

42° 44′ 49″ N   73° 48′ 16″ W   7 nm (13 km) NW of city
ICAO: KALB   IATA code: ALB   Time zone: GMT −5
Authority: County of Albany
Area: 344 hectares (850 acres)
Elevation: 285 ft (87 m)
Runways: 01/19   1,829 × 46 m (6,000 × 150 ft) asphalt
         10/28   1,829 × 46 m (6,000 × 150 ft) asphalt, grooved
         Runway 15/33 is no longer in use
Pavement strength: 01/19 200,000 lb (90,718 kg) 2,   350,000 lb
    (158,757 kg) 3; 10/28 140,000 lb (63,503 kg) 1, 169,000 lb
    (76,657 kg) 2, 280,000 lb (127,006 kg) 3.
Landing category: ICAO CAT I
Lighting:
    R/W   01/19   HIRL white edge,   10/28   MIRL white edge
    App   R/W 01   MALSR
             R/W 19   ALSF-1
             R/W 28   REIL and VASIS
    Thr   green
    Txy   blue edge
Aids: VORTAC, ASR, RVR 19, RVV 19, ILS CAT I 01/19
Twr frequency: 119.5   App frequency: 125.0/125.45/126.6
Terminals: Passenger terminal with pier and eight aircraft stands. Separate cargo terminal
Scheduled services 1978: Air North, Allegheny, American, Command Airways and Mall Airways
Main base: Mall Airways

Traffic:	1970	1975	1976	1977
Passengers (total)	968,422	1,109,834	1,143,707	1,263,627
Cargo (tonnes)	5,242	3,536	3,299	2,921
Aircraft movements	135,848	121,754	119,670	129,627
Transport movements	44,728	36,232	37,316	39,298

The first steps in creating an Albany municipal airport are somewhat uncertain and Albany County Airport in its 50th anniversary booklet gives conflicting details of the early days. One version is that the first municipal aerodrome was prepared in 1918, under the auspices of the Albany Chamber of Commerce, on the old polo grounds on the Loudonville road,

Albany County Airport.

that the aerodrome was named Quentin Roosevelt Memorial Field, but it proved unsuitable and was replaced in 1919 by a grass aerodrome on Westerlo Island, 4 miles (6.4 km) northwest of the city, which was equipped with night facilities.

Another version is that Quentin Roosevelt Field was prepared on Van Rensselaer Island (later Westerlo Island) near the Port of Albany, and there is photographic evidence of an aerodrome on this site in August 1919.

In 1926 the Westerlo site was chosen as the city airport but in October 1927 the decision was changed and the site of the present Albany County Airport was selected in the town of Colonie. In 1928 construction began on a 249-acre (100 hectare) site, two brick hangars and a brick terminal and administration building were erected and one cinder and two tarmac runways laid. The runways were 2,200 ft (671 m), 2,350 ft (716 m) and 2,500 ft (762 m) long.

It appears that Colonial Western Airways' Albany–Cleveland mail service operated from the new airport from 1 June, 1928, and that Canadian Colonial Airways' New York (Newark)–Albany–Montreal service, which began on 1 October, 1928, also used the new airport. The official opening and dedication ceremonies at Albany Municipal Airport were combined with a flying meeting and took place over the four days 3–6 October, 1928.

In 1937 it was announced that the runways were to be extended to 3,600 ft (1,097 m) but this was not done and in January 1939 the CAA closed the airport as unsuitable for use, following a long wrangle between city and federal officials over who should pay for the improvements.

Early in 1940 the City began a Works Progress Administration (WPA) project to improve the airport. Another 351 acres (142 hectares) was acquired, trees, buildings and other obstructions were removed, a new 01/19 runway of 3,500 ft (1,067 m) was built to replace the old 2,300 ft (701 m) north–south runway, and the east–west runway was widened and slightly lengthened. As a result, in December the CAA's ban was partly lifted and daylight operations allowed, to be followed on 21 January, 1942, by lifting of the night ban.

In 1947 consultants recommended runway extension, new lighting, and the removal of further obstructions. A $1.75 mn reconstruction programme was completed in 1949 after the City had tried and failed to sell the airport to New York State. The overall airport area had been increased to 800 acres (323.75 hectares), runway 01/19 extended to 5,000 ft (1,524 m), and a new east–west (10/28) runway laid. But the airport's problems were not yet over, for in 1956 the CAA threatened to close down air traffic control services because the old wooden control tower was regarded as a fire hazard. So a new tower was opened in 1957 and the old one demolished in 1960.

Albany County Airport terminal and control tower. (*County of Albany*)

In 1960 Albany County purchased the airport from the City for $4,437,000 and in 1962 completed a new terminal building, following it with cargo buildings. In 1968 runway 01/19 was extended to 6,000 ft (1,829 m) and the terminal was enlarged. A 1969 plan recommended extension of runway 01/19 to 7,000 ft (2,134 m) and 10/28 to 6,000 ft (1,829 m). The 01/19 extension was not made, but the 10/28 extension was completed in 1974 thus giving the airport two 6,000 ft (1,829 m) runways.

A new cargo terminal was completed in 1975 and in the same year a master plan was begun to cover development up to 1995. Recommendations were made late in 1977 for the early extension of runway 01/19 at its north end to give a length of 7,200 ft (2,195 m) and a three-phase upgrading of the terminal and surrounding facilities, with the first phase consisting of adding a west concourse to the terminal with upper level boarding.

The airport serves the four-county area of Albany, Rensselaer, Saratoga and Schenectady which is expected to have a population of about 860,000 people in 1995.

Albuquerque, New Mexico   Albuquerque International Airport

35° 02′ 31″ N   106° 36′ 18″ W   3.47 nm (6.4 km) SE of city
ICAO: KABQ   IATA code: ABQ   Time zone: GMT −7
Authority: City of Albuquerque
Area: 539 hectares (1,332 acres)
Elevation: 5,352 ft (1,631 m)   Ref temp: 20.5 deg C
Runways: 03/21   2,352 × 46 m   (7,717 × 150 ft)* asphalt
          08/26   4,076 × 91 m (13,373 × 300 ft)* asphalt
          12/30   1,644 × 46 m   (5,395 × 150 ft)* asphalt
          17/35   2,741 × 61 m   (8,993 × 200 ft)* asphalt
Pavement strength: 03/21 and 12/30   30,000 lb (13,608 kg) 1, 45,000 lb
(20,412 kg) 2, 80,000 lb (36,287 kg) 3;   08/26 and 17/35
100,000 lb (45,359 kg) 1, 200,000 lb (90,718 kg) 2,   350,000 lb
(158,757 kg) 3.
Landing category: ICAO CAT I
Lighting:
    R/W   03/21, 08/26 and 12/30   MIRL white edge
             17/35   HIRL white edge
    App   R/W 08   MALSR and VASIS
    Thr   green
    Txy   blue edge
Aids: VORTAC, DME, NDB, ASR, RVR, RVV, ILS CAT I 08
Twr frequency: 118.3   App frequency: 121.1/124.4

* Threshold 08 is displaced 599 ft (182.5 m), 12 is displaced 410 ft (125 m) and 21 is displaced 310 ft (94 m). Take offs are prohibited from R/W 03 and runway 35 is restricted to use by aircraft up to DC-3. There are arresting cables on R/Ws 08, 17, 26 and 35.

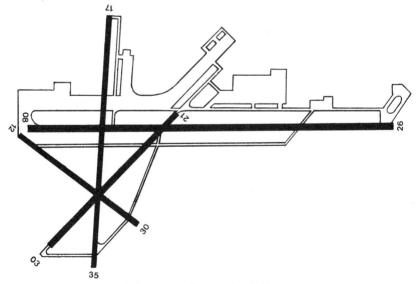

Albuquerque International Airport.

Terminals: Passenger building with west wing for wide-bodied aircraft and remote satellite, with 11 gates. International arrivals building, cargo terminal and post office building.

Scheduled services 1978: Continental, Frontier, Texas International, TWA and ZIA Airlines

Traffic:	1970	1975	1976	1977	1978
Passengers	589,896*	1,563,117	872,621*	1,949,708	2,143,114
Cargo (tonnes)	1,811	3,009*	3,151*	8,789	1,424
Aircraft movements	—	211,448	226,779	148,486	—
Transport movements	21,753†	43,839†	44,022†	108,427	—

* Embarked passengers and uplifted cargo only
† Departures only

Albuquerque is New Mexico's largest city and most important banking, industrial and communications centre. The city is situated in the fertile valley of the Rio Grande and is flanked by mesas and, to east and west, high mountains.

As in so many cases in the United States, Albuquerque obtained its first airport as a result of Lindbergh's New York–Paris flight. Two Santa Fe Railway employees, Frank G. Speakman and W. Langford Franklin, were so inspired by that flight that they learned to fly and then searched for a site for an aerodrome. They leased 140 acres (56.6 hectares) on East Mesa, now Kirtland East, and started preparing an aerodrome in their spare time. In 1928 the City helped by lending graders, scrapers and tractors, and on 15 May, 1928, a Stearman biplane, with tourists from California, made the first landing on the earth runway at Albuquerque Airport.

In mid-1928 James G. Oxnard bought Franklin's interest and began development of the facilities. A hangar and an adobe administration building had been erected by the end of 1928, in 1929 the area was increased to 480 acres (194 hectares), the runway extended to 4,000 ft (1,219 m) and given an oiled surface, and two 2,500 ft (762 m) runways prepared. The runways had green edge lights and there was a flashing beacon.

On 15 May, 1929, Western Air Express opened the first service to Albuquerque and in July it became a stopping place on the coast to coast service inaugurated by Transcontinental Air Transport (TAT).

In 1937 the City of Albuquerque decided that there should be a municipal airport and work began about 1 mile (1.6 km) south and 4 miles (6.4 km) west of the original airport, just south of what is now the intersection of Interstate Highways 25 and 40 and east of the Rio Grande and the Atchison, Topeka & Santa Fe Railway tracks.

Albuquerque Municipal Airport opened in 1939, had a small terminal and probably three runways. The original airport was then named Oxnard Field.

During the war the City sold the airport, except for the terminal and the surrounding 85 acres (34 hectares), to the Army for $1 and on 14 December, 1942, the Kirtland Air Depot and Training Command was activated. After the war TWA operated the civil part of the airport under contract to the City, but finally on 3 January, 1963, the Air Force sold the airport back to the City for $1. However, the eastern part of the airport is now Kirtland Air Force Base and it was the Air Force which built the very long 08/26 runway. On 17 April, 1963, the airport was renamed Albuquerque Sunport.

After the return of the airport to the City, work began on development and on 12 November, 1965, a new terminal, five times the size of the original, was dedicated. This terminal had an area of 160,000 sq ft (14,864 sq m), was in traditional Southwestern architectural style and in 1975 was extended by the addition of a west wing with three gates and stands for Boeing 747s. There is also a four-gate satellite connected to the main terminal by a 300 ft (91 m) tunnel. A second satellite is scheduled for 1985.

On 27 September, 1971, the airport was renamed Albuquerque International, and customs, port health and immigration facilities became operational on 1 October.

In 1978–79 a new general aviation area was constructed south of the main runway and at that time more than 200 private aircraft were based at the airport.

There are divided views on the future of the airport. Some believe that it can serve into the next century, while others feel strongly that it will reach saturation before very long and that its flight routings are too restricted by the proximity of the mountains.

Anchorage, Alaska   Anchorage International Airport

61° 10′ 11″ N   149° 59′ 20″ W   4.3 nm (7.96 km) SW of city
ICAO: PANC   IATA code: ANC   Time zone: GMT −10
Authority: State of Alaska
Area: 1,616 hectares (3,993 acres)
Elevation: 124 ft (38 m)   Ref temp: 18.7 deg C
Runways: 06L/24R   3,231 × 61 m (10,600 × 200 ft) asphalt
         06R/24L   3,321 × 46 m (10,897 × 150 ft) asphalt
         13/31   1,445 × 46 m (4,742 × 150 ft) asphalt*

* Runway 13 first 213 m (700 ft) is gravel, usable in winter only, and last 293 m (961 ft) is asphalt stopway

Pavement strength: 06L/24R   100,000 lb (45,359 kg) 1, 142,000 lb (64,410 kg) 2, 175,000 lb (79,379 kg) 3, 225,000 lb (102,058 kg) 4; 06R/24L   100,000 lb (45,359 kg) 1, 200,000 lb (90,718 kg) 2, 175,000 lb (79,379 kg) 3,   400,000 lb (181,436 kg) 4;   13/31 69,000 lb (31,298 kg) 1, 85,000 lb (38,555 kg) 2, 108,000 lb (48,988 kg) 3, 132,000 lb (53,874 kg) 4. From 1 April to 15 November runway 06L/24R is closed to aircraft above 115,000 lb (52,163 kg) except when 06R/24L is unavailable.
Landing category: ICAO CAT II
Lighting:
R/W   LIH white edge all runways. Centreline 06R/24L. TDZ 06R
App   R/W 06L ALSF-1,   R/W 06R ALSF-2. VASIS 06L/24R, 13 and 24L
Thr   green
Txy   blue edge

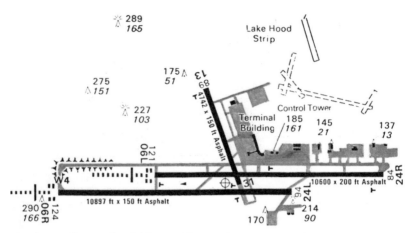

Anchorage International Airport. The seaplane lanes are shown by broken lines.
(*British Airways Aerad*)

Aids: VORTAC, NDB, L, RVR 06R/24L, ARTS III, ILS CAT II 06R
Twr frequency: 118.3   App frequency: 119.1/120.4
Terminals: Two-level passenger terminal. Adjoining international and
    domestic buildings with traffic pier and 19 aircraft stands. Terminal
    floor area 212,000 sq ft (19,695 sq m), apron area approximately 4 mn
    sq ft (371,600 sq m).
Scheduled services 1978: 19 airlines
Main base: Reeve Aleutian and Wien Air Alaska. The Alaska Air National
    Guard has a base south of the east end of runway 06R/24L.

Traffic:	1970	1975	1976	1978
Passengers (total)	1,699,376	2,454,599	2,796,048	3,249,400
Cargo (tonnes)	47,893	117,292	107,928	140,794
Aircraft movements	141,863	228,465	268,857	—
Transport movements	45,547	36,574	41,865	59,400

Western Airlines McDonnell Douglas DC-10-10 N906WA at Anchorage International Airport in 1977. (*Courtesy Airports International*)

388

Anchorage International is Alaska's main airport and a major junction for services between Europe, North America and Asia. The airport is situated on a peninsula to the southwest of the city and there are high mountains only a few miles to the east.

Immediately adjacent to the northeast section of the airport is a general aviation area comprising a gravel 14/32 runway 2,200 by 100 ft (670 by 30 m) and a seaplane area consisting of two lakes (Hood and Spenard) connected by a canal. There are four designated seaplane alighting areas: N–S 2,700 ft (823 m) and 1,300 ft (396 m), E–W 4,700 ft (1,432 m) and NW–SE 1,900 ft (579 m). Anchorage probably has the world's largest concentration of seaplanes and well over 300 are based at the airport's general aviation centre.

The movements at the international airport and general aviation complex are handled by separate controllers in the same control tower which is 150 ft (46 m) high and situated between the two areas.

A 10,500 ft (3,200 m) 14/32 crosswind runway is planned and this will be sited to the west of the existing runway 13/31.

Anchorage International was classified as a CAT II airport in April 1972.

Atlanta, Georgia
The William B Hartsfield Atlanta International Airport

33° 38′ 31″ N   84° 25′ 34″ W   7 nm (13 km) S of city
ICAO: KATL   IATA code: ATL   Time zone: GMT −5
Authority: City of Atlanta
Area: 1,518 hectares (3,750 acres)
Elevation: 1,026 ft (313 m)   Ref temp: 30 deg C
Runways: 08/26   3,048 × 46 m (10,000 × 150 ft) concrete
           09L/27R   2,438 × 46 m (8,000 × 150 ft) concrete, grooved
           09R/27L   2,743 × 46 m (9,000 × 150 ft) concrete
Pavement strength: 120,000 lb (54,431 kg) 1, 200,000 lb (90,718 kg) 2, 360,000 lb (163,293 kg) 3.
Landing category: ICAO CAT IIIa
Lighting:
     R/W   all runways HIRL edge and centreline. TDZ 08 and 09R
     App   R/W 08   ALSF-1 with CAT II waiver
              R/W 09L   REIL
              R/W 09R   ALSF-2
              R/W 26 and 27L   MALSR
              R/W 27R   REIL and VASIS
     Thr   green
     Txy   high intensity on all high-speed exits.
Aids: VOR/DME, ASR, ARTS III, RVR all runways, LLWSAS (Low Level Wind Shear Alert System), ILS CAT IIIa 09R, ILS CAT II 08, ILS CAT I 26 and 27L
Twr frequency: 119.1   App frequency: 128.9

Two of Delta Air Lines' rotunda buildings at The William B Hartsfield Atlanta International Airport. (*Delta Air Lines*)

Terminals: Passenger terminal on north side with six concourses, international arrivals building, and 67 gates. Also about 40 remote aircraft stands. Plane-Mate mobile lounges. Separate cargo terminal
Scheduled services 1978: 12 airlines
Airline base: Eastern Air Lines
Main base: Delta Air Lines and Southern Airways

Traffic:	1970	1975	1976	1977	1978
Passengers (total)	16,627,447	25,268,959	27,299,230	29,977,465	40,190,086
Cargo (tonnes)*	197,053	202,407	229,507	268,802	220,869
Aircraft movements	425,367	468,978	490,002	—	556,992
Transport movements	374,453	414,023	431,604	470,126	514,834

* Includes Express

Atlanta's William B Hartsfield International Airport is now the world's second busiest airport in terms of passengers handled, just over 40 mn in 1978, and ranks second to Chicago O'Hare. Its 1978 volume of transport aircraft movements was 514,834 compared with O'Hare's 776,471. Yet in 1958 Atlanta ranked 35th among United States continental airports.

The site of Atlanta's airport was selected in 1925 by a committee appointed by the mayor and headed by William B. Hartsfield, following a survey of all possible sites within a 25-mile (40-km) radius of the city. The site, in south Fulton County, was on the Candler Estate and consisted of 287 acres (116 hectares). This area was leased in 1926 with an option to purchase, and grading took place in 1926–27 to provide two landing strips of approximately 1,500 ft (457 m).

On 1 April, 1926, Florida Airways began operation of CAM10 between Atlanta and Miami, carrying passengers over the route in Stout 2-ATs from 1 June, but it is not certain that they used Candler Field, as Atlanta's airport was originally named. However, the new aerodrome was used by Pitcairn Aviation when it opened the Atlanta–New York CAM19 with Pitcairn Mailwings on 1 May, 1928.

During 1927–28 three private hangars were built, and the city put up two buildings on a site measuring 80 by 20 ft (24 by 6 m)—one was for soft drinks and sandwiches. In 1929 the City bought the airport site for $94,600 and began extensive grading work, and in 1931 a contract was concluded with American Airways whereby the airline paid $35,000 for a plot at the airport, in prepaid rentals, and this, plus $15,000 allocated by Fulton County, was used to build an administration and terminal building which was completed in 1932 as one of the first airport terminals of any consequence in the United States. In 1937 the runways were given an asphalt surface.

In 1941 work began on new runways and other improvements, and in 1942 the CAA installed ILS on the north–south runway—claimed as the first at a US commercial airport. Also in 1942 east and west wings were added to the terminal and a tree hazard at the south end of the north–south runway was removed.

During the war the Army acquired several sites at the airport and improved the approach areas and in 1944 the City approved preliminary plans for airport development. A new temporary terminal was constructed in 1948, runway 15/33 and its parallel taxiway and 08/26 were completed in 1951 and 03/21 and its parallel taxiway in 1952.

Construction of the present terminal began in 1959 and was dedicated on 3 May, 1961. The 8,000 ft (2,438 m) runway 09/27 (now 09L/27R) was completed in 1964, two rotundas were added to the terminal in 1968, and in 1969 runway 08/26 was reconstructed and lengthened to 10,000 ft (3,048 m). The new 9,000 ft (2,743 m) 09R/27L was opened in January 1973, and in the following year the original 09/27 runway was completely reconstructed.

However, before these last improvements, Eastern Air Lines had, on 1 July, 1971, opened Atlanta–México City services and the name of the airport was changed to The William B Hartsfield Atlanta International Airport to honour the man most responsible for Atlanta's becoming a major transport centre and to mark the airport's international status.

In October 1975 the North Cargo Building was opened. It has more than 390,000 sq ft (36,230 sq m) of ground floor area, cost $13 mn, and was claimed as the world's largest air cargo building.

Although Atlanta's airport had undergone largescale development, by the mid-1970s the terminal facilities were handling twice the traffic for which they had been designed in 1958. In the late 1960s planning began for

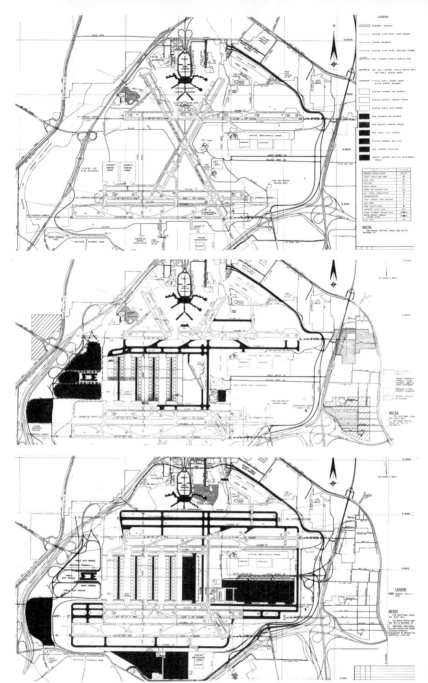

William B Hartsfield Atlanta International Airport. *Top* The existing layout, *centre* Stage I development, *bottom* Stage II development.

a major redevelopment to give the airport an annual capacity of 55 mn passengers. The final plan was agreed late in 1975 and contracts began to be placed early in 1977 for a programme costing more than \$280 mn.

The development is taking place in two phases, Stage I covering the period 1976–81 and Stage II beyond 1981. Delays are caused and fuel costs increased because aircraft using the present terminal have to cross runway 08/26 to reach the distant pair of 09/27 runways. The 03/21 and 15/33 runways have now been closed and the terminal area is to occupy the western half of the space between 08/26 and 09L/27R.

Stage I will see the building of a new terminal, some 1,000 ft (305 m) in length; a very large apron on which there will be four concourse buildings, each 2,400 ft (732 m) long and separated by aprons averaging 1,000 ft (305 m) in width, with a total of 104 stands each capable of taking a wide-bodied aircraft; a new parallel taxiway along the full length of 08/26 on its south side, with three high-speed exits; a second section of parallel taxiway in the terminal area; additional taxiways south of the terminal; a cross taxiway linking the north and south runways; a new taxiway between the North cargo terminal and the present north passenger terminal area; and extensive car parks. This phase was due to be completed in December 1980 for operation in January 1981 but brought forward to September 1980.

Stage II includes a 9,000 ft (2,743 m) 08L/26R runway with two parallel taxiways; a fifth apron concourse, bringing the number of aircraft stands to 130; a large cargo centre at the eastern end of the airport, with stands for 11 very large and 25 smaller aircraft; numerous additional taxiways including a second north–south link in the central area and a link between the runway pairs at their eastern ends; a large maintenance area in the southern part of the airport; further increase in car parking space; and the extension of runway 09L/27R to 11,889 ft (3,624 m).

The 09/27 runway centrelines are separated by 1,050 ft (320 m), the 08/26 pair will have centrelines at 1,000 ft (305 m) and the separation between the centrelines of the outer runways will be 6,450 ft (1,966 m). All approaches except 08L and 26R will have ILS.

Atlanta was the first United States airport at which a CAT III autolanding was made with passengers, by a Delta Air Lines TriStar early in 1977, and sustained CAT III operations began on 29 November, 1977, when five TriStars landed under these conditions. The airport was also one of the first to be equipped with the Low Level Wind Shear Alert System (LLWSAS).

The new Atlanta terminal will consist of two two-level buildings back to back and connected by bridges. Passengers will travel to the concourse loading buildings by underground automated 'people movers'. Very great care is being taken to safeguard the tunnel system against fire and smoke. The stations will be beneath the centre of each apron concourse building which will be a two-level structure with passenger handling on the upper level and aircraft boarding will be via aerobridges.

The main terminal will be steel-framed with exterior walls of limestone panelling, and the steel frame concourse buildings will have exterior walls of metal insulated panels. To achieve maximum energy conservation, glass areas are being kept to the minimum in all buildings, with fibreglass insulated material used as a substitute where daylight is required.

Drawing of the modified and enlarged terminal at Baltimore - Washington International Airport. (*Maryland State Aviation Administration*)

Baltimore, Maryland   Baltimore-Washington International Airport

39° 10′ 35″ N   76° 40′ 19″ W   10 nm (18.5 km) S of city
ICAO: KBAL   IATA code: BAL   Time zone: GMT −5
Authority: Maryland State Aviation Administration
Area: 1,278 hectares (3,158 acres)
Elevation: 156 ft (47 m)   Ref temp: 30 deg C
Runways: 04/22   1,830 × 46 m (6,005 × 150 ft) asphaltic concrete
           10/28   2,881 × 61 m (9,452 × 200 ft) asphaltic concrete
           15L/33R   917 × 23 m (3,010 × 75 ft)   asphalt*
           15R/33L   2,901 × 46 m (9,519 × 150 ft) asphaltic concrete
           Runways 10/28 and 15R/33L are grooved, and runway
           15L/33R is restricted to piston-engined aircraft up to 12,500 lb
Pavement strength (main runways): 100,000 lb (45,359 kg) 1, 220,000 lb
(99,790 kg) 2, 500,000 lb (226,796 kg) 3.
Landing category: ICAO CAT II
Lighting:
   R/W   10/28   HIRL, last 2,000 ft (610 m) yellow, and white
             centreline. TDZ 10
             04/22 and 15R/33L   HIRL
   App   R/W 04/22   REIL
             R/W 10   ALSF-2
             R/W 15R   SSALSR
             VASIS 28 and 33L
   Thr   10/28, 15R/33L and 22 green, 04 green with strobes
   Txy   blue edge
Aids: VORTAC, L, RVR, RVV, ILS CAT II 10, ILS CAT I 15R
Twr frequency: 119.4/121.5 App frequency: 119.7 (south), 125.9 (north)

*General aviation runway on taxiway.

394

Terminals: Three-level terminal with five traffic piers and 27 gates. Plane-Mates in use. Separate cargo facilities and two widely separated general aviation aprons

Scheduled services 1978: 11 airlines

Traffic:	1970	1975	1976	1977	1978
Passengers (total)	3,019,581	2,773,418	2,975,778	3,155,328*	3,557,139
Cargo (tonnes)	42,062	37,458	43,900	59,085	85,738
Aircraft movements	230,343	219,290	232,846	240,778	222,108
Transport movements	123,686	106,560	117,679	126,024	118,585

* Excludes transit passengers

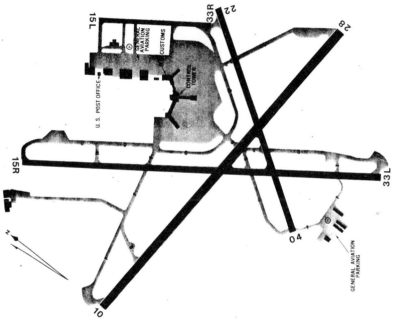

Baltimore - Washington International Airport. (*FAA*)

The first Baltimore airport, Logan Field, was opened in September 1921, but in 1928 the City announced its plans for a municipal airport to be built near Logan Field. However, the new airport, known as Harbor Field, was delayed by the economic depression and was not opened until 16 November, 1941. Soon after its opening it was realized that Harbor Field could not be expanded to handle heavier and faster aircraft and in May 1946 master plans were submitted for yet another airport, on a 3,200 acre (1,295 hectare) site near Friendship Church in Anne Arundel County.

The site chosen was a largely fog-free plateau midway between Baltimore and Annapolis and work began in 1947 to build three runways, of from 6,500 to 9,450 ft (1,981 to 2,880 m), a terminal building, and a nine-storey control tower which was the second highest in the USA when it was opened.

Named Friendship Airport, it was dedicated on 24 June, 1950, by President Truman, and when scheduled flights began a month later it was regarded as a very advanced airport. However, all was not well, for the moving of some 7 mn cubic yards of soil to build the airport had exposed a desert of light powdery material which blew away in the wind and during rain blocked the drainage system. A thorough investigation of the problem led to the planting of weeping lovegrass and other special plants to consolidate the soil. Sludge from the city's sewage plant and lime were added and by 1952 the situation had been stabilized and the airport successfully survived six inches (15½ cm) of rain in five days without damage.

In the early 1970s air traffic was increasing so rapidly that it was accepted that terminal facilities would have to be expanded although runways and navigational aids were considered adequate. It was also recognized that the improvements should be financed by the State and therefore on 26 July, 1972, the State of Maryland purchased the airport from the City of Baltimore for $36 mn.

On 16 November, 1973, the airport's name was changed to Baltimore - Washington Airport, and at the ceremony to mark the occasion details were announced of the expansion and modernization plans to meet the regional requirements of the 1980s.

The programme, costing $64.5 mn, involved increasing the terminal building area from 350,700 sq ft (32,580 sq m) to 614,837 sq ft (57,118 sq m) and its capacity from 3 mn to 11.2 mn annual passengers. Construction began in October 1974, and was completed in September 1979. The main work consisted of adding a large steel and glass canopy over the upper road along the length of the terminal, designed to admit maximum light, adding sections to the apron face of the terminal, adding a new pier at each end and increasing the area of the three original piers. Boarding gates were increased from 20 to 27 and each provided with an aerobridge. Two Plane-Mates were purchased to serve international and charter flights as well as helping out while some gates had to be closed during reconstruction.

The new piers are A and E and the old piers A, B and C have now been renamed D, C and B respectively. Pier A has three gates used by United, B has six gates used by Delta and United, C has 10 gates used by Allegheny and Piedmont, D has five gates used by American, National and TWA, E has one gate for charters and international arrivals, and there are commuter gates between piers C and D. Most gates can handle wide-bodied aircraft.

In July 1974 a new 110,000 sq ft (10,219 sq m) cargo terminal was completed, trebling the cargo area already provided by three earlier buildings. The overall cargo complex occupies 20 acres (8 hectares).

Birmingham, Alabama   Birmingham Municipal Airport

33° 33′ 47″ N   86° 45′ 19″ W   4.34 nm (8 km) NE of city
ICAO: KBHM   IATA code: BHM   Time zone: GMT −6
Authority: City of Birmingham
Area: 647 hectares (1,600 acres)
Elevation: 643 ft (196 m)   Ref temp: 16.8 deg C

Runways: 05/23   3,048 × 46 m (10,000 × 150 ft)* asphalt-concrete
        18/36   1,315 × 46 m (4,315 × 150 ft) asphalt-concrete
Pavement strength: maximum auw 500,000 lb (226,796 kg)
Landing category: ICAO CAT II
Lighting:
    R/W   05/23   HIRL and centreline. TDZ 05
           18/36   HIRL
    App   R/W 05   ALSF-2 and VASIS
           R/W 23   MALSR and VASIS
    Thr   green wing bars
    Txy   blue edge
Aids: VORTAC, NDB, VDF, ASR, RVR 05, RVV 05, ILS CAT II 05
Twr frequency: 118.7   App frequency: 119.9/124.5
Terminals: Two-level semi-circular passenger terminal with two traffic
    piers, 15 gates and aircraft stands with aerobridges. Concourse B has
    three gates for Eastern Air Lines and two for Southern Airways.
    Concourse C, with a rotunda, has seven Delta Air Lines gates and is
    also used by United Airlines. The old terminal with seven gates, is used
    for charter operations. There are two cargo gates. Separate general
    aviation area on east side of airport
Scheduled services 1978: Delta, Eastern, Southern and United. The
    Alabama Air National Guard and Alabama Army National Guard
    helicopter unit have bases at the north of the airport.

Traffic:	1970	1975	1976	1977	1978
Passengers (total)	983,405	1,206,704	1,279,360	1,420,945	1,578,934
Cargo (tonnes)	3,177	5,936	6,070	2,809†	5,565
Aircraft movements	229,096	179,694	190,368	196,461	—
Transport movements	45,219	39,759	41,905	42,015	44,647

In 1930 the City of Birmingham voted $1 mn for the acquisition of a
park, a few miles north of the city, and its development into a 323 acre (131
hectare) airport capable of obtaining the new Department of Commerce
A-1-A rating 'as ideally prepared to meet the needs of airline operators on a
large scale.'

*Threshold 23 displaced 1,770 ft (539 m). Arrester cables 05/23
†Uplifted only

Birmingham Municipal Airport terminal.

The landing ground was prepared and a terminal was built in southern colonial style based on Mount Vernon, George Washington's home in Virginia. The terminal was dedicated on 30 May, 1931. There were asphalt runways, a large hangar with the name Birmingham painted on its roof in large capitals, and the airport opened to traffic on 1 June. In 1932 Birmingham Municipal Airport achieved the distinction of being the first to be awarded the A-1-A rating.

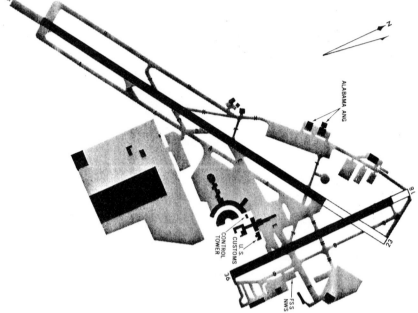

Birmingham Municipal Airport. (*FAA*)

By 1940 the airport occupied 430 acres (174 hectares). With the United States' involvement in the war, the City offered the airport to the War Department for $1 a year and for more than six years the flying area was part of the Birmingham Army Air Base. During that time additional land was purchased and three 150 ft (46 m) wide concrete runways were laid. These were almost certainly the first stages of the present 05/23 and 18/36, and the third runway, probably 08/26, is now a taxiway. The old southwest–northeast asphalt runway still exists but is in poor condition.

In 1948 the airport was returned to the City. The main all-weather runway 05/23 was extended to 8,230 ft (2,509 m) with a 1,770 ft (539 m) overrun giving it a total length of 10,000 ft (3,048 m), and runway 18/36, at present mostly used by general aviation, is to be extended south to provide 6,100 ft (1,859 m), land purchase having begun for the extension in mid-1971.

A new terminal building, alongside the original building, was dedicated on 11 February, 1962. This cost $2 mn and has seven gates and a cargo area. The original terminal then became a cargo building but it will have to be demolished when 18/36 is extended.

In mid-1965 it was recognized that new facilities would be required to keep pace with traffic growth and in August 1967 a development study was presented to the City Council. On 4 June, 1968, the voters of Birmingham approved an initial $13.2 mn in bonds to finance the development which was planned in three stages—up to 1980, 1980–85, and 1985–2000 which would see the ultimate development of the airport.

The first stage included a new terminal, dedicated on 30 November, 1973, which, with a four-level car park, cost $13 mn; a two-gate cargo terminal and apron; and extension of runway 18/36. The new terminal provided 15 gates, all with aerobridges, and was connected by a covered walkway to the previous seven-gate terminal which was redesignated Concourse A.

Stage 2 will add 10 gates to give a total of 32, and the cargo terminal will be increased to have an area of 90,000 sq ft (8,361 sq m) and three more loading gates. It is envisaged that during this stage of development there will be a need for further general aviation capacity and it is proposed to build a 4,000 ft (1,219 m) runway parallel to 05/23.

In the final stage it is planned to increase passenger gates to 36, expand the cargo terminal to 100,000 sq ft (9,290 sq m) and provide 8–10 cargo gates.

The terminal in its present stage of development has two concourses, B and C, and employs second-level loading, with each gate capable of handling wide-bodied aircraft. Great attention was given to landscaping, and magnolias, pools and coloured fountains all combine to make the terminal attractive.

Boston, Massachusetts
General Edward Lawrence Logan International Airport

42° 21′ 47″ N	71° 00′ 19″ W	1.3 nm (2.4 km) E of city
ICAO: KBOS	IATA code: BOS	Time zone: GMT −5

Authority: Massachusetts Port Authority (Massport)
Area: 1,200 hectares (2,965 acres)
Elevation: 20 ft (6 m)   Ref temp: 27 deg C

Runways:*	04L/22R	2,396 × 46 m (7,860 × 150 ft) asphalt/concrete, grooved
	04R/22L	3,048 × 46 m (10,001 × 150 ft) concrete, grooved
	09/27	2,134 × 46 m (7,000 × 150 ft) concrete, grooved
	15L/33R	752 × 38 m (2,468 × 125 ft) concrete
	15R/33L	3,073 × 46 m (10,081 × 150 ft) concrete, grooved

* Runway 04R night and IMC landings first 1,163 ft (354 m) not available. Full length available in daytime with 3 nm (5.5 km) visibility and 1,000 ft (305 m) ceiling. Runway 15R first 890 ft (271 m) not available for landings. Runway 22R first 828 ft (252 m) not available for landings. There are distance-to-go markers on 04R/22L and 15R/33L.

Pavement strength: 200,000 lb (90,718 kg) 1 and 2, 350,000 lb (158,757 kg) 3
Landing category: ICAO CAT IIIa

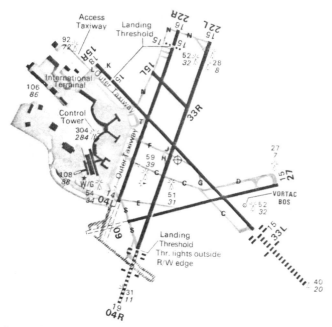

Logan International Airport, Boston. (*British Airways Aerad*)

Lighting:
R/W   04L/22R   HIRL*
            04R/22L   HIRL and centreline. TDZ 04R
            09/27   HIRL
            15L/33R   MIRL
            15R/33L   HIRL and centreline
* Last 828 ft (252 m) 04L blue edge, first 828 ft (252 m) 22R red edge

App   R/W 04L   REIL
         R/W 04R   ALSF-2
         R/W 15R and 27   VASIS
         R/W 22L   REIL and VASIS
         R/W 33L   ALSF-1 and VASIS
Thr   LIH green, with strobes on 04L, 22L and 22R
Txy   blue edge
Aids: VORTAC, NDB, RVR 04R/22L, 27 and 33L, RVV 04R/22L and
     33L, ILS CAT IIIa 04R, ILS CAT I 22L, 27 and 33L
Twr frequency: 112.71/119.1   App frequency: 120.6/126.5
Terminals: Four passenger terminals. North Terminal with three piers,
     South Terminal with two piers, Southwest Terminal with pier and
     John A Volpe International Terminal. Total of 85 gates with 67
     aerobridges. Separate cargo and general aviation areas
Scheduled services 1978: 34 airlines
Airline bases: Allegheny, American, Butler Aviation, Delta, Eastern, and
     TWA

400

Main base: Air New England

Traffic:	1970	1975	1976	1977	1978
Passengers (total)	9,389,000*	10,515,390	11,395,537	12,273,339	13,543,062
Cargo (tonnes)	132,428	129,088	147,762	161,752	211,991
Aircraft movements	323,415	258,471	265,578	281,413	299,905
Transport movements	209,379	225,461	231,887	250,191	259,813

* Rounded figure

Until 1922 Boston's aerodrome was Muster Field, at Framingham, about 20 miles (32 km) from the city, and it was used by the Army Air Corps and a few private pilots; but a search was being made for a suitable site on which to build an aerodrome at Boston—this was required by both the Massachusetts Air National Guard and the Boston Chamber of Commerce.

At the turn of the century a shipping channel had had to be dredged in Boston Harbor and the mud brought up was dumped on a spit of land jutting into the harbour from Jeffries Point in East Boston. This site on the tidal flats was selected for the aerodrome, on 12 May, 1922, the Massachusetts Legislature passed a bill authorizing the State Department of Public Works to spend money on the preparation provided an equal amount could be raised from other sources, and the Chamber of Commerce secured matching funds from prominent Bostonians. The site, measuring 189 acres (76 hectares), was leased to the US Government for 20 years on condition that the aerodrome was open to private and commercial users. Two 1,500 by 100 ft (457 by 30 m) cinder runways were laid in the form of a T, there was a small apron, a row of four hangars, and a 50 ft (15 m) wide taxiway linking the apron with the runway intersection. The aerodrome was known as East Boston Landing Field, later East Boston Airport, and later still as Boston Airport.

Some flying actually took place from the aerodrome before the official dedication on 8 September, 1923. The first commercial flying is believed to have been by the Skywriting Corporation with its S.E.5s. Colonial Air Transport, later Colonial Airways, opened CAM1 between New York and Boston on 18 June, 1926, with Curtiss Larks and from 4 April, 1927, carried passengers over the route in Fokker Universals and F.VIIs. By 1924 there was a seaplane ramp on the west side of the airport and there are reports of some services being operated by Savoia Marchetti S.55 twin-hulled flying-boats.

A Legislature Act in 1928 leased the airport to the City of Boston and the Army became tenants until 1946. On 1 December, 1941, Massachusetts Public Works Department took over the airport and major expansion plans were drawn up for postwar development. By 1941 additional land had doubled the size of the airport and a hangar had been built for American Airlines. By 1948 further dredging and filling increased the area to about 2,000 acres (809 hectares) and Apple Island and Governor's Island were levelled to become part of the airport. Four runways had been partially completed by this time together with the partly completed terminal. There were temporary hangars for American Airlines and Eastern Air Lines, a small service building for United Air Lines, and a modern hangar for National Airlines.

On 1 August, 1948, a new act put the airport under the State Airport

Management Board with a mandate for further development. A new terminal was built, but without the planned central building, and the four runways were completed.

In 1944 the airport had been renamed Commonwealth Airport, to some people's disgust, but later it was known as Logan Airport and its official title is now General Edward Lawrence Logan International Airport. General Logan, who was a First World War soldier and later a lower court judge in South Boston, had in fact had nothing to do with the airport but after his death his widow took an interest in its development and managed to get it named after the General. In 1956 a statue of General Logan was erected at the airport.

The airport now has four terminal buildings, the latest being the $33 mn Volpe International Terminal which was opened on 13 June, 1974, replacing the 1963 international terminal which had had a second floor lobby added in 1967 to provide upper-level boarding. The Volpe building has four storeys, measures 794 by 164 ft (242 by 50 m), is 69 ft (21 m) high, has 350,000 sq ft (32,515 sq m) of floor space, can handle eight Boeing 747s simultaneously and up to 1,200 arriving passengers an hour. It has a tubular space-truss roof with 64 ft (19.5 m) span plus a 31 ft (9.4 m) cantilever over the access road. A commuter airlines terminal is planned in the form of a pier from the Southwest Terminal.

Logan International Airport, Boston, in September 1973. This view looks approximately west and shows the North Terminal in the centre foreground with the South Terminal on the left. Beyond the central terminal area is the rectangular Southwest Terminal and to its right the Eastern Air Lines hangar and general aviation area. (*Aerial Photos of New England Inc*)

In 1977 a major programme was undertaken which involved runway paving and painting, installation of additional lighting and aids, and the grooving of runways 04R/22L and 09/27. After this work runway 04R was cleared for CAT IIIa operations on 23 March, 1978.

The original airport of 1922 is now occupied by part of the terminal area, mostly the car parks. The airport owes its position to Boston's harbour, and the proximity of shipping is emphasized by the fact that air traffic control notifies aircraft when shipping is known to impinge on approaches and take offs—masts of up to 207 ft (63 m) may be encountered on most approaches except 15R.

Buffalo, New York   Greater Buffalo International Airport

42° 56′ 27″ N   78° 43′ 48″ W   9.5 nm (17.6 km) E of city centre
ICAO: KBUF   IATA code: BUF   Time zone: GMT −5
Authority: Niagara Frontier Transportation Authority
Area: 244 hectares (803 acres)
Elevation: 723 ft (220 m)   Ref temp: 8.38 deg C
Runways: 05/23   2,469 × 46 m (8,100 × 150 ft) asphalt, grooved
        14/32   1,638 × 46 m (5,375 × 150 ft) asphalt/concrete
Pavement strength: 05/23 maximum auw 375,000 lb (170,097 kg)
Landing category: ICAO CAT II
Lighting:
    R/W   05/23   HIRL and distance-coded centreline. Red end lights. TDZ 05/23
           14/32   MIRL. Red end lights
    App   R/W 05   SSALR
           R/W 23   ALSF-1
           R/W 32   REIL and VASIS
    Thr   05 red and displaced threshold green and amber
           14/32 and 23 green
    Txy   blue edge
Aids: VOR/DME, NDB, L, SRE, ARTS III, RVR 05/23, ILS CAT II 23, ILS CAT I 05
Twr frequency: 120.5   App frequency: 123.8/126.5/134.05/135.35
Terminals: East Terminal with piers and 13 gates and West Terminal with eight gates. Thirteen gates have second-level aerobridges. Separate cargo buildings and general aviation terminal
Scheduled services 1978: Allegheny, American, Chautauqua Airlines, Eastern, Empire Airlines, Suburban Airlines and United

Traffic:	1970	1975	1976	1977	1978
Passengers (total)	2,195,773	2,830,605	3,107,505	3,116,388	3,527,996
Cargo (tonnes)	23,684	20,547	21,374	24,826	46,638
Aircraft movements	157,417	145,627	146,852	153,641	161,708
Transport movements	67,196	74,220	77,913	78,349	—

In 1925 the City of Buffalo purchased 194 acres (78.5 hectares) of farmland in the township of Cheektowaga for the construction of a municipal airport, and an additional 318 acres (128.7 hectares) was bought

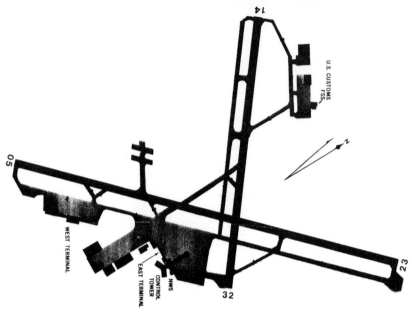

Greater Buffalo International Airport. (*FAA*)

in 1926. It was decided to lay out four 3,000 by 100 ft (914 by 30 m) cinder runways, and to erect an administrative building and hangars near the centre of the site to keep taxi-ing to the minimum.

Site clearance began in May 1926, with the help of tractors lent by the Ford Motor Company, flown in in Ford Trimotors, and assembled on the site. East–west and northeast–southwest 2,500 ft (762 m) runways were completed during 1926, work on the first of three hangars began on 26 June and on the administration building on 9 August. The corner-stone of the administration building was laid in a ceremony on 25 September and that is regarded as the inaugural date of Buffalo Airport.

The first airline operation was by Colonial Western Airways which began Buffalo–Cleveland services with a Fairchild FC-2 on 18 December, 1927.

In 1929 a further 37 acres (15 hectares) was acquired and the east–west runway was extended to 2,854 ft (870 m) and the southwest–northeast runway to 2,805 ft (855 m). The 2,378 ft (725 m) north–south and 2,490 ft (759 m) northwest–southeast runways were also constructed.

To ease the unemployment problem during the Depression, in 1935 the Works Progress Administration allocated $736,000 towards airport improvements. Thousands of men with shovels and wheelbarrows worked to improve the landing area, and a start was made on a new terminal building.

Curtiss had for some time been assembling and test flying its new aircraft at Buffalo Airport and in 1940 the Government built a new factory on land adjoining the airport. Large numbers of Curtiss military aircraft were produced and flown. Later the factory passed to Westinghouse Electric Corporation.

A Federal grant of $963,939 enabled improvements to be made in the period 1942–44. The north–south and northeast–southwest runways were given a tarmac surface, 1,900 ft (579 m) of the east–west and northwest–southeast runways were concreted, new taxiways were built and the apron extended.

Very heavy wartime use left the airport badly deteriorated and postwar priorities were making good the damage and improving and lengthening the runways. The terminal was extended, and a parallel taxiway was constructed alongside the northwest–southeast runway (by then known as 14/32). In the early postwar years piers were added to the terminal and ILS was installed on the north–south runway—the first at a US municipal airport.

In 1956 the 05/23 runway was extended to 5,642 ft (1,720 m) and in that year operation of the airport passed from the City to the newly created Niagara Frontier Port Authority. By that time the airport was known as Buffalo Municipal Airport but in May 1959 it was renamed Greater Buffalo Airport although this was changed in the following month to Greater Buffalo International Airport.

In 1963 work began on the extension to 8,100 ft (2,469 m) of runway 05/23 so that it could handle jet operations. This was a major undertaking because the Lehigh Valley Railroad tracks, Ellkott Creek and Aero Drive, all just outside the northeast boundary, had to be bridged to carry the runway and its parallel taxiway. Paving began in the spring of 1965 and the extended runway was opened for jet services on 9 October, 1965.

Looking along runway 05/23 to the northeast at Greater Buffalo International Airport. The West Terminal is in the right foreground with the East Terminal beyond. Runway 14/32 can be seen in the distance and on the left are hard stands for four jet aircraft.
(*Prior Aviation, courtesy Niagara Frontier Transportation Authority*)

The new Niagara Frontier Transportation Authority took over responsibility for the airport in 1967 and embarked on further expansion including the construction of the West Terminal to reduce pressure on the old (East) terminal. Construction began in 1970 and the terminal was opened in 1971. American Airlines and United Airlines operate from the East Terminal and Allegheny Airlines and Eastern Air Lines and the commuter airlines use the West Terminal.

Buffalo area is subject to heavy snowfalls and the airport maintains 22 pieces of snow-removal equipment including seven snowploughs, four jet brooms, five snow blowers, and a Snowblast Model RAHS-3000A rotary snow blower which was delivered in February 1978. The airport has a good reputation for snow clearance and in 1977 won the Bernt Balchen award which is given annually for outstanding performance in snow removal.

There had been plans for a completely new airport but there was much hostility to the proposals, and the regional airport studies, approved in 1977–78, concluded that the airport should continue in its present capacity until 1995. A master plan for development up to 1995 is expected to be completed in 1979–80.

Charlotte, North Carolina   Douglas Municipal Airport

35° 12′ 53″ N   80° 56′ 17″ W   4.34 nm (8 km) W of city
ICAO: KCLT   IATA code: CLT   Time zone: GMT −5
Authority: City of Charlotte
Area: 1,040 hectares (2,570 acres)
Elevation: 749 ft (228 m)   Ref temp: 32 deg C
Runways: 05/23   2,286 × 46 m (7,500 × 150 ft)* asphalt-concrete, grooved
         18/36   2,391 × 46 m (7,845 × 150 ft)† asphalt-concrete

*05 is jet preferential runway
†18 threshold displaced 645 ft (197 m)

Pavement strength: 140,000 lb (63,503 kg) 1, 170,000 lb (77,111 kg) 2, 240,000 lb (108,862 kg) 3.
Landing category: ICAO CAT I
Lighting:
    R/W   05/23 and 18/36   HIRL
    App   R/W 05   MALSR and VASIS
            R/W 18/36   REIL and VASIS
    Thr   green
    Txy   blue edge
Aids: VORTAC, NDB, ASR, RVR 05, ILS CAT I 05
Twr frequency: 118.1   App frequency: 120.5/124.0
Terminal: Passenger terminal with two piers and 16 gates. Separate general aviation area on east side with 255 tie-down spaces
Scheduled services 1978: Air Carolina, Delta, Eastern, Piedmont, Resort Commuter Airlines, Southern, United and Wheeler Flying Services

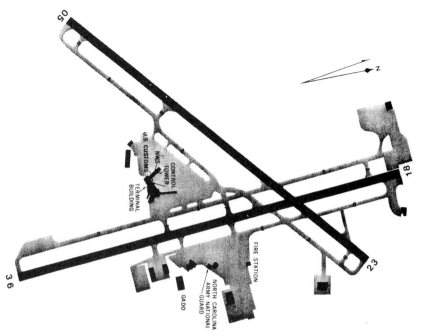

Douglas Municipal Airport, Charlotte. (*FAA*)

Main base: Air Carolina. North Carolina Air National Guard has a base
on the east of the airport

Traffic:	1970	1975	1976	1978
Passengers embarked	839,897*	1,174,200	1,312,678	2,992,954
Cargo uplifted (tonnes)	13,210*	13,613	12,180	27,851
Aircraft movements	162,783	194,826	205,329	220,376
Transport movements	62,350	66,631	69,974	76,014

* Year ended 30 June, 1970

Requests for information on this airport have been unanswered so it is
not possible to state whether this is the original site of the Charlotte Airport
of the 1920s, but the present airport is known to have been in use before
1958.

In 1977 site preparation was completed for a 10,000 ft (3,048 m)
CAT II 18R/36L runway to the west of the present 05 threshold.
Completion was planned for 1979, and there is to be a new control tower at
the north end of the airport between the pair of 18/36 runways. It is also
planned to upgrade runway 36 to CAT I standard.

Noise abatement procedures are in force between 22.00 and 07.00
when landings must be made on 05 and take offs from 23.

Chicago, Illinois　　　　Chicago O'Hare International Airport

41° 58′ 56″ N　　　87° 54′ 25″ W　　　16 nm (29.6 km) NW of city
ICAO: KORD　　　　IATA code: ORD　　　Time zone: GMT −6
Authority: City of Chicago
Area: 2,833 hectares (7,000 acres)
Elevation: 667 ft (203 m)　　　　　　　　　　Ref temp: 28.4 deg C
Runways: 04L/22R　　2,286 × 46 m　(7,500 × 150 ft) asphalt, grooved
　　　　　04R/22L　　2,460 × 46 m　(8,071 × 150 ft) asphalt, grooved
　　　　　09L/27R　　2,260 × 46 m　(7,416 × 150 ft) concrete-asphalt,
　　　　　　　　　　　　　　　　　　　　　　　　　　　　grooved
　　　　　09R/27L　　3,091 × 46 m (10,141 × 150 ft) concrete, grooved
　　　　　14L/32R　　3,049 × 46 m (10,003 × 150 ft) concrete-asphalt,
　　　　　　　　　　　　　　　　　　　　　　　　　　　　grooved
　　　　　14R/32L　　3,536 × 61 m (11,600 × 200 ft) concrete, grooved
　　　　　18/36*　　　1,628 × 46 m　(5,341 × 150 ft) asphalt

* Landings only on 18, take offs only on 36. Landings restricted to twin-propeller
aircraft when wind less than 20 kt (37 km/h), landings by all types except turbojets
when wind above 20 kt (37 km/h). Boeing 747s are restricted to 14L/32R and
14R/32L

Pavement strength: 09R/27L, 14L/32R and 14R/32L　　　LCN 100
Landing category: ICAO CAT II
Lighting:
　　R/W　　　04L/22R and 18/36　　MIRL
　　　　　　　04R/22L, 09L/27R and 09R/27L　　HIRL
　　　　　　　14L/32R　　HIRL and centreline. TDZ 14L
　　　　　　　14R/32L　　HIRL and centreline. TDZ 14R
　　App　　　R/W 04L　　SALSF and VASIS
　　　　　　　R/W 04R, 09R and 22L　　MALSR and VASIS
　　　　　　　R/W 09L　　MALSR
　　　　　　　R/W 14L and 14R　　ALSF-1 (to be ALSF-2)
　　　　　　　R/W 18　　VASIS
　　　　　　　R/W 22R　　MALSR, REIL and VASIS
　　　　　　　R/W 27L　　ALSF-1 and VASIS
　　　　　　　R/W 27R, 32L and 32R　　ALSF-1
　　Thr　　　green
　　Txy　　　blue edge, green centreline on some taxiways
Aids: VORTAC, VOR/DME, NDB, SRE, ARTS III, ASDE, RVR 09R,
　　　14L/32R, 14R/32L and 27L, ILS CAT II 14L and 14R, ILS CAT I
　　　09L/27R, 09R/27L, 04R/22L, 22R, 32L and 32R
Twr frequency: 118.1/120.75/126.2
App frequency: 119.0/124.35/125.7/126.05
Terminals: Three passenger terminals with 10 concourses and 78 gates.
　　　Terminal 1 is for international flights. Terminals linked by five
　　　tunnels, the two longest with moving walkways. Separate general
　　　aviation and commuter airline terminals. 194 acre (78.5 hectare) cargo
　　　area at east-southeast of airport with 13 cargo buildings housing 27
　　　airlines and six freight forwarders
Scheduled services 1978: 32 airlines

Airline bases: American, Continental, Delta, Eastern, TWA and United

Traffic:	1970	1975	1976	1977	1978
Passengers (total)	29,689,015	37,296,362	41,735,454	44,030,279*	49,151,449
Cargo (tonnes)	482,355	533,910	598,647	736,308	708,448
Aircraft movements	641,390	666,562	718,057	783,891	777,158
Transport movements	607,842	613,173	641,541	730,255	776,471

* Excluding transit

Chicago has for a very long time handled an enormous volume of air traffic and O'Hare International Airport is the world's busiest—it will almost certainly be the first airport to handle 50 mn passengers in a year.

Before the opening of O'Hare and its build-up of traffic, Chicago Midway Airport was the busiest, for many years recording more than a thousand aircraft movements a day—a figure regarded as in excess of the safe level. Midway, which is still in use, began in 1926 when the City of Chicago leased 120 acres (48.5 hectares), a 15-minute ride southwest of the city centre, on which to build Chicago Municipal Airport. The airport was ready for use the following year and on 1 December, 1927, the first air mail flight of Boeing Air Transport arrived from Omaha. The first terminal was completed in 1931.

The airport is approximately square and the buildings were erected along the south and east sides. Nine runways were constructed, giving parallel pairs aligned east–west, north–south, northwest–southeast and three aligned northeast–southwest. The northwest–southeast pair and the two longest northeast–southwest runways are still in use as: 04L/22R of 5,508 ft (1,679 m), 04R/22L of 6,104 ft (1,860 m), 13L/31R of 5,388 ft (1,642 m) and 13R/31L of 6,520 ft (1,987 m). A new 13R/31L is proposed and after its construction 13L/31R will be abandoned and the existing 13R/31L redesignated.

After the war the airport was renamed Chicago Midway to commemorate the Battle of Midway. In 1945 scheduled international flights began to use Midway and in 1947 the North terminal was built. Midway's peak year for passengers was 1959 when more than 10,200,000 used the airport.

For some time it was realized that Chicago would require a second major airport and the opportunity to create one came in 1946 when Orchard Place Airport was declared surplus by the War Assets Administration. Orchard Place (from which O'Hare's code is derived) had been created in 1942 when the Government built an aerodrome on farmland for aircraft assembly and testing by the Douglas Aircraft Company. This site had four runways, which are now those to the north of the terminal area.

The City of Chicago purchased Orchard Place and a considerable area of adjacent land. An 8,000 ft by 200 ft (2,438 by 61 m) 14R/32L runway was constructed to the west of the site and the first terminal building, with Y-concourse. In September 1949 it was named O'Hare Field, after Lieut-Commander Edward H. 'Butch' O'Hare, a distinguished Navy pilot from Chicago who had been killed in the Pacific war, and the name was changed to Chicago O'Hare International Airport on 8 December, 1958.

The airport was officially opened to domestic traffic in October 1955 although it had already handled about 900,000 movements and some 2 mn passengers.

The master plan for the airport envisaged a central terminal area with five Y-concourses and a tangential runway system with three parallel pairs. This plan was not strictly adhered to. In fact all the original Orchard Place

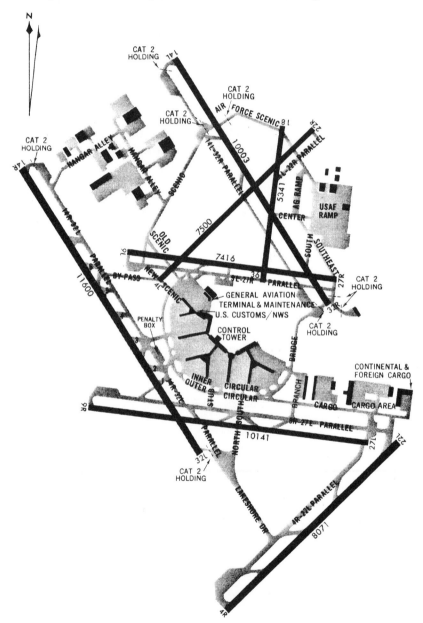

Chicago O'Hare International Airport. (*FAA*)

Chicago O'Hare International Airport terminal area with runway 14R/32L on the left and the 04L and 09L thresholds beyond the control tower.
(*Metro News Photos, courtesy City of Chicago*)

runways were lengthened except 18/36, the use of which is restricted by the terminal area, and runways 04R/22L, 09R/27L and 14R/32L were built—14R/32L before the airport opened, 09R/27L in 1964 and 04R/22L during the 1970s. The terminal area plan was also modified.

Although O'Hare was officially opened in 1955, the airport, being much further from the city, did not attract much traffic from Midway until the introduction of jet aircraft which could not be handled at the old airport because of its restricted runway lengths and the fact that it had become completely engulfed in a built-up area.

Development had continued at O'Hare, with a major expansion programme beginning in 1959, and the terminal complex was completed in 1962 after which the major airlines transferred their operations to the new airport. President Kennedy dedicated the airport on 23 March, 1963.

By 1965 O'Hare was handling more than half a million aircraft movements annually and the passenger total had reached just under 21 mn. So, apart from development at the new airport, work went on at Midway. Runways were improved and the North terminal refurbished, with most of the work completed by 1968. Airlines were encouraged to transfer some of their operations to Midway, which it was hoped would handle 5 mn passengers a year, but as a result of the fuel crisis in late 1973 services were terminated and the airport has mostly been used for general aviation although a few scheduled operations now take place and in 1976 Midway handled 177,346 aircraft movements and 547,303 passengers.

Although O'Hare is large there is considerable concern about the provision of adequate airport facilities to meet Chicago's air traffic needs. Numerous sites have been examined and consideration has been given to the construction of an offshore airport in Lake Michigan. In 1975 work began on a three-year master plan study for O'Hare and Midway to provide guidelines for the next 20 years' development of Chicago airports.

411

Cincinnati, Ohio*　　　　Greater Cincinnati International Airport

39° 03′ 30″ N　　　84° 39′ 45″ W　　　6.95 nm (12.87 km) SW of city
ICAO: KCVG　　　　IATA code: CVG　　　Time zone: GMT −5
Authority: Kenton County Airport Board
Area: 1,740 hectares (4,300 acres)
Elevation: 890 ft (271 m)　　　　　　　　　　Ref temp: 30 deg C
Runways: 09L/27R　　1,676 × 46 m (5,500 × 150 ft) asphalt
　　　　　09R/27L　　2,377 × 46 m (7,800 × 150 ft) concrete, grooved
　　　　　18/36　　　 2,896 × 46 m (9,500 × 150 ft) asphalt-concrete,
　　　　　　　　　　　　　　　　　　　　　　　　grooved
Pavement strength: auw (dual tandem) 09L/27R 150,133 lb (68,099 kg);
　09R/27L and 18/36 330,293 lb (149,818 kg)
Landing category: ICAO CAT II
Lighting:
　R/W　　　09L/27R　　MIRL
　　　　　　09R/27L　　HIRL
　　　　　　18/36　　　HIRL and centreline. TDZ 18/36
　App　　　R/W 09L/27R　　VASIS
　　　　　　R/W 09R　　MALSR and REIL
　　　　　　R/W 18　　 ALSF-1, VASIS and RAIS†
　　　　　　R/W 27L　　MALSR and VASIS
　　　　　　R/W 36　　 ALSF-1
　Thr　　　green
　Txy　　　blue edge
Aids: TACAN, VOR/DME, VDF, ASR, RVR 18/36, ILS CAT II 36,
　ILS CAT I 09R/27L and 18
Twr frequency: 118.3　　　　　　　　　App frequency: 119.7/124.9
Terminals: Three interconnected passenger terminals each with traffic pier.
　Terminal A serves Allegheny, Eastern, North Central and Piedmont
　and has an adjoining gate for charter flights; Terminal B serves
　American, Air Kentucky and TWA; Terminal C serves Delta.
　Terminals B and C have separate baggage claim buildings on the land
　side and these are connected to the terminals by covered bridges. Total
　of 25 gates with 15 aerobridges. There are separate cargo buildings
Scheduled services 1978: 11 airlines including two commuter and Federal
　Express

Traffic:	1970	1975	1976	1977	1978
Passengers (total)	2,471,971	2,555,236	2,672,916	2,782,372	3,143,423
Cargo (tonnes)	31,478	18,101	26,028	19,430	17,417
Aircraft movements	152,291	149,085	148,136	142,701	137,822
Transport movements	93,349	80,603	80,130	73,556	92,327

　　In the 1920s Lunken Municipal Airport was constructed to serve
Cincinnati and in the early 1930s three concrete runways were laid, but as
early as 1937 consideration was given to the building of a new airport
southwest of the city just south of the Ohio River. This airport was opened
on 10 January, 1947, and the first arrival, at 09.23, was an American

* The airport is at Covington in Boone County, Kentucky
† Runway Alignment Indicator System. Situated 8,630 ft (2,630 m) north, this
appears as an inverted red T.

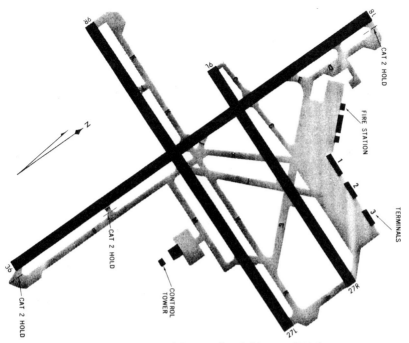

Greater Cincinnati International Airport. (*FAA*)

Airlines DC-3 from Cleveland. It was followed less than a minute later by a Delta Air Lines flight from Atlanta, with a TWA service arriving about five minutes after that. That year there were 106,116 aircraft movements, 39,111 by transport aircraft, and 302,707 passengers used the airport.

The terminal building was expanded in 1960 by which time the annual passenger figure was nearly $1\frac{1}{4}$ mn. In 1965 aircraft movements exceeded 127,000, with more than 79,000 air carrier movements and 1,805,465 passengers, and at that time planning began for major expansion of the airport to meet the region's requirements from 1975 to the end of the century.

The plan was produced but it was not until November 1971 that agreement on its implementation and financing had been reached and construction could begin. The terminal was modernized and enlarged and to its east two additional terminals were built. Each terminal has a traffic pier and there are 25 gates, 15 with aerobridges. To the north of the two new terminals is a baggage claim building with direct access to the car parks. These buildings are connected to the terminals by covered bridges. The three terminals are connected and provision has been made for a people-mover link. The new terminal complex cost $40 mn, was opened in June 1974 and has capacity for 5 mn passengers a year. There is space for an additional terminal to the west of the present buildings.

Very largescale development is planned for the remainder of the century. There are to be three new runways—18L/36R to be built to a length of 10,500 ft (3,200 m) in the period 1976–80 and extended to 12,500 ft

Greater Cincinnati International Airport looking south with the three terminals on the left, the parallel 09/27 runways beyond and runway 18/36 on the right.

(3,658 m) after 1980; 09FR/27FL, at the south of the airport, with a length of 8,400 ft (2,560 m) and a parallel taxiway to be built in the 1981–90 phase; and 18FR/36FL at the west of the airport. This will be built after 1990, have an initial length of 3,900 ft (1,189 m) and ultimately 7,200 ft (2,195 m).

The existing 09R/27L is to be extended to 8,800 ft (2,682 m) and later 10,400 ft (3,170 m); 18/36 is to become 18R/36L and sometime after 1990 is due to be lengthened to 11,600 ft (3,536 m). The present 09L/27R is to be phased out.

Runway 09FR/27FL is to be equipped for CAT I operations; 18L/36 R will be CAT II initially, and later CAT III; 18FR/36FL will not be a precision runway; and the existing 09R/27L will be upgraded to CAT III.

During the period 1976–80 there will be additions to the general aviation area south of 09R/27L and a large increase in car parking space; in the period 1981–90 there will be two more terminals and increased apron area west of the present terminals; and beyond 1990 the master plan calls for a large cargo complex west of the terminal area, second parallel taxiways for 09R/27L and 18L/36R, and new general aviation areas between the thresholds of 09R and 09FR and between 09R/27L and 09FR/27FL east of the present 18/36.

Cleveland, Ohio   Cleveland Hopkins International Airport

41° 24′ 37″ N   81° 50′ 56″ W   10 nm (18.5 km) SW of city
ICAO: KCLE   IATA code: CLE   Time zone: GMT −5
Authority: City of Cleveland Department of Port Control
Area: 652 hectares (1,610 acres)
Elevation: 792 ft (241 m)   Ref temp: 27.5 deg C
Runways: 05L/23R   1,903 × 61 m (6,242 × 200 ft) asphalt overlay
          05R/23L   2,743 × 46 m (8,998 × 150 ft) asphalt overlay, grooved
          10L/28R   1,833 × 46 m (6,015 × 150 ft) asphalt overlay, grooved
          10R/28L   1,153 × 23 m (3,783 × 75 ft)   concrete
          18L/36R   1,529 × 46 m (5,015 × 150 ft) concrete/asphalt
          18R/36L   1,954 × 46 m (6,411 × 150 ft) concrete, asphalt overlay

Pavement strength: 05R/23L 100,000 lb (45,359 kg) 1, 170,000 lb (77,111 kg) 2, 287,000 lb (130,181 kg) 3
Landing category: ICAO CAT I
Lighting:

R/W	05L/23R	HIRL
	05R	HIRL (last 2,050 ft/625 m yellow), centreline and TDZ
	23L	HIRL (last 2,250 ft/686 m yellow)
	10L/28R	HIRL (last 2,116 ft/645 m yellow)
	18L/36R and 18R/36L	MIRL
App	R/W 05R	ALSF-2
	R/W 18R	VASIS
	R/W 23L	RAIL and VASIS
	R/W 23R	MALSR
	R/W 28R	SSALSR
	R/W 36L	REIL
Thr	green	
Txy	blue edge	

Aids: VORTAC, NDB, L, RVR 05R/23L and 28R, RVV 05R/23L and 28R, ILS CAT I 05R/23L and 28R

Twr frequency: 120.9   App frequency: 124.5
Terminal: Three-concourse two-level terminal with 40 gates. Separate cargo and general aviation areas
Scheduled services 1978: 12 airlines
Airline base: United Airlines

Traffic:	1970	1975*	1976	1978
Passengers (total)	4,996,000	5,506,000	5,990,140	7,054,842
Cargo (tonnes)	112,491	74,200	109,301	87,303
Aircraft movements	218,727	197,000	204,757	236,952
Transport movements	130,048	134,000	137,990	—

* Rounded figures

Cleveland Hopkins International Airport in June 1978, with the terminal at the base of the picture. (*City of Cleveland Department of Port Control*)

415

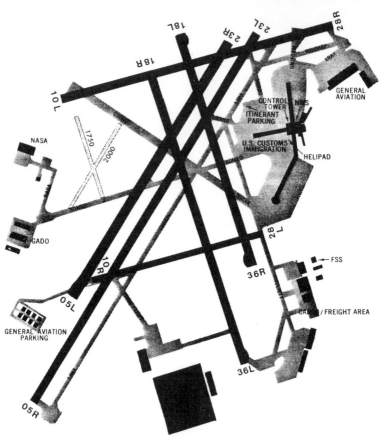

Cleveland Hopkins International Airport. (*FAA*)

Cleveland's municipal airport was opened in 1926 and by the end of that decade occupied 1,000 acres (405 hectares), had hangars and an administration building, and was claimed as the second largest in the United States. During 1931 the airport recorded 54,570 landings and 72,780 passengers.

In recent years the airport has undergone major expansion to provide capacity for more than 14 mn passengers a year. New terminal facilities were designed to handle jet aircraft and the traffic of the 1960s, and by 1973, when more than $5\frac{1}{2}$ mn passengers used the airport, facilities were barely adequate. It was then planned that an expansion programme should be undertaken to provide adequate facilities into the 1990s.

New North and South terminals were constructed; the North Concourse was modernized and provided with a new boarding level; the West Concourse was remodelled; the long South Concourse, which handles more than 60 per cent of the airport's traffic, was given moving walkways; and the immigration and customs areas were more than doubled in size. The South terminal was dedicated on 31 March, 1977, marking completion of the first phase of the overall $53 mn reconstruction programme, the entire programme being scheduled for completion by late 1978 with the opening of the new North terminal and rebuilt North Concourse.

By the autumn of 1978 the North Concourse (A) had 11 gates, used by Allegheny, Allegheny Commuter and American Airlines; the West Concourse (B) had 10 gates, customs and immigration, and was used by Air Canada, Delta, Eastern and North Central; and the South Concourse (C) had 19 gates used by Northwest and TWA.

It is planned that Cleveland's runway 05R shall be cleared for CAT III operations, but no date has been set. Runways 10R/28L and 18L/36R are for VFR daylight use only.

Columbus, Ohio   Port Columbus International Airport

39° 59′ 41″ N	82° 53′ 08″ W	7 nm (13 km) E of city
ICAO: KCMH	IATA code: CMH	Time zone: GMT −5

Authority: City of Columbus Division of Airports
Area: 722 hectares (1,785 acres)
Elevation: 816 ft (249 m)   Ref temp: 29.3 deg C
Runways: 01/19   1,082 × 46 m   (3,551 × 150 ft) asphalt*
           05/23   1,366 × 46 m   (4,483 × 150 ft) asphalt
           10L/28R   1,829 × 46 m   (6,000 × 150 ft) asphalt
           10R/28L   3,261 × 46 m   (10,700 × 150 ft) asphalt
           13/31   1,524 × 46 m   (5,001 × 150 ft) asphalt
Pavement strength: 100,000 lb (45,360 kg) 1, 150,000 lb (68,039 kg) 2, 300,000 lb (136,078 kg) 3
Landing category: ICAO CAT I

* To be abandoned

The scene at Port Columbus on 8 July, 1929, before the two TAT Ford Trimotors left for Waynoka on the inaugural westbound transcontinental service. The railway station is on the left. The aircraft in the foreground is a Fokker F.VII-3m or F-X.

417

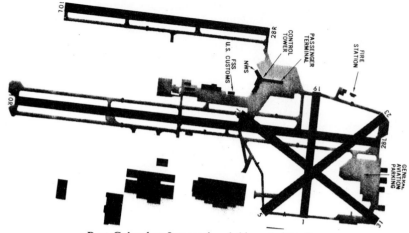

Port Columbus International Airport. (*FAA*)

Lighting:
 R/W   10L/28R and 10R/28L   HIRL
        05/23 and 13/31   MIRL
 App   R/W 10L   ALSF-1
        R/W 28R   REIL
        R/W 10R   MALSR and REIL
        R/W 28L   ALSF-1
        R/W 05/23 and 13/31 to have REIL and all runways to have
        VASIS
 Thr   green
 Txy   blue edge
Aids: VOR, RAD, RVR 10L and 28L, ASR, ILS CAT I 10L and 10R/28L.
    ILS planned for 28R
Twr frequency: 120.5   App frequency: 119.0
Terminal: Shallow-vee terminal with central projecting traffic pier and 17
    gates. Separate cargo and general aviation areas.
Scheduled services 1978: nine airlines

Traffic:	1970	1975	1976	1978
Passengers (total)	1,673,977	1,937,886	2,093,872	2,611,065
Cargo* (tonnes)	32,448	23,028	27,179	25,063
Aircraft movements	330,678	248,252	261,929	430,227
Transport movements	61,544	54,048	54,811	—

*Includes mail and air express

During 1976 Boeing 727s accounted for 52.2 per cent of transport movements, DC-9s for
25.7 per cent, BAC One-Elevens for 8.9 per cent, Boeing 707s, 737s and Convair CV-600s 3.5
per cent each, and YS-11As for 2.7 per cent.

On 16 May, 1928, Transcontinental Air Transport (TAT) was
founded, its main objective being transcontinental passenger services. The
route, planned by the airline's technical committee under the chairmanship
of Charles Lindbergh, combined railway and air travel. The New
York–Columbus section was an overnight journey in the *Airway Limited*

418

operated by the Pennsylvania Railroad, Columbus–Waynoka by air, Waynoka–Clovis by overnight train on the Atchison, Topeka & Santa Fe Railway, and Clovis–Los Angeles by air. The air sectors were operated by Ford Trimotors.

A site for the Columbus interchange was selected beside the Pennsylvania Railroad tracks about seven miles east of Columbus. Work began in April 1929, Columbus City building Port Columbus Airport immediately north of the railway, and the railway company building a special station. The administration building was quite large with two storeys and, at one corner, a 'control tower', and there were two asphalt runways, three hangars and lighting. A long covered platform was built each side of the double-track railway and a covered walkway led from the railway station to the airport administration building.

Following what would now be called proving flights, the first westbound passengers pulled out of New York's Pennsylvania Station at 18.05 on 7 July, 1929. The train arrived at Port Columbus at 07.55 the next morning and at 08.15 the Ford Trimotors *City of Columbus* and *City of Wichita* left Port Columbus for Waynoka. On the same day Lindbergh, flying the *City of Los Angeles*, took off from Grand Central Air Terminal at Glendale to inaugurate the eastbound service. The TAT coast-to-coast time was just under 48 hr.

The site of that historic Port Columbus Airport now occupies the southeast corner of the present airport and the railway line still runs along the southern boundary—but now it is the Pennsylvania Baltimore & Ohio Railroad. There are still three runways on that part of the airport, 01/19, 05/23 and 13/31 although 01/19 is to be abandoned.

What amounts to a new airport has been constructed north of the old one and much further to the west. This comprises a parallel pair of 10/28 runways and a central terminal area. The terminal has two wings, A and C concourses, and central projecting pier, B concourse. This last is to have a satellite terminal at its outer end. Also in the central area are US Customs, a general aviation area, cargo facilities and a motel. There are further general aviation facilities on the site of the original airport.

The airport layout plan drawn up early in 1977 provides for a 1,000 ft (305 m) extension to each end of runway 10L/28R to give it a length of 8,000 ft (2,438 m), additional taxiways, terminal extensions, a new cargo terminal, and a large general aviation area at the west of the airport. It was expected that work on runway extension and the construction of the Concourse B satellite would begin in 1979. When extended, runway 28R is to have approach lighting.

Dallas/Fort Worth, Texas   Dallas/Fort Worth Regional Airport

32° 53′ 49″ N   97° 02′ 26″ W
14.7 nm (27 km) from Dallas and Fort Worth
ICAO: KDFW   IATA code: DFW   Time zone: GMT −6
Authority: Dallas/Fort Worth Regional Airport Board
Area: 7,082 hectares (17,500 acres)
Elevation: 596 ft (182 m)   Ref temp: 34.6 deg C

Runways: 13L/31R   2,743 × 61 m (9,000 × 200 ft) concrete
         17L/35R   3,471 × 61 m (11,387 × 200 ft) concrete
         17R/35L   3,471 × 61 m (11,387 × 200 ft) concrete
         18R/36L   1,219 × 30 m (4,000 × 100 ft) concrete*

*Daylight VFR only, restricted to 12,500 lb (5,670 kg) auw

Pavement strength: Design strength 800,000 lb (362,874 kg)
Landing category: ICAO CAT II
Lighting:
    R/W   13L/31R, 17L/35R and 17R/35L   HIRL, centreline and
                                                            TDZ
    App   R/W 13L   VASIS
              R/W 17L/35R and 17R/35L   ALSF-2
              R/W 31R   MALSR
    Thr   green
    Txy   blue edge and green centreline
Aids: VORTAC, NDB, ASR, RVR, ILS CAT II 17L, ILS CAT I 17R/35L,
    31R and 35R
Twr frequency: 124.15/126.55   App frequency: 123.9/125.8
Terminals: Linear terminal complex on central site. Four semi-circular
    passenger terminals in use with 71 gates plus one general aviation gate
    and 77 aircraft stands. Airtrans link between terminals and to hotel
    and car parks. Separate cargo and mail buildings, including Flying
    Tiger terminal opened in 1979.
Scheduled services 1978: 19 airlines

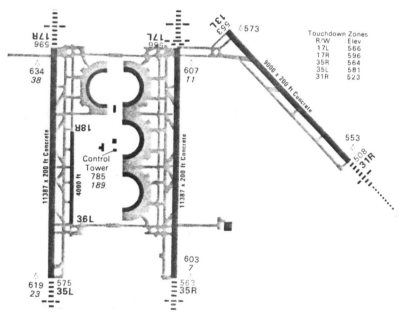

Dallas/Fort Worth Regional Airport. (*British Airways Aerad*)

420

Main base: Braniff International Airways

Traffic:	1970*	1975	1976	1977§
Passengers**	5,225,083	7,341,142	7,986,094	17,300,728
Cargo (tonnes)†	59,109	63,933	73,813	164,532
Aircraft movements	410,154	341,921	358,926	—
Transport movements	296,645	282,729	293,907	365,634

* Figures for Love Field
** Embarked passengers. Dallas/Fort Worth only records embarked passengers but for planning purposes doubles the figure and adds 10 per cent. The 1978 reported total was 19,857,416
† Includes Air Express
§ Aeroporti di Roma figures

Dallas/Fort Worth Regional Airport is an airport on an enormous scale, having an area of 17,500 acres (7,082 hectares) and, as finally planned, will extend 9 miles (14.48 km) from north to south and about 8 miles (12.87 km) from east to west. However, this vast airport was not built to serve a single city but, as its name implies, a region.

Although the airport was opened to traffic only in 1974, the idea of a single airport to serve the Dallas and Fort Worth areas goes back to 1927, the year in which Fort Worth established Meacham Field as its commercial airport. However, no action was taken and in 1928 Dallas purchased Love Field from the Army and this served as the Dallas airport until 1974, and is still used by Chaparral Airlines, Scheduled Skyways and Southwest Airlines.

Both airports were expanded and improved during the 1930s but the airlines were reluctant to serve both because of their proximity, and more discussions on the desirability of a combined regional airport took place in 1940. In 1941 the Army asked the CAA to assist in locating a training aerodrome midway between the two cities and plans were made for a 1,000 acre (404.7 hectare) Midway Airport at Arlington. There was disagreement about the layout of civil facilities and following an appeal the Secretary of Commerce said that this could be decided after the war. He asked Arlington to take over the operation, which it did in July 1943, and the Army used the aerodrome for pilot training.

After the war Dallas continued to expand Love Field and Fort Worth acquired Midway Airport in 1947. Midway was expanded and commissioned on 25 April, 1953, as Greater Fort Worth International Airport - Amon Carter Field, later Greater Southwest International Airport. In 1954 the CAB suggested that part of Greater Southwest International should be sold to Dallas and the name changed to Dallas/Fort Worth Airport but this was not followed up.

In May 1961 the Federal Government ordered hearings on the question of a single airport. The matter dragged on for several years until finally in 1965 the Dallas–Fort Worth Regional Airport Board was organized and planning of a single facility began. A bi-county authority was to be set up to develop and build the airport but in June 1967 Dallas County voters narrowly defeated the proposal. Agreement to build the airport was eventually reached in 1968, a 17,500 acre (7,082 hectare) site north of Greater Southwest International Airport was chosen, ground-breaking ceremonies were held in December 1968, and grading and

421

drainage work began in January 1969. The site chosen, almost exactly half-way between Dallas and Fort Worth, was mostly low-yield farm and ranch land, large enough for growth, well served by roads, and it involved the displacement of only 249 families and 15 small businesses.

Construction of the Dallas/Fort Worth Regional Airport was based on Phase 1 Plan–1975 and Ultimate Plan–2001 for more than 50 mn annual passengers, with the initial boundaries being those required for 2001. The airport was planned after computer simulation of total air space in northern Texas to compute the maximum possible number of aircraft that could safely be accommodated. To meet the computed requirement the airport was based on a layout capable of handling 300 VFR or 178 IFR flights an hour. It was envisaged that the total airport requirement would be needed in 2001 but actual development is based on five-year plans to ensure that capacity is available when needed.

On the ultimate plan the main core is aligned north–south, with the airport's International Parkway (the spine road) running through the centre of the site and connecting the east–west State Highways 183 (on the south) and 114 (on the north). Four miles of semi-circular terminals are to be built beside the central road, seven on the east and six on the west, with a total of more than 234 boarding gates for aircraft of at least Boeing 747 size. At the north and south ends of the airport will be cargo 'cities' each with gates for 100 of the largest aircraft at present in service.

The ultimate runway pattern comprises a pair of 17/35 runways on each side of the central terminal area, with multiple taxiways, the inner runways to be 11,387 ft (3,471 m) long and the outers 13,375 ft (4,077 m), with potential length of 20,000 ft (6,096 m); a crosswind 13/31 runway of

Dallas/Fort Worth Regional Airport, view looking northwest with Terminal 3-E in the foreground. Terminal 2-W is on the other side of the spine road and 2-E on the right. Beyond the control tower and hotel is runway 17R/35L. (*American Airlines*)

9,000 ft (2,743 m), with potential 11,000 ft (3,353 m) on the east side, and an 11,000 ft (3,353 m) 13/31 runway on the west; a 5,000 ft (1,524 m) 16/34 general aviation runway south of the east crosswind runway; and 2,000 ft (610 m) 13/31 and 16/34 STOL runways to the southwest of the west crosswind runway.

Large areas have been allocated for aircraft maintenance, an executive terminal, industrial air parks, V/STOL terminal, a world trade centre, and even a Museum of Aviation. All the main terminals, central area hotel and car parks are to be linked by the Airtrans system and there are proposals for a rapid transit system to link the airport with the central business districts of Dallas and Fort Worth.

The airport was dedicated in ceremonies on 20–23 September, 1973, during which a Concorde landed, the first on US territory by a supersonic transport, and opened to traffic at 00.01 on 13 January, 1974, an American Airlines Boeing 727 from New York, Memphis and Little Rock, being the first to land—at 00.07.

When the airport was opened much of the Plan–1975 had been completed. The inner 17/35 runways, 17L/35R and 17R/35L, each of 11,387.5 ft (3,471 m), together with dual parallel taxiways; the east crosswind runway, 13L/31R of 9,000 ft (2,743 m); and a 4,000 ft (1,219 m) general aviation runway marked out on the inner taxiway for 17R/35L and designated 18R/36L, were ready.

The terminals, to be numbered 0–W (west) to 5–W and 0–E (east) to 6–E, are to be built as required, and initially 2–W, 2–E, 3–E and 4–E were built to provide 71 boarding gates. 2–W is used by Air Canada, Braniff, Eagle Commuter, Méxicana and Rio Airways; 2–E by Air Illinois, Frontier, Ozark and Texas International; 3–E by American, Eastern and Metroflight; and 4–E by Continental and Delta. There was also a hotel and, of course, the necessary operational buildings and control tower.

Braniff transferred its main base from Love Field and has begun construction of terminal 3–W. This is to be a three-storey building built in three stages, with the first stage due for completion in 1981 and the second and third stages in 1982 and 1983. There is to be a connector building linking terminals 2–W and 3–W and at an upper level a people-mover duplicating the lower-level Airtrans. When completed, terminal 3–W will bring Braniff's investment in the airport to some $175 mn of which $45 mn will be the cost of the terminal.

The Airtrans system, which has one disadvantage—it only runs anti-clockwise, is automatic, computer-controlled, runs at a maximum speed of 17 mph (27.3 km/h), can operate with single or paired cars, and has two types of cars—enclosed passenger vehicles and open utility trucks. By mid-1976 the system had carried more than 8.5 mn passengers over 8 mn vehicle-miles and provided 98 per cent serviceability.

On 12 January, 1979, Dallas/Fort Worth became the first inland United States airport to handle supersonic transports when Braniff began operating Concordes on Washington–Dallas/Fort Worth services under interchange agreements with Air France and British Airways, the route being operated at subsonic speed.

It is of interest to record that in 1973, during the construction of one of the Dallas/Fort Worth runways, a record concrete pour was achieved for one day, with 12,630 cubic yards (9,657 cu m) in 14 hr.

Dayton, Ohio   James M Cox Dayton International Airport

39° 54′ 06″ N   84° 13′ 12″ W   10 nm (18.5 km) N of city
ICAO: KDAY   IATA code: DAY   Time zone: GMT −5
Authority: City of Dayton Department of Aviation
Area: 1,521 hectares (3,758 acres)
Elevation: 1,008 ft (307 m)   Ref temp: 22.2 deg C
Runways: 06L/24R   2,846 × 46 m (9,500 × 150 ft) concrete
        06R/24L   2,134 × 46 m (7,000 × 150 ft) concrete
        18/36   2,134 × 46 m (7,000 × 150 ft) concrete
        NE/SW   701 × 46 m (2,300 × 150 ft) grass
Pavement strength: All paved runways 100,000 lb (45,359 kg) plus ISWL
    06L/24R   200,000 lb (90,718 kg) 2, 350,000 lb (158,757 kg) 3
    06R/24L   170,000 lb (77,111 kg) 2, 305,000 lb (138,345 kg) 3
    18/36   187.000 lb (84,822 kg) 2, 340,000 lb (154,221 kg) 3
Landing category: ICAO CAT II
Lighting:
    R/W   06L/24R   HIRL and centreline. TDZ 06L
        06R/24L   HIRL
        18/36   MIRL
    App   R/W 06L   ALSF-2
        R/W 18   MALSR
        R/W 24L and 24R   REIL and VASIS
    Thr   green on all paved runways
    Txy   blue edge all taxiways
Aids: VORTAC, RVR 06L/24R, RVV 06L, ILS CAT II 06L, ILS CAT I 18
    and 24L
Twr frequency: 119.9   App frequency: 134.45
Terminals: Passenger terminal with three traffic piers and 16 gates. Three
    aerobridges in 1977 with four more planned. Separate cargo building

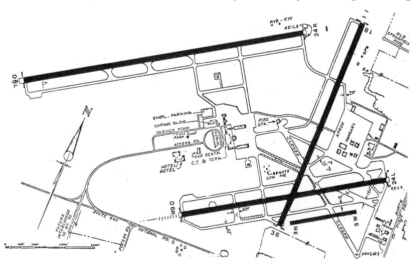

James M Cox Dayton International Airport.

424

Scheduled services 1978: Allegheny, American, Delta, North Central, TWA and United

Traffic:	1970	1975	1976	1977	1978
Passengers (total)	1,392,183	1,588,741	1,692,389	1,815,268	1,996,094
Cargo (tonnes)	27,738	24,489	26,678	25,071	—
Aircraft movements	189,766	155,520	167,751	79,154	152,865
Transport movements	59,052	52,971	51,210	50,602	—

In 1936 the City of Dayton took over a private aerodrome which had been opened in 1928. The cost, raised by public subscription, was $65,000. The Dayton Municipal Airport at that time consisted of 310 acres (125 hectares) and had three 500 by 75 ft (152 by 23 m) paved runways, two hangars and a factory building. During the war it was taken over by the USAAF and considerable development took place including the lengthening of runways and the erection of hangars and workshops. The original airport was in the southeast corner of the present site and sections of the old runways are still visible.

In July 1959 work began on a new 180,000 sq ft (16,722 sq m) terminal building and cargo building on the west of the airport. The terminal was dedicated on 28 April, 1961, and came into operation on 1 May, 1961, but subsequent runway construction expanded the airport to such an extent that it is now in a central position.

A master plan for the airport was produced in 1974 and this calls for considerable expansion. There is to be a new 18R/36L CAT II runway of 9,500 by 200 ft (2,896 by 61 m) with high-speed exits and parallel taxiway; runway 06L/24R is to be extended northeast by 2,500 ft (762 m) to provide a length of 12,000 ft (3,658 m); there are to be additional taxiways; the northwest concourse, now used by Delta, is to be doubled in length; there is to be a second northwest concourse and two new concourses are to be built south of the terminal. A large area to the west of the terminal has been allocated to a proposed cargo area with four cargo buildings. There are also plans for enlarging the general aviation areas.

High intensity lighting is to be installed on 18L/36R and both 06/24 runways are to be equipped for CAT II operations.

Denver, Colorado   Stapleton International Airport

39° 45′ 30″ N   104° 52′ 57″ W   4.3 nm (8 km) E of city
ICAO: KDEN   IATA code: DEN   Time zone: GMT −7
Authority: City and County of Denver Public Works Department
Area: 1,882 hectares (4,651 acres)
Elevation: 5,330 ft (1,625 m)   Ref temp: 31 deg C
Runways: 08L/26R   2,416 × 46 m   (7,926 × 150 ft) asphalt-concrete, grooved
          08R/26L   3,051 × 46 m   (10,010 × 150 ft) asphalt with porous friction course
          17C/35C   1,981 × 30 m   (6,500 × 100 ft) concrete*
          17L/35R   3,658 × 61 m   (12,000 × 200 ft) concrete, grooved
          17R/35L   3,505 × 46 m   (11,499 × 150 ft) asphalt-concrete

* VFR daylight only

Pavement strength: 08L/26R   150,000 lb (68,039 kg) 1, 200,000 lb (90,718 kg) 2, 320,000 lb (145,149 kg) 3;   08R/26L   200,000 lb (90,718 kg) 1 and 2, 320,000 lb (145,149 kg) 3;   17C/35C   555,000 lb (251,744 kg) 3;   17L/35R   555,000 lb (251,744 kg) 3;   17R/35L   175,000 lb (79,379 kg) 2,   285,000 lb (129,274 kg) 3

Landing category: ICAO CAT II

Lighting:

R/W	08L/26R	MIRL
	08R/26L and 17R/35L	HIRL
	17L/35R	HIRL and centreline. TDZ 35R
App	R/W 08R and 26R	VASIS
	R/W 17R	REIL and VASIS
	R/W 26L and 35L	ALSF-1
	R/W 35R	ALSF-2
Thr	green	
Txy	blue edge, with green centreline on high-speed exits from 08L/26R	

Aids: VOR/DME, ASR, RVR 17R/35L and 26L, RVV 26L, LLWSAS, ILS CAT II 35R, ILS CAT I 08R*, 26L and 35L

* glide path only

Twr frequency: 118.3/119.5   App frequency: 120.5

Terminals: Curved multi-storey terminal with four traffic piers and 59 holding rooms. 68 aircraft stands. Separate cargo building

Scheduled services 1978: 20 airlines

Airline bases: Continental, United and Western

Main base: Aspen Airways, Frontier Airlines and Rocky Mountain Airways

Traffic:	1970	1975	1976	1977	1978
Passengers (total)	7,429,150	12,026,415	13,698,742	15,281,842	18,934,054
Cargo (tonnes)	64,399	92,469	101,464	168,123	121,657
Aircraft movements	357,849	386,456	418,393	—	466,645
Transport movements	209,575	232,164	264,603	281,813	340,692

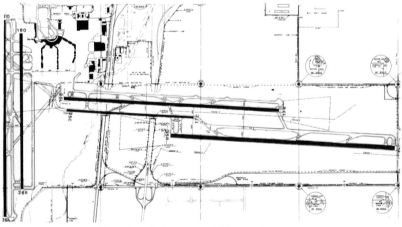

Stapleton International Airport, Denver.

The terminal and control tower at Stapleton International Airport, Denver.
(*City and County of Denver Public Works Department*)

Stapleton International Airport began with the purchase of 640 acres (259 hectares) of sagebrush 'way out in the country'—the airport is actually 5 miles (8 km) from the centre of Denver—and was regarded as 'Stapleton's Folly' when it was dedicated in October 1929, Stapleton being Mayor Benjamin F. Stapleton who foresaw Denver's future as an air transport centre.

The airport is the highest major airport in the United States and the busiest in the Rocky Mountain Region. Initially there were two unsurfaced runways, a 10-room terminal, a hangar, a garage and a wind stocking.

The original airport was on a site just south of the Union Pacific Railroad tracks where they strike out of Denver east to Kansas City. Parts of the old northeast–southwest and northwest–southeast runways can still be seen in this area, now much expanded, which also contains the parallel pair of 08/26 runways.

The present terminal, with 670,000 sq ft (62,243 sq m) of floor area, and its four concourses and 68 gates occupying another 362,000 sq ft (33,629 sq m), are on the same site as the original terminal but, together with apron and hangars, occupying a larger area than the original airport. Approximately 900 acres (364 hectares) of the airport is planted with wheat and other crops and more than 9,000 trees.

The only direction in which the airport could be expanded was northward and an 11,499 ft (3,505 m) runway 17/35 and parallel taxiway were built, with the 35 threshold about half a mile south of the railway. Construction of the runway, now 17R/35L, and taxiway involved bridging the 200 ft (61 m) wide Sand Creek, the Union Pacific Railroad and Interstate Highway 70. The bridges over the creek had to have massive abutments to withstand flood pressures.

427

In 1967 it was decided that a second 17/35 runway would be required to handle the wide-bodied and supersonic aircraft and that this runway and its associated taxiways should be capable of taking aircraft weighing 1,500,000 lb (680,388 kg). Design of runway 17L/35R began in 1968 and it was decided that it should be 13,200 ft (4,023 m) long and have its southern threshold in line with the existing 17/35 runway. Opposition from a nearby community led to the runway being located a mile (1.6 km) further north and it was decided to restrict the length to 12,000 ft (3,658 m). The relocation eased the bridging of the creek, railway and road, still necessary to take the taxiway leading to the terminal area, on which runway 17C/35C for general aviation has been provided.

The new runway was completed in 1976 and the airport area is considered sufficient to provide all required facilities to the end of the century after which a new airport will be required.

Denver has to maintain a large fleet of snow-clearance vehicles but suffers little from bad visibility, only 18 hr a year being of CAT I limitations or worse; nevertheless the airport was brought to CAT II standard in November 1976. The airport was also one of the first to introduce the Low Level Wind Shear Alert System, wind shear being a major problem because of the airport's proximity to the mountains.

Des Moines, Iowa   Des Moines Municipal Airport

41° 32′ 10″ N   93° 39′ 28″ W   3.5 nm (6.48 km) SW of city
ICAO: KDSM   IATA code: DSM   Time zone: GMT −6
Authority: City of Des Moines
Area: 435 hectares (1,075 acres)
Elevation: 957 ft (292 m)   Ref temp: 30.5 deg C
Runways: 05/23   1,981 × 46 m (6,500 × 150 ft) concrete/asphalt
           12L/30R   2,743 × 46 m (9,001 × 150 ft) concrete/asphalt
                                                      grooved*
           12R/30L   975 × 30 m (3,202 × 100 ft) concrete
           Runway 17/35 has been closed
Pavement strength: 05/23 and 12L/30R   340,000 lb (154,221 kg) 3;
     12R/30L   86,000 lb (39,009 kg) 3
Landing category: ICAO CAT I
Lighting:
     R/W   05/23 and 12R/30L   MIRL
               12L/30R   HIRL
     App   R/W 05/23   REIL and VASIS
               R/W 12L   SALS and VASIS
               R/W 30R   ALSF-1 and VASIS
     Thr   green
     Txy   blue edge
Aids: VORTAC, NDB, ASR, ILS CAT I 30R
Twr frequency: 118.3   App frequency: 118.6/123.9
Terminals: Passenger terminal with concourse and two traffic piers, having
     a total of 12 gates with holding areas, eight equipped with aerobridges.
     Separate cargo facilities.

* Arrester gear cable 500 ft (152 m) from thresholds 12L/30R

Scheduled services 1978: Air Missouri, American, Braniff, Ozark and United

Traffic:	1970	1975	1976	1978
Passengers (total)	846,896	1,023,398	1,129,438	1,376,427
Cargo (tonnes)	6,715	6,746	7,089	8,207
Aircraft movements	174,283	187,708	210,077	217,302
Transport movements	32,588	29,593	31,655	54,423

In 1976 Boeing 727s accounted for 55 per cent of transport movements and DC-9s for 37 per cent.

Des Moines first appeared on the air route maps on 15 May, 1920, when the Chicago–Omaha sector of the US Post Office's transcontinental mail route was opened, the complete coast to coast service being inaugurated on 8 September, 1920. The Des Moines aerodrome was a Government maintained field near South East 30th Street and Vandalia Road, southeast of the city. At that time there was no legislation which provided for a city to spend money on airports; but a city could legally spend money on parks outside the city limits, so the aerodrome was called Des Moines Aviation Park and the City was thus able to spend some money on it. However, the site was low lying and subject to both fog and flooding.

In 1925 the Federal Government delegated responsibility for airports to the cities, and Des Moines, realizing that a better aerodrome was necessary if it was to continue receiving the air mail service, set out to acquire both temporary and permanent airports.

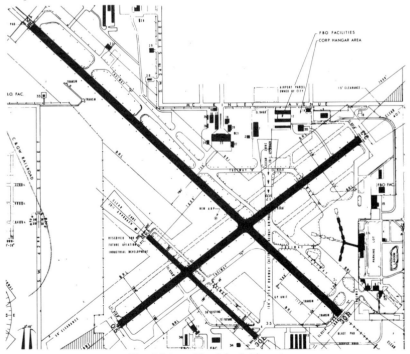

Des Moines Municipal Airport.

429

A temporary site was found on 16 acres (6.47 hectares) of land 8 miles (12.87 km) northeast of the city and near Altoona. This became the Des Moines airport in 1926 and the city's first hangar was erected there in 1928. This grass aerodrome was used by Boeing Air Transport when it began operating CAM 18 between San Francisco and Chicago, with Boeing 40A biplanes, on 1 July, 1927.

From 1928 a search was made for a permanent site and 80 locations were examined. Finally a 160 acre (64.75 hectare) tract of land at South West 21st Street (Fleur Drive) and Army Post Road was chosen. This site was easily accessible, on a hilltop with good drainage and the minimum of fog, and there was adequate room for expansion. The landowner, Truman Jones, was paid $80,000 for the land, and in April 1932 grading began on what was to become Des Moines Municipal Airport. Some 250,000 cubic yards of earth had to be moved and northeast–southwest and northwest–southeast runways were laid. These measured 1,800 by 100 ft (549 by 30 m) and were of asphalt with concrete edges. The hangar was transferred from the Altoona site and the airport opened during 1932, receiving A-1-A rating on 20 June, 1933.

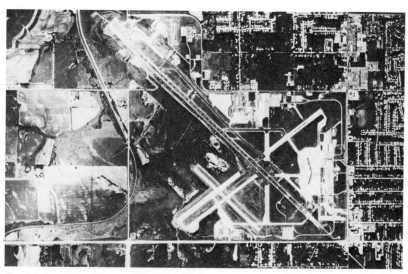

Des Moines Municipal Airport. The main runway is 12L/30R and the secondary runway 05/23. At bottom left is the short 12R/30L. The terminal is on the right. (*City of Des Moines*)

In 1935 a second storey was added to the hangar to provide space for the Weather Bureau and a restaurant, the runways were extended and a new north–south runway laid. Introduction of DC-3s necessitated further enlargement of the airport, 480 additional acres (194 hectares) of land was purchased, and work began in October 1938 which provided the airport with four runways—northwest–southeast of 5,200 ft (1,585 m) and north–south, northeast–southwest and east–west all 4,500 ft (1,372 m) long.

430

The 132nd Tactical Fighter Wing was based at the airport from 1941, in which year a temporary control tower was built, a permanent tower being commissioned in early 1943.

In 1946 Federal funds were made available for further improvements and a new 5,700 ft (1,737 m) northwest–southeast (12/30) runway was built. This became the instrument runway, with ILS, in 1947. There was still no unified terminal and the airlines were working from four separate buildings; but work began on a terminal in 1949, it was completed in December 1950 and dedicated on 23 September, 1951.

To accommodate jet aircraft of the Iowa Air National Guard, work began on extending runway 12/30 by 1,800 ft (549 m) to 7,500 ft (2,286 m). This entailed acquisition of a further 200 acres (81 hectares) of land and was completed in 1953.

Considerable changes were to take place in 1959. The old southwest–northeast runway was replaced by a new 5,000 ft (1,524 m) 05/23; part of the east–west runway was abandoned and the remainder converted to a taxiway; additional taxiways were laid; lighting was improved; additions were made to the terminal and the concourse enclosed. The instrument runway was extended to 9,001 ft (2,743 m) in 1962, bringing the airport area to 1,050 acres (425 hectares), and in 1963 runway 05/23 was extended to 6,500 ft (1,981 m).

Other improvements were made over the next few years and then in 1968 work began on a major remodelling and expansion of the terminal, increasing its area from 86,000 sq ft (7,989 sq m) to 113,000 sq ft (10,498 sq m). The old 7,500 sq ft (697 sq m) passenger concourse was replaced by a two-level concourse of 72,000 sq ft (6,689 sq m), and the original seven gates, designed for DC-6s and DC-7s, were replaced by 12 gates, eight of them with aerobridges. Provision was made for extension of the piers, with additional gates, as required.

In 1969 the 3,202 ft (975 m) 12R/30L runway was built. A master plan for the airport was completed in 1978 but no major developments are likely for some time, except to overcome the inadequacy of the cargo building which was converted in 1967 from an old United Air Lines hangar.

Detroit, Michigan   Detroit Metropolitan Wayne County Airport

42° 13′ 07″ N   83 20′ 55″ W   14.7 nm (27.2 km) WSW of city
ICAO: KDTW   IATA code: DTW   Time zone: GMT −5
Authority: Board of Wayne County Road Commissioners
Area: 2,752 hectares (6,800 acres)
Elevation: 639 ft (195 m)   Ref temp: 28.4 deg C
Runways: 03L/21R   3,200 × 61 m (10,500 × 200 ft) concrete
         03C/21C   2,591 × 61 m (8,500 × 200 ft) asphalt
         03R/21L   3,048 × 46 m (10,000 × 150 ft) concrete
         09/27   2,652 × 61 m (8,702 × 200 ft) asphalt
         Runway 15/33 is closed
Pavement strength: 100,000 lb (45,359 kg) 1, 185,000 lb (83,915 kg) 2, 350,000 lb (158,757 kg) 3

Landing category: ICAO CAT II*

Lighting:

R/W	03L/21R and 03R/21L	LIH white edge and centreline.
	03C/21C and 09/27	LIH white edge
	TDZ 03L, 03R and 21L. REIL 03C, 09 and 21C	
App	R/W 03L and 03R ALSF-2, R/W 21L and 27 MALSR, R/W 21R SSALR. RAIL 21C	
Thr	green. Strobes on 03C/21C and 09	
Txy	blue	

Aids: VORTAC, NDB, VDF, ASR, L, RVR 03L/21R and 03R, ILS CAT II 03L, ILS CAT I 03R and 21R

Twr frequency: 121.1   App frequency: 124.25/125.15

Terminals: L. C. Smith (South) and J. M. Davey (North) terminals and Michael Berry International terminal. North and South terminals have total of six traffic piers with 51 gates. The International terminal has aerobridge loading for three wide-bodied or six smaller aircraft. Separate cargo terminals.

Scheduled services 1978: 14 airlines plus five supplementals and four commuter airline/air taxi operators

Airline bases: American, Delta, Eastern, North Central, Northwest and United

Traffic:	1970	1975	1976	1977	1978
Passengers (total)	7,267,950	7,509,573	8,871,382	8,971,209	10,099,864
Cargo (tonnes)	139,722	120,453	138,292	160,219	187,203
Aircraft movements	277,947	235,131	247,320	263,300	267,862
Transport movements	193,651	160,910	159,691	166,717	—

* Runway 03L was cleared for CAT II operations in October 1968 and scheduled to be upgraded to CAT IIIa during 1979. Runway 03R was to be brought to CAT II status in the second half of 1979.

Detroit Metropolitan Wayne County Airport. North is at the right of the picture.
(*Board of Wayne County Road Commissioners*)

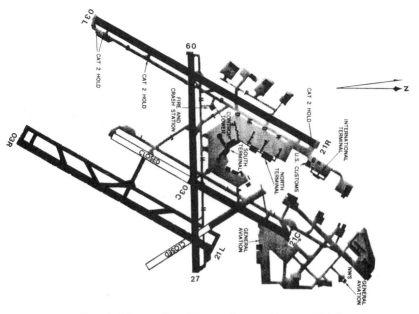

Detroit Metropolitan Wayne County Airport. (*FAA*)

The Wayne County Board of Commissioners decided to build an airport and acquired a site, approximately one mile square, at Middle Belt and Wick Roads in what was then Romulus township. A landing strip was prepared and hangars erected and the airport, known as Wayne County Airport, was opened in 1929. It is believed that when Thompson Aeronautical Corporation inaugurated its Bay City–Detroit–Cleveland night mail service on 1 April, 1929, it used the new airport.

Earlier, the Ford Motor Company and Stout Air Services had operated from Ford Airport, Dearborn, which as early as 1925 was reported to have two concrete runways of 2,600 ft (792 m) and 2,800 ft (853 m), but most other air services through Detroit were using the City Airport.

Although Wayne County Airport did not serve the prewar needs of the scheduled airlines, it was among the first to have a control tower and this had a most unusual form of communication. In October 1930 twin loudspeakers were mounted above the tower and, according to the *Aircraft Year Book 1932* the speakers had a range of over three miles (5 km).

In July 1942 the airport was leased to the Army as Romulus Field. Also during the war a new aerodrome, Willow Run, was built to serve a new aircraft factory and because of its better facilities the scheduled airlines transferred their operations there.

In September 1944 authorization was given to more than treble the size of Wayne County Airport and, in 1947, after its release by the military, money was allocated to develop the airport as a major terminal. Pan American World Airways began using the airport in May 1954 and BOAC transferred its operations from Willow Run to, what had become, Wayne Major Airport, in November 1956. But it was not until 1 October, 1958,

433

that domestic services began when American Airlines and Allegheny Airlines moved from Willow Run. Northwest Airlines followed in December 1958 and Delta Air Lines in April 1959 but it was not until 1966 that United Air Lines made the move.

A new terminal was opened to handle jet operations in December 1958 and the 09/27 runway was extended from 7,600 ft (2,316 m) to 8,500 ft (2,591 m) in 1965.

To meet the requirements of increasing traffic a second terminal was built and in August 1974 the Michael Berry International terminal was opened. Since that time further terminal expansion has taken place and the 10,000 ft (3,048 m) 03R/21L runway has been built. Terminal development restricted the usable length of the 4,330 ft (1,320 m) 15/33 runway and finally this had to be closed.

The second and third development phases envisage an entirely new terminal complex to the south of the present terminals. Under study is the development of Willow Run as a large air cargo centre, general aviation facility and reliever airport for Metropolitan Wayne County Airport.

El Paso, Texas   El Paso International Airport

31° 48′ 26″ N   106° 23′ 11″ W   5 nm (9.26 km) NE of city
ICAO: KELP   IATA code: ELP   Time zone: GMT −7
Authority: El Paso International Airport & Mass Transit Board
Area: 3,237 hectares (8,000 acres)
Elevation: 3,956 ft (1,206 m)   Ref temp: 22.2 deg C
Runways: 04/22   3,658 × 46 m (12,000 × 150 ft) asphalt
    08/26   2,746 × 46 m (9,008 × 150 ft) asphalt
    17/35   2,146 × 46 m (7,042 × 150 ft) asphalt
Pavement strength: 04/22 and 08/26   auw 100,000 lb (45,359 kg) 1, 180,000 lb (81,647 kg) 2, 350,000 lb (158,757 kg) 3; 17/35   auw 40,000 lb (18,144 kg) 1.

El Paso International Airport from 20,000 ft in May 1976. Runway 17/35 is in the foreground with 04/22 (left) and 08/26 (right) beyond. The terminal is at bottom right. (*El Paso International Airport & Mass Transit Board*)

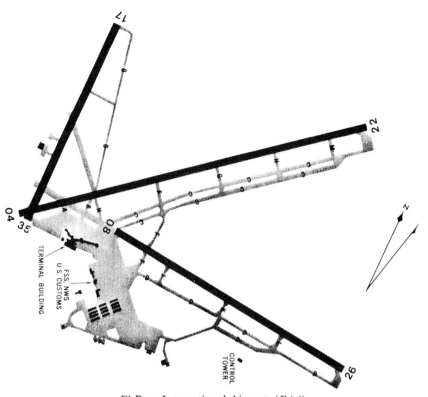

El Paso International Airport. (*FAA*)

Landing category: ICAO CAT I
Lighting:
<pre>
    R/W   04/22 and 08/26   HIRL
    App   R/W 22   ALSF-1
            R/W 26   REIL and VASIS
    Thr   green
    Txy   blue edge
</pre>
Aids: VORTAC, DME, NDB, RVV 22, ILS CAT I 22
Twr frequency: 118.3   App frequency: 118.7/119.1/119.7
Terminals: Two-level terminal with two traffic piers and 14 gates.
    Aerobridges at most gates. Separate cargo building and Military Air
    Transient Terminal
Scheduled services 1978: Airways of New Mexico, American, Continental,
    Frontier, New Mexico Air and Southwest Airlines

Traffic:	1970	1975	1976	1978
Passengers (total)	976,690	1,107,968	1,171,258	1,816,713
Cargo (tonnes)	6,207	5,705*	11,833	19,815
Aircraft movements	227,681	—	192,966	244,966
Transport movements	36,227	13,632†	26,871	—

* Uplifted only   † Departures only

During 1976 Boeing 727s accounted for 90 per cent of transport movements.

435

El Paso became a stop on the US Army Model Airway in 1926 when the New York–San Antonio route was extended to Los Angeles. The landing site was known as the Air Mail Field. In 1928 the City opened its own El Paso Airport which comprised a landing area and one building, and it received an A-1-A rating in 1933.

The city is situated on the Rio Grande over which international bridges link it to México, and it has long been a crossroads for all forms of transport—the Spanish conquistadores using Paso del Norte (Pass of the North) as early as 1591 to travel between México and Santa Fe. In the 1850s the mail coaches of John Butterfield's Overland Dispatch Line (the Butterfield Trail) passed across what is now the centre of the airport. Later, El Paso was to develop rapidly with the coming of the railway—five major railways serve the city and there is a spur into the airport.

The population of El Paso has grown from 96,810 in 1940 to well over 360,000, and annual air passenger traffic is equal to about four times the population. To meet the increasing traffic the terminal area was moved to its present site in 1942 and terminal expansion took place in 1960 and 1971.

The present terminal has an area of 200,000 sq ft (18,580 sq m) and will be capable of handling the predicted $2\frac{1}{2}$ mn passengers in 1980, but a new terminal and runway is planned to handle the $4\frac{1}{2}$ mn passengers forecast for 1990.

Two sources of useful revenue for the airport are the 330 acre (134 hectare) Industrial Park and the City-owned Military Air Transient Terminal, the latter being claimed as the only municipal facility of its kind in the United States.

Fort Lauderdale, Florida
Fort Lauderdale - Hollywood International Airport

26° 04′ 25″ N   80° 09′ 09″ W   4 nm (7.4 km) SW of city
ICAO: KFLL   IATA code: FLL   Time zone: GMT −5
Authority: Broward County Aviation Department
Area: 469 hectares (1,160 acres)
Elevation: 10 ft (3 m)   Ref temp: 32.4 deg C
Runways: 09L/27R   2,453 × 46 m (8,048 × 150 ft) bitumen, grooved
             09R/27L   1,620 × 30 m (5,316 × 100 ft) bitumen, grooved
             13/31   2,111 × 46 m (6,925 × 150 ft) bitumen
Pavement strength: 09L/27R 400,000 lb (181,437 kg) 3; 09R/27L
     30,000 lb (13,608 kg) 1; 13/31 350,000 lb (158,757 kg) 3,
     to be increased to 400,000 lb (181,437 kg).
Landing category: ICAO CAT I
Lighting:
     R/W   09L/27R   HIRL
                09R/27L and 13/31   MIRL
     App   VASIS all runways. R/W 09L is to have MALSR
     Thr   green
     Txy   blue edge
Aids: TVOR/DME, NDB, ASR, ILS CAT I 09L
Twr frequency: 119.3/120.2   App frequency: 127.65

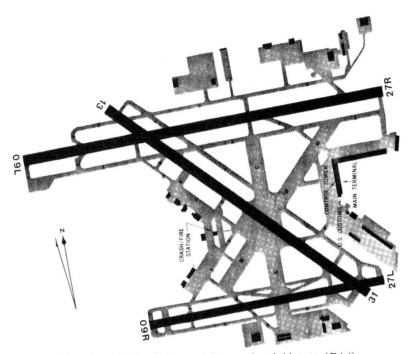

Fort Lauderdale - Hollywood International Airport. (*FAA*)

Terminals: Passenger terminal with 171,000 sq ft (15,886 sq m) floor area, five concourses and international arrival building. 16–19 aircraft stands. Three cargo buildings

Scheduled services 1978: 13 airlines

Main base: Mackey International

Traffic:	1970	1975	1976	1978
Passengers (total)	1,623,473	3,698,896	4,101,438	5,736,410
Cargo (tonnes)	3,949	8,585	10,103	22,745
Aircraft movements	518,556	331,371	319,243	357,861
Transport movements	46,348	84,102	89,364	

Fort Lauderdale - Hollywood International Airport, formerly Broward County International Airport, is approximately 2 miles (3¼ km) from the Atlantic coast and situated between the Seaboard Coastline Rail Road and Interstate Highway 95 on the west, and Florida East Coast Railway, the Old Dixie Highway and US Highway No. 1 on the east. The Dania Cut-off Canal forms the southwest boundary.

The airport was first developed in 1926 by the City of Fort Lauderdale, and named Merle Fogg Field, after a Broward County pioneer pilot. The airport was improved during the 1930s with Works Progress Administration funds, and after the attack on Pearl Harbor was acquired by the Navy, for training, as Fort Lauderdale Naval Air Station.

Four runways were laid, east–west at the north of the site, north–south, northeast–southwest and northwest–southeast. The buildings, including a wooden control tower, were on the west side.

After the war the site remained unused until 1948 when Broward

437

County acquired it under a $1 a year lease and, finally, by formal acquisition on 4 October, 1956.

Mackey Airlines began services from the airport on 1 January, 1953, and in that year the passenger total was 6,817.

In 1956 design work began for a terminal on the east of the airport and this was opened on 1 March, 1959, in which year Eastern Air Lines, National Airlines and Aerovias 'Q' began serving Fort Lauderdale. During that year there were 136,417 aircraft movements of which 12,184 were by air carrier aircraft, and passengers numbered 134,773. From then until 1965 the annual passenger figure fluctuated between 185,000 and just over a quarter of a million. Then came rapid traffic growth with 1,301,668 passengers in 1969, 2 mn in 1971, 3 mn in 1973 and 4 mn in 1976. The figures are expected to reach 8 mn in 1985 and 14½ mn in 1995.

Since 1959 the terminal has been enlarged on several occasions, with expansion stages being completed in March 1960. December 1967, January 1971 and March 1975, by which time its area was 164,000 sq ft (15,236 sq m). Since then three traffic piers have been added and there are 16–19 aircraft stands.

Traffic forecasts suggest that 624,800 sq ft (58,044 sq m) of terminal and 30 aircraft stands will be required in 1985, 732,400 sq ft (68,040 sq m) and 36 stands in 1990, 792,200 sq ft (73,595 sq m) and 42 stands in 1995, and 950,600 sq ft (88,311 sq m) and 50 stands some time after 1995.

On 26 July, 1974, Broward County Commissioners took the first step to produce a master plan covering development up to the year 2000. The airport's requirements were circulated to 37 companies in the United States but only 20 bothered to reply. Several plans were produced and finally it was decided to build a completely new terminal complex on the west side of the airport. There will be a two-level terminal, surmounted by three-level car parking, and three satellite buildings reached by some form of people-mover. Each satellite will have 10 gates with nose-in stands and provision

Fort Lauderdale - Hollywood International Airport terminal area in 1978, with the 27R threshold beyond. (*Broward County Aviation Department*)

for two extra gates when required. There is also provision for a fourth 12-gate satellite. The new terminal is due to come into service in 1981 and, based on third-quarter 1977 projections, the cost was estimated at $177 mn.

Since civil operations began the north–south runway has been abandoned and a new 09/27 runway built at the south. Further runway and taxiway improvements are planned, the 09L approach is to be equipped with MALSR, and another east–west runway has been proposed to the north of 09L/27R.

Hilo, Hawaii   General Lyman Field

19° 43′ 25″ N   155° 03′ 04″ W   1.7 nm (3.2 km) E of city
ICAO: PHTO   IATA code: ITO   Time zone: GMT − 10
Authority: State of Hawaii Department of Transportation
Area: 542 hectares (1,340 acres)
Elevation: 37 ft (11 m)   Ref temp: 28.7 deg C
Runways: 03/21   1,707 × 46 m (5,600 × 150 ft)* asphalt
        08/26   2,987 × 46 m (9,800 × 150 ft) asphalt, grooved
Pavement strength: 03/21 120,000 lb (54,431 kg) 1,   200,000 lb (90,718 kg)
        2,   360,000 lb (163,293 kg) 3;   08/26 115,000 lb (52,163 kg) 1,
        185,000 lb (83,915 kg) 2,   350,000 lb (158,757 kg) 3

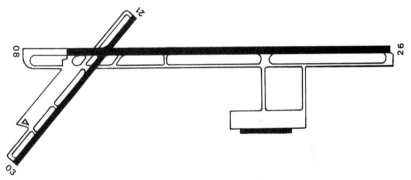

General Lyman Field, Hilo.

Landing category: ICAO CAT I
Lighting:
        R/W   03/21   LIM edge,   08/26   LIH edge
        App   R/W 26   MALSR.   VASIS 03 and 08/26
        Thr   R/W 26   green with strobes,   R/W 03/21 and 08   green
        Txy   blue edge
Aids: VORTAC, NDB, VDF, ILS 26
Twr frequency: 118.1/119.3   App frequency: 119.7
Terminals: Passenger terminal comprising departure building flanked by domestic and inter-island buildings, with 10 aircraft stands and one commuter gate. Separate cargo building

* Threshold 03 is displaced 107 m (350 ft)

General Lyman Field, Hilo, in February 1970. View from over Kuhio Bay looking southeast, with the old terminal area on the right.
(*Courtesy State of Hawaii Department of Transportation*)

Scheduled services 1978: Aloha Airlines, Continental Airlines, Hawaiian Air, Island Pacific Air, Northwest Orient Airlines, Royal Hawaiian Air Service, United Airlines and Western Airlines

Traffic:	1970	1975	1976	1977	1978
Passengers (total)	885,323	1,286,471	1,329,648	1,373,605	1,493,103
Cargo (tonnes)	13,218	27,600	29,360	29,908	29,611
Aircraft movements	52,183	51,145	52,679	60,377	52,677
Transport movements	22,843	20,056	19,916	20,216	35,793

In 1976 Boeing 737s and 747s, Douglas DC-8-62s, DC-9s and DC-10s each accounted for more than 10 per cent of total transport movements.

Under Act 257 Session Laws of the Territory of Hawaii, 1927, $25,000 was appropriated for a Hilo airport. A site was chosen on the east coast of the island of Hawaii and the airport prepared on land belonging to the Hawaiian Homes Commission. On 11 February, 1928, Clarence M. Young, Secretary of Aeronautics, US Department of Commerce, dedicated the airport, having flown to Hilo for the ceremony in the Fokker F.VII-3m *Bird of Paradise* in which Lieuts Maitland and Hegenberger had made the first successful flight from the United States to Honolulu in June 1927.

On 29 October, 1929, Inter-Island Airways* made two pre-inaugural flights to Hilo with Sikorsky S-38 amphibians and on 11 November, that year, the airline began regular Honolulu–Molokai–Maui–Hilo services.

An accelerated airport development programme began in 1937 and from then until 1941, $261,613 was invested in Hilo Airport. With the entry

* Later renamed Hawaiian Airlines (Hawaiian Air)

of the United States into the Second World War, the airport was taken over by the Army and Army Engineers constructed military installations, lengthened the runways and expanded taxiways and aprons. A fighter squadron was based at Hilo. Although the USAAF remained, in 1943 the Navy moved in and set up NAS Hilo as a carrier pilot training school. Both Services conducted largescale transport operations from Hilo and civil operations continued, but under military control. On 19 April, 1943, by Joint Resolution of the Territorial Legislature the airport was renamed General Lyman Field, in honour of a graduate of the US Military Academy who came from Hilo, died in service and was posthumously promoted from Colonel to Brigadier-General.

The airport was returned to the Territory in September 1946 although the USAAF retained operational control, the return to full civil control taking place on 8 April, 1952. Work on a new terminal, west of runway 03/21, began in July 1952 and a contract was placed for high intensity lighting for runway 08/26. The terminal was dedicated on 25 August, 1953, the dedication of the entire airport was on 5 December, 1953, and the cargo terminal was completed in 1954.

In 1965 runway 08/26 was lengthened to 9,800 ft (2,987 m) and on 1 October, 1967, Pan American World Airways and United Air Lines began operating direct services between the US mainland and Hilo. An interim overseas terminal was dedicated on 4 July, 1969.

A committee was appointed in 1970 to make long-range recommendations for development of the airport. Among its recommendations was construction of a new terminal to the south of runway 08/26, with an apron capable of handling up to eight Boeing 707s and four inter-island jets and strong enough for Boeing 747s—the first of which landed at Hilo on 6 February, 1971. Ground was broken for the new terminal in July 1974 and it was opened on 30 April, 1976, with central departure area and domestic and inter-island wings. There are 10 aircraft stands. The terminal can be expanded when required. Runway 08/26 is to be extended to 10,500 ft (3,200 m) and provided with high-speed exits.

Honolulu, Oahu   Honolulu International Airport

21° 19′ 19″ N   157° 55′ 32″ W   3.47 nm (6.42 km) NW of city
ICAO: PHNL   IATA code: HNL   Time zone: GMT − 10
Authority: State of Hawaii Department of Transportation
Area: 1,813 hectares (4,480 acres)
Elevation: 13 ft (4 m)   Ref temp: 30.8 deg C

Runways:			
04L/22R	2,119 × 61 m	(6,953 × 200 ft)	asphalt
04R/22L	2,743 × 46 m	(8,998 × 150 ft)	asphalt, grooved
04S	886 × 18 m	(2,906 × 60 ft)*	asphalt
08L/26R	3,771 × 46 m	(12,371 × 150 ft)	asphalt-concrete
08R/26L	3,658 × 61 m	(12,000 × 200 ft)	asphalt

* Runway 04S is part of the old south apron and taxiway and can only be used for take offs in VFR by aircraft of under 12,500 lb (5,670 kg) auw. Take offs and landings are not allowed on 22S

Runways 04R and 08L/26R have arresting gear

Pavement strength: 08R/26L   80,000 lb (36,287 kg) 1, 170,000 lb (77,111 kg) 2, 350,000 lb (158,757 kg) 3, 780,000 lb (353,802 kg) 4; all other runways except 04S   100,000 lb (45,359 kg) 1, 200,000 lb (90,718 kg) 2, 400,000 lb (181,437 kg) 3

Landing category: ICAO CAT I

Lighting:

R/W	04L/22R	MIRL white edge; 04R/22L, 08L/26R and 08R/26L HIRL white edge
App	R/W 08L	ALSF-1. VASIS 04L, 04R/22L, 26L and 26R. REIL 04L/22R, 04R and 26R
Thr		green, with strobes on 04L/22R and 04R and 648 ft (197 m) out from threshold 26R
Txy		blue edge

Aids: VORTAC, NDB, VDF, RVV 08L, ILS CAT I 04R and 08L

Twr frequency: 118.1   App frequency: 118.3/119.1

Terminals: John Rodgers main terminal with Y-shaped central concourse and 14 aircraft stands; Diamond Head (east) satellite with seven aircraft stands; Ewa (west) satellite with six stands; Inter-Island Terminal with 18 stands; and Commuter Terminal with four stands. Separate cargo terminals and general aviation areas

Scheduled services 1978: 22 airlines

Airline bases: Japan Air Lines, United Airlines and Western Airlines

Main base: Aloha Airlines and Hawaiian Air

Traffic:	1970	1975	1976	1977	1978
Passengers (total)	7,234,594	11,306,443	12,182,519	12,922,895	14,703,764
Cargo (tonnes)	55,155	114,815	137,948	139,747	167,788
Aircraft movements	300,629	319,776	320,565	329,926	379,106
Transport movements	122,202	108,446	108,404	114,174	—

Act 1976 Session Laws of Hawaii, 1925, appropriated $45,000 for construction of an aerodrome near Honolulu on condition that another $20,000 was raised by public subscription, and 119.3 acres (48.28 hectares) of land and 766 acres (310 hectares) under water was purchased from S. M. Damon Estate for $27,410. A small aerodrome was prepared, dedicated on 21 March, 1927, and named after the late Cmdr John Rodgers who had been commanding officer of NAS Pearl Harbor 1923–25 and who in September 1925 commanded the PN-9 flying-boat A6878 on an attempted flight from San Francisco to Hawaii. The PN-9 was forced to alight 559 miles (900 km) short of its destination, was missing for nine days but the crew, using wing fabric as sails, managed to reach Kauai. Inter-Island Airways began scheduled services between Rodgers Airport and Maui and Hilo on 11 November, 1929, with Sikorsky S-38 amphibians.

In 1941 the sum of $1,900,000 was authorized for development of the airport for both land and marine aircraft operation, and the money allowed dredging which provided earth and coral to raise the area which had previously been subject to inundation and thereby permitted future expansion.

Following the attack on neighbouring Pearl Harbor, the Army took over the airport and built runways. Then in August 1943 the Navy took over the airport as NAS Honolulu although the Army continued to use the base as a staging post. The two Services undertook most of the development work which had been planned for the civil airport.

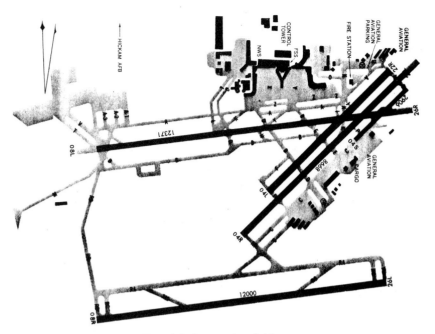

Honolulu International Airport.

When Pan American Airways began its trans-Pacific services in 1935, its Martin 130 flying-boats had operated from a base at Pearl City on the shore of Pearl Harbor but in 1943 for security reasons and because of the hazards caused by surface craft, operations were transferred to Keehi Lagoon immediately to the east of the airport, $3,300,000 having been authorized by Congress in 1940 for dredging the lagoon.

The Navy built a terminal on the southeast boundary which could serve landplanes and flying-boats, and erected a control tower and hangars, and on the north side of the airport facilities to support Navy transport operations.

At the end of the war John Rodgers Airport and Keehi Lagoon Seaplane Harbor covered 4,020 acres (1,627 hectares), had four 200 ft (61 m) wide runways of 6,150–7,650 ft (1,875–2,332 m) and three 1,000 ft (305 m) wide seaplane channels of 10,560–15,827 ft (3,219–4,824 m).

The airport was returned to the Territory of Hawaii by the Navy on 1 October, 1946, although some areas and buildings were retained, and by Act 31 Session Laws 1947 the names John Rodgers Airport and Keehi Lagoon Seaplane Harbor were changed to Honolulu Airport.

Alongside Honolulu Airport, to the west, is Hickam Air Force Base, and in March 1951 about 104 acres (42 hectares) of the Hickam reservation was leased for 20 years by the Hawaii Aeronautics Commission. This enabled the paving of a 540 ft (165 m) connecting link between Honolulu and Hickam 08/26 runways to provide a length of 13,104 ft (3,994 m), making it one of the world's longest—12,371 ft (3,771 m) is now available.

The start of the Korean War in June 1950 had a major impact on

443

Honolulu's facilities—landings increasing from 6,900 that June to 8,600 in July—and the already inadequate overseas terminal was taxed to capacity.

Plans for a new terminal, on the north side of the airport, were completed in December 1954 but Stage I construction did not begin until early 1959. So when Qantas began Boeing 707 services through Honolulu at the end of July 1959, soon followed by Pan American, the old picturesque but inadequate terminal was still in use and the seaplane lagoon was being used by Navy flying-boats.

The first stage of the new terminal was completed in December 1959 and the second stage begun. The terminal was dedicated, as the John Rodgers Terminal, on 22 August, 1962, operations were transferred to the new terminal at midnight on 14 October and the old terminal was subsequently destroyed.

Honolulu International Airport in 1978, with the 26R, 22L and 22R thresholds in the foreground, the terminal area on the right and the reef runway top left.
(*Courtesy State of Hawaii Department of Transportation*)

444

Numerous additions were made to the terminal and in 1968–69 work began on two satellite terminals to be capable of handling Boeing 747s. The first of these, the Diamond Head 'gull-wing' satellite to the east of the main building, was ready, with two aerobridges, when the first Pan American 747 service arrived on 3 March, 1970. The Ewa 'gull-wing' extension, to the west, was opened in July 1970. Also in 1970 runway 04R/22L was rebuilt and extended to 9,000 ft (2,743 m).

Terminal expansion has been almost continuous and development is expected to continue until at least 1985. Some of the planned expansion will make it necessary to replace the 1975 Inter-Island Terminal with a new building near the eastern end of the airport.

In the financial year 1970–71 model studies were made of a reef runway to be sited on reclaimed land south of the airport. This runway was intended to increase the airport's capacity and divert heavy and noisy aircraft from the city. FAA approval was given to the project in 1972 but actual construction was delayed by conservationists; work was resumed in 1974 and the new 08R/26L 12,000 ft (3,658 m) runway was opened on 14 October, 1977. This runway and its parallel taxiway blocked the approach to the Keehi Lagoon seaplane area which has now been abandoned.

Future plans call for the installation of ILS and approach lights at each end of the reef runway, installation of VASIS on 08R and closure of 04S.

Houston, Texas   Houston Intercontinental Airport

29° 59′ 08″ N   95° 20′ 46″ W   14 nm (30 km) N of city
ICAO: KIAH   IATA code: IAH   Time zone: GMT −6
Authority: City of Houston Aviation Department
Area: 3,130 hectares (7,734 acres)
Elevation: 98 ft (30 m)   Ref temp: 33.8 deg C
Runways: 08/26   2,865 × 46 m (9,400 × 150 ft) concrete, grooved
          09S/27S   610 × 23 m (2,000 × 75 ft) STOL, marked on taxiway
          13S/31S   610 × 23 m (2,000 × 75 ft) STOL, marked on taxiway
          14/32   3,658 × 46 m (12,000 × 150 ft) concrete, grooved
Pavement strength: 08/26 120,000 lb (54,431 kg) 1,   155,000 lb (70,307 kg) 2,   265,000 lb (120,202 kg) 3;   14/32 100,000 lb (45,360 kg) 1, 200,000 lb (90,719 kg) 2,   400,000 lb (181,437 kg) 3, 778,000 lb (352,895 kg) 4.
Landing category: ICAO CAT II (due to be cleared for IIIa)
Lighting:
     R/W   08/26   HIRL white edge, last 3,000 ft (914 m) amber. White centreline, last 1,000 ft (305 m) red, previous 2,000 ft (610 m) red/white. TDZ 08
             09/27   MIRL
             13/31   white edge and amber taxiway lights
             14/32   MIRL and centreline

445

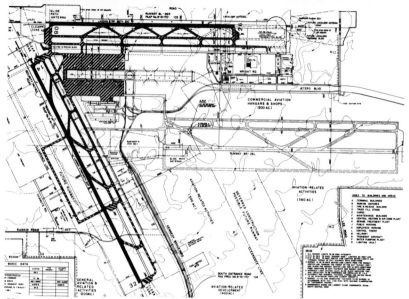

Houston Intercontinental Airport showing projected terminal and runway development.

App   R/W 08   ALSF-1
            R/W 09/27   VASIS
            R/W 14   MALSR and VASIS
            R/W 26   MALSR and VASIS
            R/W 31   VASIS
Thr   green
Txy   edge and centreline

Aids: VORTAC, NDB, LOM 08 and 14, RVR 08/26, LLWSAS, ILS CAT II 08*, ILS CAT I 14 and 26

Twr frequency: 118.1   App frequency: 120.5

Terminals: Two multi-storey passenger terminals each with concourses extending from each corner and leading to eight separate circular flight stations, each with five gates and aerobridges. Cargo area with three air carrier buildings and 11 buildings for freight forwarders. Area exceeds 331,600 sq ft (30,805 sq m).

* Due to become CAT IIIa

Scheduled services 1978: 20 airlines

Traffic:	1970	1975	1976	1977	1978
Passengers (total)	4,518,867	6,121,000	6,833,613	7,996,935	9,749,425
Cargo (tonnes)	20,668	82,953	103,194	51,602	64,523
Aircraft movements	185,133	192,953	207,519	240,497	269,641
Transport movements	47,945	152,788	161,121	—	—

In the late 1920s the City of Houston developed an airport on grazing land about 10 miles (16 km) southeast of the city. It was known as Houston Municipal Airport, later Houston International Airport, and in 1967 was renamed William P. Hobby Airport. This airport served the region's air transport needs until 1969, and is now used as a general aviation facility, but in the early 1950s it was predicted that a major new airport would be required in the late 1960s.

A site was chosen north of the city between the Interstate Highway leading north to Dallas and US 59 to Cleveland. Difficulties were encountered in acquiring the site and an ingenious method was adopted. A group of 18 citizens quietly acquired 3,000 acres (1,214 hectares) through a holding company called Jet Era Ranch Company (known, as the result of an error, as Jetero*) and held the land for the City to which it was offered for $1,900,000—the price actually paid. The City purchased the land in 1960 and later bought more land to bring the site to well over 7,000 acres (2,833 hectares).

Planning began in September 1960, the overall design was authorized on 11 October, 1961, and work on the site began about a year later.

The airport was specifically designed to meet the requirements of jet operations and was built within the budget of $110 mn. Initially there were two main runways, 08/26 of 9,400 ft (2,865 m) and 14/32 of 8,000 ft (2,438 m), two terminals and cargo facilities. Runway 14/32 has now been extended to 12,000 ft (3,658 m), there are two STOL runways of 2,000 ft (610 m) marked on taxiways, these are 09S/27S and 13S/31S, there are three air-carrier cargo buildings, several maintenance bases and, in the terminal area, a hotel.

The terminal area is linear, in the angle between the runways and parallel with 08/26. It was planned that there would be four terminal buildings and the first two, at the west of the site, were ready when the airport was dedicated on 1 June, 1969, and opened for traffic on 8 June.

* The name has been perpetuated in Jetero Boulevard.

Houston Intercontinental Airport in February 1976. The two terminals, each with four flight stations, are in the centre with the hotel on the right and runway 08/26 in the background. (*City of Houston Aviation Department*)

These terminals, which are identical, are two-level square structures above which are two levels of parking for 776 cars. The sides of the buildings measure 380 ft (116 m) and from each corner a 300 ft (91 m) second-level concourse leads to a circular satellite, known as a flight station, with five gates each with an aerobridge. The western terminal is Terminal A and its flight stations are numbered 1 to 4 anti-clockwise from the northeast corner. The adjoining building is Terminal B with flight stations 5 to 8.

For the first three years of operation the terminals were linked with each other and with the ground-level car parks, and, from 1971, with the hotel by Electronic Passenger Trains—claimed to be the first airport people-mover. This has now been replaced by the Interterminal Transportation System which is an underground fully-automated 40-ft (12 m) long train comprising three cars, each for 10 passengers. There are six of these units, running at 2-min intervals and achieving a maximum speed of 12 mph (19 km/h).

Although the Houston terminals are attractive and have proved efficient, they were designed before the advent of the large wide-bodied aircraft and do not have sufficient flexibility. It was therefore decided not to build two more identical terminals; instead there will be two similar terminals with three car-park decks, but the boarding methods will be different. Instead of the satellite flight stations there will be linear concourses and a north and south pier for each terminal. Terminal C was begun in the spring of 1978 and is due to be opened in early 1981. This building will have an area of about 690,000 sq ft (64,100 sq m), parking for 1,344 cars, a north apron for 10 wide-bodied aircraft and five commuter aircraft, and a south apron for 15 aircraft of which seven can be wide-bodied. There will be nose-in stands on the face of the linear concourses and either side of the piers. Terminal D, which will complete the terminal area as presently defined, is likely to be of the same design.

Also planned, for construction when required, is a 12,000 ft (3,658 m) 08R/26L runway which will be sited southeast of the terminal area, and there may be a 4,000 ft (1,219 m) 14R/32L runway to the west of the centre part of the present 14/32.

Indianapolis, Indiana Indianapolis International Airport

39° 43′ 36″ N	86° 16′ 59″ W	8 nm (14.8 km) SW of city
ICAO: KIND	IATA code: IND	Time zone: GMT −5

Authority: Indianapolis Airport Authority
Area: 1,000 hectares (2,471 acres)
Elevation: 797 ft (243 m)   Ref temp: 29.7 deg C
Runways: 04L/22R 3,048 × 46 m (10,000 × 150 ft) concrete, grooved
    04R/22L 1,128 × 23 m (3,701 × 75 ft)
    13/31 2,318 × 46 m (7,604 × 150 ft) concrete
Pavement strength: 04L/22R 85,000 lb (38,555 kg) 1, 120,000 lb (54,431 kg) 2, 210,000 lb (95,254 kg) 3; 13/31 80,000 lb (36,287 kg) 1, 115,000 lb (52,163 kg) 2, 200,000 lb (90,718 kg) 3.
Landing category: ICAO CAT II

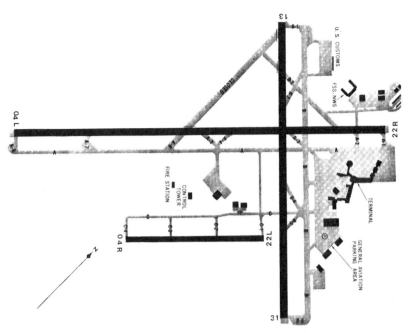

Indianapolis International Airport. (*FAA*)

Lighting:
   R/W   04L/22R   HIRL and centreline. TDZ 04L
             04R/22L   MIRL
             13/31   HIRL
   App   R/W 04L   ALSF-2
             R/W 13   REIL and VASIS
             R/W 22R   MALSR
             R/W 31   SSALSR
   Thr   green
   Txy   blue edge
Aids: VORTAC, NDB, VDF, RVR 04L/22R and 31, ILS CAT II 04L,
   ILS CAT I 31
Twr frequency: 120.9/123.95   App frequency: 119.3/121.1
Terminals: Domestic terminal with three traffic piers (one with circular
   satellite) and 16 aerobridges. Separate international arrivals building
   with 250 passengers/hour processing capability. Separate general
   aviation apron
Scheduled services 1978: Allegheny, American, Delta, Eastern, Ozark,
   Skystream Airlines and TWA

Traffic:	1970	1976	1978
Passengers (total)	2,016,404	2,666,000*	3,276,100
Cargo (tonnes)	48,211	37,623	64,812
Aircraft movements	197,938	214,979	216,229
Transport movements	91,532	101,789	109,145

     * Rounded figure

449

The City of Indianapolis appointed a committee, in 1928, to select a site for a municipal airport. At one time options were held on more than 40 but the best and the cheapest was on an area of good farmland southwest of the city, immediately south of the Pennsylvania Railroad tracks at the point where they turn north for Chicago. The City purchased 947 acres (383 hectares) for $286,000 and allocated 300 acres (121 hectares) for the landing area, keeping the remainder in reserve for future extensions.

The whole landing area was turfed and three concrete runways were laid flush with the turf so that operations were not confined to the runways, which were north–south and southwest–northeast of 2,000 ft (610 m) and northwest–southeast of 1,100 ft (335 m). All runways were 104 ft (31.7 m) wide and 6 in (15½ cm) thick. There was a combined hangar, administration and terminal building on the east side. This measured 156 by 136 ft (47.5 by 41.5 m), was surmounted by a control tower on top of which there was a 2,760,000 candlepower rotating beacon. A canopied walkway on the face of the terminal gave access to three boarding gates. There was a concrete apron, and concrete taxiways connected the apron and runways. The entire airport cost $740,000, operations began on 16 February, 1931, and the airport was the ninth to be given A-1-A rating.

From its inauguration Indianapolis Municipal Airport was equipped with lighting and radio and in the southeast corner the Government erected a radio range station. From 1931 Transcontinental and Western Air called at Indianapolis on its transcontinental services and the Embry-Riddle division of American Airways routed its Chicago–Cincinnati services through the airport.

Indianapolis International Airport in December 1976 with main terminal (right), the international apron (left) and threshold 22R (top centre).
(*Indianapolis Airport Authority*)

450

Steps were taken to safeguard future development by sterilizing 500 ft (152 m) wide safety lanes to provide for runway extensions and prevent development outside the airport which could cause obstructions. There were also plans for a possible second terminal area on the north boundary with a rail link to Union Station, and as early as 1931 provision had been made for a pair of east–west runways and three additional runways to parallel the original three.

Much of this early plan can be seen in the present layout although the terminal area now occupies the site of the first north–south runway. In 1976 a north terminal area became a reality when, on 23 July, a 13,000 sq ft (1,208 sq m) international arrivals terminal was dedicated on the site between the 13 and 22R thresholds.

At some time Indianapolis Municipal Airport was named Weir Cook Municipal Airport but in 1976, with the opening of the international arrivals building, it took its present name.

Jacksonville, Florida   Jacksonville International Airport

30° 29′ 04″ N   81° 41′ 16″ W   10 nm (18.5 km) N of city
ICAO: KJAX   IATA code: JAX   Time zone: GMT −5
Authority: Jacksonville Port Authority
Area: 2,250 hectares (5,560 acres)
Elevation: 30 ft (9 m)   Ref temp: 33.3 deg C
Runways: 07/25   2,438 × 46 m (8,000 × 150 ft)* grooved
         13/31   2,347 × 46 m (7,701 × 150 ft)†

* Arresting gear each end
† Closed to aircraft above 12,500 lb (5,670 kg)

Pavement strength: 07/25 100,000 lb (45,360 kg) 1, 208,000 lb (94,347 kg) 2, 358,000 lb (162,386 kg) 3.
Landing category: ICAO CAT II
Lighting:
R/W	07/25	HIRL and centreline. TDZ 07
	13/31	MIRL
App	R/W 07	ALSF-2
	R/W 13	MALSR
	R/W 25	VASIS
	R/W 31	REIL and VASIS
Thr	green	
Txy	blue edge	

Aids: VORTAC, NDB, ASR, RVR 07/25, ILS CAT II 07, ILS CAT I 13
Twr frequency: 118.3   App frequency: 118.0/119.0/124.9
Terminal: Square terminal building with projecting north, south and west traffic piers with 19 gates. Aerobridges at some stands. Cargo area to south of passenger terminal
Scheduled services 1978: Air Florida, Delta, Eastern, National and Southern

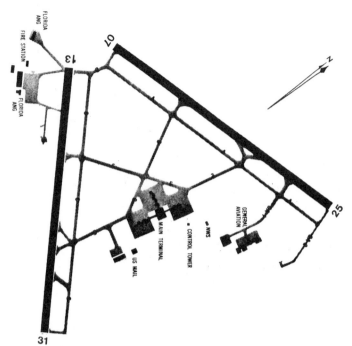

Jacksonville International Airport. (*FAA*)

Jacksonville International Airport in May 1974, looking west-northwest across the terminal area with runway 13/31 (left) and 07/25 (right). The Florida Air National Guard Base is near the 13 threshold. (*Jacksonville Port Authority*)

452

Base: The Florida Air National Guard has a base at the west of the airport, and there is a separate general aviation area

Traffic:	1970	1975	1976	1978
Passengers (total)	1,327,965	1,503,657	1,586,437	1,781,352
Cargo (tonnes)	14,004	12,266	11,700	6,547
Aircraft movements*	86,955	90,237	98,886	—

* Total movements excluding military aircraft

Established in the 1920s as Jacksonville Municipal Airport and equipped for night operations, the name was changed to Jacksonville International Airport in October 1968.

The airport has not experienced dramatic traffic growth but there are plans for both short- and long-term development. The present 07/25 runway is to be extended to 10,000 ft (3,048 m), with completion due in 1979, and there are plans for extension of 13/31 to the same length.

Longer-term plans provide for a pair of 07/25 runways south of the terminal area. These would have 1,000 ft (305 m) separation between their centrelines and each have a parallel taxiway. When constructed the northern of this pair will be the 07C/25C instrument runway of 10,000 ft (3,048 m). The southern runway, 07R/25L, will measure 7,000 ft (2,134 m). There is also a project for a 6,000 ft (1,829 m) 13L/31R runway at the north of the airport. The existing runways will become 07L/25R and 13R/31L.

The development plan also provides for extension of all three terminal piers and their loading aprons, and the cargo area.

The full implementation of runway, taxiway and terminal development is scheduled for 1992.

Kahului, Maui   Kahului Airport

20° 54′ 03″ N   156° 26′ 03″ W   2.5 nm (4.6 km) E of Kahului
ICAO: PHOG   IATA code: OGG   Time zone: GMT −10
Authority: State of Hawaii Department of Transportation
Area: 586 hectares (1,447 acres)
Elevation: 57 ft (17 m)   Ref temp: 30.4 deg C
Runways: 02/20   2,132 × 46 m (6,996 × 150 ft) asphalt
         05/23   1,521 × 46 m (4,990 × 150 ft) asphalt
         Runway 17/35 is now closed
Pavement strength: 02/20 75,000 lb (34,019 kg) 1,   100,000 lb (45,359 kg) 2,
    160,000 lb (72,575 kg) 3;   05/23 75,000 lb (34,019 kg) 1,
    106,000 lb (48,081 kg) 2
Landing category: ICAO CAT I
Lighting:
    R/W   02/20   LIM edge,   05/23   LIL edge
    App   R/W 02   MALSR.   VASIS 20
    Thr   R/W 02/20   green wing bars,   R/W 05/23   green
    Txy   blue edge
Aids: VORTAC, ASR, RVV 02, ILS CAT I 02
Twr frequency: 118.7   App frequency: 119.5

Terminals: Passenger terminal at west end of airport, with 11 aircraft stands. Cargo buildings on east apron
Scheduled services 1978: Aloha Airlines, Brandt Air, Hawaiian Air, Island Pacific Air, Midwest Aviation and Royal Hawaiian Air Service

Traffic:	1970	1975	1976	1977	1978
Passengers (total)	1,166,494	2,178,384	2,539,008	2,820,724	3,313,791
Cargo (tonnes)	—	12,128	12,248	11,975	16,768
Aircraft movements	77,451	77,062	90,455	100,655	125,291
Transport movements	38,680	35,135	37,568	40,365	88,172

On 11 November, 1929, Inter-Island Airways inaugurated services between Honolulu and Maui with Sikorsky S-38 amphibians and used an aerodrome near Maalaea Bay on the south coast. The aerodrome had no paved surfaces, was unusable in wet weather, was too small for the S-43s introduced in 1935, and its proximity to the West Maui Mountains made it hazardous.

In September 1936 wind studies began on a site at Puunene, south of Kahului, but construction of an airport did not start until 1 June, 1938. Meanwhile, in January 1938, the Chief Inspector of the Bureau of Air Commerce had condemned Maalaea Airport, granting a temporary permit for its use by small aircraft only and this left Maui without adequate air services.

Puunene Airport, with paved runways, was opened on 30 June, 1939, and it was enlarged and improved up to the time of the Japanese attack on Hawaii when it was taken over by the Navy which made further improvements. It still proved inadequate and the Navy established an air station just east of Kahului on the north coast on 1,341 acres (543 hectares) of cane land, beginning construction of Kahului Naval Air Station in 1942.

All airline operations were transferred from Puunene to Kahului on 25 May, 1951, at which time there were three runways, 02/20, 05/23 and 17/35. A passenger terminal had been constructed and one of the existing buildings converted to handle cargo. Runway lighting was installed and a new control tower was completed in October 1958. Runway 02 became the instrument runway on 9 November, 1963, and a new terminal was dedicated on 25 June, 1966. It was extended in 1970–71 and a new cargo terminal was completed on 13 February, 1970.

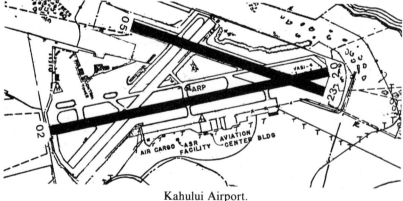

Kahului Airport.

Kahului Airport. View, taken in June 1976, looking southwest, with thresholds 23 (left) and 20 in the foreground, Kahului in the distance and the West Maui Mountains in the background.
(*Courtesy State of Hawaii Department of Transportation*)

The need for considerable terminal expansion in the decade to 1985 is foreseen, runway 02/20 is to be lengthened, and a parallel taxiway is likely to be built to serve runway 05/23. There are also plans for a general aviation area on the east apron.

Runway 02 is the designated noise abatement departure runway for large and turbine-powered aircraft but there is still a serious noise problem in Spreckelsville Beach between the airport and the coast under the climb-out paths from runways 02 and 05.

Kansas City, Missouri   Kansas City International Airport

39° 18′ 05″ N	94° 43′ 37″ W	15.6 nm (29 km) NW of city
ICAO: KMCI	IATA code: MCI	Time zone: GMT −6

Authority: City of Kansas City, Department of Aviation
Area: 2,070 hectares (5,115 acres)
Elevation: 1,025 ft (312 m)   Ref temp: 32.7 deg C

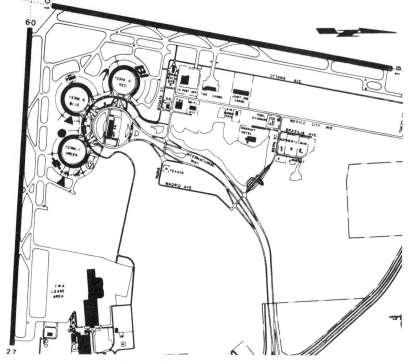

Kansas City International Airport.

Runways: 01/19   3,292 × 46 m (10,800 × 150 ft) asphalt on concrete, grooved
       09/27   2,896 × 46 m (9,500 × 150 ft) concrete, grooved
Pavement strength: 01/19 180,000 lb (81,646 kg) 2, 250,000 lb (113,398 kg) 3;   09/27 150,000 lb (68,039 kg) 2,   250,000 lb (113,398 kg) 3.
Landing category: ICAO CAT III
Lighting:

R/W	01/19	HIRL and centreline. TDZ 01/19
	09/27	HIRL
App	R/W 01	ALSF
	R/W 09	MALS and REIL
	R/W 19	ALSF-2
	R/W 27	REIL and VASIS
Thr	green	
Txy	blue edge	

Aids: VORTAC, NDB, LOM, RVR 01/19 and 09, ILS CAT III 19, ILS CAT I 01 and 09/27
Twr frequency: 118.1   App frequency: 119.35/126.6
Terminals: Three circular terminals with 51 gates. TWA and joint-user cargo terminals
Scheduled services 1978: 10 scheduled airlines and five commuter

Main base: TWA

Traffic:	1970*	1975	1976	1978
Passengers (total)	3,786,417	4,255,686	4,562,255	5,391,689
Cargo (tonnes)	54,608	36,680	45,449	74,047
Aircraft movements	232,449	176,512	178,980	195,201
Transport movements	133,572	152,774	152,064	163,965

* Figures for Kansas City Municipal Airport

During 1976 Boeing 727s accounted for 38.33 per cent of transport movements, CV-580s and DC-9s for 6.52 per cent each, Boeing 737s for 4.89 per cent and Boeing 707s for 3.37 per cent.

For more than 40 years Kansas City Municipal Airport served the airlines in spite of its proximity to the city's built-up areas, but on 11 November, 1972, the airlines began operating from the new Kansas City International Airport, and to it TWA transferred its main overhaul base.

Construction of the airport involved moving 18 mn cubic yards of earth, at a peak rate of 200,000 cubic yards a day, and 500,000 cubic yards of concrete was poured.

At present the airport is enclosed by runway 01/19 on the west, 09/27 at the south and Interstate Highway 29 on the east and north. The terminal area is in the southwest corner and there are three essentially identical three-level terminal buildings each forming 80 per cent of a circle. Measured round their outer faces the buildings are 2,300 ft (701 m) long but from the car parks within the circles to their outer faces they are only 65 ft (20 m). Combined terminal floor area is more than 1 mn sq ft (92,900 sq m).

Kansas City International Airport. The terminals, left to right, are A, B and C. In the foreground a Braniff Boeing 727 can be seen on runway 09/27, runway 01/19 is on the left with Ottawa Avenue close to the taxiway, and to the left of the lake Mexico City Avenue. The cargo area is between the two roads.
(*City of Kansas City, Department of Aviation*)

457

Terminal A (Red) has 19 gates used by Braniff and Frontier, Terminal B (Blue) has 15 gates used by Air Midwest, Delta and TWA, and Terminal C (Green) has 17 gates serving international arrivals, Continental, Méxicana, North Central, Ozark and United.

There are joint-user and TWA cargo terminals to the north of the passenger terminals and the TWA maintenance base is at the southeast corner. The roads within the airport are named after cities and include Mexico City Avenue, Brasilia Avenue, Madrid Avenue and Bogota Street.

Largescale expansion plans exist for implementation as required. These include extending runway 01/19 to 12,500 ft (3,810 m) and 09/27 to 10,250 ft (3,124 m). Both runways will have increased bearing strength and eventually will become 01L/19R and 09L/27R. A 10,130 ft (3,088 m) 09R/27L runway will be built 1,400 ft (427 m) south of the existing 09/27, and an 8,600 ft (2,621 m) 01R/19L is to be constructed to the east of the terminal area—its ultimate length is planned to be 11,750 ft (3,581 m). There are also plans for a fourth circular terminal and for considerable expansion of the cargo and maintenance areas.

It is also proposed to acquire a considerable amount of extra land, some of it outside the city limits, to the west of the airport. This would provide space for completely new and very large terminal and apron areas and the construction of two 18/36 runways—18L/36R of 10,800 ft (3,292 m) and 18R/36L of 15,100 ft (4,602 m). All runways are planned to have approach lighting, ILS, parallel taxiways and numerous high-speed exits. The 18/36 runway centrelines will be separated by 6,000 ft (1,829 m).

Las Vegas, Nevada   McCarran International Airport

36° 04′ 47″ N	115° 09′ 07″ W	5.2 nm (9.65 km) S of city
ICAO: KLAS	IATA code: LAS	Time zone: GMT −8

Authority: Clark County Commissioners
Area: 679 hectares (1,678 acres)
Elevation: 2,174 ft (663 m)   Ref temp: 40 deg C
Runways: 01L/19R   1,524 × 23 m   (5,001 × 75 ft) asphalt
         01R/19L   2,980 × 46 m   (9,777 × 150 ft)* asphalt
         07/25   3,851 × 46 m (12,636 × 150 ft)* asphalt

*01R threshold displaced 498 ft (152 m), 07 displaced 1,673 ft (510 m) and 19L displaced 867 ft (264 m)

Pavement strength: 01R/19L and 07/25 200,000 lb (90,719 kg) 1 and 2, 380,000 lb (172,365 kg) 3.
Landing category: ICAO CAT I
Lighting:
  R/W   01L/19R and 01R/19L   MIRL
          07/25   HIRL
  App   R/W 01L   REIL
          R/W 19L   VASIS
          R/W 19R   REIL and VASIS
          R/W 25   MALSR

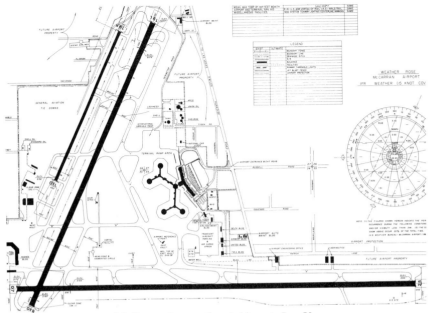

McCarran International Airport, Las Vegas.

Thr   green, with wing bars at 01R/19L and 07 displaced thresholds

Txy   blue edge on all major taxiways

Aids: VORTAC, NDB, VDF, ASR, ILS CAT I 25

Twr frequency: 119.9   App frequency: 127.15

Terminals: Two-level terminal of 525,000 sq ft (48,772 sq m) with two branching concourses each leading to two circular glass-enclosed pods or cluster buildings each of 21,615 sq ft (2,008 sq m), with total of 36 gates. Also Hughes charter terminal and separate cargo buildings

Scheduled services 1978: 13 airlines

Traffic:	1975	1976	1978
Passengers (total)	6,500,806	7,685,336	9,110,842
Cargo (tonnes)	11,018	12,252	15,022
Aircraft movements	284,766	299,997	345,711
Transport movements	90,392	138,912	153,931

On 17 April, 1926, Western Air Express began operating a Los Angeles–Las Vegas–Salt Lake City mail service, with Douglas M-2s, passengers being carried from 23 May. The WAE aircraft used a grass strip beside the Union Pacific Railroad at Spring Mountain Road, Las Vegas. Later, the airport, known as McCarran Field, was established on the site now occupied by Nellis Air Force Base, northeast of the city. Construction of a new terminal for WAE began in 1933, and during the war Las Vegas Airport was a joint-user facility.

After the war a new airport was constructed south of the city and just east of Las Vegas Boulevard South, and in 1948 airline operations were moved to the new site—now McCarran International Airport, named after the late Senator Pat McCarran.

459

In 1948 the new airport handled 35,106 passengers, and the terminal appears to have been on the west side of the airport. A new terminal, in the angle between the main runways, was opened in March 1963 and although that year the airport handled 1,284,943 passengers, the terminal was regarded as the 'white elephant basking in the desert sun.' By 1966, however, the terminal was being used to capacity and a master plan was initiated for the upgrading and expansion of the airport facilities.

The airport's annual passenger total is now equal to about 20 times the area's population and causes some special problems. Much of the rapid increase in traffic was due to liberalization of the rules governing charter flights, and Las Vegas is now handling about 60 per cent of *all* domestic charters in the United States. The requirements of charter groups are different to those of scheduled airline passengers, and counted against them is the fact that they bring very little revenue to an airport.

There is the Hughes Air Terminal, on the west of the airport, which handles charter traffic of the non-scheduled carriers, but this does not greatly help to ease the pressure on the terminal facilities because about 80 per cent of the charters are operated by the scheduled airlines.

Additions to the terminal, including four satellites, were completed in 1973 when the airport was handling about $5\frac{1}{2}$ mn passengers a year, and it was predicted that there would be sufficient terminal capacity until 1984; but the prediction proved wrong, with capacity problems being encountered as early as 1977.

McCarran International Airport, Las Vegas. View southeast across Scenic Airlines Tour Center and runways 01L/19R and 01R/19L to the terminal and runway 07/25. The aircraft is a Scenic Airlines Swearingen Metroliner (Turbo-Star 400).
(*Courtesy Clark County Commissioners*)

In March 1974 a master plan was commissioned and this was presented to the Board of County Commissioners in May 1976. The consultants forecast 445,300 aircraft movements in 1985, 554,300 in 1990, and 688,400 in 1995, with about 50 per cent being by general aviation aircraft. The forecast for embarking passengers was 7,549,000 in 1985, 10,539,000 in 1990, and 14,607,000 in 1995. Five alternate expansion plans were presented, all involving the acquisition of additional land, but the recommended plan covering the period up to 1992 involved land acquisition totalling 3,070 acres (1,242 hectares), mostly south of the existing area, and included provision of a new 12,030 ft (3,667 m) runway parallel to and 900 ft (274 m) south of the existing 07/25; a new general aviation centre with a 5,000 ft (1,524 m) 08/26 runway 3,600 ft (1,097 m) south of the existing 07/25, and a 6,000 ft (1,829 m) 02/20 runway 7,600 ft (2,316 m) east of the present 01/19. There were proposals for a new international terminal north of the present terminal and a charter terminal at the northwest of the airport.

A new master plan, approved in 1979, calls for phased development of five satellite terminals and a 07R/25L runway to provide for 30 mn passengers by 2000.

Lihue, Kauai   Lihue Airport

21° 58′ 56″ N   159° 20′ 40″ W   1.5 nm (2.7 km) E of Lihue
ICAO: PHLI   IATA code: LIH   Time zone: GMT −10
Authority: State of Hawaii Department of Transportation
Area: 74.86 hectares (185 acres)
Elevation: 149 ft (45 m)   Ref temp: 29.4 deg C
Runway: 03/21   1,829 × 30 m (6,000 × 100 ft) asphalt, grooved
Pavement strength: maximum landing weight 85,000 lb (38,555 kg) 1, 108,000 lb (48,988 kg) 2, 165,000 lb (74,843 kg) 3
Lighting:
    R/W   LIM edge
    App   VASIS 03. REIL 03/21
    Txy   blue edge
Aids: VORTAC
Twr frequency: 118.9
Terminal: Small passenger terminal and cargo building at mid-point and to north of runway, with seven aircraft stands
Scheduled services 1978: Aloha Airlines, Hawaiian Air, Island Pacific Air and Oahu and Kauai Airlines

Traffic:	1970	1975	1976	1977	1978
Passengers (total)	1,112,965	1,918,065	2,078,441	2,188,666	2,423,957
Cargo (tonnes)	—	6,412	7,496	6,307	8,374
Aircraft movements	*	53,356	58,865	65,636	74,583
Transport movements	*	23,629	24,346	25,190	57,134

* The control tower was commissioned in 1971 and previous aircraft movements were not recorded

461

Air services to Kauai began on 12 November, 1929, when an Inter-Island Airways Sikorsky S-38 amphibian made the inaugural 1 hr 15 min flight from Honolulu. The S-38s landed at Burns Field, the military aerodrome at Port Allen on the south coast. In 1931 money was allocated for a more central airport at Wailua, north of Lihue, but, opened in 1934, it proved unsafe for the S-43s which came into service in 1935. Air services were then moved back to Port Allen and, when the aerodrome was closed after the attack on Pearl Harbor, transferred to the military aerodrome at Barking Sands on the west coast.

After the war, land for an airport was acquired at Ahukini beside the ocean just south of Hanamaulu Bay and in 1948 a contract was placed for grading and paving a 3,750 ft (1,143 m) runway, taxiways and an apron. This work was not completed until December 1950 but on 1 September, 1949, the airport was opened for limited operations and the terminal was dedicated on 8 January, 1950. Night operations began on 4 April that year.

A contract for construction of a cargo terminal was placed in August 1950 and in September 1951 new medium intensity runway lights replaced the temporary lighting. In October 1952 completion of runway extension to 5,100 ft (1,554 m) made the airport ready to accept Hawaiian Airlines Convair CV-340s which were commissioned in January 1953. The terminal building was also extended in 1952 and again in 1962. The control tower was commissioned in 1971.

Development of the Lihue area as a holiday resort nearly doubled the passenger volume in the first half of the 1970s and by 1974 terminal capacity had been exceeded. By 1975 Lihue Airport was admitted to be the most overcrowded and least satisfactory of the Hawaiian airports and largescale development is projected, including a new terminal building and a second runway.

Lihue Airport. View, taken in October 1975, looking north to Hanamaulu Bay. (*Courtesy State of Hawaii Department of Transportation*)

33° 56′ 32″ N   118° 24′ 26″ W   8.69 nm (16.09 km) SW of city
ICAO: KLAX   IATA code: LAX   Time zone: GMT −8
Authority: City of Los Angeles Department of Airports
Area: 1,416 hectares (3,500 acres)
Elevation: 126 ft (38 m)   Ref temp: 24 deg C

Runwways:

Runways: 06L/24R	2,720 × 46 m	(8,925 × 150 ft) concrete
06R/24L	3,135 × 46 m	(10,285 × 150 ft) asphalt concrete, grooved
07L/25R	3,685 × 46 m	(12,090 × 150 ft) concrete asphalt
07R/25L	3,655 × 61 m	(11,992 × 200 ft) concrete asphalt
08/26*	914 × 23 m	(3,000 × 75 ft) asphalt

* 08/26 is on south taxiway and restricted to VFR daylight operation by aircraft of less than 12,000 lb (5,443 kg).

Pavement strength: auw 06L/24R   175,000 lb (79,000 kg) 1, 225,000 lb (102,000 kg) 2, 400,000 lb (181,000 kg) 3, 902,000 lb (409,000 kg) 4; 06R/24L   100,000 lb (46,000 kg) 1, 180,000 lb (82,000 kg) 2, 350,000 lb (159,000 kg) 3; 07L/25R   80,000 lb (36,000 kg) 1, 120,000 lb (54,000 kg) 2, 210,000 lb (95,000 kg) 3, 332,898 lb (151,000 kg) 4; 07R/25L   100,000 lb (46,000 kg) 1, 180,000 lb (82,000 kg) 2, 340,000 lb (154,000 kg) 4.
Landing category: ICAO CAT II
Lighting:

R/W	06L/24R	HIRL (last 2,000 ft/610 m amber) and centre-line. TDZ 24R
	06R/24L, 07L/25R and 07R/25L	HIRL (last 2,000 ft/610 m) amber
App	R/W 06L and 07R	MALSR, REIL and VASIS
	R/W 06R and 07L	MALSR and VASIS
	R/W 24L, 24R* and 25R	ALSF-1
	R/W 25L	SSALR
Thr	green all thresholds	
Txy	blue edge all taxiways	

* To become ALSF-2

Aids: VOR/DME, ASR, PAR, ARTS III, ASDE, RVR, ILS CAT II 24R* and 25L, ILS CAT I 06L, 06R, 07L, 07R, 24L and 25R

* To become CAT IIIa

Twr frequency: 118.9/120.8   App frequency: 124.9/128.5/134.65
Terminals: Central terminal area of 265 acres (107 hectares) with central Theme Building and passenger terminals on three sides. On north side are two two-level ticketing buildings and two satellites; on south side are four two-level ticketing buildings, four main satellites and a subsidiary satellite. Ticketing buildings and satellites are connected by underground channels (two having moving pavements) and the south

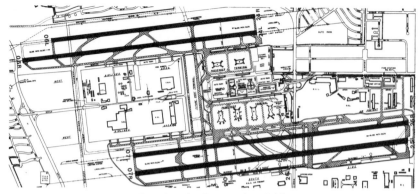

Los Angeles International Airport.

main satellites are interconnected. Commuter and air taxi operators have two terminals at the west of terminal area. Terminals are linked by a tram service. Charter flights operate from the West Imperial Terminal on the southern airport boundary close to the general aviation runway. There are 82 boarding gates. There is a 98 acre (40 hectare) cargo terminal area at the eastern end of the airport with American Airlines, Flying Tiger, TWA and United Airlines cargo terminals, an Emery Air Freight terminal and a postal centre. Airport-owned terminals serve other airlines. On the south of the airport are cargo terminals serving Airlift International, China Airlines, Japan Air Lines and Pan American

Scheduled services 1978: 40 airlines
Airline bases: American, Golden West, Pan American, TWA and United
Main base: Continental, Flying Tiger and Western

Traffic:	1970	1975	1976	1977	1978
Passengers (total)	20,780,718	23,719,028	25,983,079	28,362,485	32,900,664
Cargo (tonnes)	362,618	644,467	698,988	642,522	719,840
Aircraft movements	543,869	453,596	482,587	500,976	538,987
Transport movements	467,367	340,090	356,536	360,516	462,718

Los Angeles International Airport has a very long history, but strangely did not become an airline terminal until December 1946, when it had already, under other names, been a flying ground for more than two decades. Up to 1946 the airlines had operated from several airports, the most important being Grand Central Air Terminal at Glendale and United Airport at Burbank which later became Lockheed Air Terminal.

In a way the origin of the present airport goes back to 1894 when Andrew B. Bennett leased about 2,000 acres (809 hectares) of land near the Pacific coast and planted it with wheat, barley and beans; later, he expanded his leasehold to about 3,000 acres (1,214 hectares). In the early 1920s William M. Mines, a Canadian, leased a small section of the Bennett Rancho as a landing ground and it became known as Mines Field. The City of Los Angeles, in 1926, considered establishing a municipal airport and chose the Mines Field site which simply had an unpaved east–west landing strip, although, in September 1928, somehow the National Air Races were staged there before about 200,000 people. In October 1928 the City leased

464

640 acres (259 hectares) for 50 years at $124,800 a year and began construction on the south side of two hangars. The landing strip was extended to 2,000 ft (610 m) and given an oiled surface. Less than a year later, in August 1929, the *Graf Zeppelin* landed at Mines Field on its round-the-world flight and nearly came to grief on power lines when it left.

On 7 June, 1930, Los Angeles Municipal Airport was officially opened, and it had a hangar and administration building in Spanish style. In 1932 Douglas Aircraft moved some of its operations to the airport and in 1936 North American Aviation opened its 90,000 sq ft (8,361 sq m) factory in what was then the southeast corner of the airport.

The City of Los Angeles purchased the airport in October 1937 for $2,240,000 and extensive improvements began in 1938 under the Works Progress Administration. The initial layout and lighting was completed in January 1941, with east–west, north–south, northwest–southeast and northeast–southwest runways, and Los Angeles Airport became the official title.

In 1943 the first master plan was published. This projected an airport with 4,600 ft (1,402 m) runways and indicated future expansion. A second east–west runway, 07L/25R, was built, the original runway (redesignated 07R/25L) was extended westward to 6,000 ft (1,829 m), and 16/34 (now a taxiway) was extended to 6,753 ft (2,058 m).

View to the northwest across Los Angeles International Airport in 1976, with the 07/25 runways in the foreground, the cargo area to the right of the 25R threshold, the passenger terminal area in the centre and the 06/24 runways in the distance.
(*Los Angeles Department of Airports*)

On 1 May, 1945, a \$12½ mn bond issue was approved for purchase of 1,860 acres (753 hectares) to the west for the extension of the east–west runways to 8,000 ft (2,438 m) and for construction of a temporary terminal. The runway extension was completed by May 1953 and the terminal was built north of the 25 thresholds in what is now the cargo terminal area.

When the airport was originally developed Sepulveda Boulevard formed the western boundary and a loop road had to be built before the main east–west runway could be extended to 6,000 ft (1,829 m), and to extend the pair of 07/25 runways to 8,000 ft (2,438 m) it was necessary to sink Sepulveda Boulevard so that it would pass beneath the runway extensions. The tunnel was opened on 21 April, 1953, and by that May both runways had been extended. Runway 07L/25R was extended to 10,000 ft (3,048 m) in 1959 and later to its present 12,090 ft (3,685 m), and 07R/25L was extended to its present length in August 1960.

In June 1956 a \$59.7 mn bond issue was approved for developments to prepare the airport for the introduction of jet transports. Ground was broken in 1957 for a new terminal area to the west, the 07/25 runways were lengthened, as already mentioned, and two 06/24 runways were built on the north of the airport, 06R/24L of 8,975 ft (2,736 m) being opened in September 1959 and 06L/24R of 8,925 ft (2,720 m) in June 1970 when the ILS was moved from 24L to 24R to give greater separation from that on 25L.

The first 'jet age terminal' was dedicated by Vice President Lyndon Johnson in June 1961 and commissioned in mid-August, a new 172 ft (52 m) high control tower was commissioned in October that year, the international carriers terminal was opened on 1 June, 1962, and Satellite 6 was ready in November 1963 to complete the new terminal complex as then planned. The first unit in the 'Cargo City', on the site of the previous terminal immediately south of Century Boulevard, was completed in February 1964, and a commuter terminal at the west end of the terminal area was opened on 24 August, 1970.

In October 1976 Los Angeles International Airport became the first air carrier airport in the United States to install the Minimum Safe Altitude Warning (MSAW) altitude monitoring system.

At the end of 1978 the airport commissioners approved \$535 mn for expansion to provide capacity for 40 mn passengers a year and this programme includes two new terminals at the west of the present terminal area, one international and one for National Airlines and Pacific Southwest Airlines. There is provision for a future west terminal, runway 06L/24R extension to 10,285 ft (3,135 m) and taxiway extensions including a west link between the north and south pairs.

Three inflatable structures, to serve as temporary customs and baggage claim areas, were due to be ready for use by July 1979. They were designed to handle more than 1,500 passengers an hour.

The airport took its present name on 11 October, 1949.

Standiford Field, Louisville, with the terminal in the foreground.
(*Louisville and Jefferson County Air Board*)

Louisville, Kentucky   Standiford Field

38° 10′ 42″ N   85° 44′ 14″ W   5 nm (9.26 km) S of city
ICAO: KSDF   IATA code: SDF   Time zone: GMT −5
Authority: Louisville and Jefferson County Air Board
Area: 465 hectares (1,150 acres)
Elevation: 497 ft (151 m)   Ref temp: 31.6 deg C
Runways: 01/19   2,377 × 46 m (7,800 × 150 ft) concrete wire-combed*
06/24   1,524 × 46 m (5,000 × 150 ft) concrete wire-combed
11/29   2,210 × 46 m (7,250 × 150 ft) concrete wire-combed
Pavement strength: 82,000 lb (37,195 kg) 1, 170,000 lb (77,111 kg) 2, 360,000 lb (163,293 kg) 3.
Landing category: ICAO CAT I†
Lighting:
R/W   01/19   HIRL and centreline. TDZ 01/19
06/24   MIRL
11/29   HIRL
App   R/W 01   ALSF
R/W 11 and 19   VASIS
R/W 29   MALSR
Thr   green
Txy   blue edge
Aids: VORTAC, VDF, RAD, RVR 01, RVV 29, ILS CAT I 01, 19 and 29†
Twr frequency: 120.3   App frequency: 123.7
Terminals: Lee Terminal handles air carrier traffic with three piers and 26 gates. Eight aerobridges handle more than 60 per cent of scheduled traffic. Separate Falls City Terminal for general aviation, and a cargo terminal

*Arrester gear on runway 01/19
†Runway 01 was due to be cleared for CAT II in the winter 1978–79

467

Scheduled services 1978: Air Kentucky, Allegheny, American, Delta, Eastern, Ozark, Piedmont and TWA. There is also the Kentucky Air National Guard base

Traffic:	1970	1975	1976	1977	1978
Passengers (total)	1,795,453	1,693,732	1,822,611	1,931,618	2,163,951
Cargo (tonnes)	15,725	10,148	12,464	11,563	11,043
Aircraft movements	144,245	117,847	118,600	—	132,189
Transport movements	80,718	54,476	55,534	—	59,405

During the 1920s Louisville established a municipal airport which was also used as a US Army Air Corps aerodrome and took the name Bowman Field. A $30,000 administration building was opened in 1929, together with new hangars and parking space for 3,000 cars.

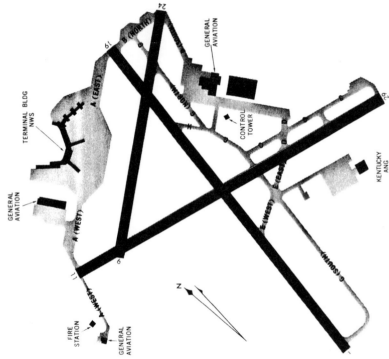

Standiford Field, Louisville. (*FAA*)

A survey of the Louisville area in 1937 undertaken during a period of extensive flooding disclosed that a large area south of the city had not been inundated and this site was chosen for a new aerodrome. In 1941 two runways, 01/19 and 11/29, were constructed, and in 1942 Standiford Field* was opened as a military aerodrome.

*The airport is named after Dr Elisha David Standiford (1831–87) whose family owned much of the land on which the airport was built. Dr Standiford, a Congressman from Louisville, had taken a great interest in transport and been connected with railways, roads, bridges and canals.

In 1947 a temporary terminal was built on the east side of the site and airline operations were transferred from Bowman Field to Standiford Field. The temporary terminal served until May 1950 when the permanent Lee Terminal was opened at the northwest of the airport.

In 1970 the main concourse was extended and the west wing (used by Allegheny Airlines) was created, and in the following year the Delta concourse and new FAA control tower were completed and radar installed. Runway 01/19 is to be extended to 9,600 ft (2,926 m).

In 1969 the Louisville and Jefferson County Air Board outlined plans for a new intercontinental airport in the Ohio valley, about 20–25 miles (32–40 km) from the city, because it was considered that Standiford Field could not be expanded to handle the 5 mn passengers forecast for 1975. The new airport, costing $250–300 mn, was not in fact built but was to have had a staggered pair of parallel runways, the longest of 15,000 ft (4,572 m), and one crosswind runway. There would have been a central spine road straddled by two square four-storey buildings each connected to a pair of 600 ft (183 m) diameter two-level circular terminals. Provision was made in the plan for two more sets of terminals and the airport was to have occupied about 15,000 acres (6,070 hectares) and been completed in 1976.

The old Bowman Field is still used for general aviation and in 1977 handled 222,645 aircraft movements.

Memphis, Tennessee   Memphis International Airport

35° 02′ 59″ N   89° 58′ 44″ W   3.47 nm (6.42 km) S of city
ICAO: KMEM   IATA code: MEM   Time zone: GMT −6
Authority: Memphis-Shelby County Airport Authority
Area: 1,355 hectares (3,350 acres)
Elevation: 332 ft (101 m)   Ref temp: 16.4 deg C

Runways:		
03/21	1,822 × 46 m (5,977 × 150 ft) asphalt	
09/27	2,721 × 46 m (8,926 × 150 ft) asphalt	
14/32	1,138 × 46 m (3,735 × 150 ft) asphalt	
17L/35R	2,560 × 46 m (8,400 × 150 ft) wire-combed concrete	
17R/35L	2,932 × 46 m (9,319 × 150 ft) wire-combed concrete	

Pavement strength: 17L/35R   100,000 lb (45,360 kg) 1, 190,000 lb (86,182 kg) 2, 337,000 lb (152,860 kg) 3; 17R/35L   100,000 lb (45,360 kg) 1, 173,000 lb (78,471 kg) 2, 338,000 lb (153,314 kg) 3.
Landing category: ICAO CAT II
Lighting:

R/W	03/21	MIRL
	09/27	HIRL
	17L/35R and 17R/35L	HIRL and centreline. TDZ 35L and 35R
App	R/W 09, 17L/35R and 17R	MALSR
	R/W 27	VASIS
	R/W 35L	ALSF-2

469

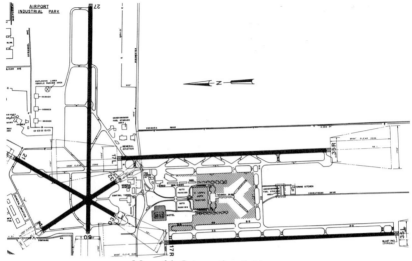

Memphis International Airport.

Thr green
Txy blue edge—possibly some centreline
Aids: VORTAC, NDB, ASR, RVR 09, 17L/35R and 35L, ILS CAT II 35L,
 ILS CAT I 09, 17L/35R and 17R
Twr frequency: 118.3   App frequency: 119.1
Terminals: Passenger terminal comprising centre, east and west units and
 five traffic piers with a total of 54 boarding gates. General aviation and
 cargo terminals
Scheduled services 1978: 10 scheduled, one commuter and one priority
 cargo airline
Airline base: Southern Airways
Main base: Federal Express. The Tennessee Air National Guard also has a
 base

Traffic:	1970	1975	1976	1978
Passengers (total)	3,333,884	4,370,181	4,833,376	5,737,916
Cargo (tonnes)	38,188	29,424	33,092	31,191
Aircraft movements	292,496	288,331	310,259	349,298
Transport movements	104,446	104,672	112,126	181,606

Memphis International Airport began as the Memphis Municipal
Airport in 1929, when it was a 200 acre (81 hectare) field, handling four
flights a day by American Airways' Ford Trimotors. The landing area
deteriorated in bad weather and in the early 1930s the airlines suspended
services through Memphis until the airport had been improved.

The first permanent terminal, a modest three-storey building
surmounted by a control tower, was built in 1938 by the Works Progress
Administration and today is the general aviation terminal.

Three asphalt runways were laid, southwest–northeast (03/21),
east–west (09/27) and northwest–southeast (14/32). During the war the
airport was an air force base, it was expanded to more than 3,000 acres
(1,214 hectares) and runway 09/27 was lengthened to 8,900 ft (2,713 m).

During the 1950s priority was given to a master plan for the airport's development. Construction of a completely new terminal, to the south of the earlier terminal area, was undertaken and a new control tower built. The control tower was completed in 1961 and the terminal was ready in 1963 at which time the airport was renamed Memphis Metropolitan Airport. A north–south runway, 17/35, was constructed to the south of the original runways.

In 1969 the airport was opened to international traffic and the present name adopted. With traffic developing rapidly it was decided to undertake a major expansion of the terminal facilities. A parallel 17/35 runway was opened late in 1972 and runway 35L was cleared for CAT II operation in May 1974.

The ground was broken for terminal expansion late in 1970 and a $36 mn programme was begun to increase the number of gates from 22 to 54. This entailed the building of two sub-terminals and connecting concourses and extensions to the southeast and southwest concourses. This expansion, plus an international arrivals facility, was completed in 1976 and a new 187 ft (57 m) high control tower was commissioned in 1977.

During the terminal construction a tunnel was made beneath the terminal area and cargo apron to accommodate some form of rapid transit system when required.

The dual north–south runways were designed for jet operations and should meet the airport's needs during the 1980s.

The terminal now consists of centre, east and west buildings with east and west concourses (each with 10 gates) and a Y pier with southwest and southeast concourses (each with 13 gates), and the link between these last two and the centre terminal has eight gates.

The impressive terminal at Memphis International Airport.
(*Jim Hilliard, courtesy Memphis-Shelby County Airport Authority*)

View west over the terminal area at Miami International Airport in the summer of 1977. Runways 09R/27L and 09L/27R are on the left and right respectively and 12/30 can be seen beyond the terminal area.
(*Miami-Metropolitan Department of Publicity and Tourism*)

Miami, Florida Miami International Airport

25° 47′ 39″ N 80° 17′ 16″ W 7.8 nm (14.48 km) NW of city
ICAO: KMIA IATA code: MIA Time zone: GMT −5
Authority: Metropolitan Dade County Aviation Department
Area: 1,306 hectares (3,228 acres)
Elevation: 10 ft (3 m) Ref temp: 32.2 deg C
Runways: 09L/27R 3,201 × 61 m (10,502 × 200 ft*) asphalt, grooved
         09R/27L 2,850 × 46 m (9,350 × 150 ft) asphalt, grooved
         12/30 2,926 × 46 m (9,601 × 150 ft) asphalt

* Marked to 150 ft (46 m)

Pavement strength: 09/27 runways 130,000 lb (58,967 kg) 1, 170,000 lb
    (77,111 kg) 2, 350,000 lb (158,757 kg) 3; 12/30 100,000 lb
    (45,359 kg) 1, 200,000 lb (90,718 kg) 2, 350,000 lb
    (158,757 kg) 3
Landing category: ICAO CAT I
Lighting:
    R/W HIRL all runways
    App R/W 09L ALSF-1
         R/W 09R MALSR and VASIS
         R/W 12 VASIS
         R/W 27L ALSF-1
         R/W 27R MALSR and VASIS
         R/W 30 REIL and VASIS
    Thr green
    Txy blue edge and on high-speed exits except from R/W 12
Aids: VORTAC, NDB, VDF, ASR, SRE, RVR 09L and 27L, ILS CAT I
    09L and 27L
Twr frequency: 118.3/123.9 App frequency: 120.5/126.85

472

Terminals: Passenger terminal with seven traffic piers and 90 gates. International satellite terminal with 12 gates. Most gates have upper level loading aerobridges. Separate west side cargo area and Delta and Northwest cargo areas.

Scheduled services 1978: 51 airlines

Airline bases: Braniff, Delta, Eastern, Northwest and Pan American

Main base: Air Florida, Airlift International, National Airlines and Southern Air Transport

Traffic:	1970	1975	1976	1977	1978
Passengers (total)	10,660,815	11,905,949	12,598,002	13,736,483	16,500,738
Cargo (tonnes)	233,070	372,726	355,545	493,993	499,496
Aircraft movements	370,327	287,565	291,634	—	355,086
Transport movements	253,813	211,430	210,594	255,363	253,243

In 1928 Pan American Field was opened to the northwest of Miami, on what is now the northeast corner of Miami International Airport. The Pan American Airways' airport, also known as 36th Street Airport, covered 230 acres (93 hectares) and was bounded on the north by 36th Street and on the east by Le Jeune Road. The site allowed room for expansion to the west but on the south was severely restricted by the tracks of the Seaboard Air Line Railroad and its marshalling yards.

A pattern of four runways was developed with one aligned east–west, one northeast–southwest and two approximately northwest–southeast. The east–west, 09/27, was eventually extended to 7,000 ft (2,134 m) and remained in use until the late 1940s or early 1950s, but the others were abandoned.

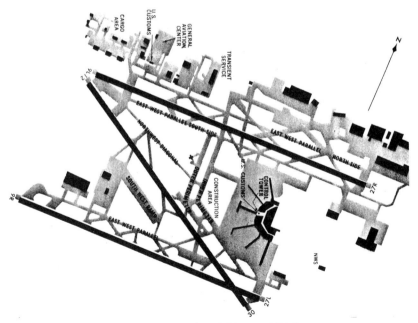

Miami International Airport. (*FAA*)

473

A second airport, known as 20th Street Airport, was established south of the railway in what is now the centre of the airport; and a 7,000 ft (2,134 m) 17/35 runway and parallel taxiway was built across the railway. This runway was later reduced to 6,081 ft (1,853 m) and then abandoned to allow for central area terminal development. On the southern part of the airport a 12/30 runway and a second 09/27 were built, both 7,000 ft (2,134 m) long. During the war a large Air Depot was established at the southwest corner of the airport to handle the large volume of military cargo.

On 1 January, 1946, the Dade County Port Authority took over the Pan American Airport as the first stage in the development of Miami International Airport, as it was named that day. By 1 January, 1948, the Authority had secured a deed to 20th Street Airport from the War Assets Administration and three months later took over the Air Depot. There were then four terminals—the International Terminal, Pan American Terminal and Eastern Air Lines Terminal, all in the northern 36th Street area, and the 20th Street Terminal which was used for non-scheduled traffic and general aviation.

Negotiations with Seaboard Air Line Railroad, now Seaboard Coast Line, led to the closing of the marshalling yards and diversion of the railway to the south of the airport. This allowed construction of a new 09/27 runway south of the original 09/27, built to a length of 9,400 ft (2,865 m) as 09L/27R. The southern, 09R/27L, was extended westward to 8,400 ft (2,560 m) and 12/30 was extended northwest to provide 8,404 ft (2,561 m). Subsequently 09L/27R was lengthened to 10,502 ft (3,201 m), 09R/27L to 9,350 ft (2,850 m) and 12/30 to 9,601 ft (2,926 m). These extensions were completed by 1959.

This major expansion had begun in 1950 with the purchase of additional land and demolition of buildings, by 1952 the airport area covered 2,878 acres (1,165 hectares), and in 1955 plans were begun for a major passenger terminal complex in the centre of the airport.

By 1959 a large central terminal, with six piers, had been opened in the central area. The advent of the wide-bodied aircraft made necessary the addition of a third storey on several of the concourses and this was completed in 1971. Then followed plans for further traffic piers and a satellite building to handle international flights. The International Satellite Terminal was built about a quarter of a mile (400 m) west of the main terminal, brought into partial operation by the end of 1976 and scheduled to be linked to the main terminal by an elevated automated shuttle by 1979. The International Satellite, known as Concourse E, has 12 gates all equipped with aerobridges. By 1978 the main terminal had seven concourses and more are planned.

There is a very large cargo terminal area on the west of the airport, Delta Air Lines and National Airlines have their own cargo terminals, and Braniff, Delta, Eastern, Northwest, National and Pan American all have large maintenance bases.

Future development plans include further terminal expansion, a tunnel to link the west cargo terminal with the central terminal area, and a westward extension of runway 09R/27L by 3,000 ft (914 m). The runway extension involves acquisition of more land and the diverting of a road and the Florida East Coast and Seaboard Coast Line railway tracks.

Milwaukee, Wisconsin   General Mitchell Field

42° 56′ 51″ N   87° 53′ 47″ W   6 nm (11 km) S of city
ICAO: KMKE   IATA code: MKE   Time zone: GMT −6
Authority: Milwaukee County
Area: 850 hectares (2,100 acres)
Elevation: 724 ft (221 m)   Ref temp: 27 deg C
Runways: 01L/19R   3,022 × 61 m (9,916 × 200 ft) concrete
          01R/19L   1,275 × 46 m (4,182 × 150 ft) concrete
          07L/25R   1,280 × 30 m (4,201 × 100 ft) asphalt
          07R/25L   2,442 × 46 m (8,011 × 150 ft) concrete
          13/31   1,789 × 46 m (5,868 × 150 ft) asphalt/concrete
Pavement strength: 01L/19R and 01R/19L auw 100,000 lb (45,359 kg) 1, 150,000 lb (68,039 kg) 2, 255,000 lb (115,666 kg) 3; 07L/25R auw 40,000 lb (18,144 kg) 1, 55,000 lb (24,948 kg) 2, 80,000 lb (36,287 kg) 3; 07R/25L auw 100,000 lb (45,359 kg) 1, 125,000 lb (56,699 kg) 2, 210,000 lb (95,254 kg) 3; 13/31 auw 50,000 lb (22,680 kg) 1, 60,000 lb (27,216 kg) 2, 90,000 lb (40,823 kg) 3.
Landing category: ICAO CAT II
Lighting:
R/W   01L/19R   LIH white edge and centreline. TDZ 01L
         07R/25L   LIH white edge. REIL 25L
         01R/19L, 07L/25R and 13/31   LIM white edge
App   R/W 01L   ALSF-2
         R/W 07R   ALSF-1
         R/W 19R   MALSR
         VASIS 13/31 and 25L
Thr   green
Txy   blue
Aids: VORTAC, NDB, RVR, ILS CAT II 01L, ILS CAT I 07R and 19R
Twr frequency: 119.1   App frequency: 123.8/126.5
Terminal: Passenger terminal with three traffic piers and 24 gates with aerobridges at some positions. There are separate general aviation facilities. Wisconsin Air National Guard has a base on the east side of the airport and there is a USAF Reserve Training Center in the southwest corner.
Scheduled services 1978: Eastern, Midstate Airlines, North Central, Northwest, Ozark and United

Traffic:	1970	1975	1976	1978
Passengers (total)	1,766,802	2,241,745	2,556,720	2,991,750
Cargo (tonnes)	28,995	24,493	24,565	41,235
Aircraft movements	226,150	210,081	229,184	247,041
Transport movements	73,817	75,121	76,914	92,130

During 1976 Douglas DC-9s accounted for 42 per cent of transport movements, Boeing 727s for 24 per cent and Convair CV-580s for 20 per cent.

In the spring of 1919 Alfred W. Lawson formed a company at Milwaukee to build the Lawson airliner and he needed an aerodrome from which to fly it. To meet this requirement the City and County allowed use of the west part of what is now James Currie Park, to the northwest of the city. The Currie Park aerodrome was ready by August 1919, as one of the first municipal airports in the United States, and on 7 June, 1926, it became an intermediate stop when Charles Dickenson began flying CAM9 from Chicago to Minneapolis - St Paul with Laird biplanes. That August Northwest Airways took over the mail operation but found the aerodrome inadequate.

If Milwaukee was to continue to have air services a new airport was urgently required, and on 11 August, 1926, the Milwaukee County Board adopted the recommendation of the County Highway Commission that all available funds should be spent on purchase of a suitable site. In 1920 Thomas F. Hamilton had purchased 56 acres (22.6 hectares) of land on East Layton Avenue, south of the city, to form a T-shaped aerodrome. He erected a small hangar and extended the area to 163 acres (66 hectares). This site was chosen for the new airport and on 5 October, 1926, the County Park Commission was directed to purchase Hamilton Field for $150,000. The name was changed to Milwaukee County Airport on 7 January, 1927.

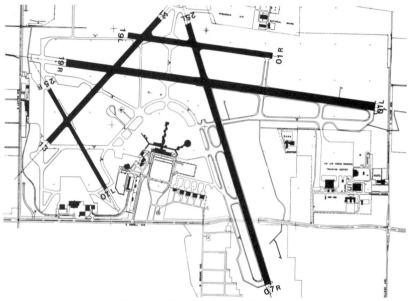

General Mitchell Field, Milwaukee.

The season was too far advanced for much work to be done on the airport in that first winter but Northwest Airways managed to keep the mail service going although pilots experienced some difficulty. Northwest Airways began passenger services over the Chicago–Milwaukee–Minneapolis - St Paul route on 5 July, 1927, with Stinson SB-1 Detroiter biplanes which were fitted with skis during winter. The first terminal was in the west wing of the hangar on the north side of the airport and later a nearby farmhouse was converted to form a terminal.

From 1928, apart from serving the airlines, Milwaukee County Airport was the site for the assembly and testing of Hamilton Metalplanes of which Northwest Airways operated nine.

Close by, another aerodrome, De Young Field, was opened on farmland beside South Howell Avenue, to the annoyance of the County Airport management, but was later absorbed by expansion.

By 1929 the airport had two larger hangars and 75 ft (23 m) wide compacted cinder runways—north–south of 2,000 ft (610 m) and northeast–southwest of 1,700 ft (518 m).

Northwest Airways had a new hangar by 1931, and the farmhouse terminal building was given an upper storey to house radio and meteorological equipment. With the growth of traffic and increase in aircraft size a new terminal was required and approval for its construction was given by the Bureau of Air Commerce in May 1938, and it was ready for use on 1 July, 1940, by which time the airport occupied 378 acres (153 hectares). Like the previous facilities, the new terminal was on the northern boundary of the airport.

On 17 March, 1941, after seven months of controversy, the Milwaukee County Board voted to change the airport's name to General Mitchell Field in honour of General William 'Billy' Mitchell who came from Milwaukee.

In 1942 the USAAF leased part of the airport as a training school for Air Transport Command and civil control was not resumed until 5 February, 1948, by which time the area had increased to 649 acres (263 hectares).

In March 1945 a master plan for postwar development was submitted to the County Board, recommending further expansion and construction of a completely new terminal complex in a central position on the west of the airport. The new terminal with three traffic piers and large apron became operational on 19 June, 1955.

General Mitchell Field, Milwaukee, looking north, with the 01L threshold in the foreground, runway 07R/25L crossing the picture, and the terminal area in the centre. (*Milwaukee County*)

Over the years the original runways were paved and lengthened and new ones built. Today only runways 07L/25R and 13/31 are on the original sites although former runways are now part of the taxiway system. The new runway 01L/19R was extended to 9,916 ft (3,022 m) and in 1958 approval was given to extend 07R/25L to 8,011 ft (2,442 m). This involved acquisition of land to the west of South Howell Avenue and the sinking of the road to pass under the extended runway and its parallel taxiway. The work was completed in December 1964. An odd feature of the airport is the fact that runways 07L/25R and 07R/25L are not parallel—their alignment differs by about 15 degrees.

Jet services began at Milwaukee in July 1961 when Northwest Airlines (successor to Northwest Airways) began operating Boeing 720Bs and in March 1972 the airline began regular operation of Boeing 747s through the airport.

An addition to the airport's facilities was made on 8 December, 1969, with the commissioning of the circular eight-gate South Concourse at the end of the south pier and in September 1975 work began on construction of the 20,101 sq ft (1,867 sq m) area International Arrivals Terminal to cater for overseas charter flights. Further extensions of the main terminal, including enlargement of the north pier, were completed during 1977 and a six-level car park opposite the terminal was finished in 1979.

A new air cargo centre is planned for the area north of runway 07R/25L, west of the South Howell Avenue, and the long-term master plan envisages considerable terminal development, with five piers each terminating in a satellite boarding concourse.

The airport was cleared for CAT II operations in February 1968.

Minneapolis - St Paul, Minnesota
Minneapolis - Saint Paul International Airport (Wold-Chamberlain Field)

44° 53′ 07″ N   93° 13′ 02″ W
  8.7 nm (16 km) SE of Minneapolis, 7.8 nm (14.4 km) SW of St Paul
ICAO: KMSP   IATA code: MSP   Time zone: GMT −6
Authority: Minneapolis - St Paul Metropolitan Airports Authority
Area: 1,214 hectares (3,000 acres)
Elevation: 840 ft (256 m)   Ref temp: 29.4 deg C
Runways: 04R/22L   2,514 × 46 m   (8,250 × 150 ft) concrete, grooved
         11L/29R   2,499 × 46 m   (8,200 × 150 ft) concrete
         11R/29L   3,048 × 61 m (10,000 × 200 ft) concrete, grooved
         There is no 04L/22R but provision has been made for such a
         runway 975 m (3,200 ft) long and 30 m (100 ft) wide.
Pavement strength: variable, but all runways ultimately to take 350,000 lb
    (158,757 kg) auw with single-wheel or dual tandem undercarriages
Landing category: ICAO CAT II
Lighting:
    R/W   04R/22L and 11L/29R   HIRL
             11R/29L   HIRL and centreline. TDZ 29L

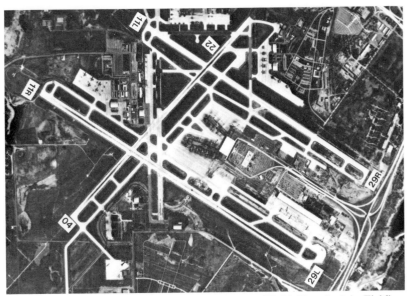

Minneapolis - Saint Paul International Airport (Wold-Chamberlain Field).

App	R/W 04R	ALSF-1
	R/W 11L	VASIS
	R/W 11R	MALSR and REIL
	R/W 22L	REIL
	R/W 29L	ALSF-2
	R/W 29R	ALSF-1 and REIL
Thr	green	
Txy	blue edge, and possibly centreline	

Aids: VORTAC, DME, NDB, RVR, PAR, ARTS III, ILS CAT II 29L, ILS CAT I 04R and 29R

Twr frequency: 118.7   App frequency: 119.3/126.35

Terminals: Main terminal with four loading piers, 39 gates and 39 nose-in aircraft stands, most with aerobridges. International/Charter Terminal with three gates and aircraft stands. Separate cargo buildings

Scheduled services 1978: nine scheduled carriers and four third-level

Main base: North Central Airlines and Northwest Airlines. There are Minnesota Air National Guard, US Air Force and US Navy areas

Traffic:	1970	1975	1976	1978
Passengers (total)	5,367,210	7,282,652	7,889,409	8,727,195
Cargo (tonnes)*	65,328	77,629	79,937	115,996
Aircraft movements	236,108	239,830	251,874	263,461
Transport movements	111,714	126,732	131,504	137,458

*Includes Air Express

Minneapolis - Saint Paul International Airport is situated immediately west of the confluence of the Mississippi and Minnesota rivers and on the site of Fort Snelling, the first US outpost in the upper Mississippi valley.

479

The 2,500 acre (1,012 hectare) Fort Snelling State Park to the east and 500 acre (202 hectare) Fort Snelling Cemetery to the south both contribute to safeguarding the airport's approaches.

The airport owes its position to the construction, in 1915, of a $2\frac{1}{2}$ mile (4 km) long motor racing track. Only one race was ever held there, but in 1920, when the Aero Club of Minneapolis was formed, the land within the track was leased as an aerodrome, providing a grass strip of about 2,000 ft (610 m) in length. A hangar was built there for the Chicago–La Crosse–Minneapolis US Post Office mail service which began on 1 December, 1920, but ceased on 30 June, 1921.

In 1923 the aerodrome was dedicated as Twin City Airport, Wold Chamberlain Field—the secondary title honouring Ernest Groves Wold and Cyrus Foss Chamberlain, both having been pilots killed in France in 1918.

On 7 June, 1926, Charles Dickenson began operating CAM9—the Chicago–Minneapolis mail route–with a Laird biplane, but he was unable to sustain the operation; on 1 October the mail service was reinstated by Northwest Airways, using borrowed aircraft until the delivery of its own Stinson SB-1 Detroiter biplanes, and occupying the Aero Club hangar.

The Minneapolis Park Board took over the airport in 1928 and renamed it Minneapolis Municipal Airport which by that time covered 325 acres (132 hectares) and had eight hangars. From the next year a Park Board warming house served as the terminal but a permanent administration and terminal building was dedicated on 19 September, 1930, and in 1931 another 100 acres (40 hectares) was added to the site. Three 3,000 ft (914 m) concrete runways were laid in 1936 under the Works Progress Administration and in 1938 a control tower was commissioned, with radio coming into use on 5 November, 1939.

The airport was given its present title on 23 August, 1948, and there has been continuous development to keep pace with increasing traffic. In 1948 the airport handled 555,307 passengers, the one million mark was passed in 1953, 2 mn in 1962, 3 mn in 1965, 4 mn in 1967, 5 mn in 1968, 6 mn in 1972, and 7 mn in 1974.

The present terminal was opened on 20 January, 1962, at a cost of $8.5 mn and having a floor area of 600,000 sq ft (55,740 sq m). Expansion was planned in 1970 to provide four piers with aerobridge boarding, and further gate improvements took place in 1977. The four piers are identified by letters and colours–Pier A (Gold Concourse) has seven gates used by NWA; Pier B (Red Concourse) has 15 gates used by NWA and North Central; Pier C (Blue Concourse) has 12 gates shared between Braniff, Ozark, United and Western; and Pier D (Green Concourse) has five gates for Allegheny, Eastern, Ozark and the commuter airlines.

The life of the main terminal was extended by the opening of the 50,000 sq ft (4,645 sq m) International/Charter Terminal, southwest of the main terminal and close to the 04R threshold. This building was designed in 1968 for overnight maintenance of United Air Lines Boeing 727s and Douglas DC-8s. When built it was the largest steel and concrete structure of its type. The building was purchased from United in the summer of 1975 and remodelled to provide three gates for international and charter flights. Shuttle buses connect the two terminal areas via a tunnel beneath runway 11R/29L.

Nashville, Tennessee   Nashville Metropolitan Airport

36° 07′ 36″ N   86° 40′ 55″ W   5.2 nm (9.63 km) SE of city
ICAO: KBNA   IATA code: BNA   Time zone: GMT −6
Authority: Nashville Metropolitan Airport Authority
Area: 1,335 hectares (3,300 acres)
Elevation: 597 ft (182 m)   Ref temp: 21.6 deg C
Runways: 02L/20R   2,347 × 46 m (7,700 × 150 ft) asphalt/concrete*
       02R/20L   1,317 × 46 m (4,320 × 150 ft) asphalt/concrete
       13/31   2,438 × 46 m (8,000 × 150 ft) asphalt/concrete

* Partly grooved

Pavement strength: 02L/20R   100,000 lb (45,359 kg) 1, 175,000 lb
    (79,379 kg) 2, 360,000 lb (163,293 kg) 3; 02R/20L   60,000 lb
    (27,216 kg) 1, 84,000 lb (38,102 kg) 2, 128,000 lb (58,060 kg) 3;
    13/31   50,000 lb (22,680 kg) 1, 77,000 lb (34,927 kg) 2, 125,000 lb
    (56,699 kg) 3.
Landing category: ICAO CAT II
Lighting:
    R/W   02L/20R   HIRL and centreline. TDZ 02L
              02R/20L and 13/31   MIRL
    App   R/W 02L   ALSF-1 and REIL
              R/W 20R   REIL and VASIS
              R/W 02R/20L   VASIS
              R/W 13   US Configuration B*, REIL and VASIS
              R/W 31   MALSR
    Thr   02L and 02R/20L green, 13/31 and 20R green with strobes
    Txy   blue edge and green centreline

* US Configuration B comprises a 2,000 ft (610 m) red bar centreline with crossbar 1,000 ft (305 m) from the threshold. Between the crossbar and the threshold are red bars from the left end of the crossbar and a single line of red lights from the right end. The threshold has green wing bars.

Terminal building at Nashville Metropolitan Airport. (*Roland C. Wolfe Jr*)

Aids: VORTAC, NDB, VDF, ASR, RVR 02L, ILS CAT II 02L, ILS CAT I 31

Twr frequency: 119.1 App frequency: 120.6/124.0

Terminals: Two-winged terminal with two aprons and 17 gates. Separate cargo building and apron

Scheduled services 1978: Air Bama, Air Kentucky, Allegheny, American, Braniff, Comair, Delta, Eastern, Ozark, Piedmont, Southern and Tennessee Airways

Traffic:	1970	1976	1977	1978
Passengers (total)	1,330,882	1,827,681	1,991,362	2,346,266
Cargo (tonnes)	17,742	16,194	17,481	27,397
Aircraft movements	182,511	214,852	217,834	227,359
Transport movements	60,282	57,426	59,022	84,173

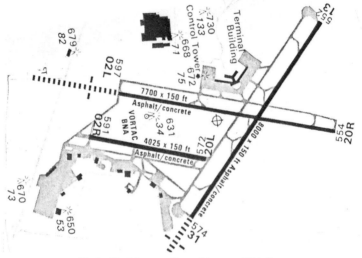

Nashville Metropolitan Airport. (*FAA*)

Nashville Metropolitan Airport serves middle Tennessee and parts of southern Kentucky and northern Alabama. It began as a 345 acre (140 hectare) aerodrome known as Berry Field* and was opened on 13 June, 1937, on what is now the southern part of the airport, now used by general aviation and the Tennessee Air National Guard.

In the summer of 1958 a major construction programme began, to provide a new terminal area to the north of the original site and this was opened in the summer of 1961 at which time the name was changed to Nashville Airport and American Airlines began serving Nashville with Boeing 707s.

The terminal, comprising a central lobby and two concourse wings, is connected to a smaller building of similar layout containing the ticketing and baggage claim areas. Originally there was an enclosed space of 149,000 sq ft (13,842 sq m) and parking space for 1,352 cars.

*Named in honour of the construction project overseer.

482

In 1973 a master plan was approved to cover development of the airport up to 1990. The first stage involved expansion and improvement of the existing terminal to provide capacity for 1.8 mn embarking passengers. Work was completed in the spring of 1977 and this added 31,152 sq ft (2,894 sq m) and 1,000 car parking spaces. In 1975 five aerobridges were ordered and there will ultimately be 12.

The second phase will provide a completely new terminal complex to handle the forecast 8 mn annual passengers by the mid-1990s. The new terminal will be located east of the intersection of runways 02L/20R and 13/31 and is due for completion in the mid-1980s. Aircraft movements are expected to reach 360,000 a year by the mid-1990s and 950 acres (384 hectares) of land is being acquired to the east of the airport to provide a new 02/20 runway of 11,000 ft (3,353 m) with dual parallel taxiways and high-speed exits. This runway is expected to come into operation in 1990.

New Orleans, Louisiana
New Orleans International Airport (Moisant Field)

29° 59′ 31″ N	90° 15′ 17″ W	10.4 nm (19.3 km) W of city
ICAO: KMSY	IATA code: MSY	Time zone: GMT −6

Authority: City of New Orleans Aviation Board
Area: 607 hectares (1,500 acres)
Elevation: 4 ft (1 m)   Ref temp: 32.6 deg C
Runways: 01/19   2,134 × 46 m (7,000 × 150 ft)* asphalt
         05/23   1,384 × 46 m (4,542 × 150 ft)** concrete
         10/28   2,812 × 46 m (9,227 × 150 ft)* concrete and asphalt

*Displaced thresholds reduce 01/19 to 5,810 ft (1,771 m) and 10/28 to 7,930 ft (2,417 m)
**05/23 is closed at night and will be phased out and used as a taxiway

New Orleans International Airport with the terminal in the foreground and Lake Pontchartrain in the distance. (*City of New Orleans Aviation Board*)

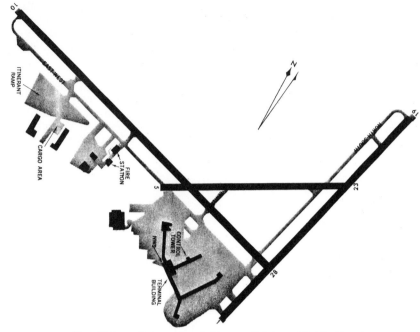

New Orleans International Airport (Moisant Field). (*FAA*)

Pavement strength: 75,000 lb (34,019 kg) single wheel all runways; dual
wheels 110,000 lb (49,895 kg) 01/19 and 10/28 and 100,000 lb (45,359
kg) 05/23; dual tandem 180,000 lb (81,647 kg) 01/19 and 10/28 and
150,000 lb (68,039 kg) 05/23
Landing category: ICAO CAT II
Lighting:
R/W	01/19	HIRL
	05/23	MIRL
	10/28	HIRL and centreline. TDZ 10
App	R/W 01	REIL
	R/W 10	ALSF-2
	R/W 19	REIL and VASIS
	R/W 28	VASIS
Thr		01/19 and 10/28 LIH green wing bars, 23 LIM green
Txy		LIM blue edge

Aids: VORTAC, RVR 10/28, ILS CAT II 10, ILS CAT I 01
Twr frequency: 119.5   App frequency: 125.5
Terminal: Passenger terminal with four pier concourses (one international)
with 31 ground-level loading gates and nine at first-floor level and 43
aircraft stands. Separate cargo area
Scheduled services 1978: 15 airlines
Airline bases: Delta Air Lines and Eastern Air Lines
Main base: TACA International

Traffic:	1970	1975	1976	1978
Passengers (total)	3,705,014	4,372,057	4,814,699	6,046,628
Cargo (tonnes)	33,675	38,655	44,702	25,009
Aircraft movements	158,051	96,444*	108,160*	180,904
Transport movements	112,116	95,502	107,416	123,704

*Aircraft movements are believed to be incomplete

New Orleans staged its first international aviation tournament at City Park in December 1910. One of the participants was John B. Moisant with a Blériot monoplane. In the period 16 August–6 September, 1910, Moisant, in a Blériot, had made the first flight from Paris to London with a passenger but on the last day of 1910 Moisant crashed at New Orleans and was killed. Today's New Orleans International Airport honours his name in its subtitle Moisant Field.

The city's prewar municipal airport was Alvin Callendar Field, but in 1929 Southern Air Transport was using Menefee Airport which had four 3,000 ft (914 m) runways and a new administration building.

In the early 1930s work began on Shushan Airport. This was built on 300 acres (121 hectares) reclaimed from Lake Pontchartrain and protected by a retaining wall. The airport, with four runways of 3,600–4,000 ft (1,097–1,219 m) and Spanish Renaissance style terminal was dedicated early in 1933 and opened in February 1934. It is now New Orleans Lakefront Airport.

New Orleans International Airport is situated in the City of Kenner, to the west of New Orleans and between the Mississippi River and Lake Pontchartrain.

The New Orleans Aviation Board began operating the airport in 1946 and the new terminal was dedicated on 11 November, 1959. The name was changed from Moisant Field to its present title on 14 December, 1971.

New York   John F Kennedy International Airport

40° 38′ 25″ N   73° 46′ 41″ W   11.29 nm (20.9 km) SE of Manhattan
ICAO: KJFK   IATA code: JFK   Time zone: GMT −5
Authority: The Port Authority of New York and New Jersey
Area: 1,995 hectares (4,930 acres)
Elevation: 12 ft (4 m)   Ref temp: 29.4 deg C
Runways: 04L/22R   3,460 × 46 m (11,352 × 150 ft) concrete, grooved
04R/22L   2,560 × 46 m (8,400 × 150 ft) concrete, grooved
13L/31R   3,048 × 46 m (10,000 × 150 ft) concrete, grooved
13R/31L   4,441 × 46 m (14,572 × 150 ft) concrete
14/32*   780 × 23 m (2,560 × 75 ft) asphalt/concrete

*General aviation and STOL runway marked on taxiway near the 22 thresholds. Usable day and night by aircraft under 12,500 lb (5,670 kg) auw

Pavement strength: All runways except 14/32 - 100,000 lb (45,359 kg) 1, 185,000 lb (83,915 kg) 2, 340,000 lb (154,221 kg) 3, 550,000 lb (249,476 kg) dual tandem with centreline unit, 778,000 lb (352,895 kg) 4

Landing category: ICAO CAT II
Lighting:
R/W   04L/22R   HIRL and centreline
            04R/22L   HIRL and centreline. TDZ 04R/22L
            13L/31R   HIRL and centreline. TDZ 13L
            13R/31L   HIRL
            14/32   MIRL
App   R/W 04L   REIL
            R/W 04R   ALSF-2
            R/W 13L   ALSF-2, VASIS and LDIN (Lead-in lighting system)
            R/W 13R   VASIS and LDIN
            R/W 22L   ALSF-1
            R/W 22R   VASIS
            R/W 31R   ALSF-1 and REIL
Thr   green
Txy   green centreline, some with blue edge

Aids: VORTAC, ASR, ASDE, RVR 04R/22L, 13R/31L and 31R, RVV 22R, ILS CAT II 04R and 13L, ILS CAT I 04L/22R, 22L, 31L and 31R, LLWSAS

Twr frequency: 119.1   App frequency: 127.4

Terminals: Port Authority International Arrival and Airline Wing Buildings and eight airline terminals. About 145 gates according to size of aircraft. Aerobridges and Plane-Mates in use. Cargo terminal comprises 19 cargo handling and cargo service buildings, three hangar/cargo buildings, animalport and US Post Office mail facility

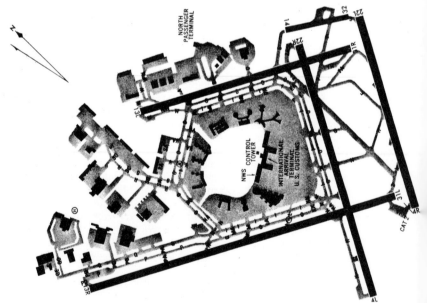

John F Kennedy International Airport, New York. (*FAA*)

486

Scheduled services 1978: 64 airlines
Airline bases: American, Eastern, Flying Tiger, Northwest, TWA and
    United
Main base: Pan American and Seaboard World

Traffic:	1970	1975	1976	1977	1978
Passengers (total)	19,096,705	19,475,761	21,032,973	22,545,497	25,056,039
Cargo (tonnes)	689,048	877,125	933,927	1,080,488	635,585
Aircraft movements	365,848	300,814	305,076	315,584	340,126
Transport movements	320,112	282,558	287,118	294,114	310,244

The original terminal and apron at John F Kennedy International Airport, New
    York, in 1947. (*Port Authority of New York & New Jersey*)

Although New York Municipal Airport - LaGuardia Field had only
opened in 1939, before the end of 1941 the City of New York was planning
a 1,200 acre (486 hectare) cargo airport on the site of Idlewild Beach golf
course adjoining tideland meadows beside Jamaica Bay, in Queens County,
some 15 miles (24 km) from 42nd Street in Manhattan. A contract for the
placing of hydraulic fill was awarded in April 1942. The cargo airport was
not built but the project grew and by 1945 the site had been increased to
4,900 acres (1,983 hectares), and the City, by 1947, spent about $60 mn on
the project.

By 1943 a plan had been produced with four pairs of runways, of
which three were to be of 10,000 ft (3,048 m), two of 8,400 ft (2,560 m), two
of 7,800 ft (2,377 m) and one 6,800 ft (2,073 m). All were to be capable of
taking aircraft weighing 250,000 lb (113,398 kg). To the northwest there
was to be a terminal area reminiscent of LaGuardia's, a very large
maintenance area was planned, and a marine air terminal. The airport built
to this layout was expected to be ready for partial use by the end of 1944.

There were numerous objections to the plan and American Airlines
suggested a tangential runway system with 10,000 ft (3,048 m) and 6,000 ft
(1,829 m) runways, surrounding a central terminal to be served by
underground railway. It was anticipated that there would always be five
take off and five landing runways all more or less into wind.

In 1944 the plan was modified to have a 13/31 pair of 10,000 ft (3,048
m) runways; 07L/25R of 6,500 ft (1,981 m) and 07R/25L of 8,200 ft (2,499
m); 01L/19R of 6,000 ft (1,829 m) and 01R/19L of 7,500 ft (2,286 m), all as
the first stage of a 12-runway tangential layout with central terminal having
a circular building with seven piers. Three runways were expected to be in
use by early 1945.

487

In August 1946 the Port of New York Authority was asked to study the possibility of assuming responsibility for development and operation of the new international airport and took over on 1 June, 1947, under a lease from the City. At that time the six runways had been built—not all to the proposed lengths, and there were a small administration building, two hangars and 70 miles (113 km) of storm sewers.

Considerable attention was given to planning the central terminal area, and by 1953 it had become apparent that a centralized terminal had numerous disadvantages and in 1954 the decision was taken to employ unit terminals. This plan, with some modifications, was adopted on a site which originally had an area of 655 acres (265 hectares).

When the Port Authority took over it expanded the small administrative building from 17,000 sq ft (1,579 sq m) to 40,000 sq ft (3,716 sq m) and provided an additional 12,800 sq ft (1,189 sq m) for Federal inspection services. The airport, named New York International but long known as Idlewild, was opened to commercial flying on 1 July, 1948, and, following test and service flights, on 9 July a Peruvian International Airways DC-4, believed to have been OB-SAF, made the first scheduled arrival. Air France began transatlantic services from the new airport on 14 July and in the following weeks many other carriers transferred their operations from LaGuardia. The airport was officially dedicated on 31 July. In its first full year, 1949, the airport handled 18,115 aircraft movements and 222,620 passengers.

When the airport opened there were six runways but only four were put into operation (01L/19R and 07L/25R were never used). None of the six runways were aligned with the instrument runways at the other New York airports and therefore the Port Authority built the 04/22 instrument runway which came into operation in 1949. Since that time 01R/19L and 07R/25L have been withdrawn, the other runways considerably lengthened, and in 1959 the 8,400 ft (2,560 m) 04R/22L instrument runway was built 3,000 ft (914 m) to the east of the original 04/22. The new runway was opened for visual use in October 1959, and in May 1960 it went into full operation for instrument landings in both directions. In October 1970 04R was cleared for CAT II operations and it has been designated to become CAT III. Runway 13L became CAT II on 18 May, 1978.

Although airports such as Dallas/Fort Worth are now bigger than John F Kennedy International, as it was renamed on 24 December, 1963, the New York International project was a brilliant concept and in September 1961 the *Architectural Record* described it as 'a lexicon of contemporary architecture', 'an encyclopedia of engineering technology' and 'a vast storehouse of information on the philosophy and practice of architecture in our time.'

The central terminal area was a rather odd shape with straight southeast face and varying radius curves for the remainder. Surrounding the area were dual taxiways, the outer to the northwest being the original 07L/25R runway.

The first permanent terminal in what became known as Terminal City was the International Arrival and Airline Wing Buildings sited on the southeast face, erected and owned by the Port Authority and dedicated on 5 December, 1957. The International Arrival Building was a three-storey structure, 640 ft (195 m) deep, with 362,000 sq ft (3,363 sq m) of floor space

The New York International Airport International Arrival and Airline Wing Buildings and control tower in November 1957.
(*Port Authority of New York & New Jersey*)

Terminal City at John F Kennedy International Airport. Clockwise from the top the terminals are the International Arrival and Airline Wing Buildings, Pan American, Northwest/Delta, Eastern, United, American, British Airways/Air Canada, National, and TWA. (*Port Authority of New York & New Jersey*)

and four double-deck arcades providing 1,000 ft (305 m) of enclosed passage leading to 24 aircraft stands. The building was originally used by all arriving flights requiring customs and immigration clearance. The centre part of the land side was dominated by a great curving-roofed concourse and this, together with the adjacent 150 ft (46 m) high control tower, became the symbol of the airport. Joining the International Arrival Building at each end were the Airline Wing Buildings, housing the non-US airlines, and the entire edifice had a length of 2,300 ft (701 m) and total floor area of 592,000 sq ft (54,997 sq m). The cost of the combined facilities was $30 mn.

Later it became necessary to more than double the size of these buildings to provide over a million square feet (92,900 sq m). To achieve this expansion, completed in 1973, the taxiways had to be relocated and the apron vastly increased in size. When finished this work increased the area of Terminal City from 655 acres (265 hectares) to 840 acres (340 hectares).

Domestic services continued to operate from the temporary terminal for many years, airlines transferring their operations to their own terminals as these were completed. The first to be ready for operation were United Air Lines in September 1959 and Eastern Air Lines the next month. United's terminal was a two-storey steel-frame building with glass and aluminium walls, two piers, 11 aircraft stands and 17 aerobridges. Eastern's building was of reinforced concrete with aluminium and glass walls, had a 30,000 sq ft (2,787 sq m) main hall, two piers and 10 stands. American Airlines and Pan American opened their terminals in 1960, TWA and the joint Braniff/Northeast/Northwest terminals opened in 1962 and later National Airlines and joint BOAC/Air Canada buildings completed the nine-terminal complex.

The Pan American and TWA terminals require special mention. Without question the most outstanding building architecturally was the TWA terminal designed by Eero Saarinen and resembling a great bird. On a single level the main building comprised four reinforced concrete intersecting barrel vaults of varying shape, supported from four Y-shaped columns, and with the exterior cased in glass. From the main building a glass-enclosed walkway led to a boarding satellite. Traffic growth and the introduction of Boeing 747s forced additions to the terminal and the construction of the satellite Flight Wing One with six boarding areas—some having four aerobridges. Flight Wing One has a greater area than the original terminal. It was the first private terminal with Federal inspection services.

Pan American World Airways JFK terminal in 1960.
(*Port Authority of New York & New Jersey*)

TWA's JFK terminal in 1971 after the addition of Flight Wing One, on the left.
(*TWA*)

The outstanding feature of the Pan American terminal was its oval cantilevered roof, with 32 prestressed steel girders radiating from a hub of 32 reinforced concrete piers, and surmounting a glass-walled building. The aircraft parked nose-in below the roof overhang. The great disadvantage of the design was that it could not be expanded and retain its original form. In fact, largescale expansion became necessary and an entire new terminal was added to the original, to provide gates for 16 aircraft. Known as Worldport Terminal this was completed in 1971 and made the Pan American building more than six times its original size.

The entire Terminal City was landscaped to form International Park with its Fountain of Liberty, and the airport is probably best seen in late evening light with, in the distance, the silhouettes of the buildings of Manhattan.

John F Kennedy has a cargo centre with more than a score of buildings; 13 aircraft hangars, of the same architectural and engineering diversity as the passenger terminals; parking for more than 13,000 cars; and storage for 32 mn gallons (more than 121 mn litres) of aviation fuel.

New York　　　LaGuardia Airport

40° 46′ 36″ N　　　73° 52′ 24″ W　　　4.34 nm (8 km) E of Manhattan
ICAO: KLGA　　　　IATA code: LGA　　　Time zone: GMT −5
Authority: The Port Authority of New York and New Jersey
Area: 263 hectares (650 acres)
Elevation: 22 ft (7 m)　　　　　　　　　　　　　Ref temp: 28.9 deg C
Runways: 04/22　　2,134 × 46 m (7,000 × 150 ft) asphalt, grooved
　　　　　13/31　　2,134 × 46 m (7,000 × 150 ft) asphalt, grooved
　　　　　14/32*　　610 × 23 m (2,000 × 75 ft)　asphalt

* Runway 14/32 is restricted to daylight VFR operations by general aviation and
STOL aircraft under 12,500 lb (5,670 kg). Take offs are only allowed to the
northwest.

Pavement strength: 80,000 lb (36,287 kg) 1, 170,000 lb (77,110 kg) 2,
　　360,000 lb (163,293 kg) 3
Landing category: ICAO CAT II
Lighting:
　R/W　　04/22　　HIRL and centreline. TDZ 22
　　　　　13/31　　HIRL and centreline
　App　　R/W 04　　ALSF-1
　　　　　R/W 13　　ALSF-1, REIL and VASIS
　　　　　R/W 22　　ALSF-2, REIL and VASIS
　　　　　R/W 31　　REIL and VASIS
　Thr　　green
　Txy　　blue edge and green centreline
Aids: VORTAC, DME, VDF, ASR, RVR 13 and 22, RVV 04, ILS CAT II
　22, ILS CAT I 04 and 13
Twr frequency: 118.7　　　　　　　　　　　App frequency: 118.0
Terminals: Four-storey curved terminal 1,300 ft (396 m) by 125 ft (38 m)
　with 650,000 sq ft (60,385 sq m) of floor space. Two 880 ft (268 m) and
　two 550 ft (168 m) piers with 36 gates. Separate Eastern Air Lines
　shuttle facilities. The old remote-sited Marine Terminal handles
　general aviation and some commuter traffic. Cargo is handled on a
　number of sites.
Scheduled services 1978: 19 airlines
Airline bases: American, Eastern, TWA and United
Main base: New York Airways

Traffic:	1970	1975	1976	1977	1978
Passengers (total)	11,980,954	13,185,753	14,088,797	15,087,530	17,279,908
Cargo (tonnes)	36,120	46,105	45,127	44,394	47,458
Aircraft movements	297,652	299,211	313,253	326,555	374,161
Transport movements	253,098	250,109	263,715	275,469	307,745

　　In 1935 New York's Mayor Fiorello LaGuardia began to look for a
site for a major airport and he chose North Beach, 8 miles (12.8 km) from
42nd Street in Manhattan, in the Borough of Queens and bordering
Flushing Bay and Bowery Bay. The site had been occupied by the Gala
Amusement Park, apparently from 1892, but in 1929 became the privately-
owned Glenn H Curtiss Airport and occupied 105 acres (42 hectares).
There were three graded runways, a few hangars and a seaplane slipway—

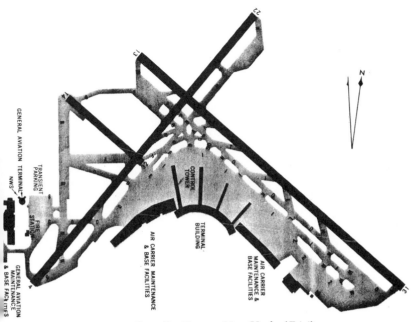

LaGuardia Airport, New York. (*FAA*)

used on one occasion by the Dornier Do X. The name North Beach Airport was later adopted.

The City of New York took a lease on North Beach Airport, with an option to buy, and in August 1937 approval was given to develop the site as the City's municipal airport. On 3 September, 1937, President Roosevelt approved the work as a WPA project and on 9 September Mayor LaGuardia lifted the first shovelfull of earth to start the project. The plan was to increase the size of North Beach Airport to 558 acres (226 hectares) of which 357 acres (144 hectares) had to be man-made.

On nearby Rikers Island there were huge Department of Sanitation dumps, and a trestle bridge was built between the island and the airport over which to carry the cinders, ash and rubbish which was used to fill portions of Flushing Bay and Rikers Island Channel. About 5,000 men worked three shifts a day, six days a week on this job. There was some satisfaction that this work reclaimed land for the airport while removing an eyesore—but the future problems it was to cause were not foreseen. By the early part of 1939 there were 23,000 working on the airport.

New York Municipal Airport was dedicated, with 320,000 people present, on 15 October, 1939, the name was changed to New York Municipal Airport - LaGuardia Field on 2 November, and opened to traffic on 2 December.* There were four asphalt runways: No. 1 (later 13/31) of 6,000 ft (1,829 m), No. 2 (later 04/22) of 5,000 ft (1,524 m), No. 3 (later 09/27) of 4,500 ft (1,372 m), and No. 4 (later 18/36) of 3,532 ft (1,077 m). On the south side was a 6,200 ft (1,890 m) by 400 ft (122 m) curved

* The first commercial service was a TWA DC-3 from Chicago which landed at 00.01.

LaGuardia Airport in 1977. This view clearly shows the runway extensions built over Flushing Bay. (*Port Authority of New York & New Jersey*)

concrete apron. Near the centre of the apron was the administration building and control tower with a 1,500 ft (457 m) long curved covered platform leading to 15 aircraft positions. On each side of the terminal were three large hangars. On the west of the airport was the Marine Terminal. Construction of the airport involved 17.3 mn cubic yards (13.2 mn cu m) of fill, 450,000 cubic yards (344,050 cu m) of crushed rock, 102,100 cubic yards (77,985 cu m) of concrete, and 3 mn US gallons (1.13 mn litres) of asphalt. There were 9,012 concrete piles beneath the buildings. The entire project cost $40 mn.

It was from LaGuardia's Marine Terminal that Pan American Airways operated its North Atlantic Boeing 314 services, and after the Second World War landplane transatlantic services also used LaGuardia.

There was some development in the Marine Terminal area and a few extra hangars were built, but for several years LaGuardia remained much as it was when originally opened. On 1 June, 1947, the Port of New York Authority leased the airport from the City, became responsible for its operation and changed the name to LaGuardia Airport.

The Port Authority was faced with enormous problems. Traffic increased from 145,444 aircraft movements and 2.7 mn passengers in 1948 to 245,340 movements and nearly 5.8 mn passengers in 1957. But apart from the traffic growth LaGuardia suffered from flooding during spring tides and from subsidence. The rubbish with which the airport had originally been claimed contained material, such as tins, which disintegrated, resulting in undulations in runways and buildings and the buildings had regularly to be jacked up. The Port Authority cured the flooding and then in 1961 built a new 5,965 ft (1,818 m) 13/31 runway.

There then followed a complete rebuilding of the terminal area with a new central terminal with four two-level arcades leading to 36 gate positions. A two-level roadway served the terminal and parking spaces were provided for more than 5,000 cars. The terminal was dedicated on 17 April, 1964, and the new 150 ft (46 m) control tower beside the west arcade came into operation that May. This new terminal complex transformed LaGuardia from a run-down makeshift facility to a modern and attractive airport—and amazingly the work was done while the airport continued to handle about 3 mn passengers a year.

In order to handle jet aircraft it was necessary to extend the runways. This involved building a 50 acre (20 hectare) L-shaped platform over Flushing Bay. Runway 04/22 was extended by 2,000 ft (610 m) to 7,000 ft (2,134 m) and opened to its full length in March 1966. Runway 13/31 was extended from 5,965 ft (1,818 m) to 7,000 ft (2,134 m) and opened in November 1966. Taxiway extensions and holding pads were also built, 3,000 ft (914 m) piers were constructed to take the approach lighting and it was necessary to dredge a new shipping channel between Rikers Island and South Brother Island.

Runways 09/27 and 18/36 were abandoned but in October 1966 a 2,000 ft (610 m) by 75 ft (23 m) general aviation runway was opened at the west of the airport, for VFR daylight take offs only, and in 1968 an 835 ft (254 m) 01/19 STOL runway was opened, but this is no longer listed as active.

The Marine Terminal, at one time called the Overseas Terminal, is now used by Air New England, commuter airlines, air taxis and private aircraft.

On 30 April, 1961, Eastern Air Lines began operating its LaGuardia–Boston Air-Shuttle and passengers on this and the New York–Washington shuttle have been handled in Hangar 8 at the east of the airport, but on 8 March, 1979, work began on a $25 mn Air-Shuttle Terminal adjacent to Hangar 8. This is to be a two-storey building with second-level aerobridge loading and capacity for 3 mn passengers a year. It is due to come into service in the autumn of 1980.

The Air-Shuttle Terminal is being financed by the Port Authority under a 25-year lease to Eastern Air Lines. From the time it took over LaGuardia in 1947 up to March 1979, the Port Authority had invested about $228 mn in its development.

New York/New Jersey Newark International Airport

40° 41′ 36″ N 74° 10′ 07″ W 2.6 nm (4.8 km) S of Newark
ICAO: KEWR IATA code: EWR Time zone: GMT −5
Authority: The Port Authority of New York and New Jersey
Area: 930 hectares (2,300 acres)
Elevation: 18 ft (5 m) Ref temp: 30.6 deg C

Runways: 04L/22R   2,499 × 46 m (8,200 × 150 ft) asphalt, grooved
        04R/22L   2,987 × 46 m (9,800 × 150 ft) asphalt, grooved
        11/29   2,073 × 46 m (6,800 × 150 ft) asphalt, to be
                                    grooved
Pavement strength: 350,000 lb (150,745 kg) 3, 650,000 lb (294,835 kg) 4
Landing category: ICAO CAT II
Lighting:
    R/W   04L/22R   HIRL and centreline
            04R/22L   HIRL and centreline. TDZ 04R/22L
            11/29   HIRL
    App   R/W 04L   ALSAF
            R/W 04R   ALSF-2
            R/W 22L   ALSF-1
            R/W 22R and 29   REIL and VASIS
    Thr   green
    Txy   blue edge and green centreline
Aids: VDF, ASR, RVR, ASDE, ILS CAT II 04R, ILS CAT I 04L and 22L
Twr frequency: 118.3   App frequency: 125.5
Terminals: Central terminal area of 425 acres (172 hectares), with two
    multi-level terminals each 800 ft (244 m) by 165 ft (50 m), and a third
    terminal, construction of which has been deferred. Each terminal has
    three two-level satellite gate buildings with total of 55 gates. North
    Terminal handles international flights. The Air Cargo Center,
    completed in December 1954, has three cargo terminals and one
    service building
Scheduled services 1978: 16 airlines
Airline base: United Airlines

Traffic:	1970	1975	1976	1977	1978
Passengers (total)	6,460,489	6,265,797	6,752,726	7,303,604	8,628,613
Cargo (tonnes)	142,702	101,778	109,574	98,586	68,564
Aircraft movements	204,595	166,099	172,822	179,473	206,121
Transport movements	160,597	125,369	144,996	150,543	179,375

Newark International Airport is situated in the southern part of the
City of Newark and adjacent to Elizabeth. Immediately to its east are the
New Jersey Turnpike, the tracks of the Central Railroad of New Jersey,
and the Port of Newark.

The first development of the airport took place in what is now its
northeast corner, and it seems to owe its existence to the enthusiasm for
aviation generated by Lindbergh's New York–Paris flight in 1927. The City
of Newark chose this unlikely site on an expanse of marshland and began
construction in January 1928 of a 68 acre (27.5 hectare) municipal
aerodrome.

In nine months and at a cost of $1.75 mn Newark Municipal Airport
was created with a 1,600 ft (488 m) northeast–southwest asphalt-surfaced
runway and a 120 ft (36.5 m) square hangar. It was claimed that Newark's
runway was the first hard-surfaced strip at any commercial airport in the
United States; this claim may be justified by inclusion of the term
commercial but the Ford Airport at Dearborn had concrete runways of
2,600 ft (792 m) and 2,800 ft (853 m) in 1925.

Newark Metropolitan Airport, as it was called for a time, was opened on 1 October, 1928, but a Ryan monoplane had made the first landing that August. The airport was designated as the New York metropolitan air mail terminus in 1929 and mail operations were transferred from Hadley Field. In the same year four airlines began scheduled passenger services to and from Newark and built combined hangars and passenger terminals in a row along the eastern boundary. United Air Lines' terminal was in Southern Colonial style with high slender-columned portico. By the autumn of 1930 Newark was claimed to be the world's busiest airport and in that year there were some 28,000 landings and about 20,000 passengers.

By 1934 traffic had reached a level which the airlines felt required an adequate central terminal. In February 1934 President Roosevelt cancelled the air mail contracts and on the 20th the Army Air Corps began carrying the mail. At Newark work was begun on construction of an administration building, at the north of the airport, for the use of Army pilots. The Army made its last mail flights on 1 June, 1934, and the Newark building was modified to become the terminal, with operation starting on 15 May, 1935.

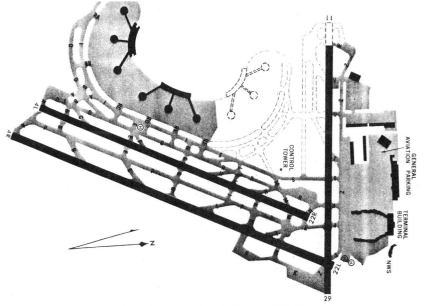

Newark International Airport. (*FAA*)

The old Newark airport was equipped for night operations and centreline lights were installed at an early stage. Another early innovation was a crude instrument landing system introduced in 1932. Wires were stretched at right angles to the runway and emitted signals which the pilot received to indicate his position on the approach.

The Army took over the airport during the war and expanded its facilities which by the war's end included three runways—east–west (designated 10/28 and now 11/29), north–south and northeast–southwest—and the site then occupied 1,400 acres (566.5 hectares).

Following a consultant's report on the operation and development of the airport, a lease for its operation was agreed with the Port of New York Authority which took over on 22 March, 1948. By that time the airport was in a dense industrial and residential area and none of its runways was suitable for modern aircraft. Three aircraft crashed in residential areas and there was intense pressure to close the airport. This was overcome and the Port Authority undertook a major reconstruction programme. The north–south and northeast–southwest runways were closed and a new 04/22 instrument runway of 7,000 ft (2,134 m) was opened in November 1952 on the east side of the airport. A modern terminal building, with 500 ft (152 m) long concourse and two 575 ft (175 m) covered arcades, was opened to the west of the old terminal on 29 July, 1953. Later the arcades were nearly doubled in length to provide 32 gates. The new control tower, of striking design, was completed in January 1960.

It was in this first development stage that sequenced flashing centreline approach lights were developed at Newark. The system was installed in 1952 on the new 04/22 instrument runway and subsequently became the approved CAA/FAA standard.

By 1963 Newark was handling more than 4 mn passengers a year and it became clear that simple expansion would not meet future needs. Instead the decision was taken to build what amounted to a new airport on the site which had been enlarged to 2,300 acres (930 hectares).

The development plan included a completely new central terminal area, a new 04/22 runway, lengthening of the earlier 04/22 runway and runway 11/29, and provision of a 3,200 ft (975 m) general aviation 10/28 runway. The estimated cost of the development was $200 mn. The redevelopment was based on the assumption that there would be more than 300,000 aircraft movements and 12 mn passengers in 1975 and 19 mn passengers by 1980, but in fact only about half the forecast volume was recorded in 1975, even lower than the 1970 traffic.

Site preparation began in September 1963 with construction of a large drainage ditch extending for 4 miles (6½ km) round the airport to take storm water into Elizabeth Channel. Then, beginning in the autumn of 1965, more than 14 mn cubic yards of coarse sand was pumped from an underwater site off Swinburne Island in New York Harbor, loaded into barges and taken to Port Newark from where it was pumped 2 miles (3.2 km) to reclaim the marshland between the 04/22 runway and US Highway No. 1 to the west. On this reclaimed land, within a 425 acre (172 hectare) oval area, two terminals were built and a third started.

The terminals are curved structures measuring 800 ft (244 m) by 165 ft (50 m) and having piers leading to circular satellites with upper-level boarding via aerobridges. The main terminals are hyperbolic paraboloid structures of pleasing appearance. The anticipated three-terminal complex would have had capacity for more than 12 mn passengers and been served by 83 gates, but because of the stagnation of air traffic the third terminal has not yet been completed and there are only 55 gates in use. Terminal A, the southern unit, and Terminal B, the centre unit, were officially opened on 12 September, 1973, although Terminal A was operational from 8 August, 1973. The former terminal, now known as the North Terminal, was remodelled and in May 1975 opened for international and supplemental airline traffic.

Newark International Airport in 1977, with Terminal A in the foreground and Terminal B beyond. The twin towers of the World Trade Center on Manhattan can be seen in the background. (*Port Authority of New York & New Jersey*)

Construction of the 8,200 ft (2,499 m) 04L/22R runway began in December 1967 and it was opened in March 1970 after which 04R/22L was rehabilitated, extended to 9,800 ft (2,987 m), and reopened in August 1973.

The present title, Newark International Airport, was adopted in 1972. The creation of a new airport on this crowded corner of New Jersey was a magnificent achievement. It may have been disappointing that fuel costs and the economic recession drastically restricted traffic growth but now that traffic expansion has begun Newark International is among the few airports with surplus capacity ready for use. A pointer to the future was the agreement between World Airways and the Port Authority that from 11 April, 1979, that airline would transfer all its operations from John F Kennedy International to Newark International.

Norfolk, Virginia   Norfolk International Airport

36° 53' 40" N   76° 12' 05" W   5.6 nm (10.4 km) NE of city centre
ICAO: KORF   IATA code: ORF   Time zone: GMT −5
Authority: Norfolk Port and Industrial Authority
Area: 486 hectares (1,200 acres)
Elevation: 27 ft (8 m)   Ref temp: 30 deg C
Runways: 05/23   2,286 × 46 m (7,499 × 150 ft) concrete and asphalt
         13/31   1,486 × 46 m (4,876 × 150 ft) asphalt
Pavement strength: 05/23   95,000 lb (43,091 kg) 1, 200,000 lb
    (90,718 kg) 2, 510,000 lb (231,332 kg) 3;   13/31 95,000 lb (43,091 kg) 1,
    135,000 lb (61,235 kg) 2
Landing category: ICAO CAT I
Lighting:
    R/W   05/23   HIRL
            13/31   MIRL
    App   R/W 05   ALSF-1
            R/W 13 and 31   REIL
            R/W 23   MALSR
    Thr   green
    Txy   blue edge
Aids: VORTAC, DME, VDF, ASR, RVR 05, ILS CAT I 05/23
Twr frequency: 120.8   App frequency: 119.45
Terminals: Separate domestic and international terminals. Two traffic
    piers with 13 gates and aerobridges. Separate general aviation
    terminal
Scheduled services 1978: Allegheny, National, Piedmont and United
Airline bases: National Airlines and Piedmont Airlines

Traffic:	1970	1975	1976	1978
Passengers (total)	1,167,052	1,349,255	1,488,048	1,799,224
Cargo (tonnes)	7,613	5,959	6,229	14,541
Aircraft movements	166,757	150,816	170,131	167,659
Transport movements	37,800	32,620	34,900	50,409

The Norfolk International Airport terminal opened in January 1974.
(*Lawrence S. Williams Inc, courtesy Norfolk Port and Industrial Authority*)

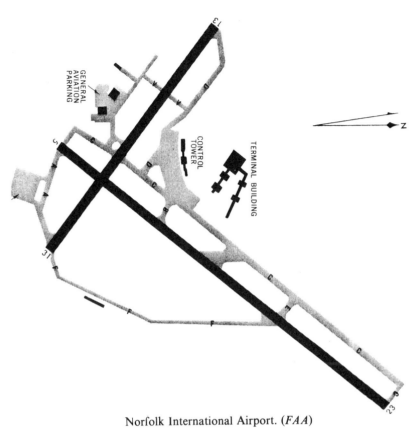

Norfolk International Airport. (*FAA*)

The present Norfolk airport came into operation in 1938, but the city was first served by scheduled air services in 1926, when from 10 October to 30 November, Philadelphia Rapid Transit Service operated CAM15 between Philadelphia and Norfolk with Fokker F.VII-3ms. Then in 1929 Ben Epstein began a Norfolk–Richmond air taxi service from his aerodrome on Granby Street and it was this that was used in 1931 when Luddington Line and Eastern Air Transport, respectively, began Norfolk–Washington and Norfolk–Richmond services. Granby Street aerodrome could not be expanded because of its proximity to Norfolk Naval Air Station and commercial operations were transferred to Glenrock Airport. Traffic declined and for a few years there were no air services but Pennsylvania-Central Airlines planned to open services when there was a suitable airport.

The City of Norfolk owned the Truxton Manor Golf Course, northeast of the city, and 456 acres (184.5 hectares) of this was approved by PCA in 1938 as suitable for an airport. This site was prepared as the Norfolk Municipal Airport, with a 3,500 ft (1,067 m) runway and a very simple wooden chalet-type terminal, and PCA began service there that year with Boeing 247s. The equally simple two-storey 'permanent' terminal was

501

dedicated in 1940. The USAAF took over the airport during the Second World War, extended the runway and built two more, officially returning the airport to the City in 1947 although National Airlines opened services there in 1945.

After the war a much larger terminal was constructed and this was dedicated in 1951. It was later doubled in area by the addition of two curved wings, and a canopied concourse was erected on the apron side. To meet jet requirements the 05/23 runway was lengthened and many other improvements made.

In 1968 the Southeastern Regional Planning Commission designated the airport as southern Tidewater's official regional airport and the name was changed to Norfolk Regional Airport.

In spite of the additions and improvements it was realized that the airport would require new facilities for it to be adequate for the traffic into the 21st century and a plan was made which involved land exchange with the neighbouring Norfolk Botanical Gardens, the remodelling of both the airport and the gardens and including construction of a new terminal, aprons and taxiways, and runway extensions. An attractive two-level modern terminal with two piers and 13 gates was dedicated on 18 January, 1974. The 325,000 sq ft (30,192.5 sq m) terminal has been set in a wooded area and thousands of azaleas, camellias and rhododendrons make an attractive setting. Both piers can be extended and a third pier added. Ultimately it is planned to extend the 05/23 runway to the southwest to give it a length of 9,000 ft (2,743 m) and to extend 13/31 southeast to a length of 6,519 ft (1,987 m).

The 13/31 extension will mean relocating the tracks of the Norfolk Southern Railway and Pennsylvania Railroad. The master plan also allows for a 4,100 ft (1,250 m) 05R/23L runway which would involve some land reclamation, and further taxiways, maintenance and cargo areas and general aviation facilities. Runway 13/31 is to be re-equipped with high intensity lighting.

Oakland, California
Metropolitan Oakland International Airport

37° 43′ 25″ N	122° 12′ 56″ W	4.3 nm (7.96 km) S of city
ICAO: KOAK	IATA code: OAK	Time zone: GMT −8

Authority: City of Oakland Board of Port Commissioners
Area: 5,316 hectares (13,135 acres)
Elevation: 6 ft (1.8 m)   Ref temp: 23.3 deg C

Runways:	09L/27R*	1,662 × 46 m	(5,452 × 150 ft) asphalt
	09R/27L	1,893 × 46 m	(6,210 × 150 ft) asphalt
	11/29	3,048 × 46 m	(10,000 × 150 ft) asphalt
	15/33†	1,679 × 46 m	(5,510 × 150 ft) asphalt

*Closed to air carrier aircraft
†Threshold 33 displaced 2,115 ft (645 m)

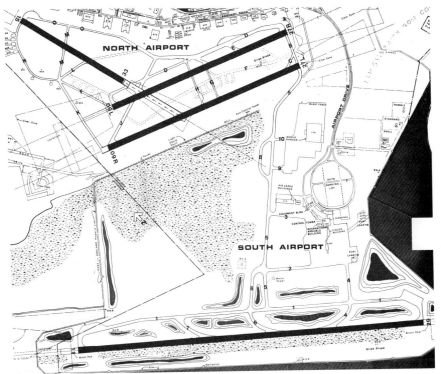

Metropolitan Oakland International Airport.

Pavement strength: 09L/27R   40,000 lb (18,144 kg) 1, 50,000 lb (22,680 kg) 2,
77,000 lb (34,927 kg) 3;   09R/27L 110,000 lb (49,895 kg) 1,   140,000 lb
(63,503 kg) 2,   230,000 lb (104,326 kg) 3;   11/29 200,000 lb (90,718
kg) 1 and 2,   400,000 lb (181,437 kg) 3;   15/33 50,000 lb
(22,680 kg) 1,   65,000 lb (29,483 kg) 2,   100,000 lb (45,359 kg) 3
Landing category: ICAO CAT II
Lighting:
R/W   09L/27R, 09R/27L and 15/33   HIRL
           11/29   HIRL and centreline. TDZ 29
App   R/W 27R   ALSF-1
           R/W 29   ALSF-2
Thr   09L/27R, 09R/27L and 11/29   green
Txy   blue edge all taxiways, some centreline and high-speed exit
           lights
Aids: VORTAC, DME, NDB, ASR, RVR 11/29, RVV 27R, ILS CAT II
29, ILS CAT I 27R
Twr frequency: 127.2
App frequency: 135.1 south complex, 135.4 north complex
Terminals: Passenger terminal with 18 gates. Separate cargo buildings.
General aviation area at north
Scheduled services 1978: 11 airlines plus supplemental carriers

503

Airline base: Air California
Main base: Trans International Airlines and World Airways

Traffic:	1970	1975	1976
Passengers (total)	2,055,180	2,083,687	2,164,243
Cargo (tonnes)	6,975	6,094	6,477
Aircraft movements	366,455	333,575	398,954
Transport movements	—	—	48,909

On 26 November, 1926, the City of Oakland accepted an offer to buy part of Bay Farm Island, on the east side of San Francisco Bay, for development of a municipal airport. The transaction was completed on 14 January, 1927, and planning began—the title Oakland Municipal Airport being adopted on 13 April, 1927.

In June 1927 planning was disrupted when the Assistant Secretary for War announced that Oakland had been chosen as the starting point for the Army Air Corps' attempt to fly to Hawaii, provided the runway was ready by 24 June. A runway, 7,200 ft (2,195 m) long, 600 ft (183 m) wide at the starting end and 300 ft (91 m) at the far end, was built in less than a month and on 28 June Lieuts Lester J. Maitland and Albert F. Hegenberger took off in the Fokker F.VII-3m *Bird of Paradise* and reached Honolulu 25 hr 50 min later. Roads at the present airport bear the names Maitland Drive and Hegenberger Road, while others are named after Amelia Earhart and Jimmy Doolittle.

A further interruption came in August 1927 when the contestants in the Dole race to Hawaii used Oakland as their departure point. After the race flying was restricted while construction continued.

An administration building and hangars were erected on the north side of the site, a channel from the Bay was dredged for seaplanes, and on 17 September, 1927, the airport was officially dedicated by Charles Lindbergh.

From that autumn Pacific Air Transport began calling at Oakland on its Seattle–Los Angeles services and Boeing Air Transport began using the airport on 15 December, 1927.

Completion of the airport as initially planned was announced in February 1930.

In August 1928 the Navy had established a reserve base at the airport; and in 1934, when for a time the Army took over the mail services, Oakland was its western terminal.

Considerable improvements were made under WPA projects from 1934 and the airport was enlarged. There were four runways, east–west (now 09L/27R), northwest–southeast (now 15/33), a parallel but much shorter northwest–southeast (now abandoned), and a northeast–southwest (now a taxiway).

In 1939 there were 254,393 aircraft movements, 11,039 of them by air carriers, and 68,770 airline passengers, and in 1940 it became necessary to extend the administration building.

After the Japanese attack on Pearl Harbor the Army took over the airport and based Curtiss P-40s there for the defence of the Bay area, and at the northwest of the airport the Navy established an air station. In 1942 the Army built additional taxiways and hardstandings and some of them are now used by general aviation aircraft.

In 1944/45 extensive improvements were made by the CAA and the

Metropolitan Oakland International Airport with North Airport on the right and South Airport on the left. (*City of Oakland Board of Port Commissioners*)

Army. A dyke was built along the south of the airport, fill was dredged from the Bay and runway 09R/27L constructed. Runways 09L/27R and 15/33 were strengthened and the latter was extended southeast for 900 ft (274 m) to intersect with the new 09R/27L.

Parts of the airport were returned to the City in September 1945. A year later the City remodelled an ex-military building to handle the growing number of overseas flights. Non-scheduled carriers were moved to the prewar hotel which was then described as the International Terminal.

Much expansion was undertaken in the original terminal area but in 1953 it was decided that a master plan should be produced to develop the airport and, to represent its role in serving the whole East Bay area, the name was changed to Metropolitan Oakland International Airport. The plan was submitted in July 1954 and called for what was virtually a second airport with a new 8,600 ft (2,621 m) 11/29 runway about a mile out in the Bay and a new terminal complex, all to be built on land to be created by fill from the Bay. As a result of the plan the last major additions to the old north site terminal were authorized in January 1956 and completed in June 1959.

The contract for building the southern dyke was let in July 1955 and by March 1958 it had been completed, and the fill had settled sufficiently for contracts to be awarded for the rock base and drainage. Work began on the new terminal on 26 September, 1960, and the runway, lengthened to 10,000 ft (3,048 m), and its parallel taxiway were completed on 4 June, 1962. With the South Airport substantially completed, dedication and opening ceremonies took place on 15/16 September, 1962, although the terminal building was not accepted from the contractors until 5 October.

Work continued on both the North and South Airports. In 1962 runway 09R/27L was levelled and resurfaced and 09L/27R received the same treatment in 1965. General aviation facilities were increased at the North Airport in 1968, and in 1969 work began on two cargo buildings at the east of the airport. A new parallel taxiway, with connecting links, for runway 09L/27R was completed in July 1969. In July 1971 work began on a hangar for World Airways capable of housing four Boeing 747s.

In December 1971 work started on a dyke to extend runway 11/29 to the northwest to give a length of 12,500 ft (3,810 m), and filling of the area began in 1972.

In spite of the new terminal, Customs and Immigration complained that international facilities were inadequate, so in August 1972 work began on an international arrivals building beside the main terminal. This was opened in January 1973.

The South Airport terminal consists of four main units. There is a 500 ft (152 m) glass-fronted curved ticket and baggage claim building opposite the 3,200 vehicle car park. This building has a floor area of 44,000 sq ft (4,088 sq m) and 372 ft (113 m) of counters. It is connected to the square terminal building, with 41,600 sq ft (3,865 sq m) ground area, which in turn has a finger building with 18 gates. The international arrivals building is connected to the main terminal. Close to the terminal buildings is a 100 by 75 ft (30 by 23 m) helipad.

Oklahoma City, Oklahoma   Will Rogers World Airport

35° 23′ 37″ N   97° 35′ 58″ W   6 nm (11 km) SW of city
ICAO: KOKC   IATA code: OKC   Time zone: GMT −6
Authority: City of Oklahoma City
Area: 3,035 hectares (7,500 acres)
Elevation: 1,294 ft (394 m)   Ref temp: 21.7 deg C
Runways: 12/30   1,990 × 46 m (6,528 × 150 ft) asphalt-concrete
           17L/35R   2,987 × 46 m (9,801 × 150 ft) asphalt-concrete
           17R/35L   2,987 × 46 m (9,800 × 150 ft) concrete, grooved
           18/36*   907 × 23 m (2,975 × 75 ft)   asphalt

* Part of taxiway 600 ft (183 m) west of 17R/35L. Daylight VFR only. Used as taxiway when not being used for take offs and landings

Pavement strength: 12/30   50,000 lb (22,680 kg) ISWL, 200,000 lb (90,718 kg) 2, 350,000 lb (158,757 kg) 3; 17L/35R   50,000 lb (22,680 kg) 1, 200,000 lb (90,718 kg) 2, 350,000 lb (158,757 kg) 3; 17R/35L   50,000 lb (22,680 kg) 1, 200,000 lb (90,718 kg) 2, 400,000 lb (181,437 kg) 3; 18/36   50,000 lb (22,680 kg) 1, 150,000 lb (68,039 kg) 2, 240,000 lb (108,862 kg) 3
Landing category: ICAO CAT II
Lighting:
   R/W   12/30   MIRL
            17L/35R   HIRL and centreline. TDZ 35R
            17R/35L   HIRL
            18/36   blue edge taxiway lights

App   R/W 12   REIL and VASIS
            R/W 17L, 30 and 35L   VASIS
            R/W 17R   MALSR
            R/W 35R   ALSF-2
Thr   green
Txy   blue edge

Aids: VORTAC, NDB, ARTS III, LLWSAS, RVR 17L/35R, ILS CAT II 35R, ILS CAT I 17R

Twr frequency: 118.3   App frequency: 119.3/121.05/124.2/124.6

Terminal: 200,000 sq ft (18,580 sq m) area passenger terminal with two piers. Helipad near terminal

Scheduled services 1978: American, Braniff, Continental, Frontier, Metro Airlines and TWA

Base: Oklahoma Air National Guard has a base at the northwest corner of the airport

Traffic:	1970	1975	1976	1977	1978
Passengers (total)	1,264,152	1,541,277	1,671,348	1,827,722	2,084,829
Cargo (tonnes)	9,135	7,646	9,284	10,044	—
Aircraft movements	186,108	139,871	154,581	163,978	167,142
Transport movements	49,139	48,037	47,670	51,076	60,529

Oklahoma City's 'first municipal airpark' began in 1928 with construction on a 660 acre (267 hectare) site. Purchase of the land, engineering, drainage, construction of runways, a three-storey terminal,

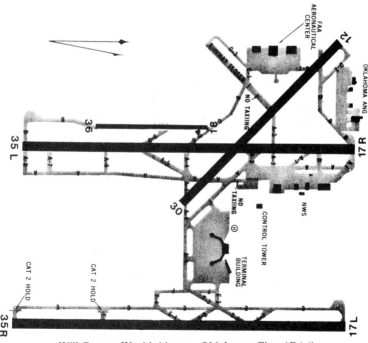

Will Rogers World Airport, Oklahoma City. (*FAA*)

507

View across the FAA's Mike Monroney Aeronautical Center at Will Rogers World Airport, Oklahoma City, to the runways and terminal area. The Oklahoma Air National Guard Base is on the left. (*City of Oklahoma City*)

apron, and 120 ft (36.5 m) square hangar cost $500,000, of which $53,000 was spent on the terminal. The original airport occupied part of what is now the present airport's northwest corner and there appear to have been four runways—north–south, east–west, northwest–southeast and northeast–southwest. The airport was dedicated on 1 April, 1932, and officially opened that June.

In June 1941 the name was changed from Oklahoma City Airport to Will Rogers Field and in February 1956 became Will Rogers World Airport.

To meet traffic requirements considerable extension took place, including the lengthening of runway 17/35 to the south, and construction of a new terminal and runway 17L/35R to the east greatly extended the airport to give its present configuration. The new terminal was opened on 10 December, 1966, and the old one was demolished in 1967.

The present three-storey terminal has three concourses and 200,000 sq ft (18,580 sq m) of floor space. Two of the concourses are in the form of traffic piers with rotundas at their extremities. These are used by the five scheduled airlines and one commuter airline and can handle 12 scheduled aircraft at the same time, although only two of Braniff's aerobridges can handle Boeing 747s. The third concourse, on the east of the terminal, is used for general aviation and one commuter airline. It will probably be extended to form a third full-length pier. The terminal was designed to limit walking to a maximum of 300 ft (91 m). Three-quarters of the basement forms a storm and fall-out shelter.

At the north of the airport is the Oklahoma Air National Guard base and on the west the FAA's large Mike Monroney Aeronautical Center.

Omaha, Nebraska   Eppley Airfield

41° 17′ 59″ N   95° 53′ 35″ W   4 nm (7.4 km) NE of city
ICAO: KOMA   IATA code: OMA   Time zone: GMT −6
Authority: Omaha Airport Authority
Area: 1,113 hectares (2,750 acres)
Elevation: 983 ft (300 m)   Ref temp: 10.8 deg C
Runways: 14L/32R 1,326 × 23 m (4,350 × 75 ft) general aviation R/W

    14R/32L 2,591 × 46 m (8,500 × 150 ft) concrete with asphaltic
      17/35 1,829 × 46 m (6,000 × 150 ft) concrete grooved overlay

Pavement strength: 384,000 lb (174,179 kg) dual tandem
Landing category: ICAO CAT I
Lighting:
    R/W   14L/32R   MIRL
             14R/32L* and 17/35   HIRL
    App   R/W 14R   ALSF-1
            R/W 17   VASIS
            R/W 32L   MALSR and VASIS
            R/W 35   REIL and VASIS
    Thr   green
    Txy   blue edge

* It was planned that 14R should have centreline and TDZ lights by the winter 1978–79, bringing it to CAT II standard, but no funds were available for ALSF-2 approach lights

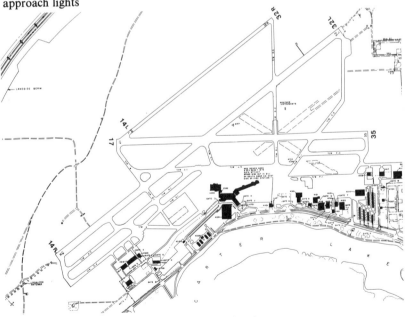

Eppley Airfield, Omaha.

The terminal at Eppley Airfield with the buildings of Omaha immediately behind.
(*Omaha Airport Authority*)

Aids: VORTAC, NDB, RVR, ILS CAT I 14R/32L
Twr frequency: 119.1/134.95   App frequency: 119.8/124.5
Terminals: Two-level passenger terminal with traffic piers, nine gates and
    16 aircraft stands. Separate cargo buildings
Scheduled services 1978: Air Nebraska, American, Braniff, Eastern,
    Frontier, Hughes Airwest, North Central, Ozark, Pioneer Airways
    and United

Traffic:	1970	1975	1976	1978
Passengers (total)	1,341,705	1,515,980	1,647,907	1,867,527
Cargo (tonnes)	15,803	8,298	9,798	9,721
Aircraft movements	221,699	159,533	177,174	171,884
Transport movements	47,587	40,839	46,238	55,723

Omaha was among the first cities in the United States to receive air
services, when on 15 May, 1920, the Post Office transcontinental air mail
reached the city with the extension of the New York–Chicago sector. The
mail service was flown by D.H-4s, and at Omaha there was a hangar with
sliding doors and the inscription 'U.S. Post Office Dept. Omaha Aerial
Mail'.

The present airport began as a grass field known as Omaha Legion
Airport and was first used as an airport in 1925. Boeing Air Transport
began using it in 1927, and in 1928 the American Legion constructed its first
hangar, which also served as the terminal. The airport, which became
Omaha Municipal Airport, was in open country northeast of the city and
completely within a loop of the Missouri River. On its west was the
U-shaped Carter Lake. A low-frequency radio range station was installed
in 1932, a two- and three-storey brick terminal building was constructed in
1935, and in the following year asphaltic-concrete surfacing of the runways
began, with completion in 1938.

A military ILS was installed in 1944 and in 1946 runways 14/32 and
17/35 were reconstructed with Portland concrete. In 1959 the Omaha
Airport Authority was established and the airport renamed Eppley
Airfield.

510

Continuous improvement has taken place. In 1961 a new terminal was constructed, lighting improved and approach lighting installed on runway 14; approach lights were installed on runway 32 in 1963; a 4,350 ft (1,326 m) 14L/32R general aviation runway was constructed in 1969; major terminal expansion was completed in 1971; a cargo building was completed in 1972 and a second in 1974. A new control tower and large multi-storey garage were completed in 1975.

The airport had always had to be protected from flooding by a levee; in 1976 a much more substantial one was built, forming a great semi-circle around the east of the airport from south to north, and its construction has enlarged the airport area.

The background to the terminal, with its aerobridges, is no longer fields and trees but close-in high-rise buildings.

The general aviation facilities at the southwest of the airport are to be transferred to the east side thus allowing additional space for terminal development.

Orlando, Florida   Orlando International Airport

28° 25′ 53″ N   81° 19′ 28″ W   7 nm (13 km) SE of city
ICAO: KMCO   IATA code: MCO   Time zone: GMT −5
Authority: Greater Orlando Aviation Authority
Area: 2,711 hectares (6,700 acres)
Elevation: 96 ft (29 m)   Ref temp: 21.8 deg C
Runways: 18L/36R   3,658 × 61 m (12,002 × 200 ft) bitumen
          18R/36L   3,658 × 91 m (12,002 × 300 ft) concrete
Pavement strength: 18L/36R   165,000 lb (74,843 kg) 1, 200,000 lb (90,718 kg) 2, 400,000 lb (181,437 kg) 3; 18R/36L   100,000 lb (45,359 kg) 1. Dual wheel and dual tandem as 18L/36R
Landing category: ICAO CAT II
Lighting:
     R/W   18L/36R   HIRL and centreline. TDZ 36R
           18R/36L   HIRL

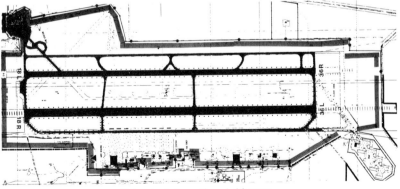

Orlando International Airport.

App   R/W 18R   US Configuration B, REIL and VASIS
          R/W 36L   ALSF-1
          R/W 36R   ALSF-2
Thr   green
Txy   blue edge

Aids: TACAN, VOR/DME, ASR, ARTS III, RVR 36R, ILS CAT II 36R, ILS CAT I 36L

Twr frequency: 124.3   App frequency: 124.8

Terminals: Passenger terminal at extreme northeast corner of airport. Y traffic pier (North/South Concourse) with 15 gates and West Concourse (international) with three gates. Also charter terminal. Cargo building south of main terminal

Scheduled services 1978: 12 airlines

Traffic:	1970	1975	1976	1977	1978
Passengers (total)	1,287,540	3,344,011	3,678,346	4,154,781	5,182,264
Cargo (tonnes)	—	9,945	11,668	13,956	16,720
Aircraft movements	—	65,952	74,094	80,308	86,298
Transport movements	19,989*	60,892	71,116	78,494	83,682

* Departures only

In 1976 Boeing 727s, Douglas DC-9s and DC-10s and Lockheed TriStars each accounted for more than 10 per cent of transport movements.

Orlando is situated in mid-Florida about halfway between Jacksonville and West Palm Beach and a little under 50 miles (80 km) west of Cape Canaveral. Eight miles (13 km) southeast of the city McCoy Air Force Base was built for the operation of Boeing B-52s and two 12,002 ft (3,658 m) runways were laid.

From April 1961 McCoy became a joint-user facility, serving as Air Force Base and Orlando Airport, the civil facilities being known as Orlando Jetport. The City of Orlando took over the entire airport from the USAF in 1975.

The space programme and the proximity of Cape Canaveral led to a rapid increase in Orlando's traffic, passengers increasing from about 250,000 in 1964 to more than 500,000 in 1966 and 1¼ mn in 1970. In October 1971 Walt Disney World was opened some 15-minutes' drive from the airport and this attraction doubled Orlando's traffic in two years.

When commercial traffic began using Orlando, the terminal comprised two 200 by 180 ft (61 by 55 m) missile storage buildings connected by a small concourse, with eight boarding gates. To meet the rapidly increasing traffic the building was remodelled in 1974, and in 1977 a charter terminal was opened. These improvements provided 19 gates.

In 1976 Disney World announced that it planned to open in October 1979 the Experimental Prototype Community of Tomorrow and this is expected to increase Orlando area's visitors to about 25 mn by 1980.

The remodelling of the airport terminal and some taxiway and apron improvements were Phase II and I of a much bigger development plan for long-term expansion. It was decided to increase the area of the airport, if possible to at least 12,000 acres (4,856 hectares), and to develop in such a way that the present site can serve as Orlando's airport for at least 75–80 years.

Drawing of the new Orlando International Airport terminal with the first two boarding centres. (*Greater Orlando Aviation Authority*)

Orlando's airport, it became Orlando International Airport in December 1976 after being declared a port of entry on 1 November that year, has some unique problems apart from its rapid traffic growth. From 1970 to 1976 the number of passengers embarked increased by 261 per cent but only about 35 per cent of this traffic was generated in the area. Most of the passengers are one-flight-a-year inexperienced travellers who need special guidance. Their use of the airport is unusual, too,—they use buses, courtesy transport and a large number of rented cars; only a small percentage of ground transport is represented by private cars.

Taking all these factors into account the planners submitted their master plan to the City and to the airlines in January 1977. The new terminal complex is being constructed on a 6,247 acre (2,528 hectare) site southeast of the present interim terminal and east of the present parallel runways. There will be a central terminal consisting of a transfer station flanked by two ticketing and baggage claim units, and north and south of these there will be vehicle parking areas. The entire area will be landscaped with sub-tropical plants and lakes.

To the west of the central, landside, terminal will be two, airside, boarding centres, initially with 30 gates although later this can be increased to 48. Curved elevated ways will link the boarding centres with the west face of the landside terminal and on these elevated ways will run an enclosed automated Westinghouse people-mover system.

The official ground-breaking ceremonies took place on 15 September, 1978, site clearance began on 2 October, and the new terminal is scheduled to come into operation in January 1981. The 30-gate terminal as planned for 1981 will have capacity for 8 mn passengers a year.

As part of the development there is a water quality control programme which will revitalize existing natural flora, provide a stormwater retention system which will slowly release fresh water to the surrounding area with the aim of benefiting natural vegetation and animal life.

513

Looking further ahead there is provision for two more boarding centres to the east, bringing the number of gates to 96, and a third parallel runway with additional taxiways. This runway, to be designated 18L/36R, would be on the east side of the airport, located somewhat further south than the present pair, and would be 10,050 ft (3,063 m) long by 200 ft (61 m) wide; the existing 18L/36R would then become 18C/36C.

Even when the entire terminal complex with four boarding units is complete there will still be room, to the south, for another terminal area of at least the same size. East of the projected 18L/36R runway a large area has been designated as a possible reliever area for general aviation.

Philadelphia, Pennsylvania   Philadelphia International Airport

39° 52′ 12″ N   75° 14′ 43″ W   6 nm (11 km) SW of city
ICAO: KPHL   IATA code: PHL   Time zone: GMT −5
Authority: City of Philadelphia
Area: 931 hectares (2,300 acres)
Elevation: 23 ft (7 m)   Ref temp: 30.4 deg C
Runways: 09L/27R   2,896 × 46 m   (9,501 × 150 ft) asphalt, grooved
        09R/27L   3,200 × 61 m (10,499 × 200 ft) asphalt, grooved
        17/35   1,664 × 46 m   (5,460 × 150 ft) asphalt
Pavement strength: auw 09R/27L   100,000 lb (45,359 kg) 1, 350,000 lb
    (158,757 kg) 3;   17/35   75,000 lb (34,019 kg) 1, 240,000 lb (108,862
    kg) 3.
Landing category: ICAO CAT II
Lighting:
    R/W   09L/27R and 09R/27L   HIRL and centreline. TDZ 09R
        17/35   MIRL
    App   R/W 09L   ALSF-1
        R/W 09R   ALSF-2
        R/W 35   VASIS
    Thr   green, displaced 500 ft (152 m) on 17/35
    Txy   blue edge
Aids: VOR, RVR 09R/27L and 27R, RVV 09R and 27R, ILS CAT II 09R,
    ILS CAT I 27L
Twr frequency: 118.5   App frequency: 126.6/128.4

Allegheny Airlines Boeing 727 and Convair CV-580 on the apron at Philadelphia International Airport. (*City of Philadelphia*)

514

Terminals: Four domestic terminal units, with five traffic piers, in angle between runways 09L/27R and 17/35; overseas and charter terminal to east of 17 threshold and beside Island Avenue. Separate cargo areas including Cargo City
Scheduled services 1978: 16 airlines
Airline bases: American, Eastern and TWA. Pennsylvania Air National Guard base to south of overseas terminal

Traffic:	1970	1975–76	1976–77	1977–78
Passengers (total)	6,592,527	7,906,191	8,201,573	9,034,406
Cargo (tonnes)	107,047	108,445	110,944	127,062
Aircraft movements	272,831	300,967	324,337	329,511
Transport movements	195,035	140,462	142,425	145,291

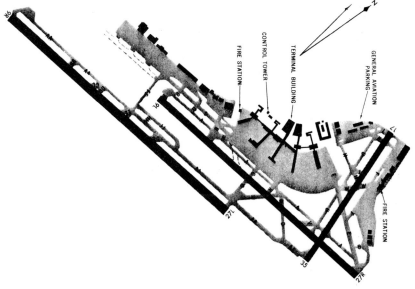

Philadelphia International Airport. (*FAA*)

Philadelphia International Airport, situated beside the Delaware River, has served the city since 1940; but the first air activity on the site began in 1925 when the city provided 125 acres (51 hectares) of land for the training of Pennsylvania National Guard pilots, and that site is now part of the airport's northeast corner. The adjoining 1,000 acre (405 hectare) Hog Island site had housed large wartime emergency shipbuilding yards, and in 1930 the City of Philadelphia bought Hog Island from the Federal Government to provide for airport expansion but, because of the Depression, construction of the landing ground and buildings did not begin until 1937. From 1926 the aerodrome had been known as the Municipal Aviation Landing Field but the airport was officially opened on 20 June, 1940, as Philadelphia Municipal Airport, and from that time American Airlines, Eastern Air Lines, TWA and United Air Lines transferred their operations from Central Airport, Camden, New Jersey, to the new airport. About 40,000 passengers were handled during the first year.

In 1945 the title became Philadelphia International Airport when American Overseas Airlines inaugurated transatlantic services from Philadelphia.

A new terminal was opened on 15 December, 1953, and the 09R/27L instrument runway was dedicated on 11 December, 1972. An overseas terminal, 1½ miles (2.4 km) from the main terminal, was opened in April 1973, and spring 1977 saw completion of the modernized and expanded domestic terminal area, with four unit terminals replacing the earlier central terminal.

Phoenix, Arizona
Phoenix Sky Harbor International Airport

33° 26′ 07″ N	112° 00′ 43″ W	2.6 nm (4.8 km) E of city
ICAO: KPHX	IATA code: PHX	Time zone: GMT −7

Authority: City of Phoenix
Area: 822 hectares (2,031 acres)
Elevation: 1,128 ft (344 m)   Ref temp: 40.5 deg C
Runways: 08L/26R   2,668 × 46 m   (8,753 × 150 ft) asphaltic-concrete
              08R/26L   3,139 × 46 m (10,300 × 150 ft) asphaltic-concrete
Pavement strength: auw 08L/26R   80,000 lb (36,287 kg) 1, 150,000 lb (68,039 kg) 2, 280,000 lb (127,006 kg) 3; 08R/26L   100,000 lb (45,360 kg) 1, 200,000 lb (90,719 kg) 2, 350,000 lb (158,757 kg) 3.
Landing category: ICAO CAT I
Lighting:

R/W	08L/26R	MIRL
	08R/26L	HIRL
App	R/W 08L	REIL and VASIS
	R/W 08R	MALSR
	R/W 26L	VASIS
	R/W 26R	REIL
Thr	green	
Txy	blue edge	

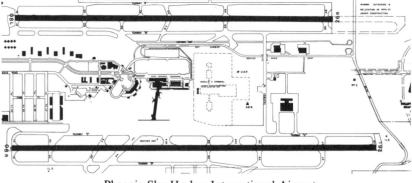

Phoenix Sky Harbor International Airport.

Phoenix Sky Harbor International Airport with the terminal in the foreground, runway 08L/26R on the right and the city in the background. (*City of Phoenix*)

Aids: VOR/DME, NDB, ASR, RVR 08R, ILS CAT I 08R
Twr frequency: 118.7/120.9
App frequency: 119.2/120.4/124.1/124.9/126.8
Terminals: East and West passenger terminals and international building, with 32 gates. Additional terminals under construction. Separate cargo centre and general aviation terminal.
Scheduled services 1978: American, Cochise Airlines, Continental, Delta, Frontier, Hughes Airwest, Scenic Airlines, TWA and Western
Airline base: Hughes Airwest. The Arizona Air National Guard has a base on the southern boundary

Traffic:	1970	1975	1976	1978
Passengers (total)	2,869,842	3,846,424	4,414,625	5,931,806
Aircraft movements	346,249	434,256	425,773	405,651
Transport movements	92,114	95,927	99,813	—

The first Phoenix municipal airport was on a 400 acre (162 hectare) site 8 miles (12.8 km) west of the city centre. It appears to have borne the name Sky Harbor, this title having appeared in a list of airports as early as 1929 and showing it as already equipped for night operations.

The present airport was initiated when, in 1935, the City of Phoenix spent $70,000 on the purchase of 235 acres (95 hectares) about 4 miles (6.4 km) east of downtown Phoenix.

The airport became an international port of entry on 6 October, 1970, and serves more than a million people in the Phoenix metropolitan area as well as being a major terminal for the southwestern United States.

The West Wing terminal was dedicated on 13 September, 1952, and the East Wing terminal came into public use on 16 April, 1962, being dedicated on 26 May that year. The East Wing terminal was designed to handle 1,800,000 passengers annually but major expansions have been made, including the addition of a rotunda building which increased the number of boarding gates from 14 to 22.

517

In 1972 the City Council approved a master plan for phased construction of six new terminals with 96 boarding gates and an annual capacity of 24 mn passengers—to be completed in 2015.

Contracts for Phase 1A of the master plan were awarded in November 1976 and these called for the construction by 1979 of the three-level Module III terminal to the east of the existing terminals. This has a planned floor area of 384,000 sq ft (35,674 sq m) and two separate north and south concourses with 15 boarding gates, 10 of them suitable for wide-bodied aircraft. Also under this phase the 08L/26R runway is to be extended by 2,250 ft (686 m) at its eastern end to provide a length of 11,000 ft (3,353 m).

When the Module III terminal is complete, the West Wing terminal and the old control tower will be demolished.

Phoenix enjoys extremely good weather, with about 7 in (18 cm) of rain annually and an average wind strength of less than 5 mph (8 km/h). In more than 30 years the airport has only been closed for a total of about 15 hr; nevertheless, runway 08R is equipped with CAT I lighting and ILS.

Pittsburgh, Pennsylvania   Greater Pittsburgh International Airport

40° 29′ 35″ N   80° 13′ 51″ W   14 nm (30 km) NW of city
ICAO: KPIT   IATA code: PIT   Time zone: GMT −5
Authority: County of Allegheny Department of Aviation
Area: 4,047 hectares (10,000 acres)
Elevation: 1,203 ft (367 m)   Ref temp: 28.1 deg C
Runways: 05/23   1,200 × 46 m (3,939 × 150 ft)
          10L/28R   3,201 × 46 m (10,502 × 150 ft) concrete, grooved
          10R/28L   3,048 × 46 m (10,001 × 150 ft) concrete, grooved
          14/32   2,469 × 46 m (8,101 × 150 ft) concrete, grooved
Pavement strength: 100,000 lb (45,360 kg) 1, 225,000 lb (102,058 kg) 2, 400,000 lb (181,437 kg) 3; 14/32 maximum auw 410,000 lb (185,972 kg) dual tandem
Landing category: ICAO CAT II
Lighting:
      R/W   05/23   MIRL
               10L/28R   HIRL and centreline. TDZ 10L/28R
               10R/28L and 14/32   HIRL
      App   R/W 10L   ALSF-1
               R/W 28L   ALSF-1 and VASIS
               R/W 28R   VASIS
               R/W 32   REIL (to have approach lighting)
      Thr   green
      Txy   blue edge
Aids: VORTAC, VDF, RVR 10L/28R and 28L, RVV 10L/28R and 28L, ILS CAT II 10L, ILS CAT I 28L and 32
Twr frequency: 119.1   App frequency: 118.7/124.15
Terminal: Two -level terminal with three traffic piers known as East, West and South Docks. 37 domestic gates and one international, and 19 aerobridges. Separate general aviation and cargo areas.

Greater Pittsburgh International Airport, view looking south across the terminal and runways. Runway 10L/28R is out of the picture to the right.
(*County of Allegheny Department of Aviation*)

Scheduled services 1978: Aeromech, Allegheny, American, Cumberland Airlines, Eastern, Northwest, Nordair, Seaboard World, TWA and United

Main base: Allegheny Airlines. The Pennsylvania Air National Guard has a base.

Traffic:	1970	1975	1976	1978
Passengers (total)	6,086,344	7,359,631	8,182,063	9,664,404
Cargo (tonnes)	24,330	18,311	20,790	39,519
Aircraft movements	274,444	285,165	310,150	336,366
Transport movements	179,082	226,561	246,932	278,474

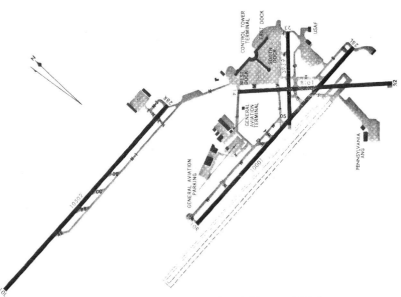

Greater Pittsburgh International Airport. (*FAA*)

519

Greater Pittsburgh Airport was dedicated on 31 May, 1952, and handled 1,176,364 passengers during its first year of operation. The terminal, at the north of the airport, comprised a three-level building with a central projecting traffic pier (known as South Dock) and 20 boarding gates. In 1959 the East Dock was added and in 1971 the West Dock, International Terminal, and rotundas at the ends of the East and South Docks, bringing the number of gates to 38.

A master plan for the development of the airport was produced in November 1972 and revised in January 1975, calling for a new 10R/28L runway of 11,000 by 200 ft (3,353 by 61 m) at the south of the airport, with parallel taxiway and high-speed exits, with completion at the end of 1979.

A further review of the master plan began late in 1977.

With the opening of the International Terminal in 1971 the airport was renamed Greater Pittsburgh International Airport.

Portland, Oregon   Portland International Airport

45° 35′ 21″ N	122° 35′ 36″ W	4.34 nm (8 km) NE of city
ICAO: KPDX	IATA code: PDX	Time zone: GMT −8

Authority: Port of Portland
Area: 1,214 hectares (3,000 acres)
Elevation: 26 ft (8 m)   Ref temp: 26 deg C
Runways: 02/20   2,134 × 46 m (7,000 × 150 ft) asphalt*
          10L/28R   2,440 × 46 m (8,004 × 150 ft) asphalt
          10R/28L   3,357 × 61 m (11,014 × 200 ft) asphalt

*Threshold 20 displaced 530 ft (162 m)

Pavement strength: 02/20   auw 170,000 lb (77,000 kg) 1,   200,000 lb (91,000 kg) 2, 340,000 lb (154,000 kg) 3; 10L/28R   130,000 lb (59,000 kg) 1, 190,000 lb (86,000 kg) 2, 350,000 lb (159,000 kg) 3; 10R/28L   170,000 lb (77,000 kg) 1, 200,000 lb (91,000 kg) 2, 360,000 lb (163,000 kg) 3
Landing category: ICAO CAT II

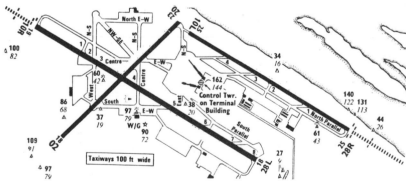

Portland International Airport. (*British Airways Aerad*)

520

Lighting:
```
R/W     02/20      MIRL
        10L/28R    HIRL
        10R/28L    HIRL and centreline. TDZ 10R
App     R/W 10L    VASIS
        R/W 10R    ALSF-2 and REIL
        R/W 20 and 28L    VASIS
        R/W 28R    ALSF-1
Thr     green all runways, strobes on 20
Txy     blue edge all taxiways
```
Aids: VORTAC, NDB, VDF, LOC/DME, ASR, SRE, RVR 10R/28L
    and 28R, RVV 10R and 28R, ILS CAT II 10R, ILS CAT I 28R
Twr frequency: 118.7/126.2   App frequency: 111.8/119.8
Terminals: Two-level passenger terminal with two long and one short
    traffic piers and 26 gates. Separate cargo and mail buildings
Scheduled services 1978: 13 airlines including two all-cargo and three
    commuter
Bases: The Oregon Air National Guard has its fighter base on the south
    side of the airport and there is a USAF Reserve search and rescue
    helicopter squadron

Traffic:	1970	1975	1976	1977	1978
Passengers (total)	2,473,836	3,087,198	3,357,087	3,716,807	4,187,846
Cargo (tonnes)	26,690	38,202	40,477	43,304	44,447
Aircraft movements	173,735	200,960	217,083	246,166	230,425
Transport movements	83,325	75,880	78,593	82,159	82,361

In 1976 Boeing 727s accounted for 55 per cent of transport movements and DC-9s for 16 per cent.

Portland's first municipal airport was opened in 1920 in the area now known as Westmoreland Park, but by the mid-1920s pressure was being exerted for construction of a larger airport on Swan Island, which had been acquired by the Port of Portland in 1921 in connection with dredging and filling operations on the Willamette River.

An aerodrome was prepared and the first landing was made in July 1927, by a military D.H-4. The first public use of the aerodrome was when Charles Lindbergh, on 14 December, 1927, landed his Ryan monoplane *Spirit of St Louis* as part of the dedication ceremonies. Ryan M-1s had been used when Pacific Air Transport had begun service through the original airport in 1926. A two/three-storey terminal was built and in 1930 the airport handled 5,830 passengers and 125 tons of cargo. In 1931 the airport was regarded as essentially complete but the traffic growth showed the need for expanded facilities and longer runways, and in 1935 the Bureau of Air Commerce notified the Port of Portland that it would not approve operation of larger aircraft at Portland Airport on the Swan Island site.

A search was made for a new airport site and early in 1936 the Portland voters approved purchase of 700 acres (283 hectares) of land in the Columbia Bottoms area adjacent to the Columbia River northeast of the city. Dredging and filling was completed by the end of the year and in 1940 the new Portland Columbia Airport was opened. In 1942 Swan Island was leased to the Federal Government for shipbuilding and the airport terminal was incorporated in the shipyard—it was finally demolished in 1964.

The terminal building at Portland International Airport. (*Port of Portland*)

Portland Columbia's first control tower was commissioned in 1941—a 15 ft (4.5 m) square tin box on top of 40 ft (12 m) steel legs. During the war the airport was used by military transports as well as civil aircraft and at present both the Oregon Air National Guard and a USAF Reserve search and rescue helicopter squadron have bases on the south of the airport. A pattern of paved runways was laid at what is now the northwest area of the airport, and these included east–west, northwest–southeast and northeast–southwest runways. It is believed that the last of these was extended and rebuilt to form the present 02/20.

For three months during 1948 the airport was closed by a devastating flood but in the following year airport expansion began with the start on construction of runway 10/28 of 8,800 ft (2,682 m), now the 11,014 ft (3,357 m) 10R/28L. The 10/28 runway was completed in 1952, giving the airport four operational runways and an area of 1,506 acres (609 hectares). That year the airport was renamed Portland International.

Facilities soon proved inadequate and in July 1956 work began on a new $4.25 mn terminal which was dedicated in September 1958 and was designed to handle 1½ mn passengers a year. In 1962 an 8,000 ft (2,438 m) 10L/28R runway was completed close to the river. In the same year the airport handled the volume of traffic which had been predicted for nearly 10 years later.

In 1966 the Port Commission authorized production of a master plan and various alternate developments were evaluated over the next six years. A plan for reclaiming a portion of the Columbia River was abandoned but it was decided to extend runway 10R/28L to its present length, to double the size of the terminal and provide 5 mn passengers annual capacity, increase car parking and improve airport access. The expanded terminal was dedicated on 16 May, 1977, and is expected to meet the airport's needs well into the 1980s when it is planned to build a second terminal.

In 1977 a new master plan was commissioned. Known as Airplan 2000 it was expected to take two years to complete, it will consider the airport and its vicinity and lay out the airport's development over the next 20 years. One study to be undertaken is the feasibility of a multi-modal cargo facility at or near the airport for air/road/rail/marine interchange.

Portland International Airport's runway 10R was cleared for CAT II operations in November 1974 and upgrading to CAT III is planned.

Raleigh-Durham, North Carolina   Raleigh-Durham Airport

35° 52′ 20″ N   78° 47′ 02″ W
10 nm (18.52 km) NW of Raleigh and 8.69 nm (16 km) SE of Durham
ICAO: KRDU   IATA code: RDU   Time zone: GMT −5
Authority: Raleigh-Durham Airport Authority
Area: 1,619 hectares (4,000 acres)
Elevation: 436 ft (133 m)
Runways: 05/23   2,286 × 46 m (7,500 × 150 ft) asphalt
         14/32   1,371 × 46 m (4,498 × 150 ft) asphalt and concrete
Pavement strength: 85,000 lb (38,555 kg) 1, 200,000 lb (90,718 kg) 2,
    400,000 lb (181,437 kg) 3
Landing category: ICAO CAT I
Lighting:
    R/W   05/23 and 14/32   HIRL
    App   R/W 05   ALSF-1
               R/W 23   MALSR and VASIS
               R/W 32   REIL and VASIS
    Thr   green
    Txy   blue edge
Aids: VORTAC, NDB, VDF, RVR 05, RVV 05, ILS CAT I 05 and 32
Twr frequency: 119.3   App frequency: 118.05/125.3
Terminal: Passenger terminal with two traffic piers and eight gates.
    Separate cargo area
Scheduled services 1978: Colgan Airways, Delta, Eastern, Piedmont,
    Resort Commuter Airlines, United, and Wheeler Flying Service

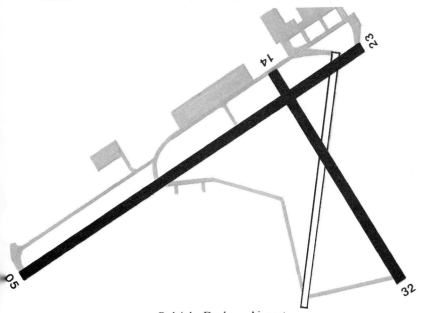

Raleigh-Durham Airport.

Airline bases: Delta, Eastern, Piedmont and United
Main base: Wheeler Flying Service

Traffic:	1970	1975	1976	1978
Passengers (embarked)	491,416	597,281	635,107	809,917
Cargo (tonnes)*	1,172	606	738	—
Aircraft movements	140,588	183,147	197,620	209,244

* Cargo figures may be for uplifted cargo, although supplied by the airport as total.

Requests for information on the history of this airport were unanswered. The airport may have been developed on the site of the original Raleigh Airport established during the 1920s.

Reno, Nevada   Reno International Airport

39° 29′ 51″ N   119° 46′ 02″ W   4 nm (7.4 km) SE of city
ICAO: KRNO   IATA code: RNO   Time zone: GMT −8
Authority: City of Reno Department of Airports
Elevation: 4,412 ft (1,345 m)   Ref temp: 33.3 deg C
Runways: 07/25   1,860 × 46 m (6,101 × 150 ft) concrete
          16R/34L   2,743 × 46 m (9,000 × 150 ft) concrete*

* Arrester cables on 16R/34L

Pavement strength: 75,000 lb (34,019 kg) 1, 185,000 lb (83,915 kg) 2,
    350,000 lb (158,757 kg) 3
Landing category: ICAO CAT I

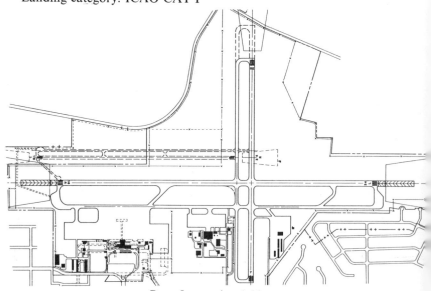

Reno International Airport.

The terminal area at Reno International Airport with a Boeing 727 and 737 on the apron. (*City of Reno Department of Airports*)

Lighting:

R/W	07/25	MIRL
	16R/34L	HIRL
App	R/W 16R	ALSF-1
	R/W 25	REIL
	R/W 34L	VASIS
Thr	green	
Txy	blue edge	

Aids: VORTAC, DME, NDB, RVV 16R, ILS CAT I 16R
Twr frequency: 118.7   App frequency: 119.2
Terminal: Passenger terminal with 10 gate positions. Separate general
    aviation area with facilities for three fixed-base operators
Scheduled services 1978: Hughes Airwest, United and Western

Traffic:	1975	1976	1978
Passengers (total)	1,044,716	1,268,678	2,302,423
Cargo (tonnes)	2,893	3,230	6,294
Aircraft movements	119,986	127,943	195,201
Transport movements	21,544	24,696	53,320

The airport was opened in 1929 as Boeing Field, soon renamed Hubbard Field, and then Reno Municipal Airport in 1960, the year that the present terminal was completed. The terminal is to be doubled in size and have a T-shaped pier by June 1980; a general aviation 16L/34R runway is planned to be operational by June 1985; and runway 07/25 is to be extended at its eastern end.

The Nevada Air National Guard has a base on the west side of the airport.

The airport is closed to Boeing 747s.

525

Rochester, New York   County of Monroe Airport-Rochester

43° 07′ 11″ N   77° 40′ 18″ W   4 nm (7.4 km) SW of city
ICAO: KROC   IATA code: ROC   Time zone: GMT −5
Authority: County of Monroe
Area: 438 hectares (1,083 acres)
Elevation: 560 ft (171 m)
Runways: 04/22   2,438 × 46 m (8,000 × 150 ft) concrete
         07/25   1,342 × 46 m (4,403 × 150 ft) asphalt
         10/28   1,676 × 46 m (5,500 × 150 ft) asphalt
Pavement strength: 126,000 lb (57,153 kg) 1, 160,000 lb (72,575 kg) 2,
     265,000 lb (120,202 kg) 3
Landing category: ICAO CAT I

County of Monroe Airport-Rochester. (*FAA*)

Lighting:
    R/W   04/22   HIRL and centreline. TDZ 04
            07/25   MIRL
            10/28   HIRL
    App   R/W 04   ALSF-2
            R/W 22   MALSR and VASIS
            R/W 28   ALSF-1
    Thr   green
    Txy   blue edge
Aids: VORTAC, NDB, ASR, RVR 04 and 28, ILS CAT I 04/22 and 28
Twr frequency: 118.3   App frequency: 123.7
Terminals: Passenger terminal with two concourses and 12 gates. Separate
     general aviation terminal
Scheduled services 1978: Allegheny, American, Commuter Airlines and
     United

526

An unpleasant day at County of Monroe Airport - Rochester. (*British Aerospace*)

Traffic:	1970	1975	1976
Passengers (total)	1,302,642	1,507,915	1,595,880
Cargo (tonnes)	—	4,582	8,449
Aircraft movements	252,684	247,987	218,475
Transport movements	41,685	43,759	45,384

This is possibly the Rochester Municipal Airport established in the 1920s and which in the early 1930s extended its two runways, installed a new beacon and rebuilt its waiting room; but all requests for information on the history of County of Monroe Airport have been unanswered.

It was planned that runway 04 should be cleared for CAT II operations during 1979.

St Louis, Missouri   Lambert-St Louis International Airport

38° 45′ 54″ N   90° 21′ 47″ W   9.5 nm (17.6 km) NW of city
ICAO: KSTL   IATA code: STL   Time zone: GMT −6
Authority: City of St Louis Airport Authority
Area: 890 hectares (2,200 acres)
Elevation: 589 ft (180 m)   Ref temp: 31.3 deg C
Runways: 06/24   2,317 × 61 m   (7,602 × 200 ft) concrete, grooved
         12L/30R   2,018 × 46 m   (6,621 × 150 ft) concrete
         12R/30L   3,053 × 61 m   (10,018 × 200 ft) asphalt
         17/35   1,219 × 46 m   (4,000 × 150 ft) concrete
    Runways 06/24 and 12R/30L have arresting devices at each end
Pavement strength: All runways 100,000 lb (45,359 kg) 1, 184,000 lb
    (83,460 kg) 2, 346,000 lb (156,943 kg) 3
Landing category: ICAO CAT I

Lighting:
- R/W   All runways HIRL
- App   R/W 06   SALS
  - R/W 12L and 30R   REIL and VASIS
  - R/W 12R   SSALSR
  - R/W 24   ALSF-1
  - R/W 30L   MALSR
- Thr   green
- Txy   blue edge

Aids: VORTAC, NDB, RVR 12R and 24, ILS CAT I 12R and 24

Twr frequency: 118.5   App frequency: 126.5

Terminals: Passenger terminal with three piers and international wing and 45 gates. Separate cargo buildings and general aviation areas

Scheduled services 1978: 16 airlines

Airline base: TWA. Missouri Air National Guard has a base

Main base: Ozark Air Lines

Traffic:	1970	1975	1976	1978
Passengers (total)	6,661,000	6,353,900	6,772,000	8,294,747
Cargo (tonnes)	59,874	43,635	49,240	80,660
Aircraft movements	322,142	314,400	321,055	341,296
Transport movements	188,410	174,200	175,377	239,479

St Louis International Airport began as the 169 acre (68 hectare) Lambert Field in 1920. The aerodrome was temporarily enlarged for the Pulitzer Trophy and International Air Races of 1923. Air mail services to

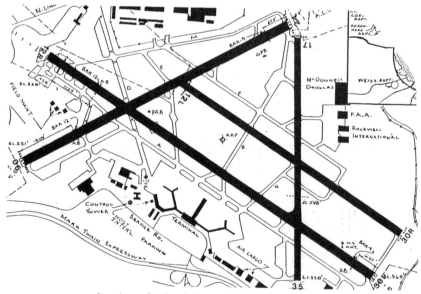

Lambert-St. Louis International Airport. (*FAA*)

528

View looking north across the terminal at Lambert-St Louis International Airport, with the cargo terminal in the right foreground and the McDonnell Douglas factory beyond the runways. (*City of St Louis Airport Authority*)

and from Chicago began in 1925 and in 1928 approval was given for the City's purchase of the aerodrome for development as the Municipal Airport. Five runways were laid and in 1933 a modern terminal was constructed. Lambert was Major Albert B. Lambert, a pioneer aviator and one of the first St Louis citizens to give financial backing to Charles Lindbergh for his New York–Paris flight in the Ryan NYP *Spirit of St Louis*. From 1939 the airport was the home of McDonnell Aircraft, now McDonnell Douglas.

After the Second World War a very fine terminal building was constructed,* consisting of arched segments, but traffic growth has forced the addition of long traffic piers at either end.

In 1969 there was a plan to build a new airport at Columbia - Waterloo in Illinois but this was cancelled because it was considered that Lambert could handle the forecast traffic at least until 1995 when the airport is expected to absorb 237,000 aircraft movements and 11.4 mn passengers.

In 1974 two 125-passenger Plane-Mates were purchased for use at the international terminal.

At the end of 1974 a plan was produced which called for two new parallel runways, of 11,000 and 10,000 ft (3,353 and 3,048 m), a considerable expansion of the terminal, new taxiways and relocation of the cargo terminal. This plan has been modified and the existing 12L/30R will be lengthened to 9,500 ft (2,896 m), reconstructed, equipped with centreline lighting and 30R upgraded to CAT II. Runway 12R/30L will be extended by 1,000 ft (305 m). Much of the redevelopment work was in hand by early 1979.

*The terminal was opened in 1956 but the old terminal was not demolished until 1978.

The terminal area at Salt Lake City International Airport with the 16/34 runways beyond and the 14 threshold near the centre of the picture.
(*Salt Lake City Airport Authority*)

Salt Lake City, Utah   Salt Lake City International Airport

40° 47′ 03″ N   111° 58′ 01″ W   2.6 nm (4.8 km) W of city
ICAO: KSLC   IATA code: SLC   Time zone: GMT −7
Authority: Salt Lake City Airport Authority
Area: 3,035 hectares (7,500 acres)
Elevation: 4,226 ft (1,288 m)   Ref temp: 33.3 deg C
Runways: 14/32   1,614 × 46 m (5,295 × 150 ft) asphalt
          16L/34R   2,925 × 46 m (9,596 × 150 ft)⎫ asphalt with porous
          16R/34L   3,018 × 46 m (9,902 × 150 ft)⎭ friction course
Pavement strength: 14/32 and 16L/34R   60,000 lb (27,215 kg) 1, 170,000 lb (77,111 kg) 2, 320,000 lb (145,149 kg) 3; 16R/34L 60,000 lb (27,215 kg) 1, 200,000 lb (90,718 kg) 2, 350,000 lb (158,757 kg) 3. Weights for 14/32 apply to centre 75 ft (23 m) only
Landing category: ICAO CAT II
Lighting:
       R/W   14/32   MIRL
                  16L/34R   HIRL
                  16R/34L   HIRL and centreline. TDZ 34L
       App   R/W 16L   MALSR
                  R/W 16R and 34R   VASIS
                  R/W 34L   ALSF-2
       Thr   green
       Txy   blue edge and LIH on high-speed exits

Aids: VORTAC, DME, VDF, ASR, RVR 16R and 34L, ILS CAT II 34L, ILS CAT I 16L

Twr frequency: 118.3 App frequency: 124.3

Terminals: Main terminal on west side of airport with two traffic piers serving 25 loading gates. North pier includes international arrivals area. Executive and general aviation terminal on east side of airport. Separate cargo and freight forwarding buildings

Scheduled services 1978: American, Frontier, Hughes Airwest, Key Airlines, Sky West Aviation, Texas International, United and Western

Main base: Key Airlines. Utah Air National Guard has its base on the east of the airport

Traffic:	1975	1976	1977	1978
Passengers	1,373,950*	1,564,835*	3,517,534	4,221,778
Cargo (tonnes)	8,801†	9,503†	33,543‡	35,256‡
Aircraft movements	—	255,475	260,277	262,396
Transport movements	30,164§	66,156	62,000‖	103,536

* Embarked only † Uplifted only ‡ Includes Air Express § Departures only ‖ Approximate

Salt Lake City established its municipal airport in the 1920s, dedicated its terminal in 1933 and constructed three paved runways in 1937.

In 1952 the City began planning today's facilities but meanwhile improved the old terminal building and extended the north–south runway from 5,500 ft (1,676 m) to 6,700 ft (2,042 m). In 1954 westward development of the airport began with the construction of the 8,300 ft (2,530 m) 16R/34L main instrument runway. In the following year the old runways, taxiways and aprons were resurfaced, and in 1956 filling began on

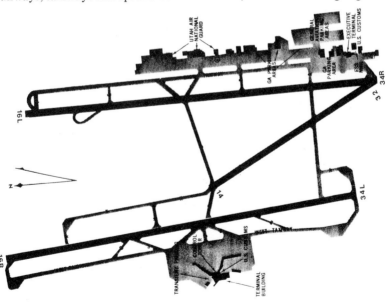

Salt Lake City International Airport. (*FAA*)

531

the west side of the airport for the new terminal on which construction began in 1959. Runway 16R/34L was also extended to its present length and a parallel taxiway laid down.

The new terminal was dedicated on 17 June, 1961, and in 1978 Unit No. 2 was added for use by Western Airlines.

1977 saw the addition of an apron for large aircraft adjacent to the cargo terminal and the construction of an executive and corporate terminal.

In 1979 work began to put an upper deck on Unit No. 1 of the terminal for second-level boarding and remodelling of the apron side of this unit. In 1980 the land side of Unit No. 1 is to be remodelled to match No. 2.

Looking further ahead, Boeing Aerosystems International has been awarded programme management for an expansion which envisages a terminal with six traffic piers and a greatly increased number of boarding gates.

San Antonio, Texas   San Antonio International Airport

29° 31′ 59″ N   98° 28′ 11″ W   6.95 nm (12.87 km) N of city
ICAO: KSAT   IATA code: SAT   Time zone: GMT −6
Authority: City of San Antonio
Area: 933 hectares (2,305 acres)
Elevation: 809 ft (246 m)   Ref temp: 35 deg C
Runways: 03L/21R   762 × 23 m (2,500 × 75 ft) asphalt*
         03R/21L   2,287 × 61 m (7,502 × 200 ft) asphalt/concrete
         12L/30R   1,098 × 30 m (3,601 × 100 ft) asphalt
         12R/30L   2,591 × 46 m (8,500 × 150 ft) asphalt/concrete,
                                                      grooved

*On taxiway

Pavement strength: 03L/21R   60,000 lb (27,216 kg) 1, 75,000 lb (34,019 kg) 2, 130,000 lb (58,967 kg) 3; 03R/21L   95,000 lb (43,091 kg) 1, 120,000 lb (54,431 kg) 2, 180,000 lb (81,647 kg) 3; 12L/30R   17,000 lb (7,711 kg) 1; 12R/30L   95,000 lb (43,091 kg) 1, 190,000 lb (86,182 kg) 2, 270,000 lb (122,470 kg) 3
Landing category: ICAO CAT II
Lighting:
    R/W   03L/21R and 12L/30R   MIRL
               03R/21L   HIRL
               12R/30L   HIRL and centreline. TDZ 12R
    App   R/W 03L/21R and 12L   VASIS
               R/W 03R   MALS
               R/W 12R   ALSF-2
               R/W 21L   REIL and VASIS
               R/W 30L   MALSR
    Thr   green all runways, strobes on 21L
    Txy   blue edge

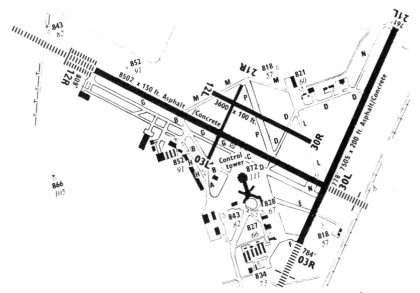

San Antonio International Airport. (*British Airways Aerad*)

Aids: **VORTAC, NDB, VDF, SRE, RVR 12R and 30L, ILS CAT II 12R, ILS CAT I 03R**

Twr frequency: 119.8   App frequency: 121.2

Terminal: 200,000 sq ft (18,580 sq m) terminal with traffic piers with 17 gates, to south of intersection of 12R and 03R. Separate cargo terminal

Scheduled services 1978: American, Braniff, Continental, Eastern, Méxicana, Southwest Airlines, Texas International and Trans Regional Airlines

Traffic:	1970*	1975	1976	1978
Passengers (embarked)	778,897	838,736	894,182	1.514,979
Cargo uplift (tonnes)	6,185	3,956	4,054	4,762
Aircraft movements	—	208,491	194,921	253,645
Transport movements	27,231	47,643	49,676	75,321

* Year ended 30 June, 1970

All requests for information on this airport have remained unanswered. It is possible that the airport was originally Winburn Field which was the San Antonio municipal airport opened during the 1920s. The airport is bordered on the west by US Highway 281, to the south by Loop Expressway 410, and on the east by the Missouri Pacific Rail Road.

Since the mid-1960s runway 03/21, now 03R/21L, has been extended at its northeast end from 5,301 ft (1,616 m) to 7,502 ft (2,287 m); the 5,452 ft (1,662 m) runway 17/35 has been closed, its northern half being used as a taxiway; the 3,601 ft (1,098 m) runway 12L/30R has been constructed; the 2,500 ft (762 m) 03L/21R has been made from a former taxiway; and the terminal apron has been considerably enlarged. There is either a new terminal or the old one has been enlarged and had concourses added.

San Diego International Airport-Lindbergh Field with the terminal area near the far end of the main runway and the Naval Air Station on North Island at top left.
(*Port of San Diego*)

San Diego, California
San Diego International Airport-Lindbergh Field

32° 43′ 58″ N   117° 11′ 14″ W   1.73 nm (3.2 km) W of city
ICAO: KSAN   IATA code: SAN   Time zone: GMT −8
Authority: San Diego Unified Port Authority
Area: 283 hectares (700 acres) approximately
Elevation: 15 ft (5 m)   Ref temp: 25.2 deg C
Runways: 09/27   2,865 × 61 m (9,400 × 200 ft)* concrete†
          13/31   1,353 × 23 m (4,439 × 75 ft)* asphalt-concrete

*Threshold displacements are: 09 703 ft (214 m); 27 1,816 ft (553 m); 13 550 ft (168 m); 31 400 ft (122 m)
† Non-standard grooving on west end

Pavement strength: 09/27   100,000 lb (45,359 kg) 1, 150,000 lb (68,039 kg) 2, 250,000 lb (113,399 kg) 3; 13/31   30,000 lb (13,608 kg)1*

*Airport allows all-up weight on 09/27 of 180,000 lb (81,647 kg) dual wheel and 350,000 lb (158,757 kg) dual tandem

Landing category: ICAO CAT I
Lighting:
R/W	09/27	HIRL
	13/31	MIRL
App	R/W 09	ALSF-1
	R/W 27	REIL and VASIS
Thr	green all runways	
Txy	blue edge	

534

Aids: VOR/DME, VDF, RVR 09/27, ILS CAT I 09
Twr frequency: 118.3/133.3 App frequency: 119.6
Terminal: East passenger terminal with 144,000 sq ft (13,378 sq m) floor
    space, two traffic piers with 16 gates and 18 aircraft stands; West
    terminal with 11 gates. Separate cargo buildings to east of terminals
Scheduled services 1978: 11 airlines
Main base: Pacific Southwest Airlines

Traffic:	1966	1970	1975	1976	1978
Passengers (total)	2,048,034	3,341,291	4,490,668	4,912,368	6,185,583
Cargo (tonnes)	5,074	11,438	14,023	14,852	25,045
Aircraft movements	181,469	217,130	195,016	207,401	203,808
Transport movements	46,233	77,609	70,722	73,883	—

San Diego International Airport, located at the northeast corner of
San Diego Bay, is just north of North Island where, at the end of December
1910, the first US Navy pilot began learning to fly at the Curtiss flying
school—the San Diego Naval Air Station is still on North Island.

It was also from San Diego that the first regular passenger air services
to be operated wholly over the mainland of the United States began, when
on 1 March, 1925, Ryan Airlines opened its service to Los Angeles. This
operated from 'Dutch Flats' north of the Marine Corps Base which is
immediately west of the present airport.

The present airport, Lindbergh Field, traces its beginning to a 1927
bond issue of $650,000 for the deepening of part of the Bay for harbour
development. The site of the airport was a large area of mud flats which
were sometimes covered by water at high tide. The excavated Bay mud was
used to reclaim 142 acres (57 hectares) of the tidelands and on this San
Diego Municipal Airport was constructed, dedication being on 16 August,
1928.

In 1931 Pacific Air Transport, a predecessor of United Airlines, leased
land at the airport and built a combination hangar/office/depot. On 16
October, 1934, the airport was given an A-1 rating by the Department of
Commerce and made a permanent international port of entry.

As traffic and the area's population increased, a larger airport became
necessary, and the City, Harbor Department, Navy, Army Corps of

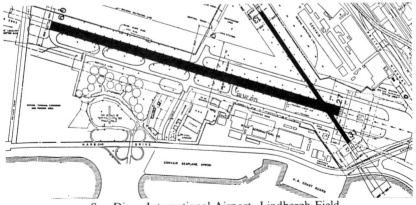

San Diego International Airport - Lindbergh Field.

535

Engineers and the WPA all sponsored dredging projects which provided additional tidal mud to bring the airport to 450 acres (182 hectares). The two runways were east–west, of 5,000 ft (1,524 m), and northwest–southeast, of 4,450 ft (1,356 m). Ryan and Consolidated both leased areas at the airport, and in 1942 the USAAF took over control of the site, making it imperative that runways be improved to handle heavy bombers. In 1944 the Federal Government placed contracts for the complete reconstruction of the runways. The northwest–southeast runway, 13/31, was lengthened to 4,719 ft (1,438 m), and the east–west runway, 09/27, was extended westward to provide 8,750 ft (2,667 m). The extension of 09/27 was built across the Marine Corps Base, and in 1949 the City received about 245 acres (99 hectares) of the Base for further airport expansion.

San Diego's traffic rapidly increased and the eight-gate terminal had to be replaced. Construction was authorized late in 1964, ground for the new terminal was broken in November 1965 on a site at the southwest of the airport and it was opened for traffic on 5 March, 1967, with 16 gates. A second terminal, immediately to its west, was opened in 1979.

The main, 09/27, runway was lengthened to 9,400 ft (2,865 m) but it has been necessary to displace all runway thresholds, and the proximity of built-up areas immediately to the east of the airport has meant that the 27 threshold has had to be displaced by 1,816 ft (553 m).

General Dynamics/Convair and Ryan still occupy large sites at the airport and at the southeast corner is a Coast Guard Station with seaplane ramp and heliport.

For more than 30 years there have been proposals for construction of a new airport, but in 1964 the Stanford Research Institute completed an 18-month study of Southern California airports and concluded that the present airport was 'unusually convenient' and only needed improvements. However, strong feeling was aroused in support of a new airport and the closure of Lindbergh Field when, on 25 September, 1978, a Pacific Southwest Airlines Boeing 727-200, on approaching the airport, collided with a Cessna 172 on a training flight from one of the numerous aerodromes in the area, and 136 people were killed, 13 of them on the ground by the falling wreckage.

San Francisco, California   San Francisco International Airport

37° 37′ 07″ N   122° 22′ 35″ W   7.8 nm (14.48 km) SE of city
ICAO: KSFO   IATA code: SFO   Time zone: GMT −8
Authority: City and County of San Francisco
Area: 2,107 hectares (5,207 acres) including about 1,012 hectares (2,500 acres) under water
Elevation: 12 ft (4 m)   Ref temp: 23.1 deg C
Runways: 01L/19R   2,134 × 61 m   (7,000 × 200 ft) asphalt
            01R/19L   2,896 × 61 m   (9,500 × 200 ft) asphalt
            10L/28R   3,618 × 61 m   (11,870 × 200 ft) asphalt
            10R/28L   3,231 × 61 m   (10,600 × 200 ft) asphalt
            11/29*   1,219 × 23 m   (4,000 × 75 ft)   asphalt

* Temporary general aviation runway marked on taxiway

Pavement strength: 60,000 lb (27,216 kg) 1, 190,000 lb (86,182 kg) 2, 350,000 lb (158,757 kg) 3
Landing category: ICAO CAT IIIa
Lighting:
R/W	01L/19R and 01R/19L	HIRL
	10L/28R	HIRL and centreline. TDZ 28R
	10R/28L	HIRL and centreline. TDZ 28L
App	R/W 10L	REIL
	R/W 10R	VASIS
	R/W 19L	SALSF-1
	R/W 28L	ALSF-1
	R/W 28R	ALSF-2
Thr	green	
Txy	blue edge on some taxiways	

Aids: VOR/DME, RVR all main runways, RVV, ILS CAT IIIa 28R, ILS CAT I 19L and 28L

Twr frequency: 120.5/128.65   App frequency: 123.85/124.4

Terminals: Central, South and North passenger terminals with eight piers and international rotunda building. 86 gates. Separate cargo areas
Scheduled services 1978: 27 airlines
Airline bases: American, Flying Tiger, Pacific Southwest, Pan American, TWA and United. Also US Coast Guard Air Station
Main base: Hughes Airwest

Traffic:	1970	1975	1976	1977	1978
Passengers (total)	14,447,929	17,503,778	18,765,087	19,498,146	23,040,603
Cargo (tonnes)	287,278	294,817	310,260	337,168	469,333
Aircraft movements	386,674	326,677	342,509	344,786	355,896
Transport movements	306,520	285,269	293,522	290,742	295,993

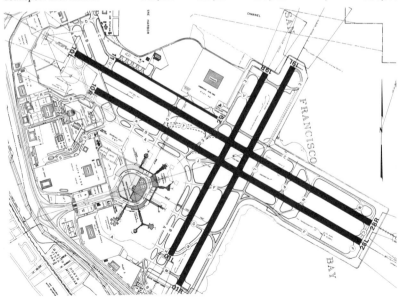

San Francisco International Airport.

Flying began in the San Francisco area at the beginning of 1911, various sites being used including a bayside strip at the Presidio, by the Golden Gate, which later became Crissy Field. After the First World War flying again took place from numerous sites, including Crissy Field which was often affected by fog or crosswinds, but there was a demand for provision of a municipal aerodrome.

No suitable site for airport development could be found within the city limits and in November 1926 San Francisco's voters approved a Charter amendment authorizing acquisition of land outside the city. A site of 155 acres (62.7 hectares) on Ogden Mills estate, in San Mateo county between the old Bayshore Boulevard and the Bay eastward from San Bruno, then a small country village, was selected, and in March 1927 approval was given to leasing the site for 3–5 years and the spending of $100,000 on development. Eight sites had been considered and of these six were between the Southern Pacific railway tracks and the Bay and most have since been incorporated in the present airport.

A grass aerodrome was prepared, a wooden administration building was built which included a public waiting room and a forest of lights above the roof, and there was a 10,000 sq ft (929 sq m) hangar, an apron, and boundary lighting. The aerodrome was dedicated on 7 May, 1927, as Mills Field Municipal Airport of San Francisco and was fully operational from 7 June. Following the opening, work began on three more hangars and preparation of a 1,700 ft (518 m) graded earth runway.

The first transport aeroplane, owned by Boeing Air Transport, landed at Mills Field on 21 September, 1927. By the end of the year there had been 2,895 landings and 4,562 passengers used the airport. In 1928 there were 19,457 landings and 33,740 passengers.

Three macadam-surfaced 200 ft (61 m) wide runways were prepared: nevertheless, the airport was described as a 'mud hole' and the competitors in the Dole race to Honolulu in 1927 preferred Oakland across the Bay.

In May 1928 West Coast Air Express, Western Air Express and Maddux Airlines decided to base their Bay Region activities at Mills Field, but airport development over the next three years was minimal although authorization to purchase 1,100 acres (445 hectares) of pasture and tidelands was given and a master plan produced. In 1931 Mills Field was renamed San Francisco Airport but the airlines, except for Century Pacific, had left. However, Pacific Air Transport moved in in December 1932 and Transcontinental & Western Air in February 1933.

Almost the entire development of San Francisco Airport has taken place on land reclaimed from the Bay. In November 1935 the first expansion of the operating area had been completed with a 38 acre (15 hectare) triangular area of fill and this provided sufficient space for two 3,000 ft (914 m) paved runways. In 1937 a two-storey Spanish-style steel and concrete terminal, measuring 225 ft (68.6 m) by 90 ft (27.4 m), was opened and in that year the Coast Guard selected the airport for a land-sea-air rescue base.

In the mid-1930s a revised master plan was produced calling for a much expanded area which would allow extension of the main runway (north-northwest–south-southeast) to 5,000 ft (1,524 m), the extension of the northwest–southeast runway, described as the east–west instrument runway, to 6,000 ft (1,829 m), and the building of a 5,000 ft (1,524 m)

538

San Francisco International Airport, looking east. The 10/28 runways run from the left edge. The terminal occupies the centre of the picture with the Central terminal facing the main access road and the curved South terminal to the right. The International Rotunda is to the right of the access road. The North terminal had not been built. To the left of the access road are the United Airlines maintenance base and cargo building. To the right of the road are the Pan American and TWA bases. American Airlines base is to the left of the 19 thresholds, with to its left the seaplane harbour. (*Courtesy Airport Forum*)

north–south runway and a 4,200 ft (1,280 m) east-southeast–west-northwest runway. It was also proposed to provide a 2,300 ft (701 m) diameter seaplane harbour and terminal in the hope that Pan American Airways would transfer its Pacific-operations base from Yerba Buena Island*, near the Bay Bridge.

By 1938 the airport area had been expanded to 2,265.33 acres (916.76 hectares) but the total airport staff was only 21. Development was slow but the north–south runway was completed and the dredging to a depth of 10 ft (3 m) of the seaplane harbour began at the end of 1936. After the Japanese attack on Pearl Harbor the airport came under military control but restricted civil operations were allowed. The Navy commandeered PAA's Yerba Buena base and also developed the airport's seaplane base where it

* It is of interest to recall that in planning the Golden Gate International Exposition which took place in 1939 on the manmade Treasure Island beside Yerba Buena Island, three of the principal buildings were designed for airport use and it was proposed that after the exhibition closed the San Francisco Airport should be built on the Yerba Buena shoals and that it would have provided 4,000 ft (1,219 m) runways aligned in any desired directions.

built hangars and a terminal—the base becoming operational in 1944. Runways, taxiways and aprons were enlarged and strengthened to accommodate multi-engined military aircraft.

In 1939–40 the airport had handled 126,546 passengers but in spite of wartime restrictions the 1945 figure was 521,568. To meet the rapidly growing traffic a new master plan was produced and in 1945 a crash programme was begun for major expansion. This included the grading of enough land to provide 3,000 acres (1,214 hectares) above high tide and acquisition of about 2,200 acres (890 hectares) of tidelands to be reserved as clearways to protect the approaches to the most-used runways. Operations were to take place from two sets of parallel runways at right angles (01/19 and 10/28). The Bayshore Highway was relocated a mile to the west and a new terminal built to handle an estimated 5 mn passengers which would use the airport in the late 1960s.

The new central terminal, with two traffic piers, was dedicated on 27 August, 1954, when it appears that the name was changed to San Francisco International Airport. The new runways were all operational from 1 September, 1954, and were: 01L/19R of 7,000 ft (2,134 m), 01R/19L of 7,750 ft (2,362 m), 10L/28R of 8,870 ft (2,704 m) and 10R/28L of 6,500 ft (1,981 m). Additional taxiways had also been constructed to serve the new runway pattern.

Traffic grew faster than predicted and the airport actually handled more than 5 mn passengers in 1960, and the curved South terminal was built, and dedicated on 15 September, 1963. The new terminal was designed to handle 7 mn passengers a year and the Central terminal was expanded to handle a similar number.

Almost continuous development has been taking place, with terminal additions, enlarged car parks, new roads and runway extensions. Runway 01R/19L was extended to 9,500 ft (2,896 m), 10R/28L to 10,600 ft (3,231 m) and in July 1974 the extension of 10L/28R to 12,000 ft (3,658 m) was completed and equipped for CAT II operation, being cleared for CAT IIIa on 26 February, 1976. To a large extent the 10/28 extensions had been made to reduce noise nuisance to the west of the airport.

The nine-gate International Rotunda (Pier G) was built onto the South terminal and dedicated on 3 April, 1974, bringing the number of piers to six and gates to 55. By that time, for more than six years the airport had been handling a passenger volume in excess of its design capacity. In 1968 the Airports Commission had proposed construction of a two-pier four-storey North terminal to provide the airport with a total of 86 gates, 70 for wide-bodied aircraft, and capacity for 24 mn passengers a year. Although provision of this terminal did not involve any overall expansion of the airport, it was violently opposed and its construction was delayed for three years—the original completion schedule for 1975 had to be amended to December 1978, with opening in 1979.

In spite of the objections to the North terminal, San Francisco is not unduly restrained because of noise, it being possible to handle 98–99 per cent of all approaches over the Bay and to make nearly 70 per cent of take offs towards the Bay.

Seattle-Tacoma International Airport looking north-northwest. The South satellite terminal is at the near end of the apron and the hangar with the tail cut-out is that of Northwest Airlines. (*Port of Seattle*)

Seattle, Washington   Seattle-Tacoma International Airport

47° 26′ 55″ N   122° 18′ 28″ W   10.4 nm (19.3 km) S of Seattle
ICAO: KSEA   IATA code: SEA   Time zone: GMT −8
Authority: Port of Seattle
Area: More than 809 hectares (2,000 acres)
Elevation: 428 ft (130 m)   Ref temp: 24 deg C
Runways: 16L/34R   3,627 × 46 m (11,900 × 150 ft) asphalt
         16R/34L   2,873 × 46 m (9,425 × 150 ft) concrete, grooved
         17/35*   876 × 23 m (2,875 × 75 ft) concrete

*General aviation and STOL runway on taxiway for VFR daylight operations by aircraft under 12,500 lb (5,670 kg)

Pavement strength: 16L/34R   160,000 lb (72,575 kg) 1, 200,000 lb (90,718 kg) 2, 320,000 lb (145,150 kg) 3, 800,000 lb (362,874 kg) 4·
     16R/34L   100,000 lb (45,359 kg) 1, 200,000 lb (90,718 kg) 2. 350,000 lb (158,757 kg) 3, 800,000 lb (362,874 kg) 4
Landing category: ICAO CAT II
Lighting:
    R/W   16L/34R   HIRL
            16R/34L   HIRL and centreline. TDZ 16R
    App   R/W 16L   MALS (F) and VASIS
            R/W 16R   ALSF-2
            R/W 34L   VASIS
            R/W 34R   ALSF-1
    Thr   green
    Txy   blue edge, centreline on main taxiways and high-speed exits
Aids: VORTAC, NDB, ASR, ASDE, RVR 16L/34R and 16R/34L, ILS CAT II 16R, ILS CAT I 34R

Twr frequency: 119.9 App frequency: 119.2/119.5/120.4/123.9

Terminals: 835,000 sq ft (77,571 sq m) main passenger terminal with four concourses and two satellites with 1,915,000 sq ft (177,903 sq m) of floor space. 9,050 ft (2,758 m) of underground automated railway links the terminal and satellites. 58 loading gates in use at autumn 1978. Separate cargo and mail handling buildings. Flying Tiger has major cargo terminal

Scheduled services 1978: 17 airlines

Airline bases: Alaska Airlines, Northwest Airlines, Pan American and Western Airlines

Traffic:	1970	1975	1976	1978
Passengers (total)	4,653,443	6,112,423	6,806,748	8,364,446
Cargo (tonnes)	75,196	152,641	162,804	211,368
Aircraft movements	150,676	163,759	173,525	194,991
Transport movements	104,414	109,962	114,998	—

Seattle - Tacoma International Airport

By 1922 the Duwamish River, south of Seattle, had been straightened and dredging and filling completed, and farms began to flourish on the reclaimed flood plain. But filling continued and the valley was raised 18 ft (5.48 m) and given a cinder top-dressing. On part of this site an aerodrome was established, with a south-southwest–north-northeast cinder runway of about 2,000 ft (610 m) and two hangars, one belonging to Boeing. In 1928 King County acquired the aerodrome and on 26 July that year there was an official dedication ceremony with 50,000 people and numerous aeroplanes present. On the following day the first Boeing 80 made its maiden flight from the site. The Boeing Field administration building was dedicated on 21 April, 1930, and for the rest of the decade Boeing Field served as the Seattle airport. Boeing built up its factories on the west side of the airport and the civil facilities on the east became King County Airport. Now known as Boeing Field/King County International Airport it still serves Boeing and some commercial operations and has a 10,000 ft (3,048 m) runway.

During the Second World War, however, the demands by military aviation on Boeing Field made it necessary to find a site for a new civil airport. A 906 acre (367 hectare) site was selected in the Bow Lake area 14

542

miles (22.5 km) south of downtown Seattle and 18 miles (29 km) north of Tacoma, and in 1944 the Seattle-Tacoma Airport was opened, consisting of a runway, a quonset hut and a shack. Cost of the land and construction was $5 mn.

In 1947 a temporary passenger terminal was built and in 1949 this was replaced by a large glass-fronted terminal. Considerable expansion took place to accommodate increasing traffic and meet the demands of the jet era which for the United States had been initiated by Boeing only a few miles away at the old Boeing Field.

In the period 1969–72 Sea-Tac International Airport, as it is now generally known, underwent largescale development to bring it to its present state, with two parallel runways and a temporary general aviation runway providing for up to 300,000 annual aircraft movements, and its terminal complex, with automated underground railway, being capable of handling up to 12 mn passengers a year.

Sites have been allocated for considerable development of cargo and maintenance areas and there are plans for taxiway extensions. It is also planned to upgrade the airport for CAT III operations. It is considered that the airport can serve the area's requirements for the rest of the century and will be capable of handling 20 mn passengers annually.

Spokane, Washington   Spokane International Airport

47° 37′ 12″ N   117° 31′ 58″ W   5.2 nm (9.65 km) SW of city
ICAO: KGEG   IATA code: GEG   Time zone: GMT −8
Authority: Spokane International Airport Board
Area: 1,120 hectares (2,767 acres)
Elevation: 2,372 ft (723 m)   Ref temp: 29.1 deg C
Runways: 03/21   2,743 × 46 m (9,000 × 150 ft) concrete
           07/25   2,499 × 46 m (8,199 × 150 ft) asphalt/concrete
           Runway 16/34 has been closed
Pavement strength: 03/21   100,000 lb (45,359 kg) 1, 200,000 lb (90,718 kg) 2, 350,000 lb (158,757 kg) 3; 07/25   40,000 lb (18,144 kg) 1, 80,000 lb (36,287 kg) 2, 150,000 lb (68,039 kg) 3
Landing category: ICAO CAT II
Lighting:
     R/W   03/21   HIRL, centreline and distance to go markers. TDZ 21
               07/25   MIRL
     App   R/W 03, 07 and 25   VASIS
             R/W 21   ALSF-1 (to have ALSF-2)
     Thr   03/21   green
     Txy   blue edge
Aids: VORTAC, DME, NDB, ASR, RVR 03/21, RVV 03/21, ILS CAT II 21
Twr frequency: 118.3   App frequency: 124.7
Terminals: Terminal to northwest of 03/21 with two piers and 11 gates. Separate cargo terminal

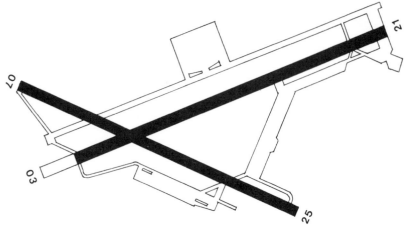

Spokane International Airport.

Scheduled services 1978: Cascade Airways, Columbia Pacific Airlines, Frontier, Hughes Airwest, Northwest and United
Main base: Cascade Airways

Traffic:	1970*	1975	1976	1978
Passengers (embarked)	436,326	551,756	633,087	677,488
Cargo uplift (tonnes)	1,354	2,374	2,744	10,037§
Aircraft movements	73,389	130,572	142,731	—
Transport movements†	14,717	27,672	29,619	45,722§

* Year ended 30 June, 1970 † Departures § Total

Spokane's prewar municipal airport was Felts Field, to the east of the city. This was opened during the 1920s and by 1930 was said to be one of the best equipped airports in the United States.

The present Spokane International Airport, southwest of the city, may have been a wartime military aerodrome with three runways, but the 16/34 runway has been withdrawn from use.

CAT II operations began on runway 21 in December 1977, a waiver having been granted on rock penetration of the approach light system and non-standard threshold lights but RVR is limited to 1,600 ft (488 m) pending installation of ALSF-2.

No requests for information on this airport have been answered.

Syracuse, New York   Syracuse Hancock International Airport

43° 06′ 41″ N   76° 06′ 29″ W   5 nm (9.2 km) E of city
ICAO: KSYR   IATA code: SYR   Time zone: GMT −5
Authority: City of Syracuse Department of Aviation
Area: 809 hectares (2,000 acres)
Elevation: 421 ft (86 m)   Ref temp: 27.8 deg C

Runways: 06/24*   994 × 46 m (3,261 × 150 ft) concrete
        10/28   2,748 × 46 m (9,005 × 150 ft) asphalt
        14/32   2,286 × 46 m (7,500 × 150 ft) asphalt

* Closed to air carrier operations, restricted to aircraft of 12,500 lb (5,670 kg) auw

Pavement strength: 10/28   91,000 lb (41,277 kg) 2;   14/32   80,500 lb
    (36,514 kg) 2
Landing category: ICAO CAT I
Lighting:
    R/W   06/24   MIRL
             10/28   HIRL and centreline. TDZ 28
             14/32   HIRL
    App   R/W 10   MALSR and REIL
             R/W 14   REIL
             R/W 28   ALSF-1
             R/W 32   VASIS
    Thr   green
    Txy   blue edge

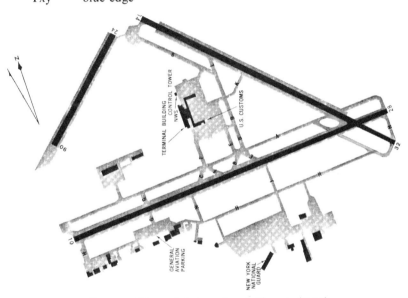

Syracuse Hancock International Airport. (*FAA*)

Aids: VORTAC, NDB, ASR, RVR 28, RVV 28, ILS CAT I 28
Twr frequency: 120.3   App frequency: 118.85/124.6
Terminals: Passenger terminal with North and South Fingers. Allegheny
    Airlines operates from North Finger and American Airlines and
    Eastern Air Lines from South Finger which contains customs and
    immigration. Separate cargo terminal and general aviation area
Scheduled services 1978: Allegheny, American, Eastern, Flying Tiger,
    Otonabee Airways and Wagner Aviation

Syracuse Hancock International Airport in June 1978. South is at the base of the photograph. (*City of Syracuse Department of Aviation*)

Traffic:	1970	1975	1976	1977	1978
Passengers (total)	1,303,628	1,381,698	1,474,813*	1,560,849*	1,750,340
Cargo (tonnes)	9,323	8,733	8,195	6,449	5,599
Aircraft movements	158,339	162,165	157,633	189,358	—
Transport movements	—	—	44,016	44,723	39,773

* Excluding transit

Syracuse's first municipal airport was opened in 1929 near the small village of Amboy, west of the city, and remained in operation until 1949.

During the war a bomber base was constructed at Mattydale, east of the city. This had three runways, 06/24 and 10/28 each of 5,500 ft (1,676 m) and 14/32 which appears to have been of the same length. After the war the military base was taken over by the City of Syracuse as Hancock Airport, named after Congressman Clarence E. Hancock. An old machine shop was converted to serve as a passenger terminal.

A new terminal, with two traffic piers, was opened in the centre of the airport in 1962 and its approach road had to be constructed across the southern end of runway 06/24 which is now the 3,261 ft 994 m) general aviation runway. Runway 10/28 has been extended three times; runway 14/32 was extended to 6,480 ft (1,975 m) and then in 1977 to 7,500 ft (2,286 m).

A new cargo terminal with separate apron and taxiways was completed in 1972–73.

Category II ILS for runway 28 was installed in 1978 and an FAA lighting waiver was given for 150 ft (46 m) decision height and 1,600 ft (488 m) RVR; but the system had not been commissioned by mid-January 1979.

Planned for the period 1977–80 was an upgrading of runways and taxiways, including high-speed exits from 10/28, and at the north of the airport a 3,650 ft (1,113 m) 10/28 general aviation runway with parallel taxiway and large general aviation and transient apron and tie-down area. Construction of these new general aviation facilities, planned for 1980, will necessitate the closing of runway 06/24.

With the opening of scheduled services to and from Canada and the increasing use of the airport by supplemental charter airlines, the airport's name was changed in 1970 from Clarence E. Hancock to Syracuse Hancock International.

There is a New York Air National Guard base on the southern boundary.

Tampa, Florida   Tampa International Airport

27° 58′ 25″ N   82° 31′ 57″ W   3.47 nm (6.4 km) W of city
ICAO: KTPA   IATA code: TPA   Time zone: GMT −5
Authority: Hillsborough County Aviation Authority
Area: 1,335 hectares (3,300 acres)
Elevation: 27 ft (8 m)   Ref temp: 32 deg C
Runways: 09/27   2,134 × 46 m (7,000 × 150 ft) asphalt/concrete*
           18L/36R   2,530 × 46 m (8,300 × 150 ft) asphalt/concrete*
           18R/36L   2,652 × 46 m (8,700 × 150 ft) concrete, grooved

* 75 ft (23 m) concrete centre is wire combed

Pavement strength: 09/27   70,000 lb (32,000 kg) 1, 85,000 lb (39,000 kg) 2, 140,000 lb (64,000 kg) 3; 18L/36R unlimited ISWL, 200,000 lb (91,000 kg) 2, 780,000 lb (340,000 kg) 3; 18R/36L   unlimited ISWL, 210,000 lb (95,000 kg) 2, 400,000 lb (181,000 kg) 3, 850,000 lb (386,000 kg) 4
Landing category: ICAO CAT II
Lighting:
    R/W   09/27   MIRL
             18L/36R   HIRL
             18R/36L   HIRL and centreline. TDZ 36L
    App   R/W 09/27   REIL and VASIS
             R/W 18L   ALSF-1 and VASIS
             R/W 18R and 36R   VASIS
             R/W 36L   ALSF-2 and VASIS
    Thr   green
    Txy   blue edge on major taxiways and high-speed exit 36L
Aids: VOR/DME, NDB, ARTS-8, RVR 18L and 36L, LLWSAS, ILS CAT II 36L, ILS CAT I 18L
Twr frequency: 119.5   App frequency: 118.5
Terminals: Multi-level landside building with four airside buildings connected by elevated Westinghouse automatic passenger shuttle system. Provision in plan for two more airside buildings. 60 gates. Separate general aviation and cargo areas
Scheduled services 1978: 14 airlines

Traffic:	1970	1975	1976	1978
Passengers (total)	2,740,538	5,163,284	5,476,712	6,984,037
Cargo (tonnes)	16,429	24,700*	27,231	45,644
Aircraft movements	155,749	193,650	192,037	223,155
Transport movements	80,229	117,434	128,966	150,065

* Rounded figure

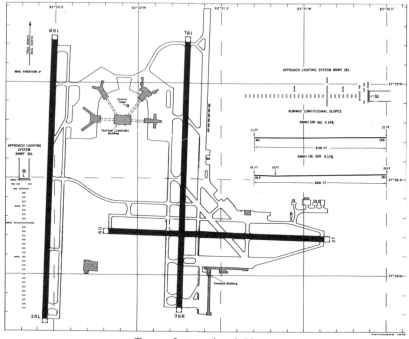

Tampa International Airport.

At 10.23 on 1 January, 1914, a small Benoist flying-boat operated by St Petersburg -Tampa Airboat Line, piloted by Anthony Jannus and carrying one passenger, alighted at Tampa after a 23-minute flight from St Petersburg. That was the world's first scheduled air service.

But Tampa's early association with air transport was not sustained and the city's first steps in acquiring an airport were not taken until 1927 when 160 acres (64.75 hectares) of land were leased from John H. Drew. Named Drew Field, the aerodrome was used as a flying school and for flying meetings, the first hangar being built in 1929; in 1935, however, the city's first airport to be used by air services was developed for land and marine aircraft on Davis Island. Named Peter O. Knight Airport, this remained the commercial airport until the spring of 1946.

In 1933 the City's lease of Drew Field ended but following protracted negotiations it acquired the site, for $11,654, on 10 February, 1934. Two weeks later the Federal Government allocated $31,000 for long-range development of airport facilities, and a further $47,000 was allocated in 1935. Three 7,000 ft (2,134 m) runways were laid out to form a triangle, lighting was installed, hangars built and a small paved apron provided, but the airlines stayed at Peter O. Knight Airport—now used for general aviation.

Drew Field, by then 240 acres (97 hectares), was leased to the Federal Government in 1940 for the duration of the war or 25 years, and as Drew Army Air Force Base it was used for aircrew training. On 1 March, 1946, the airport was formally returned to the City of Tampa and custody was transferred to the Hillsborough County Aviation Authority. At that time the site had been extended to 1,733 acres (701 hectares).

Various improvements were made and National Airlines began scheduled services through Tampa on 25 April, or 1 May, 1946, and Eastern Air Lines followed on 1 or 15 May.* The one- and two-level wooden terminal had been adapted from the old USAAF administration building. A new terminal was constructed in stages south of runway 09/27 and east of the south end of the 18/36 runway (now 18L/36R). The west section of the terminal was opened in 1952 together with an apron with 10 aircraft stands. The east section was completed in December 1958, and the open-air baggage-claim area between the two sections was enclosed to form one continuous unit which was opened in the spring of 1961. Runway 18R/36L was commissioned on 15 July, 1963, and 18L/36R was extended to 8,300 ft (2,530 m).

* Hillsborough County Aviation Authority give both sets of inaugural dates

Tampa International Airport central terminal and airside buildings. The tracks for the automatic shuttle system are clearly visible.
(*Hillsborough County Aviation Authority*)

549

Almost continuous runway, taxiway and lighting improvements took place but in April 1961 the FAA advised that Tampa's airport should continue on its present site or be developed at MacDill Air Force Base. Subsequently it was ruled that MacDill should remain as a military base, and the decision was taken to develop the existing Tampa International Airport, as it had been renamed on 15 October, 1947.

Detailed planning for a new terminal began in 1965 and, to prevent airport sprawl, a new concept was devised. This consisted of a central building known as the Landside building, with full passenger facilities and surmounted by three levels of car parking, and a series of satellite or 'Airside' buildings located in a circle round the Landside building and connected to it by double elevated roads, 30 ft (9 m) apart, on each of which runs an automated electric shuttle.

The new terminal complex, between the north–south runways, was opened on 15 April, 1971. The four satellites, each of different design and now having 15 gates each, are Airside B (No. 2) with three concourses; Airside C (No. 3) with customs and immigration, a main and two branch concourses; Airside D (No. 4) with two concourses; and Airside E (No. 5) with two concourses. Aircraft park nose-in with the noses under cover. When required, Airside A (No. 1) and F (No. 6) will be built south of the Landside building and the total of at least 72 gates is expected to be adequate to handle 20 mn passengers a year.

The Airside buildings are 1,000 ft (305 m) from the Landside building and the Westinghouse 100–125-passenger air-conditioned track-guided vehicles cover the distance in 40 seconds. Each satellite is served by two vehicles, each capable of handling 5,040 passengers an hour.

Space has been allocated for the northward extension of runway 18L/36R to 10,500 ft (3,200 m) and 18R/36L to 11,100 ft (3,383 m). Runway 09/27 can be extended eastward to 8,200 ft (2,499 m) and there is a proposal for a 3,700 by 75 ft (1,128 by 23 m) north–south general aviation runway to the west of 18R/36L.

Tucson, Arizona   Tucson International Airport

32° 07′ 08″ N   110° 56′ 36″ W   6 nm (11 km) S of city
ICAO: KTUS   IATA code: TUS   Time zone: GMT −7
Authority: Tucson Airport Authority
Area: 1,011 hectares (2,500 acres)
Elevation: 2,630 ft (802 m)   Ref temp: 37.2 deg C
Runways: 03/21   2,134 × 46 m   (7,000 × 150 ft) asphalt*
           11L/29R   3,658 × 46 m   (12,000 × 150 ft) asphalt†
           11R/29L   1,585 × 23 m   (5,200 × 75 ft) asphalt‡

* Threshold 03 displaced 851 ft (259 m) and 21 displaced 500 ft (152 m). Arrester gear on 21 and 11L/29R

† Runway 11L/29R has 1,000 ft (305 m) asphalt overrun each end

‡ Runway 11R/29L is listed by the FAA as being 9,105 ft (2,775 m) long. It is in fact a 75 ft (23 m) wide taxiway being used as a temporary general aviation runway. Threshold 11R is displaced 2,143 ft (653 m) and 29L is displaced 1,762 ft (537 m).

Pavement strength: 190,000 lb (86,182 kg) 1, 200,000 lb (90,718 kg) 2, 350,000 lb (158,757 kg) 3
Landing category: ICAO CAT I
Lighting:

R/W	03/21	MIRL
	11L/29R	HIRL
App	R/W 11L	MALSR
	R/W 21	REIL and VASIS
	R/W 29R	VASIS
Thr	03/21 and 11L/29R	green
Txy	blue edge on most taxiways	

Aids: VORTAC, NDB, VDF, RAD, ILS CAT I 11L
Twr frequency: 118.3/119.0   App frequency: 118.5/125.1
Terminals: Three-level terminal with two piers, 11 air carrier stands and one commuter stand. Separate general aviation and cargo terminals
Scheduled services 1978: Aeroméxico, American, Cochise Airlines, Continental, Frontier, Hughes Airwest and TWA
Main base: Cochise Airlines. Arizona Air National Guard has base

Traffic:	1970	1975	1976
Passengers (embarked)	463,201	615,986	665,240
Cargo (tonnes)	6,473	8,106	7,585
Aircraft movements	190,829	223,250	256,669
Transport movements	38,026	33,905	35,450

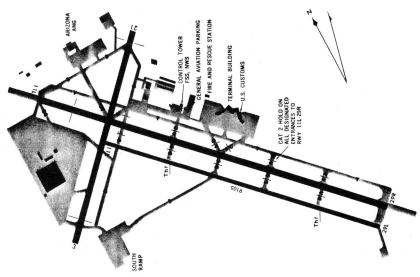

Tucson International Airport. (*FAA*)

The site of Tucson International Airport, immediately east of the Tucson–Nogales Highway and Southern Pacific railway tracks, was selected in 1940 but the airport did not receive scheduled air services until 1948.

The City had opened a municipal airport as early as 1919. In May of

551

The Tucson International Airport terminal with American Airlines and Continental Airlines Boeing 707s on the apron. (*Tucson Airport Authority*)

that year the US Army Air Service wrote to the Mayor asking that the city should build a permanent aerodrome. A site was chosen on an 82.64 acre (33.4 hectare) tract of land four miles (6.4 km) south of the city on Nogales Highway where the Rodeo Grounds are now situated. The site was approved by General Billy Mitchell, the aerodrome was named New Macauley Field, and the first landing, almost certainly by a Curtiss Jenny, was on 20 November, 1919. New Macauley Field was claimed to be the first municipal aerodrome in the United States and in 1920 it was renamed Fishburn Field.

However, a larger aerodrome was needed and this was prepared southeast of the city and dedicated in 1927 by Charles Lindbergh as Davis-Monthan Field. It was said to be the largest municipal airport in the USA and in 1928 received its first scheduled services, operated by Standard Airlines. There was a considerable build-up of military traffic at, what became, Davis-Monthan Air Force Base and, in anticipation of civil operations being forced out, the City selected a new site in 1940, purchased about 4,000 acres (1,619 hectares) of land and reserved 2,500 acres (1,012 hectares) for a new airport sited about two miles (3.2 km) south of the original airport and three miles (4.8 km) southwest of Davis-Monthan.

Soon after the start of the Second World War Consolidated-Vultee Aircraft Corp built three hangars at the new aerodrome to undertake B-24 bomber modifications and subsequent military activities brought numerous improvements.

Three runways were built, all about 6,000 ft (1,981 m) in length. These were the 03/21 and 11/29 runways which are still in use and a north–south runway which has since been abandoned.

In late 1947 American Airlines was finally told that it would have to cease operations through Davis-Monthan AFB and on 15 October, 1948, became the first airline to operate scheduled services from Tucson Municipal Airport, as the new site had been named.

In 1950 Grand Central Aircraft Co moved from California to Tucson Municipal Airport and took on the work of reconditioning and modifying B-29s, which had been stored at Davis-Monthan, for the Korean War. Later the company did similar work on B-47s and this necessitated lengthening runway 11/29 from 6,300 ft (1,920 m) to 12,000 ft (3,658 m).

Hughes Aircraft Co moved to the airport in 1951 and in 1954 Douglas Aircraft Co set up facilities for modifying RB-66s. In May 1956 the 162nd Fighter Group of the Arizona Air National Guard took up occupation of a site at the north of the airport. In 1960 a number of airlines, including Aer Lingus, Ansett-ANA, BOAC, Lufthansa, Qantas and TAA, selected Tucson for their jet conversion training.

When Tucson Municipal Airport was first used by scheduled air services a terminal building was added to the side of a hangar on the western boundary but late in 1962 construction was begun of the present terminal on the east of the airport. This was a three-storey building of 130,000 sq ft (12,077 sq m) in Southwestern architectural style, and 90,000 people attended the dedication ceremonies in November 1963. In March that year the airport had been made a port of entry and renamed Tucson International.

In July 1973 the 1994 Airport Master Plan was commissioned and this was completed, with recommendations, by August 1974. This forecast that aircraft movements would be 277,000 in 1984, 313,000 in 1989 and 358,000 in 1994, and that the number of embarking passengers would be 1,228,000 in 1984, 1,560,000 in 1989 and 1,912,000 in 1994. To meet this traffic growth and overcome the airport's severe noise problems a three-phase development programme was recommended.

Stage 1 (1974–79) called for the acquisition of another 6,300 acres (2,550 hectares) of land; the construction of an 11,000 ft (3,353 m) runway 11R/29L, as far southeast as possible to reduce noise, for use by air carriers, with general aviation being transferred to 11L/29R; construction of associated taxiways and other work.

Stage 2 (1980–84) called for a further 25 acres (10 hectares) and a 63,000 sq ft (5,853 sq m) northwestward expansion of the terminal with three additional gates.

Stage 3 (1985–94) called for 62,000 sq ft (5,760 sq m) southeast extension of the terminal with three more gates, and additional taxiways.

Beyond 1994 it is proposed that runway 11L/29R should be 11,000 ft (3,353 m) on its same alignment but relocated to the southeast, and that provision should be made to the east of the 11/29 runways for a general aviation area with two 5,600 ft (1,707 m) 11/29 runways. It is also considered that the terminal should be expanded to 350,000 sq ft (32,515 sq m) with 18–28 aircraft stands. The master plan allows for considerable expansion of cargo facilities and the possibility of building a second passenger terminal.

A November 1976 chart (reproduced here) shows CAT II holding points at all designated entrances to runway 11L/29R but at October 1978 CAT II ILS and lighting had not been installed.

Tulsa, Oklahoma   Tulsa International Airport

36° 11′ 55″ N   95° 53′ 14″ W   5.2 nm (9.65 km) NE of city
ICAO: KTUL   IATA code: TUL   Time zone: GMT −6
Authority: Tulsa Airport Authority
Area: 2,428 hectares (6,000 acres)
Elevation: 676 ft (206 m)   Ref temp: 33.88 deg C

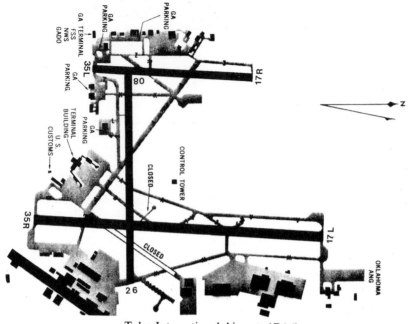

Tulsa International Airport. (*FAA*)

Runways: 08/26   2,347 × 46 m (7,700 × 150 ft) asphalt concrete, grooved
          17L/35R   3,047 × 61 m (9,999 × 200 ft) concrete*
          17R/35L   1,676 × 46 m (5,498 × 150 ft) asphalt

* 17L/35R has arrester cables at each end

Pavement strength: 08/26   75,000 lb plus (34,019 kg plus) 1, 170,000 lb (77,111 kg) 2, 290,000 lb (131,542 kg) 3; 17L/35R   50,000 lb plus (22,680 kg plus) 1, 200,000 lb (90,718 kg) 2, 400,000 lb plus (181,437 kg plus) 3; 17R/35L   16,500 lb (7,484 kg) 1—general aviation use only
Landing category: ICAO CAT II
Lighting:
    R/W   08/26 and 17R/35L   MIRL
           17L/35R   HIRL and centreline. TDZ 35R
    App   R/W 17L   SSALSR
           R/W 17R and 26   REIL and VASIS
           R/W 35L   VASIS
           R/W 35R   ALSF-1
    Thr   green all runways
    Txy   blue edge and green centreline
Aids: VORTAC, NDB, ASR, RNAV, RVR 17L/35R, ILS CAT II 35R, ILS CAT I 17L
Twr frequency: 118.7 (west), 121.2 (east)
App frequency: 120.7 (west), 119.1 (east)

554

Terminal: Centralized terminal with two piers, 19 loading gates and eight
    aerobridges. Separate general aviation areas
Scheduled services 1978: American, Braniff, Continental, Delta, Frontier,
    Metroflight Airlines, Ozark, Scheduled Skyways System and TWA.
Airline bases: American Airlines engineering centre for Boeing 707 and
    727. Also houses the airline's central computer system. Oklahoma Air
    National Guard has base

Traffic:	1970	1975	1976	1977	1978
Passengers (total)	1,019,944	1,373,352	1,516,462	1,659,180	1,922,185
Cargo (tonnes)	3,835	6,209	6,319	6,752	12,089*
Aircraft movements	207,036	188,351	192,718	197,437	215,190
Transport movements	47,761	42,784	44,475	46,898	—

* Includes mail

Tulsa Airport was opened on 3 July, 1928. It had a grass landing area
and in 1930 was claimed as the world's busiest airport, 175,000 passengers
using it that year. During 1930 three steel and concrete hangars were
completed and they were linked by about a mile of concrete taxiway. There
was a small administration building, a restaurant and an aircraft apron.

The cost of acquiring the site for the airport had been underwritten by
the Tulsa Airport Corporation, comprising 47 individuals and companies,
but the city's voters approved a bond issue for the purchase of the airport
and it was transferred to the City Park Department, the name being
changed to Tulsa Municipal Airport on 5 December, 1930.

In 1931 Tulsa Municipal Airport recorded 21,900 aircraft movements
and 93,844 passengers on non-scheduled flights, no records apparently
being kept of passengers on scheduled flights. By 1932 the airport had a
modern passenger terminal which was described as 'one of the finest air
passenger terminals in the Southwest.'

The Tulsa Airport Authority was created on 7 May, 1958, and took
over the airport from the Park Board.

In November 1961 the present terminal building was completed, on 28
August, 1963, the airport took its present name, in July 1976 CAT II
operations were authorized and in 1977 runway 08/26 was lengthened from
6,785 ft (2,068 m) to 7,700 ft (2,347 m).

Tulsa International Airport terminal area—looking approximately northeast.
(*Tulsa Airport Authority*)

The terminal building and control tower at Dulles International Airport.
(*US Department of Transportation*)

Washington, D.C.   Dulles International Airport

38° 56′ 39″ N   77° 27′ 24″ W   4 nm (7.4 km) NW of Chantilly, Va
ICAO: KIAD   IATA code: IAD   Time zone: GMT − 5
Authority: Metropolitan Washington Airports, FAA
Area: 4,047 hectares (10,000 acres)
Elevation: 313 ft (95 m)   Ref temp: 30.2 deg C
Runways: 01L/19R   3,505 × 46 m (11,500 × 150 ft) concrete, grooved
      01R/19L   3,505 × 46 m (11,500 × 150 ft) concrete, grooved
      12/30   3,048 × 46 m (10,000 × 150 ft) concrete, grooved
1,500 ft (457 m) of the west parallel taxiway has been designated as
STOL runway 01S/19S. VFR daylight operations by propeller aircraft
of less than 12,500 lb (5,670 kg) are allowed on taxiways—designated
18L 3,332 ft (1,016 m) near north end; 36R 3,132 ft (955 m) near south
end; 11-29 3,080 ft (939 m).
Pavement strength: 200,000 lb (90,718 kg) 1, 250,000 lb (113,398 kg) 2,
450,000 lb (204,116 kg) 3.
Landing category: ICAO CAT IIIa*
Lighting:
  R/W   01L/19R, 01R/19L and 12/30   HIRL and centreline.
                                                            TDZ 01R and 19R
          01S/19S   MIRL
  App   R/W 01L   MALSR
          R/W 19R   SSALSR
          R/W 01R   ALSF-2
          R/W 19L   MALSR
          R/W 12   MALSR and VASIS
          R/W 30   REIL and VASIS
  Thr   green
  Txy   blue edge, plus green centreline on high-speed exits and first
          1,600 ft (488 m) of taxiways adjoining exits

*Dulles International Airport was the first in the United States to be cleared for
CAT IIIa operations.

Aids: VORTAC, DME, ARTS III, ASDE, RVR 01R, 19L and 19R, ILS CAT IIIa 01R, ILS CAT I 01L, 12, 19L and 19R
Twr frequency: 120.1   App frequency: 119.2/126.1
Terminals: Two-level passenger terminal, separate general aviation terminal and three cargo buildings
Scheduled services 1978: 14 airlines plus two commuter airlines

Traffic:	1970	1975	1976	1977	1978
Passengers (total)	2,157,463	2,528,407	2,841,495	2,867,782	3,189,954
Cargo (tonnes)	16,926	30,297	30,764	32,071	34,145
Aircraft movements	184,226	177,673	187,720	186,391	177,121
Transport movements	62,100	54,464	57,364	55,876	54,747

The need for a second Washington airport was realized soon after the end of the Second World War, and the Second Washington Airport Act of 7 September, 1950, as amended by the Congressional Act of 11 July, 1958, provided for 'the construction, protection, operation, and maintenance of a public airport in or in the vicinity of the District of Columbia.'

A study was made of many sites and in 1958 President Eisenhower decided on a 10,000 acre (4,047 hectare) site in farming country in northern Virginia, partly in Loudoun County and partly in Fairfax County.

Construction began on 2 September, 1958, the airport was dedicated on 17 November, 1962, and opened for traffic on 19 November. During the four years of construction some 3,000 acres (1,214 hectares) was graded, 1,200 acres (486 hectares) of woodland cleared, 11½ mn cubic yards of earth excavated, and 675,000 cubic yards of top soil redistributed. About 1½ mn seedlings were planted to form a 1,000 ft (305 m) wide belt of trees encircling the airport, and there is at least 8,000 ft (2,438 m) between each runway threshold and the airport boundary.

Dulles International Airport, Washington, looking south, with the terminal centred between the 01/19 runways and on the right runway 12/30.
(*US Department of Transportation*)

557

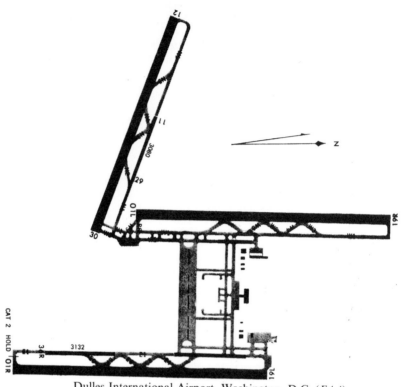

Dulles International Airport, Washington, D.C. (*FAA*)

Two 11,500 ft (3,505 m) 01/19 staggered parallel runways were built with 6,700 ft (2,042 m) separation, and a 10,000 ft (3,048 m) 12/30 runway. Provision has been made for a second 10,000 ft (3,048 m) 12/30 runway with 3,000 ft (914 m) separation between the pair.

The terminal area is between the two north–south runways. Eero Saarinen was chosen to design the terminal building, control tower and service buildings, and he considered the terminal to be his best work. It was decided to separate the terminal from the jet aircraft and use mobile lounges as the links between gates and aircraft. The terminal is a two-level structure, 600 ft (183 m) long and 150 ft (46 m) deep and can be doubled in size by equal extension at each end. The building is completely walled in glass and has a spectacular sculptured roof sweeping down from tapered supporting columns on the road side and then slightly up to a lower level facing the apron.

From the centre point of the terminal the south concourse projects towards the apron, is surmounted by the 193 ft (58.8 m) high control tower, and leads to 10 feederline, regional and commuter gates. Along the face of the terminal there are 12 boarding gates each side of the south concourse. Mobile lounges serve each gate and take 3 min to reach the jet parking apron south of the terminal. The apron is 4,100 ft (1,250 m) long by 750 ft (229 m) and has 30 aircraft stands at 246 ft (75 m) centres. There is provision for two more aprons further south to bring the number of stands to about 90.

Dulles International was the first airport to use mobile lounges, as distinct from buses, and initially there were 21 Chrysler units measuring 54 ft (16.45 m) in length, 16 ft (4.8 m) in width and 17 ft 6 in (5.3 m) in height. They weigh 76,000 lb (34,473 kg), have 172 hp engines, operate at 20 mph (32 km/h), and can carry 102 passengers, 71 seated. To meet the requirements of the wide-bodied aircraft 12 second-generation mobile lounges—Plane-Mates—were acquired. These are 49 ft (14.93 m) long, weigh 75,000 lb (34,019 kg), have 195 hp Diesel engines, can travel at 19 mph (30.5 km/h), have a capacity of 150 passengers with 94 seated, and when fully raised can withstand a 100 kt (185 km/h) wind or jet blast.

Washington, D.C.   Washington National Airport

38° 51′ 08″ N   77° 02′ 15″ W   3 nm (5.5 km) S of city
ICAO: KDCA   IATA code: DCA   Time zone: GMT −5
Authority: Metropolitan Washington Airports, FAA
Area: 275 hectares (680 acres)
Elevation: 15 ft (4 m)
Runways: 03/21   1,440 × 46 m (4,724 × 150 ft) asphalt, grooved
         15/33   1,589 × 61 m (5,212 × 200 ft) asphalt, grooved
         18/36   2,094 × 61 m (6,870 × 200 ft) asphalt, grooved
Pavement strength: 110,000 lb (49,895 kg) 1, 200,000 lb (90,718 kg) 2, 360,000 lb (163,293 kg) 3.
Landing category: ICAO CAT II
Lighting:
    R/W   03/21   MIRL
               15/33   HIRL
               18/36   HIRL and centreline. TDZ 36
    App   R/W 03/21 and 15/33   REIL and VASIS
               R/W 18   MALS, REIL and VASIS
               R/W 36   ALSF-2
    Thr   green
    Txy   blue edge
Aids: VOR/DME, NDB, RVR 36, RVV 18, ILS CAT II 36, ILS CAT I 18, MLS 18 (evaluation)
Twr frequency: 119.1/120.75   App frequency: 119.85/124.2
Terminals: Connected three-level main and north terminals with three piers, one connected to a circular satellite with eight aerobridges. Total of 39 gates. Separate general aviation terminal used by commuter airlines.
Scheduled services 1978: 15 airlines

Traffic:	1970	1975	1976	1977	1978
Passengers (total)	9,768,375	11,369,061	12,336,534	13,258,200	14,176,233
Cargo (tonnes)	35,480	31,865	37,799	37,729	38,595
Aircraft movements	319,449	306,494	326,083	345,452	352,044
Transport movements	212,353	197,882	206,712	212,406	208,748

Washington National Airport with the Potomac on the right.
(*US Department of Transportation*)

The first airport to serve Washington was Hoover Field, named after President Herbert Hoover, which opened in 1926 on a site beside the Potomac almost opposite the Lincoln memorial. In the following year another airport, named Washington National, was opened beside Hoover Field. The operation of two airports side by side was obviously impossible and in 1930 the two were merged as Washington Hoover Airport. This airport was very convenient to the city but had no other advantages. It was crossed by a much used military road, had a very small terminal, was flanked by electricity poles, had a tall chimney on one approach, and on the site was a refuse dump which almost continually sent up clouds of smoke.

The first legislation for the present Washington National Airport was submitted in 1927 and re-submitted every year for 10 years before being approved. Numerous sites were considered but on 26 September, 1938, President Franklin Roosevelt announced that he was 'tired of waiting for Congress' to select a site and that the new airport would be built on the mudflats on a bend of the Potomac at Gravelly Point, $4\frac{1}{2}$ miles ($7\frac{1}{4}$ km) south of the city. On 21 November, 1938, the first shovelful of earth was moved to signal the start of construction.

Funds were available from the Works Progress Administration and Public Works Administration, and the Civil Aeronautics Act of 1938, effective from 22 August that year, gave the Federal Government authority, for the first time, to construct and own commercial airports. The newly created Civil Aeronautics Authority was responsible for construction and also for operation of the airport until it was taken over by the Federal Aviation Administration (FAA). Washington National is today one of the only two Federally owned and operated US airports—the other being Dulles International Airport.

560

The boundaries of the airport enclose 680 acres (275 hectares) of which 180 acres (73 hectares) are beneath the Potomac. 425 acres (172 hectares) was reclaimed from the river. The first task was erection of a dyke on the river side and clearing of silt from the runway area so that sand and gravel could be pumped in on top of a stable base.

Exactly two years after site selection President Roosevelt laid the corner-stone of the terminal and gave the dedication address, and the airport was opened for traffic on 16 June, 1941.

When the airport was opened there were four runways, north–south (now 18/36) of 6,855 ft (2,089 m), northwest–southeast (now 15/33) of 5,210 ft (1,588 m), northeast–southwest (now 03/21) of 4,892 ft (1,491 m), and east–west (later 09/27) of 4,100 ft (1,250 m). Since that time there have been only slight changes in runway length, 09/27 has been closed and is used as a taxiway and for aircraft parking, and in 1967 runway 18/36 became the first in the United States to be grooved.

The very impressive curved terminal was designed in Southern Colonial style and had 115,000 sq ft (10,683 sq m) of floor space. When completed many considered that it was too big and would never be used to capacity and even during the late stages of its design 300 ft (91 m) was eliminated from the north end for this reason. In 1942, the first full year of operation, 459,396 passengers were handled, and 1,230,480 passengers used the airport in 1946.

In November 1950 the first major expansion was completed with the addition of 25,110 sq ft (2,333 sq m) at the south end of the terminal. In 1955 the 587 ft (179 m) long south finger was added, providing badly needed extra gates and loading positions. The North Terminal, of 7,264 sq ft (675 sq m), was opened in mid-October 1958, and in 1961 the 772 ft (235 m) passageway between the two terminals was covered and enclosed on the airport side.

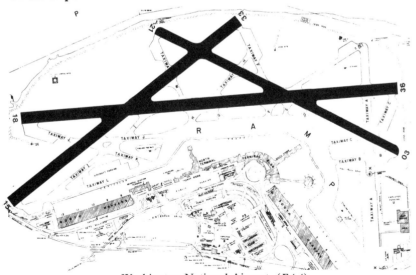

Washington National Airport. (*FAA*)

561

The airport has not been without its problems. In 1846 the Federal Government had retroceded the portion of Virginia which had been contributed to the original District of Columbia and the boundary was then established by the mean high water mark along the Virginia shore of the Potomac. The fill on which the airport was constructed altered that boundary and resulted in legal problems. The matter was solved in 1945, the airport being placed within the territory of Virginia but federal jurisdiction retained, with some rights, such as the taxing of motor fuel and oil sold on the airport, going to the State.

The restricted size of the airport and its proximity to the city also imposed problems. These resulted in some limits to nonstop flights, a maximum of 60 aircraft movements an hour (40 scheduled, 12 general aviation and eight air taxi), and strict noise abatement procedures.

In November 1959 the FAA banned all jet operations at Washington National but from 24 April, 1966, twin- and three-engined jet aircraft operating scheduled services were allowed. Four-engined jet aircraft are not allowed to use the airport, and it was the high capacity of the jet aircraft which made necessary the limitation on movements.

The Pentagon now occupies much of the site of the old Washington Hoover Airport.

West Palm Beach, Florida   Palm Beach International Airport

26° 41′ 01″ N   80° 05′ 40″ W   2.6 nm (4.8 km) W of West Palm Beach
ICAO: KPBI   IATA code: PBI   Time zone: GMT − 5
Authority: Palm Beach County Department of Airports
Area: 858 hectares (2,120 acres)
Elevation: 19 ft (6 m)   Ref temp: 32.3 deg C
Runways: 09L/27R   2,436 × 61 m (7,991 × 200 ft) asphalt
             09R/27L   961 × 23 m (3,152 × 75 ft)   asphalt
             13/31   2,112 × 46 m (6,930 × 150 ft) asphalt
Pavement strength: 09L/27R   85,000 lb (38,555 kg) 1, 200,000 lb
    (90,718 kg) 2,   400,000 lb (181,437 kg) 3
Landing category: ICAO CAT I
Lighting:
    R/W   09L/27R   HIRL
               13/31   MIRL*
    App   R/W 09L   ALSF-1
               R/W 13/31   REIL and VASIS
    Thr   green
    Txy   blue edge

*Southeast 428 ft (130 m) not lighted

Aids: VORTAC, NDB, SRE, L, RVR 09L, ILS CAT I 09L
Twr frequency: 119.1   App frequency: 128.3
Terminals: Domestic and international terminals in northeast corner of
    airport, with 9,500 sq ft (882.5 sq m) floor area and 17 gates. Cargo
    terminal and three general aviation aprons

562

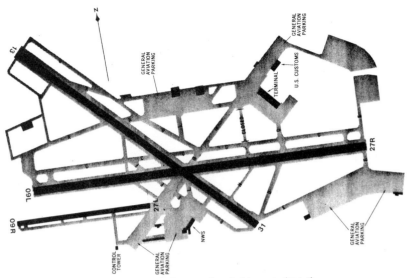

Palm Beach International Airport. (*FAA*)

Scheduled services 1978: Air Florida, Delta, Eastern, Mackey International, National and United

Traffic:	1970	1975	1976
Passengers (embarked)	342,229	666,153	731,674
Cargo (tonnes)†	934	1,362	1,510
Aircraft movements	260,424	212,291	219,729
Transport movements	33,149	33,310	35,489

† Uplifted only

Palm Beach International Airport is believed to be the old West Palm Beach Airport which was opened in the 1920s. It would seem that east–west, northwest–southeast and northeast–southwest runways were built and it is possible that there may have been a north–south runway. It has not proved possible to verify these assumptions because all requests for information were unanswered.

The northeast–southwest runway has been abandoned and is part of the taxiway system.

The terminal is at the northeast of the airport, and the Delta, Eastern and National gates are equipped with aerobridges. There is a large general aviation apron on the north side and two more on the south, where the control tower is also located. The international terminal is situated adjacent to the northwest end of the main terminal.

Mohawk Airlines BAC One-Eleven *Ontario* at the multi-named Bradley Field before it took its present title. (*British Aerospace*)

Windsor Locks, Connecticut   Bradley International Airport

41° 56′ 19″ N   72° 41′ 01″ W   2.6 nm (4.8 km) W of Windsor Locks
ICAO: KBDL   IATA code: BDL   Time zone: GMT −5
Authority: State of Connecticut Department of Transportation
Area: 1,012 hectares (2,500 acres) approximately
Elevation: 173 ft (53 m)   Ref temp: 28.9 deg C
Runways: 01/19   1,599 × 61 m (5,246 × 200 ft) concrete-asphalt
         06/24   2,896 × 61 m (9,500 × 200 ft) concrete-asphalt
         15/33 .   2,087 × 61 m (6,846 × 200 ft) concrete-asphalt
         There are jet barriers 45 ft (13.7 m) beyond the thresholds of
         06/24 and 15/33
Pavement strength: 01/19   128,000 lb (58,060 kg) ISWL;   06/24
    and 15/33   350,000 lb (158,757 kg) 3
Landing category: ICAO CAT II
Lighting:
     R/W   01/19   MIRL
              06/24   HIRL and white centreline. TDZ 06/24
              15/33   HIRL
     App   R/W 06   ALSF-2
            R/W 24   MALSR and VASIS
            R/W 33   MALS, REIL and VASIS
     Thr   green on all runways, with strobes on 33
     Txy   blue edge
Aids: TACAN, VORTAC/DME (proposed), ASR, LOM 06, ARTS III,
    RVR 06/24, RVV 06/24, ILS CAT II 06, ILS CAT I 24 and 33
Twr frequency: 120.3   App frequency: 121.2 (east), 123.85 (west)
Terminals: Francis S. Murphy two-level terminal with main concourse,
    two domestic piers and international concourse. Twelve gate houses
    with bypasses for arriving passengers (25 planned) and 16 aircraft
    stands (25 planned). United Airlines and general cargo terminals

Scheduled services 1978: Allegheny, American, Cumberland Airlines, Delta, Eastern and Pilgrim Airlines
Base: Headquarters of Connecticut Air National Guard

Traffic:	1970	1975	1976
Passengers (total)	1,810,026	2,447,863	2,726,476
Cargo (tonnes)	45,486	38,415	42,947
Aircraft movements	153,549	138,189	140,461
Transport movements	61,137	70,401	63,811

During 1976 Boeing 727s and 737s, DC-9s, Electras and Convair CV-580s accounted for 29 per cent of transport movements and Boeing 707s, DC-8s and wide-bodied aircraft for 16 per cent.

Bradley International Airport, now playing an increasing role as an international terminal, is about midway between New York and Boston and only a 12 mile (19 km) drive from Hartford. It plays an important role as diversion airport during bad weather.

The aerodrome was opened as a USAAF fighter base in 1941, the first landing being made by a Bell P-39 on 18 August, 1941. It was originally known as Windsor Locks Air Force Base but was renamed in memory of Lieut Eugene Bradley who was killed there in a crash in 1942. The base had three runways of adequate length for Republic P-47s.

In 1946 the State of Connecticut took over the aerodrome, converted some of the buildings into a terminal, and reconditioned runways and taxiways. In 1947 Eastern Air Lines opened the first commercial services to the airport.

High intensity lighting was switched on for the first time on 20 June, 1950, and that same night assisted the landings of a number of aircraft diverted from New York.

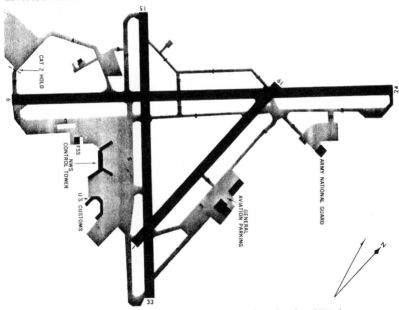

Bradley International Airport, Windsor Locks. (*FAA*)

The corner-stone of the Francis S. Murphy Terminal was laid in 1951 and the building was completed in 1952. Additions were made to the terminal in 1957, and in 1958 construction began of the temporary international terminal. The international and itinerent concourses were opened in 1967.

To meet the requirements of ANG jet aircraft, runway 06/24 was extended to 6,825 ft (2,080 m), later it was again lengthened, to 7,800 ft (2,377 m), and in 1958 an extension to the northeast gave it a length of 9,500 ft (2,896 m). Runway 15/33 was increased from 5,000 ft (1,524 m) to its present length in 1960.

To provide easy access between the terminal and large car parking areas the Ford Motor Company designed a fully-automated monorail transport system of rubber-tyred 30-passenger vehicles running at 30 mph (48 km/h) on elevated guideways.

Uruguay

Montevideo   Aeropuerto Nacional de Carrasco

ICAO: SUMU   IATA: MVD
34° 49′ 58″ S   56° 01′28″ W   Elevation: 95 ft (29 m)
Longest runway: 06/24   2,450 m (8,038 ft)   ART   VASI 06
Aids: VOR/DME, NDB, SRE/PAR, GCA, L, ILS 24

	1970	1975	1976	1977
Passengers	591,878*	741,128	660,722	597,694
Transport movements	18,922	18,267	20,841	—

* Excluding transit

Scheduled services 1978: 13 airlines
Main base: Aerolineas Colonia SA (ARCO) and Pluna

A Fokker F.28 at Carrasco National Airport, Montevideo. (*Fokker-VFW*)

USSR

It is not possible to deal with Soviet airports in the same manner as for those of most other countries. Very few Soviet traffic figures are available and therefore one cannot categorize the airports. The few figures available indicate that in 1967 Krasnodar was handling more than a million passengers; in 1969 Simferopol was handling 383,000 and Adler (for Sochi) more than half a million—these figures covering only the traffic to and from Moscow; Moscow's Bykovo Airport is known to have handled about three million passengers in 1976, and the ICAO figures for 1977 traffic at Moscow's Sheremetyevo Airport are 3,564,511 passengers, 29,846 tonnes of cargo and 59,091 transport aircraft movements, but these may only be the figures for international services. Sukhumi handled 624,000 passengers in 1976 and is expected to handle 750,000 in 1980. The estimated passenger total for Simferopol Tsentralny (Central) Airport in 1977 was two million.

The Soviet airline Aeroflot serves some 3,500 cities, towns, villages and settlements within the Soviet Union and there is considerable variation in the quality of the airports used, but for several years a very large airport building and modernization programme has been in course of implementation and, looking ahead, calls for 220 new All-Union airports and 1,000 local airports by 1990 and 400 All-Union and 1,600 local airports by the year 2000.

Since the war many Soviet cities have had to make do with inadequate airports, and with terminal buildings which are unsuitable although some are of architectural interest and worth preservation.

About 70 airport terminals with the capability of handling a total of 40 million passengers annually were built under the 1971–75 Five Year Plan and a similar number was planned for the period 1976–80.

Moscow is served by four airports, Bykovo, Domodedovo*(opened on 20 May, 1965), Sheremetyevo (opened in June 1961) and Vnukovo (opened on 2 July, 1941). A fifth airport, to handle up to 40 mn passengers a year, is to be built and this will probably come into operation in 1990. Meanwhile the four existing airports are to be expanded to handle a total of 20–38 mn passengers a year and Sheremetyevo is having largescale extensions to cope with the 1980 Olympic Games traffic.

Kiev's Borispol International Airport came into service on 19 May, 1965, and it appears that new terminals were opened at Baku, Simferopol and Sverdlovsk during the late 1960s.

During the first three years of the 1971–75 Five Year Plan, modern terminals, and perhaps in some cases new airports, were constructed at Aktyubinsk, Alma Ata, Anadyr', Arkhangel'sk (Archangel), Chardzhou, Chelyabinsk, Dnepropetrovsk, Donetsk, Izhevsk, Kaunas, Kirov, Kishenev, Leningrad - Pulkovo (this may have been a new airport), Magadan, Palanga, Pskov, Riga, Surgut, Tbilisi (Tiflis), Tyumen, Ulyanovsk, Volgograd and Voronezh. During the latter part of the period new terminals were under construction at Anapa, Astrakhan, Brest (Brest-

* A Soviet report gave Domodedovo's 1976 passenger total as 8.4 mn.

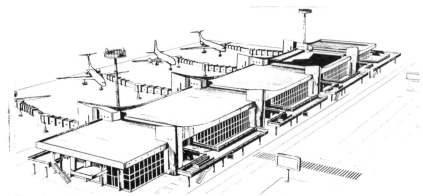

Drawing of the new terminal at Rostov on Don. Capable of handling 1,500 passengers an hour, this terminal is believed to have been opened in 1978. (*Aeroflot*)

Litovsk), Frunze, Grosnyy, Irkutsk, Kazan, Komsomol'sk, Kustanay, Moscow - Bykovo, Murmansk, Nizhne-Vartovsk, Orenburg, Rostov on Don, and Stavropol.

By the mid-1970s designs had been completed for new terminals at Khabarovsk, Kiev-Borispol, Moscow-Vnukovo, Sochi (Adler), Tashkent, and Yerevan South. Plans had also been started for new airports at Krasnoyarsk and Minsk. New terminal projects for the period 1976–80 are known to include Batumi, Kazan, Khabarovsk and Nalchik, and there is to be a new airport at Tallinn.

The terminals which have been opened in recent years are of modern design and pleasing appearance. The airports for which information is available mostly have approach, runway and threshold lighting (ART).

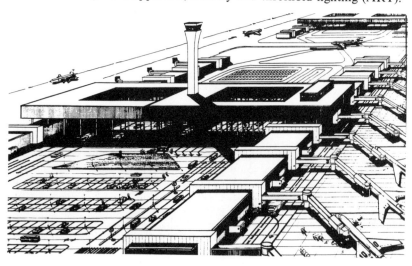

Drawing of the new Kazan Airport terminal. (*Aeroflot*)

568

The airports in this section are those which appear in the published Soviet AIP, with the exception of Ust'-Ordynskiy which is believed to handle only a small amount of traffic. All Soviet airports are State-owned.

Additional abbreviations used in this section are KGSP, a Soviet ILS not compatible with ICAO specifications, PA precision approach lights, SA simple approach lights.

Aktyubinsk, Kazakh SSR   Aktyubinsk Airport

50° 15′ N   57° 13′ E   ICAO: UATT   IATA: AKX
Elevation: 722 ft (220 m)   Ref temp: 24.6 deg C   GMT plus 5
Runway: 13/31   3,100 × 60 m (10,171 × 197 ft) concrete   ART
Aids: NDB, VDF, PAR, SRE, KGSP 13/31
Pavement loading: 14,500 kg (31,967 lb) ISWL
In the southern suburbs of the city. Served by Aeroflot only.

Alma Ata, Kazakh SSR   Alma Ata Airport

43° 21′ N   77° 01′ E   ICAO: UAAA   IATA: ALA
Elevation: 2,215 ft (675 m)   Ref temp: 25.5 deg C   GMT plus 6
Longest runway: 05/23   4,400 × 56 m (14,436 × 184 ft) concrete
          PA 05/23   RT
Aids: PAR, SRE, ILS 23, KGSP 05
Pavement loading: 23,000 kg (50,706 lb) ISWL
In the northeast suburbs of the city. Served by Aeroflot only
Main base: Aeroflot Kazakhstan Directorate

The old Alma Ata Airport terminal, in 1964. This has been replaced by a modern building, as have many Soviet airport terminals. One hopes that some of the old terminals have been preserved for their architectural interest.

569

Chita, RSFSR   Kadala International Airport

52° 02′ N   113° 18′ E   ICAO: UIAA   IATA: CHT
Elevation: 2,231 ft (680 m)   Ref temp: 21.3 deg C   GMT plus 9
Runway: 11/29   2,800 × 56 m (9,186 × 184 ft) concrete   PA 29   RT
Aids: NDB, VDF, PAR, SRE, KGSP 11/29
Pavement loading: 90,000 kg (198,416 lb) auw
7.3 nm (13.5 km) west of city

Dushanbe (Dyushambe), Tadzhik SSR   Dushanbe Airport

38° 33′ N   68° 49′ E   ICAO: UTDD   IATA: DYU
Elevation: 2,569 ft (783 m)   Ref temp: 30.4 deg C   GMT plus 6
Longest runway: 09/27   3,100 × 60 m (10,170 × 197 ft) concrete
    SA 09/27   RT
Aids: NDB, PAR, SRE, KGSP 09
Pavement loading: 11,300 kg (24,912 lb) ISWL
3.8 nm (7 km) south of city.   Served by Aeroflot only
Main base: Aeroflot Tadzhik Directorate

Dushanbe Airport terminal.

Irkutsk, RSFSR   Irkutsk Airport

52° 15′ N   104° 23′ E   ICAO: UIII   IATA: IKT
Elevation: 1,640 ft (500 m)   Ref temp: 20 deg C   GMT plus 8
Runway: 12/30   2,750 × 60 m (9,022 × 197 ft) concrete
Lighting:
    R/W   white edge, last 600 m (1,968 ft) yellow, red end lights

An Aeroflot Yak-40 at Irkutsk. (*Aeroflot*)

App	R/W 12	simple LIL
	R/W 30	LIH centreline and six crossbars
Thr	green	
Txy	blue edge	

Aids: VDF, PAR, SRE, KGSP 12/30
Pavement loading: 16,000 kg (35,274 lb) ISWL
3.5 nm (6.5 km) SE of city.   Served by Aeroflot and Air Mongol
Main base: Aeroflot Eastern Siberia Directorate

Khabarovsk, RSFSR   Novy International Airport

48° 31′ N   135° 10′ E   5.7 nm (10.5 km) NE of city
ICAO: UHHH   IATA code: KHV
Elevation: 243 ft (74 m)   Ref temp: 22.6 deg C   GMT plus 10
Runways: 05/23   3,500 × 78 m (11,483 × 256 ft) concrete/asphalt
          05/23   2,500 × 60 m   (8,202 × 197 ft) grass
          The main runway has a width of 68 m (233 ft) over the northeast
          1,000 m (3,281 ft). The grass runway is adjacent to the southeast
          edge of the main runway
Pavement loading: Main runway LCN 95
Landing category: ICAO CAT I
Lighting:
    Main R/W   white edge with yellow last 610 m (2,000 ft) with wing
                 bars at 305 m (1,000 ft). Take-off aiming lights.
                 Red wing bars 290 m (951 ft) beyond end of 05 and
                 457 m (1,499 ft) beyond end of 23
    App   R/W 05/23   LIH white centreline and five
                 crossbars
    Thr   green
    Txy   edge

571

Khabarovsk's Novy International Airport terminal. (*Aeroflot*)

Aids: NDB, VDF, PAR, SRE, ILS 05, KGSP 05/23
Twr frequency: 122.5/128.0   App frequency: 126.0
Terminals: Passenger and cargo terminals to west of runways, with 86
    aircraft stands including three for cargo loading and three for aircraft
    requiring maintenance. Nine grass parking positions for winter use
    only.
Scheduled services 1978: Aeroflot, CAAK (North Korea), International
    Air Cargo and Japan Air Lines
Main base: Aeroflot Far East Directorate

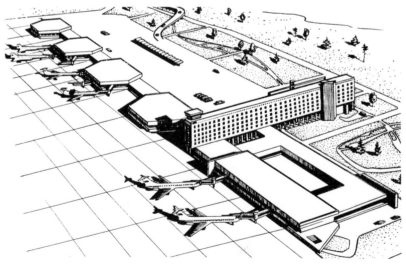

Drawing of the new Khabarovsk Novy terminal. (*Aeroflot*)

Kiev, Ukrainian SSR   Borispol International Airport

50° 21′ N   30° 55′ E   ICAO: UKBB   IATA: KBP
Elevation: 410 ft (125 m)   Ref temp: 21.6 deg C   GMT plus 3
Runways: 18L/36R   2,500 × 80 m   (8,202 × 262 ft) concrete
        18R/36L   3,500 × 63 m (11,483 × 207 ft) concrete
Lighting:
   R/W   white edge with yellow ends and white centreline
   App   R/W 18L and 36R   LIL simple
        R/W 18R and 36L   LIH centreline and five crossbars*
   Thr   red/green
   Txy   edge
Pavement loading: 18R/36L   LCN 96
Aids: NDB, PAR, SRE, ILS CAT II 18R, KGSP 18L/36R and 36L
15.66 nm (29 km) E of city
Scheduled services 1978: Aeroflot, Balkan, ČSA, Interflug, JAT, LOT and
   Malév
Joint main base: Aeroflot Ukraine Directorate
The airport was opened on 19 May, 1965

* Approach lighting on R/W 18R is CAT II and on 36L CAT I

The terminal and control tower at Borispol International Airport, Kiev. (*Aeroflot*)

Kiev, Ukrainian SSR   Zhulyany Airport

50° 24′ N   30° 27′ E   ICAO: UKKK   IATA: IEV
Elevation: 574 ft (175 m)   Ref temp: 21.6 deg C   GMT plus 3
Runway: 08/26   1,800 × 80 m (5,905 × 262 ft) concrete   ART
Aids: PAR, SRE, KGSP 08/26
Pavement loading: 6,500 kg (14,330 lb) ISWL
3.24 nm (6 km) SW of city.   Served by Aeroflot and Interflug
Joint main base: Aeroflot Ukraine Directorate

573

Kuybyshev, RSFSR   Kurumoch Airport

53° 30′ N   50° 10′ E   ICAO: UWWW   No IATA code
Elevation: 453 ft (138 m)   Ref temp: 23.6 deg C   GMT plus 4
Runway: 05/23   2,500 × 60 m (8,202 × 197 ft) concrete
    SA 05/23   RT
Aids: VDF, PAR, SRE, KGSP 05/23
Pavement loading: 15,000 kg (33,069 lb) ISWL
19 nm (35 km) N of city   Served by Aeroflot only
Main base: Aeroflot Volga Directorate

Leningrad, RSFSR   Pulkovo International Airport

59° 49′ N   30° 18′ E   8.1 nm (15 km) S of city
ICAO: ULLL   IATA code: LED   Time zone: GMT plus 3
Elevation: 59 ft (18 m)   Ref temp: 18.5 deg C
Runways: 10/28   3,400 × 70 m (11,155 × 230 ft) concrete
    13/31   2,500 × 60 m   (8,202 × 197 ft) concrete
Pavement strength: LCN 80
Landing category: ICAO CAT I
Lighting:
   R/W   10/28   LIH and LIL white edge and centreline, last 610 m (2,000 ft) yellow. TDZ each end and distance wing bars. Red end lights
        13/31   white edge, last 610 m (2,000 ft) yellow. Also take-off aiming lights, and mid-point lights
   App   R/W 10/28   LIH white centreline with five yellow crossbars and barrettes on inner 305 m (1,000 ft) of R/W 10
        R/W 13/31   LIL red centreline with crossbar and double lights on inner 305 m (1,000 ft)
   Thr   10/28 green wing bars, 13/31 green
   Txy   edge
Aids: VOR, VDF, PAR, SRE, ILS CAT I 10, KGSP 13/31 and 28

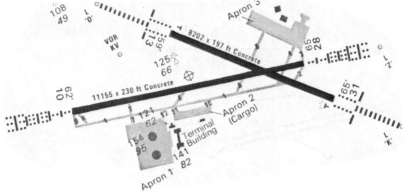

Pulkovo International Airport, Leningrad. (*British Airways Aerad*)

574

Aeroflot Tupolev Tu-134s at Pulkovo International Airport, Leningrad. (*Aeroflot*)

The main hall at Pulkovo International Airport, Leningrad. (*Aeroflot*)

Twr frequency: 118.1/119.0/128.0   App frequency: 120.3/125.2
Terminal: Modern passenger terminal with more than 30 aircraft stands
    and cargo terminal with 18 aircraft stands
Scheduled services 1978: Aeroflot, Air France, Balkan, ČSA, Finnair,
    Interflug, JAT, LOT, Malév and SAS
Main base: Aeroflot Leningrad Directorate
Leningrad is also served by Smolny Airport 2.7 nm (5 km) SW of city

Lvov, Ukrainian SSR   Snilow Airport

49° 49′ N   23° 57′ E   ICAO: UKLL   IATA: LWO
Elevation: 1,063 ft (324 m)   Ref temp: 19.3 deg C   GMT plus 3
Runway: 13/31   2,510 × 45 m (8,235 × 148 ft) concrete   ART
Aids: NDB, VDF, PAR, SRE, KGSP 31
Pavement loading: 13,000 kg (28,660 lb) ISWL
In southwest suburbs of city.   Served by Aeroflot only

Minsk, Byelorussian SSR   Loshitsa International Airport

53° 52′ N   27° 33′ E   1.6 nm (3 km) S of city
ICAO: UMMM   IATA code: MSQ   Time zone: GMT plus 3
Elevation: 741 ft (226 m)   Ref temp: 19.9 deg C
Runways: 12/30   2,000 × 60 m (6,562 × 197 ft) concrete
           12/30   2,000 × 65 m (6,562 × 213 ft) grass
Pavement strength: 10,500 kg (23,148 lb) ISWL
Landing category: ICAO CAT I
Lighting:
     R/W   main runway white edge, last 610 m (2,000 ft) yellow. Red
             end lights
     App   R/W 12   LIL centreline and one crossbar
             R/W 30   LIH white centreline with six crossbars
     Thr   green with wing bars
     Txy   blue edge
Aids: NDB, VDF, PAR, SRE, KGSP 12/30
Twr frequency: 119.0/128.0   App frequency: 126.0
Scheduled services 1978: Aeroflot and Interflug
Main base: Aeroflot Byelorussia Directorate

Moscow's Domodedovo Airport terminal, with three Tupolev Tu-104s

Moscow, RSFSR   Sheremetyevo International Airport

55° 58′ N   37° 25′ E   15.1 nm (28 km) NW of city
ICAO: UUEE   IATA code: SVO   Time zone GMT plus 3
Elevation: 623 ft (190 m)   Ref temp: 20 deg C

Aeroflot Tupolev Tu-134 at Sheremetyevo International Airport, Moscow.
(*Aeroflot*)

Runways: 07L/25R   3,530 × 80 m (11,581 × 262 ft) concrete
           07R/25L   3,700 × 60 m (12,139 × 197 ft) concrete
           Runways are only about 60 m (197 ft) apart
Pavement strength: 07L/25R LCN 100
Landing category: ICAO CAT II
Lighting:
    R/W   LIH and LIL white edge, last 610 m (2,000 ft) yellow, and white centreline, last 900 m (2,953 ft) red. Red take-off aiming lights 457 m (1,500 ft) beyond end of 25R and 500 m (1,640 ft) beyond end of 07L. TDZ 25L and 25R. Wing bars 305 m (1,000 ft) from thresholds 07L/25R
    App   R/W 07L   LIH white centreline and six crossbars
               R/W 07R   LIH white centreline and five crossbars
               R/W 25L   LIH white centreline and five crossbars, red barrettes on inner 275 m (902 ft)
               R/W 25R   LIH white centreline and six crossbars, red barrettes on inner 275 m (902 ft)
        VASIS 07L/25R and 07R
    Thr   green
    Txy   edge
Aids: VOR/DME, NDB, VDF, L, PAR, SRE, ILS CAT I 07L and 07R, ILS CAT II 25L and 25R
Twr frequency: 118.1/131.5   App frequency: 119.3/123.7

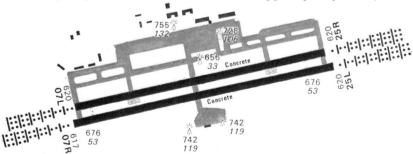

Sheremetyevo International Airport, Moscow. (*British Airways Aerad*)

577

Model of new terminal at Sheremetyevo International Airport, being built to handle Olympic Games traffic. This terminal bears the title Sheremetyevo-2—also borne by an earlier terminal.

Terminals: Sheremetyevo 1 and 2 with total of 64 aircraft stands. Sheremetyevo 2, with eight stands, may be VIP terminal. On 17 November, 1977, the foundation stone was laid for a new international terminal due for completion at the end of 1979 in time for the 1980 Olympic Games. Designed by Dipl Ing Heinz Wilke, and mostly prefabricated in Germany, the terminal will have three passenger levels (ground floor arrivals, first floor departures, second floor transit) and be capable of handling up to 6 mn passengers a year with peak hour capacity of 2,100. There will be 19 aerobridges to handle 19 aircraft of any major type simultaneously.

Scheduled services 1978: 28 airlines
Main base: Aeroflot TsUMVS

	1975	1976	1977
Passengers	2,543,512	4,101,244	3,564,511
Cargo (tonnes)	44,507	60,117	29,846
Transport movements	43,418	67,908	59,091

The airport was opened for traffic in June 1961.

Moscow, RSFSR   Vnukovo Airport

55° 34′ N   37° 16′ E   15.1 nm (28 km) SW of city
ICAO: UUWW   IATA code: VKO   Time zone: GMT plus 3
Elevation: 669 ft (204 m)   Ref temp: 20 deg C

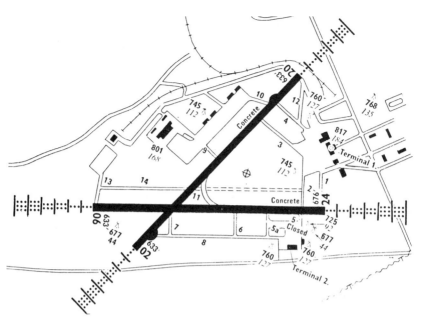

Vnukovo Airport, Moscow. (*British Airways Aerad*)

A Finnair Convair CV-340 at Vnukovo Airport, Moscow, on 10 February, 1956. (*Finnair*)

Runways: 02/20   3,050 × 60 m (10,006 × 197 ft) concrete
         06/24   3,000 × 80 m (9,842 × 262 ft) concrete
Pavement strength: 30,000 kg (66,139 lb) ISWL
Landing category: ICAO CAT I
Lighting:
    R/W   02/20   white edge, last 610 m (2,000 ft) yellow
             06/24   white edge and centreline. Last 280 m (919 ft) of
                       06 yellow, last 250 m (822 ft) of 24 yellow. White TDZ 24
    App   LIH centreline with six crossbars for all runways
    Thr   02/20 green, 06/24 green with wing bars
    Txy   blue edge
Aids: NDB, PAR, SRE, ILS CAT I 24, KGSP 06 and 02/20
Twr frequency: 121.0/126.0   App frequency: 134.2
Terminals: Passenger terminals Vnukovo 1 and 2. 52 aircraft stands (32 in
    front of terminal) at Vnukovo 1 with six start-up positions
Scheduled services 1978: Aeroflot only

The airport was opened on 2 July, 1941, and in 1976 is reported to
have handled nine million passengers. A new terminal is to be built, with
aerobridge loading, capable of handling 5,300 passengers an hour.

Novosibirsk, RSFSR   Tolmachevo Airport

55° 01′ N   82° 37′ E   ICAO: UNNN   IATA: OVB
Elevation: 358 ft (109 m)   Ref temp: 20.7 deg C   GMT plus 7
Runway: 07/25   3,600 × 70 m (11,811 × 230 ft) concrete
Lighting:
    R/W   white/yellow edge and red end lights
    App   R/W 07 and 25   LIH white centreline with six crossbars.
             VASI 07
    Thr   green
    Txy   blue edge
Aids: VDF, KGSP 07/25
Pavement loading: 110,000 kg (242,508 lb) auw
9.2 nm (17 km) W of city.   Served by Aeroflot only
Main base: Aeroflot Western Siberia Directorate

The terminal at Tolmachevo Airport, Novosibirsk. (*Aeroflot*)

Tsentralny Airport, Odessa, with an Antonov An-24 on the left. (*Aeroflot*)

Odessa, Ukrainian SSR   Tsentralny (Central) Airport

46° 26′ N   30° 41′ E   ICAO: UKOO   IATA: ODS
Elevation: 164 ft (50 m)   Ref temp: 24.4 deg C   GMT plus 3
Runway: 16/34   2,800 × 56 m (9,186 × 184 ft) concrete
Lighting:
    R/W   white/yellow edge and red end lights
    App   R/W 16 LIL simple, 34 LIH white centreline with six
           crossbars
    Thr   green
    Txy   blue edge
Aids: VDF, PAR, SRE, KGSP 16/34
Pavement loading: 9,500 kg (20,944 lb) ISWL
In southwest suburbs of city.   Served by Aeroflot only.
Passengers in 1976–1,236,700.

Riga, Latvian SSR   Spilve Airport

56° 59′ 30″ N   24° 03′ 30″ E   3.78 nm (7 km) NW of city
ICAO: UMRR   IATA code: RIX   Time zone: GMT plus 3
Elevation: 7 ft (2 m)   Ref temp: 18.7 deg C
Runways: 08/26   550 × 70 m   (1,804 × 230 ft) grass
          14/32   1,700 × 50 m   (5,577 × 164 ft) concrete
          17/35   1,500 × 100 m (4,921 × 328 ft) grass
Pavement strength: R/W 14/32   5,000 kg (11,023 lb) ISWL
Lighting:
    R/W   14/32   LIL white edge, last 610 m (2,000 ft) yellow. White
           wing bars 350 m (1,148 ft) after threshold of 14 and 137 m
           (449 ft) after threshold of 32. Red end lights
    App   R/W 14   LIL white centreline with two crossbars
           R/W 32   nil

581

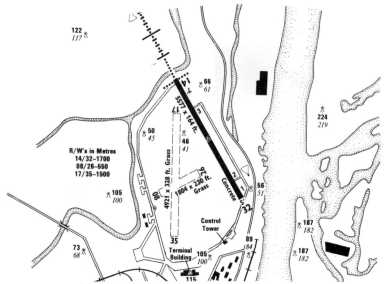

Spilve Airport, Riga. (*British Airways Aerad*)

Thr   R/W 14   green wing bars,   R/W 32   green wing bars
         with yellow wing bars 183 m (600 ft) before threshold
Txy   blue edge

Aids: VOR, PAR, SRE, GCA 32, KGSP 14
Twr frequency: 118.1/128.0   App frequency: 126.0/134.6
Terminal: No information but claimed as largest in Soviet Baltic countries
Scheduled services 1978: Aeroflot, Air France and KLM
Main base: Aeroflot Latvia Directorate
The airport was expected to handle more than a million passengers in 1977

A new airport, Skulte, handles All-Union traffic.

Ryazan, RSFSR   Dyagilevo Airport

54° 38′ N   39° 34′ E   ICAO: UUWR   No IATA code
Elevation: 440 ft (134 m)   Ref temp: 20.8 deg C   GMT plus 3
Runways: 06/24   3,000 × 70 m (9,842 × 230 ft) concrete
         06/24   3,000 × 100 m (9,842 × 328 ft) grass
Lighting:
    R/W   white edge, last 610 m (2,000 ft) yellow
    App   R/W 06/24 (concrete)   LIL white
    Thr   green wing bars
    Txy   no detail
Aids: PAR, SRE, L, KGSP 06/24
Pavement loading: 7,000 kg (15,432 lb) ISWL
5.4 nm (10 km) WNW of city.   Served by Aeroflot local services
Ryazan is a designated alternate for Moscow-Sheremetyevo.

582

Samarkand, Uzbek SSR   Samarkand Airport

39° 42' N   66° 59' E   ICAO: UTSS   IATA: SKD
Elevation: 2,201 ft (671 m)   Ref temp: 28.7 deg C   GMT plus 6
Runway: 09/27   2,400 × 49 m (7,874 × 161 ft) concrete PA09 RT
Aids: NDB, VDF, L, PAR, SRE, KGSP 09
Pavement loading: 80,000 kg (176,370 lb) auw
2.9 nm (5.5 km) NE of city.   Served by Aeroflot only

Main hall of Samarkand Airport. (*Aeroflot*)

Tashkent, Uzbek SSR   Yuzhnyy International Airport

41° 15' N   69° 17' E   ICAO: UTTT   IATA: TAS
Elevation: 1,394 ft (425 m)   Ref temp: 28.8 deg C   GMT plus 6
Runway: 08/26   3,500 × 60 m (11,483 × 197 ft) concrete
Lighting:
    R/W   edge white/yellow
    App   R/W 08   LIH white centreline with six yellow crossbars
            R/W 26   LIH white centreline with three yellow
                      crossbars
    Thr   green/red
    Txy   blue
Aids: VOR, VDF, PAR, SRE, ILS CAT II 26, KGSP 08/26
Pavement loading: LCN 52

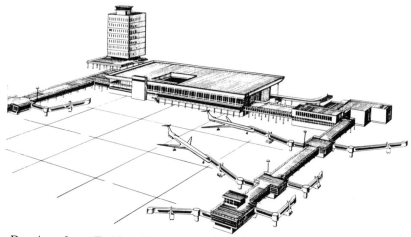

Drawing of new Tashkent Yuzhnyy International Airport terminal. (*Aeroflot*)

Terminals: Three terminals with 81 aircraft stands
1.6 nm (3 km) S of city.
Served by Aeroflot, Ariana Afghan Airlines and Finnair
Main base: Aeroflot Uzbek Directorate

Tbilisi (Tiflis), Georgian SSR   Novo-Alekseyevka Airport

41° 40′ N   44° 57′ E   ICAO: UGGG   IATA: TBS
Elevation: 1,555 ft (474 m)   Ref temp: 26.2 deg C   GMT plus 4
Runway: 13/31   2,500 × 60 m (8,202 × 197 ft) concrete
Lighting:
    R/W   white edge and red end lights
    App   R/W 31   LIH white centreline and five crossbars
            R/W 13   nil
    Thr   green with wing bars
    Txy   blue edge
Aids: VDF, PAR, SRE, ILS CAT I 13, KGSP 13/31
Pavement loading: 16,000 kg (35,274 lb) ISWL
7.56 nm (14 km) ESE of city.   Served by Aeroflot only
Main base: Aeroflot Georgia Directorate

Termez, Uzbek SSR   Termez Airport

37°17′ N   67° 20′ E   ICAO: UTST   IATA: TMZ
Elevation: 1,014 ft (309 m)   Ref temp: 37.7 deg C   GMT plus 6
Runway: 06/24   1,500 × 42 m (4,921 × 138 ft) concrete   No lights
Aids: VOR, NDB
Pavement loading: 9,000 kg (19,842 lb) ISWL
4.3 nm (8 km) NE of city.   Served by Aeroflot only

584

Ulan-Ude, RSFSR   Mukhino Airport

51° 48′ N   107° 28′ E   ICAO: UIUU   IATA: ULU
Elevation: 1,663 ft (507 m)   Ref temp: 21.6 deg C   GMT plus 8
Runway: 08/26   2,200 × 42 m (7,218 × 138 ft) concrete   RT
Aids: NDB, VDF, L
Pavement loading: 64,000 kg (141,096 lb) auw
5.1 nm (9.5 km) SW of city.   Served by Aeroflot only

Velikiye-Luki, RSFSR   Velikiye-Luki Airport

56° 21′ N   30° 33′ E   ICAO: ULOL   IATA: VEK
Elevation: 328 ft (100 m)   GMT plus 3
Runway: 15/33   1,420 m (4,659 ft)   ART
Aids: VOR, NDB, VDF, L, KGSP 33
3.8 nm (7 km) NE of city.   Served by Aeroflot only

Vil'nyus, Lithuanian SSR   Vil'nyus International Airport

54° 38′ N   25° 17′ E   ICAO: UMWW   IATA: VNO
Elevation: 623 ft (190 m)   Ref temp: 19.8 deg C   GMT plus 3
Runways: 02/20   2,500 × 50 m (8,202 × 164 ft) concrete   ART
          17/35   1,600 × 50 m (5,249 × 164 ft) asphalt/concrete ART
Aids: NDB, VDF, L, PAR, SRE, GCA 17, KGSP 02/20
Pavement loading: 8,000 kg (17,637 lb) ISWL
2.7 nm (5 km) south of city.   Served by Aeroflot only
Main base: Aeroflot Lithuania Directorate

Vil'nyus International Airport terminal in 1964, with Ilyushin Il-14s of Aeroflot
and Interflug.

585

Model of the new terminal for Yerevan Zapadnyy Airport.

Yerevan, Armenian SSR   Zapadnyy (West) Airport

40° 07′ N   44° 27′ E   ICAO: UGEE   IATA: EVN
Elevation: 2,805 ft (855 m)   Ref temp: 30 deg C   GMT plus 4
Runway: 09/27   3,100 × 57 m (10,170 × 187 ft) concrete
Lighting:
    R/W   white/yellow edge
    App   R/W 09   LIH white centreline with six crossbars
            R/W 27   nil
    Thr   red
    Txy   blue edge
Aids: NDB, L, PAR, SRE, KGSP 09
Pavement loading: 12,000 kg (26,455 lb) ISWL
5.4 nm (10 km) west of city.
Served by Aeroflot and Syrian Arab Airlines
Main base: Aeroflot Armenia Directorate

Major reconstruction is in hand. A new terminal is being built to handle more than 18 mn passengers a year with a peak rate of 2,100 an hour. There will be a circular terminal with three sections—two handling All-Union traffic and one for foreign tourists. The central block will contain traffic handling services, transit facilities, ticket offices, post office and other services. There will be decentralized handling with minimum walking distances. A tower restaurant will provide views of Yerevan and Mount Ararat. The new terminal was due to open in 1979.
    A completely new airport is also to be built at Leninakan.

Venezuela

Carácas
Aeropuerto Internacional de Maiquetía - Simón Bolívar

10° 36′ 23″ N   66° 59′ 23″ W
2.6 nm (4.8 km) W of Puerto La Guaira
ICAO: MVMI   IATA code: CCS   Time zone: GMT −4
Authority: Instituto Autónomo, Aeropuerto de Maiquetía
Area: 809 hectares (2,000 acres) approximately
Elevation: 233 ft (71 m)   Ref temp: 32 deg C
Runways: 08/26   3,000 × 60 m (9,842 × 197 ft)* asphaltic concrete
         09/27   3,500 × 45 m (11,483 × 148 ft) asphaltic concrete

* Threshold 08 displaced 1,200 m (3,937 ft). Take offs on 26 limited to 1,200 m (3,937 ft). Runways 26 and 27 take offs VFR only

Pavement strength: 08/26 auw 70,000 kg (154,324 lb); 09/27 auw 333,000 kg (734,139 lb)
Landing category: ICAO CAT I
Lighting:
    R/W   08/26 and 09/27   LIH white edge, last 600 m (1,968 ft) yellow. TDZ 09/27
    App   R/W 09   LIH white bar centreline and crossbar. VASIS
             R/W 26 and 27   VASIS
    Thr   green, with wing bars on 09
    Txy   blue edge
Aids: VOR/DME, NDB, SRE, ASR, ILS CAT I 09
Twr frequency: 118.1/118.4   App frequency: 120.1

An Avianca Boeing 707 in front of the new international terminal at Carácas.
(*A. G. Heape*)

Terminals: Three-level international terminal with seven gates and 16 stands. Aerobridges for close-in stands and Plane-Mates for remote stands. Separate domestic terminal, to be replaced by new building. Cargo and general aviation areas at eastern end of airport

Scheduled services 1978: 24 airlines

Main base: Aeropostal, Avensa and VIASA

Traffic:	1970	1975	1976	1977	1978
Passengers (total)	1,469,166*	3,008,160	3,367,205	4,240,531	4,912,519
Cargo (tonnes)	47,963	72,122	79,508	112,947	100,475
Aircraft movements	—	80,458	67,760	78,951	83,011
Transport movements	48,627	61,647	60,085	73,359	79,210

*Excluding transit

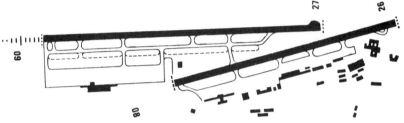

Maiquetía - Simón Bolívar International Airport, Carácas.

Simón Bolívar International Airport, still generally referred to as Maiquetía, is situated on the narrow coastal strip between the Caribbean and high mountains, some 12 miles (19.3 km) from Carácas to which it is joined by a six-lane highway through the mountains.

Known originally as La Guaira Airport, it was constructed in 1930 by Pan American Airways and by 1949 had a 5,000 ft (1,524 m) runway, which was later extended to 3,000 m (9,842 ft). The original terminal building, towards the eastern end of the airport, was opened in 1948.

In the late 1960s a master plan was produced for the airport, which is being developed in stages. In 1970 an international arrivals building was completed near the centre of the present layout, just south of the western end of runway 08/26, and work began on a permanent international terminal and a second runway. The new 09/27 runway 'is between the original 08/26 runway and the sea and extends to the west of the earlier site. Its construction involved moving about 24 mn cubic yards of earth, and its turning area at the 27 threshold is very close to the reinforced embankment which separates it from the sea. This runway came into operation in 1972.

In 1978 the first section of the new terminal at the west of the airport came into operation for international services. It is a three-storey steel and concrete building with seven aerobridge-equipped gates and a presidential gate. Plane-Mates are used for remote stands. The terminal has a peak-hour capacity of 1,200 passengers and is expected to be adequate until the mid-1980s.

In 1979 domestic operations were transferred to the temporary international terminal and later these will be moved to a new domestic section to the east of the new terminal. The general aviation and cargo areas are at the eastern end of the airport.

Maiquetía - Simón Bolívar International Airport, Carácas, looking west along the 08/26 runway with the new 09/27 on the right. (*A. G. Heape*)

There is no alternative site available for a new airport and it was therefore necessary to build all the new facilities without disrupting traffic. Runway 08/26 is almost in line with the new terminal and is restricted to use by piston-engined and small jet aircraft, with the 26 direction being limited to 1,200 m (3,937 ft).

A second 3,500 m (11,483 ft) 09/27 runway is to be built about 215 m (705 ft) to the north and west of the present 09/27. This will have a full-length parallel taxiway and its construction will involve the removal of a series of hills beside the shore. This runway is due for completion in the early 1980s and the 08/26 runway will almost certainly be closed.

The expansion programme is designed to provide capacity for 15 mn passengers a year by 2000 AD.

Maracaibo   Aeropuerto Internacional La Chinita

ICAO: MVMC   IATA: MAR
10° 33′ 40″ N   71° 43′ 32″ W   Elevation: 213 ft (65 m)
Longest runway: 02L/20R   3,000 m (9,842 ft)   ART   VASI 02L
Aids: VOR/DME, NDB, ILS 02L

	1970	1975	1976	1977
Passengers	304,059*	520,790	559,246	650,042
Transport movements	13,514	13,752	13,647	13,189

* Excluding transit

Scheduled services 1978: Aeropostal, Avensa, Delta, LACSA, Pan
    American, Transporte Aéreo de Carga and VIASA

Margarita
    Aeropuerto Internacional del Caribe General Santiago Mariño

ICAO: MVMG   IATA: PMV
10° 55′ 00″ N   63° 57′ 44″ W   Elevation: 88 ft (27 m)
Runway: 09/27   3,182 m (10,439 ft)   ART   VASI 09
Aids: VOR/DME, NDB

	1970	1975	1976	1977
Passengers	152,483*	558,437	647,252	827,924
Transport movements	8,144	13,537	14,288	16,784

* Excluding transit

Scheduled services 1978: Aeropostal, Avensa and Transporte Aéreo de
    Carga

Virgin Islands (USA)

Charlotte Amalie, St Thomas   Harry S Truman Airport

ICAO: MIST   IATA: STT
18° 20′ 26″ N   64° 58′ 11″ W   Elevation: 11 ft (3 m)
Runway: 09/27   1,420 m (4,658 ft)   ART   VASI 09
Aids: VOR/DME, ILS 09

	1970	1976	1977
Passengers	952,371	730,039	803,081
Transport movements	—	6,324	6,460

Scheduled services 1978: 10 airlines
Airline bases: Aero Virgin Islands, All Island Air, and Virgin Air

Yemen Arab Republic

San'a   San'a International Airport

ICAO: OYSN   IATA: SAH
15° 28′ 48″ N   44° 13′ 15″ E   Elevation: 7,238 ft (2,206 m)
Runway: 18/36   3,252 m (10,669 ft)   RT   VASI 18/36
Aids: VOR, NDB, VDF, L

	1976
Passengers	256,271
Transport movements	6,703

Scheduled services 1978: 11 airlines
Main base: Yemen Airways

The airport was officially opened on 26 September, 1973

Yugoslavia

Belgrade (Beograd)   Aerodrom Beograd - Surcin

44° 49′ 09″ N   20° 18′ 44″ E
6.5 nm (12 km) W of city railway station
ICAO: LYBE   IATA code: BEG   Time zone: GMT plus 1
Authority: Preduzeće za aerodromske usluge aerodrom "Beograd"
Elevation: 331 ft (101 m)   Ref temp: 24 deg C
Runway: 12/30   3,000 × 60 m (9,842 × 197 ft) concrete
Pavement strength: LCN 100
Landing category: ICAO CAT I
Lighting:
R/W   LIH white edge, last 750 m (2,461 ft) yellow

Belgrade - Surcin Airport with a JAT Caravelle. (*JAT*)

591

App   R/W 12   900 m (2,953 ft) LIH Calvert white centreline
           with six crossbars and LIL red centreline with six crossbars
           R/W 30   420 m (1,381 ft) simple LIL red centreline with
           one crossbar. VASIS 12/30
Thr   LIH green
Txy   LIL blue edge
Aids: VOR/DME, NDB, VDF, PAR, SRE, L, RVR 12, ILS CAT I 12
Twr frequency: 118.1   App frequency: 119.1/119.5
Terminal: Two-level terminal on south side of airport. Two concrete
    aprons, 300 by 85 m (984 by 279 ft) and 375 by 60 m (1,230 by 197 ft),
    with 18 aircraft stands
Scheduled services 1978: 23 airlines
Main base: Air Jugoslavia, Aviogenex and JAT

Traffic:	1970	1975	1976	1977
Passengers (total)	867,996	2,076,061	2,103,245	2,350,358
Cargo (tonnes)	6,491	15,866	17,267	22,915
Aircraft movements	29,810	50,552	45,834	45,376
Transport movements	27,020	46,496	41,910	42,328

From at least the early 1930s Belgrade was served by Zemun Airport,
but on 28 April, 1962, President Tito officially opened the new Belgrade -
Surcin international jet airport.

A new terminal building with an annual passenger capacity of 5 mn
was due to be completed during the summer of 1978. Lighting is to be
brought to ICAO standard and will include runway and taxiway centreline
lights, runway end lights and touchdown zone lighting.

Dubrovnik   Aerodrom Dubrovnik - Cilipi

                   ICAO: LYDU   IATA: DBV
42° 33′ 45″ N   18° 16′ 10″ E   Elevation: 528 ft (161 m)
Runway: 12/30   3,300 m (10,827 ft)   ART   VASI 12/30
Aids: NDB, VDF, SRE, L, GCA, ILS 12

	1970	1975	1976	1977
Passengers	693,000*	818,312	871,126	843,511
Transport movements	10,726	12,280	12,751	12,107

* Round figure

Scheduled services 1978: Aeroflot, Interflug, JAT, LOT and Malév

Pula   Aerodrom Pula   ICAO: LYPL   IATA: PUY

44° 53′ 38″ N   13° 55′ 38″ E   Elevation: 276 ft (84 m)
Runway: 09/27   2,950 m (9,678 ft)   ART   VASI 27
Aids: NDB, SRE, L, PAR, ILS 27

	1970
Passengers	262,000*

* Round figure

Scheduled services 1978: JAT

Split   Aerodrom Split - Kaštel   ICAO: LYSP   IATA: SPU

43° 32′ 20″ N   16° 17′ 59″ E   Elevation: 79 ft (24 m)
Runway: 05/23   2,550 m (8,366 ft)   ART
Aids: VOR, NDB, VDF, L, ILS 05

	1970
Passengers	298,257
Transport movements	7,072

Scheduled services 1978: JAT, LOT and Malév

Zagreb   Aerodrom Zagreb - Pleso

45° 44′ 35″ N   16° 04′ 25″ E   9.18 nm (17 km) NW of city
ICAO: LYZA   IATA code: ZAG   Time zone: GMT plus 1
Authority: Aerodrom "Zagreb" poduzeće za aerodromske usluge
Area: 300 hectares (741 acres)
Elevation: 351 ft (107 m)   Ref temp: 22.1 deg C
Runway: 05/23   3,250 × 45 m (10,663 × 148 ft) asphalt
Pavement strength: LCN 90
Landing category: ICAO CAT I
Lighting:
    R/W   LIH white edge
    App   R/W 05   900 m (2,953 ft) LIL red centreline with one crossbar
        R/W 23   900 m (2,953 ft) LIH white centreline with one crossbar
    Thr   LIH green
    Txy   LIL blue edge
Aids: VOR, NDB, VDF, SRE, L, RVR 05/23, ILS CAT I 05
Twr frequency: 118.3   App frequency: 118.5/120.7

Zagreb - Pleso Airport with a JAT Convair-Liner. (*JAT*)

593

Terminal: Terminal at south end of airport to east of runway. Two concrete/asphalt aprons, 390 by 70 m (1,280 by 230 ft) and 320 by 75 m (1,050 by 246 ft), with eight aircraft stands
Scheduled services 1978: 11 airlines
Airline base: JAT
Main base: Pan Adria

Traffic:	1970	1975	1976
Passengers (total)	669,000*	1,484,963	1,500,080
Cargo (tonnes)	5,588	10,202	10,430
Aircraft movements	20,400	32,548	32,042
Transport movements	—	30,676	30,004

* Rounded figure

In 1976 DC-9s accounted for 63.2 per cent of transport aircraft movements, Boeing 727s for 11.58 per cent and Tu-134s for 4.99 per cent.

In 1959 the Yugoslav Air Force gave JAT permission to use Pleso military aerodrome instead of the grass surfaced Lučko which had been used for several years.

There is a two-level passenger terminal with 4,500 sq m (48,438 sq ft) area and this is to be extended to 7,600 sq m (81,806 sq ft) to provide capacity for up to 2,000 passengers an hour.

République du Zaïre

Kinshasa   Aéroport de Kinshasa/Ndjili

ICAO: FZAA   IATA: FIH
04° 23′ S   15° 26′ E   Elevation: 1,014 ft (309 m)
Runway: 07/25   4,700 m (15,420 ft)   ART
Aids: VOR/DME, ILS CAT I 25

	1970	1975	1976	1977
Passengers	283,309	434,427	369,697*	494,393
Aircraft movements	12,407	14,529	23,429	26,157

* The ICAO passenger figure for 1976 was 533,793

Scheduled services 1978: 13 airlines
Main base: Air Zaïre

Zambia

Lusaka Lusaka International Airport

ICAO: FLLS IATA: LUN
15° 19′ 36″ S 28° 27′ 21″ E Elevation: 3,779 ft (1,152 m)
Longest runway: 10/28 3,962 m (12,998 ft) ART VASI 10/28
Aids: VOR/DME, NDB, L, TAR, ILS 10

	1970	1975	1976	1977
Passengers (terminal)	280,744	356,123	374,834	402,906
Transport movements	10,721	16,117	15,831	15,036

Scheduled services 1978: 12 airlines
Main base: Zambia Airways

Zimbabwe

Salisbury Salisbury Airport ICAO: FRSB IATA: SAY

17° 55′ 54″ S 31° 05′ 38″ E Elevation: 4,901 ft (1,494 m)
Longest runway: 06/24 4,725 m (15,502 ft) ART VASI 06/24
Aids: VOR/DME, NDB, VDF, L, SRE, ILS CAT I 06

	1970	1975	1976	1977
Passengers	374,497	631,811	537,777	529,820
Transport movements	13,403	16,910	13,702	13,271

Scheduled services 1978: Air Rhodesia and South African Airways
Main base: Air Rhodesia

Opened as Southern Rhodesia Air Force base 2 January, 1953.
Opened as civil airport 30 June, 1956.

Appendix

International Airports

known to have handled 100,000 or more passengers in 1975, 1976 or 1977, but less than 250,000.

Country/City	Airport	Longest Runway	Passengers 1975	Passengers 1976	Passengers 1977
Afghanistan					
Kabul	Kabul	11/29	2,800 m	105,908*	118,506*	151,277
Argentina					
Corrientes	Corrientes	01/19	2,100 m	121,386	111,049	123,514
Resistencia	Resistencia	03/21	2,770 m	142,250	115,845	142,723
Salta	Salta	05/23	2,400 m	141,018	138,784	158,091
Belgium					
Antwerp	Deurne	11/29	1,475 m	115,787	138,030	131,473
Ostend	Ostend/Middelkerk	08/26	3,200 m	119,570	129,540	118,037
Belize					
Belize City	Belize International	07/25	1,920 m	140,733	—	142,163
Cameroon, United Rep. of					
Yaoundé	Yaoundé	03/21	2,000 m	—	210,100	—
Congo, People's Rep. of					
Brazzaville	Maya-Maya	06/24	3,300 m	117,414	132,178	169,520

Country/City	Airport	Longest Runway	1975	Passengers 1976	1977
Djibouti, Rep. of Djibouti	Ambouli	09/27 3,140 m	—	203,900	—
Ethiopia Addis Ababa	Bole International	07/25 3,700 m	206,396	212,431	—
France Beauvais Clermont-Ferrand Le Touquet Nîmes	Tillé Aulnat Paris-Plage Garons	13/31 2,430 m 09/27 3,015 m 14/32 2,250 m 18/36 2,440 m	167,041 131,958 98,064 89,534	121,380 146,062 100,395 110,628	170,519 128,902 112,445 137,540
German Fed. Republic Saarbrücken	Ensheim	09/27 2,000 m	150,192*	125,855	138,194
Honduras San Pedro Sula Tegucigalpa	Ramón Villeda Morales Toncontín	03/21 2,803 m 01/19 2,000 m	101,904* 144,155**	112,000*† 143,000*†	178,136 210,429
Madagascar (Malagasy) Tamatave Tananarive	Tamatave Ivato	01/19 2,200 m 11/29 3,100 m	61,916 178,314	84,294 216,865	103,752 192,475
Mali Bamako	Sénou	07/25 2,700 m	96,645	108,575	131,267

Country/City	Airport	Longest Runway		Passengers 1975	1976	1977
Mauritania						
Nouakchott	Nouakchott	05/23	3,000 m	68,915	98,867	106,027
Morocco						
Marrakech	Ménera	10/28	3,100 m	197,784	203,115	236,977
Oujda	Angad	06/24	3,000 m	142,849	143,648	—
Netherlands Antilles						
Kralendijk,						
Bonaire Is	Flamingo	10/28	1,750 m	90,639	85,000*†	121,202
New Caledonia						
Noumea	La Tontouta	11/29	3,250 m	—	—	237,422
Niger						
Niamey	Niamey	09/27	3,000 m	120,108	127,609	146,568
Sierra Leone						
Freetown	Lungi	12/30	3,200 m	101,329	107,336	119,967
Spain						
Almería	Almería	08/26	2,400 m	118,540*	170,839	191,642
Aviles	Asturias	12/30	2,200 m	200,082*	209,973	247,191
Granada	Granada	10/28	2,900 m	107,459*	123,741	146,562
Reus	Reus	07/25	2,200 m	166,219*	136,125	152,357
Zaragoza	Zaragoza	13R/31L	3,720 m	132,935*	145,039	171,274

Country/City	Airport	Longest Runway	1975	Passengers 1976	1977
Togo Lomé	Tokoin	05/23 3,000 m	115,552	122,163	147,042
United Kingdom					
Blackpool	Squire's Gate	10/28 1,829 m	123,411	103,297	104,044
Bournemouth	Hurn	08/26 1,838 m	117,117	106,878	131,787
Cardiff	Cardiff - Wales	13/31 2,134 m	208,524	217,429	208,450
Inverness	Inverness (Dalcross)	06/24 1,887 m	124,748	136,059	133,579
Middlesbrough	Tees-side	06/24 2,291 m	187,176	220,602	236,305
Norwich	Norwich	10/28 1,842 m	119,742	135,866	167,928
Southend-on-Sea	Southend (Rochford)	06/24 1,605 m	202,713	218,427	242,181
USA Niagara Falls	Niagara Falls Int'l	10L/28R 2,780 m	69,879	131,185	—
US Samoa Pago Pago	Pago Pago Int'l	05/23 2,743 m	—	233,284	170,633‡
Upper Volta Ouagadougou	Ouagadougou	04/22 2,500 m	74,411	90,376	102,204
Venezuela Maturín	Maturín	05/23 2,100 m	163,126	185,341	212,774

*Excludes transit passengers   †ICAO estimate   ‡Nine months only

Addis Ababa - Bole International Airport was formerly Haile Salassie 1st International. Cardiff - Wales Airport was formerly Rhoose Airport. Norwich Airport was formerly RAF Station Horsham St Faith. Tees-side Airport also serves Bishop Auckland, Darlington, Hartlepool and Stockton-on-Tees.

INDEX OF AIRPORTS

McDonnell Douglas Aircraft since 1920

RENÉ J. FRANCILLON

This important work traces the history of two great United States aircraft manufacturers and their predecessor companies. The two companies, Douglas and McDonnell, have made significant contributions to the development of world air transport and to the defence of many countries.

Each product of these companies is described in detail, and its history of development and service is fully covered. Among the Douglas types are the first Douglas transport, the Cloudster; the World Cruisers which made the first flight round the earth; numerous pre-war military types; the DC-1, DC-2 and DC-3, of which well over 10,000 were built in civil and military versions. The Second World War Devastator, Dauntless and Boston series are well recorded and lead on to the great series of four-engined transports, the DC-4, DC-6 and DC-7.

The post-war jet aircraft include the DC-8, DC-9 and DC-10 jetliners and such types as the Skyray, Skyhawk and Skylancer. Also dealt with at length are the very high-speed research aircraft, the present-day F-15 Eagle, F-18 Hornet, AV-8B Harrier and the YC-15 STOL transport. Some of the more important projects are included and there is a full production list of Douglas aircraft.

The McDonnell types include the early Phantom, the Banshee, Goblin and Voodoo. The later Phantom, of which more than 5,000 have been built, is recorded in great detail and there are such little-known types as the Whirlaway and Little Henry.

'An important addition to the range . . . For the serious student of aviation history, this new title is an obvious "must" . . . no one can accuse either publisher or author of cutting corners.'

Air International